IMAGINARY PEOPLE

IMAGINARY PEOPLE

A Who's Who of Modern
Fictional Characters

DAVID PRINGLE

WORLD ALMANAC

AN IMPRINT OF PHAROS BOOKS • A SCRIPPS HOWARD COMPANY
NEW YORK

Copyright © 1987 by David Pringle

First published in 1987 in Great Britain by Grafton
Books, a division of the Collins Publishing Group, 8
Grafton Street, London W1X 3LA

Library of Congress Cataloging-in-Publication Data

Pringle, David.
Imaginary people.

Bibliography: p.
1. Characters and characteristics in literature –
Dictionaries. I. Title
PN56.4.P75 1988   809'.927   88-60375

ISBN 0-88687-364-9

Photoset in Linotron Trump Mediaeval by Rowland
Phototypesetting Ltd., Bury St. Edmunds, Suffolk
Printed and bound in Great Britain by Hartnolls Ltd,
Bodmin, Cornwall

World Almanac
An Imprint of Pharos Books
A Scripps Howard Company
200 Park Avenue
New York, New York 10166

10 9 8 7 6 5 4 3 2 1

CONTENTS

ACKNOWLEDGMENTS

I have discussed the contents of this book with many friends and acquaintances whose suggestions have been most valuable. I should particularly like to thank Phyllis McDonald for reading an early version of the manuscript and pointing out numerous errors and omissions. I also owe a great (and, I trust, obvious) debt to those critics, commentators and bibliographers whose works are listed at the end of this volume. My heartfelt thanks to them all.

INTRODUCTION

We have all been touched by fictitious persons at numerous points in our lives. They have moved or amused, horrified or inspired us since early childhood. Story-telling is one of the most fundamental of human activities – probably as necessary to our mental health as eating, drinking and breathing are to our physical well-being. Story-telling is inconceivable without characters. In some cases those 'characters' are scarcely human, and take the forms of supernatural beings or anthropomorphized animals. Usually, however, the characters in stories are imaginary human beings. They range from the larger-than-life (frequently omnipotent) heroes and heroines of myth, legend, folk tales and popular fiction, to the all-too-human (often ironically limited) persons who populate realistic novels, plays and films. We first meet them in the nursery, and we continue to meet versions of them throughout our lives. Like it or not, such characters form part of the furniture of our minds.

This book contains short entries which provide information on more than 1,300 modern fictional characters. The characters I have selected range in time from Daniel Defoe's Robinson CRUSOE (created in 1719) to such present-day equivalents of Robinson as Paul Theroux's Allie Fox (who appeared in *The Mosquito Coast*, 1981). I began with Robinson Crusoe because it seemed to me that he is a character who stands squarely at the beginning of a modern tradition. Defoe has often been described as 'the father of the English novel', and even if that label is disputed there can be no doubt that his best-known work has exercised a huge influence on subsequent fiction of various kinds. Not just Allie Fox, but many of the other characters listed in this book are 'sons of' Robinson Crusoe. So I have concentrated on the period of the modern novel, from Defoe to the present. This seems appropriate, since the novel was the first mass art-form, manufactured and distributed by commercial interests to an 'invisible' public of indeterminate extent. But this is not to say that I have considered novels alone: in fact, I have included noteworthy characters from all sources within the period in question – novels, plays, short stories, opera, ballet, comic-strips, songs, films, radio and television. The emphasis is on the fictional creations of the

English-speaking world, although I have also included many foreign
characters who have become well known to English speakers.

With one or two partial exceptions (ALICE, D'ARTAGNAN,
HIAWATHA), I have tried to limit my entries to the strictly fictional.
Actual persons – particularly military heroes and political leaders
ranging from Alexander the Great to John F. Kennedy – have often
been the subjects of novels and films, but such fictional treatments
of the real are not listed here. Nor have I attempted in any
systematic way to point to the 'real' people who are sometimes
alleged to lie behind the fictional – partly because this has already
been done (by Alan Bold and Robert Giddings in their *True
Characters*, 1984, and by William Amos in his *The Originals*,
1985), and partly because this seems in any case to be a dubious
enterprise, one which reduces the products of the creative imagination
to mundane (and often fallacious) reportage. By and large, the present
volume is a *Who's Who* of people who never were: figments,
phantasms, the *dramatis personae* of a modern mythology.

The traditional characters of myth and legend, those of the
Classical, medieval and Renaissance periods, are also excluded – even
though many of them, from Gilgamesh and Theseus through King
Arthur and Robin Hood to Falstaff and Dr Faustus, continue to lead
vigorous lives in the story-telling media of the late twentieth
century. There are already many dictionaries of mythology and
literature, of phrase and fable, which provide information about
these traditional characters. My object was to produce a guidebook to
the *modern* myth-figures, those household names which are almost
entirely the products of recent imaginations.

It follows that this is an eclectic selection. Leopold and Molly
BLOOM rub shoulders with BATMAN and WONDER WOMAN. My
main criterion for including a particular character was that he or
she should have lived beyond the original source. That is to say, the
vast majority of characters included here have been perpetuated by
the original author from work to work, or have been perpetuated by
other authors and by adaptations to different media, or have names
which have entered the language for one reason or another. Some of
the now-forgotten characters were household names in their day;
others became household names only in particular types of household.
Nevertheless, all the characters included here have some claim to
fame – even if in a number of cases that fame was fleeting, or
limited to certain sections of society.

I have attempted in each entry to give a brief outline of the character's 'career' through the years, decades, centuries. This is where my book differs considerably from the only previous attempt to cover a similar field: *Everyman's Dictionary of Fictional Characters* by William Freeman (1963; revised by Fred Urquhart in 1973). Freeman's ground-breaking reference book mentioned the first appearances of many literary characters, but did not attempt to follow those characters through their incarnations in other media. Nor did Freeman choose to mention figures who *originated* in films, comic-strips, and other non-bookish forms.

One feature which I hope proves useful is the listing of 'sequels by other hands'. To the best of my knowledge, no previous reference book has tried to list this peculiar species of fiction – although recent editions of a standard British work, *Sequels* (published by the Association of Assistant Librarians since 1922), make a few half-hearted stabs at it. I have mentioned every sequel by another hand which I came across in the course of my research; but no doubt there are many more that I have not discovered. Sequels by other hands constitute a form of fiction which has flourished in recent years – Nicholas Meyer (and many others) have written Sherlock HOLMES novels, John Gardner has perpetuated James BOND (not to mention Professor MORIARTY), George Macdonald Fraser has resurrected Harry FLASHMAN, and so on – so perhaps the time has come to essay a map of the territory.

Think of it as a working map of the fictional landscapes of our time rather than as a work of literary criticism. I have made the occasional 'value judgement' in order to vary the tone, but such judgements are not the purpose of this book. Rather, I have attempted to show the remarkable longevity and pervasiveness of certain fictional creations, and this has necessitated a degree of neutrality, of openness to the facts. My approach has been all-embracing, 'democratic' and anti-élitist. Conan Doyle was a lesser writer than Leo Tolstoy, yet Sherlock HOLMES demanded a much longer entry in this book than Anna KARENINA. The creations of Edgar Rice Burroughs loom larger than those of Marcel Proust, and this was unavoidable. The great fictional characters – the most fully rounded, the most heart-breakingly human – are not necessarily the most successful. And it is the cultural success of certain imaginary people which interests me here, not their intrinsic value as truthful symbols of the human condition.

Yet there may be truths of a sort to be gained from my quantitative rather than qualitative approach. The fact that Sherlock HOLMES has become the best-known fictional character of the past two centuries is a fact worth pondering. To borrow a phrase from Kingsley Amis, 'unreal policemen' of various kinds – detectives, spies, quasi-criminals, agents and enforcers – seem to constitute the most numerous group in the long list of characters which follows. I trust that this does not reflect a bias towards crime fiction on my own part so much as it reflects an inescapable cultural fact. It may be that the detective/policeman/spy *is* the quintessential fictional character of our time, and if this is so the realization should tell us something about ourselves.

But readers may wish to draw their own conclusions from the mass of evidence which I have accumulated here. I am aware that this evidence is still imperfect and incomplete; there is no definite point at which one can declare a project of this nature 'finished', and I shall be interested to hear from readers concerning any omissions and inaccuracies which strike them as obvious (after all, *everyone* is an expert in this field). Knowing just where to draw the line was my major problem in organizing this book – for example, there are hundreds of other long-lived detectives, policemen and spies that I could have included, not to mention thousands of interesting characters from other forms of fiction – but I offer the results for what they are worth, in the hope that they may prove informative, entertaining and, just possibly, enlightening.

David Pringle
Brighton, 1987

NOTE ON USING THIS BOOK

The characters are arranged in alphabetical order. Each may be found under the best-known form of his or her name. Surnames precede forenames, except in those cases where a character's surname is unknown or very rarely used. Thus we have entries for ADAMS, Alice (the Booth Tarkington character) and for ALICE (the Lewis Carroll character). I have included copious cross-references from well-known forenames to lesser-known surnames. Ranks, titles and other formal indications of status also follow the surname, in those cases where it seems appropriate to cite them – for example BROWN, Father; DRACULA, Count; EASY, Captain; VALIANT, Prince; and WHO, Doctor. Exceptions to these rules are the animal characters – KING KONG, MICKEY MOUSE, MOBY DICK, RUPERT BEAR and so on – who are alphabetized according to the first elements of their names.

There are just two abbreviations which are used repeatedly throughout this book. They are 'dir.', which means 'directed by' (in the case of films), and 'vt', which means 'variant title' (in the case of books). The cross-references are of two kinds: 'see' references, and 'see under' references. The purpose of the latter is to direct readers to information about the lesser characters who have not been given full entries of their own. Where I have cited books by critics and commentators, the details of the works concerned may be found in the bibliography at the end of this volume.

For my wife, Ann, and my son, James

Also for Philip José Farmer,
Leslie A. Fiedler and Leslie Halliwell,
who collectively inspired this book

A

ABBOTT, JUDY Full name Jerusha Abbott, an American orphan who is sent to college by a mysterious gentleman, 'Mr Smith', whom she later meets, loves and marries. It turns out that Mr Smith is a rich philanthropist called Jervis Pendleton. Judy's story is told in Jean Webster's sentimental novel *Daddy Long-Legs* (1912) and its sequel, *Dear Enemy* (1915). The first of these books has been dramatized and filmed several times. In the silent movie *Daddy Long-Legs* (1919; dir. Marshall Neilan) Mary Pickford played Judy. The first talkie version (1931; dir. Alfred Santell) starred Janet Gaynor. In the musical remake (1955; dir. Jean Negulesco) Leslie Caron took the role. The stage musical *Love from Judy* (1953) was also based on the story.

ABEL, GUEVEZ DE ARGENSOLA See under RIMA

ABNER, UNCLE Bible-quoting nineteenth-century backwoods 'detective', a highly respected moral figure in American mystery fiction. He was created by Melville Davisson Post, in short stories which appeared from 1911 and were collected in the book *Uncle Abner: Master of Mysteries* (1918). A posthumous volume, *The Methods of Uncle Abner* (1974), collects later stories by Post first published in magazines of the 1920s.

ABSOLUTE, CAPTAIN JACK Son of Sir Anthony Absolute, and hero of Richard Brinsley Sheridan's play *The Rivals* (1775). He is in love with Lydia Languish, the niece of Mrs MALAPROP, and after many complications he succeeds in winning her hand. According to *Brewer's Dictionary of Phrase and Fable*, Captain Absolute's name is synonymous with 'a bold despotic man determined to have his own way'.

ADAMANT, ADAM Edwardian dandy who is frozen into suspended animation and subsequently thawed out in the 1960s. Played by Gerald Harper, he was the hero of the mid-1960s BBC television series, 'Adam Adamant', created by Verity Lambert and Tony Williamson.

ADAMS, ABRAHAM Parson in Henry Fielding's novel *The Adventures of Joseph Andrews, and of his Friend Mr Abraham Adams* (1742). A delightful quixotic hero, Parson Adams is learned, pugilistic, warm-hearted and very innocent of the ways of the world. J. B. Priestley has written at length about the Parson in his book *The English Comic Characters*: 'Few humorous characters have been so heartily praised as Parson Adams; critic after critic has added to the chorus of praise, and his various oddities, his absent-mindedness and innocent vanity, have been noted in a score of famous volumes.' In the film *Joseph Andrews* (1977; dir. Tony Richardson) Adams was played by Michael Hordern. See Joseph ANDREWS.

ADAMS, ALICE Small-town heroine of Booth Tarkington's novel *Alice Adams* (1921). She is an ambitious girl, but prone to romantic self-deception. The novel was filmed in 1923, with Florence Vidor in the leading role, and again in 1935 (dir. George Stevens), with Katharine Hepburn giving one of her first memorable performances.

ADAMS, HILDA Nurse who doubles as a private detective. Her admiring friend, Inspector Patton, nicknames her 'Miss Pinkerton'. She appears in novels and short stories by the popular American author Mary Roberts Rinehart, including such titles as *Miss Pinkerton* (1932; vt *Double Alibi*), *Mary Roberts Rinehart's Crime Book* (1933) and *The Haunted Lady* (1942). In the film *Miss Pinkerton* (1932; dir. Lloyd Bacon) the heroine was played by Joan Blondell.

ADAMS, NICK Hero of a number of near-autobiographical short stories by Ernest Hemingway which appeared in the collections *In Our Time* (1925), *Men Without Women* (1927) and elsewhere. They were recombined in a posthumous volume entitled *The Nick Adams Stories*. A film, *Hemingway's Adventures of a Young Man* (1962; dir. Martin Ritt) had Richard Beymer in the role of Nick.

ADDAMS FAMILY, THE Spooky family in *New Yorker* cartoons by the artist of the comic/macabre, Charles Addams (who began to produce his characteristic work in 1935). An amusing television series, *The Addams Family* (1964–6), starred John Astin as

Gomez Addams, Carolyn Jones as Morticia, and an ageing and grotesque Jackie Coogan as Uncle Fester. The characters also appeared in a subsequent cartoon series and in a one-off television show, *Halloween with the Addams Family* (1979). In the mid-1980s drawings of the Addams Family were used on London advertising posters to sell the telephone services of British Telecom.

ADELAIDE, MISS   See under Nathan DETROIT

ADLER, IRENE   See under Sherlock HOLMES

ADVERSE, ANTHONY   Hero of the historical novel *Anthony Adverse* (1934) by the American writer Hervey Allen. This book was a huge bestseller in its time (it rivalled Margaret Mitchell's *Gone with the Wind* in the public's affections). Adverse has various adventures in early nineteenth-century Europe and America. He was played by Fredric March in the film of the same title (1936; dir. Mervyn Le Roy).

AELITA   Princess of the planet Mars (more accurately, the daughter of the chairman of the Martian Supreme Council), in an early Soviet science fiction novel, Alexei Tolstoy's *Aelita* (1922). The silent film of the book (1924; dir. Yakov A. Protazanov) starred Yulia Solntseva and was noted for its expressionist technique.

AGENT 99   See under Maxwell SMART

AHAB, CAPTAIN   One-legged master of the whaling-ship *Pequod* in Herman Melville's great novel *Moby Dick, or, The Whale* (1851). Obsessed with killing the elusive white whale, he drives himself and most of his crew to doom. In films, the 'monomaniacal Ahab' has been played twice by John Barrymore – in the silent movie *The Sea Beast* (1926), and in the talkie *Moby Dick* (1930; dir. Lloyd Bacon) – and, rather less convincingly, by Gregory Peck (1956; dir. John Huston). There has also been a notable stage presentation of *Moby Dick* (1955), written and directed by Orson Welles. See also ISHMAEL, MOBY DICK and QUEEQUEG.

AÏDA   Heroine of Giuseppe Verdi's classic opera *Aïda* (1871). She is an Ethiopian princess who is taken for a slave-girl in Egypt at the time of the Pharaohs. She hides away in the crypt where her lover, Radames, is to be buried alive, and the opera ends with her dying in his arms. The libretto is by Antonio Ghislanzoni, based on a French story by Camille du Locle and A. E. Mariette. A film version of the opera (1954; dir. Clemente Fracassi) starred Sophia Loren (but not her singing voice).

ALBERT THE ALLIGATOR   See under POGO

ALBRIGHT, CAPTAIN   See Captain MIDNIGHT

ALDRICH, HENRY   Accident-prone middle-American teenager created by Clifford Goldsmith for his play *What a Life!* (1938). Its success soon led to a radio series, in which actor Ezra Stone, who had played Henry on stage, gave voice to the character. Goldsmith's play was filmed under its original title (1939; dir. Theodore Reed), with Jackie Cooper taking the lead role. A second film, with much the same cast, was *Life With Henry* (1941). Actor Jimmy Lydon then replaced Jackie Cooper for a further nine films, including such titles as *Henry Aldrich for President* (1941), *Henry Aldrich, Editor* (1942), *Henry Aldrich Haunts a House* (1943) and *Henry Aldrich Plays Cupid* (1944). One of the earliest regular comedy series on American television was *The Aldrich Family* (1949–53). This starred Robert Casey as Henry (later replaced by Bobby Ellis, among others). The film critic Leonard Maltin describes Henry Aldrich as 'America's dumbest high-schooler – dumb, yet in an odd way, endearing'.

ALEX   Juvenile anti-hero of Anthony Burgess's comic/horrific novel *A Clockwork Orange* (1962). Alex is a mugger, a rapist and a murderer. He is also a lover of classical music. While in prison, he is conditioned to behave meekly – and is devastated to find that he can no longer enjoy Beethoven. The novel formed the basis of a remarkable film (1971; dir. Stanley Kubrick), in which Malcolm McDowell played Alex.

ALEXIS   See Alexis Carrington COLBY

ALFIE   See Alfie ELKINS

ALGERNON See under Charlie GORDON

ALGY PUG See under RUPERT BEAR

ALICE Little girl of Victorian times who has some very odd
experiences in strange realms of the imagination. She appears in
Alice's Adventures in Wonderland (1865) and *Through the
Looking-Glass and What Alice Found There* (1871) by Lewis
Carroll (Charles Lutwidge Dodgson), where she encounters such
delightfully memorable characters as the White Rabbit, the
Cheshire Cat, the Mad Hatter, the Mock Turtle, and the Red
Queen and White Queen. As all the world now knows, Alice was
modelled on a real-life girl of Dodgson's acquaintance, Alice
Liddell – but since the author never mentions her surname, and
since her adventures are wholly fantastic, she counts for our
purposes as a fictional character. Indeed, she is one of the most
famous characters in the whole of English-language fiction, an
everlasting childhood favourite who retains an enormous appeal for
adults. The literature on Alice is vast, ranging from the meticulous
scholarship of *The Annotated Alice* (1960) by Martin Gardner,
through such studies as *Alice in Many Tongues* (1964) by Warren
Weaver (the Alice books have been translated 'more often and
into more languages than almost any other work except the Bible',
according to *The Oxford Companion to Children's Literature*)
to the critical compendium *Aspects of Alice* (1972) edited by
Robert Phillips. There have also been modern sequels by other
hands; one recent example is *Alice Through the Needle's Eye*
(1984) by Gilbert Adair.

   Our conceptions of Alice over the decades owe a great deal to
the illustrators of Carroll's books, first and foremost among them
John Tenniel. Other artists who have drawn distinctive pictures
to accompany the texts include Arthur Rackham, Mabel Lucie
Attwell, Mervyn Peake, Ralph Steadman and even Salvador Dali.
There have been countless stage adaptations of Alice's
adventures, beginning with an operetta, *Alice in Wonderland*
(1886), by Henry Savile Clarke. There have also been many
films since the first short silent version was made in 1903. (Unless
otherwise indicated, all of the adaptations mentioned in the
following paragraph are called *Alice in Wonderland*, although in
fact many of them use material from *Through the Looking-Glass*.)

Silent movies were produced in 1910, 1915 and 1927. The first
Hollywood sound version (1933; dir. Norman Z. McLeod) starred
Charlotte Henry as Alice. It was followed by a full-length Disney
cartoon (1951; dir. Clyde Geronimi, Hamilton Luske and Wilfred
Jackson); this almost coincided with a lesser-known British
version (1950; dir. Dallas Bower) which had Carole Marsh as Alice
amidst a cast of puppets. Versions since then include a remarkable
BBC television adaptation (1966; dir. Jonathan Miller), starring
Anne-Marie Malik, which reinterpreted the books as a child's-

Alice as drawn by *John Tenniel*

eye view of a nightmarishly threatening Victorian society; and an insipid musical film, *Alice's Adventures in Wonderland* (1972; dir. William Sterling), with Fiona Fullerton. A recent five-part adaptation for British independent television (1985; dir. Harry Aldous) had Giselle Andrews as Alice, with puppets as the other characters. An American 'mini-series' version (also 1985), with Natalie Gregory as Alice, is described by Leslie Halliwell as 'mind-boggling' and a 'travesty'. (The film *Dreamchild* [1986; dir. Gavin Millar] starred Coral Browne as the real-life Alice Liddell.)

ALLARD, KENT   See The SHADOW

ALLEY OOP   Comic-strip caveman invented by the American cartoonist V. T. Hamlin in 1933. Alley's girlfriend is named Oola, and he has a pet dinosaur called Dinny. Hamlin continued to draw the strip until 1971, and Alley Oop and his friends were still going strong a decade later.

ALLEYN, RODERICK   Old-Etonian policeman in more than thirty crime novels by the New Zealand writer Ngaio Marsh, commencing with *A Man Lay Dead* (1934). Alleyn's later cases include *Enter a Murderer* (1935), *The Nursing Home Murder* (1935), *Death in Ecstasy* (1936), *Artists in Crime* (1938), *Overture to Death* (1939), *Death at the Bar* (1940), *Surfeit of Lampreys* (1940; vt *Death of a Peer*), *Died in the Wool* (1945), *Swing, Brother, Swing* (1949; vt *A Wreath for Rivera*), *Spinsters in Jeopardy* (1953; vt *The Brides of Death*), *Death of a Fool* (1956; vt *Off With His Head*), *Singing in the Shrouds* (1958), *Killer Dolphin* (1966; vt *Death at the Dolphin*), *Clutch of Constables* (1968), *When in Rome* (1970) and *Black as He's Painted* (1974). Alleyn ages realistically throughout the series, and in *Last Ditch* (1977) his son Ricky takes over the role of detective. The last Alleyn novels are *Photo Finish* (1980) and *Light Thickens* (1982).

ALLNUTT, CHARLIE   Hero of C. S. Forester's exciting novel *The African Queen* (1935). A good-for-nothing riverboat engineer in Africa at the outbreak of World War I, he comes under the influence of a missionary's wife, Rose Sayer, who persuades him to join the fray. They turn their leaky old craft into a 'torpedo', and eventually ram and sink a German gunboat. The novel was

filmed, very successfully, from a script by James Agee (1951; dir.
John Huston), and the role of Charlie Allnutt provided
Humphrey Bogart with one of his most memorable parts. Years
later, Warren Oates played Allnutt in the pilot for a proposed
US television series (1977).

ALLWORTHY, SQUIRE   See under Tom JONES

ALMAYER, KASPAR   European trader in the Dutch East Indies,
desirous of riches and inordinately proud of his half-caste daughter.
He appears, along with another recurring character, Captain Tom
Lingard, in Joseph Conrad's early novels *Almayer's Folly* (1895)
and *An Outcast of the Islands* (1896). In the film of the latter title
(1951; dir. Carol Reed) Almayer was played by Robert Morley.

ALOMA   Beautiful Polynesian heroine of a popular American play,
Aloma of the South Seas by John B. Hymer and Leroy Clemens. In
the silent film of the same title (1926; dir. Maurice Tourneur) she
was played by Gilda Gray. The talkie remake (1941; dir. Alfred
Santell) starred Dorothy Lamour.

ALVIN CHIPMUNK   Leader of 'The Chipmunks', an imaginary
singing trio which had an enormous success in America and
elsewhere with a novelty record called 'The Chipmunk Song'
(1958). This was followed by various other hits. The Chipmunks'
high-pitched voices were in fact provided by David Seville (Ross
Bagdasarian). Alvin was the mischievous leader of the group;
his brothers were named Simon and Theodore. The three appeared
in an animated television series, 'The Alvin Show' (1961–2).

AMBER   See Amber ST CLAIR

AMBROSIO   Villain of Matthew Gregory Lewis's gothic horror
novel *The Monk* (1796). Ambrosio is a Spanish monk who is led
astray by his sexual urges. He pursues a young woman, kills her,
and is eventually arrested and tortured by the Inquisition. He makes
a pact with the devil to escape the stake, and is utterly damned.
This unpleasant sado-masochistic farrago was one of the most
popular novels of its day, and is regarded by some critics as the
greatest of the English 'Gothics'.

AMELIA   See Amelia Booth

AMERICA, CAPTAIN   Costumed superhero created by Joe Simon
and Jack Kirby for a comic-book which first appeared in March
1941. The Captain began life as a weakling called Steve Rogers.
Injected with a wonder drug, he gains mighty muscles and sets
about bashing Nazis. Clad in a Stars-and-Stripes costume and a
tight-fitting hood with a big letter 'A' on the brow, he proceeds to
win World War II almost single-handed (he has some help from a
boy sidekick named Bucky). His principal enemy is a spy-leader
known as the Red Skull. After the war ended, Captain America
lost his *raison d'être* and the comic-book went downhill. 'The
greatest champion of democracy' was revived briefly in 1954 in
order to fight the Communist Menace. He came to life again
during the new superhero boom of the late 1960s, and has appeared
sporadically in various Marvel Comics titles ever since. A
cinema serial, *Captain America* (1944), starred Dick Purcell as
the hero ('Purcell's serial role was strenuous . . . Only a few
weeks after completing *Captain America*, Purcell collapsed in
the locker room of a Los Angeles country club and died. The
strain of his vigorous assignment had taxed his heart too heavily'
– R. W. Stedman, *The Serials*). Decades later two TV movies,
Captain America (1978) and *Return of Captain America* (1979),
were made as pilots for a series which failed to materialize. These
starred Reb Brown as the original Captain's supposed son. Novels
which feature Captain America include *The Great Gold Steal*
(1968) by Ted White, and *Holocaust for Hire* (1979) by Joseph Silva.

AMES, JANET   See Sheena

AMOS AND ANDY   Amos Jones and Andy Brown, a pair of blackface
clowns in a very popular American radio series, 'Amos 'n' Andy',
broadcast from the 1920s to the 1940s. The white comedians who
impersonated Amos and Andy were Freeman S. Gosden and Charles
V. Correll. They also played the characters in one feature film,
Check and Double Check (1932; dir. Melville Brown). An
'Amos 'n' Andy' series appeared on American television in
1951–3, but by this time the material was regarded as offensive,
even though the latter series featured black actors (Alvin Childress
and Spencer Williams) in the lead roles.

ANCIENT MARINER, THE   Aged sailor with a compelling eye, who
is obliged to tell his horrific story over and over again. He
appears in Samuel Taylor Coleridge's magical poem 'The Rime of
the Ancient Mariner' – first published in *Lyrical Ballads* (1798), a
volume of verse by Coleridge and William Wordsworth. The
Mariner is sole survivor of a voyage to the south seas, during which
he committed the crime of killing a friendly albatross (symbol of
good fortune). The bird's carcass is hung around the Mariner's
neck by his horrified shipmates; nevertheless every man on the
voyage comes to woe. Written in the style of a traditional ballad,
the poem is packed with wonderful romantic imagery and
hauntingly memorable lines. The Mariner's influence has been
immense – a great deal of the imaginative writing of the past

The Ancient Mariner is relieved of his burden

century and a half abounds with references to him – and over
the years the poem has been illustrated by Gustave Doré and
Mervyn Peake among many others.

ANDERSON, JIM AND MARGARET   Good-humoured, level-
headed, middle-American parents in the radio comedy series 'Father
Knows Best' (from 1949). Their lively offspring were named Betty,
Bud and Kathy Anderson. The wise Jim Anderson was played
by Robert Young, who also took the role when the series was
transferred to television (1954–60). On TV, Margaret Anderson
was played by Jane Wyatt. The show is fondly remembered as 'the
classic wholesome family situation comedy' (in the words of
Tim Brooks and Earle Marsh).

ANDERSON, PEPPER   Attractive blonde police sergeant played by
Angie Dickinson in the popular American television series 'Police
Woman' (1974–8). The series was a spin-off from the slightly
earlier 'Police Story', and both series were produced by David
Gerber.

ANDREWS, ARCHIE   Puppet teenager who appeared on BBC radio
from 1944 to 1960. Even though it seemed a contradiction in terms
to present a ventriloquist's dummy on the air, the series 'Archie
Takes the Helm' (later replaced by 'Educating Archie' and
'Archie's the Boy') proved extremely popular. Archie's voice was
provided by Peter Brough, and the character was conceived by
scriptwriter Ted Kavanagh. Comedians and singers who played
opposite young Archie Andrews during his long run include
Hattie Jacques, Max Bygraves, Julie Andrews, Tony Hancock,
Alfred Marks, Harry Secombe, Bernard Miles, James Robertson
Justice, Beryl Reid, Dick Emery, Warren Mitchell, Bernard
Bresslaw, Bruce Forsyth and Sidney James. At the height of the
character's popularity an Archie Andrews stage show toured
Britain and a waxwork model of the puppet was displayed in
Madame Tussaud's. (For a completely different Archie Andrews
see ARCHIE.)

ANDREWS, JOSEPH   Likeable young hero of Henry Fielding's novel
*The Adventures of Joseph Andrews and of his Friend Mr
Abraham Adams* (1742). Joseph is supposed to be the brother of

Pamela ANDREWS (Samuel Richardson's heroine), and the novel was originally intended as a parody of *Pamela*. It soon takes on a life of its own, however, when Joseph sets out on his travels in the company of the wonderful Parson Abraham ADAMS. In the film *Joseph Andrews* (1977; dir. Tony Richardson) Joseph was played by Peter Firth.

ANDREWS, PAMELA   Suffering heroine of Samuel Richardson's first novel *Pamela, or Virtue Rewarded* (1740). Determined to protect her virginity from an aristocratic seducer, she suffers all manner of persecution up to and including attempted rape. Intolerably frustrated, and impressed by her moral steadfastness, her persecutor offers to marry her; after some prevarication, she consents, and her middle-class 'virtue' is duly rewarded. This story proved very popular indeed, and anonymous parodies, pastiches and continuations by other hands began to appear almost immediately (the most famous of these is *Shamela* by Henry Fielding). To forestall such plagiarism, Richardson himself continued the story in *Pamela, Part II* (1741), which deals interminably with his heroine's married life. His rival Fielding was to produce another mocking 'sequel', however; the latter's *Joseph Andrews* purports to be about Pamela's handsome brother (see Joseph ANDREWS). Latterly, *Pamela* has been dramatized for the British stage by Giles Havergal (1985).

ANDY PANDY   Puppet in a blue-striped suit who appeared in the BBC television programme 'Watch with Mother' during the 1950s. His friends are a Teddy bear and a rag doll, Looby Loo. He also appears in a long series of little books, written by Maria Bird and illustrated by Marvyn Wright (1954 onwards). (Andy Pandy should not be confused with the American cartoon character Andy Panda, created by animator Walter Lantz in the late 1930s.)

ANGELIQUE   Seventeenth-century female picaroon who features in a series of bawdy historical novels by the French husband-and-wife writing team Serge and Anne Golon (writing as 'Sergeanne Golon'). According to the blurb on the British Pan Books edition Angélique is 'the most ravishing – and surely the most ravished – heroine of all time'. The books have been international bestsellers since the late 1950s. They have been translated into English as *Angélique I: The Marquise of Angels* (1958), *Angélique II: The Road to Versailles* (1958), *Angélique and the King* (1960), *Angélique and the Sultan* (1961), *Angélique in Revolt* (1962), *Angélique in Love* (1963), *The Countess Angélique* (1965), *The Temptation of Angélique* (1969), *Angélique and the Demon* (1973) and *Angélique and the Ghosts* (1977). A series of French films has been based on the character. It began with *Angélique* (1964; dir. Bernard Borderie), which starred Michèle Mercier as the lovely wanton.

ANGSTROM, HARRY   Known as 'Rabbit', middle-American anti-hero of John Updike's novels *Rabbit, Run* (1960), *Rabbit Redux* (1971) and *Rabbit is Rich* (1981). Once a basketball champion, Angstrom has become a well-to-do car-dealer, limited and complacent in his attitudes, something of a latter-day George F. BABBITT. *Rabbit, Run* was filmed (1970; dir. Jack Smight), with James Caan in the principal part.

ANN VERONICA   See Ann Veronica STANLEY

ANNE OF GREEN GABLES   See Anne SHIRLEY

ANNIE   See LITTLE ORPHAN ANNIE

ANVILLE, EVELINA   English débutante, in Fanny Burney's epistolary novel *Evelina, or The History of a Young Lady's Entrance into the World* (1778). Although her parentage is mysterious, Evelina is introduced into London society and is courted by various eligible young men. All ends happily when her true lineage is established and she marries Lord Orville. Fanny Burney's sprightly novel was much admired and imitated.

APPLEBY, HUMPHREY   See under Jim HACKER

APPLEBY, JOHN   Erudite police detective created by Michael Innes (J. I. M. Stewart) for a long series of novels commencing with *Death at the President's Lodging* (1936; vt *Seven Suspects*). Appleby must be the best-read policeman in fiction, always able to come up with an apt literary quotation – the books in which he

appears are the archetypal 'donnish' detective novels (see also
Gervase FEN and Nigel STRANGEWAYS). Other titles are *Hamlet,
Revenge!* (1937), *Lament for a Maker* (1938), *Stop Press* (1939; vt
The Spider Strikes) and almost thirty more, among them a number
which feature the detective's name in the title: *Appleby on Ararat*
(1941), *Appleby's End* (1945), *Appleby Talking* (1954; vt *Dead
Man's Shows*), *Appleby Talks Again* (1957), *Appleby Plays Chicken*
(1957; vt *Death on a Quiet Day*), *Appleby at Allington* (1968; vt
Death by Water), *Appleby's Answer* (1973), *Appleby's Other Story*
(1974) and *The Appleby File* (1976). Later Appleby novels are *The
Ampersand Papers* (1978), *Sheiks and Adders* (1982) and *Appleby
and the Ospreys* (1986 – published on its author's eightieth
birthday). By now the hero is a grand old man of the British
police force, and has received a knighthood.

AQUAMAN   See under SUB-MARINER

ARAGORN   See under Frodo BAGGINS

ARAMIS   See under D'ARTAGNAN

ARBUTHNOT, SANDY   Full name the Hon. Ludovick Gustavus
Arbuthnot (later Baron Clanroyden) – a dashing young man-about-
the-Empire in John Buchan's *Greenmantle* (1916) and other
novels. It is said of Sandy Arbuthnot that 'he rode through Yemen,
which no white man ever did before . . . He's blood-brother to
every kind of Albanian bandit' and 'he used to take a hand in
Turkish politics'. He helps Richard HANNAY to solve the mystery
of the Islamic prophet known as Greenmantle, and later plays
a prominent part in other adventures which are chronicled in the
books *The Three Hostages* (1924), *The Courts of the Morning* (1929),
and *The Island of Sheep* (1936). Sandy appears briefly as a friend
of Sir Edward LEITHEN in *Sick Heart River* (1941; vt *Mountain
Meadow*). He also makes several appearances in Buchan's short
story collection *The Runagates Club* (1928).

ARCHER, DAN AND DORIS   Farming couple in the BBC's long-
running radio serial 'The Archers' (from 1950). The programme was
announced as 'an everyday story of country folk', and part of its
original purpose was to provide sugar-coated advice on better

farming techniques. Dan and Doris live on Brookfield Farm near the village of Ambridge, somewhere in the western shires of England. Their neighbours include the gravel-voiced Walter GABRIEL. In the original cast Harry Oakes was Dan and Gwen Berryman was Doris. Other actors who have played Dan Archer over the years include Monte Crick, Edgar Harrison and Frank Middlemass. A novelization of the early scripts is *The Archers of Ambridge* (1955) by Geoffrey Webb and Edward J. Mason. A novel which serves as a 'prequel' to the main story is *Spring at Brookfield* (1975) by Brian Hayles: this tells how the young Dan Archer woos and wins Doris Forest in the years shortly after World War I. There have been several other books which celebrate the radio series in various ways. A recent example is *The Archers: The Official Companion* (1985) by William Smethurst. Dan Archer finally died at the age of eighty-nine, in 1986 (although the radio programme goes on). The character's autobiography, *The Ambridge Years* (1986), was 'ghosted' by William Smethurst and Anthony Parkin.

ARCHER, ISABEL   American girl in Europe, heroine of Henry James's novel *The Portrait of a Lady* (1881). Wooed by various eligible men, she 'affronts her destiny' by marrying the unworthy Gilbert Osmond, who brings her unhappiness. The novel, which has been described as one of Henry James's finest by F. R. Leavis, Graham Greene and others, was dramatized for the London stage in 1883, and has been serialized on BBC television (1968).

ARCHER, LEW   Thoughtful private-eye hero of a series of novels by Ross Macdonald (Kenneth Millar), starting with *The Moving Target* (1949). He haunts the same Californian landscape as Chandler's Philip MARLOWE, finding skeletons in many a wealthy family's closet. His subsequent adventures are recounted by Macdonald in *The Drowning Pool* (1950), *The Way Some People Die* (1951), *The Ivory Grin* (1952), *Find a Victim* (1954), *The Name is Archer* (1955), *The Barbarous Coast* (1956), *The Doomsters* (1958), *The Galton Case* (1959), *The Wycherley Woman* (1961), *The Zebra-Striped Hearse* (1962), *The Chill* (1964), *The Far Side of the Dollar* (1965), *Black Money* (1966), *The Instant Enemy* (1968), *The Goodbye Look* (1969), *The Underground Man* (1971), *Sleeping Beauty* (1973), *The Blue Hammer* (1976) and *Lew Archer,*

Private Investigator (1977). Archer has been played by Paul
Newman in two movies (where, irritatingly, the character's name
is changed to 'Harper'): *Harper* (1966; vt *The Moving Target*;
dir. Jack Smight) and *The Drowning Pool* (1975; dir. Stuart
Rosenberg). Peter Graves played him in the TV movie *The
Underground Man* (1974; dir. Paul Wendkos); and Brian Keith
essayed the role in the follow-on TV series, 'Archer' (1975).

ARCHIE   Red-headed teenager at Riverdale High School
(somewhere in the USA). He was created by editor John L.
Goldwater and artist Bob Montana for *Pep Comics* in 1941. (His
surname is Andrews, but he should not be confused with Archie
ANDREWS, the British puppet character.) Within a few years Archie
had his own comic-book, the first of a proliferating family of
titles issued by Archie Comic Publications Inc. Drawn by a
number of different artists, Archie and his host of friends have
continued their high-jinks for over forty years. In recent times
Archie has doubled as a costumed superhero, Pureheart the
Powerful.

ARDEN, DALE   See under Flash GORDON

ARDEN, ENOCH   Central character of a narrative poem by Alfred,
Lord Tennyson (1864). Enoch is shipwrecked, and after ten years
on a desert island returns to England to find that his beloved wife
has remarried. Rather than spoil her new happiness, he does not
reveal himself, and dies. This touching Victorian fable has been
dramatized and filmed several times (the great American director
D. W. Griffith made two silent movie versions). The Hollywood
comedy *My Favourite Wife* (1940; dir. Garson Kanin) is about a
certain Mrs Arden, played by Irene Dunne, who is stranded on an
island for several years; when she returns to America she
discovers that her handsome husband (Cary Grant) has married
another woman . . .

ARMITAGE, JO   Middle-class Englishwoman whose marriage goes
sadly awry, in Penelope Mortimer's novel *The Pumpkin Eater*
(1960). In the powerful film of the book (1964; dir. Jack Clayton),
which was scripted by Harold Pinter, Jo was played by Anne
Bancroft.

ARMSTRONG, JACK   Hero of 'Jack Armstrong, the All-American Boy', a radio series which was broadcast in the United States from 1933 to 1951. He was the creation of scriptwriter Robert Hardy Andrews, and the first actor to provide his voice was Jim Ameche (brother of Don Ameche). A latter-day Frank MERRIWELL (or Jack HARKAWAY), Jack Armstrong begins as a sports-loving schoolboy but soon embarks on globe-trotting adventures with the help of his Uncle Jim (owner of a hydroplane, an autogyro, a dirigible and other marvellous vehicles). The vigorous young hero also appeared in a 1940s comic-book (where his All-American Motto was: 'To keep myself straight and strong and clean, in mind as well as in body') and in a Columbia Pictures serial, *Jack Armstrong* (1947).

ARN   See under Prince VALIANT

ARNOUX, MARIE   See under Frédéric MOREAU

ARON, SIMON   See under Duke DE RICHLEAU

ARROWSMITH, MARTIN   Idealistic man of medicine, in Sinclair Lewis's novel *Arrowsmith* (1925). He begins his career in a small American town, exhausts himself in research, and later fights disease on a Caribbean island. Lewis was offered the Pulitzer Prize for this book, but refused to accept it because he objected to a clause which suggested winning novelists should depict 'the wholesome atmosphere of American Life'. In the film of the novel (1932; dir. John Ford) Dr Arrowsmith was played by Ronald Colman.

ARTFUL DODGER, THE   See under FAGIN

ASCH, HERBERT   Soldier in Hitler's army whose impertinent, deceitful ways are the subject of a series of comic novels by Hans Helmut Kirst. In English, the series consists of *The Revolt of Gunner Asch* (1955), *Forward Gunner Asch!* (1956), *The Return of Gunner Asch* (1957), and *What Became of Gunner Asch* (1964).

ASCHENBACH, GUSTAVE VON   Ailing German writer who goes south for the sake of his health. In Venice he is smitten with love

for a beautiful young boy, Tadzio. A plague breaks out;
Aschenbach lingers too long in the city, contracts the disease,
and dies. The story is told in Thomas Mann's moving novella
Death in Venice (1912). In the notable film version (1971; dir.
Luchino Visconti) Aschenbach is reimagined as a composer
(transparently based on Gustav Mahler). He was played, with
sensitivity, by Dirk Bogarde. Mann's tale has also formed the basis
of an opera by Benjamin Britten (1973).

ASHENDEN   Secret agent in short stories by W. Somerset
Maugham, collected in the book *Ashenden, or The British Agent*
(1928). The episodes are set during World War I, and are based on
Maugham's own experience in British Intelligence. Ashenden
is a new sort of spy in English fiction, devoted to a rather humdrum
routine far from the heroics imagined by more romantic writers.
He also makes an appearance in Maugham's novel *Cakes and Ale*
(1930). The film *The Secret Agent* (1936; dir. Alfred Hitchcock),
with John Gielgud, is based on Ashenden's exploits.

ASHLEY, LADY BRETT   See under Jake BARNES

ASHTON, LUCY   Heroine of Sir Walter Scott's novel *The Bride of
Lammermoor* (1819), which is set in seventeenth-century Scotland.
Her father is an enemy of the powerful Ravenswood family,
despite which Lucy falls in love with Edgar, the young Master
of Ravenswood. Their love is thwarted, however, when Lucy's
parents force her to marry another. She stabs her new husband,
goes mad, and dies. This grisly story forms the basis of Gaetano
Donizetti's opera *Lucia di Lammermoor* (1835), which has a libretto
(freely adapted from the Scott novel) by Salvatore Cammarano.
(Donizetti was a prolific composer of operas, and seems to have
been drawn to British themes; another of his works has the exotic
title *Emilia di Liverpool*.) Scott's novel has been serialized on
BBC radio (1982), with Gerda Stevenson as Lucy Ashton.

ASLAN   Magnificent lion who acts as an unlikely Christ-figure in
C. S. Lewis's children's novel *The Lion, the Witch and the Wardrobe*
(1950). He presides over the land of Narnia – which Peter, Susan,
Lucy and Edmund reach by way of an old wardrobe. Aslan
reappears in the later books of the series: *Prince Caspian* (1951),

The Voyage of the 'Dawn Treader' (1952), *The Silver Chair* (1953), *The Horse and His Boy* (1954), *The Magician's Nephew* (1955) and *The Last Battle* (1956). He is a character who has made some adult readers uneasy. Margery Fisher writes: 'To many adults, whether they think of Christ as man, archetypal scapegoat or the Son of God, Aslan remains an inadequate and in some ways a distasteful character. He is, besides, a character who strikes at the very root of the adventure story. Virtue, in the Narnia books, is seen ultimately to lie in obedience and not in brave, hazardous free decision . . .' An animated TV movie, *The Lion, the Witch and the Wardrobe* (1978; dir. Bill Melendez) won an Emmy Award. There has also been a successful UK stage production of the novel.

ASPERN, JEFFREY   See under Juliana BORDEREAU

ASTA   See under Nick and Nora CHARLES

ASTERIX   An ancient Gaul, short of stature but with a most impressive moustache, created by artist Albert Uderzo and writer René Goscinny for strip cartoons published in France since 1959. Asterix and his friends – who include Obelix the muscle-man and Getafix the Druid – have become internationally famous, and the many books of their amusing adventures have been translated widely. There have been several French animated films, including *Asterix the Gaul* (1967), *Asterix and Cleopatra* (1970) and *The Twelve Labours of Asterix* (1975). Asterix has also appeared on BBC radio, and has featured as a 'character' in computer games.

ATHOS   See under D'ARTAGNAN

ATREIDES, PAUL   Also known as Muad'Dib, a prince who inherits the planet Arrakis (Dune) from his murdered father and has to fight long and hard to secure his rights. With the help of the Fremen, hardy desert-dwellers, and the Sandworms, spectacular monsters which are the source of a spice that confers longevity, Paul becomes a charismatic leader. All this is narrated in Frank Herbert's bestselling science fiction novel *Dune* (1965). Paul's later career is recounted in the sequel *Dune Messiah* (1969), and the generations-long saga of the Atreides family and the planet

Arrakis is extended over several more books: *Children of Dune* (1976), *God-Emperor of Dune* (1981), *Heretics of Dune* (1984) and *Chapter-House Dune* (1985). Biographies of Paul and the members of his family are provided in an impressively detailed secondary tome, *The Dune Encyclopedia* (1984) compiled by Willis E. McNelly. A film, *Dune* (1984; dir. David Lynch), starred Kenneth McMillan as Paul.

AUBREY, JACK   English sea-faring hero of the Napoleonic Wars, introduced by Patrick O'Brian in his novel *Master and Commander* (1970). Aubrey is large, clumsy and enthusiastic – and something of a foil to Dr Stephen Maturin, his quick-witted ship's surgeon. The other titles in the series are *Post Captain* (1972), *H.M.S. Surprise* (1975), *The Mauritius Command* (1977), *Desolation Island* (1978), *The Fortune of War* (1979), *Surgeon's Mate* (1980), *The Ionian Mission* (1981), *Treason's Harbour* (1983), *The Far Side of the World* (1985) and *The Reverse of the Medal* (1986). Many critics find Jack Aubrey the most entertaining of the sons of HORNBLOWER (others include Richard BOLITHO, Richard DELANCEY and Nicholas RAMAGE).

AUDLEY, DAVID   British intelligence operative who has appeared in some sixteen spy thrillers by Anthony Price, beginning with *The Labyrinth Makers* (1970). Audley is a backroom boy who nevertheless finds himself dragged into the action. He has been described as 'formidably intelligent'. Other titles in the series include: *The Alamut Ambush* (1971), *Colonel Butler's Wolf* (1972), *The October Men* (1973), *Other Paths to Glory* (1974), *Our Man in Camelot* (1975), *War Game* (1976), *The '44 Vintage* (1977 – this one tells of Audley's early career during World War II), *Tomorrow's Ghost* (1979), *The Hour of the Donkey* (1980), *Soldier No More* (1981), *The Old Vengeful* (1982), *Gunner Kelly* (1983), *Here Be Monsters* (1985) and *For the Good of the State* (1986). Dr David Audley has been played by David Hemmings in a short-lived series on British television (early 1980s).

AUDLEY, LADY LUCY   Real name Helen Maldon, later Mrs George Talboys, who adopts the name Lucy Graham and bigamously marries Sir Michael Audley. She is the conniving, mentally unstable woman of mystery in Mary Elizabeth Braddon's novel *Lady*

Audley's Secret (1862). Her most notorious act is the attempted murder of her first husband, Mr Talboys, whom she pushes down a well. Miss Braddon's melodramatic novel was immensely popular, and has been described as 'one of the top two bestsellers in English nineteenth-century fiction' (the other is Mrs Henry Wood's *East Lynne* – see Lady Isabel VANE). There were several silent movie versions of *Lady Audley's Secret*, including one which starred Theda Bara (1915).

AURA, PRINCESS   See under MING THE MERCILESS

AUSTIN, STEVE   'Bionic man', protagonist of Martin Caidin's novel *Cyborg* (1972). Austin is a test pilot who crashes, is badly injured, and is rebuilt as part man, part machine. As he adjusts to his new body he discovers that he has wonderfully enhanced physical powers. He uses these to pursue various villains. Sequels, also by Caidin, are *Operation Nuke* (1973), *High Crystal* (1974) and *Cyborg IV* (1975). The first novel formed the basis of a very successful television series, 'The Six Million Dollar Man' (1973–8), with Lee Majors as Austin. This in turn led to a spin-off series, *The Bionic Woman* (scc Jaime SOMMERS). There was also a *Six Million Dollar Man* comic-book in the late 1970s.

AXEL, COUNT   Young aesthete who immures himself in a lonely Black Forest castle, in Villers de L'Isle Adam's symbolist play *Axel* (1890). He has much in common with Huysmans' Duc Jean DES ESSEINTES, and when he is exhorted to use his great wealth to pursue a full and active life, he replies, famously: 'Live? Our servants will do that for us . . .' Edmund Wilson's influential book about modernism in literature, *Axel's Castle* (1931), is named in honour of this strange character and his creator. The hero of J. G. Ballard's short story 'The Garden of Time' (1962) is also called Count Axel: he attempts to halt the passage of time by plucking the crystalline 'time flowers' which grow in the garden of his villa.

AYACANORA   See under Amyas LEIGH

AYESHA   See SHE-WHO-MUST-BE-OBEYED

AYLA   Stone-age blonde in the bestselling novels of Jean M. Auel (described by one reviewer as 'paleolithic soap opera'). Ayla is a well-developed Cro-Magnon who falls in with a tribe of hairy Neanderthals. Her uplifting story is told in *The Clan of the Cave Bear* (1980) and its sequels *The Valley of the Horses* (1982) and *The Mammoth Hunters* (1985). In the movie *The Clan of the Cave Bear* (1986; dir. Michael Chapman) Ayla was played by Daryl Hannah.

AZIZ, DOCTOR   Sympathetic Indian doctor of medicine, in E. M. Forster's novel *A Passage to India* (1924). He is accused of assaulting the Englishwoman Adela Quested in the Marabar caves, and is made to stand trial. Although acquitted, he is permanently embittered. A BBC television adaptation (1965) had Zia Moyheddin as the doctor. In the later film of the novel (1984; dir. David Lean) Aziz was played very effectively by Victor Bannerjee.

Dr Aziz (Victor Bannerjee) in the film *A Passage to India*

B

B.D.   See under DOONESBURY

BABAR   Well-dressed African elephant in books for young children written and illustrated by Jean de Brunhoff (published in French from 1931 onwards). In English the titles are: *The Story of Babar* (1934), *Babar's Travels* (1935), *Babar the King* (1936), *Babar's Friend Zephir* (1937), *Babar's ABC* (1937), *Babar at Home* (1938) and *Babar and Father Christmas* (1940). After the author's death his son Laurent de Brunhoff continued the series with *Babar and That Rascal Arthur* (1947) and many other titles. Babar has appeared in a television series, and has also provided inspiration for Francis Poulenc, the French composer: 'Poulenc added a new and illuminating dimension to Babar when he composed a sequence of piano pieces that illustrated the first stories gracefully and expressively and subtly suggested Babar's pachydermatous moods and movements' – Margery Fisher. The Marxist critic Ariel Dorfman has written at length about Babar in his book *The Empire's Old Clothes* (1983).

BABBITT, GEORGE F.   Small-town real-estate agent, protagonist of the novel *Babbitt* (1922) by Sinclair Lewis. He is a devoted businessman, a patriotic optimist, and a member of the 'Elks'. He rebels, all too briefly, before reaffirming his lot in life. His creator views him sardonically, and Babbitt's name has become a byword for American middle-class philistinism. The novel was a great success, and a silent movie version of the story was released in 1924. It was remade as a talkie under the same title (1934; dir. William Keighley), with the plump actor Guy Kibbee in the leading role.

BABY DUMPLING   See under BLONDIE

BABY JANE   Grotesque ageing film actress, a former child star, played by Bette Davis in the film *Whatever Happened to Baby Jane?* (1962; dir. Robert Aldrich). This unpleasant story, in which

Baby Jane torments her sister, has been described as 'a sado-
gerontophilic exercise in Hollywood *Grand Guignol*' (John Baxter,
Hollywood in the Sixties). The script is based on a novel by
Henry Farrell.

BACKBITE, SIR BENJAMIN   See under Charles and Joseph SURFACE

BADGER   See under TOAD OF TOAD HALL

BAGGINS, BILBO   Small, hairy-footed creature, apparently
cowardly but with hidden reserves of intelligence and courage.
Bilbo is the hero of J. R. R. Tolkien's children's novel *The Hobbit,
or There and Back Again* (1937). In the company of the wizard
GANDALF and a dozen 'dwarves', he helps slay a dragon and recover
a treasure-hoard. Bilbo reappears in Tolkien's three-volume
novel *The Lord of the Rings* (1954–5). His adventures have been
dramatized on BBC radio and in the animated television movie
The Hobbit (1977; dir. Arthur Rankin and Jules Bass). He also
appears in the cartoon feature film *Lord of the Rings* (1978; dir.
Ralph Bakshi).

BAGGINS, FRODO   Young hobbit, cousin and heir to Bilbo
BAGGINS. He plays the hero's role in J. R. R. Tolkien's epic fantasy
novel *The Lord of the Rings* (1954–5). With the aid of GANDALF
and assorted characters (including the mysterious Aragorn, also
known as Strider), Frodo succeeds in destroying the One Ring
which is sought by Sauron, the Dark Lord who wishes to spread his
evil rule over all 'Middle-Earth'. In the animated film *Lord of the
Rings* (1978; dir. Ralph Bakshi) Frodo's voice was provided by
Christopher Guard. He was played by Ian Holm in the BBC radio
serialization of the same story (1981; scripted by Brian Sibley).
During the first great Tolkien boom of the late 1960s the phrase
'Frodo lives!' became a familiar graffito on subway walls across
America.

BAGHEERA   See under MOWGLI

BAILEY, GEORGE   American small-town businessman, hero and
narrator of Frank Capra's classic populist movie *It's a Wonderful
Life* (1946). Bailey, played by James Stewart, is on the verge of

suicide. He is saved from death by an angel named Clarence. The
latter convinces Bailey of his own worth by showing him the
town's life as it might have been had Bailey never been born.
The film was scripted by Capra in collaboration with Frances
Goodrich and Albert Hackett. It is a marvellous movie – arguably
the most effective tearjerker ever to come out of Hollywood – but
Bailey would not have merited an entry in the present volume
were it not for the curious fact that David Thomson chose to use
him as the central character in his 'novel' *Suspects* (1985). In this
book George Bailey is made to narrate the biographies of about a
hundred other characters from the cinema – mostly from crime
thrillers and *films noirs*, and including such people as Norman
BATES, Rick BLAINE, Norma DESMOND, Jay GATSBY, Laura
HUNT, Harry LIME, Dolly Schiller (LOLITA) and Jack TORRANCE.
Thomson's George Bailey also reveals that he has a number of close
family relationships with characters from other films: three of
them, Harry Moseby from *Night Moves* (1975), Travis Bickle from
Taxi Driver (1976), and Sally Bailey from *Atlantic City* (1982), are
supposed to be his children.

BAILEY, STUART   See under KOOKIE

BAINES, CONSTANCE AND SOPHIA   Draper's daughters
from the Five Towns of northern England (see also Anna
TELLWRIGHT). The story of their divergent lives is told in *The Old
Wives' Tale* (1908), a long novel which is generally regarded as
Arnold Bennett's masterpiece. Constance is the sensible stay-at-
home sister, Sophia the more romantic and ambitious girl who
elopes to Paris. After many years they end their lives together
back where they began, at home in the Five Towns.

BAINES, SCATTERGOOD   'Shrewd, fat Yankee promoter' invented
by Clarence Budington Kelland for his book *Scattergood Baines*
(1921) and many magazine stories. The sequels are *Scattergood
Pulls the Strings* (1941) and *Scattergood Baines Returns*. The
character appeared in an American radio series (1937–42), where
he was voiced by the actor Jess Pugh. In the film *Scattergood
Baines* (1941; dir. Christy Cabanne) he was played by Guy Kibbee,
who also took the role in five low-budget sequels, concluding with
Cinderella Swings It (1943).

BALBOA, ROCKY   Professional boxer created by actor-writer-director Sylvester Stallone in his films *Rocky* (1976; dir. John G. Avildsen), *Rocky II* (1979; dir. Stallone), *Rocky III* (1982; dir. Stallone) and *Rocky IV* (1985; dir. Stallone). The first of these, though judged to be sentimental and old-fashioned, won an Oscar as the best movie of its year. Critics have been less kind to the sequels, despite which the whole series has been extremely popular. Rocky may not be very bright, but his muscular build and dogged determination to win have brought him the admiration of all but the most sophisticated cinema audiences.

BALFOUR, DAVID   Young Scotsman of the eighteenth century, hero and narrator of Robert Louis Stevenson's adventure novels *Kidnapped* (1886) and *Catriona* (1893). At the mercy of his villainous Uncle Ebenezer, David is borne away on a ship. He befriends the Jacobite rebel Alan Breck, and the two make their escape across the Scottish Highlands. The first of these novels has been filmed several times – in 1938 (dir. Alfred L. Werker), with Freddie Bartholomew as David; in 1959 (dir. Robert Stevenson [no relation to the author]), with James MacArthur; and in the 1971 (dir. Delbert Mann), with Lawrence Douglas. Both novels have been serialized on BBC radio (1985), with David Rintoul as Balfour.

BALOO   See under MOWGLI

BAMBI   Young deer who lives in a German forest – created by Felix Salten (Sigmund Salzmann) for his gentle, moving children's novel *Bambi* (1926). It is a realistic depiction of forest life, dealing with birth, death and courtship among the animals. The story formed the basis of one of the most famous of the Walt Disney studio's feature-length cartoon films (1942; dir. David Hand and Perce Pearce). However, not all admirers of the book approve of this adaptation. According to Margery Fisher: 'In a long history of falsifying, Walt Disney made no more drastic or mistaken change than when he showed Bambi as a cute, lisping celluloid puppet titupping through a rainbow-hued landscape. A child who came to the book after seeing Disney's cartoon would find it hard to believe that Salten's young deer was the same character.'

BANDELLO, RICO   Prohibition-era gangster in W. R. Burnett's
hardboiled novel *Little Caesar* (1929). The story is obviously
based on the real-life career of Al Capone. In the film of the book
(1930; dir. Mervyn LeRoy) he was played by Edward G. Robinson
(a performance which turned that diminutive actor into a star).
Bandello's famous last line is: 'Mother of mercy, is this the end
of Rico?'

BANNER, BRUCE   See The INCREDIBLE HULK

BARACUS, B.A.   Giant bejewelled tough guy played by the ex-
wrestler Mr T in the American television series 'The A-Team', a
hit since 1983. The A-Team consists of four veterans of the
Vietnam War who have set themselves up as an extra-legal vigilante
group. Their leader is the grizzled Colonel John 'Hannibal' Smith
(played by George Peppard). Hi-tech Robin Hoods, they set the
world to rights with considerable violence – though the series is
played for laughs. 'B.A.' is the most memorable character of the
four, and is particularly popular with children. It is alleged that
his initials stand for 'Bad Attitude'.

BARBARELLA   Delectable blonde spacefarer in a comic-strip by
Jean-Claude Forest, originally published in the French *V
Magazine* from 1962. Her spicy adventures proved very popular
and were collected in the book *Barbarella* (1964) which has been
widely translated. A film of the same title (dir. Roger Vadim) was
produced in 1967, with a screenplay by Terry Southern and
others. Barbarella was played, rather spectacularly, by Jane Fonda.

BARDELL, MRS   (1) See under Samuel PICKWICK; (2) see under
Sexton BLAKE

BARKLEY, CATHERINE   See under Frederic HENRY

BARLOW, CHARLIE   Heavy-set, authoritative policeman in the
long-running British television series 'Z Cars' (1960–78). Initially
famed for its low-life realism, the series was devised by
scriptwriter Troy Kennedy Martin. Inspector Barlow (its most
famous character) was played by Stratford Johns. Later spin-off

series were 'Softly, Softly' (1966–76) and 'Barlow' (mid-1970s).
Elwyn Jones has written a series of novels about Inspector Barlow:
it includes such titles as *Barlow* (1972), *The Barlow Casebook* (1975)
and *Barlow Down Under* (1978).

BARNABY   Five-year-old boy who wishes for a fairy godmother,
and gets a cigar-smoking fairy godfather instead. Barnaby and
his godfather, Mr O'Malley, were invented by Crockett Johnson
for his popular comic-strip *Barnaby* (1942–52). The strip has
been reissued in America in paperback in the 1980s.

BARNES, JAKE   Impotent hero of Ernest Hemingway's celebrated
first novel *The Sun Also Rises* (1926; vt *Fiesta*). A war-wounded
American living in Paris, he becomes entangled with the
fascinating Lady Brett Ashley. Both are archetypal figures of the
'Lost Generation'. In the film, *The Sun Also Rises* (1957; dir.
Henry King), Jake was played by Tyrone Power. There has also
been a television mini-series based on the story (1985; dir. James
Goldstone).

BARON, THE   Also known as John Mannering (and, in America, as
'Blue Mask') – a jewel-thief who changes his ways and becomes a
crime-buster. He is the hero of some forty-seven novels by
Anthony Morton (John Creasey), beginning with *Meet the Baron*
(1937; vt *The Man in the Blue Mask*). Later titles in the series
include *The Baron Returns* (1937; vt *The Return of the Blue
Mask*), *The Baron at Bay* (1938; vt *The Blue Mask at Bay*), *Alias
the Baron* (1939; vt *Alias Blue Mask*), *The Baron Comes Back*
(1943), *Shadow the Baron* (1951), *Salute to the Baron* (1960), *Sport
for the Baron* (1966) and *The Baron, King-Maker* (1975). A British-
produced television series, 'The Baron' (1965–6), starred Steve
Forrest as an updated (and Americanized) version of the hero.

BARRY, REDMOND   See Barry LYNDON

BARTLEBY   New York clerk who one day says to his employer 'I
would prefer not to' – and who goes on refusing to obey until
he dies. He is the hero of Herman Melville's oddly Kafkaesque
short story 'Bartleby the Scrivener' (1856). A British film
version, *Bartleby* (1970; dir. Anthony Friedmann), starred Paul

Scofield. Bartleby retains a fascination for modern literary
critics: a recent volume by Elizabeth Hardwick is entitled
Bartleby in Manhattan and Other Essays (1983).

BARTON, AMOS Curate of Shepperton, Middlesex, in George
Eliot's touching novella 'The Sad Fortunes of the Rev. Amos Barton'
(included in *Scenes of Clerical Life*, 1858). The death of his wife,
Milly, brings him the sympathy of all his parishioners.

BARTON, DICK 'Special Agent' – muscular hero of a British radio
series which was aired from 1946 to 1951. Dick was created by
scriptwriters Edward J. Mason and Geoffrey Webb, and his voice
was provided by actors Noel Johnson and Duncan Carse. For a short
time the character achieved phenomenal popularity, and three
low-budget films were made: *Dick Barton, Special Agent* (1948),
Dick Barton Strikes Back (1949) and *Dick Barton at Bay* (1950),
all starring Don Stannard. Although he was notably high-
minded and clean-living, Dick attracted criticism from
correspondents to *The Times* and elsewhere as a potential bad
influence on Britain's youth. Such critics drew a riposte from a
government minister, Herbert Morrison, who said: 'I like Dick
Barton and listen to him when I get the chance. I listen because I
like it, which seems a good reason for doing a thing provided you
don't get yourself into trouble. There are too many people going
round publicly trying to psycho-analyse other people' (quoted in
E. S. Turner's *Boys Will Be Boys*). Dick Barton was revived by the
BBC in 1978, for a short-lived television series which starred Tony
Vogel.

BARTON, MARY Working-class heroine of Elizabeth Gaskell's
novel *Mary Barton: A Tale of Manchester Life* (1848). She is torn
between love of a rich employer's son, Henry Carson, and a young
man of her own class, Jem Wilson. Carson is murdered, and
suspicion falls on Wilson, whom Mary strives to save from the
gallows. Notable for its sympathetic portrayal of industrial
workers' lives, the novel was vilified by mill-owners and right-
wing critics of the day, but it proved very popular.

BASTABLE, OSWALD Boy narrator of the children's novels *The
Story of the Treasure Seekers* (1899), *The Would-be-Goods*

(1901) and *The New Treasure Seekers* (1904) by E. Nesbit. Oswald
has five siblings, and together they try to restore their family's
fortunes by seeking 'treasure'. Nesbit's books have remained
popular, and deservedly so, since they are richly comic and inventive
works. *The Story of the Treasure Seekers* was dramatized on BBC
television in 1981–2, with Simon Hill in the part of Oswald.
(Michael Moorcock borrowed the name of Oswald Bastable for
the time-travelling hero of his science fiction novels *The Warlord
of the Air* [1971], *The Land Leviathan* [1974] and *The Steel Tsar*
[1981].)

BATES, MISS   See under Emma WOODHOUSE

BATES, NORMAN   Insane murderer in charge of a lonely motel, in
Robert Bloch's novel *Psycho* (1959). Bates believes that he is
his own mother, and in a fit of sexual frenzy he kills a young
woman who has unknowingly aroused him. The story became
the basis of one of Alfred Hitchcock's most memorable films
(1960), in which Anthony Perkins gave an admirably twitchy
performance as Bates. Twenty years later Bates escapes from the
hospital for the criminally insane and goes on the rampage
again. These events are recounted in *Psycho 2* (1982), Bloch's
sequel to his original novel. The film which was vaguely based on
this second book (1983; dir. Richard Franklin) also starred
Anthony Perkins, as did a third movie, *Psycho 3* (1986; dir.
Perkins). Norman Bates's early life is described in David
Thomson's collection of fictitious biographies, *Suspects* (1985;
see under George BAILEY).

BATMAN   Costumed superhero of American comic-books, second
in fame only to SUPERMAN himself. He was conceived and drawn
by Bob Kane (with the uncredited help of writer Bill Finger) for
Detective Comics, beginning in May 1939. Batman's real name is
Bruce Wayne; he is a Gotham City socialite and philanthropist
who dons his grey-and-blue bat-suit (with cape and mask) in
order to fight villains incognito. His assistant is Robin the Boy
Wonder, alias Dick Grayson. These energetic vigilantes use a range
of marvellous vehicles and technological artifacts in their struggle
against such baddies as The Joker (a recurrent character who 'smiles
a smile without mirth, a smile of death'). From 1940 Batman had

Batman as played by Adam West in the 1960s TV series

his own comic-book, and before long he was appearing in the
cinema. The film serial *Batman* (1943; dir. Lambert Hillyer)
starred Lewis Wilson, while the later *Batman and Robin* (1949; dir.
Spencer Bennett) had Robert Lowery as the hero. A distinctly
tongue-in-cheek television series (1966–8) starred Adam West as
Batman and Burt Ward as Robin. It was a considerable success,
and a feature film, *Batman* (1966; dir. Leslie Martinson), had
the same cast. There have also been two TV cartoon series of
Batman adventures (1973 and 1977–8). A spin-off character is
Batgirl, alias Babs Gordon, who appeared in *Detective Comics*
from 1967 and also featured in later episodes of the 1960s TV series.
A novel, *Batman and the Three Villains of Doom* (1966) by

William Lyons, was published at the time of Batman's peak popularity on television. Latterly, Batman has been given a whole new lease of life by the talented comic-book artist Frank Miller. In a recent series of strips, collected in the book *Batman: The Dark Knight Returns* (1986), Miller reimagines Batman as a rather sad, superannuated figure in a world which no longer has a place for costumed superheroes.

BATSON, BILLY   See Captain MARVEL

BATTLE   See under G-8

BATTY, NORA   See under COMPO

BAZAROV, YEVGENY VASIL'EVICH   Young Russian revolutionary in Ivan Turgenev's novel *Fathers and Sons* (1862). He is a representative of the radical intelligentsia of the 1860s, in revolt against the aristocracy. The novel caused heated controversy in its day, and Turgenev felt obliged to leave the country.

BECK, MARTIN   Swedish policeman in a series of crime novels by the wife-and-husband writing team Maj Sjöwall and Per Wahlöö. In English they are known as: *Roseanna* (1967), *The Man on the Balcony* (1968), *The Man Who Went Up in Smoke* (1969), *The Laughing Policeman* (1970), *The Fire Engine That Disappeared* (1970), *Murder at the Savoy* (1971), *The Abominable Man* (1972), *The Locked Room* (1973), *Cop Killer* (1975) and *The Terrorists* (1976). Martin Beck was played by Walter Matthau in the film *The Laughing Policeman* (1974; dir. Stuart Rosenberg).

BEDE, ADAM   Upright, honest carpenter who loves Hetty SORREL, in the novel *Adam Bede* (1859) by George Eliot (Mary Ann Evans). He eventually loses Hetty, but gains the love of her cousin, Dinah Morris. A notable comic character in this novel is the farmer's wife, Mrs Rachel Poyser.

BEDFORD, MR   See under CAVOR

BEEBLEBROX, ZAPHOD   See under Arthur DENT

BELL, PETER   Travelling potter who tries to steal an ass, is taken
for a magical ride, and subsequently becomes a new man. The
tale is told in William Wordsworth's narrative poem 'Peter Bell'
(1819), which promptly inspired a number of parodies by other
hands. These include the amusing 'Peter Bell the Third' (1819) by
Percy Bysshe Shelley.

BELLAMY FAMILY, THE   See under Mr HUDSON

BELVEDERE, MR   Unlikely babysitter, a self-dubbed 'genius',
played by the waspish actor Clifton Webb in the Hollywood
comedy *Sitting Pretty* (1948; dir. Walter Lang; based on the novel
Belvedere by Gwen Davenport). Two film sequels, also starring
Webb, are *Mr Belvedere Goes to College* (1949; dir. Elliot Nugent)
and *Mr Belvedere Rings the Bell* (1951; dir. Henry Koster).

BEN ADHEM, ABOU   Arabian gentleman who is visited by an angel,
in Leigh Hunt's best-known poem 'Abou Ben Adhem' (1834;
republished in *The Book of Gems*, 1838). Ben Adhem assures his
visitor that he is a lover of his fellow-men. The following night, the
angel shows him 'the names whom love of God had blest/And lo!
Ben Adhem's name led all the rest'. The poem has long been
one of the most familiar of English anthology pieces.

BEN HASSAN, AHMED   See The SHEIK

BEN-HUR, JUDAH   Romano-Jewish hero of General Lew Wallace's
historical novel about ancient Rome and the coming of Christianity,
Ben-Hur: A Tale of the Christ (1880). The novel was made into a
spectacular film in 1926 (dir. Fred Niblo), with Ramon Novarro
in the leading role. It was remade in 1959 (dir. William Wyler),
with Charlton Heston. The scriptwriter of the latter film, Karl
Tunberg, has also written a sequel to Wallace's original novel,
The Quest of Ben-Hur (1981).

BENNET, ELIZABETH   High-spirited heroine of Jane Austen's
classic novel of courtship *Pride and Prejudice* (1813). Her 'prejudice'
against the proud Fitzwilliam DARCY is gradually overcome, and
the book ends with their happy marriage. Among the notable
characters in the novel are the foolish clergyman, William Collins,

and his overbearing patron, Lady Catherine de Bourgh. Sequels
by other hands include *The Ladies* by E. Barrington (Lily Adams
Beck) and *Pemberley Shades* by D. Bonavia-Hunt. The
Hollywood film *Pride and Prejudice* (1940; dir. Robert Z. Leonard)
was scripted by Aldous Huxley, and Greer Garson took the part of
Elizabeth. A BBC radio serialization of the story (1984) had
Elizabeth Counsell as the heroine. The novel has also been adapted
for the stage, a recent example being David Pownall's version
which was performed at the Old Vic theatre in 1986.

BENNY   Woolly-hatted simpleton played by Paul Henry in the
British television soap opera 'Crossroads' (from 1964). He has
become the best-known character from the series (apart from the
matriarchal Meg RICHARDSON), his name recurring in comedians'
jokes and in TV advertising ('as simple as Benny').

BENWAY, DOC   Sinister man of medicine in *The Naked Lunch*
(1959) and other books of the satirical grotesque by William S.
Burroughs, including *The Soft Machine* (1961) and *Nova Express*
(1964). He is 'a manipulator and co-ordinator of symbol systems,
an expert on all phases of interrogation, brainwashing and control'.
At one stage in his ghastly career, however, he was a ship's surgeon
aboard 'as filthy a craft as ever sailed the seas. Operating with one
hand, beating the rats offa my patient with the other . . .'

BERESFORD, TOMMY AND TUPPENCE   Detective couple
invented by Agatha Christie. They appear in one of her earliest
titles, *The Secret Adversary* (1922), and in such later books as
Partners in Crime (1929; vt *The Sunningdale Mystery*), *N or M?*
(1941), *By the Pricking of My Thumbs* (1968) and *Postern of Fate*
(1973). In the British television series *Agatha Christie's Partners
in Crime* (1983) Tommy and Tuppence were played by James
Warwick and Francesca Annis.

BERKELEY-WILLOUGHBY, ARCHIBALD   See P.C.49

BERRY   See Berry PLEYDELL

BERTRAM, EDMUND AND SIR THOMAS   See under Fanny PRICE

BERTRAM, HARRY   See under Guy MANNERING

BESTE-CHETWYNDE, MARGOT   See Lady Margot METROLAND

BEULAH   Jolly black housemaid who first appeared in the
American radio show 'Fibber McGee and Molly' in 1944 (see Fibber
and Molly McGEE). She soon graduated to her own radio series,
and then to television. Beulah's voice was in fact provided by a
white male actor, Marlin Hurt. In the TV series 'Beulah' (1950–53)
she was played initially by Ethel Waters, later by Louise Beavers.
As with AMOS AND ANDY, the characterization of Beulah is now
remembered as a rather insulting racial stereotype; nevertheless she
was 'one of the most popular comedy characters of the 1940s and
1950s' (Tim Brooks and Earle Marsh).

BEVERLY HILLBILLIES, THE   See Jed CLAMPETT

BEVIS   Hero of Richard Jefferies' bucolic novels *Wood Magic* (1881)
and *Bevis, the Story of a Boy* (1882). Bevis is a resourceful
Wiltshire lad, expert in hunting and in making things. In the
second novel he goes rafting and boating with his friend Mark,
and together they dream of themselves as adventurers and
explorers. Although Bevis has not quite gained the status of an
English Tom SAWYER or Huckleberry FINN, the books are regarded
as classic expressions of the themes of boyhood and country life.

BEZUKHOV, PIERRE   One of the principal male characters in
Count Leo Tolstoy's massive novel *War and Peace* (1864–9).
He is captured by the French and takes part in the terrible retreat
from Moscow of 1812. After the death of his friend and rival,
Prince Andrei Bolkonsky, Pierre marries Natasha ROSTOVA. In
films and television serializations of the novel Bezukhov has
been played by Henry Fonda (1956), Sergei Bondarchuk (1967) and
Anthony Hopkins (1972), among others.

BHAER, FRIEDRICH   See under Jo MARCH

BICKLE, TRAVIS   See under George BAILEY

BIG BROTHER   Nameless dictator of 'Oceania' in George Orwell's nightmarish dystopian novel *Nineteen Eighty-Four* (1949). The book's hero, Winston SMITH, learns to 'love' Big Brother – that is, to obey him. A sequel by another hand is *1985: A Historical Report (Hong Kong 2036)* (1982) by the Hungarian writer György Dalos. This gives an account of the historical development of Oceania after Big Brother's death.

BIG EARS   See under NODDY

BIGGER THOMAS   Black anti-hero of Richard Wright's moving novel *Native Son* (1940). The victim of racial prejudice, he is eventually condemned to death for a double murder. The character's name is no doubt an ironic comment on Mrs Harriet Beecher Stowe's Uncle TOM. James Baldwin once stated: 'No American negro exists who does not have his private Bigger Thomas living in the skull' (quoted in Leslie A. Fiedler, *What Was Literature?*).

BIGGLES   Full name James Bigglesworth, DSO, DFC, MC – the most famous aviator in boys' fiction. He was invented by Captain W. E. Johns for a number of magazine stories which first appeared in the early 1930s. Biggles starts his heroic flying career during World War I, eventually becoming the commander of a fighter squadron. He makes bosom friends of such daring young men as Algy Lacy and Ginger Hebblethwaite, who remain his companions in adventure for many years to come. After the war Biggles becomes a flying crime-fighter, but when World War II arrives he naturally plays a major role in the Battle of Britain. He takes up his crime-busting career again after 1945, remaining a daredevil adventurer until his author's death in 1968. W. E. Johns was editor of the magazine *Popular Flying* when he wrote the early Biggles stories, swiftly collected in the book *The Camels are Coming* (1932; vt *Biggles, Pioneer Air Fighter*). These first stories have a realistic edge which is missing from the later Biggles novels, since Johns was drawing on genuine memories of his experiences in the Royal Flying Corps during World War I. The later books, almost 100 of them, are gung-ho yarns for boys, full of old-fashioned imperialist sentiments. Some of the titles are: *The Cruise of the Condor: A Biggles Story* (1933), *Biggles of the Camel*

The pipe-smoking Biggles with two of the chaps

Squadron (1934), *Biggles Flies Again* (1934), *Biggles Flies East* (1935), *Biggles in France* (1935), *Biggles and Co.* (1936), *Biggles in Africa* (1936), *Biggles Flies West* (1937), *Biggles, Air Commodore* (1937), *Biggles Flies South* (1938), *Biggles Goes to War* (1938), *Biggles Flies North* (1939), *Biggles in Spain* (1939), *Biggles in the Baltic* (1940), *Biggles Defies the Swastika* (1941), *Biggles Sweeps the Desert* (1942), *Biggles in the Orient* (1945), *Biggles and the Black Raider* (1953), *Biggles and the Leopards of Zinn* (1960), *Biggles and the Dark Intruder* (1967) and *Biggles and the Little Green God* (1969). John Pearson has written an entertaining book, *Biggles: The Authorized Biography* (1978), which gives an 'adult' account of the character's life. Many of the Biggles stories were dramatized on BBC radio, where the first actor to give voice to the character was Jack Watson (from 1948). The air ace made a long-delayed movie debut in *Biggles* (1986; dir. John Hough), starring Neil Dickson.

BILBO   See Bilbo BAGGINS

BILKO, ERNEST G.   Bespectacled Master Sergeant in the American army, played by Phil Silvers in the anarchic television comedy series 'You'll Never Get Rich' (1955–9; later known as 'The Phil Silvers Show' and 'Bilko'). Ernie Bilko is a loveable, loud-mouthed conman who is for ever fooling his superior officers. The inventor of Bilko, Private Duane Doberman and the rest was scriptwriter Nat Hiken. Over the years the show has become something of a cult, and some enthusiasts believe Sergeant Bilko to be the most memorable comic creation on American TV. Silvers played a similar character, Harry Grafton, in *The New Phil Silvers Show* (1963–4), but this was less successful. A book about Sergeant Bilko and the original series is *Bilko: The Fort Baxter Story* (1985) by David Thomas and Ian Irvine.

BILL BADGER   See under RUPERT BEAR

BILLINA   See under Dorothy GALE

BINDLE, JOSEPH   Henpecked husband in a series of comic domestic novels by the British writer Herbert Jenkins. Poor Bindle is often on the dole, and Mrs Bindle is for ever crying 'Lorst yer job?' in an accusatory tone. The series includes: *Bindle* (1916), *The Night Club* (1917), *The Adventures of Bindle* (1918), *Mrs Bindle* (1921) and *The Bindles on the Rocks.*

BINGHAM, SERGEANT   See under Inspector HORNLEIGH

BINGO THE BRAINY PUP   See under RUPERT BEAR

BIONIC WOMAN, THE   See Jaime SOMMERS

BIRABEAU, PIERRE   Alias the Red Shadow, a young French officer who becomes the secret leader of a band of Moroccan rebels, the Riffs, in Sigmund Romberg's popular musical play *The Desert Song* (1926; book and lyrics by Otto Harbach, Oscar Hammerstein and Frank Mandel). The story was filmed in 1929 (dir. Roy del Ruth), with John Boles; in 1943 (dir. Robert Florey), with Dennis Morgan; and in 1953 (dir. H. Bruce Humberstone), with Gordon Macrae.

BIRKIN, RUPERT   Lover and eventual husband of Ursula BRANGWEN in D. H. Lawrence's major novel *Women in Love* (1920). His virtues are contrasted with the faults of the other main male character, Gerald Crich. It has commonly been assumed that Birkin is very much a self-portrait of Lawrence. In the film *Women in Love* (1969; dir. Ken Russell) the part was taken by Alan Bates.

BLACK BEAUTY   Horse who is the narrator and central character of Anna Sewell's well-loved novel *Black Beauty* (1877). We follow Beauty's life from birth, as he passes through the hands of a number of owners, good and bad. At one point he joins the stables of an earl, but his knees are injured by an incompetent groom and he is sold as a cab horse. After a period of honest toil as a working horse, Beauty is sold to a vicious new owner who treats him cruelly and ruins his health. Luckily, he falls into the hands of a kindly farmer, regains his strength, and is finally reunited with one of his original grooms. This touching *Bildungsroman* is one of the most effective animal stories ever penned. The Royal Society for the Prevention of Cruelty to Animals once used it as a propaganda weapon, and indeed the book is thought to have done much to better the treatment of carriage horses in late Victorian times. One could make the claim that it has served as the *Uncle Tom's Cabin* for the equine race. There have been a number of sequels by other hands, for example *Son of Black Beauty* (1954) by Phyllis Briggs. Black Beauty's story has been filmed at least five times – in 1921, in 1933 (dir. Phil Rosen), in 1946 (dir. Max Nosseck), in 1957 (dir. Harold Schuster) and in 1971 (dir. James Hill). There have also been several television versions, including a British series called 'The Adventures of Black Beauty' (1972), which had little in common with the book.

BLACK BOB   Heroic sheepdog of the Scottish Borders. He has featured in British newspaper strips and annual volumes. Family legend has it that the very first book which the present compiler read was a *Black Bob* annual (*circa* 1954).

BLACKETT, NANCY AND PEGGY   See under The WALKER FAMILY

BLACKHAWK   American vigilante hero who appeared in *Military Comics*, and in his own comic book, *Blackhawk*, from 1941 to 1969. He began his adventurous career as an anti-Nazi freedom-fighter, and ended it as a CIA agent. Created by Chuck Cuidera, Blackhawk was perpetuated by Reed Crandall and other artists. The character appeared on the radio during the 1940s, and was played by Kirk Allyn in a cinema serial, *Blackhawk* (1952).

BLACKSHIRT   Real name Richard Verrell, a gentleman thief or amateur cracksman in the tradition of A. J. RAFFLES. He first appeared in *Blackshirt* (1925) by Bruce Graeme (Graham Montague Jeffries), a book which sold a million copies in Britain in the succeeding decade or so. According to William Vivian Butler, Verrell 'is so scrupulous that he has never been known to carry a gun, and so sartorially sensitive that he not only wears an evening suit on all his escapades, complete with black hood, black silk gloves, black shoes, black socks and, of course, black shirt, but he also has a special pocket in his coat from which he can "spring out" an opera hat, to be set rakishly on his head as, a "gentleman of the world" again, he sets out for home.' Other books by Bruce Graeme which feature this elegant hero include

The Return of Blackshirt (1927), *Blackshirt Again* (1929; vt
Adventures of Blackshirt), *Alias Blackshirt* (1932), *Blackshirt the
Audacious* (1935), *Blackshirt the Adventurer* (1936), *Blackshirt
Takes a Hand* (1937), *Blackshirt, Counter-Spy* (1938), *Blackshirt
Interferes* (1939) and *Blackshirt Strikes Back* (1940). Blackshirt's
son, Anthony Verrell, becomes the hero in *Son of Blackshirt*
(1941), *Lord Blackshirt: The Son of Blackshirt Carries On* (1942)
and *Calling Lord Blackshirt* (1943). After World War II, the
author's son, writing as Roderic Graeme, revived the original
Blackshirt, Richard Verrell, for a new series which commenced
with *Concerning Blackshirt* (1952) and ran for another eighteen
volumes, concluding with *Blackshirt Stirs Things Up* (1968).

BLADE   See under EDGE

BLAINE, RICK   American night-club owner in French Morocco,
and a former soldier of fortune. He is the central character of an
unsuccessful stage play, *Everybody Comes to Rick's* by Murray
Burnett and Joan Alison, which was made into one of the most
successful movies that Hollywood ever produced – *Casablanca*
(1942; dir. Michael Curtiz). The eminently quotable script,
based on the original play, was by Philip and Julius Epstein in
collaboration with Howard Koch. The story concerns a love
triangle in the early days of World War II. Victor Laszlo, a heroic
resistance fighter, flees from Nazi-occupied Europe to
supposedly neutral Casablanca, and Rick Blaine is persuaded to
help him – even though the man is married to Ilsa Lund, the woman
whom Rick loves. In the film Blaine was played, most memorably,
by the world-weary Humphrey Bogart (with Ingrid Bergman as Ilsa
and Paul Henreid as Laszlo). There have been two American
television series based on the movie: one in 1955–6, starring
Charles McGraw as Rick, and one in 1983, with David Soul.
Blaine features as a prominent character in David Thomson's
odd book *Suspects* (1985), as do the other members of the triangle,
Ilsa Lund and Victor Laszlo (see under George BAILEY).

BLAISE, MODESTY   Newspaper strip-cartoon adventuress created
by Peter O'Donnell for the London *Evening Standard* in 1963. Her
loyal sidekick is the Cockney Willie Garvin. Often regarded
(inaccurately) as a female version of James BOND, she rose to

fame during the spy-fiction boom of the 1960s and soon graduated from comic-strips to the unadorned printed word. Her first novel, written by O'Donnell, was *Modesty Blaise* (1965). It was followed by over ten sequels, including *Sabre Tooth* (1966), *I, Lucifer* (1967), *A Taste for Death* (1969), *The Impossible Virgin* (1971), *Pieces of Modesty* (1972), *The Silver Mistress* (1973), *Last Day in Limbo* (1976), *The Dragon's Claw* (1978), *The Xanadu Talisman* (1981), *The Night of Morningstar* (1982) and *Dead Man's Handle* (1985). A beautiful and extremely active heroine of lowly origins, she is 'one of the first truly liberated women of mystery fiction', in the words of critic Otto Penzler. She has appeared in one rather uncharacteristic film, *Modesty Blaise* (1966; dir. Joseph Losey), where she was played by Italian actress Monica Vitti. Meanwhile, her cartoon adventures continue to be syndicated in newspapers around the world.

BLAKE, SEXTON Long-lived detective hero of boys' fiction – the English equivalent of Nick CARTER. The first Blake story, 'The Missing Millionaire', was written by Hal Meredith (Harry Blyth) and it appeared in Harmsworth's *Halfpenny Marvel* in 1893. After a few months Blake was transferred to another boys' paper published by Harmsworth, the *Union Jack*, and it was within the pages of this well-loved periodical that he grew to fame (although he was to make guest appearances in many other magazines). Over the next eighty years almost 200 authors contributed to the Blake saga – some of the better-known are William Murray Graydon, Edwy Searles Brooks (see also Nelson LEE), John Newton Chance, W. Howard Baker, Jack Trevor Story and Michael Moorcock. When the *Union Jack* ceased to appear in 1933 Blake's adventures continued in *Detective Weekly* and in his own regular publication, the *Sexton Blake Library*. The latter series of novellas lasted until 1963. Since that date new Blake adventures have appeared sporadically in paperback, and in hardcover from the Howard Baker Press. The same publisher has issued such reprint volumes as *Sexton Blake – The Star of 'Union Jack'* (1972).

By the early years of the twentieth century Sexton Blake had become established as the poor man's Sherlock HOLMES (there is a marked physical resemblance between the two). He has a boy assistant called Tinker and a treasure of a landlady called Mrs

Bardell. Like the greater detective, he inhabits rooms in Baker Street, whence he ventures forth to tackle all manner of master criminals. Blake's opponents over the decades have included the glamorous Mademoiselle Yvonne, the deadly Dr Huxton Rymer, Prince Wu Ling (Chief of the Brotherhood of the Yellow Beetle), and such talented eccentrics as Waldo the Wonder Man and Zenith the Albino. Unlike Holmes, Blake relies more on his muscles than his brains; his powers of endurance, in every sense of the term, are prodigious. Dorothy L. Sayers once wrote that 'blood-and-thunders' such as the exploits of Sexton Blake are our 'nearest approach to a national folk-lore, conceived as the centre for a cycle of loosely connected romances in the Arthurian manner' (quoted in E. S. Turner's *Boys Will be Boys*). As well as in many millions of words of pulp fiction, the hero has appeared in low-budget British films since 1914. A number of silent movies of the late 1920s starred Langhorne Burton as Blake. Later the detective was played by George Curzon, in such titles as *Sexton Blake and the Bearded Doctor* (1935) and *Sexton Blake and the Hooded Terror* (1938); and by David Farrar, in *Meet Sexton Blake* (1943) and other films. There have also been occasional appearances by Sexton Blake on British radio and television. A BBC TV serial, *Sexton Blake and the Demon God* (1978), was scripted by Simon Raven.

BLAKENEY, MARGUERITE   Gorgeous, high-spirited wife of Sir Percy Blakeney in Baroness Orczy's novel *The Scarlet Pimpernel* (1905) and its sequels. She was played by Merle Oberon in the film *The Scarlet Pimpernel* (1934), by Margaret Leighton in *The Elusive Pimpernel* (1950), and by Jane Seymour in the television remake of the first title (1982). Lately, her solo adventures have been recounted by novelist C. Guy Clayton in *Daughter of the Revolution: The Blakeney Papers, Volume 1* (1984), *Such Mighty Rage: The Blakeney Papers, Volume 2* (1985) and *Bordeaux Red: The Blakeney Papers, Volume 3* (1986). See also The SCARLET PIMPERNEL.

BLAKENEY, PERCY   See The SCARLET PIMPERNEL

BLANDISH, BARBARA   Millionaire's daughter who is kidnapped, tortured and raped by a villain known as Slim Grissom. The surprising thing is that she likes it. James Hadley Chase's salacious novel *No Orchids for Miss Blandish* (1939) sold some half million copies in Britain during the early years of World War II. Chase was the pseudonym of an Englishman, René Raymond, who attempted to write in American vernacular. As George Orwell pointed out in his famous essay 'Raffles and Miss Blandish' (1944), the plot of Chase's book owes much to William Faulkner's *Sanctuary* (see Temple DRAKE). The story of Miss Blandish's sufferings became a stage play and then a film (1948; dir. St John L. Clowes). The latter starred Linden Travers as Miss Blandish, and is 'one of the worst films ever made', according to Leslie Halliwell. It has been remade as *The Grissom Gang* (1971; dir. Robert Aldrich), with Kim Darby as the heroine. Discussing Aldrich's movie in the *New Statesman* (5 November 1971), Philip French wrote: 'Miss Blandish belongs forever in the Forties schoolboys' prurient pantheon as part of the unholy trinity completed by Fanny Hill and Lady Chatterley: to be joined shortly after the war by Amber St Clair. Their names were enough to raise a laugh in any desperate music-hall comedian's act . . .'

BLANE, TORCHY   Girl newspaper reporter played by Glenda Farrell in a series of seven Hollywood movies beginning with *Smart Blonde* (1936). She was also played by Lola Lane in one film, *Torchy Blane in Panama* (1938), and by Jane Wyman in another, *Torchy Plays with Dynamite* (1939).

BLIMP, COLONEL   Archetypal English reactionary, a bewhiskered military man who berates the younger generation for its lax ways. Colonel Blimp was a newspaper cartoon figure created by David Low in the 1930s. An ambitious film, *The Life and Death of Colonel Blimp* (1943; dir. Michael Powell and Emeric Pressburger), starred Roger Livesey as Colonel Clive Candy, a Blimp-like soldier (sympathetically portrayed). The film follows his career from the Boer War to World War II.

BLISS, DAVID ALEXANDER   Carefree bachelor in the BBC radio comedy series 'A Life of Bliss' which ran (with breaks) from 1953 to 1969. The scriptwriter was Godfrey Harrison, and actors who played David Bliss include David Tomlinson, George Cole and

Carleton Hobbs. The series also appeared briefly on BBC television (1956), with George Cole in the lead.

BLOCK, ELZEVIR   See under John TRENCHARD

BLOFELD, ERNST   See under James BOND

BLONDIE   Once upon a time she was Blondie Boopadoop, a flapper girl; later she became wife to the hapless Dagwood Bumstead and mother of the precocious Baby Dumpling. This comedy of everyday American life was unfolded by newspaper strip-cartoonist Chic Young in his long-running *Blondie* (from 1930). A film, also called *Blondie* (1938; dir. Frank Strayer), had Penny Singleton in the title role. It proved to be the first of a series of more than twenty movies, which included such titles as *Blondie Brings Up Baby* (1939), *Blondie Goes to College* (1942), *Blondie Knows Best* (1945), *Blondie's Reward* (1948) and came to an end with *Blondie's Hero* (1950). In 1957 Blondie moved to television, where she was played by Pamela Britton. A later TV series (1968–9) starred Patricia Harty. According to Victor Neuburg, *Blondie* is 'probably the most widely circulated comic strip in the world . . . Its international audience numbers hundreds of millions.' It has been claimed elsewhere, however, that Charles M. Schulz's *Peanuts* is the world's number one comic strip (see Charlie BROWN and SNOOPY).

BLOOD, PETER   Medical doctor turned pirate captain in Rafael Sabatini's rousing historical novel *Captain Blood* (1922) and its sequels *The Chronicles of Captain Blood* (1931; vt *Captain Blood Returns*) and *The Fortunes of Captain Blood* (1936). Unjustly sentenced by Judge Jeffreys, Doctor Blood is transported to the Spanish Main, but there he escapes captivity and becomes a privateer. A silent movie (1925) had J. Warren Kerrigan as Peter Blood. The sound film *Captain Blood* (1935; dir. Michael Curtiz) was a great success and made a star of its leading man, Errol Flynn. Later films based on the character include *The Fortunes of Captain Blood* (1950) and *Captain Blood, Fugitive* (1952), both starring Louis Hayward; and *Son of Captain Blood* (1962), with the appropriately-cast Sean Flynn (Errol's son).

BLOODNOK, MAJOR   See under ECCLES

BLOOM, LEOPOLD   Jewish Dubliner, *l'homme moyen sensuel*, created by James Joyce in his great novel *Ulysses* (1922). Like the heroic Greek invoked in the book's title, Bloom is quite a traveller – but his journeyings do not take him beyond Dublin's labyrinthine streets. For a twenty-four-hour period in June 1904, we see him wending his way through the pleasures and perils of Ireland's capital city, finding a surrogate son in Stephen DEDALUS, and eventually coming home to the warm bed of his Penelope, the faithless Molly BLOOM. Leopold Bloom is a most endearing character – decent, peace-loving, a trifle cowardly but ever inquisitive – and the reader is privy to all his passing thoughts. More than any other character in modern fiction, he is the twentieth-century Everyman. To the best of my knowledge, Bloom is the only (modern) fictional person to have a calendar-date named after him: 'Bloomsday', celebrated by Joyce scholars the world over, is 16 June. The film, *Ulysses* (1967; dir. Joseph Strick), scarcely does justice to the book, though Milo O'Shea made a tolerably attractive Bloom. There have been several other adaptations of the novel, including a BBC radio musical, *The Blooms of Dublin* (1982), by Anthony Burgess. A 'biography' of Leopold Bloom has been written by Peter Costello (1981).

BLOOM, MOLLY   Wife to Leopold BLOOM in James Joyce's novel *Ulysses* (1922), and a famous fictional creation in her own right. She does not leave her bed during the course of the book, dallying there with her lover, Blazes Boylan, while Bloom is doing his daily rounds. She comes into her own in the last chapter of the novel, which consists of her notorious night-time 'monologue'. This unpunctuated *tour de force* represents her flow of thoughts as she drifts into sleep – a flow which becomes so majestic that she seems to attain the status of an Earth-goddess. Molly was played by Barbara Jefford in the 1967 film based on the book.

BLUEBOTTLE   Zany character voiced by Peter Sellers on 'The Goon Show', on BBC radio from 1953. He is devoted to his 'Capting', Neddie Seagoon, and is wont to exclaim at the end of every appearance: 'You rotten swine! You have deaded me!' See also ECCLES.

BLUTO   See under POPEYE

BOBBSEY TWINS, THE   Two sets of twins in a long series of books for young children written by Laura Lee Hope, beginning with *Bobbsey Twins, or, Merry Days Indoors and Out* (1904). The older pair are called Bert and Nan, while the younger two are Freddie and Flossie. The books about the Bobbsey family, described as 'nursery soap-opera' in the slightly caustic phrase of Margery Fisher, have been read by generations of American children. Laura Lee Hope revised her first book in 1950, amending its genteel racism (which centred on the mammy figure of Dinah the cook) and generally updating the circumstances of the twins' lives.

BODIE, CHEYENNE   Tall hero played by Clint Walker in a long-running Western series on American television, 'Cheyenne' (1955–63). He was notable for being the first TV cowboy who was a true loner: he had no buddy, sidekick or pardner. The series began life in a package entitled 'Warner Brothers Presents', where it alternated with episodes of 'Casablanca' and 'Kings Row' (see Rick BLAINE and Parris MITCHELL). Like those other, less successful, series it was originally inspired by a Warner Brothers movie – in this case, *Cheyenne* (1947; dir. Raoul Walsh), which starred Dennis Morgan. A spin-off character from the 'Cheyenne' TV series was Bronco Layne (played by Ty Hardin), who soon appeared in his own series, 'Bronco' (1958–62).

BODIE AND DOYLE   Tough secret agents played by Lewis Collins and Martin Shaw in the British television series 'The Professionals' (1978–83). At the height of its popularity this series was watched by 'one-third of the nation'.

BOLAN, MACK   See The EXECUTIONER

BOLITHO, RICHARD   Englishman who joins the Royal Navy as a twelve-year-old midshipman in 1768, and eventually attains the rank of Admiral before dying in action in 1815. He is the hero of a series of popular novels by Alexander Kent, beginning with *To Glory We Steer* (1968). Bolitho is one of the many 'sons of' Horatio HORNBLOWER (see also Jack AUBREY, Richard DELANCEY and Nicholas RAMAGE). His other adventures are recounted in

Form Line of Battle! (1969), *Enemy in Sight!* (1970), *The Flag Captain* (1971), *Sloop of War* (1972), *Command a King's Ship* (1973), *Signal – Close Action!* (1974), *Richard Bolitho – Midshipman* (1975), *Passage to Mutiny* (1976), *In Gallant Company* (1977), *Midshipman Bolitho and the Avenger* (1978), *The Inshore Squadron* (1979), *Stand Into Danger* (1981) and *A Tradition of Victory* (1982).

BOLKONSKY, PRINCE ANDREI   See under Pierre Bᴇᴢᴜᴋʜᴏᴠ and Natasha Rᴏsᴛᴏᴠᴀ

BOMBA   Hero of the novel *Bomba the Jungle Boy* (1926) by 'Roy Rockwood' (a house name of Edward L. Stratemeyer's writing syndicate), and its many sequels which include such titles as *Bomba at the Moving Mountain, Bomba at the Giant Cataract, Bomba at Jaguar Island* and *Bomba in the Abandoned City.* Bomba, who lives in the Amazon basin, is perhaps the best known of all the pseudo-Tᴀʀᴢᴀɴs (others include Kᴏʀᴀᴋ, Sʜᴇᴇɴᴀ, Otis Adelbert Kline's Jan of the Jungle, Marvel Comics' Ka-Zar, William L. Chester's Kioga of the Wilderness, and Republic Pictures' serial heroine Nyoka). According to Richard A. Lupoff, 'not only are the Bomba books poorly written, [but] they reek of the most blatant racism'. Bomba was played by Johnny Sheffield in the low-budget film *Bomba the Jungle Boy* (1949; dir. Ford Beebe) and eleven sequels. These movies were later re-edited to make a television series. Bomba has also appeared in comic-books.

BONAPARTE, INSPECTOR NAPOLEON   See Bᴏɴʏ

BOND, JAMES   Secret agent 007, created by Ian Fleming for his novel *Casino Royale* (1953). Bond has been the most successful of all post-World War II fictional characters. Although his creator died in 1964, Bond has gone on and on, perpetuated in book form by other authors, as well as in films and comic-strips. He is a great modern myth figure – at once an obedient enforcer of international law, and a vaunting hero exempt from all moral restraints ('licensed to kill'); simultaneously a conscientious organization man, and a heroic, libidinous loner. He works for the British secret service and is under the strict command of his boss, 'M', but is best known for his luxurious life-style – fast cars, smart clothes, martinis and beautiful girls, with extended sojourns in the Caribbean, the Far East and other exotic places. His adventures usually bring him into conflict with some world-menacing villain – Sir Hugo Drax, Dr No, Ernst Blofeld, Auric Goldfinger and the like – whom he overcomes not so much by his wits as by sheer endurance and mere luck. Bond's later exploits as chronicled by Fleming are to be found in *Live and Let Die* (1954), *Moonraker* (1955), *Diamonds are Forever* (1956), *From Russia with Love* (1957), *Dr No* (1958), *Goldfinger* (1959), *For*

James Bond (Roger Moore) with a beautiful friend in *Live and Let Die*

Your Eyes Only (1960), *Thunderball* (1961), *The Spy Who Loved Me* (1962), *On Her Majesty's Secret Service* (1963), *You Only Live Twice* (1964), *The Man with the Golden Gun* (1965) and *Octopussy and The Living Daylights* (1966). Sequels by other hands are *Colonel Sun* (1968) by 'Robert Markham' (Kingsley Amis); *James Bond: The Authorized Biography of 007* (1973) by John Pearson; and *Licence Renewed* (1981), *For Special Services* (1982), *Icebreaker* (1983), *Role of Honour* (1984) and *Nobody Lives Forever* (1986) by John Gardner.

The first Bond film, *Doctor No* (1962; dir. Terence Young) starred the saturnine Scottish actor Sean Connery as Bond. It was an immense success and has been followed by an unending series of sequels: *From Russia with Love* (1963; dir. Terence Young), *Goldfinger* (1964; dir. Guy Hamilton), *Thunderball* (1965; dir. Terence Young), *Casino Royale* (1967; dir. John Huston *et al.* – a spoof, with David Niven as Bond), *You Only Live Twice* (1967; dir. Lewis Gilbert), *On Her Majesty's Secret Service* (1970; dir. Peter Hunt – with George Lazenby as Bond), *Diamonds are Forever* (1971; dir. Guy Hamilton), *Live and Let Die* (1973; dir. Guy Hamilton – with Roger Moore as Bond, a role which he has repeated in all but one of the subsequent films), *The Man with the Golden Gun* (1974; dir. Guy Hamilton), *The Spy Who Loved Me* (1977; dir. Lewis Gilbert), *Moonraker* (1979; dir. Lewis Gilbert), *For Your Eyes Only* (1981; dir. John Glen), *Octopussy* (1983; dir. John Glen), *Never Say Never Again* (1983; dir. Irvin Kershner; with Sean Connery making a comeback in the leading role) and *A View to a Kill* (1985; dir. John Glen; Roger Moore's last appearance in the part). The latest Bond film, *The Living Daylights*, is scheduled for release in 1987; it has a new leading man, Timothy Dalton (a former screen HEATHCLIFF). Many of these movies, particularly the later ones, fantasticate Bond's adventures to such an extent as to turn them into science fiction. They are full of advanced gadgetry and hi-tech furniture, and it is not unusual for the plots to come to a climax in outer space. Non-fiction books about the Bond phenomenon include *The James Bond Dossier* (1965) by Kingsley Amis, *James Bond in the Cinema* (1972) by John Brosnan, and *Bond and Beyond: The Political Career of a Popular Hero* (1986) by Tony Bennett and Janet Woollacott.

BONES   See under Mr Commissioner SANDERS

BONES, NORMAN AND HENRY   Juvenile detectives, the British
equivalents of Frank and Joe HARDY. They appeared regularly
on the BBC radio programme 'Children's Hour' from the late
1940s, and in a series of books by Anthony C. Wilson which includes
such titles as *Norman Bones, Detective* (1949) and *Norman and
Henry Bones, the Boy Detectives* (1952).

BONY   Inspector Napoleon Bonaparte, the grandly-named semi-
Aboriginal detective, usually known as 'Bony', created by
Australian writer Arthur W. Upfield. Bony works for the
Queensland police, and most of his adventures are set in the
outback. They are chronicled in the books *The Barakee Mystery*
(1929; vt *The Lure of the Bush*), *The Sands of Windee* (1931)
and almost thirty others, including such titles as *Wings Above
the Diamantina* (1936; vt *Wings Above the Claypan*), *The Bone is
Pointed* (1938), *The Mystery of Swordfish Reef* (1939), *Death of a
Swagman* (1945), *An Author Bites the Dust* (1948), *Death of a Lake*
(1954), *Man of Two Tribes* (1956), *Bony and the Black Virgin*
(1959), *The Will of the Tribe* (1962) and *The Lake Frome Monster*
(1966 – completed by the author's widow). An Australian
television series of the 1970s, 'Boney' (sic), was based on the
Upfield books; the hero was played by James Laurenson.

BONZO   Loveable, lop-eared puppy dog created by British cartoonist
George E. Studdy. According to comics expert Denis Gifford, Bonzo
appeared in 'almost every popular medium during the 1920s and
1930s; picture postcards, cigarette cards, pictures, posters,
children's picture and story books, magazine illustrations, stuffed
dolls, toys, souvenirs, ashtrays'. The little dog also existed in
newspaper and magazine strips, and in a series of short animated
films (mid-1920s). The character may have been forgotten, but the
name lives on. An eccentric British pop group of the late 1960s
and early 1970s was called The Bonzo Dog Doo-Dah Band.
(Another Bonzo was a chimpanzee who appeared in two
Hollywood movies: *Bedtime for Bonzo* [1951; dir. Frederick de
Cordova] and *Bonzo Goes to College* [1952]. This beast's co-star
was the future President of the United States, Ronald Reagan.)

BOO-BOO   See under YOGI BEAR

BOOP, BETTY   Sexy star of short animated films produced by Max Fleischer in the 1920s and 1930s. She had big eyes, a squeaky voice, and frequently appeared in states of undress. Betty was the first cartoon character to be censored (by the American cinema industry's Hays Office). She actually began life as a cute little dog, created by animator Grim Natwick, but from 1930 onwards she was fully human and her voice was provided by actress Mae Questal. Betty's immensely successful short cartoons included such titles as 'Boilesk' (1933), 'Red Hot Mama' (1934) and 'Zula Hula' (1937). Many of these films were revived for American television in the 1970s, and Ms Boop's career was the subject of a lengthy TV documentary, 'Boop-Oop-a-Doop!' (1985; dir. Vernon P. Becker).

BOOPADOOP, BLONDIE   See BLONDIE

BOOT, WILLIAM   Hero of Evelyn Waugh's comic novel *Scoop* (1938). Boot is an obscure writer of nature essays who is mistakenly sent to Africa as a war correspondent for the London newspaper *The Beast*. This error has very amusing consequences. The novel has been adapted for British television a couple of times, the latest production being a two-hour TV movie (1987; dir. Gavin Millar) with Michael Maloney as William Boot.

BOOTH, AMELIA   Loving wife of Captain Billy Booth, in Henry Fielding's mellow last novel *Amelia* (1751). Although her soldiering, gambling husband causes her much distress, their love remains true, and eventually the couple achieve wealth and happiness. Extremely popular in its day, *Amelia* has become Fielding's 'forgotten' novel: its virtuous heroine has something in common with Samuel Richardson's equally virtuous Sir Charles GRANDISON.

BOOTSIE AND SNUDGE   Private soldier and his choleric sergeant, played by Alfie Bass and Bill Fraser in the popular British television series 'The Army Game' (1957–62). The critic Philip Purser has commented: 'Snudge is a towering comic creation . . . a bully and a coward and a social climber.' The characters also appeared in the feature film *I Only Arsked* (1958). They were revived for a later TV series, 'Bootsie and Snudge', which dealt with their lives as civilians. A decade later they came back again for a shorter series (1974).

BORDEREAU, JULIANA   Former mistress of the romantic poet Jeffrey Aspern, in Henry James's novella *The Aspern Papers* (1888). The narrator visits her in Venice, in the hope of procuring the long-dead poet's literary remains, and discovers the once-beautiful Juliana to be an extremely wizened old lady. The story has been dramatized for the stage, and also forms the basis of an effective Hollywood movie, *The Lost Moment* (1947; dir. Martin Gabel) – in which 'Agnes Moorehead enjoys the chance of being 105, with a face wrinkled into old parchment' (according to Geoff Brown, *Radio Times*, 11 February 1984). A later film version of the story, *Aspern* (1983; dir. Eduardo de Gregorio), transferred the action to Lisbon. Alida Valli played the aged Miss Bordereau.

BORROWERS, THE   Homily, Pod and little Arriety – a family of tiny people who live beneath the floorboards, in Mary Norton's highly-regarded children's novel *The Borrowers* (1952). The sequels are *The Borrowers Afield* (1955), *The Borrowers Afloat* (1959), *The Borrowers Aloft* (1961) and *The Borrowers Avenged* (1982). The first of these books has formed the basis of an American television movie (1973; dir. Walter C. Miller).

BOSAMBO   See under Mr Commissioner SANDERS

BOSTON BLACKIE   Crook turned crime-fighter who began life in *Cosmopolitan* magazine stories which were collected in the book *Boston Blackie* (1919) by Jack Boyle. The character soon became well known in the cinema. A silent movie, *Boston Blackie's Little Pal*, appeared in 1919 and was followed in the 1920s by a couple of other films about the hero. Blackie was revived in the 1940s for a series of fourteen 'B' movies which starred Chester Morris. The first of these was *Meet Boston Blackie* (1941; dir. Robert Florey) and the last was *Boston Blackie's Chinese Venture* (1949; dir. Seymour Friedman). Morris also played Blackie on the radio. The reformed bank-robber later appeared in an American television series, 'Boston Blackie' (1951–3), where he was played by Kent Taylor.

BOTT, VIOLET ELIZABETH   See under William BROWN

BOUNDERBY, JOSIAH   See under Thomas GRADGRIND

BOVARY, EMMA   The most famous heroine in nineteenth-century
French fiction, a classic example of the bored middle-class wife
who dreams of romance and endeavours to find it through
adultery. She appears in Gustave Flaubert's masterly novel
Madame Bovary (1857). There have been numerous stage, film
and television adaptations of the story. An early talkie was
entitled *Unholy Love* (1932). The later Hollywood version
Madame Bovary (1949; dir. Vincente Minnelli) starred Jennifer
Jones. There have been two BBC TV serials based on the novel:
one in 1964, with Nyree Dawn Porter, and another in 1975,
with Francesca Annis. The story has also been adapted for the
stage by Edna O'Brien (1987).

BOWLES, SALLY   English night-club singer in Germany just before
the coming of the Nazis. Although she is very young, she has
green-painted fingernails and cultivates an outrageous air of
sexual knowingness. She appears in Christopher Isherwood's
novella *Sally Bowles* (1937), which was later incorporated in the
volume *Goodbye to Berlin* (1939). This was subsequently
turned into a stage play (1951, by John Van Druten) and a film
(1955; dir. Henry Cornelius), both entitled *I am a Camera.* The
film starred Julie Harris as Sally. After another title change, to
Cabaret, the slight story became a stage musical (1961, with
lyrics by Fred Ebb and music by John Kander) and a much-lauded
musical film (1972; dir. Robert Fosse). Liza Minnelli played Sally
Bowles in the latter production, and in view of her barnstorming
performance it is amusing to note that Isherwood originally wrote
of Sally: 'She sang badly, without any expression, her hands
hanging down at her sides . . .'

BOYLAN, BLAZES   See under Molly BLOOM

BOYLE, JUNO   Strong, resourceful heroine of Sean O'Casey's tragi-
comic play *Juno and the Paycock* (1924). The action is set during
the Irish civil war of 1922, and the 'paycock' of the title is Juno's
drunken, posturing husband, Jack Boyle. The play was filmed by
Alfred Hitchcock (1930), with Sara Allgood as Juno.

BRACKETT, HILDA   See HINGE AND BRACKETT

BRACKLEY, SIR DANIEL   See under Dick SHELTON

BRACKNELL, LADY AUGUSTA   Formidable dowager aunt in Oscar
Wilde's witty play *The Importance of Being Earnest: A Trivial
Comedy for Serious People* (1895). The plot concerns the
tribulations of two young men who assume false identities in
the pursuit of love. They eventually discover that they are
brothers, one of them having been 'mislaid' in a handbag on
Victoria Station,when he was a baby. In the film of the play (1952;
dir. Anthony Asquith) Lady Bracknell was played by Dame Edith
Evans, who placed inimitable scorn on the line 'a *hand*bag . . .?'
A musical version of Wilde's comedy, with a score by Vivian Ellis,
is entitled *Half in Earnest*. In her essay on the play, 'The
Unimportance of Being Oscar' (1947), Mary McCarthy says of Lady
Bracknell: 'When she is on the stage – during the first and the
third acts – the play opens up . . . Into this splendid creation, Wilde
surely put all the feelings of admiration and despair aroused in
him by Respectability.'

BRADDOCK, BENJAMIN   Young man who graduates from college,
suffers an identity crisis, and becomes amorously entangled
with his parents' friend, Mrs Robinson, and her beautiful daughter.
His anti-heroic story is told in Charles Webb's novel *The
Graduate* (1963). This was made into one of the most successful
films of its decade (1967; dir. Mike Nichols), with Dustin Hoffman
as Benjamin.

BRADFORD, BRICK   Spaceman hero of American newspaper
comic-strips and a cinema serial. He is one of the rivals to Buck
ROGERS. Bradford was created by author William Ritt and artist
Clarence Gray, and appeared from 1933. The serial *Brick Bradford*
(1947) starred Kane Richmond.

BRADLEY, BEATRICE LESTRANGE   Enduring female detective
who has appeared in some sixty novels by Gladys Mitchell,
beginning with *Speedy Death* (1929). Mrs Bradley, later Dame
Beatrice, is a consultant psychiatrist to the British Home Office.
She resembles a witch, and is known affectionately as 'Mrs Croc'.

Later novels in the series include *The Mystery of a Butcher's Shop* (1929), *The Longer Bodies* (1930), *The Saltmarsh Murders* (1932), *Dead Man's Morris* (1936), *The Worsted Viper* (1942), *The Rising of the Moon* (1945), *Tom Brown's Body* (1949), *Merlin's Furlong* (1953), *Watson's Choice* (1955), *Adders on the Heath* (1963), *Late, Late in the Evening* (1976), *Here Lies Gloria Mundy* (1982) and *The Crozier Pharaohs* (1984).

BRAMBLE, COLONEL British army officer during World War I, an amiable version of Colonel BLIMP as seen through foreign eyes. He appears in the humorous novel *Les Silences du Colonel Bramble* (1918) by André Maurois (Emile Herzog). A sequel is entitled *Colonel Bramble* (1921). Bramble's name endeared itself to Anglophiles in the years between the two world wars. In Saul Bellow's novel *Mr Sammler's Planet* (1970) the elderly Polish-born protagonist Artur Sammler recalls how 'he fell in love with England. Most of that nonsense had been knocked out of him. He had reconsidered the whole question of Anglophilia, thinking sceptically about Salvador de Madariaga, Mario Praz, André Maurois and Colonel Bramble. He knew the phenomenon.'

BRANDSTETTER, DAVE Homosexual detective who works for a Californian insurance company. He is the sympathetic lead character of highly praised crime novels by Joseph Hansen: *Fadeout* (1970), *Death Claims* (1973), *Troublemaker* (1975), *The Man Everybody Was Afraid Of* (1978), *Skinflick* (1979), *Gravedigger* (1982) and *Nightwork* (1984).

BRANESTAWM, PROFESSOR Absent-minded professor who is always building crazy, impractical machines – perfectly illustrated by W. Heath Robinson in Norman Hunter's book *The Incredible Adventures of Professor Branestawm* (1933). Hunter went on to write more Branestawm stories over a period of almost fifty years. The crack-brained inventor was still going strong in *Professor Branestawm's Perilous Pudding* (1980). He has also appeared on BBC radio and in a television series (1969).

BRANGWEN, URSULA Strong-willed woman who tries on several men for size before finding satisfaction with Rupert BIRKIN. She and her sister, Gudrun Brangwen, appear in D. H. Lawrence's major

novels *The Rainbow* (1915) and *Women in Love* (1920). In the
film of the latter title (1969; dir. Ken Russell) Ursula was played
by Jennie Linden.

BRECK, ALAN See under David BALFOUR

BRECKINRIDGE, MYRA Trans-sexual heroine and narrator of
Gore Vidal's amusing novel about Hollywood myths, *Myra
Breckinridge* (1968). He/she is fond of quoting the film critic
Parker Tyler (author of *Magic and Myth of the Movies*), who is 'our
age's central thinker, if only because *in the decade between 1935
and 1945, no irrelevant film was made in the United States.*
During those years, the entire range of human (which is to say,
American) legend was put on film, and any profound study of
those extraordinary works is bound to make crystal-clear the
human condition.' Vidal's sequel is called *Myron* (1975). The
film *Myra Breckinridge* (1970; dir. Mike Sarne) starred Raquel
Welch (the female Charlton Heston).

BREED See under EDGE

BRER RABBIT AND BRER FOX See under Uncle REMUS

BREWSTER, MONTGOMERY Young man who is given the
delightful but awkward task of spending a million dollars before the
expiry of a tight deadline. He is the hero of George Barr
McCutcheon's comic novel *Brewster's Millions* (1902), which
was turned into a successful stage play by Winchell Smith and
Byron Ongley. There have been several movie versions of this
understandably popular story. It was filmed in 1921 with Fatty
Arbuckle as Brewster; in 1935 (dir. Thornton Freeland) with
Jack Buchanan; in 1945 (dir. Allan Dwan) with Dennis O'Keefe;
in 1961 (retitled *Three on a Spree*; dir. Sidney J. Furie) with Jack
Watling; and in 1985 (dir. Walter Hill) with Richard Pryor.
(Montgomery Brewster should not be confused with Mortimer
Brewster, the bemused hero of Joseph Kesselring's play *Arsenic
and Old Lace*, which was also filmed [1944; dir. Frank Capra], with
Cary Grant in the lead.)

BRIDEHEAD, SUE See under Jude FAWLEY

BRIDGES, MRS See under Mr HUDSON

BRIGHTEYES, ERIC Icelandic hero of H. Rider Haggard's historical adventure novel *Eric Brighteyes* (1891). It is a bloodthirsty tale told in the manner of the Norse sagas. A modern sequel by another hand is *Eric Brighteyes 2: A Witch's Welcome* (1979) by Sigfriour Skaldaspillir (the American fantasy writer Mildred Downey Broxon).

BRODIE, JEAN Middle-aged Edinburgh school teacher of the 1930s, in Muriel Spark's novel *The Prime of Miss Jean Brodie* (1961). She is romantically attracted to Mussolini's fascism, and exerts a charismatic hold over the minds of her girl pupils – although certain of them learn to reject her. The story was turned into a play and a film. Miss Brodie was played by Maggie Smith in the movie (1969; dir. Ronald Neame). In a later television serial, also entitled 'The Prime of Miss Jean Brodie' (1978), the role was taken by Geraldine McEwan.

BRONCO See under Cheyenne BODIE

BROOK, ROGER British secret agent during the period of the Napoleonic Wars. He was invented by popular novelist Dennis Wheatley for the series of books which began with *The Launching of Roger Brook* (1947). Part naval adventure, part spy story, part bawdy romp, the first episode ends with its roguish hero being exonerated by the English Prime Minister. Brook returns to his espionage (and his amorous exploits) in *The Shadow of Tyburn Tree* (1948), *The Rising Storm* (1949), *The Man Who Killed the King* (1951), *The Dark Secret of Josephine* (1955), *The Rape of Venice* (1959), *The Sultan's Daughter* (1963), *The Wanton Princess* (1966), *Evil in a Mask* (1969), *The Ravishing of Lady Mary Ware* (1971), *The Irish Witch* (1973) and *Desperate Measures* (1974).

BROOKE, DOROTHEA Heroine of George Eliot's greatest novel, *Middlemarch: A Study of Provincial Life* (1871–2). An intellectual girl, she makes the mistake of marrying the pedantic Rev. Edward Casaubon. After his death she finds true love with the much younger and more virile Will Ladislaw. The novel has been serialized on BBC television.

BROOKS, CONNIE   School teacher played by Eve Arden in the
American radio series 'Our Miss Brooks' (from 1948). She taught
English at Madison High School, under the eye of the
cantankerous principal Osgood P. Conklin. The series also ran on
television (1952–6), and formed the basis of a feature film of the
same title (1956). Both of these starred Eve Arden, who 'was
much in demand to speak to educational groups and at PTA
meetings, and even received a dozen offers of positions as an English
teacher at real high schools' (according to Tim Brooks and Earle
Marsh).

BROOKS, THEODORE MARLEY   See under Doc SAVAGE

BROWN, ANDY   See AMOS AND ANDY

BROWN, BUSTER . Mischievous American schoolboy created in
1902 by newspaper cartoonist Richard F. Outcault (previously
celebrated for his creation in 1895 of The Yellow Kid, one of the
first strip-cartoon heroes). The adventures of Buster and his
grinning bulldog Tige (a beast which had made its debut in The
Yellow Kid strip) ran in various papers until the 1920s, and have
been revived sporadically since. For many decades an American
footware company has used the name Buster Brown for its
popular line of children's shoes.

BROWN, CHARLIE   Central character, along with his dog SNOOPY,
of Charles M. Schulz's hugely successful strip-cartoon series
Peanuts (from 1950). Charlie is an ordinary American kid,
somewhat diffident and 'wishy-washy', whose pals include the
bossy-boots Lucy and the blanket-clutching Linus. The strips
have been reprinted copiously in paperback and have been translated
into numerous animated films for television (beginning with
'A Charlie Brown Christmas' (1965). There has been a stage musical,
You're a Good Man, Charlie Brown (1967), and there have also
been at least three cartoon feature films: *A Boy Named Charlie
Brown* (1969), *Snoopy, Come Home* (1972) and *Race for Your Life,
Charlie Brown* (1977), all directed by Bill Melendez.

BROWN, FATHER   Brilliant priest-cum-detective invented by
G. K. Chesterton for a series of short stories collected in *The*

Innocence of Father Brown (1911) and other books. The good
Father is apparently the meekest and most unassuming of men, but
he has an uncanny comprehension of the criminal mind. His most
agile and demanding opponent is the French thief Flambeau. The
critic Otto Penzler has written: 'Just as Holmes has Dr Watson
... Father Brown has his own indispensable assistant – God.'
Chesterton's other books about the canny Father are *The Wisdom
of Father Brown* (1914), *The Incredulity of Father Brown* (1926),
The Secret of Father Brown (1927) and *The Scandal of Father
Brown* (1935).

There have been a number of attempts to capture the lyrical,
paradoxical atmosphere of the Father Brown stories on film and
television: *Father Brown, Detective* (1934; dir. Edward Sedgwick)
starred Walter Connolly; *Father Brown* (1954; vt *The Detective*;
dir. Robert Hamer) had Alec Guinness in the part; two German
films of the 1960s had Heinz Ruhmann. On TV the priest has been
played most successfully by Kenneth More in the British series
'Father Brown' (1974). In the American TV movie *The Girl in the
Park* (1980; dir. John Llewellyn Moxey) Barnard Hughes took the
role. The moon-faced detective also appeared in several BBC radio
series of the 1940s. Latterly he has been played by Andrew Sachs
in yet another BBC radio series entitled 'Father Brown Stories'
(1984–5).

BROWN, TOM Boy hero of the novel *Tom Brown's Schooldays*
(1857) by Thomas Hughes. A pupil at Rugby School, under the
headmastership of the famous Dr Arnold, he is the first notable
character in a long tradition of English school fiction. His sufferings
(at the hands of the bully Harry FLASHMAN), and his subsequent
triumphs in the classroom and on the sports field, have fascinated
readers for well over a century. Hughes wrote a less successful
sequel called *Tom Brown at Oxford* (1861). Film versions of the
original novel were made in 1940 (dir. Robert Stevenson), with
Jimmy Lydon as Tom, and in 1951 (dir. Gordon Parry), with John
Howard Davies. A BBC television serial was aired in the 1970s.
There has also been a stage musical version of the story, performed
in Britain in 1972.

BROWN, VELVET Little girl who loves horses, in the novel
National Velvet (1935) by Enid Bagnold. In his book *Bestseller*,

Claud Cockburn summarizes the plot as follows: 'Fourteen-year-old lower-middle-class girl dreams of entering piebald gelding won in shilling raffle for Grand National and riding it herself. Does so. Wins. Becomes national heroine. End story.' Velvet was played by the young Elizabeth Taylor in the film of the novel (1944; dir. Clarence Brown), and by Lori Martin in an American television series (1960–62). A long-delayed sequel to Enid Bagnold's original story was the film *International Velvet* (1978; dir. Bryan Forbes), in which Nanette Newman played Velvet as a middle-aged woman. The latter movie has also been novelized by Bryan Forbes.

BROWN, VICTOR Young working-class Yorkshireman in Stan Barstow's novel *A Kind of Loving* (1960). He is forced into an early marriage when his girlfriend falls pregnant, and this ends unhappily. In the film of the same title (1962; dir. John Schlesinger) Victor was played by Alan Bates. Stan Barstow has since written a couple of sequels to his original novel, *The Watchers on the Shore* (1966) and *The Right True End* (1976). Material from all three books was used in the television serial 'A Kind of Loving' (1982), which starred Clive Wood as Vic Brown.

BROWN, WILLIAM Grubby eleven-year-old who appears in a long series of delightfully comic stories by Richmal Crompton. William lives in a nice middle-class home in an archetypal English village, surrounded by piping hedgerows, vicarage tea parties and slow country policemen. Into this stuffily quaint setting he brings a large dose of juvenile anarchy and fantasy – for William is a latter-day Don Quixote, for ever planning grandiose adventures and for ever falling foul of an unaccommodating reality. He has a band of friends known as the Outlaws – Ginger, Henry and Douglas. Their regular 'enemies' include William's moony older brother Robert, his gloopy sister Ethel, and a spoiled brat called Violet Elizabeth Bott (whose famous line is, 'I'll thkweam and thkweam until I make myself thick'). The first magazine story about William appeared in 1917. It and the succeeding stories were collected in the books *Just – William* (1922), *More William* (1922), *William Again* (1923), *William the Fourth* (1924), and more than thirty others, ending with *William the Lawless* (1970). Most of these volumes were very effectively

William Brown as drawn by *Thomas Henry*

illustrated by Thomas Henry. There have been several films about William, including *Just William's Luck* (1947; dir. Val Guest) and *William Comes to Town* (1948; dir. Guest). A BBC radio series ran from 1945 until the early 1950s. The later British television series, 'Just William' (1976–7), starred Adrian Dannatt.

BRUIN BOYS, THE   See under TIGER TIM

BUCHANAN   See under EDGE

BUCHANAN, DAISY   See under Jay GATSBY

BUCK, JOE   Country boy who tries to make his way as a gigolo in New York City. Fundamentally an innocent, he soon comes to grief. 'Joe Buck' is the assumed name of the hero of James Leo Herlihy's novel *Midnight Cowboy* (1965). It was filmed under the same title (1969; dir. John Schlesinger), with Jon Voight as the unfortunate Buck.

BUCKET, CHARLIE   See under Willy WONKA

BUCKET, INSPECTOR   One of the earliest police detectives to be portrayed in English fiction. He appears in *Bleak House* (1852–3)

by Charles Dickens, where he investigates the murder of the old
lawyer, Tulkinghorn. Inspector Bucket is a comparatively
minor figure in this populous novel, but he is cherished by
aficionados of detective fiction as the first character of his kind.
He was played by Ian Hogg in the BBC television serial based on
Dickens's book (1985). See also Esther SUMMERSON.

BUCKY   See under Captain AMERICA

BUDD, BILLY   Innocent sailor of the eighteenth-century British
navy, in Herman Melville's posthumously published novella *Billy
Budd, Foretopman* (1924). He strikes an officer who has provoked
him cruelly, and for this offence he is hanged by the agonized,
conscience-stricken ship's captain. The story formed the basis of
a play by Louis Osborne Coxe and Robert H. Chapman. It also
inspired Benjamin Britten's successful opera *Billy Budd* (1951),
which has a libretto by E. M. Forster and Eric Crozier. In the film
Billy Budd (1962; dir. Peter Ustinov) Terence Stamp played the
title role.

BUDD, LANNY   Rich young American, son of an armaments
manufacturer, who attempts to put the world to rights. He
features in a series of books by the crusading novelist Upton
Sinclair: *World's End* (1940), *Between Two Worlds* (1941),
Dragon's Teeth (1942), *Wide is the Gate* (1943), *Presidential Agent*
(1945), *Dragon Harvest* (1945), *A World to Win* (1946),
Presidential Mission (1947), *One Clear Call* (1948), *O Shepherd,
Speak* (1949) and *The Return of Lanny Budd* (1953).

BUENDÍA FAMILY, THE   José Arcadio Buendía and his offspring,
inhabitants of the remote South American town of Macondo, are
the chief characters of Gabriel García Márquez's great novel *One
Hundred Years of Solitude* (1967). This has frequently been
described as the quintessential work of Latin American 'magic
realism'.

BUGGINS, GRANDMA   Tiresome and 'cussed' old lady played by
Mabel Constanduros on BBC radio from 1925 until the late 1940s.
The Bugginses, who included Mr and Mrs Buggins and their three
children, were Britain's first 'radio family', and they appeared in

various different shows, one of which was entitled 'The Adventures of Grandma'. Mabel Constanduros not only wrote the scripts but provided most of the voices.

BUGS BUNNY Cartoon rabbit with a famous Brooklyn accent. He made his first appearance in a Warner Brothers animated short in 1937, and soon launched into a long series of films in which he played the starring role. Bugs was created by animators Chuck Jones and Tex Avery, and was given voice by the ubiquitous Mel Blanc. The adventures of this streetwise bunny have also been

Bugs Bunny

published in comic-books and newspaper strips. Since the 1970s
Bugs has appeared regularly on television. His catch-phrase, 'What's
up, Doc?', was used by Peter Bogdanovich for the title of a crazy-
comedy film made in 1972. Bugs has also appeared in his own
feature-length movies (mostly compilations of old material)
which bear such titles as *Bugs Bunny, Superstar* (1975) and *The
Bugs Bunny/Road Runner Movie* (1979).

BULBA, TARAS   Cossack chieftain whose story is told in Nikolai
Gogol's novella *Taras Bulba* (1835) – a work which attempts to
do for the Russian steppes what Fenimore Cooper did for the
American prairies. In the film *Taras Bulba* (1962; dir. J. Lee
Thompson) the hero was played by Yul Brynner.

BULL, JOHNNY   See under Harry WHARTON

BULLWINKLE   Cartoon moose created by producer Jay Ward and
writer Bill Scott for the American television show 'Rocky and His
Friends' (1959–61). Bullwinkle appeared with his friend Rocket J.
Squirrel (also known as Rocky the Flying Squirrel), in short
adventurous tales which pitted them against the dastardly Boris
Badenov. The characters were subsequently seen in a long-
running series, 'The Bullwinkle Show' (1961–73), and have been
revived in the 1980s. There have also been *Bullwinkle* comic-books
and newspaper strips.

BULMAN, GEORGE   Burly British policeman played by Don
Henderson in the television series 'The XYY Man' (1977),
'Strangers' (1980–82) and 'Bulman' (1985–6).

BULTITUDE, DICK   Boy who exchanges bodies with his father, a
stern Victorian *pater familias*, with the help of a magic stone.
Their story is told in the humorous novel *Vice-Versa, or a Lesson
to Fathers* (1882) by F. Anstey (Thomas Anstey Guthrie). The novel
was filmed as *Vice Versa* (1947; dir. Peter Ustinov), with Anthony
Newley as young Dick, and has since been serialized on British
television.

BUMPPO, NATTY   Also known as 'Hawkeye' or 'Leatherstocking',
the American frontiersman hero of novels by J. Fenimore

Cooper. The sequence began with *The Pioneers, or The Sources of the Susquehanna* (1823), and continued with *The Last of the Mohicans* (1826), *The Prairie* (1827), *The Pathfinder, or The Inland Sea* (1840) and *The Deerslayer, or The First War-Path* (1841). Natty Bumppo is at his youngest in the last of these books (the series chronicles his life in approximately the reverse order of events), and it is in this volume that he first meets CHINGACHGOOK, his loyal Mohican friend. A modern single-volume abridgment of the series is entitled *The Leatherstocking Saga* (1954; edited by Allan Nevins). 'Natty has taken on mythic significance in the history of the American imagination,' according to William Rose Benét; he is 'the natural man uncorrupted by civilization'. There have been numerous film versions of Natty Bumppo's adventures. The silent movie *The Last of the Mohicans* (1920; dir. Maurice Tourneur) had George Hackathorne as Natty; and the sound remake (1936; dir. George B. Seitz) starred Randolph Scott. The TV movie of the same title (1977; dir. James L. Conway) had Steve Forrest. A follow-up TV movie, *The Deerslayer* (1978; dir. Dick Friedenberg) also starred Forrest. The Canadian-made television series, 'Hawkeye and the Last of the Mohicans' (1956), had John Hart as the hero. A BBC TV serialization of *The Last of the Mohicans* (1971) was filmed in Scotland and received much praise.

BUMSTEAD, BLONDIE AND DAGWOOD   See BLONDIE

BUNKER, ARCHIE   American version of Alf GARNETT. Played by Carroll O'Connor, he appeared in the very successful television comedy series 'All in the Family' (1971–9), which was later revamped and continued as 'Archie Bunker's Place' (1979–83). Like his English cousin, Alf Garnett, Archie is a loud-mouthed bigot who has low opinions of all ethnic minorities. The ignorant Mr Bunker's impact on the American TV-viewing public was electrifying, and despite (or because of) much controversy the show gained first place in the ratings for five years running. The producer was Norman Lear, who was also responsible for a number of other hit series of the 1970s (see, for example, Mary HARTMAN). Spin-off series from 'All in the Family' include the popular 'Maude' (1972–8), about Mrs Bunker's outspoken liberal cousin Maude Findlay (played by Beatrice Arthur).

BUNTER, BILLY   Fat, bespectacled, check-trousered schoolboy, one of the best known and best loved characters in the whole of English fiction, created by Frank Richards (Charles Hamilton) for an immensely long series of stories which appeared from 1908 onwards. William George Bunter is greedy, cowardly, foolish and inane – his characteristic exclamation is 'Yarooooh!' – and yet his adventures are deliciously funny, and remembered with great affection. He attends Greyfriars School, where he is known to his friends, Harry WHARTON *et al.*, as the Fat Owl of the Remove. He has a sister, Bessie Bunter, whose adventures Hamilton chronicled for another paper under the pseudonym Hilda Richards. In the world of Greyfriars 'everything is safe, solid and unquestionable', according to George Orwell's famous essay, 'Boys' Weeklies' (*Horizon*, 1940). 'Everything will be the same for ever and ever.' That, undoubtedly, is a large element of the Bunter saga's appeal. Now, almost fifty years after Orwell first attempted to analyse it, the timeless world of Greyfriars retains its charm for many readers. The stories originally appeared in an ephemeral boys' paper, the *Magnet*; nowadays they are reprinted in handsome hardbound volumes. It would seem that Bunter has achieved literary immortality.

The *Magnet* ceased publication in 1940, but after World War II Charles Hamilton continued to write original Bunter novels until his death in 1961. The first book was *Billy Bunter of Greyfriars School* (1947), and it was followed by many others. Bunter soon reached television: for ten years from 1952 there was a BBC television series which starred the plump Gerald Campion. There were also a number of Billy Bunter stage plays in the late 1950s. Of course not everyone felt an affection for the bloated anti-hero. When the novel *Bunter's Last Fling* appeared in 1965 the humorist Arthur Marshall wrote (prematurely): 'At long last it is the end of the road for the monstrous Billy Bunter, the revolting, chortling fatty in the tightest trousers in Greyfriars . . .' Recently, a couple of novels by other hands have been appended to the huge corpus of Bunter fiction. They are *But for Bunter* (1985) by David Hughes, in which Billy is discovered still hale at the age of eighty-nine; and *A White Man's Burden: The Early Adventures of Bunter Sahib* (1985) by Daniel Green, which deals with the exploits of the Fat Owl's great-great-grandfather.

BUNTER, MERVYN   See under Lord Peter WIMSEY

BUNTHORNE, REGINALD   Described by his creators as 'a Fleshly
Poet', a young aesthete who carries 'a poppy or a lily' in his
'medieval hand'. He appears in the comic opera *Patience, or
Bunthorne's Bride* (1881) by W. S. Gilbert and Arthur S.
Sullivan. It is commonly supposed that Bunthorne is a caricature
of the young Oscar Wilde.

BURKE, AMOS   Smooth Beverly Hills police chief (and millionaire)
played by Gene Barry in the American television series 'Burke's
Law' (1963–6). The character was actually created a couple of
years earlier, for an episode of 'Dick Powell Theatre' (in which
Powell took the role). In its last season the title of the series was
changed to 'Amos Burke – Secret Agent'.

BURKE, TOMMY   See under Dixon HAWKE

BURLINGTON BERTIE   Swanky young man-about-town who
features in a British music-hall song, 'Burlington Bertie of Bow'.
The number was originally performed by Vesta Tilley. In the
parlance of the late nineteenth century, Bertie is a 'masher',
which is to say a 'swell' or a 'lady-killer'. A similar character,
from another music-hall song, is Gilbert the Filbert, 'the colonel
of the Knuts'.

BURMA   See under Terry LEE

BURNS, WALTER   See under Hildy JOHNSON

BUTLER, RHETT   Southern gentleman at the time of the American
Civil War. He is the hero of Margaret Mitchell's Pulitzer Prize-
winning novel *Gone with the Wind* (1936), which sold many
millions of copies in the years immediately following its
publication. Rhett vies with Ashley Wilkes for the love of Scarlett
O'HARA, eventually marries her, and finds unhappiness. In the
celebrated film of the novel (1939; dir. Victor Fleming) he was
played by Clark Gable.

BUTTERFLY, MADAME   Also known as Cho-cho-san, a Japanese
beauty who marries Lieutenant B. F. Pinkerton of the US Navy. She
commits suicide three years after he deserts her. Her sad story
was told in David Belasco's play *Madame Butterfly* (1898),
which was based on a short story by John Luther Long. The Italian
composer Giacomo Puccini saw the play shortly after it opened
in London, and determined to make it the basis of an opera. His
Madama Butterfly (1904), with a libretto by Giuseppe Giacosa
and Luigi Illica, swiftly became one of the most famous of all
operas. There have been many film adaptations, including a silent
movie which starred Mary Pickford. The first talkie version (1932;
dir. Marion Gering) starred Sylvia Sidney, *sans* Puccini's music.
A more recent film of the opera (1974; dir. Jean Pierre Ponnelle)
had Mirella Freni as Madame Butterfly and Placido Domingo as
Pinkerton.

C

C-3PO   See under Luke SKYWALKER

CADFAEL, BROTHER   Twelfth-century Welsh monk who lives at Shrewsbury Abbey, where he tends the herb garden and occasionally uses his great powers of deduction to solve murder mysteries. He appears in a series of historical detective novels by Ellis Peters (Edith Pargeter): *A Morbid Taste for Bones* (1977), *One Corpse Too Many* (1979), *Monk's-Hood* (1980), *Saint Peter's Fair* (1981), *The Leper of Saint Giles* (1981), *The Virgin in the Ice* (1982), *The Sanctuary Sparrow* (1983), *The Devil's Novice* (1983), *Dead Man's Ransom* (1984), *The Pilgrim of Hate* (1984), *An Excellent Mystery* (1985), *The Raven in the Foregate* (1986), *The Rose Rent* (1986) and *The Hermit of Eyton Forest* (1987).

CAGNEY AND LACEY   Female cops, the 'First Ladies of the New York Police Department', played by Loretta Swit and Tyne Daly in the American television movie *Cagney and Lacey* (1981; dir. Ted Post). In the subsequent popular series Loretta Swit, who played Christine Cagney, was replaced by Meg Foster, who in turn was replaced by Sharon Gless, while Tyne Daly continued to play the part of Mary Beth Lacey. Cagney and Lacey are attractive, capable professionals, approaching forty years of age. They have made a strong impression on the viewing public: on 5 April 1986 the *Radio Times* gave the addresses of two Cagney and Lacey fan clubs active in Britain. The series was conceived by producer Barry Rosenzweig, with more than a little help from scriptwriter Barbara Avedon.

CAINE, KWAI CHANG   Chinese-American priest who is exiled from China to nineteenth-century USA, where his martial-arts skills stand him in good stead. A strong man of few words, he is the hero of the very successful American television series 'Kung Fu' (1971–5), which starred David Carradine. The series was created by producer/director Jerry Thorpe and writer Ed Spielman.

CALAF   See under Princess Turandot

CALIGARI, DOCTOR   Mysterious villain of the celebrated German horror film *The Cabinet of Dr Caligari* (1919; dir. Robert Weine). He is a magician and hypnotist who uses a sleepwalking victim to commit murders on his behalf. Caligari was played by Werner Krauss. A much later American film, *The Cabinet of Caligari* (1962; dir. Roger Kay), starred Dan O'Herlihy as a psychiatrist called Dr Caligari but it bears very little relation to the earlier movie.

CALLAHAN, HARRY   Violent hero played by Clint Eastwood in the film *Dirty Harry* (1971; dir. Don Siegel). Callahan is a San Francisco cop of decidedly authoritarian views. Armed with a huge Magnum pistol, he flouts the law in pursuit of his own version of justice. He reappears in the movies *Magnum Force* (1973; dir. Ted Post) and *The Enforcer* (1976; dir. James Fargo), both of which also starred Eastwood. In addition to the usual paperback novelizations of these three films, a series of 'original' Dirty Harry novels has been published in the following decade: the first of these is *Duel for Cannons* (1981) by Dane Hartman.

CALLAHAN, SLIM   See under Lemmy Caution

CALLAN, DAVID   Tough, dour secret agent, the low-life antithesis of James Bond, in the British television series 'Callan' (1967–73). Callan was played by Edward Woodward, and the series was created by James Mitchell. The feature film *Callan* (1974; dir. Don Sharp) was based on the first episode of the series. Callan was revived for the TV movie *Wet Job* (1981), also starring Woodward. James Mitchell has written novels based on the original TV scripts, including such titles as *A Magnum for Schneider* (1969; vt *A Red File for Callan*), *Russian Roulette* (1973), *Death and Bright Water* (1974) and *Smear Job* (1975).

CAMERON, DOCTOR   See under Doctor Finlay

CAMERON, EWEN   Scottish highlander who supports Bonnie Prince Charlie in the 1745 rising. He appears in Dorothy Kathleen Broster's romantic historical novel *The Flight of the Heron* (1925), and its sequels, *The Dark Mile* and *The Gleam in the North*.

CAMILLE Marguerite Gautier, a courtesan who spurns her lover, Armand Duval, for his own good, and eventually dies of consumption in Paris. She first appeared in the novel *La Dame aux Camélias* (1848) by Alexandre Dumas, *fils* (not the author of *The Three Musketeers*, but his illegitimate son). Dumas turned his story into a very successful stage play (1852). (Giuseppe Verdi based his opera *La Traviata* [1853] on this play, but the lovers' names were changed to Violetta and Alfredo.) The play was filmed, under the title *Camille*, in 1915, with Clara Kimball Young; in 1917, with Theda Bara; in 1921, with Nazimova; and in 1936 (dir. George Cukor), with Greta Garbo giving one of her most famous performances (she dies beautifully). In a two-part BBC television production entitled *Lady of the Camellias* (1976) the heroine was played by Kate Nelligan. Latterly, the story has been turned into a glossy Anglo-American TV movie, once more called *Camille* (1984; dir. Desmond Davis), with Greta Scacchi as the seductive Marguerite. There has also been a ballet by Sir Frederick Ashton entitled *Marguerite and Armand* (1963).

CAMILLO, DON Muscular village priest in a series of humorous short stories by Giovanni Guareschi. Camillo's adversary is the local communist mayor, Peppone. The stories first appeared in the Italian magazine *Candido*, in the late 1940s, and they have been collected in several books. In English the titles of the volumes are *The Little World of Don Camillo* (1950), *Don Camillo and the Prodigal Son* (1952), *Don Camillo's Dilemma* (1954), *Don Camillo and the Devil* (1957), *Comrade Don Camillo* (1964) and *Don Camillo Meets the Flower Children* (1969). The films, *The Little World of Don Camillo* (1951; dir. Jules Duvivier), *The Return of Don Camillo* (1953; dir. Duvivier) and *Don Camillo Monseigneur* (1961) all starred the French comic actor Fernandel as the battling priest. A BBC television series, 'Don Camillo' (1980), had Mario Adorf in the title role.

CAMPION, ALBERT Upper-class detective who appears in the crime novels of Margery Allingham, beginning with *The Crime at Black Dudley* (1929; vt *The Black Dudley Murder*). In the first book he is a minor figure, but in the following novels, *Mystery Mile* (1929) and *Look to the Lady* (1931; vt *The Gyrth Chalice Mystery*), Allingham turned him into a heroic, if somewhat foppish, character (she was to describe the early Mr Campion as a 'zany, or goon, laughing inanely at danger . . .'). In the series of novels which followed, Campion grows and matures. The later titles are *Police at the Funeral* (1932), *Sweet Danger* (1933; vt *Kingdom of Death*), *Death of a Ghost* (1934), *Flowers for the Judge* (1936), *The Case of the Late Pig* (1937), *Mr Campion and Others* (1937; vt *Mr Campion, Criminologist*), *Dancers in Mourning* (1937), *The Fashion in Shrouds* (1938), *Black Plumes* (1940), *Traitor's Purse* (1941), *Coroner's Pidgin* (1945; vt *Pearls Before Swine*), *The Case Book of Mr Campion* (1947), *More Work for the Undertaker* (1948), *The Tiger in the Smoke* (1952), *The Beckoning Lady* (1955; vt *The Estate of the Beckoning Lady*), *Hide My Eyes* (1958; vt *Tether's End*), *The China Governess* (1962), *The Mind Readers* (1965) and the posthumous *Cargo of Eagles* (1968). After Allingham's death in 1966 her husband, Philip Youngman Carter, wrote two more Campion books: *Mr Campion's Farthing* (1968) and *Mr Campion's Falcon* (1969; vt *Mr Campion's Quarry*). One of Allingham's Campion novels has been filmed: *Tiger in the Smoke* (1956; dir. Roy Baker). The same book has been dramatized for BBC radio (1984), with Basil Moss as Albert Campion.

CANDIDE   Innocent hero of the celebrated novella *Candide, ou L'optimisme* (1759) by Voltaire (François-Marie Arouet). Candide wanders the world with his tutor, Dr PANGLOSS, experiences disaster after disaster, and eventually settles down quietly to cultivate his own garden. The satirical film *Candide* (1960; dir. Norbert Carbonneaux) had Jean-Pierre Cassel as an updated version of the hero. The television movie of the same title (1973; dir. James McTaggart) starred Ian Ogilvy in a straight rendition of the tale. The story has also been rendered as a stage musical (1957), with music by Leonard Bernstein and lyrics by Richard Wilbur.

CANDY   Delectable heroine of the comic-pornographic novel *Candy* (1958) by Terry Southern and Mason Hoffenberg. Candy is an innocent, a female CANDIDE for a sexually-liberated era. The book was filmed (1968; dir. Christian Marquand), with Ewa Aulin as the much-molested Candy.

CANDY, CLIVE   See Colonel BLIMP

CANNON, FRANK   Fat private-eye played by William Conrad in the American television series 'Cannon' (1970–76). A gourmet with great ratiocinative skills, he is an unacknowledged substitute of sorts for Rex Stout's Nero WOLFE (whom the same actor went on to play in a later series). Cannon himself was revived for the TV movie *The Return of Frank Cannon* (1980; dir. Corey Allen), in which William Conrad once more played the semi-retired detective.

CAPP, ANDY   Cloth-capped working man who hails from the north-east of England. He is the lazy, belligerent anti-hero of Britain's most successful newspaper comic-strip. Reg Smythe first drew Andy Capp and his nagging wife Flo for the *Daily Mirror* in 1957, since when the strip has been syndicated widely and is reportedly 'the second biggest cartoon in the world, next to *Peanuts*' (see Charlie BROWN and SNOOPY). A stage musical, *Andy Capp* (1982), was written by Trevor Peacock and had songs by Alan Price. A British television series, with James Bolam as the truculent Mr Capp, has been announced for 1987.

CARELLA, STEVE   Detective of the '87th Precinct', in a long series of *romans policiers* by Ed McBain (Evan Hunter). In a city which may or may not be New York, Carella and his many colleagues crack a succession of tough cases. The first of these are recounted in the books *Cop Hater*, *The Mugger* and *The Pusher* (all 1956). There have been more than thirty-five titles in all, including *Killer's Choice* (1957), *Killer's Wedge* (1959), *Give the Boys a Great Big Hand* (1960), *Ax* (1964), *Doll* (1965), *Fuzz* (1968), *Hail, Hail, the Gang's All Here!* (1972), *Bread* (1974), *Long Time No See* (1977), *Heat* (1981), *Lightning* (1984) and *Eight Black Horses* (1985). Lieutenant Carella's wife, 'Teddy', is a deaf-mute. An American television series, '87th Precinct' (1961–2), starred Robert Lansing. Carella also appeared in the film *Fuzz* (1972; dir. Richard A. Colla), where he was played by Burt Reynolds.

CAREY, PHILIP   Hero of W. Somerset Maugham's semi-autobiographical novel *Of Human Bondage* (1915). Philip has a club-foot, and suffers a lonely childhood. He becomes a doctor, but his infatuation for a waitress leads to trouble. Despite its length, the story has been filmed several times: in 1934 (dir. John Cromwell), with Leslie Howard in the lead; in 1946 (dir. Edmund Goulding), with Paul Henreid; and in 1964 (dir. Ken Hughes), with Laurence Harvey.

CARMEN   Flirtatious Spanish gypsy who entices an army corporal, Don José, away from his fiancée and his duty. She drives him to distraction, and he stabs her when she attempts to abandon him for another man, the bullfighter Escamillo. This quintessential *femme fatale* first appeared in Prosper Mérimée's novel *Carmen* (1852), which formed the basis of Georges Bizet's rousing opera of the same title (1875). Bizet's masterpiece, which has a libretto by Henri Meilhac and Ludovic Halévy, was badly received in its day but has since proved to be the most popular of all operas. During the twentieth century it has been staged, filmed and televised in countless productions. Movies include the silents *Carmen* (1915; dir. Raoul Walsh), with Theda Bara, and *The Loves of Carmen* (1927; dir. Walsh), with Dolores Del Rio. A talkie, also entitled *The Loves of Carmen* (1948; dir. Charles Vidor) starred Rita Hayworth. Oscar Hammerstein II wrote the lyrics for an updated version of Bizet's opera, with the action transposed to America; this was filmed as *Carmen Jones* (1954; dir. Otto Preminger), with Dorothy Dandridge in the title role. Several new film or television versions of *Carmen* have been released in the 1980s, including three by the noted British theatrical director Peter Brook, and another by the French film-maker Jean-Luc Godard. An outstanding French-Italian co-production (1984; dir. Francesco Rosi) had Julia Migenes-Johnson as Carmen and Placido Domingo as Don José.

CARMILLA   Beautiful female vampire in J. Sheridan Le Fanu's novella 'Carmilla' (included in the collection *In a Glass Darkly*, 1872). Her story has formed the basis of several films, including *Vampyr* (1931; dir. Carl Dreyer) with Sybille Schmitz; *Blood and Roses* (1960; dir. Roger Vadim) with Elsa Martinelli; and *The Vampire Lovers* (1970; dir. Roy Ward Baker) with Ingrid Pitt.

CARNACKI   Detective who specializes in supernatural cases. He is the hero of nine short stories by the English writer William

Hope Hodgson. These are collected in the book *Carnacki, the Ghost Finder* (1913; expanded edition 1947). Carnacki is a psychic investigator who utilizes a combination of ancient lore and modern technology. 'Although the stories are rather badly written, Carnacki remains a memorable figure, if only for his human admission to being "in a sheer funk" in the face of the unknown' (Julia Briggs, *Night Visitors*). See also John SILENCE.

CARNELIAN, JHEREK   See under Jerry CORNELIUS

CARR, KATY   High-spirited, 'naughty' heroine of *What Katy Did* (1872) by Susan Coolidge (Sarah Chauncy Woolsey). She is confined to a wheelchair as a result of a spinal injury, and by the time she can walk again she has learned, through the 'school of pain', how to accept domestic discipline. Her later adventures, at boarding school and abroad, are recounted in the same author's *What Katy Did at School* (1873) and *What Katy Did Next* (1886). The books have become perennial favourites.

CARRADOS, MAX   Blind detective created by Ernest Bramah (E. B. Smith) for a series of short stories collected in the books *Max Carrados* (1914), *The Eyes of Max Carrados* (1923) and *Max Carrados Mysteries* (1927). Carrados also appears in one short story included in *The Specimen Case* (1924) and in the novel *The Bravo of London* (1934). His extremely acute hearing and sense of smell help him solve various criminal cases.

CARRIE   (1) See Carrie MEEBER; (2) see Carrie WHITE

CARRINGTON, ALEXIS   See Alexis Carrington COLBY

CARRUTHERS   Hero and narrator of Erskine Childers's novel *The Riddle of the Sands: A Record of Secret Service* (1903). While on a yachting holiday in the North Sea, he and his friend Arthur Davies discover evidence of a German plot to invade England. In the film of the book (1978; dir. Tony Maylam) Carruthers was played by Michael York.

CARSON, HENRY   See under Mary BARTON

CARTER, JOHN   Plain-named but well-bred hero of Edgar Rice
Burroughs's swashbuckling interplanetary fantasy *A Princess
of Mars* and its nine sequels. Carter is a nineteenth-century
confederate army officer who finds himself translated by
magical means to Barsoom (the planet Mars). There he fights giant
green men and other monstrosities, and falls in love with a red-
skinned princess, Dejah Thoris. The novel was first published in
All-Story magazine in 1912, eventually reaching book form in
1917. Its immediate sequels, *The Gods of Mars* (1918) and *The
Warlord of Mars* (1919), continue the story of Carter's rise to power
in Barsoomian society. The later novels in the series often relegate
him to a secondary role, although he does come to the fore again in
a number of them. The rest of the series consists of: *Thuvia, Maid
of Mars* (1920), *The Chessmen of Mars* (1922), *The Master Mind of
Mars* (1928), *A Fighting Man of Mars* (1931), *Swords of Mars*
(1936), *Synthetic Men of Mars* (1940), *Llana of Gathol* (1948),
and the posthumous *John Carter of Mars* (1964 – one of the two
stories in this volume is probably not by Burroughs). Oddly enough,
there have been no cinema or television adaptations of John
Carter's adventures (perhaps his time will come) but he has had
several incarnations as a character in newspaper strips and
comic-books. Burroughs's son, John Coleman Burroughs, drew
a strip version of *A Princess of Mars* in 1941, and this was followed
by a comic-book in the 1950s. Following the great revival of
Burroughs's popularity in the 1960s and 1970s, Marvel Comics
launched their *John Carter, Warlord of Mars* in 1977.

CARTER, NICK   Extremely long-lived detective hero who made his
first appearance in the *New York Weekly* in 1886, in a story entitled
'The Old Detective's Pupil'. He is boyish, clean-living and all-
American. He is also an expert at disguise. Carter was created
by Ormond G. Smith (publisher) and John Russell Coryell (writer).
The character was soon taken over by writer Frederic Van
Rensselaer Dey, who produced almost 500 novellas about Carter
over a period of twenty-one years. These range from *The Piano
Box Mystery* (1892) to *The Spider's Parlor* (1913). As with Britain's
Sexton BLAKE, Carter has been perpetuated by many other
writers. Among the earlier authors were William Wallace Cook,
who also wrote science fiction, and Johnston McCulley, the
creator of ZORRO. At one time the hero had his own magazines,

the *Nick Carter Detective Library* and the *Nick Carter Weekly*. In his latest incarnation Nick Carter is the 'author' and tough-guy protagonist (now known as the 'Killmaster') of a series of cheap paperback novels which bear such titles as *The China Doll* (1964), *The Inca Death Squad* (1972), *The Devil's Dozen* (1973), *The Green Wolf Connection* (1976), *The Mendoza Manuscript* (1982) and *The Caribbean Coup* (1984). Among the authors who have written these latter-day Nick Carter adventures anonymously are Michael Avallone, Willis Todhunter Ballard, Michael Collins and Martin Cruz Smith. The character has also appeared in cinema serials (several of which were made in France, between 1906 and 1910) and on the radio. An American TV movie, *The Adventures of Nick Carter* (1972; dir. Paul Krasny), starred Robert Conrad as the master detective.

CARTON, SYDNEY   English wastrel who becomes a self-sacrificing hero in Charles Dickens's novel about the French Revolution and its aftermath, *A Tale of Two Cities* (1859). He is in love with Lucie Manette, but she marries Charles Darnay (who happens to bear a strong physical resemblance to Carton). When Darnay is condemned to the guillotine Carton very nobly takes his place, uttering the famous line: 'It is a far, far better thing that I do, than I have ever done; it is a far, far better rest that I go to than I have ever known.' The story has been adapted to the stage, where a long-running Victorian production was entitled *The Only Way*. It has also formed the basis of an opera, *A Tale of Two Cities* (1953) by Arthur Benjamin. A more recent stage musical version, called *Two Cities* (1969), was less successful. Silent movie versions of Dickens's novel were made in 1917, with William Farnum in the lead, and in 1926, with Martin Harvey. In the sound film *A Tale of Two Cities* (1936; dir. Jack Conway) Carton was played by Ronald Colman; in the remake (1958; dir. Ralph Thomas) the dual role of Carton and Darnay was taken by Dirk Bogarde. The TV movie of the same title (1980; dir. Jim Goddard) starred Chris Sarandon, and a more recent BBC television serial version had Paul Shelley in the main part.

CARTWRIGHT, BEN   Owner of the Ponderosa ranch, played by Lorne Greene in the long-running American television series *Bonanza* (1959–73). A combination of Western adventure and soap opera, the series was created by David Dortort. The all-male Cartwright family consists of the wise elder, Ben, and his sons Adam, Hoss and Little Joe.

CASAMASSIMA, THE PRINCESS   Under her maiden name, Christina Light, she is the principal female character in Henry James's first novel, *Roderick Hudson* (1876). She reappears more famously in James's *The Princess Casamassima* (1886), where she decides to study the lives of the London poor and becomes involved with a young radical called Hyacinth Robinson.

CASAUBON, EDWARD   See under Dorothea Brooke

CASEY, BEN   Young doctor played by Vince Edwards in the American television series 'Ben Casey' (1961–6). He is a harder, more realistic (and more hairy-armed) version of Dr James Kildare. His mentor (his 'Dr Gillespie') is one Dr David Zorba. The series was created by James E. Moser.

CASPER   Cute little ghost, in search of an hospitable American family to haunt. He first appeared in a short animated film entitled *The Friendly Ghost* (1945; dir. Isador Sparber; based on a short story by Seymour Reitt). Soon Casper appeared in more films, and in his own long-lived comic-book (from 1949). There have been many spin-off comic-book titles, including such items as *Casper's Ghostland*, *Casper's Space Ship* and *Casper's TV Showtime*.

CASS, EPPIE   See under Silas Marner

CASSIDY, HOPALONG   Black-clad hero of the Old West created by writer Clarence E. Mulford for his novel *Hopalong Cassidy* (1910). Sequels by Mulford include such titles as *Hopalong Cassidy Returns*, *Hopalong Cassidy's Protégé*, *Hopalong Cassidy and the Eagle's Brood* and *Hopalong Cassidy Serves a Writ*. Cassidy became famous as the leading character played by William Boyd in a series of more than sixty cheap films, beginning with *Hopalong Cassidy* (1935) and petering out in 1948. The old movies became very popular when they were reshown on American television, and Boyd played Hopalong again in a new

made-for-TV series (1949–51). According to TV historians Tim
Brooks and Earle Marsh, 'Hoppy, silver-haired and dressed all in
black, [chased] villains to their doom on his faithful horse Topper.
He was a true Knight of the West – and a far cry from the profane,
unwashed, gimpy-legged cowpoke originally created in the stories
of Clarence E. Mulford.' There was also a radio series of
Hopalong Cassidy adventures. Sequels by other hands in book
form include *Hopalong Cassidy and the Mothers of West Fork*
(1950) and *Hopalong Cassidy and the Trail to Seven Pines* (1951)
by Tex Burns (Louis L'Amour).

CASTLEWOOD, LADY RACHEL   See under Henry ESMOND

CASTORP, HANS   Young man who spends seven years at a
tuberculosis sanatorium in the Swiss Alps, in Thomas Mann's
philosophical novel *The Magic Mountain* (1924). He engages in
intellectual debate with people of various nationalities, and
eventually is granted a vision which seems to reconcile the
conflicting forces of rationality and irrationality within himself
and within European society as a whole.

CATHERINE   Beautiful, violet-eyed French girl of the fifteenth
century. Her adventures, during which she meets Joan of Arc, Gilles
de Rais and other famous folk of the period, are recounted in a
series of salacious historical novels by Juliette Benzoni. In
English, the first five titles are: *One Love is Enough* (1964),
Catherine (1965), *Belle Catherine* (1966), *Catherine and
Arnaud* (1967) and *Catherine and a Time for Love* (1968). These
novels belong to much the same genre as Sergeanne Golon's
books about ANGÉLIQUE.

CAULFIELD, HOLDEN   Juvenile protagonist of J. D. Salinger's
highly esteemed novel *The Catcher in the Rye* (1951). A Huckleberry
FINN of the post-World War II generation, Holden runs away from
his school and has sundry adventures in New York. Aware of the
'phoniness' all around him, he narrates his slender story in a part-
cynical, part-naïve style which captivated a large readership and
helped prepare the world for the drop-out ethos of 1960s youth.
Salinger, who is one of the most mysterious and reclusive of writers,
has not permitted the book to be adapted for the movies or

television. Holden Caulfield also appears in some of the tales included in Salinger's *Nine Stories* (1953; vt *For Esmé, with Love and Squalor*).

CAUTION, LEMMY 'G-man' hero of a series of pseudo-American thrillers by the British writer Peter Cheyney. The titles are *This Man is Dangerous* (1936), *Poison Ivy* (1937), *Dames Don't Care* (1937), *Can Ladies Kill?* (1938), *Don't Get Me Wrong* (1939), *You'd Be Surprised* (1940), *Mr Caution – Mr Callaghan* (1941; in which Lemmy Caution meets Cheyney's other principal series character, Slim Callaghan), *Your Deal, My Lovely* (1941), *Never a Dull Moment* (1942), *You Can Always Duck* (1943), *I'll Say She Does!* (1945) and *G Man at the Yard* (1946). Caution is notable for his readiness to employ violence. He was played by Ben Wright in the BBC radio series 'Lemmy Caution Calling' (from 1940). According to Donald McCormick, 'during the war years Cheyney became compulsive reading for millions and by the end of the war he was topping one and a half million sales a year, with editions of his books regularly published in the US and France'. He must have made an impression in the latter country, because Lemmy Caution appeared in several French movies of the 1950s, where he was played by the flinty-faced actor Eddie Constantine. Indeed, the character has been 'immortalized' by director Jean-Luc Godard in his curious science fiction film *Alphaville* (1965). In this Pop-Art movie Eddie Constantine played Lemmy Caution as a lone trench-coated hero in a futuristic totalitarian city.

CAVARADOSSI, MARIO See under Floria TOSCA

CAVOR 'Short, round-bodied, thin-legged little man, with a jerky quality in his motions', who chooses 'to clothe his extraordinary mind in a cricket cap, an overcoat, and cycling knickerbockers and stockings'. He is the inventor of 'Cavorite', a substance which counters gravity. By enclosing themselves in an airtight sphere which is coated with this remarkable material, Cavor and his friend Mr Bedford are able to fly to the Moon. Their terrifying adventure is recounted in H. G. Wells's novel *The First Men in the Moon* (1901). Bedford eventually returns to Earth, but Cavor is stranded in caverns beneath the Moon's surface where he confronts the Grand Lunar, ruler of all the Selenites. The unsatisfactory film of the novel (1964; dir. Nathan Juran) starred Lionel Jeffries as Cavor.

CECIL, BERTIE See under CIGARETTE

CELIE Suffering heroine of Alice Walker's Pulitzer Prize-winning novel *The Color Purple* (1982). A black girl growing up in the American South, she is cruelly treated by her father and husband, and eventually finds solace in female companionship. In the successful film of the novel (1985; dir. Steven Spielberg) Celie was played by Whoopi Goldberg.

Celie (Whoopi Goldberg) in the film *The Color Purple*

CHALLENGER, GEORGE EDWARD   Black-bearded British
scientist of ferocious temperament, created by Arthur Conan
Doyle for his novel *The Lost World* (1912). Together with the
eminent explorer Lord John Roxton and the young newspaper
reporter Edward Malone, Professor Challenger goes in search of
'Maple White Land', a mysterious plateau in South America. There
they discover living dinosaurs and ape-men. Doyle revived the
irascible and opinionated Professor for two later novels, *The Poison
Belt* (1913) and *The Land of Mist* (1926), as well as a couple of
short stories – all of which are collected in the omnibus volume
The Professor Challenger Stories. The silent-movie version of *The
Lost World* (1925; dir. Harry Hoyt) starred Wallace Beery as
Challenger, and was celebrated in its day for its advanced special
effects. The remake (1960; dir. Irwin Allen), with Claude Rains, was
less impressive.

CHAMPION   Wild horse of the American West who is befriended
by a young boy. Champion is the hero of an American comic-book
and a television series, *The Adventures of Champion* (1956; also
known as *Champion the Wonder Horse*), which was shown many
times around the world. Originally, Champion was the name
given to a series of horses ridden by the singing cowboy Gene
Autry in the numerous Western movies he made from 1935.

CHAMPION, JANE   Plain heroine of Florence Barclay's popular
romantic novel *The Rosary* (1909), a work which 'was said to have
been read and wept over by every housemaid in the British Isles'
(Rachel Anderson). Jane refuses to marry the artist Garth Dalmain
for fear that his love will turn cold. When he is blinded in a
shooting accident she tends to him, under the alias of 'Nurse
Rosemary Gray', and gains his love anew: 'He lifted his sightless
face to hers, for one moment. "You?" he said. "*You!* You – all
the time?" Then he hid his face in the soft lace at her breast.'

CHAN, CHARLIE   Chinese-American detective who works for the
Honolulu Police. Wise, unflappable, aphoristic, Chan solves
many murder mysteries, usually with the enthusiastic help of his
'Number-One Son'. Charlie Chan was created by Earl Derr Biggers,
who featured him in six novels: *The House Without a Key* (1925),
The Chinese Parrot (1926), *Behind That Curtain* (1928), *The Black*

Camel (1929), *Charlie Chan Carries On* (1930) and *Keeper of the Keys* (1932). A sequel by another hand is *Charlie Chan Returns* (1974) by Dennis Lynds (Michael Collins). The Chinese detective went on to become an immensely successful character in the movies, and has appeared in over fifty films. The most famous screen Chan was the Swedish actor Warner Oland, who first played the part in *Charlie Chan Carries On* (1931; dir. Hamilton McFadden). Oland starred in another fifteen Chan films, ending with *Charlie Chan at Monte Carlo* (1937; dir. Eugene Forde). He was replaced by Sidney Toler, who took the role in a further twenty-two films, beginning with *Charlie Chan in Honolulu* (1938; dir. H. Bruce Humberstone) and concluding with *The Trap* (1946; dir. Howard Bretherton). Roland Winters then played Chan in another six films, from *The Chinese Ring* (1947; dir. William Beaudine) to *Sky Dragon* (1949; dir. Lesley Selander). There have been sporadic attempts to revive the character since, for instance the TV movie *Happiness is a Warm Clue* (1971; vt *The Return of Charlie Chan*; dir. Leslie Martinson), with Ross Martin; and the spoof feature film *Charlie Chan and the Curse of the Dragon Queen* (1981; dir. Clive Donner), which had Peter Ustinov as the inscrutable one. Chan has also appeared in a British-produced television series, 'The New Adventures of Charlie Chan' (1956–7), where he was played by J. Carrol Naish; and in an animated TV series, 'Charlie Chan and the Chan Clan' (1972), with Keye Luke (who played Number-One Son in the films of the 1930s) providing the detective's voice.

CHANCE   Reclusive gardener, a *tabula rasa* whose knowledge of the wide world is entirely gleaned from television. When his elderly employer dies Chance is cast out into the world, where his blank innocence is interpreted as great depth of character and subtlety of purpose. He introduces himself as 'Chance the gardener', is misheard, and becomes 'Chauncey Gardiner' – a sage, a media hero and a possible candidate for the presidency of the United States. Chance's unlikely story is told in Jerzy Kosinski's slim novel *Being There* (1970). In the film of the book (1979; dir. Hal Ashby) he was played by Peter Sellers.

CHANCELLOR, OLIVE   Strong-willed feminist who demands the love and allegiance of a beautiful girl, Verena Tarrant, in Henry

James's novel *The Bostonians* (1886). Verena is also loved by Basil Ransom, a Southern gentleman of conventional views, and the plot concerns the tug of war between Olive and Basil with Verena as the prize. Recent critics have assumed that Olive Chancellor is partly motivated by lesbian feelings. In the film of the novel (1984; dir. James Ivory) she was played by Vanessa Redgrave.

CHANDOS, RICHARD WILLIAM   Known as Bill to his friends (who include the redoubtable Jonah MANSEL), a young gentleman-adventurer in the novels of Dornford Yates (Cecil William Mercer). Chandos and his pal George Hanbury are sent down from Oxford for beating up communists; they meet Jonah Mansel in a London club, and set out together to retrieve buried treasure in Austria. Chandos recounts this exciting story in *Blind Corner* (1927), the first of a series of thrillers which he narrates. Other titles in which he appears are: *Perishable Goods* (1928), *Blood Royal* (1929), *Fire Below* (1930), *She Fell Among Thieves* (1935), *Gale Warning* (1939), *An Eye for a Tooth* (1943), *Red in the Morning* (1946) and *Cost Price* (1949). The British TV movie *She Fell Among Thieves* (1978; dir. Clive Donner) had a script by Tom Sharpe and starred Malcolm McDowell as Richard Chandos.

CHANG   See under Hugh CONWAY

CHANNING, MARGO   Glamorous but ageing actress of the Broadway stage who is elbowed aside by a ruthless newcomer. She appears in Joseph L. Mankiewicz's multi-Oscar-winning film *All About Eve* (1950), where she is played with acid brilliance by Bette Davis. A stage musical, *Applause*, was based on the film.

CHARLES, NICK AND NORA   Husband-and-wife detective team, created by Dashiell Hammett for his sparkling mystery novel *The Thin Man* (1934). They live in a luxurious New York apartment, drink large quantities of liquor, and have a pampered dog named Asta. Hammett wrote no more stories about them, but Mr and Mrs Charles soon took on a life of their own in the movies. *The Thin Man* (1934; dir. W. S. Van Dyke) starred William Powell and Myrna Loy. It was a great success and was followed by five more films, all with the same stars: *After the Thin Man* (1936; dir. Van Dyke), *Another Thin Man* (1939; dir. Van Dyke),

Shadow of the Thin Man (1941; dir. Van Dyke), *The Thin Man Goes Home* (1944; dir. Richard Thorpe) and *Song of the Thin Man* (1947; dir. Edward Buzzell). (The 'Thin Man' of the titles is a character who appears in the first story only.) A television series, also called 'The Thin Man' (1957–8), starred Peter Lawford and Phyllis Kirk.

CHARTERS AND CALDICOTT   Two Englishmen abroad, played by Basil Radford and Naunton Wayne in the comedy thriller *The Lady Vanishes* (1938; dir. Alfred Hitchcock). Charters and Caldicott are cricket-loving gents of limited intelligence, but fundamentally decent and courageous. They were the happy creations of scriptwriters Frank Launder and Sidney Gilliat. The characters as embodied by Radford and Wayne proved very popular, and they reappeared in the film *Night Train to Munich* (1940; dir. Carol Reed) and in the BBC radio serials 'Crook's Tour' (1941) and 'Secret Mission 609' (1942) (the first of these serials was filmed [1941; dir. John Baxter]). Decades later, *The Lady Vanishes* was remade (1979; dir. Anthony Page) with Arthur Lowe as Charters and Ian Carmichael as Caldicott. An amusing television series, 'Charters and Caldicott' (1985), was written by Keith Waterhouse. It starred Robin Bailey and Michael Aldridge as the ageing pair.

CHATTERLEY, LADY CONSTANCE   Repressed upper-class woman who finds carnal satisfaction with her game-keeper, Oliver Mellors, in D. H. Lawrence's notorious and oft-misunderstood novel *Lady Chatterley's Lover* (1928). Long banned, the book became a *cause célèbre* in 1960, when Penguin Books were unsuccessfully prosecuted for publishing a full version for the first time in Britain. The paperback edition became a huge bestseller, and Lady Chatterley's name entered the language as a schoolboys' dirty joke. A much inferior sequel by another hand is *Lady Chatterley's Daughter* (1961) by Patricia Robins. Also of inferior quality are the French-made films based on Lawrence's novel – the tame *Lady Chatterley's Lover* (1955; dir. Marc Allégret), with Danielle Darrieux, and the more explicit remake (1981; dir. Just Jaeckin), with Sylvia Kristel. The story of Lady Chatterley and her lover has recently been retold in a salacious comic-book version by Hunt Emerson (1986).

CHAUVELIN, CITIZEN   See under The SCARLET PIMPERNEL

CHEE CHEE   See under John DOLITTLE

CHERRINGTON, EUSTACE AND HILDA   Brother and sister whose young lives are described in L. P. Hartley's trilogy of novels *The Shrimp and the Anemone* (1944; vt *The West Window*), *The Sixth Heaven* (1946) and *Eustace and Hilda* (1947). Eustace is a gentle, pliable, hedonistic boy who is emotionally bullied by his elder sister. There have been BBC television adaptations of the three novels (1977–8), with Grant Bardsley as the young Eustace and Sarah Webb as Hilda (Christopher Strauli and Susan Fleetwood played the characters as adults).

CHERRY, BOB   See under Harry WHARTON

CHESHIRE CAT, THE   See under ALICE

CHESTER   See under Matt DILLON

CHICHIKOV, PAVEL IVANOVICH   Swindling anti-hero of Nikolai Gogol's novel *Dead Souls* (1842). He plans to buy recently deceased serfs from rich landowners (who wish to be relieved of the tax burden), so that he can then mortgage this impressive property (which will exist only on paper) in order to set himself up with his own estate. But his grotesque scheme to traffic in 'dead souls' goes awry, to blackly humorous effect. The novel was hailed as a masterpiece, and Gogol began work on a sequel which he left incomplete at his death. A sequel by another hand is 'The Adventures of Chichikov' (1922) by Mikhail Bulgakov (who also adapted Gogol's original story to the stage in 1932).

CHINGACHGOOK   Also known as John Monhegan, a Mohican Indian chief who becomes the lifelong friend of Natty BUMPPO (Hawkeye) in J. Fenimore Cooper's novels *The Pioneers* (1823), *The Last of the Mohicans* (1826), *The Pathfinder* (1840) and *The Deerslayer* (1841). Chingachgook has been played in films and on television by Lon Chaney, Jr (1956) and Ned Romero (1977), among others.

CHIPMUNKS, THE   See ALVIN CHIPMUNK

CHIPS, MR   Full name Arthur Chipping, a much-loved
schoolmaster created by James Hilton in the waning days of the
English public-school story. Hilton's sentimental novella,
Goodbye, Mr Chips (1934), recounts its elderly hero's life in
flashback. He has worked at Brookfield School all his days. Long
a bachelor, he once met a young woman while on a
mountaineering holiday; she became his wife, but died after two
years. Since that tragedy, Chips has devoted himself entirely to
the school. In retirement, he lives close by and still provides tea
and crumpets for visiting boys. James Hilton provides some
more anecdotes from Chips's life in a sequel volume, *To You, Mr
Chips* (1938), which also contains a long essay in which the
author justifies his creation of the character. 'There was no
schoolmaster I ever knew who was entirely Mr Chips, but there
were several who had certain of his attributes and achieved that
best reward of a well-spent life – to grow old beloved. One of them
was my father.' Hilton's original story has been adapted to the
stage and film. Chips was incarnated memorably by Robert
Donat in the movie *Goodbye, Mr Chips* (1939; dir. Sam Wood).
This was remade, rather less successfully, as a musical film starring
Peter O'Toole (1969; dir. Herbert Ross). Tales of Mr Chips have
also been broadcast on BBC radio. The BBC television serial
'Goodbye, Mr Chips' (1984) had Roy Marsden as the old
schoolmaster.

CHO-CHO-SAN   See Madame BUTTERFLY

CHOCKY   Disembodied alien intelligence which invades a young
boy's mind, in the novel *Chocky* (1968) by John Wyndham
(originally published in shorter form in *Amazing Stories* magazine
in 1963). The story was dramatized successfully by Anthony Read
for British independent television (1984), with Glynis Brooks
providing Chocky's voice. It was followed by two sequels,
Chocky's Children (1985) and *Chocky's Challenge* (1986), also
written by Anthony Read.

CHRISTIAN, PAUL   American country doctor played by Jean
Hersholt in a series of six Hollywood 'B' movies which began

with *Meet Dr Christian* (1939; dir. Bernard Vorhaus) and ended with *They Meet Again* (1941). Jean Hersholt also gave voice to the character on the radio. A television series, *Dr Christian* (1956), starred Macdonald Carey.

CHRISTIE, ANNA   Full name Anna Christopherson, the daughter of a Swedish sea captain. She falls in love with an Irish seaman and gains her father's disapproval and eventual forgiveness, in Eugene O'Neill's play *Anna Christie* (1922). The first film of the play (1923) starred Blanche Sweet; the second (1930; dir. Clarence Brown) had Greta Garbo in her first talking part. A musical comedy version of the story, entitled *New Girl in Town* (1957), was written by George Abbott.

CHRISTOPHER ROBIN   See under WINNIE-THE-POOH

CHUZZLEWIT, MARTIN   Youthful hero of Charles Dickens's long novel *The Life and Adventures of Martin Chuzzlewit* (1843–4). Dismissed from his employment as a trainee architect with the odious Mr Seth PECKSNIFF, he goes to seek his fortune in America. Martin is accompanied on his travels by an ever-optimistic servant, Mark Tapley (a man of the sunniest disposition). After various terrifying and comical adventures they return to England, where Martin wins the hand of his loved one, Mary Graham. Another memorable character who appears in this novel, which some critics regard as Dickens's comic masterpiece, is the disreputable midwife Mrs Sarah GAMP. According to William Rose Benét, 'the section of the book which takes place in the US was extremely offensive to the American public'.

CIGARETTE   Bar girl in *Under Two Flags* (1867), a romantic novel about the French Foreign Legion by Ouida (Marie Louise de la Ramée). She falls in love with the Englishman Bertie Cecil. Cigarette has been described as a 'swearing, killing, fighting, laughing, dancing bastard heroine' (Rachel Anderson). Silent movie versions of the story were made in 1917, with Theda Bara, and in 1922. In the later Hollywood film of the novel (1936; dir. Frank Lloyd) she was played by Claudette Colbert.

CIO-CIO-SAN   See Madame BUTTERFLY

CISCO KID, THE   Latinate hero of the American west, originally
an unsavoury Mexican bandit who appeared in 'The Caballero's
Way', a short story by O. Henry (William Sydney Porter). The
character became a long-running hero of Hollywood films. After
various appearances in silent movies, he was played by Warner
Baxter in the talkie *In Old Arizona* (1929; dir. Raoul Walsh —
the part was to have been played by Walsh himself, but he lost
an eye during filming and had to be replaced by Baxter) and its
sequels *The Cisco Kid* (1931) and *The Return of the Cisco Kid*
(1937). Cesar Romero took on the role for *The Cisco Kid and the
Lady* (1939) and six subsequent movies. He was followed by
Duncan Renaldo, who starred in *The Cisco Kid Returns* (1945)
and seven more films. Finally Gilbert Roland played the part of
Cisco in *The Gay Cavalier* (1946) and five later titles. In the popular
television series, 'The Cisco Kid' (1950–56), Duncan Renaldo
returned to the part (with Leo Carrillo as his fat, aged sidekick,
Pancho). There was also a Cisco Kid radio show during the 1940s,
and a comic-strip during the 1950s and 1960s.

CLAMPETT, JED   Poor farmer from the Ozark mountains who
strikes oil, becomes rich, and moves his family to California,
where they are hilariously out of place. He was played by Buddy
Ebsen in the exceedingly popular television series 'The Beverly
Hillbillies' (1962–71). The series was created by Paul Henning,
and its theme song, 'The Ballad of Jed Clampett' by Lester Flatt
and Earl Scruggs, was a hit when released as a record in 1963.
Ebsen also played Jed Clampett in the TV movie *The Return of the
Beverly Hillbillies* (1981; dir. Robert Leeds). The Clampett family
has much in common with the earlier Ma and Pa KETTLE, and with
the television McCoy family (who appeared in 'The Real McCoys',
1957–63) and Duke family ('The Dukes of Hazzard', from 1979).

CLANCY, PETER   Hero of a lengthy series of detective novels by
the American writer Lee Thayer (Emma Redington Lee). Clancy
is a private-eye of the old school: he enjoys the services of an
English valet called Wiggar. The series consists of about sixty
books, beginning with *The Mystery of the Thirteenth Floor* (1919).
Later titles include *The Unlatched Door* (1920), *The Sinister Mark*
(1923), *Dead Men's Shoes* (1929), *The Scrimshaw Millions* (1932),
Dark of the Moon (1936; vt *Death in the Gorge*), *X Marks the*

Spot (1940), *Accident, Manslaughter, or Murder?* (1945), *Pig in a Poke* (1948; vt *A Clue for Clancy*), *Blood on the Knight* (1952), *Guilt is Where You Find It* (1957) and *Dusty Death* (1966; vt *Death Walks in Shadow*).

CLANROYDEN, LORD   See Sandy ARBUTHNOT

CLARE, ANGEL   See under Tess DURBEYFIELD

CLARISSA   See Clarissa HARLOWE

CLAUDIA   See Claudia NAUGHTON

CLAUDINE   Lively young heroine of four semi-autobiographical novels by Colette (Sidonie Gabrielle Colette). The books are known in English as *Claudine at School* (1900), *Claudine in Paris* (1901), *Claudine Married* (1902; vt *The Indulgent Husband*) and *Claudine and Annie* (1903; vt *The Innocent Wife*). A later book, *La Maison de Claudine* (1922), does not concern the character but merely uses her name.

CLAYHANGER, EDWIN   Protagonist of a trilogy of novels by Arnold Bennett: *Clayhanger* (1910), *Hilda Lessways* (1911) and *These Twain* (1916). He grows up in the Five Towns (Staffordshire), enters the family business, quarrels with his father, and eventually marries his beloved, Hilda. The trilogy is unusual in that the second volume is a reprise of the events of the first, seen this time from the woman's point of view. *The Roll Call* (1918) is a related novel, not a part of the trilogy proper. The British television serial 'Clayhanger' (1976) starred Peter McEnery as Edwin.

CLAYTON, JACK   See KORAK

CLAYTON, JOHN   See TARZAN

CLEEK, HAMILTON   Chameleon-like hero of a series of fantastic detective stories by the American writer Thomas W. Hanshew. Cleek is able to disguise himself merely by altering the expression on his face. He appears in the books *The Man of the Forty Faces* (1910; vt *Cleek, the Man of the Forty Faces*), *Cleek of Scotland*

Yard (1914) and *Cleek's Greatest Riddles* (1916; vt *Cleek's Government Cases*).

CLEGG, CAPTAIN   See Dr Syn

CLEGG AND FOGGY   See under Compo

CLENNAM, ARTHUR   See under Amy Dorrit

CLOUSEAU, JACQUES   Accident-prone French police inspector played by Peter Sellers in the slapstick comedy film *The Pink Panther* (1963; dir. Blake Edwards). The sequels are *A Shot in the Dark* (1964; dir. Edwards), *Inspector Clouseau* (1968; dir. Bud

Inspector Jacques Clouseau (Peter Sellers)

Yorkin), *The Return of the Pink Panther* (1974; dir. Edwards), *The Pink Panther Strikes Again* (1976; dir. Edwards) and *The Revenge of the Pink Panther* (1978; dir. Edwards), all but one of which starred the irreplaceable Sellers (Alan Arkin played the hero in *Inspector Clouseau*). After Peter Sellers's death, a final Clouseau film, *Trail of the Pink Panther* (1982), was stitched together from leftover footage of the previous movies. Inspector Clouseau has also been seen in television cartoons (where he appeared alongside the animated Pink Panther which had originally featured in the credit sequences of the live-action films).

CLUFF, CALEB   Police sergeant in a small Yorkshire town. He is the down-to-earth hero of a series of crime novels by Gil North (Geoffrey Horne): *Sergeant Cluff Stands Firm* (1960), *The Methods of Sergeant Cluff* (1961), *Sergeant Cluff Goes Fishing* (1962), *More Deaths for Sergeant Cluff* (1963), *Sergeant Cluff and the Madmen* (1964), *Sergeant Cluff and the Price of Pity* (1965); *The Confounding of Sergeant Cluff* (1966), *Sergeant Cluff and the Day of Reckoning* (1967), *The Procrastination of Sergeant Cluff* (1969), *No Choice for Sergeant Cluff* (1971) and *Sergeant Cluff Rings True* (1972). There was a British television series about the character in 1964.

COFFEY, GINGER   Full name James Francis Coffey, a penniless Irishman adrift in Canada. His comical but sad tale is told in Brian Moore's novel *The Luck of Ginger Coffey* (1960). In the film of the book (1964; dir. Irvin Kershner) he was played by Robert Shaw.

COGBURN, ROOSTER J.   Ageing one-eyed marshal in Charles Portis's Western novel *True Grit* (1969). He assists a young girl, Mattie Ross, to avenge her murdered father. In the film of the book (1970; dir. Henry Hathaway) Cogburn was played by John Wayne, who won an Oscar for his efforts. There have been two film sequels: *Rooster Cogburn* (1975; dir. Stuart Miller), also with Wayne, and a TV movie *True Grit: A Further Adventure* (1978; dir. Richard T. Heffron), with Warren Oates in the lead role.

COLBY, ALEXIS CARRINGTON   Vampish leading lady of the American television soap opera 'Dynasty' (from 1981). A member of the oil-rich set, she has an intense rivalry with Krystle

Carrington, the new wife of her former husband, Blake. Played by the middle-aged English actress Joan Collins, Alexis became almost as much of a household name as J. R. EWING (of 'Dallas' fame). A spin-off series is 'Dynasty II: The Colbys' (from 1985).

COLLIER, TERRY See The LIKELY LADS

COLLIN, JACQUES See VAUTRIN

COLLINS, WILLIAM See under Elizabeth BENNET

COLLYER, CLAYTON See under Kitty FOYLE

COLUMBO, LIEUTENANT Dishevelled Italian-American cop played by the squint-eyed actor Peter Falk in the television movie *Prescription Murder* (1967; dir. Richard Irving), and in the subsequent series 'Columbo' (originally part of the 'Mystery Movie' series, 1971–7). The character was created by writers Richard Levinson and William Link. Apropos Columbo, Clive James has remarked: 'That Kojak can dress so well and Columbo so badly on what must basically be the same salary is one of the continuing mysteries of American television.' (See Theo KOJAK.).

COMPO Ragged, unshaven old Yorkshireman in the oddball BBC television series 'Last of the Summer Wine' (from 1974). When he is not paying court to the fearsome, raucous-voiced Nora Batty (his old flame), Compo has mildly amusing adventures in the company of his friends Clegg and Foggy: they are the three ageing musketeers of their small West Riding town. Despite Compo's personal unsavouriness, the programme was described as mellow and charming, and it gradually gained the approval of a mass audience. Compo was played by Bill Owen, and the series was created by scriptwriter Roy Clarke. The latter is also the author of a series of original novels known as the 'Summer Wine Chronicles': the first of these was *Gala Week* (1986).

COMPSON, QUENTIN Suicidal scion of the decaying Compson family of Yoknapatawpha County, in William Faulkner's novels *The Sound and the Fury* (1929) and *Absalom, Absalom!* (1936). The first of these books is divided into four sections, one of which is narrated by Quentin (another is told by his idiot brother Benjy, whose madness provides the 'sound and fury' of the novel's title). A student at Harvard University, Quentin is haunted by his love for his sister Caddy, who has married unwisely. In the second novel Quentin features as one of the narrators of the tragic life-story of Thomas Sutpen, a man of low birth who had thought to elevate himself to the Southern 'aristocracy'. In the film *The Sound and the Fury* (1959; dir. Martin Ritt) the lead role was played by Yul Brynner.

CONAN THE BARBARIAN   Mighty-thewed warrior from a land named Cimmeria (which now lies beneath the North Sea) in the so-called Hyborian Age (shortly after the fall of Atlantis). Created by the Texan writer Robert E. Howard, Conan is the original sword-and-sorcery hero, long in brawn and short in brain, hacking his way through a pseudo historical never-never world of magic and monsters. He first appeared in short stories written for *Weird Tales* magazine in the early 1930s. The only novel-length Conan story which Howard wrote, 'The Hour of the Wolf' (scrialized 1935–6), eventually became the first Conan book, *Conan the Conqueror* (1950 – published well after its author's death). More Conan volumes followed, cobbled together by various editors (the most notable being L. Sprague de Camp) from Howard's magazine stories and unpublished fragments: *The Sword of Conan* (1952), *The Coming of Conan* (1953), *King Conan* (1953), *Conan the Barbarian* (1955), *Tales of Conan* (1955), and numerous later revisions and recombinations of the material contained in these books.

The first of many sequels by other hands was *The Return of Conan* (1957; vt *Conan the Avenger*) by L. Sprague de Camp and Bjorn Nyberg. Others include: *Conan of the Isles* (1968) by de Camp and Lin Carter; *Conan the Buccaneer* (1971) by de Camp and Carter; *Conan of Aquilonia* (1977) by de Camp and Carter; *The Road of Kings* (1979) by Karl Edward Wagner; *Conan the Rebel* (1980) by Poul Anderson; *Conan and the Spider God* (1980) by de Camp; the aptly-titled *Conan the Mercenary* (1980) by Andrew J. Offutt (commenting on which the sf/fantasy news magazine *Locus* said somewhat sourly: 'This is part of Ace's original Conan series, not to be confused with Bantam's original Conan series or de Camp's editing of Howard's original Conan series or the original Conan series comics, movies, or wind-up dolls'); *Conan the Invincible* (1982) by Robert Jordan; *Conan the Defender* (1982) by Jordan; *Conan the Unconquered* (1983) by Jordan; *Conan the Triumphant* (1983) by Jordan; *Conan the Magnificent* (1984) by Jordan; *Conan the Victorious* (1984) by Jordan; *Conan the Valorous* (1985) by John Robert Maddox; *Conan the Fearless* (1986) by Steve Perry; *Conan the Renegade* (1986) by Leonard Carpenter; and no doubt many more to come.

Conan seemed to reach the highest pitch of his popularity in the early 1980s, fifty years after his creation – and almost as long after the suicide of his creator (Robert E. Howard never lived to see what a monstrous figment he had unleashed on the world). The character has also appeared in comic-books, with at least three different Marvel Comics series, *Conan the Barbarian* (from 1970), *The Savage Sword of Conan* (from 1974) and *King Conan* (from 1980). The first Conan movie, *Conan the Barbarian* (1982; dir. John Milius), was a blood-soaked fantasy made ponderous by references to Nietzsche. It starred body-builder Arnold Schwarzenegger in the title role – and no actor ever looked the part of an established fictional character more convincingly. He played the hero again in *Conan the Destroyer* (1984; dir. Richard Fleischer).

CONCHIS   See under Nicholas URFE

CONKLIN, OSGOOD P.   See under Connie BROOKS

CONQUEST, NORMAN   Dashing desperado, from the same mould as BLACKSHIRT or the SAINT, invented by Berkeley Gray (the veteran boys'-story writer Edwy Searles Brooks). Not surprisingly, Norman Conquest's nickname is '1066'. He first appears in the novel *Mr Mortimer Gets the Jitters* (1937), where he is described as having 'a laugh in his lilting baritone voice and a deadly purpose in his heart'. Through almost fifty novels Conquest keeps up the good cheer while he biffs the baddies. Later books in the series include *Vultures, Ltd.* (1938), *Conquest Marches On* (1939), *Miss Dynamite* (1939), *Conquest Takes All* (1940), *Six Feet of Dynamite* (1941), *Cavalier Conquest* (1944), *The Conquest Touch* (1948), *Conquest in Scotland* (1951), *Conquest Goes West* (1954),

Conquest in Command (1956), *Conquest on the Run* (1960), *Curtains for Conquest?* (1966) and *Conquest in Ireland* (1969).

CONRAD   Hero of the narrative poem *The Corsair* (1814) by George Gordon, Lord Byron. He is a chivalrous Mediterranean pirate who rescues a beautiful slave from the Turkish pasha's harem. At the end of the poem he disappears – to reappear in the immediate sequel, *Lara* (1814), where it transpires that Conrad is really Lara, a mysterious Spanish landowner. Both poems were bestsellers in their day, and helped establish the popular image of the romantic, brooding 'Byronic' hero (see also Childe HAROLD and MANFRED).

CONTINENTAL OP, THE   Operative of the 'Continental Detective Agency' – the nameless, self-effacing hero of tough crime stories by Dashiell Hammett. As the critic Steven Marcus says, there is nothing glamorous about the Op: he is 'short, thick-set, balding, between thirty-five and forty', yet he lives according to a code and is 'a special case of the Protestant ethic, for his entire existence is bound up in and expressed by his work, his vocation'. The first Op story appeared in *Black Mask* magazine in 1923. He later featured in the novels *Red Harvest* and *The Dain Curse* (both 1929), and in the collection *Blood Money* (1943). A posthumous collection of the best of Hammett's Op stories, selected and introduced by Steven Marcus, was published as *The Continental Op* (1974). An overlong TV-movie version of *The Dain Curse* (1978; dir. E. W. Swackhamer) starred James Coburn as the hero. The Op also makes an appearance alongside his real-life creator in Joe Gores's book *Hammett: A Novel* (1975), which has been filmed (1982; dir. Wim Wenders).

CONWAY, HUGH   English adventurer who visits the peaceful valley of Shangri-La, in James Hilton's novel *Lost Horizon* (1933). There he meets a wise Chinese gentleman called Chang, and a mysterious High Lama who claims to be hundreds of years old. 'Shangri-La' has entered the language, to denote a tranquil haven far from the anxiety and violence of twentieth-century life. In the exciting film of the book (1937; dir. Frank Capra) Conway was played by Ronald Colman. The movie has been remade less effectively in a musical version (1972; dir. Charles Jarrott), with Peter Finch.

COOL, BERTHA   Fat, formidable private detective in a series of twenty-nine crime novels by A. A. Fair (Erle Stanley Gardner), beginning with *The Bigger They Come* (1939). With her partner Donald Lam, a disbarred lawyer, she runs an agency known as Bertha Cool – Confidential Investigations. Later books in the series include *Gold Comes in Bricks* (1940), *Double or Quits* (1941), *Owls Don't Blink* (1942), *Crows Can't Count* (1946), *Bedrooms Have Windows* (1949), *Some Women Won't Wait* (1953), *You Can Die Laughing* (1957), *Bachelors Get Lonely* (1961) and *All Grass Isn't Green* (1970).

COPPELIUS, DOCTOR   Spectacles-maker who helps the inventor Spalanzani to build a lovely female automaton, in E. T. A. Hoffmann's story 'The Sandman' (1816). Dr Coppelius and his living doll have been perpetuated in two famous works based on Hoffmann's tale: the ballet *Coppélia, ou La Fille des Yeaux d'Émail* (1870) by Léo Delibes and Arthur Saint-Léon; and the opera *Les Contes d'Hoffmann* (1881) by Jacques Offenbach (with a libretto by Jules Barbier and Michel Carré). The ballet simplifies Hoffmann's story, and changes the puppet's name from Olympia to Coppélia. The opera complicates the original narrative by making Hoffmann a character in his own story. A film, *The Tales of Hoffmann* (1951; dir. Michael Powell and Emeric Pressburger) is based on Offenbach's opera, although it also contains some ballet scenes.

COPPERFIELD, DAVID   Young writer-hero of Charles Dickens's ever-popular novel *David Copperfield* (1849–50). The outline of his career bears resemblances to Dickens's own life. Orphaned at an early age, David is sent by his cruel stepfather to work in a London factory. He runs away to Dover and seeks help from his eccentric aunt, Betsy Trotwood. She enables him to complete his education and gain employment with a legal firm. He marries a pretty but empty-headed girl, Dora Spenlow, and begins to gain a reputation as a writer. Dora dies, and David eventually marries the beautiful and virtuous Agnes Wickfield. Along the way, he encounters such vivid characters as the rakish James Steerforth, Wilkins MICAWBER, the simple-minded Mr Dick, Daniel Peggotty and his Little Em'ly, and the villainous Uriah HEEP. Hollywood made a memorable film of *David Copperfield* (1935; dir. George

Cukor), with Freddie Bartholomew and Frank Lawton playing David at different ages. The book has been a particular favourite on television: a TV movie version (1970; dir. Delbert Mann) had Robin Phillips as David. Of the many BBC serializations, the most recent were shown in 1975, with David Yelland in the lead, and in 1986, with Colin Hurley.

CORINTHIAN TOM   See TOM AND JERRY

CORKRAN, ARTHUR   Known as 'Stalky' – leader of a remarkable trio of schoolboys in Rudyard Kipling's short-story collection *Stalky and Co.* (1899). Corkran and his friends, M'Turk and Beetle, are pupils at a small public school in Devon. Although they regard their headmaster as a friend, they have a general contempt for school discipline, for organized sports, and for most of their teachers. They play cruel practical jokes and indulge in ritual 'gloats' (triumphal nonsense-recitations which express their high feelings on defeating various enemies). In later life Stalky becomes an army hero in India. Kipling's strange blend of schoolboy anarchism and imperial virtues has often been condemned as a glorification of bullying: H. G. Wells was to remark that *Stalky and Co.* 'lights up the political psychology of the British Empire'. Kipling wrote several more stories about Corkran and his friends, and these were eventually brought together in the volume entitled *The Collected Stalky and Co.* (1929). A BBC television serial, 'Stalky and Co.' (1982), was scripted by Alexander Baron, with Robert Addie as Corkran.

CORLEONE, MICHAEL   Son of Don Vito Corleone, Mafia leader, in Mario Puzo's bestselling novel *The Godfather* (1968). Michael is a sensitive, well-educated young man who at first shuns his father's criminal line of business. However, when his brother is killed by a rival gang, and his ageing father's life is threatened, Michael assumes the leadership of the family and proves just as ruthless as the old Don. The novel was filmed, brilliantly, by Francis Ford Coppola in 1972, with Al Pacino as Michael. A filmed sequel, *The Godfather Part II* (1974; dir. Coppola), continues the story of Michael's inexorable rise to power (again he was played by the excellent Pacino). Mario Puzo, the author who originally created the characters, has returned to the Corleone story in another novel, *The Sicilian* (1985).

CORNELIUS, JERRY Chameleon-like anti-hero of a series of Pop-Art science fiction novels by Michael Moorcock, beginning with *The Final Programme* (1968; vt *The Last Days of Man on Earth*). A long-haired, pill-popping young man of ambivalent sexuality, he has the ability to travel through the many parallel worlds of the 'Multiverse'. Later Cornelius titles by Moorcock are *A Cure for Cancer* (1971), *The English Assassin* (1972), *The Adventures of Una Persson and Catherine Cornelius in the Twentieth Century* (1976), *The Lives and Times of Jerry Cornelius* (1976), *The Condition of Muzak* (1977 – winner of the *Guardian* fiction prize), *The Great Rock 'n' Roll Swindle* (1980 – in which Jerry meets the Sex Pistols), *The Entropy Tango* (1981) and *The Opium General and Other Stories* (1984). A number of short sequels by other hands are collected in the anthology *The Nature of the Catastrophe* (1971), edited by Moorcock and Langdon Jones. The character also makes guest appearances in some of Moorcock's 'Eternal Champion' fantasies (see ELRIC OF MELNIBONÉ and EREKOSË). Other avatars of Cornelius are Jerry Cornell in the comedy-thrillers *The Chinese Agent* (1970) and *The Russian Intelligence* (1980), and Jherek Carnelian in the *Dancers at the End of Time* trilogy (1972–6) and related books. Jerry's Cockney mother, the redoubtable Honoria Cornelius, reappears in Moorcock's most ambitious novels, *Byzantium Endures* (1981) and *The Laughter of Carthage* (1984) – the first two volumes in a tetralogy which the author originally said would be collectively entitled 'Mrs Cornelius Between the Wars'. (Moorcock's work is exceedingly complex; characters recur and series overlap with joyous abandon.) Jerry Cornelius has also featured in a comic-strip, initially drawn by Mal Dean, later by R. Glyn Jones, which was published in the 'underground' paper *International Times*, circa 1969–70. The film *The Final Programme* (1973; dir. Robert Fuest), which was released in America as *The Last Days of Man on Earth*, starred Jon Finch as the mercurial Jerry.

CORRIGAN, PHIL See X-9

CORUM, PRINCE See under ELRIC OF MELNIBONÉ and EREKOSË

COSWAY, ANTOINETTE   See under Edward ROCHESTER

COUPEAU, ANNA   See NANA

COVENANT, THOMAS   Leper who enters the magical world of the
Land and comes into conflict with Lord Foul the Despiser. He is
the hero of Stephen R. Donaldson's odd, pretentious, yet
bestselling fantasy series, 'The Chronicles of Thomas Covenant the
Unbeliever'. The titles in the sequence are *Lord Foul's Bane*
(1977), *The Illearth War* (1977), *The Power That Preserves* (1977),
The Wounded Land (1980), *The One Tree* (1982) and *White Gold
Wielder* (1984).

COWARDLY LION, THE   See under Dorothy GALE

COWPERWOOD, FRANK   Ruthless, power-hungry businessman in
Theodore Dreiser's novels *The Financier* (1912), *The Titan*
(1914) and *The Stoic* (1947 – published posthumously).
Cowperwood eventually comes to realize that 'even giants are
but pigmies, and that an ultimate balance must be struck'.

CRABB, JACK   One-hundred-and-eleven-year-old survivor of the
Battle of Little Big Horn, in Thomas Berger's serio-comic Western
Little Big Man (1964). According to the narrator, 'Jack Crabb was
either the most neglected hero in the history of this country or a
liar of insane proportions'. In the film of the novel (1970; dir.
Arthur Penn) Crabb was played by Dustin Hoffman.

CRANE, ICHABOD   Ungainly schoolmaster who appears in
Washington Irving's short story 'The Legend of Sleepy Hollow'
(1819; included in his *Sketch Book of Geoffrey Crayon, Gent.*).
Ichabod's courting of a local girl is interrupted when his jealous
rival disguises himself as a ghostly headless horseman. The
misadventures of Ichabod Crane are almost as celebrated in
America as Rip VAN WINKLE's, and the character has been
perpetuated in cartoon films – for example, the Walt Disney
compendium *Ichabod and Mr Toad* (1949).

CRANSTON, LAMONT   See The SHADOW

CRATCHIT, BOB   See under Ebenezer SCROOGE

CRAWFURD, DAVID   Hero and narrator of John Buchan's exciting
novel of African adventure, *Prester John* (1910). David helps foil
a black rebellion which is led by the awe-inspiring John LAPUTA.

CRAWLEY, RAWDON   See under Becky SHARP

CREATURE, THE   Man-like aquatic monster which is found far up
the river Amazon, in the Hollywood movie *The Creature from
the Black Lagoon* (1954; dir. Jack Arnold). The Creature was
played by stuntman Ricou Browning in a rubber suit. The film
was a commercial success and spawned two sequels, *Revenge of
the Creature* (1955; dir. Arnold) and *The Creature Walks Among
Us* (1956; dir. John Sherwood).

CRIBB, SERGEANT   Bowler-hatted police detective who features
in a series of pastiche-Victorian crime novels by Peter Lovesey:
Wobble to Death (1970), *The Detective Wore Silk Drawers* (1971),
Abracadaver (1972), *Mad Hatter's Holiday* (1973), *Invitation
to a Dynamite Party* (1974; vt *The Tick of Death*), *A Case of
Spirits* (1975), *Swing, Swing Together* (1976) and *Waxwork* (1978).
Most of the stories are set against a background of nineteenth-
century sports and outdoor pastimes. The British TV series,
'Cribb' (1979–81), starred Alan Dobie.

CRICH, GERALD   See under Rupert BIRKIN

CRICHTON, BILL   Manservant to the shipwrecked Lord Loam in
J. M. Barrie's play *The Admirable Crichton* (1902). Because of his
resourcefulness and wide practical knowledge he proves himself
to be much the most able survivor in the marooned group. In the
film of the play (1957; dir. Lewis Gilbert) Crichton was portrayed
by Kenneth More. There has also been a stage musical version
of the play, retitled *Our Man Crichton*.

CRIME DOCTOR, THE   Robert Ordway, a psychological detective
created by Max Marcin for an American radio series (from 1940).
Ordway, himself a one-time criminal and amnesia victim, solves
mysteries with the help of his Freudian patter. He was played

by Warner Baxter in a series of ten films, beginning with *The Crime Doctor* (1943; dir. Michael Gordon) and ending with *The Crime Doctor's Diary* (1949; dir. Seymour Friedman).

CROCKETT, SONNY   Cool, laid-back policeman played by Don Johnson in the American television series 'Miami Vice' (from 1984). With his sidekick Ricardo Tubbs, he tackles drug-dealers and other peddlers of vice. Crockett has become a male sex symbol of the mid-1980s. He favours an unshaven look (what one might call the 'near-beard'), though he is always impeccably dressed. The series was created by Anthony Yerkovitch.

CROUCHBACK, GUY   Middle-aged Catholic hero of Evelyn Waugh's trilogy about World War II, known collectively as *Sword of Honour.* The individual novels are: *Men at Arms* (1952), which tells how Guy enlists in the army and is sent abroad; *Officers and Gentlemen* (1955), which describes the Blitz on London and combat in Crete; and *Unconditional Surrender* (1961; vt *The End of the Battle*), in which Guy sees out the war in Yugoslavia and London. Edward Woodward played Crouchback in a BBC television serial, Sword of Honour (1967). The novels have also been dramatized on BBC radio (1984), with Hugh Dickson as Guy.

CROW   See under EDGE

CRUSOE, ROBINSON   Pious English seafarer who is cast away on a desert island for twenty-eight years, keeps his sanity, builds a comfortable life for himself, and eventually gains a native 'subject' whom he calls Man FRIDAY. He was created by Daniel Defoe in the novel *The Life and Strange Surprizing Adventures of Robinson Crusoe* (1719), a book which has never gone out of print and which has been translated, abridged, pirated, bowdlerized, and otherwise disseminated in countless guises ever since. Crusoe is undoubtedly the most celebrated fictional character of them all: both his names, separately or together, have become bywords around the world, the French having named a whole genre after him – the *Robinsonnade*. Defoe himself wrote two sequels to the original book: *The Farther Adventures of Robinson Crusoe* (1719), in which Crusoe revisits his island as

Robinson Crusoe

a colonial overseer, and *Serious Reflections During the Life and Surprizing Adventures of Robinson Crusoe* (1720), which is a sequence of dull tracts rather than a work of fiction proper. A modern sequel by another hand is *The Return of Robinson Crusoe* (1958) by Henry Treece. Crusoe and Friday also appear in J. M. Coetzee's novel *Foe* (1986).

Defoe's tale is one of the most influential works of fiction ever penned. In his book *The Rise of the Novel* Ian Watt has gone so far as to say: '*Robinson Crusoe* falls most naturally into place, not with other novels, but with the great myths of Western civilization, with *Faust, Don Juan*, and *Don Quixote*.' Those who have admired it, and drawn different morals from it, include Jean-Jacques Rousseau and Karl Marx. Numerous lesser writers have contributed to the tradition of *Robinsonnades* – 277 imitations were counted by one German scholar up to the year 1898. Some of the better-known, limiting ourselves to those which actually mention Crusoe in their titles, are: *Robinson der Jungere* (1779) by Joachim Campe, *Der schweizerische Robinson* (1812) by Johann Wyss (initially translated into English as *The Family Robinson Crusoe*, later called *The Swiss Family Robinson*), *Dog Crusoe* (1861) by R. M. Ballantyne and *L'École des Robinsons* (1882) by Jules Verne (translated as *The School for Crusoes*). One could also adduce the modern science fiction film *Robinson Crusoe on Mars* (1964; dir. Byron Haskin). None of these works actually features Defoe's Robinson Crusoe as a character, but they invoke the magic of his name to give authenticity to their own paler creations.

There have been many stage adaptations of Defoe's original novel. According to Humphrey Carpenter and Mari Prichard in *The Oxford Companion to Children's Literature*, 'one of the earliest productions was a version by Sheridan, *Robinson Crusoe; or Harlequin Friday*, which was performed as a pantomime at Drury Lane in 1781. Sheridan treated Defoe's story with great respect until the finale, when, upon Crusoe's rescue, contemporary custom obliged him to transform Friday into Harlequin, who "receives his final reward in the hand of Columbine".' In the nineteenth century Jacques Offenbach wrote an operetta, *Robinson Crusoe*, which has been revived in recent years. There have also been numerous film versions of the story, including silent movies made in 1913, 1917, 1924 and 1929. Perhaps the most notable film is *The Adventures of Robinson Crusoe* (1954) by the great Spanish director Luis Bunuel. It starred Dan O'Herlihy as Robinson. A Russian-made film, *Robinson Crusoe* (1972; dir. Stanislas Govorukin), had Leonid Duravlev in the role. A British TV-movie version (1974; dir. James MacTaggart) had Stanley Baker as the castaway. Robinson has also been played by Peter O'Toole in the feature film *Man Friday* (1975; dir. Jack Gold).

CTHULHU   Terrifying god of the elder days created by the American horror-story writer H. P. Lovecraft for such magazine stories as 'The Call of Cthulhu' (1928). He (or It) is the focus of the so-called 'Cthulhu Mythos', as elaborated after Lovecraft's death by August Derleth and other writers. Books by Derleth include *The Lurker at the Threshold* (1945; based on notes left by Lovecraft), *The Mask of Cthulhu* (1958) and *The Trail of Cthulhu* (1962). The anthology *Tales of the Cthulhu Mythos* (1969; edited by Derleth) contains stories by various hands. Authors who have contributed to the Mythos include Frank Belknap Long, Robert E. Howard, Clark Ashton Smith, Robert Bloch, Henry Kuttner, Ramsey Campbell, Brian Lumley, Colin Wilson and Lin Carter.

CUFF, RICHARD   Scotland Yard detective-sergeant in Wilkie Collins's novel *The Moonstone* (1868). He is a sharp-faced, grey-haired man, whose passion is rose-growing. Although he was preceded by Dickens's Inspector BUCKET, Sergeant Cuff is generally regarded as the first true detective-story hero in English fiction. In his introduction to a 1967 reprint of the novel Anthony Burgess wrote: 'When James Bond is forgotten Sergeant Cuff . . . will shine as brightly as he did more than a hundred years ago.' A film of *The Moonstone* was released in 1934, and the novel has been serialized on British television.

CURTIS, SIR HENRY   See under Allan QUATERMAIN

CURTIS, OLIVIA   Heroine of Rosamond Lehmann's novels *Invitation to the Waltz* (1932) and *The Weather in the Streets* (1936). The latter, in which she has an unhappy love-affair with a man named Rollo, has been described as 'one of those rare novels which enters into a woman's mind fully and intimately without being obscure. Olivia appeals to anyone who has ever loved foolishly and recklessly' (Nicola Beauman, *A Very Great Profession*). In the BBC television film of *The Weather in the Streets* (1984; dir. Gavin Millar) Olivia was played by Lisa Eichhorn.

CUSINS, ADOLPHUS   See under Barbara UNDERSHAFT

D

DACIER, PERCY See under Diana WARWICK

DAISY MAE See under L'IL ABNER

DAKER, JOHN See EREKOSË

DALE, JIMMIE Also known as the Gray Seal, a sophisticated 'Robin Hood of Crime' – the American equivalent of A. J. RAFFLES. He was created by Frank L. Packard for a series of short stories which inspired a silent movie serial, *Jimmie Dale, Alias the Gray Seal* (1916). Packard's stories were collected in the books *The Adventures of Jimmie Dale* (1917), *The Further Adventures of Jimmie Dale* (1917), *Jimmie Dale and the Phantom Clue* (1922), *Jimmie Dale and the Blue Envelope Murder* (1930) and *Jimmie Dale and the Missing Hour* (1935).

DALE, LAETITIA See under Sir Willoughby PATTERNE

DALE, MARY Doctor's wife in the long-running BBC radio serial 'Mrs Dale's Diary' (from 1948; later called simply 'The Dales'). Mary Dale and her husband James live with their children Robert and Gwen in the town of Exton. The series was created by scriptwriters Jonquil Anthony and Ted Willis, and for many years the part of Mrs Dale was played by Ellis Powell (she was replaced by Jessie Matthews in 1963). A novel based on the scripts is *The Dales: The Story of a Family* (1969) by Rex Edwards.

DALEKS, THE Tin-can aliens on wheels whose monotonous voices, threatening to 'exterminate' all who cross their path, became one of the most familiar sounds on British television. They were invented by scriptwriter Terry Nation for the BBC series 'Doctor Who' (from 1963). According to Nigel Robinson (*Time Out*, 1 January 1982), 'the Daleks were not the sole reason for the show's early success, but they did push the audience from three million to eight million'. See also Dr WHO.

DALEY, ARTHUR   'Arfur', an ageing Cockney spiv played by
George Cole in the British television series 'Minder' (1979–85). The
epitome of seediness, shadiness and all things dodgy, Daley
became a well-loved comic figure in the early 1980s. His fame
exceeded that of the series' hero, Terry MᶜCᴀɴɴ, and was even
celebrated in a pop song – 'Arfur Daley, He's All Right'. Daley
and his long-suffering 'Minder' were created by scriptwriter Leon
Griffiths. The latter has also written a humorous book entitled
Arthur Daley's Guide to Doing it Right (1985).

DALGLEISH, ADAM   Scotland Yard policeman in the crime novels
of P. D. James. He writes poetry on the side, so he is evidently
one of the thoughtful breed so common in English detective
fiction. The first Dalgleish book was *Cover Her Face* (1962) and the
later titles are *A Mind to Murder* (1963), *Unnatural Causes* (1967),
Shroud for a Nightingale (1971), *An Unsuitable Job for a Woman*
(1972 – this one is mainly about private-eye Cordelia Gʀᴀʏ, to
whom Dalgleish is attracted), *The Black Tower* (1975), *Death of an
Expert Witness* (1977), *The Skull Beneath the Skin* (1982) and *A
Taste of Death* (1986). Several of the Dalgleish novels have been
dramatized for British independent television, including *Death of
an Expert Witness* (1983), *Shroud for a Nightingale* (1983),
Cover Her Face (1985) and *The Black Tower* (1985), all with Roy
Marsden as the detective.

DALLAS, STELLA   Self-sacrificing heroine, a paragon of American
motherhood, in Olive Higgins Prouty's weepy novel *Stella Dallas*
(1923). The book was dramatized for the stage and then made into
a silent film (1925; dir. Henry King), with Belle Bennett in the part
of Stella. The talkie remake (1937; dir. King Vidor) starred Barbara
Stanwyck (according to Leslie Halliwell, '1937 audiences came to
sneer and stayed to weep'). Following the success of the second
film Stella Dallas became a long-lasting heroine of American
radio (1935–55), where she was played by Anne Elstner.

DALLOWAY, CLARISSA   Central character of Virginia Woolf's
novel *Mrs Dalloway* (1925). She is a society hostess, married to
a Member of Parliament. The book describes her thoughts and
memories during the course of one day in London. Clarissa
Dalloway had first appeared as a minor character in Woolf's earlier

novel *The Voyage Out* (1915). She also features in seven short stories which were collected posthumously in the book *Mrs Dalloway's Party* (1973).

DALMAIN, GARTH   See under Jane CHAMPION

DAMIEN   See Damien THORN

DANGERFIELD, SEBASTIAN   American law student in Ireland, the rambunctious, two-fisted, hard-drinking hero of J. P. Donleavy's novel *The Ginger Man* (1955). The journalist Stanley Reynolds has written: 'it is a grand book, particularly in the wonderful writing which recalls just what it was like to be a young American and come suddenly into this strange post-war world of Britain and Ireland. How cold and damp and grey and how marvellously old-fashioned and genteel it was, like some old great aunt who had seen better days' (*Guardian*, 26 June 1986). Sebastian also appears in Donleavy's own stage version of the novel (1959).

DANTÈS, EDMOND   See The Count of MONTE CRISTO

DANVERS, LINDA LEE   See SUPERGIRL

DANVERS, MRS   See under Rebecca DE WINTER

DARBISHIRE   See under John Christopher Timothy JENNINGS

DARCY, FITZWILLIAM   Nephew of the monstrous Lady Catherine de Bourgh, in Jane Austen's best-loved novel *Pride and Prejudice* (1813). He is attracted to the beautiful Elizabeth BENNET, who initially spurns him because of his apparent pride and *hauteur*. But Darcy is a young man who learns better; he sheds his condescending manner, woos Elizabeth with genuine feeling and eventually wins her hand, despite the opposition of his aunt. In the Hollywood film of the novel (1940; dir. Robert Z. Leonard) Darcy was played by Laurence Olivier.

DARE, DAN   Space pilot featured in the lead comic-strip of the British boys' paper *Eagle* from 1950 to 1967. Dan is a wholesome, strong-jawed hero with rather Satanic eyebrows; in effect, he is an updated version of the ideal Battle-of-Britain pilot. He serves as a colonel in the Interplanetary Space Fleet, and with his 'batman' Digby, he has adventures on the planet Venus and further afield. His arch-enemy is the dome-headed MEKON. The strips were conceived, drawn and written by Frank Hampson, and later carried on by other hands. Dan Dare proved immensely popular, and his adventures were adapted for the radio and children's books. Noel Johnson (formerly the BBC's Dick BARTON) played Dan Dare on Radio Luxembourg from 1951 to 1956. According to James Slattery, in his introduction to the reprint volume *Dan Dare, Pilot of the Future, in the Man from Nowhere* (1979): '*everybody* read Dan Dare – Cabinet ministers along with Rhondda Valley schoolboys. And in the 50s the exploitation of the characters and craft in the strip by commercial concerns was almost ridiculous – the young fanatic could skip out of his Dan Dare pyjamas, into his Dan Dare slippers and dressing gown, brush his teeth with Calvert's Dan Dare toothpaste, all before checking that it was time (on his Dan Dare watch) to kit up in his Dan Dare T-shirt, belt, scarf, spacesuit, etc . . . etc . . . Hulton Press's company secretary estimated in 1957 that the total value of the sales and merchandizing royalties on the strip was about £1,000,000 a year.' There have been attempts to revive a Dan Dare strip in the 1970s (in *2,000 AD* comic) and in the 1980s (in a new *Eagle*) but, lacking the visual flair of Frank Hampson, Dan's later adventures have proved disappointing. A recent book, *The Man Who Drew Tomorrow* (1985) by Alastair Crompton, tells the story of Hampson's career; it is amusing to note that the *Eagle*, begun by the Rev. Marcus Morris, was intended as a Christian propaganda comic.

DARLING, WENDY   Little girl who befriends PETER PAN and flies away to Never-Never Land, in J. M. Barrie's play *Peter Pan* (1904). The name 'Wendy' was an invention of Barrie's and has since become popularly accepted as a girl's Christian name.

DARNAY, CHARLES   See under Sydney CARTON

DARRELL, LARRY   Truth-seeking hero of W. Somerset Maugham's novel *The Razor's Edge* (1944). He abandons a life of carnal pleasure and goes to India in order to study Vedanta. Anthony Burgess has commented that 'Larry is very nearly the sole example in all [Maugham's] work of a personage wholly good – even wholly holy.' Despite this unusually ascetic theme, the novel has been made into a successful Hollywood film (1946; dir. Edmund Goulding), with Tyrone Power as Larry.

D'ARTAGNAN   Swashbuckling hero of Alexandre Dumas's popular historical novel *The Three Musketeers* (1844). Strictly speaking, he is not a fictional character, since it seems there really was a Sieur d'Artagnan who served Louis XIV as a captain of musketeers and eventually died in battle in the year 1673. Dumas based his tale on an account of this man's life. However, it is as a character in fiction rather than as a historical personage that D'Artagnan is remembered. Dumas perpetuated him and his trio of musketeer friends – Athos, Porthos and Aramis – in two sequels, *Twenty Years After* (1845) and *The Vicomte de Bragelonne* (1847). The last-named novel is extremely long, and has often been published in several volumes under different titles, the best-known segment being *The Man in the Iron Mask*. Sequels by other hands include the 'Years Between' series by P. Féval and M. Cassez, which consists of such titles as *The Mysterious Cavalier*, *Martyr to the Queen*, *The Secret of the Bastille*, *The Heir to Buckingham*, *Comrades at Arms* and *Salute to Cyrano*. There have been many films based on Dumas's books, including *The Three Musketeers* (1921) and *The Iron Mask* (1928), with Douglas Fairbanks as D'Artagnan; a remake of *The Three Musketeers* (1935; dir. Rowland V. Lee), with Walter Abel; a comic version of the same title (1939; dir. Allan Dwan), with Don Ameche (and the Ritz Brothers); *The Man in the Iron Mask* (1939; dir. James Whale), with Warren William; *The Three Musketeers* (1948; dir. George Sidney), with Gene Kelly; *The Three Musketeers (The Queen's Diamonds)* (1973; dir. Richard Lester) and *The Four Musketeers (The Revenge of Milady)* (1974; dir. Lester), both starring Michael York; and *The Fifth Musketeer* (1978; dir. Ken Annakin), with Cornel Wilde as an ageing D'Artagnan. The TV movie *The Man in the Iron Mask* (1977; dir. Mike Newell) had Louis Jourdan as the hero. Dumas's D'Artagnan also has the distinction of being the first famous literary character to appear in an American 'Classics Illustrated' comic-book (*The Three Musketeers*, 1941).

DASHWOOD, ELINOR   Heroine of Jane Austen's novel, *Sense and Sensibility* (1811). Elinor's good sense is contrasted with the fashionable 'sensibility' of her sister Marianne (an early, unpublished version of the novel was entitled 'Elinor and Marianne'). A sequel by another hand is *Margaret Dashwood* by Mrs F. Brown.

DA SILVA, JOSÉ   Brazilian police captain in a series of crime novels by the American writer Robert L. Fish: *The Fugitive* (1962), *Isle of the Snakes* (1963), *The Shrunken Head* (1963), *The Diamond Bubble* (1965), *Brazilian Sleigh Ride* (1965), *Always Kill a Stranger* (1967), *The Bridge That Went Nowhere* (1968), *The Xavier Affair* (1969), *The Green Hell Treasure* (1971) and *Trouble in Paradise* (1975).

DAVIES, ARTHUR   See under CARRUTHERS

DAWES, RUFUS   Real name Richard Devine, an Englishman who is transported to Australia for a crime he did not commit, in Marcus Clarke's powerful novel *For the Term of His Natural Life* (1874). In the Australian-produced television mini-series (1983) Rufus Dawes was played by Colin Friels.

DEADEYE, DICK   Sailor in W. S. Gilbert and Arthur Sullivan's operetta *H.M.S. Pinafore, or The Lass that Loved a Sailor* (1878). An animated feature film, *Dick Deadeye, or Duty Done* (1982; dir. Bill Melendez), features many of the Gilbert and Sullivan characters and has Dick as its hero.

DEADWOOD DICK   Western hero of nineteenth-century dime novels, mostly written by Edward L. Wheeler. As with the better-known Buffalo Bill and Calamity Jane, he is supposed to have been based on a real-life character – in this case, a pony-express rider called William Clark; however, 'it may be assumed that any resemblance between [Clark's] life and the Deadwood Dick of Wheeler's creation was negligible' (E. S. Turner). Dick's adventures are recounted in such titles as *Deadwood Dick's Dream, or The Rivals of the Road: A Mining Tale of 'Tombstone'* (1881) and *Deadwood Dick's Protégée, or Baby Bess, the Girl Gold Miner* (1887). Like Frank READE and Tom SWIFT, he has a son,

Deadwood Dick Jr, who becomes virtually indistinguishable
from his father.

DEANS, JEANIE   Woman who walks from Edinburgh to London in
order to secure a pardon for her half-sister Effie (who is wrongly
convicted of infanticide). The story is told in Sir Walter Scott's
novel *The Heart of Midlothian* (1818), long regarded as one of his
most effective works. At the time of the book's first publication
an English admirer wrote to Scott in glowing terms: 'I have not only
read it myself, but am in a house where everybody is tearing it
out of each other's hands, and talking of nothing else . . . Had
this story been conducted by a common hand, Effie would have
attracted all our concern and sympathy – Jeanie only cold
approbation. Whereas Jeanie, without youth, beauty, genius,
warm passions, or any other novel-perfection, is here our object
from beginning to end. This is "enlisting the affections in the
cause of virtue" ten times more than ever Richardson did; for whose
male and female pedants, all-excelling as they are, I never could
care half so much as I found myself inclined to do for Jeanie
before I finished the first volume' (quoted in the introduction to
the Everyman edition, 1906).

DE BOURGH, LADY CATHERINE   See under Elizabeth BENNET and
Fitzwilliam DARCY

DE CRÉCY, ODETTE   See under Charles SWANN

DEDALUS, STEPHEN   Central character of James Joyce's novel *A
Portrait of the Artist as a Young Man* (1916). He grows up in late
nineteenth-century Dublin, rebels against family, religion and
nation, and finally sets sail for France where he will live as a poet
in 'silence, exile and cunning' and forge 'the uncreated conscience'
of the Irish people. Dedalus is very evidently Joyce's self-portrait,
although viewed with an ironical detachment. He reappears in
Joyce's masterpiece *Ulysses* (1922), where he acts as a surrogate son
for that universal man Leopold BLOOM. An earlier, partial version
of Joyce's first novel was published after the author's death as
Stephen Hero (1944); this is quite different from *A Portrait of the
Artist* and deals with Stephen's university days in Dublin. In
the film *Ulysses* (1967; dir. Joseph Strick) Stephen was played by

Maurice Roeves. The German composer Hans Zender has adapted part of Joyce's *Ulysses* as an opera entitled *Stephen Climax* (1986).

DEDLOCK, SIR LEICESTER AND LADY   See under Esther SUMMERSON

DEEDS, LONGFELLOW   Good-hearted down-home hero played by Gary Cooper in the film *Mr Deeds Goes to Town* (1936; dir. Frank Capra). He inherits some wealth and goes to New York, where he devastates the city-dwelling cynics with his simple, honest charity (one old lady describes him as 'pixilated'). The movie was scripted by Robert Riskin, from a story, 'Opera Hat', by Clarence Budington Kelland. A television series, also entitled 'Mr Deeds Goes to Town' (1969–70), starred Monte Markham.

DEERING, WILMA   See under Buck ROGERS

DE GRANDIN, JULES   Occult detective in the tradition of Dr John SILENCE or CARNACKI the Ghost Finder. The Frenchman de Grandin and his amanuensis, Dr Trowbridge, were created by the American writer Seabury Quinn for a series of more than ninety stories which appeared in *Weird Tales* magazine from 1925 to 1951. A few of these stories were included in Quinn's book *The Phantom-Fighter* (1966), but the majority were not reprinted until well after their author's death, when they appeared in such volumes as *The Adventures of Jules de Grandin*, *The Casebook of Jules de Grandin*, *The Hellfire Files of Jules de Grandin*, *The Skeleton Closet of Jules de Grandin*, *The Devil's Bride* and *The Horror Chambers of Jules de Grandin* (all 1976).

DEJAH THORIS   See under John CARTER

DELANCEY, RICHARD   British naval hero of a series of novels by C. Northcote Parkinson (Horatio HORNBLOWER's biographer). Delancey's adventures commence in the year 1794, and are recounted in *Devil to Pay* (1973), *The Fireship* (1975), *Touch and Go* (1977), *Dead Reckoning* (1978) and *So Near, So Far* (1981).

DE NERAC, GASTON   See Berzelius Nibbidard PARAGOT

DENISOVICH, IVAN   Prisoner in a Soviet labour camp at the time
of Stalin's dictatorship. He appears in Alexander Solzhenitsyn's
short novel *One Day in the Life of Ivan Denisovich* (1962). In the
British-made film of the book (1971; dir. Caspar Wrede) he was
played by Tom Courtenay.

DENNIS THE DACHSHUND   See under LARRY THE LAMB

DENNIS THE MENACE   There are two versions of Dennis the
Menace. (1) A cartoon kid created by American comic-strip
artist Hank Ketcham in 1951. This four-year-old brat has been
described as 'the equivalent of Hans and Fritz rolled into one'
(see the KATZENJAMMER Kids). He later appeared in a television
series, 'Dennis the Menace' (1959–63), where he was played by Jay
North (the character's full name was Dennis Mitchell).
  (2) Another little terror created almost simultaneously by British
cartoonist David Law for the weekly comic *The Beano* (from
1951). This Dennis has a shock of black hair, wears a red striped
jersey, and is accompanied in his pranks by a fearsome dog called
Gnasher.

DENRY   See Denry MACHIN

DENT, ARTHUR   Bemused Englishman who becomes the
involuntary hero of a space epic when the Earth is threatened with
demolition in order to make way for a hyperspace bypass. Dent
first appeared in Douglas Adams's humorous BBC radio series
'The Hitch-Hiker's Guide to the Galaxy' (1978–80), where he was
played by Simon Jones. Other notable characters from the series
are Zaphod Beeblebrox, Marvin the Paranoid Android, and the
unfortunately-named Slartibartfast – not to mention a mighty
computer called Deep Thought. Douglas Adams went on to write
a bestselling book, also entitled *The Hitch-Hiker's Guide to the
Galaxy* (1980), which has been followed by three sequels, *The
Restaurant at the End of the Universe* (1981), *Life, the Universe
and Everything* (1982) and *So Long, and Thanks for All the Fish*
(1983). A BBC television series (1981) was based on the original
radio serial, with Simon Jones repeating his role as Arthur Dent.
There have also been *Hitch-Hiker's* records, stage shows and
computer games.

DE RICHLEAU, DUKE   Aristocratic hero of thrillers by Dennis Wheatley, beginning with the author's first book *The Forbidden Territory* (1933). De Richleau's usual comrades in arms are Richard Eaton, Simon Aron and Rex Van Ryn (the 'modern musketeers'). They make their most notable appearances in the occult shocker *The Devil Rides Out* (1934) and its direct sequel *Strange Conflict* (1941). The Duke also features in *The Golden Spaniard* (1938), *Three Inquisitive People* (1940), *The Second Seal* (1944), *Code-Word Golden Fleece* (1946), *The Prisoner in the Mask* (1957), *Vendetta in Spain* (1961), *Dangerous Inheritance* (1965) and *Gateway to Hell* (1970). In the film *The Devil Rides Out* (1967; dir. Terence Fisher) De Richleau was played by Christopher Lee.

DERONDA, DANIEL   See under Gwendolen HARLETH

DESBOROUGH, LUCY   See under Richard FEVEREL

DESENEX, PHILBERT   See WONDER WART-HOG

DES ESSEINTES, DUC JEAN   Perverse aesthete in Joris-Karl Huysmans' influential novel *À Rebours* (1884; translated into English as *Against the Grain* or *Against Nature*). Weary of the conventional pleasures of Paris, Des Esseintes shuts himself away from the world in order to enjoy an artificial nocturnal life surrounded by his favourite works of art and literature. Huysmans' novel was to have a major influence on Oscar Wilde's hero Dorian GRAY. The latter muses: 'It was the strangest book that he had ever read. It seemed to him that in exquisite raiment and to the delicate sound of flutes, the sins of the world were passing in dumb show before him.'

DES GRIEUX, CHEVALIER   See under Manon LESCAUT

DESMOND, NORMA   Ageing movie star memorably portrayed by Gloria Swanson in the film *Sunset Boulevard* (1950; dir. Billy Wilder). She ensnares Joe Gillis, a penniless scriptwriter who becomes her gigolo, and together they watch her old silent films projected by the mysterious manservant who was once her director. (The casting of the film is exquisitely ironic, since the

servant is played by Erich Von Stroheim who had in fact directed
Gloria Swanson in *Queen Kelly*, an unfinished film from which
extracts are used in *Sunset Boulevard*). The film was written by
Wilder in collaboration with Charles Brackett and D. M. Marshman
Jr. Norma Desmond appears in David Thomson's book *Suspects*
(1985; see under George BAILEY), where she is imagined as giving
birth (at the age of fifty-one) to Julian Kay, the character played
by Richard Gere in the film *American Gigolo* (1980).

DESPERATE DAN   Beefy, stubble-chinned westerner created by
British comic-strip artist Dudley D. Watkins for the weekly
paper *The Dandy* (from 1937). Dan's favourite repast is cow pie,
with the horns protruding from the pastry. He is still popular after
nearly fifty years of continuous publication.

DESTROYER, THE   Real name Remo Williams, hero of a paperback
thriller series by Warren Murphy and Richard Ben Sapir,
beginning with *Created, the Destroyer* (1971). Williams is a tough
cop who has become a master of unarmed combat, thanks to the
training he has received from an eighty-year-old Korean guru. He
now works as a special agent for the President of the USA, and is
prepared to go anywhere and kill anybody. Over fifty novels about
The Destroyer have been published (later titles in the series are
written by Warren Murphy only). The film *Remo – Unarmed and
Dangerous* (1985; dir. Guy Hamilton) starred Fred Ward, and
its script has been turned into a new novel by Murphy and Sapir.
(There was also a comic-book character called the Destroyer [alias
Keen Marlow]. He was created by Stan Lee and, like his brother-
in-arms Captain AMERICA, he fought Nazis from 1941 to 1946.)

DESTRY, TOM   Sheriff of the town of Bottleneck in the Old West.
He drinks sarsaparilla and refuses to carry a gun, much to the
consternation of the townsfolk. This unusual lawman was created
by Max Brand (Frederick Faust) for his novel *Destry Rides Again*
(1930). In the entertaining film of the book (1939; dir. George
Marshall) Destry was played by James Stewart. In the inferior
remake, simply entitled *Destry* (1954; dir. Marshall), the role was
taken by Audie Murphy. There was also a short-lived television
series called 'Destry' (1964), which starred John Gavin as Harrison
Destry, Tom's supposed son. A stage musical, *Destry Rides*

Again, with music and lyrics by Harold Rome, was first performed on Broadway in 1959 (with Andy Griffith in the lead part) and was revived in Britain in 1982.

DETROIT, NATHAN   Broadway hustler, owner of the longest established floating crap game in New York, who appears in various short stories by Damon Runyon (including 'The Idyll of Miss Sarah Brown', better known as 'Guys and Dolls'). Nathan has been engaged to his girlfriend, Miss Adelaide, for fourteen years. These characters feature, along with Sky MASTERSON, in Frank Loesser's stage musical *Guys and Dolls* (1950); and in the film of the musical (1955; dir. Joseph L. Mankiewicz), where Nathan was played by Frank Sinatra.

DE VERE, RICHARD   See under Audrey FFORBES-HAMILTON

DE VIL, CRUELLA   Aristocratic villainess of Dodie Smith's children's novel *One Hundred and One Dalmatians* (1956).

Cruella De Vil with her minions and captives
Copyright Walt Disney Productions

She kidnaps a huge brood of puppies in order to turn their fur into coats for humans. The story was made into a full-length animated film by the Disney organization (1961; dir. Wolfgang Reitherman, Hamilton S. Luske and Clyde Geronimi) – described by Leslie Halliwell as 'Disney's last really splendid feature cartoon' – since when the name of Cruella De Vil has been a byword for female heartlessness.

DEVINE, RICHARD   See Rufus DAWES

DE WINTER, REBECCA   Deceased wife of Maximilian de Winter, mysterious owner of a romantic Cornish house called Manderley. She gives her name to one of the most popular novels of this century, Daphne du Maurier's *Rebecca* (1938). The nameless heroine and narrator of the book becomes de Winter's second wife, but she is persecuted by the sinister housekeeper, Mrs Danvers ('tall and gaunt, dressed in deep black, whose prominent cheekbones and great, hollow eyes gave her a skull's face'), and continually haunted by reminders of the glamorous and high-spirited Rebecca. It transpires that Rebecca was murdered by Max de Winter, who was driven to distraction by her unfaithfulness to him. The novel was rapidly turned into a stage play and then a very successful film (1940; dir. Alfred Hitchcock). It has since been adapted for BBC television (1979). In an entertaining essay (*Guardian*, 15 March 1982) Jill Tweedie has claimed that '*Rebecca* is the incarnation of the Electra myth, embodying all daughters' infantile fears that they cannot compete for their fathers' attention with a certain mature hussy who appears to have some sort of hold over Dad, the nature of which is hazy but definitely distasteful. She was there first, before we came, she plays all the trumps and everyone compares us with her, to our detriment.' An operatic version of *Rebecca*, written by Wilfred Josephs, was first performed in 1983.

DICK, MR   See under David COPPERFIELD

DIGBY   See under Dan DARE

DiGRIZ, SLIPPERY JIM   See The STAINLESS STEEL RAT

DILLON, MATT   Dodge City marshal played by James Arness in the long-running television series 'Gunsmoke' (1955–75; later known as 'Gun Law'). Dillon's lame, whiny-voiced deputy Chester Goode (played by Dennis Weaver from 1955 to 1964) became almost as much of a household name as the marshal himself. The characters had actually originated on CBS radio, in 1952. On the air Matt Dillon was voiced by William Conrad (who later became famous as the fat TV detectives Frank CANNON and Nero WOLFE). The singer Bob Dylan (Robert Zimmerman) is said to have taken his name from Matt Dillon (not Dylan Thomas).

DIME, MIKE   See under Jack LEVINE

DIMMESDALE, ARTHUR   See under Hester PRYNNE

DIMSIE   Full name Dorothy Maitland, a sports-loving schoolgirl who forms an 'Anti-Soppist Society' which is opposed to love, sentiment and the use of make-up. This may sound like clear-eyed, conscious feminism on her part, but in fact she is the quintessential English girl of the 'jolly hockey sticks' type. She appeared in a long series of school stories by Dorita Fairlie Bruce, beginning with *The Senior Prefect* (1921; vt *Dimsie Goes to School*). The books were very popular with girls throughout the 1920s and 1930s. Later titles include: *Dimsie Moves Up* (1921), *Dimsie Moves Up Again* (1922), *Dimsie Goes Back* (1927) and *Dimsie Carries On* (1942).

DINMONT, DANDIE   See under Guy MANNERING

DINSMORE, ELSIE   Exceedingly virtuous little girl who appears in a series of twenty-six books by the American writer Martha Finley (Martha Farquharson), beginning with *Elsie Dinsmore* (1867). Later books in the series, including such titles as *Elsie's Girlhood*, *Elsie's Womanhood* and *Elsie's Widowhood*, show the pious Elsie growing to maturity and even old age. These tales were very popular with young readers in America and Britain.

DIRTY DEN   See Angie and Den WATTS

DIRTY HARRY   See Harry CALLAHAN

DIVER, DICK   Psychiatrist whose principal patient is his deranged
wife, Nicole, in F. Scott Fitzgerald's most ambitious novel, *Tender
is the Night* (1934). In the film of the novel (1961; dir. Henry King)
Diver was played by Jason Robards Jr. A lavish television serial
(1985), scripted by Dennis Potter, starred Peter Strauss as the rich,
handsome and long-suffering Diver.

DIXON, GEORGE   Policeman played by Jack Warner in the film
The Blue Lamp (1949; dir. Basil Dearden). Dixon is very much
the reliable English bobby: a middle-aged, comforting, level-
headed, and at times servile authority-figure. Developed by
scriptwriter Ted Willis for BBC television, he became the leading
character in the long-running series 'Dixon of Dock Green'
(1955–76). Jack Warner continued to play the part until he was
eighty years old. Dixon also appears in several novels by Ted Willis:
The Blue Lamp (1950), *Dixon of Dock Green: My Life* (with
Charles Hatton, 1960) and *Dixon of Dock Green: A Novel* (with
Paul Graham, 1961).

DIXON, JIM   Hilarious anti-hero of Kingsley Amis's bestselling first
novel *Lucky Jim* (1954). He is a young academic at a provincial British
university. Surrounded by pedants and ageing authority-figures, he
pulls faces, gets drunk, plays practical jokes and generally acts in
a most unseemly manner (considered shocking by some at the time
of the book's first publication). A film, *Lucky Jim* (1957; dir. John
Boulting), starred Ian Carmichael as Dixon. The character has also
recurred in two BBC television series, 'The New Adventures of Lucky
Jim' (1967), with Keith Barron, and 'The Further Adventures of
Lucky Jim' (1982), with Enn Reitel.

DOASYOUWOULDBEDONEBY, MRS   See under TOM

DOBERMAN, DUANE   See under Ernest G. BILKO

DOBBIN, WILLIAM   See under Becky SHARP

DOBSON, ZULEIKA   Divine young woman who wins the hearts of
Oxford's undergraduates in Max Beerbohm's fantastic novel *Zuleika
Dobson* (1911). So smitten are the young men that they all drown
themselves in sorrow. With a suitably altered ending, the story

was turned into a musical play by James Ferman and Peter Tranchell (1957).

DODD, LEWIS   See under Tessa SANGER

DOLITTLE, ELIZA   Cockney heroine of George Bernard Shaw's play *Pygmalion* (1914). She is a humble flower-seller until Professor Henry Higgins takes her in hand, gives her intensive elocution lessons, and introduces her to high society. In the film of the play (1938; dir. Anthony Asquith) Eliza was played by Wendy Hiller. The story was adapted as a stage musical, *My Fair Lady* (1956), with lyrics by Alan Jay Lerner and music by Frederick Loewe, and this in turn was filmed (1964; dir. George Cukor), with Audrey Hepburn in the leading role. Shaw's original play has been televised many times. A recent American TV movie version of *Pygmalion* (1984) starred Margot Kidder.

DOLITTLE, JOHN   Doctor who communes with animals, and eventually gives up his human practice to become a full-time 'animal doctor'. He lives in Puddleby on the Marsh, but his adventures take him all over the world and even as far as the Moon. His companions include Polynesia the Parrot, Chee Chee the Monkey and Gub Gub the Pig – as well as a few token humans such as Matthew Mugg, the cat's-meat man. They appear in Hugh Lofting's *The Story of Doctor Dolittle* (1920) and its sequels: *The Voyages of Doctor Dolittle* (1922), *Doctor Dolittle's Post Office* (1923), *Doctor Dolittle's Circus* (1924), *Doctor Dolittle's Zoo* (1925), *Doctor Dolittle's Caravan* (1926), *Doctor Dolittle's Garden* (1927), *Doctor Dolittle in the Moon* (1928), *Gub Gub's Book* (1932), *Doctor Dolittle's Return* (1933), and the posthumous books *Doctor Dolittle and the Secret Lake* (1948), *Doctor Dolittle and the Green Canary* (1950) and *Doctor Dolittle's Puddleby Adventures* (1952). The middle volumes of the series are generally thought to be the best (according to *The Oxford Companion to Children's Literature*, 'Lofting is almost unique in children's literature in being the author of a series which improves rather than deteriorates as it goes on'). An unsuccessful musical film, *Doctor Dolittle* (1967; dir. Richard Fleischer), starred Rex Harrison as the gentle Doctor. There has also been an animated television series of the same title (1970).

DOMBEY, PAUL   Sensitive boy who is sent to a harsh school, where he falls ill and dies. The story of Paul and his father is told in Charles Dickens's novel *Dealings with the Firm of Dombey and Son* (1847–8). 'The death of the little Dombey moved the nation nearly as much as the death of Little Nell,' according to *The Oxford Companion to English Literature* (see LITTLE NELL). The remainder of the novel deals with the elder Dombey's second marriage, his cruelty to his daughter Florence, and the eventual collapse of his business. *Dombey and Daughter* (1847) by Renton Nicholson is not so much a sequel as an attempt to cash in on the popularity of Dickens's title. A genuine sequel by another hand is *The Gay Dombeys* (1919) by Sir Harry Johnston (a sometime African explorer and travel writer who turned to novels late in life and wrote several sequels to famous works: see also Mr and Mrs VENEERING and Vivie WARREN). There was a silent movie version of *Dombey and Son* (1917; dir. Maurice Elvey), and the sound film *Rich Man's Folly* (1931; dir. John Cromwell) is an updated version of Dickens's story. The BBC television serialization of the novel (1983) starred Julian Glover as Dombey Senior, with Barnaby Buik as young Paul.

DONALD DUCK   Bad-tempered cartoon duck who dresses in a sailor suit – created by the Walt Disney studios in 1934. His first appearance was in an animated film called *The Wise Little Hen*, where he was drawn by Art Babbit and Dick Huemer and voiced by Clarence Nash. Donald is second in fame only to MICKEY MOUSE, and has appeared in many newspaper strips and comic-books as well as short cinema and television films. He has a trio of uncontrollable nephews named Huey, Dewey and Louie who made their cinematic debut in 1938. The Chilean Marxist critic Ariel Dorfman has written a widely-translated book entitled *How to Read Donald Duck: Imperialist Ideology in the Disney Comic* (1975).

DONNITHORNE, ARTHUR   See under Hetty SORREL

DONOVAN, DICK   Victorian police detective, narrator of some 200 short stories by Joyce Emmerson Preston Muddock (writing under the pseudonym of 'Dick Donovan'). Donovan's adventures were collected in the following books: *The Man-Hunter: Stories from* *the Note-Book of a Detective* (1888), *Caught at Last! Leaves from the Note-Book of a Detective* (1889), *Who Poisoned Hetty Duncan? and Other Detective Stories* (1890), *Tracked and Taken: Detective Sketches* (1890), *A Detective's Triumphs* (1891), *Wanted! A Detective's Strange Adventures* (1892), *In the Grip of the Law* (1892), *From Information Received* (1893), *Link by Link* (1893), *From Clue to Capture* (1893), *Suspicion Aroused* (1893), *Found and Fettered* (1894), *Dark Deeds* (1895), *Riddles Read* (1896) and *Tales of Terror* (1899). Dick Donovan was one of the most popular detective heroes in the days immediately prior to the arrival of Sherlock HOLMES.

DOONE, LORNA   Heroine of R. D. Blackmore's historical novel *Lorna Doone, a Romance of Exmoor* (1869). The Doones are a band of brigands who live in a remote part of Devon at the time of the Duke of Monmouth's rebellion against the crown. Young Lorna saves the life of John Ridd, a sworn enemy of the Doones. He falls in love with her, and eventually discovers that she is the lost daughter of a nobleman. Silent film adaptations of *Lorna Doone* were made in 1912, 1915, 1920 and 1922. Sound versions were made in 1934 (dir. Basil Dean), with Victoria Hopper as Lorna, and in 1951 (dir. Phil Karlson), with Barbara Hale. The story has also been serialized on BBC television (1963).

DOONESBURY   Titular hero of Garry Trudeau's satirical comic-strip about American college graduates (originally entitled *Bull Tales*, from 1968). In addition to the ineffectual Doonesbury, the strip features a host of characters, including the hero's erstwhile campus friends, the sports-loving B.D. and the would-be radical Megaphone Mark. Since 1970 *Doonesbury* has enjoyed wide syndication, and has been reprinted in book form. In recent years Trudeau's strip has appeared in the British 'quality' newspaper, the *Guardian*.

DOROTHY   See Dorothy GALE

DORRIT, AMY   Devoted daughter of William Dorrit, an imprisoned debtor who is known as the 'Father of the Marshalsea', in Charles Dickens's novel *Little Dorrit* (1855–7). She falls in love with Arthur Clennam, whom she tends when he too is jailed in the

Marshalsea, and, after many vicissitudes, they marry. A German-made film of the novel (1933) had Anny Ondra in the principal role. A new two-part film adaptation (dir. Christine Edzard), with Sarah Pickering as Amy Dorrit, is due for release in 1987.

DOUGAL   Long-haired dog who is the central character of the television puppet series 'The Magic Roundabout' (from 1965). His name and personality were created by Eric Thompson, who also wrote the books based on the series. The short puppet films around which Thompson spun his charmingly naïve fantasies were originally made by Serge Danot for French TV (under the title 'Le Manège Enchanté'). Dougal's friends include the guitar-playing rabbit Dylan, the bee Zebedee and the little girl Florence. Although intended for small children, 'The Magic Roundabout' became a cult programme in Britain among young adults (particularly students) during the late 1960s and early 1970s. The books by Eric Thompson include *The Adventures of Dougal* (1971), *The Misadventures of Dougal* (1972) and other titles. The feature film *Dougal and the Blue Cat* (1972; dir. Danot) includes a trip to the moon; standing on the lunar surface, Dougal pronounces: 'One small step for a dog but a great step for dogkind.'

DOVER, WILFRED   Anti-heroic detective-inspector, known as the 'Shame of Scotland Yard', who appears in a series of comic crime novels by Joyce Porter: *Dover One* (1964), *Dover Two* (1965), *Dover Three* (1966), *Dover and the Unkindest Cut of All* (1967), *Dover Goes to Pott* (1968), *Dover Strikes Again* (1970), *It's Murder with Dover* (1973), *Dover and the Claret Tappers* (1977), *Dead Easy for Dover* (1978) and *Dover Beats the Band* (1980). Dover also appears in a series of short stories which Joyce Porter has contributed to *Ellery Queen's Mystery Magazine*. He is fat, lazy and ill-tempered, yet somehow he manages to catch his man.

DOWD, ELWOOD P.   See under HARVEY

DOYLE, POPEYE   Slovenly New York police detective who tackles a drug-smuggling ring in Robin Moore's novel *The French Connection* (1970). The story is supposed to be based on a real-life case. Other, related books by Moore are *The Fifth Estate* (1973), *French Connection II* (1975), *The Terminal Connection* (1978) and *The New York Connection* (1979). Popeye Doyle was memorably played by Gene Hackman in the Oscar-winning film *The French Connection* (1971; dir. William Friedkin) and its sequel *French Connection II* (1975; dir. John Frankenheimer).

DRACULA, COUNT   Near-immortal Transylvanian vampire in Bram Stoker's immensely successful horror novel *Dracula* (1897). Like the vampire bat and the *nosferatu* of Romanian legend, he feeds on blood – preferably the blood of beautiful young women such as Lucy Westenra and her friend Mina Harker (two of the novel's several narrators). After one of his ghastly feasts Dracula is described by Stoker as 'looking as if his youth had been half renewed . . . the cheeks were fuller, and the white skin seemed ruby-red underneath; the mouth was redder than ever, for on the lips were gouts of fresh blood, which trickled from the corners of the mouth and ran over the chin and neck. Even the deep, burning eyes seemed set amongst swollen flesh, for the lids and pouches underneath were bloated. It seemed as if the whole awful creature were simply gorged with blood; he lay like a filthy leech, exhausted with his repletion.' It takes all the arcane skills of the vampire-hunter Dr Abraham VAN HELSING, with his deployment of crucifixes, garlic and wooden stakes, finally to defeat Dracula. The undead Count is one of the half-dozen best-known fictional characters of modern times, and he has pursued a long and active career on the stage, in films, on television, in comic-books, advertising, merchandizing, jokes and popular lore. Stoker revived him for just one short story, included in *Dracula's Guest and Other Stories* (1914), but many others have been tempted to pen sequels (or imitations). Recent sequels by other hands include *The Dracula Archives* (1971) by Raymond Rudorff; *Dracula Returns* (1973) by Robert Lory; *The Dracula Tape* (1975) by Fred Saberhagen; *Dracula Unborn* (1977) and *The Revenge of Dracula* (1978) by Peter Tremayne; *The Holmes-Dracula File* (1978) by Saberhagen (in which the Count meets a certain famous consulting detective); and *Sherlock Holmes Versus Dracula* (1978) by Loren D. Estleman (in which the two most famous fictional characters of their era clash once more).

   The first notable film to be based on Stoker's novel was the German *Nosferatu* (1921; dir. F. W. Murnau). It starred Max Schreck as the vampire, but for copyright reasons the character was not

named 'Dracula' in this production. A stage adaptation of
Dracula, by Hamilton Deane and John L. Balderston, opened in
New York in 1927 with the Hungarian actor Bela Lugosi in the
lead. Lugosi was invited to perpetuate the role in the film of the
play (1931; dir. Tod Browning), and the success of this movie
led to an entire Dracula film industry. Direct Hollywood sequels
are *Dracula's Daughter* (1936; dir. Lambert Hillyer), with Gloria
Holden as the eponymous lady, *Son of Dracula* (1943; dir. Robert
Siodmak), with Lon Chaney, Jr as the said son, and *House of Dracula*
(1945; dir. Erle C. Kenton), with John Carradine (in which Dracula
meets FRANKENSTEIN's monster and the WOLF MAN). Later films
include the British-made *Dracula* (1958; dir. Terence Fisher; also
known as *Horror of Dracula*), with Christopher Lee as the Count,
and its Hammer Films sequels, most of which also star Lee: *Brides
of Dracula* (1960; dir. Fisher), *Dracula, Prince of Darkness*
(1965; dir. Fisher), *Dracula Has Risen from the Grave* (1968; dir.
Freddie Francis), *Taste the Blood of Dracula* (1969; dir. Peter
Sasdy), *Scars of Dracula* (1970; dir. Roy Ward Baker), *Dracula AD
1972* (1972; dir. Alan Gibson) and *The Satanic Rites of Dracula*
(1973; dir. Gibson). Other recent productions include the TV
movies *Dracula* (1973; dir. Dan Curtis), with Jack Palance, and
Count Dracula (1977; dir. Philip Saville), with Louis Jourdan, and
a new feature film, again entitled *Dracula* (1979; dir. John
Badham), with Frank Langella as a smoothly romantic version of
the Count. In addition to all the foregoing, there have been scores
of foreign-language films, ranging from a Hungarian *Drakula*,
made around the same time as Murnàu's *Nosferatu*, to the
Greek *Dracula Tan Exarchia* (1983). *Nosferatu* itself has been
remade in Germany (1979; dir. Werner Herzog), with Klaus
Kinski giving a notably ghoulish performance.

DRAGON LADY, THE   See under Terry LEE

DRAKE, JOHN   Suave secret agent, hero of the British television
thriller series 'Danger Man' (1959–63). He was played by Patrick
McGoohan. Later episodes of this series had a successful run in
America under the title 'Secret Agent'. See also The PRISONER.

DRAKE, PAUL   See under Perry MASON

DRAKE, TEMPLE   College girl who runs around with gangsters in William Faulkner's violent novel *Sanctuary* (1931). She is raped by Popeye Vitelli, murderous leader of the bandits, who places her in a Memphis brothel. Faulkner continues her story in *Requiem for a Nun* (1951), in which Temple is now married with children. A film based on *Sanctuary* is *The Story of Temple Drake* (1933; dir. Stephen Roberts), which starred Miriam Hopkins. A later version is *Sanctuary* (1961; dir. Tony Richardson), with Lee Remick.

DRAX, HUGO   See under James BOND

DREDD, JUDGE   Joe Dredd, a muscular law-enforcer of the futuristic Mega-City One. His adventures are recounted in a British science fiction comic-strip which has appeared in *2000 AD* magazine since 1977. The violent judge is the creation of artist Brian Bolland and writer John Wagner, whose strips have been reprinted in large-format paperback books. Judge Dredd has become the most admired of contemporary comic-book characters in the UK, a cynical Dan DARE for the 1980s.

DREW, NANCY   Girl detective whose father is a former district attorney. Like Frank and Joe HARDY, she was created by Edward Stratemeyer, boss of a celebrated American children's fiction factory which is usually known as the 'Stratemeyer syndicate'. Her adventures are the product of a number of different writers, among them Stratemeyer's daughter Harriet Adams. They have appeared over many decades in a long series of books which all bear the house name 'Carolyn Keene'. Early books about Nancy Drew include *The Hidden Staircase*, *The Bungalow Mystery* and *The Secret of the Old Clock* (all 1930). Further episodes in her eventful life continue to be published up to the present day. She was played by Bonita Granville in four 'B' movies, beginning with *Nancy Drew, Detective* (1938; dir. William Clemens). In the American television series 'The Hardy Boys and Nancy Drew Mysteries' (1977–9) she was played initially by Pamela Sue Martin, later by Janet Louise Johnson.

DROOD, EDWIN   Young man who disappears and is presumed dead, in Charles Dickens's unfinished novel *The Mystery of Edwin Drood* (1870). Suspicion of foul play has often fallen upon John

JASPER, Edwin's uncle, who is the evident villain of the piece. Because the book is incomplete, and because the nature of the mystery itself (much less its outcome) remains uncertain, the novel has attracted many 'conclusions' by other hands. One which appeared soon after Dickens's death is *John Jasper's Secret* (1871–2) by H. Morford and others. A recent ingenious example is *The Mystery of Edwin Drood . . . Concluded* (1980) by Leon Garfield. A film, *The Mystery of Edwin Drood* (1935; dir. Stuart Walker), had Douglass Montgomery as Drood and Claude Rains as Jasper: the script was by John L. Balderston and others. Dickens's incomplete story has even formed the basis of a stage musical, *Edwin Drood* (1985), with music, lyrics and 'book' by Rupert Holmes.

DRUMMOND, HUGH 'BULLDOG'   Beefy hero of a very popular series of thrillers by 'Sapper' (H. C. McNeile), beginning with *Bulldog Drummond* (1920). Drummond is a young ex-army captain in search of adventure. He advertises his services in a newspaper, and is soon deeply embroiled in a world of international crooks, fiendish spies and other enemies of the Empire. He is a fine example of 'the Breed' – those jolly, sports-loving clubmen from English public schools who uphold the British code in the face of all things furtive, foreign and foul-smelling. He has an understanding and energetic wife called Phyllis. He also has a gang of slavishly admiring followers, who in effect constitute a private army dedicated to the chastisement of 'Bolshevik Jews' and other undesirables. Their arch-enemies are Carl Peterson, a foreigner of obscure origin, and Peterson's mistress, Irma. Needless to say, Bulldog Drummond is now deeply out of fashion, his author condemned as a racist and proto-fascist, but in the 1920s and 1930s Sapper's books enjoyed as wide a readership as Ian Fleming's did later (Drummond is certainly the main prototype for James BOND, although he is a heartier character than Bond, much given to joshing and japing). Sapper's other titles about Hugh Drummond and his friends are *The Black Gang* (1922), *The Third Round* (1924), *The Final Count* (1926), *The Female of the Species* (1928), *Temple Tower* (1929), *Bulldog Drummond Returns* (1932), *Knock-Out* (1933; vt *Bulldog Drummond Strikes Back*), *Bulldog Drummond at Bay* (1935) and *Challenge* (1937; vt *Bulldog Drummond Hits Out*). Immediately after Sapper's death the

Bulldog Drummond (Ronald Colman) biffs the baddies

series was continued by his friend Gerard Fairlie. Titles by the latter are *Bulldog Drummond on Dartmoor* (1938), *Bulldog Drummond at War* (1940), *Captain Bulldog Drummond* (1945), *Bulldog Drummond Stands Fast* (1947), *Hands off Bulldog Drummond* (1949), *Calling Bulldog Drummond* (1951) and *The Return of the Black Gang* (1954). Drummond has also been perpetuated by Jack Smithers in his amusing novel *Combined Forces* (1985) – wherein hearty Hugh makes common cause with such superannuated contemporaries as Richard HANNAY and Jonah MANSEL.

The first actors to play Bulldog Drummond in films were Carlyle Blackwell (1922) and Jack Buchanan (1925). Ronald Colman played him with great success in *Bulldog Drummond* (1929; dir. F. Richard Jones) and *Bulldog Drummond Strikes Back* (1934; dir. Roy del Ruth). He was also portrayed by Kenneth McKenna (1930); Ralph Richardson (1934); Jack Hulbert (in a spoof called *Bulldog Jack*, 1935); John Lodge (1937); and Ray Milland (1937). The longest-lasting of the screen Drummonds was American actor John Howard, who played the character in eight films beginning with *Bulldog Drummond Comes Back* (1937; dir. Louis King). Ron Randell later took the lead in two Drummond films (1947), and Tom Conway in two more (1948). *Calling Bulldog Drummond* (1951; dir. Victor Saville) starred Walter Pidgeon; and *Deadlier Than the Male* (1967; dir. Ralph Thomas) and *Some Girls Do* (1969; dir. Ralph Thomas) had Richard Johnson as a sleekly updated version of the hero. Richard Usborne has written very entertainingly about Drummond in his book *Clubland Heroes* (1953). He says: 'Sapper's Bulldog Drummond is the Monarch of Muscle, the Sultan of Swat. He is the huge, ugly, cheerful, apparently brainless hunk of a man, who slaps you on the back with a hand the size of a leg of mutton, picks you up, gives you several tankards of beer to drink, and then takes you off in a Sports Bentley to help him gatecrash on the Moated Grange.' Other critics take a less affectionate view.

DUBIN, WILLIAM   Staid middle-aged biographer who falls into an affair with a young woman while he is working on a book about D. H. Lawrence (high priest of sex). His tragi-comic story is told in Bernard Malamud's novel *Dubin's Lives* (1979).

DUBOIS, BENSON   See under Jessica TATE

DUBOIS, BLANCHE   Faded southern belle in Tennessee Williams's
   bitter play *A Streetcar Named Desire* (1947). She goes to live with
   her sister and brother-in-law (Stanley Kowalski) in New Orleans,
   and provokes the latter into raping her. Still dreaming of a life of
   romantic gentility, she is later committed to a mental home. In
   the film of the play (1951; dir. Elia Kazan) Blanche was played
   by Vivien Leigh – an appropriate piece of casting in view of the
   fact that Leigh had played the most famous of southern belles,
   Scarlett O'HARA, some twelve years earlier. In a later TV movie
   version (1984; dir. John Erman) Ann-Margret played Blanche.

DUKE FAMILY, THE   See under Jed CLAMPETT

DUPIN, C. AUGUSTE   Well-bred but impoverished French
   detective created by Edgar Allan Poe. The Chevalier Dupin appears
   in just three short stories – 'The Murders in the Rue Morgue'
   (1841), 'The Mystery of Marie Rogêt' (1842) and 'The Purloined
   Letter' (1844) – yet he is a towering figure in the history of
   detective fiction, a worthy antecedent of Sherlock HOLMES and
   hundreds of lesser sleuths. (When Dr WATSON first meets Holmes
   in *A Study in Scarlet* [1887] he says: 'You remind me of Edgar
   Allan Poe's Dupin. I had no idea that such individuals did exist
   outside of stories.') As Julian Symons has written, Dupin 'solves the
   problems presented to him by pure analytic deduction.
   Aristocratic, arrogant and apparently omniscient, Dupin is what
   Poe often wished he could have been himself, an emotionless
   reasoning machine.' Poe may have been sparing in his use of
   the character, but other writers have exploited Dupin at greater
   length. A modern sequel by another hand is *The Exploits of
   Chevalier Dupin* (1968) by Michael Harrison (expanded as *Murder
   in the Rue Royale*, 1972).
      The first of Poe's three stories has been filmed several times.
   Versions include *Murders in the Rue Morgue* (1932; dir. Robert
   Florcy); *Phantom of the Rue Morgue* (1954; dir. Roy Del Ruth),
   with Steve Forrest as 'Prof. Paul Dupin'; and *Murders in the Rue
   Morgue* (1971; dir. Gordon Hessler). None of these is particularly
   faithful to the original work. In the film *The Man with a Cloak*
   (1951; dir. Fletcher Markle), the central character, played by

Joseph Cotten, calls himself 'Dupin' but actually turns out to be Edgar Allan Poe.

DURBEYFIELD, TESS   Simple country girl who is seduced by her rich cousin, Alec D'Urberville, and bears his child. The baby dies, and poor Tess's sufferings continue. She marries a rector's son, Angel Clare, but he abandons her after hearing about her sinful past. Tess is driven to murder Alec D'Urberville, and is condemned to death. Thomas Hardy's tragic novel *Tess of the D'Urbervilles* (1891) was considered shocking on first publication, especially as Hardy provoked his Victorian public by referring to Tess as 'a Pure Woman'. In the film *Tess* (1979; dir. Roman Polanski) she was played by Nastassia Kinski.

DURWARD, QUENTIN   Dashing young Scotsman who serves the King of France in Sir Walter Scott's novel of the fifteenth century, *Quentin Durward* (1823). In the film *The Adventures of Quentin Durward* (1955; dir. Richard Thorpe) the hero was played by a slightly over-age Robert Taylor.

DUVAL, ARMAND   See under CAMILLE

DYLAN   See under DOUGAL

E.T. A 'little squashy guy' from outer space who befriends the children of a Californian household in Steven Spielberg's film *E.T.: The Extra-Terrestrial* (1982). E.T. is a gentle soul who has come to Earth in search of plant specimens; he gets stranded and is afraid. Given refuge by the children, he returns their kindness by showing them how to fly. Eventually he jury-rigs an apparatus which enables him to phone home. He falls ill, apparently dies, and is reborn shortly before the spacecraft returns to carry him away. It is a remarkably moving story, perhaps the only film of recent times which has reduced a large proportion of its worldwide audience to tears. 'E.T. phone home' became a catch-phrase of 1982–3, when the movie rapidly established itself as the most commercially successful in Hollywood's history. E.T.'s grotesque but endearing looks were designed by special-effects man Carlo Rambaldi. The script was novelized by William Kotzwinkle, who later wrote a sequel, 'based on an original story by Steven Spielberg', called *E.T.: The Book of the Green Planet* (1985).

EARNSHAW, CATHERINE Heroine of Emily Brontë's powerful romantic novel *Wuthering Heights* (1847). She falls in love with HEATHCLIFF, a mysterious boy who has been adopted by her father. Both assume that they will marry one day, but Heathcliff overhears Catherine telling the housekeeper that such a marriage would 'degrade' her – and he runs away for three years. In the interim Catherine marries Edgar Linton, but her passion for Heathcliff does not wane. Shortly after the latter's return she dies while giving birth to a daughter, Cathy. Heathcliff lives on, heartbroken. In the film of the novel (1939; dir. William Wyler) Catherine was played by Merle Oberon. The remake (1970; dir. Robert Fuest) starred Anna Calder-Marshall. A BBC television serialization of the novel (1978) had Kay Adshead as the heroine. Catherine Earnshaw also features in a pop song of the late 1970s, 'Wuthering Heights' by Kate Bush.

EARWICKER, HUMPHREY CHIMPDEN   Dublin publican who becomes an Everyman when he sleeps – which is what he does throughout the considerable length of James Joyce's 'novel' *Finnegans Wake* (1939), a formidable work written almost entirely in multilingual puns. The book is the transcript of a night's dreaming, a cascade of fantasies which draw upon all of human history. Earwicker, his wife (known in the dream-language as Anna Livia PLURABELLE), his two sons and his daughter all feature in countless roles. The principal *motif* is a cyclical Rise-and-Fall: like Adam in the Garden of Eden, like Finnegan in the Irish ballad, Earwicker is for ever falling – only to rise again.

EASY, CAPTAIN   Hook-nosed adventurer created by artist Roy Crane for American newspaper comic-strips. He describes himself as 'beach-comber, boxer, cook, aviator, seaman, explorer, and soldier of artillery, infantry and cavalry'. At first Easy was a sidekick for the boy hero Washington Tubbs II, but within a few years of his creation in 1929 he had a strip of his own, *Captain Easy, Soldier of Fortune*. He became one of the most popular comic-strip characters of the 1930s, and after Roy Crane abandoned him in 1943 his career was perpetuated by Leslie Turner and other artists. Drawn by Bill Crooks, Easy was still going strong in the 1980s.

EASY, JACK   Likeable young hero of Frederick Marryat's novel *Mr Midshipman Easy* (1836). He joins the Royal Navy, has sundry adventures and learns all about the virtues of hierarchy and discipline. In the film *Midshipman Easy* (1935; dir. Carol Reed) he was played by Hughie Green.

ED, MR   Talking horse voiced by Allan Lane in the American television series 'Mister Ed' (1961–5). He is a TV equivalent of the movies' FRANCIS THE MULE. The series was created by Arthur Lubin, who also had a hand in the Francis films.

EDEN, MARTIN   Left-wing writer who goes to sea in Jack London's semi-autobiographical novel *Martin Eden* (1909). He is rejected by his fiancée, among others, but when he becomes famous his former friends try to ingratiate themselves once more. In the film *The Adventures of Martin Eden* (1942; dir. Sidney Salkow) the unhappy hero was played by Glenn Ford.

EDGE   Hero of a long series of violent Westerns by George G. Gilman, all published as paperback originals. There are over forty Edge novels, and they carry such titles as *The Loner*, *Ten Thousand Dollars American*, *Apache Death* and *Killer's Breed* (these four first published in Britain in 1972). This series is representative of many others which have appeared in recent decades. Other examples are Gilman's 'Adam Steele' series; Matt Chisholm's 'Blade'; J. A. Muir's 'Breed'; Jonas Ward's 'Buchanan'; John J. McLaglen's 'Herne the Hunter'; Tabor Evans's 'Longarm'; William S. Brady's 'Hawk'; James W. Marvin's 'Crow'; and J. T. Edson's 'Ole Devil Hardin', 'Dusty Fog', 'Ysabel Kid' and 'Waco' series. Hundreds of these books continue to fill the paperback racks in the 1980s, proving that the cheap Western novel is far from dead.

EDWARD BEAR   See WINNIE-THE-POOH

EDWARD TRUNK   See under RUPERT BEAR

EEYORE   See under WINNIE-THE-POOH

ELAINE   See under Craig KENNEDY

ELASTIC LAD   See under Jimmy OLSEN

ELIOT, LEWIS   Civil servant in C. P. Snow's long sequence of novels known collectively as 'Strangers and Brothers'. Like his creator, Eliot serves his country as lawyer, academic and government mandarin, and his life-story covers the period from World War I until the 1960s. The individual volumes are:

Strangers and Brothers (1940; vt *George Passant*), *The Light and the Dark* (1948), *Time of Hope* (1950), *The Masters* (1951), *The New Men* (1954), *The Homecoming* (1956), *The Conscience of the Rich* (1958), *The Affair* (1960), *The Corridors of Power* (1964), *The Sleep of Reason* (1968) and *Last Things* (1970). One of these titles, *The Affair*, was turned into a successful stage play by Ronald Miller, and this was shown on BBC television in 1963. The much later BBC TV serial, 'Strangers and Brothers' (1984), was dramatized by Julian Bond and featured Shaughan Seymour as Lewis Eliot.

ELIZA (1) Mulatto girl who flees with her baby across the ice-floes of the Ohio river, in one of the most famous scenes of Harriet Beecher Stowe's novel *Uncle Tom's Cabin* (1851–2).

(2) Heroine of a series of comic novels by the English writer Barry Pain: *Eliza* (1900), *Eliza's Husband* (1908), *Eliza Getting On* (1911), *Exit Eliza* (1912) and *Eliza's Son* (1913).

(3) See Eliza DOLITTLE.

ELKINS, ALFIE Cockney philanderer in Bill Naughton's play *Alfie Elkins and His Little Life*, which was rewritten as *Alfie* (1963). Naughton has also written two novels about the character: *Alfie* (1968) and *Alfie Darling* (1970). Alfie is a glib and likeable lad, but his lecherous escapades soon land him in trouble. He was played by Michael Caine in the popular film of the play (1966; dir. Lewis Gilbert) and by Alan Price in the inferior sequel *Alfie Darling* (1975; dir. Ken Hughes).

ELLIE MAY See under Jeeter LESTER

ELLIOT, ANNE Twenty-seven-year-old heroine of Jane Austen's last novel, the mellow *Persuasion* (1818). On the advice of a friend, she has broken with her fiancé, Frederick Wentworth, but this has brought her unhappiness and a keen sense of regret. Some years have gone by; Wentworth is now a captain in the navy, and appears to be drawn to another young woman. However, he soon rediscovers his love for Anne and the two are finally betrothed. In the British television serial based on the novel (1969) the level-headed heroine was played by Ann Firbank.

ELLIOTT, CHRISTINA   See under Archie WEIR

ELRIC OF MELNIBONÉ   Albino hero of sword-and-sorcery tales by
  Michael Moorcock. A more introspective version of CONAN the
  Barbarian, ruled by his half-living sword Stormbringer, Elric first
  appeared in the pages of *Science Fantasy* magazine in 1961. His
  adventures are collected in the books *The Stealer of Souls* (1963),

Stormbringer (1965), *The Singing Citadel* (1970), *The Sleeping Sorceress* (1971; vt *The Vanishing Tower*), *Elric of Melniboné* (1972; vt *The Dreaming City*), *The Sailor on the Seas of Fate* (1976) and *Elric at the End of Time* (1984). Some of the contents of these books have been recombined under different titles, including *The Weird of the White Wolf* and *The Bane of the Black Sword* (both 1977). Moorcock eventually tied the Elric stories into his 'Eternal Champion' cycle, which encompasses the adventures of other sword-and-sorcery heroes such as EREKOSË, Hawkmoon and Corum, and the anti-hero Jerry CORNELIUS. Elric has also appeared in comic-books; one such is *Elric: The Return to Melniboné* (1973), illustrated by Philippe Druillet.

ELSMERE, ROBERT   English clergyman who becomes obsessed with social issues, and eventually leaves the church in order to pursue good works in London's East End. His story is told in Mrs Humphry Ward's best-known novel *Robert Elsmere* (1888). 'The novel sold extremely well, was reviewed by Gladstone, and initiated much debate' (*The Oxford Companion to English Literature*).

EMERSON, GEORGE   See under Lucy HONEYCHURCH

EMIL   See Emil TISCHBEIN

EMILE   Boy whose model upbringing is the subject of Jean-Jacques Rousseau's novel *Emile, ou l'Education* (1762), a work which is said to have influenced pedagogical theory across Europe. Emile is educated according to 'natural' principles, with due consideration for each stage of his psychological development. Rousseau also wrote a sequel, *Emile et Sophie*, which deals with his hero's less-than-happy married life.

EMMANUEL, PAUL   See under Lucy SNOWE

EMMANUELLE   'Liberated' heroine of the French semi-pornographic film *Emmanuelle* (1974; dir. Just Jaeckin). She was played by the former model Sylvia Kristel, who also took the role in several soft-core sequels, including *Emmanuelle II* (1975) and *Goodbye Emmanuelle* (1978). Emmanuelle has also appeared as a character in a series of paperback novels.

EMSWORTH, LORD   Clarence Threepwood, the ninth Earl of
Emsworth – a pig-loving peer who resides at Blandings Castle, in
the novels and short stories of P. G. Wodehouse. Lord Emsworth
and his idiotic son, the Hon. Freddie Threepwood, first appear in
the novel *Something Fresh* (1915; vt *Something New*). They
reappear in *Leave it to Psmith* (1923), in which Wodehouse's
delightfully grandiloquent hero PSMITH visits Blandings Castle,
and in a series of books which followed: *Summer Lightning*
(1929; vt *Fish Preferred*), *Heavy Weather* (1933), *Blandings Castle*
(1935), *Lord Emsworth and Others* (1937; vt *The Crime Wave
at Blandings*), *Uncle Fred in the Springtime* (1939), *Full Moon*
(1947), *Pigs Have Wings* (1952), *Service With a Smile* (1962),
Galahad at Blandings (1965; vt *The Brinkmanship of Galahad
Threepwood*), *A Pelican at Blandings* (1969; vt *No Nudes is Good
Nudes*) and the unfinished *Sunset at Blandings* (1977). Many of
the stories involve dastardly plots to abduct the Empress of
Blandings, Lord Emsworth's prize pig. The worthy Earl has been
played by Ralph Richardson on BBC television (in some episodes of
the series 'The World of Wodehouse', *circa* 1967) and by Michael
Hordern in a BBC radio dramatization of *Leave it to Psmith* (1981).
Blandings the Blest (1968) by Geoffrey Jaggard is a useful guide
to the dotty but idyllic world of Lord Emsworth.

ENDERBY, F. X.   Peripatetic poet in Anthony Burgess's serio-comic
novels *Inside Mr Enderby* (1963 – first published under the
pseudonym Joseph Kell), *Enderby Outside* (1968), *The Clockwork
Testament, or Enderby's End* (1974) and *Enderby's Dark Lady,
or No End to Enderby* (1984). He attains his greatest heights of
inspiration when seated on the toilet, scribbling away to the
sound of such 'posterior ripostes' as 'pfffrrrummmp' and
'perrrrrp'.

ENITHARMON   See under URIZEN

EREKOSË   Also known as John Daker, the reluctant sword-
swinging hero of Michael Moorcock's fantasy novel *The Eternal
Champion* (1970) and its various sequels. A shorter version of the
story first appeared as a magazine novella in 1962. It describes
how the twentieth-century John Daker is summoned by dream
voices to serve as champion to a beleaguered people of the far future

(or distant past). He takes the name Erekosë, and eventually sides with humanity's enemies, the morally superior Eldren. His adventures are continued in *Phoenix in Obsidian* (1970; vt *The Silver Warriors*), *The Quest for Tanelorn* (1975) and *The Dragon in the Sword* (1986). In the course of these books his destiny becomes entangled with those of other Moorcock heroes, including ELRIC OF MELNIBONÉ, Dorian Hawkmoon and Prince Corum. It is revealed that all these (and others) are aspects of the same Eternal Champion, doomed to fight throughout the ages in the everlasting war of Law against Chaos.

ERICSON, GEORGE EASTWOOD   Captain of the Royal Navy corvette *Compass Rose* during World War II. His long and gruelling war is described in Nicholas Monsarrat's bestselling novel *The Cruel Sea* (1951). Lieutenant-Commander Ericson is first introduced to the reader as 'a big man, broad and tough, a man to depend on, a man to remember: about forty-two or -three, fair hair going grey, blue eyes as level as a foot-rule . . .' He was played by Jack Hawkins in the film of the novel (1952; dir. Charles Frend).

ERIK   See The PHANTOM OF THE OPERA

ERNEST THE POLICEMAN   See under LARRY THE LAMB

ERROL, CEDRIC   See Lord FAUNTLEROY

ESCAMILLO   See under CARMEN

ESMERALDA   See under QUASIMODO

ESMOND, HENRY   Hero and narrator of W. M. Thackeray's novel, set at the time of Queen Anne, *The History of Henry Esmond, Esquire* (1852). He fights in various wars and becomes involved in the Jacobite cause. After being disappointed in his love for his flighty cousin, Beatrix, he marries her mother, Lady Rachel Castlewood, and emigrates to Virginia. Thackeray's *The Virginians* (1857–9) deals with the fortunes of Esmond's grandsons in America. Henry Esmond has been described as 'courageous, courteous, generous [and] loyal. He has an even keener eye for his own weaknesses than for those of other people, but he has an equally keen eye for excellence, and he is incapable of envy. He is, in short, a great gentleman' (M. R. Ridley, introduction to the Everyman edition, 1963).

ESTELLA   Young *femme fatale* in Charles Dickens's novel *Great Expectations* (1860–61). She has been raised by the jilted and half-mad Miss HAVISHAM to break men's hearts with her flighty beauty. Pip (Philip PIRRIP) falls in love with her, but at first she spurns him for another man. It turns out in the end that she is not Estella Havisham, but Estella Magwitch, daughter of the runaway convict Abel MAGWITCH. Modern sequels by other hands include *Estella, Her Expectations* (1982) by Sue Rowe, a novel which reimagines the character as a twentieth-century girl; and *Estella* (1986) by Alanna Knight, a 'straight' sequel. Estella has been played by Jane Wyatt (1934), Jean Simmons (1946) and Sarah Miles (1975) in film and television versions of Dickens's story.

ESTRAGON   See VLADIMIR AND ESTRAGON

EUSTACE, ETHNE   See under Harry FEVERSHAM

EUSTACE AND HILDA   See Eustace and Hilda CHERRINGTON

EVELINA   See Evelina ANVILLE

EVERAGE, EDNA   Monstrous Australian matron who wears butterfly-winged spectacles and loves to discuss her husband's prostate-gland problems. She styles herself 'Dame Edna Everage, Superstar'. Edna is a *persona* of the comedian Barry Humphries. She made an appearance in the film *The Adventures of Barry Mackenzie* (1972; dir. Bruce Beresford), and was frequently to be seen on British television during the 1970s and 1980s. (See also Sir Les PATTERSON.)

EVERDENE, BATHSHEBA   Country lass who is wooed by the worthy shepherd Gabriel Oak but is led astray by the handsome ne'er-do-well Sergeant Francis Troy, in Thomas Hardy's novel *Far From the Madding Crowd* (1874). This, one of the few Hardy novels with a happy ending, was turned into a stage play by the

author (first performed 1924). In the film of the novel (1967;
dir. John Schlesinger) Bathsheba was played by Julie Christie.

EWING, J. R.   Machiavellian businessman in the American
television series 'Dallas' (from 1979). Full name John Ross
Ewing, son of Jock and Eleanor ('Miss Ellie') Ewing, he is brother
of the handsome Bobby and husband to the beautiful but erring Sue
Ellen. He wears a broad-brimmed hat decorated with what appear
to be 'crushed budgerigars' (in the words of TV critic Clive
James). J.R. is heir to a Texas oil fortune, and he is determined to
keep every penny of it. Played by Larry Hagman (who also directed
some of the episodes), J.R. is a man you love to hate – despite
which he became astonishingly popular in the early 1980s,
especially in Britain. There have been several novels about the
Ewing family, an example being *The Ewings of Dallas* (1980)
by Burt Hirschfeld, 'based on the series created by David Jacobs'.
A book which delves deep into the family's imagined past is *Dallas:
The Complete Ewing Family Saga, 1860–1985* (1985) by Laura
Van Wormer. During the 1985–6 season viewers feared that J.R.
was becoming too 'nice'; the show's scriptwriters realized all was
not well, and in the following season J.R. was just as mean and
nasty as he had ever been. There has also been a TV movie
'prequel', *Dallas: The Early Years* (1986), which includes
glimpses of J.R. as a teenager.

EXECUTIONER, THE   Real name Mack Bolan, but known as 'The
Executioner' – a revenge-seeking Vietnam veteran who appears
in a long series of violent thrillers by Don Pendleton, beginning
with *War Against the Mafia* (1969). He travels from city to city
in the USA in pursuit of the Mafia criminals who murdered his
parents; when he catches up with them his methods of settling the
score are ruthless in the extreme. Bolan is a one-man killing
machine, the ultimate vigilante. The Executioner, and Don
Pendleton, are credited with initiating the whole 'aggressor' sub-
genre of modern American crime fiction: many other series
characters have been created in emulation of this one. Over sixty
paperback original novels in The Executioner series have now
appeared. Most are by Pendleton, although at least one, *Sicilian
Slaughter* (1973), was written by Jim Peterson.

EYRE, JANE   Plain but sensitive heroine of Charlotte Brontë's well-
loved novel *Jane Eyre* (1847). An orphan, she is sent by her
uncaring aunt to Lowood Institution, where she endures a harsh
education. Eventually she is appointed governess to the 'ward' of
Edward ROCHESTER at Thornfield Hall. She wins Rochester's love,
and they are about to be married when it is revealed that he already
has a wife. After various vicissitudes, and the death of Mrs
Rochester, Jane and Rochester are united in marriage. (By this time
the sinister Rochester has been symbolically castrated – he has
lost his sight in the fire which destroyed Thornfield Hall.) The
film *Jane Eyre* (1934) starred Virginia Bruce. In the superior remake
(1943; dir. Robert Stevenson) the heroine was played by Peggy
Ann Garner (as a little girl) and by Joan Fontaine (as a young
woman). In the TV movie of the same title (1971; dir. Delbert Mann)
the part of the grown-up Jane was taken by Susannah York. A
stage version of *Jane Eyre*, adapted by Peter Coe, was performed in
Britain in 1986.

F

FABULOUS FURRY FREAK BROTHERS, THE Frankling, Fat
Freddy and Phineas – three long-haired, doped-up hippies of the late
1960s, continually on the run from the Pigs (or Fuzz). Along with
Fat Freddy's cat, they appear in Gilbert Shelton's underground
comic-strip, *The Fabulous Furry Freak Brothers*. Shelton's other
celebrated creation, WONDER WART-HOG, would not have approved
of the Freak Brothers.

FAFHRD AND THE GRAY MOUSER Pair of swashbuckling
adventurers in Fritz Leiber's series of sword-and-sorcery tales
set in the imaginary world of Newhon. Fafhrd is a giant brawling
barbarian, a good-humoured CONAN, while the Mouser is a small
wily sneak-thief, expert with a knife. Their first exploit was
recorded in the pages of *Unknown* magazine in 1939, although their
first book, *Two Sought Adventure* (1957; vt *Swords Against
Death*), did not appear until almost two decades later.
Subsequent books in the series are *The Swords of Lankhmar*
(1968), *Swords Against Wizardry* (1968), *Swords in the Mist*
(1968), *Swords and Deviltry* (1970) and *Swords and Ice Magic*
(1977).

FAGIN Master of the London pick-pockets, including the Artful
Dodger and young Oliver, in Charles Dickens's novel *Oliver Twist*
(1838–9). After Shakespeare's Shylock, Fagin is perhaps the best-
known stereotype of the villainous Jew in English literature. In
films he has been played by Alec Guinness (1948) and Ron Moody
(1968), among others. On television he has been played by Eric
Porter, in a BBC serialization of the novel (1985). See also Oliver
TWIST and Bill SIKES.

FAIRCHILD FAMILY, THE Lucy, Emily and Henry Fairchild, with
their zealously religious parents, are the model English family
who appear in Mary Martha Sherwood's very popular children's
novel *The Fairchild Family* (1818). Additions to the novel were
published in 1842 and 1847, the third part being a collaboration

Fagin as drawn by *George Cruikshank*

between Mrs Sherwood and her daughter Sophia. The work remained in vogue throughout the nineteenth century. A modern critic, Gillian Avery, has described *The Fairchild Family* as 'an extraordinary compilation of Calvinistic sentiments, cruelty, necrophily and cant'.

FAIRLIE, LAURA   See under Count FOSCO

FAIRSERVICE, ANDREW   See under Francis OSBALDISTONE

FALCON, THE   Real name Michael Waring, a roguish crime-buster invented by Michael Arlen for his short story 'Gay Falcon' (1940). Played by George Sanders, he soon became a popular hero of the American cinema in *The Gay Falcon* (1941; dir. Irving Reis) and three later films. In the fourth film the original Falcon dies and is replaced by his brother. George Sanders's real-life brother, Tom Conway, went on to play the role of the Falcon's brother in *The Falcon Strikes Back* (1943; dir. Edward Dmytryk) and eight further films. The role was then taken on by John Calvert for a final three films (1948–9). The Falcon was also popular on the radio in the late 1940s, and appeared in a US television series, 'The Adventures of the Falcon' (1954), where he was played by Charles McGraw.

FALKLAND   See under Caleb WILLIAMS

FAMOUS FIVE, THE   (1) See Harry WHARTON
    (2) Four middle-class children and a dog who have far-fetched adventures in various holiday locations around the coast of Britain. The group consists of two brothers and a sister (Julian, Dick and Anne), their tomboy cousin Georgina (known as 'George'), and their mutt Timmy. They are the creations of the twentieth-century's most popular writer of children's books, Enid Blyton, who first introduced them in her novel *Five on a Treasure Island* (1942). She went on to recount later exploits of the Famous Five in a further twenty volumes, including such titles as *Five Run Away Together* (1944), *Five Go Off in a Caravan* (1946), *Five Go Off to Camp* (1948), *Five Fall Into Adventure* (1950), *Five Go to Demon Rocks* (1951), *Five Go to Mystery Moor* (1954), *Five Have a Mystery to Solve* (1962) and *Five Are Together Again* (1963;

the last of the series). In the early 1970s, several years after the author's death, there appeared the first sequels by another hand: surprisingly, they were by a French writer, Claude Voilier. This new series of books was translated into English from 1981, commencing with *The Famous Five and the Mystery of the Emeralds* and *The Famous Five and the Stately Homes Gang*. Later additions to the series include such exciting-sounding titles as *The Famous Five and the Golden Galleon* (1982) and *The Famous Five and the Inca God* (1984). Although execrated by critics and librarians, Blyton's creations remain stubbornly popular. At least one Famous Five film has been released by a British producer: *Five on Treasure Island* (1957). In 1978 a thirteen-episode set of Famous Five adventures appeared on independent television. The success of this TV series led to the publication of a *Famous Five Annual* which reused Blyton's stories together with other matter. The characters were lampooned rather wickedly in 'Five Go Mad in Dorset' (1982) and 'Five Go Mad on Mescalin' (1983), thirty-minute farces in the 'Comic Strip Presents . . .' series on Channel Four Television.

FANE, MICHAEL   Hero of Compton Mackenzie's *Bildungsroman*, *Sinister Street* (1913–14; the first part was published in the USA as *Youth's Encounter*). Michael and his sister Stella are illegitimate, but nevertheless privileged. Michael goes to Oxford university, and later mixes with members of London's theatrical world (including Sylvia SCARLETT). Three quasi-sequels are *Guy and Pauline* (1917; vt *Plasher's Mead*), *Sylvia Scarlett* (1918) and *Sylvia and Michael* (1919). In a BBC television serialization of *Sinister Street* (1969) Michael was played by Brett Usher.

FANNY   Heroine of a trilogy of plays by Marcel Pagnol. The setting is Marseilles, where Fanny is abandoned by her lover, Marius, when he goes to sea. She marries another (much older) man in order to provide her child with a father. The three plays were made into successful French films: *Marius* (1931; dir. Alexander Korda), *Fanny* (1932; dir. Marc Allégret) and *César* (1936; dir. Marcel Pagnol), with Orane Demazis as Fanny. The storyline was compressed for a Hollywood movie, *Port of Seven Seas* (1938; dir. James Whale), which starred Maureen O'Sullivan. Twenty years later the same story formed the basis of a stage musical,

Fanny, by Harold Rome and S. N. Behrman. This in turn was filmed (1961; dir. Joshua Logan), with Leslie Caron in the lead. (See also Fanny HILL and Fanny HOOPER.)

FANSLER, KATE   Professor of English literature who doubles as an amateur detective, in a series of mystery novels by Amanda Cross (Carolyn G. Heilbrun). The titles are: *In the Last Analysis* (1964), *The James Joyce Murder* (1967), *Poetic Justice* (1970), *The Theban Mysteries* (1971), *The Question of Max* (1976), *Death in a Tenured Position* (1981; vt *A Death in the Faculty*), *Sweet Death, Kind Death* (1984) and *No Word from Winifred* (1986). Professor Fansler is the most 'donnish' of American donnish detectives.

FANTASTIC, MR   Real name Reed Richards, a comic-book superhero whose body and limbs seem to be infinitely stretchable. He has gained his elasticity as a result of bombardment by cosmic rays. Richards is the leader of the Fantastic Four (the others being Sue Storm, alias the Invisible Girl, Johnny Storm, alias the Human Torch, and Ben Grimm, alias The Thing). The characters have appeared in Marvel Comics' popular title *The Fantastic Four* since 1961. Originally the creations of writer Stan Lee and artist Jack Kirby, they have featured in two animated television series (1967–70; and 1978). Mr Fantastic and his unlikely friends appear in the paperback novel *Doomsday* (1979) by Marv Wolfman. (An earlier comic-book hero, Plastic Man – in DC Comics from 1941 – also had the power of stretchability.)

FANTOMAS   French master criminal who has a change of heart and decides to use his nefarious skills for good causes. He first appeared in the novel *Fantomas* (1911) by Pierre Souvestre and Marcel Allain. It was followed by at least a dozen sequels, with titles such as *Fantomas Captured* and *The Revenge of Fantomas*. The character rose to international fame when he was played by René Navarre in five silent film serials directed by the great Louis Feuillade (1913–14). An American cinema serial about the adventures of Fantomas was made in 1921. There have been several later French feature films, the most recent being *Fantomas Against Scotland Yard* (1965; dir. André Hunebelle), starring Jean Marais. There have been numerous European comic-strips and comic-books devoted to Fantomas's exploits.

FAT FREDDY'S CAT   See under The Fabulous Furry Freak
Brothers

FAUNTLEROY, LORD   Cedric Errol, an American boy who
discovers himself to be heir to the English Earl of Dorincourt.
Plucked from his New York home and transplanted to England,

Mary Pickford in the dual role of Little Lord Fauntleroy
and his 'Dearest'

he charms everyone with his honest, open, democratic ways.
He features in the novel *Little Lord Fauntleroy* (1886) by Frances
Hodgson Burnett. This was soon turned into a popular stage play,
in which Cedric appeared with long curly hair and clad in velvet
knickerbockers. The apparently effete aristocratic image of the
character has lingered on in the public consciousness, blurring
the fact that the Lord Fauntleroy of the book is in reality a
hardy, self-reliant American lad. The story has been filmed several
times – in 1914 (a British production); in 1921 (dir. Jack Pickford
and Alfred E. Green), with Mary Pickford as both Cedric and his
mother (it sounds appalling, but in fact it is one of Pickford's
most effective films); in 1936 (dir. John Cromwell), with Freddie
Bartholomew; and in 1980 (dir. Jack Gold), with Ricky Schroder.

FAWLEY, JUDE   Thwarted intellectual hero of Thomas Hardy's
tragic novel *Jude the Obscure* (1895). After his wife deserts him he
sets up home with his unhappily married cousin, Sue Bridehead,
and is ostracized by society. They have two children, but these are
murdered by their half-brother (Jude's son by his former wife).
Sue returns to her husband, and Jude dies in drunken misery. This
novel was very badly received by late Victorian readers and critics,
and as a result Hardy wrote no more fiction. *Jude the Obscure* has
been serialized on British television.

FAWLTY, BASIL   Impatient, accident-prone hotelier played by John
Cleese in the BBC television comedy series 'Fawlty Towers'
(1975–9). Basil is totally unsuited to his job, and the hotel's staff
(especially the Spanish waiter, Manuel), his wife Sybil and the guests
regularly send him into paroxysms of rage which he expresses in
a hilariously physical manner. The series was written by John
Cleese and Connie Booth.

FELIX THE CAT   Cartoon character, one of the earliest
and most successful to appear in the American
cinema. Feline Felix was created in 1919 by the
animator Otto Messmer, and a series of short silent
films featuring the beast was produced by Pat Sullivan
in the 1920s. Felix also appeared in newspaper comic-
strips from 1923, and in comic-books from 1943. The
character was revived for a new series of animated

films made for American television in the 1950s, and continues to be popular in comic-strips around the world. Otto Messmer has stated that he based his black tomcat's mannerisms on those of Charlie Chaplin.

FELL, GIDEON   Larger than life, beer-drinking, private detective, an expert in the solution of locked-room murder mysteries, created by the American-born novelist John Dickson Carr. Dr Gideon Fell is a decidedly Chestertonian figure, and his relish for paradoxes and miraculous revelations is reminiscent of Father BROWN's. He first appeared in the novel *Hag's Nook* (1933), and his further adventures are recounted in *The Mad Hatter Mystery* (1933), *The Eight of Swords* (1934), *The Blind Barber* (1934), *Death-Watch* (1935), *The Three Coffins* (1935; vt *The Hollow Man*), *The Arabian Nights Murder* (1936), *To Wake the Dead* (1938), *The Crooked Hinge* (1938), *The Problem of the Green Capsule* (1939; vt *The Black Spectacles*), *The Problem of the Wire Cage* (1939), *The Man Who Could Not Shudder* (1940), *The Case of the Constant Suicides* (1941), *Death Turns the Tables* (1941; vt *The Seat of the Scornful*), *Till Death Do Us Part* (1944), *He Who Whispers* (1946), *The Sleeping Sphinx* (1947), *Dr Fell, Detective, and Other Stories* (1947), *Below Suspicion* (1949), *The Dead Man's Knock* (1958), *In Spite of Thunder* (1960), *The House at Satan's Elbow* (1965), *Panic in Box C* (1966) and *Dark of the Moon* (1967). Dr Fell also appears in a few scattered short stories and radio plays by Carr.

FELLOWS, FRED C.   Tobacco-chewing, small-town police chief who features in a series of detective novels by the American writer Hillary Waugh. The titles are: *Sleep Long, My Love* (1959; vt *Jigsaw*), *Road Block* (1960), *That Night it Rained* (1961), *The Late Mrs D.* (1962), *Born Victim* (1962), *Death and Circumstances* (1963), *Prisoner's Plea* (1963), *The Missing Man* (1964), *End of a Party* (1965), *Pure Poison* (1966) and *The Con Game* (1968).

FELSON, EDDIE   Sharp professional pool-player known to his friends and rivals as 'Fast Eddie'. He is the eponymous hero of Walter Tevis's novel *The Hustler* (1959), which was effectively filmed (1961; dir. Robert Rossen) with Paul Newman as Eddie. Twenty-five years later Tevis revived the character for a sequel,

The Color of Money (1984). This too has been filmed (1986; dir. Martin Scorsese), with Newman again in the leading role. Both director and star of the latter film received much praise for their portrayal of the ageing Eddie Felson, a man who has refused to 'curl up and die'.

FEN, GERVASE   Professor of English at Oxford University who works as a private detective in his spare time. He appears in a series of nine 'donnish' crime novels and two collections of short stories by Edmund Crispin (Bruce Montgomery), beginning with *The Case of the Gilded Fly* (1944; vt *Obsequies at Oxford*). He reappears in *Holy Disorders* (1945), and his most admired exploit is recounted in *The Moving Toyshop* (1946). Fen's remaining appearances are in *Swan Song* (1947; vt *Dead and Dumb*), *Love Lies Bleeding* (1948), *Buried for Pleasure* (1949), *Frequent Hearses* (1950; vt *Sudden Vengeance*), *The Long Divorce* (1951), *Beware of the Trains* (1962), *The Glimpses of the Moon* (1977) and *Fen Country* (1980).

FENWICK, IRIS   Wild girl of the 1920s, who drives a Hispano-Suiza car described as 'a huge yellow insect that had dropped to earth from a butterfly civilization', in the fashionable bestseller *The Green Hat: A Romance for a Few People* (1924) by Michael Arlen (Dikran Kouyoumdjian). After her husband kills himself on their wedding night, Diana travels widely in search of love. The story was filmed as *A Woman of Affairs* (1928; dir. Clarence Brown), with Greta Garbo as the reckless heroine (whose name was changed to 'Diana Merrick').

FERDINAND THE BULL   Gentle, peace-loving bull in the children's fable *The Story of Ferdinand* (1936) by Munro Leaf. Because of his size, he is chosen for the bull-ring, but the matador is disappointed when it turns out that all Ferdinand wants to do is to appreciate the odour of the flowers in the women spectators' hair. The Disney studios' animated film, *Ferdinand the Bull* (1938), won an Academy Award.

FERRIS, BOB   See The Likely Lads

FEVEREL, RICHARD   Erring hero of George Meredith's novel *The Ordeal of Richard Feverel: A History of Father and Son* (1859). Under the tutelage of his domineering but idealistic father, Richard endures a very strict education. However, he falls in love with Lucy Desborough, a girl of lowly origins, and marries her. His father forces them apart, with tragic consequences.

FEVERSHAM, HARRY   Hero of A. E. W. Mason's popular novel *The Four Feathers* (1902). Harry is a Lieutenant in the British army at the time of the war in the Sudan. Scion of a family with a long military history, he is a sensitive soul with no real stomach for warfare. He resigns his commission just as his regiment is about to embark for Africa. Three of his comrades each send him a white feather; worst of all, he receives a fourth feather from his beloved, Ethne Eustace. Grimly determined to prove his courage, he follows his regiment to the Sudan, where he eventually covers himself with glory. This poignant tale of Victorian honour has been 'seven times a major film', according to a recent paperback blurb. An early talkie version (1929; dir. Lothar Mendes, Merian C. Cooper and Ernest Schoedsack) starred Richard Arlen, but the best-remembered celluloid version is the lavish Alcxander Korda production (1939; dir. Vincent Korda), with John Clements. Since then it has been remade as *Storm Over the Nile* (1955; dir. Terence Fisher), with Anthony Steel, and as a TV movie, *The Four Feathers* (1976; dir. Don Sharp), with Beau Bridges. In both the film versions which I have seen the hero's name is changed to Faversham.

FFORBES-HAMILTON, AUDREY   Well-bred widow played by Penelope Keith in the BBC television comedy series 'To the Manor Born' (1979–81). She is obliged to move out of the manor house into more modest accommodation, whence she wages a running battle with the manor's new owner, the *nouveau riche* Richard De Vere. A fearsome comic heroine fit for Margaret Thatcher's Britain, she proved very popular for a few seasons.

FIGARO   Wily comic servant who utters seditious statements, in the plays *The Barber of Seville* (1775) and *The Marriage of Figaro* (1784) by Beaumarchais (Pierre Augustin Caron). The latter play was considered revolutionary in its day, and caused

Beaumarchais to be imprisoned for a short time. Needless to say, it had an enormous popular success – 'possibly the greatest any play has ever had in the history of French theatre' (William Rose Benét). Shorn of its more dangerous sentiments, *The Marriage of Figaro* formed the basis of an opera by Wolfgang Amadeus Mozart (1786, libretto by Lorenzo da Ponte). The first of Beaumarchais's Figaro plays, *The Barber of Seville*, has also been turned into a celebrated opera – initially by Giovanni Paisiello (1782), with a later and more enduring version by Gioacchino Rossini (1816, libretto by Cesare Sterbini). Beaumarchais wrote a third Figaro play, *La Mère Coupable* (1792; known in English as *A Mother's Guilt*); this is a more melodramatic work than the earlier plays, and has never gained their popularity. All three pieces were broadcast on BBC radio (1985), in new translations by comedian John Wells. A famous French newspaper, *Le Figaro*, is named after the character.

FILIPPOVNA, NATASHA   See under Prince Myshkin

FINCH, ATTICUS   Southern lawyer, the father of 'Scout' and Jem, in Harper Lee's bestselling novel *To Kill a Mockingbird* (1960). He defends a black man against a charge of murder – and has to cope with the consequent social prejudices, especially as they affect his two motherless children. In the film of the novel (1962; dir. Robert Mulligan) he was played by Gregory Peck.

FINDLAY, MAUDE   See under Archie Bunker

FINLAY, DOCTOR   Medical hero of *Beyond This Place* (1953) by A. J. Cronin. He lives with his elder and mentor, Dr Cameron, and their housekeeper, Janet, in the Scottish highland village of Tannochbrae. The book formed the basis of a popular BBC television series, 'Dr Finlay's Casebook' (1959–66), which starred Bill Simpson as Finlay and Andrew Cruickshank as Cameron. Although it had a long run, the series did not win universal approval: Philip Purser has described Dr Finlay as 'one of the few utterly detestable characters in television fiction. He is . . . smug, self-satisfied, self-righteous. He is also a bully.' A late book by A. J. Cronin is *Doctor Finlay of Tannochbrae* (1978).

FINN, HUCKLEBERRY   Pipe-smoking ragamuffin boy, a friend of
Tom SAWYER, created by Mark Twain (Samuel Langhorne
Clemens) for his books *The Adventures of Tom Sawyer* (1876)

and *The Adventures of Huckleberry Finn (Tom Sawyer's Comrade)* (1884). Of the two works, the second is generally regarded as the greater. Vividly narrated by Huck in his Mississippi dialect, it describes how the boy runs away from his guardian in the company of NIGGER JIM, an escaped slave. They travel down the great river on a raft, encountering confidence tricksters and other perils. At the end Huck is taken in by a good family, but promises himself that he will 'light out for the Territory' again some day. Mark Twain never told us that subsequent story, but a modern sequel by another hand, *The Further Adventures of Huckleberry Finn* (1983) by Greg Matthews, recounts how Huck and Jim head west in the 1849 Gold Rush. T. S. Eliot paid a great tribute to Twain's creation when he asserted that Huckleberry Finn is 'one of the permanent symbolic figures of fiction not unworthy to take a place with Ulysses, Faust, Don Quixote, Don Juan, Hamlet and other discoveries which man has made about himself'.

Huck Finn appears in the many film versions of *The Adventures of Tom Sawyer*. Cinema versions of his own book include *Huckleberry Finn* (1931; dir. Norman Taurog), with Jackie Coogan; *The Adventures of Huckleberry Finn* (1939; dir. Richard Thorpe), with Mickey Rooney; a remake of the same title (1960; dir. Michael Curtiz), with Eddie Hodges; and the musical *Huckleberry Finn* (1974; dir. J. Lee Thompson), with Jeff East. There have also been several television movies, including *Huckleberry Finn* (1975; dir. Robert Totten), with Ron Howard, and *The Adventures of Huckleberry Finn* (1981; dir. Jack B. Hively), with Kurt Ida. The semi-animated series 'The New Adventures of Huck Finn' (1968–9) starred Michael Shea. A TV series of the early 1980s, 'Huckleberry Finn and His Friends', had Ian Tracey as Huck.

FINN, PHINEAS Irish Member of Parliament who features in several of Anthony Trollope's 'Palliser' novels: *Phineas Finn* (1869), *Phineas Redux* (1874), *The Prime Minister* (1876) and *The Duke's Children* (1880). He has various love-affairs, and at one point is tried for murder (and acquitted). See also Plantagenet PALLISER.

FIRMIN, GEOFFREY   Former British consul who drinks himself to
death in a Mexican town. The story of the last day of his life is told
in Malcolm Lowry's remarkable novel *Under the Volcano* (1947)
– a 'Faustian masterpiece', according to Anthony Burgess. In
the film of the book (1984; dir. John Huston) Firmin was played
by Albert Finney.

FISHER, BILLY   Young working-class day-dreamer in Keith
Waterhouse's novel *Billy Liar* (1959). Billy works as an
undertaker's clerk in a dull northern town, but he has vivid
fantasies of much greater things in store for him. In fact, his life
becomes a chapter of comical accidents caused by his propensity
to tell lies. He has frequently been compared to another modern
quixotic dreamer, Walter MITTY. Waterhouse continued Billy's
story in a second novel, *Billy Liar on the Moon* (1975), but prior to
that he collaborated with playwright Willis Hall on a successful
stage version of the first novel (1960). The latter was filmed (1963;
dir. John Schlesinger), with Tom Courtenay in the part of Billy.
This was followed by a British television series, also called 'Billy
Liar' and also scripted by Waterhouse and Hall (1973–4). The
character has since been Americanized for a US TV series, 'Billy'
(1979), which starred Steve Guttenberg.

FITZBOODLE, GEORGE SAVAGE   London clubman, narrator of a
series of sketches and stories which W. M. Thackeray contributed
to *Fraser's Magazine* in 1842–3. These were collected as *The
FitzBoodle Papers* and *Men's Wives*. Thackeray also used the
name FitzBoodle as his byline on the first publication of his novel
The Luck of Barry Lyndon (1844).

FIVER   See under HAZEL (2)

FLAGG, CAPTAIN, AND SERGEANT QUIRT   Brawling American
soldiers during World War I. They become rivals for the love of
a French girl, in the play *What Price Glory?* (1924) by Maxwell
Anderson and Laurence Stallings. The popular silent film of the
play (1926; dir. Raoul Walsh) starred Victor McLaglen and Edmund
Lowe as the two-fisted, hard-drinking duo (the movie became
infamous because of the obscenities which were noticed by lip-
readers). McLaglen and Lowe played Flagg and Quirt again in three

film sequels (all directed by Walsh): *The Cock-Eyed World* (1929), *Women of All Nations* (1931) and *Under Pressure* (1935). Later, *What Price Glory?* was remade (1952; dir. John Ford) with James Cagney and Dan Dailey in the leading roles.

FLAMBEAU   See under Father BROWN

FLANDERS, MOLL   Sharp-witted lady of doubtful virtue, heroine of Daniel Defoe's picaresque novel *The Fortunes and Misfortunes of the Famous Moll Flanders* (1722). This book is 'the most authentic portrait of a prostitute in English literature', according to critic Kenneth Rexroth. After a long succession of husbands and lovers she is convicted of theft and transported to Virginia – following which she 'at last grew Rich, liv'd Honest, and Died a Penitent'. A mediocre film, *The Amorous Adventures of Moll Flanders* (1965; dir. Terence Young), had Kim Novak in the title role. Latterly, there has been a stage musical, *Moll Flanders* (1986), by Claire Luckham.

FLASHMAN, HARRY   School bully in Thomas Hughes's novel *Tom Brown's Schooldays* (1857). He 'roasts' young Tom BROWN in front of an open fire. Eventually the cowardly Flashman is bested by Tom and his friend East, and is later expelled from Rugby School for drunkenness. This dislikable cad has since become the hero of a series of comic historical novels by George Macdonald Fraser, beginning with *Flashman: From the Flashman Papers 1839–1842* (1969). Fraser's Flashman cheerfully admits that he is 'a scoundrel, a liar, a cheat, a thief, a coward – and, oh yes, a toady'. Nevertheless, as a result of many happy accidents and much low cunning he becomes a Victorian army hero, the recipient of a knighthood and a VC. His later adventures, both military and amorous, are recounted in *Royal Flash* (1970), *Flash for Freedom* (1971), *Flashman at the Charge* (1973), *Flashman in the Great Game* (1975), *Flashman's Lady* (1977), *Flashman and the Redskins* (1982) and *Flashman and the Dragon* (1985). In the film *Royal Flash* (1975; dir. Richard Lester) he was played by Malcolm McDowell.

FLAVIA, PRINCESS   See under Rudolf RASSENDYLL

FLEMING, HENRY   Young American who becomes a battlefield
hero despite himself, in Stephen Crane's novel *The Red Badge
of Courage: An Episode of the American Civil War* (1895). Fleming
also appears in a couple of short stories by Crane, collected in the
volume *Whilomville Stories* (1900). In the film *The Red Badge of
Courage* (1951; dir. John Huston) he was played by a real-life
war-hero turned actor, Audie Murphy. In the television movie
remake (1974; dir. Lee Philips) Richard Thomas took the role.

FLETCHER, IRWIN MAURICE   Known as 'Fletch', an American
newspaper reporter who becomes embroiled in various crimes
and capers, in the novels of Gregory Mcdonald. He first appears
in *Fletch* (1974). Later titles include *Confess, Fletch* (1976), *Fletch's
Fortune* (1978), *Fletch and the Widow Bradley* (1981), *Fletch's
Moxie* (1982), *Fletch and the Man Who* (1983), *Carioca Fletch* (1984),
Fletch Won (1985) and *Fletch, Too* (1986). In the film *Fletch* (1985;
dir. Michael Ritchie) the hero was played by Chevy Chase.

FLETCHER, NORMAN STANLEY   Old lag played by Ronnie Barker
in the BBC television comedy 'Porridge' (1974–7). This very
funny series about prison life was conceived and written by Ian
La Frenais and Dick Clement. A follow-up series, 'Going
Straight' (1978), showed Fletcher trying to adjust to life on the
outside once more.

FLINTSTONE, FRED AND WILMA   Stone-age couple in the
animated television series 'The Flintstones' (1960–66), produced by
Hanna-Barbera. The Flintstones and their neighbours, Barney and
Betty Rubble, lead a typical suburban existence in a world of
paleolithic automobiles and dinosaur-powered gadgets. Fred was
voiced by Alan Reed and Wilma by Jean Vander Pyle. The series
became very popular in America and Britain, and has been
repeated many times. There have been Flintstones comic-strips and
comic-books, and an animated feature film, *A Man Called
Flintstone* (1966; dir. Joseph Barbera and William Hanna). Fred
is remembered for his jubilant cry: 'Yabba dabba doo!'

FLOOK   Strip-cartoon creature, invented for the British *Daily Mail*
by artist Wally Fawkes ('Trog') in 1949. Flook is a cuddly bear-
like beast with an extended snout.

FLORENCE   See under DOUGAL

FLYTE, SEBASTIAN   Younger son of Lord Marchmain, and friend
of Charles RYDER, in Evelyn Waugh's novel *Brideshead Revisited*
(1945). An outrageous dandy while at Oxford, he eventually
becomes an alcoholic living in obscurity in North Africa. He was
played very effectively by Anthony Andrews in the British
television serialization of the novel (1981).

FOG, DUSTY   See under EDGE

FOGG, PHILEAS   Eccentric English traveller who goes *Around the
World in 80 Days*, in Jules Verne's novel of that title (1872). The
story was successfully dramatized for the stage, and many decades
later was made into a blockbusting film (1956; dir. Michael
Anderson) with David Niven as Fogg. A curious sequel by another
hand is *The Other Log of Phileas Fogg* (1973) by Philip José
Farmer, in which it is revealed that Mr Fogg has dealings with
alien beings from outer space. In the 1980s Phileas Fogg's name has
been used to merchandise snack foods.

FONZ, THE   Arthur Fonzarelli, also known as Fonzie, a cool teenage
hero of the 1950s, played by Henry Winkler in the American
television series 'Happy Days' (1974–84). Although he began life
as a minor character, low down the cast list, the leather-jacketed
Fonz became a major cult figure of the mid-to-late 1970s. The
series was created by Gary Marshall. According to TV historians
Tim Brooks and Earle Marsh, 'In its later years "Happy Days"
became something of an institution. In 1980 it was announced that
the Fonz's leather jacket was being enshrined in the Smithsonian
Institution.' The series has since been re-created in animated
cartoon form (1980–83).

FORD, JACK   Dour working-class hero of the 1930s played by
James Bolam in the BBC television series 'When the Boat Comes
In' (1975–7). The character was created by scriptwriter James
Mitchell, who has also written a series of novels based on the
scripts: *When the Boat Comes In* (1975), *The Hungry Years* (1976)
and *Onward and Upward* (1977).

FORSYTE, SOAMES   English solicitor whose tangled family affairs, and especially his relationship with his beautiful wife Irene, are the subject of a trilogy of novels by John Galsworthy. *The Man of Property* (1906), *In Chancery* (1920) and *To Let* (1921) were republished, with new bridging episodes, as one volume entitled *The Forsyte Saga* (1922). Two later trilogies continue the chronicle of the Forsyte family. They consist of *The White Monkey* (1924), *The Silver Spoon* (1926) and *Swan Song* (1928) – known collectively as *A Modern Comedy* (1929); and *Maid in Waiting* (1931), *The Flowering Wilderness* (1932) and *Over the River* (1933) – known collectively as *The End of the Chapter* (1935). There is also a collection of short stories about the family, *On Forsyte 'Change* (1930). Soames dies at the end of the second trilogy, and the final three novels deal with younger Forsytes. The books enjoyed considerable popularity, and 'Soames's death at the end of *Swan Song* was front-page material for London newspapers in 1928' (according to Janet Husband). The first novel in the sequence formed the basis of a film, *That Forsyte Woman* (1949; dir. Compton Bennett), with Errol Flynn as Soames. The BBC television serial 'The Forsyte Saga' (1967) starred Eric Porter. The latter was a tremendous success, won various awards, and has been shown all over the world. John Fisher's *The World of the Forsytes* (1976) is a book about Galsworthy's characters and their milieu.

FORTUNE, DAN   One-armed private detective who has appeared in a series of mystery novels by the American author Michael Collins (Dennis Lynds). The titles are: *Act of Fear* (1967), *The Brass Rainbow* (1969), *Night of the Toads* (1970), *Walk a Black Wind* (1971), *Shadow of a Tiger* (1972), *The Silent Scream* (1973), *Blue Death* (1975), *The Blood-Red Dream* (1976), *The Nightrunners* (1978), *The Slasher* (1980) and *Freak* (1983). Fortune is not a private investigator of the usual hard-boiled type: he is philosophical, non-violent, and wears a beret and duffel-coat.

FORTUNE, REGGIE   Upper-class sleuth who appears in a series of short stories and novels by H. C. Bailey. His adventures were very popular in Britain between the wars, although a latter-day critic, Julian Symons, professes to find Fortune 'intolerably facetious and whimsical'. The first book about Reggie Fortune was a collection of short stories, *Call Mr Fortune* (1920), and it was followed by another twenty-one titles: *Mr Fortune's Practice* (1923), *Mr Fortune's Trials* (1925), *Mr Fortune, Please* (1927), *Mr Fortune Speaking* (1929), *Mr Fortune Explains* (1930), *Case for Mr Fortune* (1932), *Mr Fortune Wonders* (1933), *Shadow on the Wall* (1934), *Mr Fortune Objects* (1935), *Clue for Mr Fortune* (1936), *Black Land, White Land* (1937), *This is Mr Fortune* (1938), *The Great Game* (1939), *Mr Fortune Here* (1940), *The Bishop's Crime* (1940), *No Murder* (1942; vt *Apprehensive Dog*), *Mr Fortune Finds a Pig* (1943), *Dead Man's Effects* (1945), *The Life Sentence* (1946), *Save a Rope* (1948) and *Shrouded Death* (1950).

FOSCO, COUNT Italian gentleman living in England, the apparently amiable villain of Wilkie Collins's mystery novel *The Woman in White* (1860). He is the 'first fat villain in English literature' (according to William Freeman). The plot concerns the unjust incarceration of an heiress, Laura Fairlie, by the avaricious Sir Percival Glyde – an evil scheme which is aided and abetted by the smoothly duplicitous Count Fosco. The story was turned into a stage play in 1871, and filmed in 1912, 1913, 1918 and 1929. Sidney Greenstreet played Fosco in the later Hollywood film version of the novel (1948; dir. Peter Godfrey). In the British television serialization (1982) he was played by Alan Badel.

FOSTER, JUDY Bobby-soxer who appeared in a popular American radio series entitled 'A Date with Judy' (from 1941). She also had her own comic-book (from 1947), which featured such subsidiary characters as Judy's crew-cut boyfriend Oogie Pringle and her 'bosom enemy' Tootsie. The musical film *A Date with Judy* (1948; dir. Richard Thorpe) starred Elizabeth Taylor. A television series of the same title (1951–3), had Patricia Crowley, later replaced by Mary Linn Beller, as the carefree teenage heroine.

FOUQUE, ADELÄIDE See under ROUGON-MACQUART

FOUR JUST MEN, THE Criminal quartet who conspire to murder the British Foreign Secretary in order to prevent the passage of a law which will restrict civil liberties. This risqué tale is told in Edgar Wallace's thriller *The Four Just Men* (1905). The Just Men's motives may be fine, but their means are vile – despite which Wallace revived them as the 'heroes' of several more novels and short-story collections: *The Council of Justice* (1908), *The Just Men of Cordova* (1917), *The Law of the Four Just Men* (1921), *The Three Just Men* (1925) and *Again the Three Just Men* (1928). In the film *The Four Just Men* (1939; dir. Walter Forde) the four were played by Hugh Sinclair, Francis L. Sullivan, Frank Lawton and Griffith Jones. A BBC television series of the late 1950s starred Jack Hawkins, Richard Conte, Dan Dailey and Vittorio de Sica as updated (and anaemic) versions of the just ones.

FOX, ALLIE   Crazed American *pater familias* who wishes to escape the ills of modern civilization. He takes his family to the jungles of Honduras, where he becomes obsessed with building a huge rerrigeration machine. Allie, who resembles a cross between Robinson CRUSOE and Captain AHAB, is the anti-hero of Paul Theroux's novel *The Mosquito Coast* (1981). Harrison Ford played him in the film of the book (1986; dir. Peter Weir).

FOYLE, KITTY   Irish-American girl from the wrong side of the tracks. She falls in love with Clayton Collyer, scion of one of Philadelphia's richer families. Her story is told in Christopher Morley's popular novel *Kitty Foyle* (1939). In the film of the book (1940; dir. Sam Wood) she was played by Ginger Rogers. The success of the movie led to an American radio series, 'Kitty Foyle' (1942–4), with Julie Stevens giving voice to Kitty.

FOZZIE BEAR   See under KERMIT THE FROG

FRANCIS THE MULE   Talking mule voiced by Chill Wills in a popular series of seven low-budget Hollywood films, beginning with *Francis* (1950; dir. Arthur Lubin). The last of the series was *Francis in the Haunted House* (1956; dir. Charles Lamont). Arthur Lubin, who was mainly responsible for these movies, went on to create television's Mr ED.

FRANKENSTEIN, VICTOR   Scientific researcher who creates a man, or monster, which he disowns – and which then turns on him, killing those he loves and making his life a misery. This fable of over-reaching ambition and fatal retribution was invented by the nineteen-year-old Mary Shelley in her novel *Frankenstein, or the Modern Prometheus* (1818). The name 'Frankenstein' has become part of modern mythology, and in popular parlance the scientist, Victor Frankenstein, is often confused with his creation, the monster sewn together from bits of various corpses. The macabre story of Frankenstein's hubris and its monstrous nemesis has been immensely influential, and indeed Brian Aldiss and others have claimed it as the inspiration for most subsequent science fiction. Within a few years of the book's first publication it had become a favourite in the form of sensationalized stage adaptations. Such nineteenth-century melodramas are the direct ancestors of the twentieth-century movie versions of the story. Modern sequels by other hands include the novels *Frankenstein Unbound* (1973) by Brian Aldiss, *The New Adventures of Frankenstein* (1977) by Donald F. Glut and *The Frankenstein Papers* (1986) by Fred Saberhagen.

Early film versions of the story were made in 1910 and 1915, but it seems they no longer exist. Our latter-day conceptions of Frankenstein and his monster owe almost everything to the first Hollywood talkie version, *Frankenstein* (1931; dir. James Whale). This starred Colin Clive as the scientist and Boris Karloff as his creation. Karloff's shambling creature, both menacing and pathetic, has never been forgotten: it is part of the indelible visual iconography of the twentieth century. The movie has spawned countless sequels – *The Bride of Frankenstein* (1935; dir. Whale), *Son of Frankenstein* (1939; dir. Rowland V. Lee), *The Ghost of Frankenstein* (1942; dir. Erle C. Kenton) and so on and on. More recent examples are the British Hammer Films remakes, beginning with *The Curse of Frankenstein* (1957; dir. Terence Fisher), which starred Peter Cushing as Frankenstein and Christopher Lee as the monster. There have also been many spoofs, ranging from *Abbott and Costello Meet Frankenstein* (1948; dir. Charles Barton) to *Young Frankenstein* (1974; dir. Mel Brooks). Two American TV movie versions were made in the same year, 1973; one of them, which had the benefit of a script by Christopher Isherwood, was rather inaccurately titled *Frankenstein: The True Story*. A British independent television version (1984) had Robert Powell as Frankenstein and David Warner as his creature.

White-coated Dr Frankenstein (Colin Clive)
with his monster looming above

FRANNY AND ZOOEY See under Seymour GLASS

FREAK BROTHERS, THE See The FABULOUS FURRY FREAK BROTHERS

FRENCH, JOSEPH Police inspector in over thirty detective novels by Freeman Wills Crofts, beginning with *Inspector French's Greatest Case* (1924). Connoisseurs of crime fiction now regard Crofts as a 'humdrum', and inevitably his Inspector French has come to seem something of a plodder. Later books in which this worthy detective appears include *The Cheyne Mystery* (1926), *The Sea Mystery* (1928), *Mystery in the English Channel* (1931), *Man Overboard!* (1936), *Enemy Unseen* (1945) and *Anything to Declare?* (1957). The character also appeared in the BBC radio series 'Chief Inspector French's Cases' (1943–5), where he was played by Milton Rosmer.

FRIDAY Companion and servant to the castaway Robinson CRUSOE in Daniel Defoe's famous novel *The Life and Strange Surprizing Adventures of Robinson Crusoe* (1719). Presumably a South American Indian, he is known to his master as 'Man Friday'. In Defoe's sequel, *The Farther Adventures of Robinson Crusoe* (also 1719), poor Friday is killed while defending Crusoe from savages. There have been at least two modern retellings by other hands, both of which concentrate on the character of Friday rather than that of Crusoe (who has been top-dog long enough in this particular fictional relationship). They are *Vendredi ou La Vie Sauvage* (1971) by Michel Tournier (translated into English as *Friday or The Other Island*), in which Friday, humorous and wise, teaches the half-mad Robinson how to live happily; and *Man Friday* (1972), a play by Adrian Mitchell, which points up the implicitly racist and imperialist nature of Defoe's original work. The Mitchell play (which was televised in 1972) has been filmed under the same title (1975; dir. Jack Gold), with Richard Roundtree as Friday and Peter O'Toole as Crusoe. Defoe's Man Friday has given his name to the English language as a handy term for a personal assistant or secretary (more often 'Girl Friday', as in the title of the Hollywood movie *His Girl Friday* [1940 – see Hildy JOHNSON]).

FRIDAY, JOE   Los Angeles sergeant played by Jack Webb in the long-running police-procedural television series 'Dragnet' (1951–8; new series 1967–9). The character was created by Jack Webb and writer Richard L. Breen. The same team also collaborated on the feature film *Dragnet* (1954; dir. Jack Webb) and the TV movie *Dragnet* (1969; vt *The Big Dragnet*; dir. Webb).

FRITZ THE CAT   Lewd feline created by cartoonist Robert Crumb for the American *Cavalier* magazine and for underground comics (or 'comix') of the late 1960s. Animator Ralph Bakshi brought the obscene beast to the movie screen in an X-rated feature, *Fritz the Cat* (1972), where he was voiced by Skip Hinnant. A cartoon sequel is entitled *The Nine Lives of Fritz the Cat* (1974).

FRODO   See Frodo BAGGINS

FROLLO, CLAUDE   See under QUASIMODO

FROME, ETHAN   New England farmer who tires of his nagging wife and falls in love with her cousin. He makes a suicide pact with the latter, but their plans go awry. The story is told in Edith Wharton's glum little novel *Ethan Frome* (1911).

FU MANCHU, DOCTOR   Chinese master villain, head of the secret society known as the 'Si-Fan'. A cold-eyed calculating expert in conspiracy, torture and murder, Fu operates all over the globe, his apparent aim the ultimate mastery of the world. He is described as having 'a brow like Shakespeare and a face like Satan'. However, his nefarious plans are repeatedly foiled by the stout Britisher Dennis Nayland SMITH. Fu was created by Sax Rohmer (Arthur Sarsfield Ward) in a series of short stories which ran in the *Story-Teller* magazine from 1912. These were soon cobbled together into bestselling novels: *The Mystery of Dr Fu Manchu* (1913; vt *The Insidious Dr Fu Manchu*), *The Devil Doctor* (1916; vt *The Return of Dr Fu Manchu*), and *The Si-Fan Mysteries* (1917; vt *The Hand of Fu Manchu*). For several years Sax Rohmer tried to escape from the loom of his most famous character, but following the success of Fu Manchu in silent films during the 1920s he was driven to resume the series and to continue it throughout the remainder of his long writing career. The later novels are:

Daughter of Fu Manchu (1931), *The Mask of Fu Manchu* (1932), *Fu Manchu's Bride* (1933; vt *The Bride of Fu Manchu*), *The Trail of Fu Manchu* (1934), *President Fu Manchu* (1936), *The Drums of Fu Manchu* (1939), *The Island of Fu Manchu* (1941), *Shadow of Fu Manchu* (1948), *Re-enter Fu Manchu* (1957) and *Emperor Fu Manchu* (1959). *The Wrath of Fu Manchu* (1973) is a posthumous collection of short stories.

The actor Harry Agar Lyons played Fu Manchu in the short silent movies of the 1920s. The first talkie to feature the Devil Doctor, *The Mysterious Dr Fu Manchu* (1929), starred Warner Oland, who repeated the part in two subsequent films. However, the most memorable Fu on celluloid proved to be Boris Karloff in *The Mask of Fu Manchu* (1932; dir. Charles Brabin and Charles Vidor). He was followed by Henry Brandon, who took on the role in the serial *Drums of Fu Manchu* (1939). Decades later, a new series of five Fu Manchu films was made in Britain, with Christopher Lee filling the part splendidly; *The Face of Fu Manchu* (1965; dir. Don Sharp) was the first of these, and *The Castle of Fu Manchu* (1970; dir. Jesus Franco) was the last. An unsuccessful spoof movie, *The Fiendish Plot of Dr Fu Manchu* (1980; dir. Piers Haggard), starred Peter Sellers.

In the 1930s and 1940s Fu was very popular on American radio and in comic-strip adaptations. He also appeared on Radio Luxembourg, broadcast to a British audience, from 1936 to 1938. An American television series, 'The Adventures of Fu Manchu' (1955–6), starred Glen Gordon. Probably the most famous villain in twentieth-century popular fiction, Fu Manchu has remained a byword: he is the 'Yellow Peril incarnate', one of the best-known embodiments of a racial stereotype. A new Fu Manchu novel appeared as recently as 1984 – *Ten Years Beyond Baker Street* by Rohmer's friend and biographer Cay Van Ash. In this the deadly doctor is pitted against Sherlock HOLMES, who has been summoned from retirement to help rescue the unfortunate Nayland Smith from the arch-fiend's clutches.

FUGITIVE, THE   Dr Richard Kimble, the long-running hero of a long-running American television series, 'The Fugitive' (1963–7). This modern avatar of Jean VALJEAN was played by David Janssen, and the series was conceived by producer Roy Huggins. Falsely accused of his wife's murder, Kimble is in flight from his nemesis,

Lieutenant Philip Gerard; at the same time he is pursuing a mysterious one-armed man who may or may not be the real murderer. When all was revealed in the last episode the show attracted record audiences across America.

FUNGUS THE BOGEYMAN   Loveable but at the same time repulsive hero of Raymond Briggs's illustrated book for children, *Fungus the Bogeyman* (1977). Fungus and his family live underground, in a dank smelly world where all things dry and clean are abhorred. The book is full of 'dirty jokes' and horrid inversions which have made it appealing to adults as well as kids. Briggs reworked the material for his *Fungus the Bogeyman Plop-Up Book* (1982).

FURILLO, FRANK   Hard-working captain in the American television police-procedural series 'Hill Street Blues', a critical hit of the early 1980s. The creators of the series were Steven Bochco and Mike Kozoll, and Furillo was played by Daniel J. Travanti. Furillo and his fast-talking crew of cops have much in common with Ed McBain's Steve CARELLA and colleagues.

FURTER, FRANK N.   Transvestite villain of *The Rocky Horror Show*, a spoof of all things kinky and Transylvanian. He 'entertains' an innocent couple called Janet and Brad in his old dark house. With songs and lyrics by Richard O'Brien, the show became a cult success on the British stage. It was soon transferred to film: *The Rocky Horror Picture Show* (1975; dir. Jim Sharman) starred Tim Curry as Frank N. Furter. A semi-sequel is the film *Shock Treatment* (1981; dir. Sharman).

FUTURE, CAPTAIN   Real name Curt Newton, the spacefaring hero of the science fiction pulp magazine *Captain Future* (1940–44). He pursues interstellar criminals, accompanied by three unlikely helpers – a robot, an android and a 'living brain'. Most of the short novels featuring these characters were written by Edmond Hamilton (sometimes under the pseudonym Brett Sterling). After the title folded Hamilton wrote later adventures of Captain Future for the magazine *Startling Stories*. A number of the novellas were reprinted in paperback in the late 1960s.

G

G-8 Nameless grey-eyed hero of the American pulp magazine *G-8 and His Battle Aces*, which ran for 110 issues (1933–44). G-8 is a flying spy; he has a manservant called Battle, and both are in the service of the US government. 'He once jumped 100 feet from a window, catching a tree limb on the way down "like a crazy ape". Likewise, he thought nothing of hanging onto wheels and wings of flying planes, once fighting with the ghastly Professor Unger while clinging to the landing gear' (Jeff Rovin, *The Encyclopedia of Superheroes*). Most of the stories were written by Robert J. Hogan, and some of the novellas were reprinted as paperbacks in 1969–71. The character also appeared in an unsuccessful comic-book (1966). Philip José Farmer introduces G-8 as a minor character in his novel *The Adventure of the Peerless Peer* (1974), where he helps fly Sherlock HOLMES to Africa to meet TARZAN. Farmer seems to be of the opinion that G-8 was utterly insane.

GABLER, HEDDA Neurotic heroine of Henrik Ibsen's harrowing play *Hedda Gabler* (1890). Bored by her husband, the ineffectual Tesman, Hedda toys with a former lover and drives the latter to suicide. Another man tries to blackmail her into becoming his mistress, but she forestalls him by shooting herself. The play has often been televised. An Anglo-American co-production (1963) starred Ingrid Bergman as Hedda. Later British television versions had Janet Suzman (1972) and Diana Rigg (1980). The feature film *Hedda* (1975; dir. Trevor Nunn) starred Glenda Jackson. The play also forms the basis of an opera by Edward Harper (1985).

GABRIEL, WALTER Gravel-voiced oldster played by Robert Mawdesley in the long-lived BBC radio serial, 'The Archers' (from 1950). At one time he was probably the best known radio character in Britain. After his wife's death Walter Gabriel let his farm run down, until he eventually gave it up entirely in 1957. 'Since then, shed of all his responsibilities, Walter has played havoc in Ambridge with a whole string of entrepreneurial ventures that have left the villagers variously bemused, bothered and bewildered' (according to the BBC publication *Twenty-Five Years of the Archers: A Who's Who of Ambridge*, 1975).

GALE, DOROTHY   Little girl who is carried away by a cyclone to the magical world of Oz in L. Frank Baum's children's novel *The Wonderful Wizard of Oz* (1900). In her journey down the

Dorothy Gale (Judy Garland)
with the Tin Woodman and the Scarecrow

Yellowbrick Road to the Emerald City, Dorothy meets the
Scarecrow, the Tin Woodman, the Cowardly Lion and eventually
the Wizard of Oz himself. It proved an immensely popular story,
America's most celebrated modern fairy tale. Baum went on to
write thirteen sequels: *The Marvellous Land of Oz* (1904), which
has a curious trans-sexual theme – it is mainly about a boy called
Tip who is changed into a beautiful princess; *Ozma of Oz*
(1907), which reintroduces Dorothy along with such new
characters as Billina the hen and Tik-Tok the mechanical man;
Dorothy and the Wizard of Oz (1908); *The Road to Oz* (1909);
The Emerald City of Oz (1910), in which Dorothy brings her Aunt
Em and Uncle Henry from Kansas to Oz; *The Patchwork Girl of
Oz* (1913); *Tik-Tok of Oz* (1914); *The Scarecrow of Oz* (1915);
Rinkitink in Oz (1916); *The Lost Princess of Oz* (1917); *The Tin
Woodman of Oz* (1918); *The Magic of Oz* (1919) and the posthumous
Glinda of Oz (1920). All of these books except the first were
illustrated by John R. Neill. At least three of the stories were turned
into stage plays in Baum's lifetime, and the author himself
experimented in making short films about the Oz characters.

By the time of Baum's death Oz had become an American
institution, and his publishers swiftly commissioned another writer
to continue the series. Ruth Plumley Thompson wrote twenty-
one Oz books in all, of which the first half dozen are: *The Royal
Book of Oz* (1921); *Kabumpo of Oz* (1922); *The Cowardly Lion
of Oz* (1923); *Grampa in Oz* (1924); *The Lost King of Oz* (1925);
and *The Hungry Tiger of Oz* (1926). After Thompson ceased
writing in 1939 the illustrator John R. Neill wrote another three
titles in the series. Since then there have been occasional sequels
by other hands. A recent example (intended for adults) is *A
Barnstormer in Oz* (1982) by Philip José Farmer, which purports
to be about the adventures of Dorothy's son, Hank. In movies,
Dorothy has been immortalized by the young Judy Garland, who
played her in the musical film *The Wizard of Oz* (1939; dir. Victor
Fleming). 'Over the Rainbow', and the other songs by Harold
Arlen and E. Y. Harburg which were written for this colourful
production, have been used in stage versions of the story ever
since. The animated film *Journey Back to Oz* (1974; dir. Hal
Sutherland) featured the voice of Liza Minnelli (Judy Garland's
daughter) to characterize Dorothy. *The Wiz* (1978; dir. Sidney
Lumet) was based on a stage musical which transposes the action

of the original Oz story to New York; it had an all-black cast, with Diana Ross as Dorothy. The recent Disney blockbuster *Return to Oz* (1985) starred a young actress called Fairuza Balk.

GALE, MRS   See under Emma Peel

GAMP, SARAH   Known as 'Sairey', a nurse of low repute in Charles Dickens's novel *Martin Chuzzlewit* (1843–4). A large, gin-tippling woman, she is fond of quoting her all-knowing but ever-absent friend, 'Mrs Harris'. At one time Sairey Gamp gave her name to a type of umbrella, although use of the word 'gamp' is now uncommon. See also Martin Chuzzlewit.

GANDALF   Ageless wizard with a long white beard. He first appears in J. R. R. Tolkien's children's book *The Hobbit* (1937), where he assists Bilbo Baggins to retrieve a great treasure. He reappears in Tolkien's lengthy master work *The Lord of the Rings* (1954–5) where he plays a crucial and heroic role in helping to defeat Sauron, the Dark Lord. Gandalf became something of a cult figure in the late 1960s, when a British 'underground' magazine, *Gandalf's Garden*, was named after him. He appears in the animated television movie *The Hobbit* (1977) and the cartoon feature film *Lord of the Rings* (1978; dir. Raph Bakshi). In the BBC radio adaptation of *The Lord of the Rings* (1981) Gandalf was voiced by Michael Hordern.

GANT, EUGENE   Hero of Thomas Wolfe's quasi-autobiographical novels *Look Homeward, Angel: A Story of the Buried Life* (1929) and *Of Time and the River: A Legend of Man's Hunger in His Youth* (1935). He grows up in a provincial American town, attends Harvard university, and dedicates himself to a literary career. Wolfe's later novels, *The Web and the Rock* (1939) and *You Can't Go Home Again* (1940), are effectively sequels, though in these books the very similar hero is called George Webber.

GANTRY, ELMER   Fiery but dishonest preacher who founds an evangelical church, in Sinclair Lewis's novel *Elmer Gantry* (1927). In the film of the book (1960; dir. Richard Brooks) he was played by Burt Lancaster. A recent stage musical version of the story (1986) had music and lyrics by Steve Brown.

GARDINER, CHAUNCEY See CHANCE

GARFIELD Fat, ginger pussy-cat in newspaper comic-strips by the American cartoonist Jim Davis (from 1978). Garfield, who has also appeared in television 'specials', is one of the most popular comic characters of the past decade. Since 1980 Davis's strips have been reprinted in paperback books which have sold in the millions, and the Tubby Tabby's image has appeared on greetings cards and other merchandise.

GARNETT, ALF Prejudiced, irascible working-class Londoner in the BBC television comedy series 'Till Death Us Do Part' (1964–74). Alf is a royalist, a racist and a loudmouth, and he has succeeded in becoming something of an English national institution. The series was written by Johnny Speight, and the bald-headed Alf was played by Warren Mitchell. The feature films *Till Death Us Do Part* (1968; dir. Norman Cohen) and *The Alf Garnett Saga* (1972; dir. Bob Kellett) also starred Mitchell. Alf and his long-suffering wife Else were revived for a new BBC television series 'In Sickness and in Health' (1985–6), also written by Johnny Speight. (The American equivalent of Alf Garnett is Archie BUNKER.)

GARP, T. S. Mother-dominated hero of the bestselling novel *The World According to Garp* (1978) by the American writer John Irving. The book has been described by one reviewer as 'a social tragi-comedy of such velocity and hilarity that it reads rather like a domestic sequel to *Catch-22*' (see YOSSARIAN). 'T.S.' stands for Technical Sergeant, which was the rank of Garp's father at the time the child was conceived. In the film of the novel (1982; dir. George Roy Hill) Garp was played by James McCall (as a boy) and Robin Williams (as a young man).

GARVIN, WILLIE See under Modesty BLAISE

GATSBY, JAY Rich American with a shady past, in F. Scott Fitzgerald's novel *The Great Gatsby* (1925). He buys a house on Long Island in order to be close to Daisy Buchanan, the woman he has long worshipped from afar. Gatsby's passion for Daisy leads to tragedy. In films of the novel he has been played by Warner Baxter (1926), Alan Ladd (1949; dir. Elliott Nugent) and Robert Redford (1974; dir. Jack Clayton). Jay Gatsby's early life is described in David Thomson's book *Suspects* (1985; see under George BAILEY).

GAUTIER, MARGUERITE See CAMILLE

GEORDIE See Geordie MACTAGGART

GEPETTO See under PINOCCHIO

GERARD, ETIENNE Hero of Napoleon's army, in a series of historical adventure stories by A. Conan Doyle. The tales are collected in *The Exploits of Brigadier Gerard* (1896) and *The Adventures of Gerard* (1903). In some respects a latter-day Don Quixote, Gerard is brave, egotistical, naïve, accident-prone and, above all, lucky. Doyle based a play, *Brigadier Gerard* (1906), on some of his own stories. In the film *The Adventures of Gerard* (1970; dir. Jerzy Skolimowski) the half-lunatic hero was played by Peter McEnery.

GERARD, PHILIP See under The FUGITIVE

GERT AND DAISY Pair of Cockney ladies created by Elsie and Doris Waters for a gramophone record which was released in 1930. The comic duo soon became very popular on BBC radio, where they continued to appear for many years. Perhaps their best-remembered wireless programme is 'Petticoat Line' (from 1949).

GESCHWITZ, COUNTESS See under LULU

GESTE, BEAU Proper name Michael Geste – a bold young Englishman who joins the French Foreign Legion and has gruelling adventures in North Africa. The story is told in P. C. Wren's bestselling romantic novel *Beau Geste* (1924). There are three Geste brothers, Michael, Digby and John, and the first two die gallantly at the end of the novel. The sequels are mainly concerned with the adventures of John, the surviving younger brother: *Beau Sabreur* (1926), *Beau Ideal* (1928), *Good Gestes* (1929; short stories set in the period before Beau's death) and *Spanish Main* (1935; vt *Desert Heritage*). The first book has been adapted to the stage, cinema and television. In a 1929 theatrical version the lead role was taken by Laurence Olivier. In films Beau Geste has been played by Ronald Colman (1926; dir. Herbert Brenon); by Gary Cooper (1939; dir. William Wellman); and by Guy Stockwell (1966; dir. Douglas Heyes). In the BBC television serial (1982) Benedict Taylor starred as Beau. There has also been a spoof movie, *The Last Remake of Beau Geste* (1977; dir. Marty Feldman), in which Michael York played the hero, with the bug-eyed Mr Feldman as his supposed twin brother.

GETAFIX   See under ASTERIX

GETHRYN, ANTHONY   Hero of an intermittent series of detective stories by British novelist/screenwriter Philip MacDonald. Colonel Gethryn first appears in *The Rasp* (1924). Later titles which feature him are: *The White Crow* (1928), *The Link* (1930), *The Noose* (1930), *The Choice* (1931; vt *The Polferry Riddle*), *Persons Unknown* (1931; vt *The Maze*), *The Wraith* (1931), *The Crime Conductor* (1931), *Rope to Spare* (1932), *The Nursemaid Who Disappeared* (1938; vt *Warrant for X*) and – after a gap of twenty-one years – *The List of Adrian Messenger* (1959). The last of these novels has been filmed (1963; dir. John Huston) with George C. Scott as the detective.

GHOTE, GANESH   Indian police detective invented by H. R. F. Keating for his novel *The Perfect Murder* (1964). Inspector Ghote lives and works in Bombay. He is an unassuming chap, easily bullied, but he always cracks his cases. The later novels in the series are *Inspector Ghote's Good Crusade* (1966), *Inspector Ghote Caught in Meshes* (1967), *Inspector Ghote Hunts the Peacock* (1968), *Inspector Ghote Plays a Joker* (1969), *Inspector Ghote Breaks an Egg* (1970), *Inspector Ghote Goes by Train* (1971), *Inspector Ghote Trusts the Heart* (1972), *Bats Fly Up for Inspector Ghote* (1974), *Filmi, Filmi, Inspector Ghote* (1976),

Inspector Ghote Draws a Line (1979), *Go West, Inspector Ghote* (1981), *The Sheriff of Bombay* (1984) and *Under a Monsoon Cloud* (1986). In the BBC television serial 'Hunt the Peacock' (1969) the character was played by Zia Mohyeddin. The part has since been taken by Sam Dastor in another TV adaptation called 'Inspector Ghote Moves In' (1983).

GIDEON, GEORGE   Police superintendent at Scotland Yard, in a series of crime novels by J. J. Marric (John Creasey). The titles are: *Gideon's Day* (1955), *Gideon's Week* (1956), *Gideon's Night* (1957), *Gideon's Month* (1958), *Gideon's Staff* (1959), *Gideon's Risk* (1960), *Gideon's Fire* (1961), *Gideon's March* (1962), *Gideon's Ride* (1963), *Gideon's Vote* (1964), *Gideon's Lot* (1964), *Gideon's Badge* (1965), *Gideon's Wrath* (1967), *Gideon's River* (1968), *Gideon's Power* (1969), *Gideon's Sport* (1970), *Gideon's Art* (1971), *Gideon's Men* (1972), *Gideon's Press* (1973), *Gideon's Fog* (1974), *Gideon's Buy* (1975) and *Gideon's Drive* (1976). Two further novels, *Gideon's Force* (1978) and *Gideon's Law* (1981), were written by William Vivian Butler after Creasey's death. In the film *Gideon of Scotland Yard* (1958; dir. John Ford) Gideon was played by Jack Hawkins. The British television series 'Gideon's Way' (1964) starred John Gregson.

GIDGET   Full name Francine Lawrence, a lively, squeaky-clean teenager played by Sandra Dee in the movie *Gidget* (1959; dir. Paul Wendkos; based on a novel by Frederick Kohner). The character proved popular enough to appear in two film sequels – *Gidget Goes Hawaiian* (1961; dir. Wendkos), with Deborah Walley, and *Gidget Goes to Rome* (1962; dir. Wendkos), with Cindy Carol – as well as a television series (1965–6) which starred Sally Field, and three TV movies: *Gidget Grows Up* (1969; dir. James Sheldon), with Karen Valentine; *Gidget Gets Married* (1971; dir. E. W. Swackhamer), with Monie Ellis; and *Gidget's Summer Reunion* (1985; dir. Bruce Bilson), with Caryn Richman. Gidget has been described as a female Andy HARDY.

GIGI   Gilberte, the charming young heroine of Colette's novella *Gigi* (1944). She is a Parisian girl who is trained by her aunt to become a courtesan. In the film of the novel (1948; dir. Jacqueline Audry) Gigi was played by Daniele Delorme. The story also formed the basis of a successful stage musical, with music and lyrics by Frederick Loewe and Alan Jay Lerner, and this was filmed (1958; dir. Vincente Minnelli) with Leslie Caron in the lead role.

GILBERT THE FILBERT   See under Burlington Bertie

GILDA   See under Rigoletto

GILDERSLEEVE, THROCKMORTON P.   See under Fibber and Molly McGee

GILLESPIE, DOCTOR   See under James Kildare

GILLIS, DOBIE   American college student invented by writer Max Shulman. He appeared in the musical film *The Affairs of Dobie Gillis* (1953; dir. Don Weis), where he was played by Bobby Van, and in the television series 'The Many Loves of Dobie Gillis' (1959–63), which starred Dwayne Hickman. The girl-crazy Dobie's principal friend and co-conspirator is a rather disreputable youth called Maynard Krebs. *Whatever Happened to Dobie Gillis?*, a failed pilot for a proposed new TV series, was broadcast in 1977.

GILLIS, JOE   See under Norma Desmond

GILPIN, JOHN   Middle-aged London draper whose uncontrollable horse takes him for an unwelcome twenty-mile ride, in William Cowper's narrative poem 'The Diverting History of John Gilpin' (1782). The poem was reprinted in chapbook form and became exceedingly well known.

GINGER   See Ginger Meggs

GLASS, SEYMOUR   Intellectual member of the talented Glass family (his siblings are Franny, Zooey and Buddy) of New York. Seymour commits suicide in J. D. Salinger's short story 'A Perfect Day for Bananafish' (collected in *Nine Stories*, 1953; vt *For Esmé, with Love and Squalor*). Other books about the half-Irish half-Jewish Glass family are *Franny and Zooey* (1961) and *Raise High the Roof Beam, Carpenters, and Seymour: An Introduction*

(1963). Mary McCarthy has written an entertaining essay, 'J. D. Salinger's Closed Circuit', in which she deprecates the clubby, cosy, 'insider' atmosphere of these undeniably well-written stories: 'Unlike the average genius, the Glass kids are good guys; they love each other and their parents and their cat and their goldfish, and they are expert phony-detectors. The dead sage Seymour has initiated them into Zen and other mystical cults.'

GLENCORA, LADY   See under Plantagenet PALLISER

GLICK, SAMMY   Jewish kid from New York who rises in the motion-picture industry to become a movie mogul. He appears in Budd Schulberg's powerful novel *What Makes Sammy Run?* (1941).

GLUM FAMILY, THE   Tipsy Pa Glum, his brainless unemployed son Ron, and the latter's ever-hopeful fiancée Eth were played by Jimmy Edwards, Dick Bentley and June Whitfield in the BBC radio comedy series 'Take it From Here' (1953–60). The shows were scripted by Frank Muir and Denis Norden – 'it occurred to us that as the airwaves were becoming clogged with everyday stories of good-hearted, decent folk like the Archers and the Huggetts . . . we might redress the balance by writing the everyday doings of a really *awful* family.' The characters were revived for an independent television series, 'The Glums' (1979). Jimmy Edwards continued to play Pa, while Ian Lavender and Patricia Brake were Ron and Eth.

GLYDE, SIR PERCIVAL   See under Count FOSCO

GNASHER   See under DENNIS THE MENACE

GODFATHER, THE   See Michael CORLEONE

GODOT   See under VLADIMIR AND ESTRAGON

GODZILLA   Known as Gojira in Japanese – an enormous dinosaur which threatens to destroy Tokyo, in the movie *Godzilla, King of the Monsters* (1955; dir. Inoshiro Honda). The creature is awakened from its sleep, deep in the primordial ooze, by an H-bomb test. (An earlier American film which used much the same idea is *The Beast from 20,000 Fathoms* [1953; dir. Eugene Lourie], based on a story by Ray Bradbury.) Godzilla has appeared in many subsequent Japanese films and television cartoon series. Movie sequels include *King Kong vs. Godzilla* (1962), *Godzilla vs. the Thing* (1964) and *Destroy All Monsters* (1969).

GOLDBERG, MOLLY   Good-hearted but gossip-prone matriarch played by Gertrude Berg in the long-running American radio soap opera 'The Goldbergs' (1933–48). She and her husband Jake (who is in the New York clothing business) live in a Bronx apartment with their children Sammy and Rosalie. Gertrude Berg continued in the role of Molly when the series was transferred to television (1949–55). Philip Loeb, the actor who played Jake, was less lucky: in 1951 he was blacklisted because of alleged left-wing views, and subsequently committed suicide (in the TV series, he was replaced initially by Harold J. Stone, later by Robert H. Harris).

GOLDFINGER, AURIC   See under James BOND

GOLIGHTLY, HOLLY   Eighteen-year-old *femme fatale* at large in New York. Her calling card states: 'Miss Holiday Golightly, Travelling.' It turns out that she is a Midwestern farmer's child-bride, on the run. Holly is the fascinating heroine of Truman Capote's novella *Breakfast at Tiffany's* (1958). In the film of the story (1961; dir. Blake Edwards) she was played by Audrey Hepburn. Capote's story has also been adapted to the stage by playwright Edward Albee (1966).

GOLLANTZ, EMMANUEL   German-Jewish businessman who founds a dynasty in England. The story of his family is told in Naomi Jacob's 'Gollantz Saga', which consists of *Young Emmanuel* (1932), *The Founder of the House* (1935) and other novels. Later titles include *That Wild Lie, Four Generations, Private Gollantz, Gollantz: London, Paris, Milan* and *Gollantz and Partners* (1957).

GOLLIWOGG, THE   Black-faced doll which became a popular children's plaything and a merchandising motif (usually spelled 'golliwog'). It actually began life as a character in a picture book,

The Adventures of Two Dutch Dolls and a 'Golliwogg' (1895) by Bertha and Florence Upton. The Uptons wrote and illustrated twelve more books about the Golliwogg's adventures, the last being *Golliwogg in the African Jungle* (1909). This innocently racist stereotype soon became a nursery favourite, perpetuated not only by toy manufacturers but by other writers and artists – for example, Ruth Ainsworth has written a series of little tales about a golliwog called Rufty Tufty.

GOOD, JOHN   See under Allan QUATERMAIN

GOOD, TOM AND BARBARA   Suburban husband and wife who opt for an ecologically sound life-style, much to the disgust of their conventionally middle-class neighbours, in the BBC television comedy series 'The Good Life' (1974–8). The series was written by Bob Larbey and John Esmonde, and starred Richard Briers and Felicity Kendal as the oddball but endearing couple.

GOODE, CHESTER   See under Matt DILLON

GOODE, JOHNNY B.   Guitar-strumming backwoods boy, in the rock'n'roll song 'Johnny B. Goode' by Chuck Berry (*circa* 1957). Berry was rock music's first 'poet', and several of his songs contain sharply-delineated characters as well as witty observations of American teenage culture. Berry's 'Johnny B. Goode' gained a new generation of fans when it was used on the soundtrack of the hit movie *Back to the Future* (1985).

GOODWIN, ARCHIE   See under Nero WOLFE

GOODY TWO-SHOES   Little girl in a nursery story published by John Newbery in 1765. The full title is *The History of Little Goody Two-Shoes; Otherwise Called Mrs Margery Two-Shoes, With the Means by Which She Acquired Her Learning and Wisdom, and in Consequence Thereof Her Estate.* It is possible that the tale was written by Oliver Goldsmith, who was working for Newbery at the time. Margery is a ragged orphan who is given a pair of shoes by a kindly benefactor. She subsequently teaches herself to read, becomes a schoolmistress, and marries well. This small book was an enormous success, much read and much imitated. A sequel by another hand is *The Adventures of Thomas Two-Shoes* (1818) by Mary Elliott (the story of Goody's sailor brother). The original story has formed the basis of a pantomime, frequently staged since 1803.

GOOFY See under MICKEY MOUSE

GORDON, BABS See under BATMAN

GORDON, CHARLIE Man of low intelligence whose mental capacities are increased to genius level through surgery. He first appeared in Daniel Keyes's short story 'Flowers for Algernon' (1959). The 'Algernon' of the title is a laboratory mouse with which Charlie identifies. The tale was later expanded to novel length under the same title (1966). In the film *Charly* (1968) the unfortunate hero was played by Cliff Robertson. In a stage musical version, called *Flowers for Algernon*, he was played by Michael Crawford.

GORDON, FLASH Brawny spaceman-hero, created (in imitation of Buck ROGERS) by the newspaper-strip cartoonist Alex Raymond. Flash's adventures with his girlfriend Dale Arden on the planet Mongo and elsewhere were chronicled by Raymond for ten years after the strip's inception in 1934. Since 1944 *Flash Gordon* has been drawn by many other hands. The cinema serial *Flash Gordon* (1936) starred Buster Crabbe as the blond hero and Charles Middleton as his arch-enemy, MING THE MERCILESS. Crabbe perpetuated the role in two further serials, *Flash Gordon's Trip to Mars* (1938) and *Flash Gordon Conquers the Universe* (1940). Flash has also appeared in an American television series (1953–4), where he was played by Steve Holland. The extravagant feature film *Flash Gordon* (1980; dir. Mike Hodges) starred Sam J. Jones. An earlier movie, *Flesh Gordon* (1974), is a pornographic spoof. There has also been an animated TV movie of Flash's exploits (1981; dir. Gwen Wentzler). In the 1970s a series of Flash Gordon novels appeared under the byline of Alex Raymond (presumably adapted from Raymond's comic-strips). Another series of Flash Gordon books has been written by Con Steffanson (Ron Goulart) and includes such titles as *The Lion Men of Mongo*, *The Plague of Sound* and *The Space Circus* (all 1974).

GORIOT, PÈRE Suffering father of ungrateful daughters, in Honoré de Balzac's novel *Le Père Goriot* (1834; sometimes translated into English as *Old Goriot*). His two daughters marry rich men and become contemptuous of their old father, even though they still turn to him for money. Goriot bears more than a passing resemblance to King Lear. Other notable characters who appear in the novel, which is a part of Balzac's *Comédie Humaine*, include Eugène de RASTIGNAC and VAUTRIN.

GOULD, CHARLES See under NOSTROMO

GRADGRIND, THOMAS Flinty-hearted industrialist in Charles Dickens's novel *Hard Times* (1854). An inhabitant of Coketown in the north of England, Gradgrind is a personification of Victorian harshness and 'utilitarian' meanness. He marries his unfortunate daughter to Josiah Bounderby, an old manufacturer. The novel has been serialized on British television (1977), in a highly-praised production which starred Patrick Allen.

GRAFTON, HARRY See under Ernest G. BILKO

GRAHAM, LUCY See Lady Lucy AUDLEY

GRAHAM, MARY See under Martin CHUZZLEWIT

GRAND INQUISITOR, THE See under Dmitri, Ivan and Alexei KARAMAZOV

GRANDCOURT, HENLEIGH See under Gwendolen HARLETH

GRANDET, EUGÉNIE Girl whose love affair with her cousin Charles is forbidden by her overbearing father. The story is told in Honoré de Balzac's novel *Eugénie Grandet* (1833), a part of his *Comédie Humaine* series (see also Père GORIOT and VAUTRIN). A Hollywood film of the novel, with Alice Terry as Eugénie, was entitled *The Conquering Power* (1922; dir. Rex Ingram).

GRANDISON, CHARLES Exceedingly virtuous hero of Samuel Richardson's epistolary novel *Sir Charles Grandison* (1753). He falls in love with a girl he has rescued from a villain; however, he is already betrothed to another, and determines to do the honourable thing. In its day, this novel was almost as popular as *Clarissa* (see Clarissa HARLOWE), but it is seldom read now. It was Jane Austen's favourite among Richardson's books; and in Tchaikovsky's opera *Eugene Onegin* (1879) one of the female characters exclaims: 'Oh, Grandison! . . . Oh, Richardson!'

GRANT, LOU Rugged-featured, amiable newspaperman with a marked social conscience. He is the City Editor of the *Los Angeles Tribune*. Played by Edward Asner, Lou Grant first appeared in the American television series 'The Mary Tyler Moore Show' (1970–77), where he was the boss of Mary Richards (the careerwoman played by Mary Tyler Moore). He proved such a memorable character that he was revived for his own series, 'Lou Grant' (1977–82). The show was eventually dropped by CBS television, allegedly because Edward Asner's clearly expressed opinions were too liberal to suit the prevailing political climate in the United States. Shortly after the series' cancellation, the *Guardian* newspaper commented (28 October 1982): 'The end of *Lou Grant* means the loss of the only issues-oriented drama series on American TV. In the last year the programme moved further and further away from the newspaper office that is its nominal setting and delved more deeply into political and social issues than is usual on American television. Gun control, neo-Nazism, world hunger, the boat people, and nuclear war were among the subjects squeezed into the *Lou Grant* format in the 1981–2 season.'

GRAY, CORDELIA Lady detective who appears in P. D. James's novels *An Unsuitable Job for a Woman* (1972) and *The Skull Beneath the Skin* (1982). According to Carolyn G. Heilbrun in *Twentieth-Century Crime and Mystery Writers*, the author provides 'a satisfying portrait of a woman private detective who is a rare creature even in a genre notable for its interesting women. Cordelia Gray is independent, autonomous, self-supporting, and intelligent; she is, moreover . . . absolutely without guilt.' In the television movie *An Unsuitable Job for a Woman* (1985; dir. Christopher Petit) the heroine was played by Pippa Guard. (See also Adam DALGLEISH.)

GRAY, DORIAN   Handsome young man who remains physically
unaffected by time, dissipation and sin. His magical portrait
absorbs all these malign influences: when the painting is
destroyed Dorian withers and dies. His story is told in Oscar
Wilde's witty and 'decadent' novel *The Picture of Dorian Gray*

Dorian Gray (Hurd Hatfield) in the 1945 film (with Donna Reed)

(1890). In the film of the book (1945; dir. Albert Lewin) Dorian was played by Hurd Hatfield. A subsequent BBC television version (1976; dir. John Gorrie) had Peter Firth in the part.

GRAY, FIELDING Central character of Simon Raven's novel sequence *Alms for Oblivion* (1964–76). A former British army officer turned writer, Fielding Gray has been described by more than one reviewer as 'loathsome'. The novels in the sequence are: *The Rich Pay Late* (1964), *Friends in Low Places* (1965), *The Sabre Squadron* (1966), *Fielding Gray* (1967), *The Judas Boy* (1968), *Places Where They Sing* (1970), *Sound the Retreat* (1971), *Come Like Shadows* (1972), *Bring Forth the Body* (1974) and *The Survivors* (1976). In the 1980s Raven has begun to produce a new series of novels under the general title *The First-Born of Egypt*: this also features Fielding Gray and many of his old associates.

GRAY, PETERKIN See under Ralph ROVER

GRAY SEAL, THE See Jimmie DALE

GRAYSON, DICK See under BATMAN

GREEN, VERDANT Innocent undergraduate at an ancient university, in the three-part comic novel *The Adventures of Mr Verdant Green, an Oxford Freshman* (1853–7) by Cuthbert Bede (Edward Bradley). This work has been reprinted in the 1980s, and is regarded as a minor classic of English humour.

GREEN HORNET, THE Real name Britt Reid (he is a relative of John Reid, the LONE RANGER), a masked crime-fighter created by producer George W. Trendle and writer Fran Striker for an American radio show, 'The Green Hornet' (1936–52). The Hornet never kills; he uses a gas gun to render criminals unconscious. His sidekick is a Japanese youth called Kato, and together they drive around in a heavily-armed car known as the Black Beauty. His voice was provided by the actor Al Hodge, and later by Donovan Faust, Bob Hall and Jack McCarthy. The Hornet was a great success on the radio, and soon appeared in cinema serials: *The Green Hornet* (1940), starring Gordon Jones, and *The Green Hornet Strikes Again* (1941), starring Warren Hull. The television series, 'The Green Hornet' (1966–7), had Van Williams as the Hornet and Bruce Lee as Kato (because of Bruce Lee's later popularity as a practitioner of the martial arts, several of the TV episodes were cobbled together as a feature film in 1974). There have been at least four series of Green Hornet comic-books, published from the 1940s to the 1960s, and a novel about the character: *The Infernal Light* (1966) by Ed Friend.

GREEN LANTERN   Real name Alan Scott (later changed to Hal Jordan), a comic-book superhero created in 1940 by artist Martin Nodell and writer Bill Finger. His fantastic 'power ring' enables him to fly and to summon up forces which can defeat all villainy. Originally a member of the 'Justice Society of America' (along with such worthies as the Flash and Hawkman), Green Lantern was revamped by DC Comics in 1959 and remained popular for many years.

GREENER, FAYE   See under Tod HACKETT

GREY, AGNES   Unassuming, virtuous heroine of Anne Brontë's novel *Agnes Grey* (1847; published at the same time as her sister Emily's *Wuthering Heights*). Agnes becomes a governess and is treated badly – but is eventually rewarded by marriage to a kindly curate, Edward Weston.

GREYSTOKE, LORD   See TARZAN

GRIFFIN, DOCTOR   See The INVISIBLE MAN

GRIFFITHS, CLYDE   Young man on the make, in Theodore Dreiser's novel *An American Tragedy* (1925). He is from a poor background, and is bedazzled by the wealth and opportunity he sees around him when he goes to work in New York State. But his social ambitions are put at risk when a factory girl threatens to reveal to the world that she is carrying his child. They are involved in a boating accident, and Clyde allows the girl to drown. He is accused of murder, tried, and executed. This bitter story of thwarted ambition has been filmed twice – in 1931 (dir. Josef von Sternberg), with Phillips Holmes in the lead; and in 1951 as *A Place in the Sun* (dir. George Stevens), with Montgomery Clift.

GRIMES, MR   See under TOM

GRIMES, PETER   Poor fisherman, a loner in a small community, who is suspected of murdering his boy apprentices. His story is told in George Crabbe's long poem *The Borough* (1810). He became the subject of Benjamin Britten's opera *Peter Grimes* (1945), which has a libretto by Montague Slater.

GRIMM, BEN   See under Mr FANTASTIC

GRISSOM, SLIM   See under Barbara BLANDISH

GROAN, TITUS   Youthful seventy-seventh Earl of Groan, who inherits Gormenghast Castle and eventually leaves to seek the wider world, in Mervyn Peake's great fantasy trilogy *Titus Groan* (1946), *Gormenghast* (1950) and *Titus Alone* (1959). Titus is still a baby at the end of the first volume, and the action principally concerns the machinations of a villainous underling called STEERPIKE. The trilogy is full of memorably eccentric characters who are depicted in Dickensian fashion. The first two Titus novels have been dramatized on BBC radio (1984), with Julian Firth as Titus Groan.

GROVE FAMILY, THE   Britain's first television soap-opera family. The lower-middle-class Groves appeared in the BBC series 'The Grove Family' (1953–6), which was created by producer John Warrington and scriptwriter Michael Pertwee. The programme was among the first to provide news-material for the popular press. According to Philip Purser, 'Gran Grove, played by Nancy Roberts as a testy old matriarch, became a folk heroine much in demand for opening fetes and new department stores. When a new actress took over the part of pretty daughter Pat it attracted as much attention as a Cabinet change' (*Halliwell's Television Companion*).

GRUNDEIS, HERR   See under Emil TISCHBEIN

GRUNDY, MRS   Character in a now obscure English play, *Speed the Plough* (1798) by Thomas Morton. Mrs Grundy became famous as a symbol of rigid social convention, and her name has entered the language (meaning 'a narrow-minded person who keeps critical watch on the propriety of others', according to one recent dictionary).

GRYCE, EBENEZER   New York policeman whose exploits are celebrated in a series of mystery novels by 'the mother of the detective story', Anna Katherine Green. The titles are: *The Leavenworth Case: a Lawyer's Story* (1878), *A Strange Disappearance* (1880), *Hand and Ring* (1883), *Behind Closed Doors* (1888), *A Matter of Millions* (1890), *The Doctor, His Wife, and the Clock* (1895), *That Affair Next Door* (1897), *Lost Man's Lane* (1898), *The Circular Study* (1900), *One of My Sons* (1901), *Initials Only* (1911) and *The Mystery of the Hasty Arrow* (1917). The first of these novels became exceedingly famous: although he is forgotten today, Ebenezer Gryce was a household name ten years before Sherlock HOLMES.

GUB GUB   See under John DOLITTLE

GULLIVER, LEMUEL   Sailor hero of Jonathan Swift's great satire *Travels Into Several Remote Nations of the World, by Lemuel Gulliver* (1726), familiarly known as *Gulliver's Travels*. Gulliver is a surgeon aboard a merchant ship which is wrecked off the coast of Lilliput, an island where the inhabitants are just six inches tall. In the book's most famous scene Gulliver awakes from his exhausted sleep on the beach to find that he has been tied to the ground by a horde of curious and fearful LILLIPUTIANS. He soon befriends his tiny captors – they call him the 'man mountain' – and aids them in their war against a neighbouring state. In later episodes Gulliver visits Brobdingnag, a land of giants, and Laputa, an island of impractical men of science. He encounters the immortal but unhappy Struldbrugs, and a race of intelligent horses, the Houyhnhnms, who are contrasted to the brutish and all-too-human Yahoos. *Gulliver's Travels* gained instant popularity, and it has been read and disseminated ever since in dozens of variant forms. Swift's friend Alexander Pope wrote several 'Gulliver' poems. Among other things, the book has become a classic of children's literature: suitably bowdlerized and abridged, Gulliver's Lilliputian and Brobdingnagian adventures have been presented to the young in countless editions. The book

Lemuel Gulliver with the Lilliputians

has also been used as a model for later satires and tall tales intended
for adults, including some science fiction. Modern sequels by
other hands include two novellas by the Hungarian writer Frigyes
Karinthy, *Voyage to Faremido* (1917) and *Capillaria* (1921). In the
first of these Gulliver visits a land of machines where organic
life is regarded as an abomination; in the second he finds himself
in a country where women rule and men are eaten. Another latter-
day sequel is the BBC radio play *Gulliver Five* (1986) by Brian Wright.

   Films about Gulliver include the animated feature *Gulliver's
Travels* (1939; dir. Dave Fleischer); the live-action *The Three
Worlds of Gulliver* (1960; dir. Jack Sher), starring Kerwin
Mathews; the Japanese cartoon *Gulliver's Travels Beyond the Moon*
(1966; dir. Yoshio Kuroda); and the live-action *Gulliver's Travels*
(1977; dir. Peter Hunt), with Richard Harris as the hero. There have
been many television adaptations, including a Hanna-Barbera
cartoon series, 'The Adventures of Gulliver' (1980), and a BBC serial,
'Gulliver in Lilliput' (1982), which had Andrew Burt in the leading
role. Frank Finlay has played Gulliver on BBC radio (1981).

GUMMIDGE, WORZEL   Scarecrow who stands in the Ten-acre Field
at Scatterbrook Farm. He comes to life, much to the astonishment
of the children Susan and John. Worzel – who speaks with a ripe
country accent, carries an old umbrella and has birds nesting
in his pockets – becomes involved in many comical adventures.
They are recounted in Barbara Euphan Todd's books *Worzel
Gummidge, or The Scarecrow of Scatterbrook Farm* (1936),
Worzel Gummidge Again (1937), *More About Worzel
Gummidge* (1938), *Worzel Gummidge and Saucy Nancy* (1947),
Worzel Gummidge Takes a Holiday (1949), *Earthy Mangold and
Worzel Gummidge* (1954), *Worzel Gummidge and the Railway
Scarecrows* (1955), *Worzel Gummidge at the Circus* (1956), *Worzel
Gummidge and the Treasure Ship* (1958) and *Detective Worzel
Gummidge* (1963). Worzel's adventures became popular on BBC
radio's 'Children's Hour', and, decades later, they were also
adapted to television by Keith Waterhouse and Willis Hall. The
TV series, 'Worzel Gummidge' (1978–81), starred Jon Pertwee,
and its success led to a new series of books by Waterhouse and Hall.
In the early 1980s the leader of the British Labour Party, Michael
Foot, was nicknamed 'Worzel Gummidge' because of his dishevelled
appearance.

GUMP, ANDY   Comic-strip *pater familias* created by American cartoonist Sidney Smith for his newspaper strip *The Gumps* (from 1917). Andy, with his wife Min and son Chester, enjoyed immense popularity throughout the 1920s and 1930s. They became as well-known as any soap-opera characters, and soon made the transition to low-budget films. The hero's 'autobiography' (written by Smith) was entitled *Andy Gump: His Life Story* (1924). Sidney Smith died in a car crash in 1935, but his strip was perpetuated by Gus Edson until 1959.

GUNGA DIN   Loyal Indian water-carrier in Rudyard Kipling's poem 'Gunga Din' (in *Barrack-Room Ballads*, 1892). He is killed while tending a wounded English soldier. 'Of all them blackfaced crew/The finest man I knew/Was our regimental bhisti, Gunga Din/ . . . You're a better man than I am, Gunga Din!' says the grateful soldier after the Indian has sacrificed his life. In the rousing adventure film *Gunga Din* (1939; dir. George Stevens), which is very loosely based on Kipling's piece, Gunga Din was played by Sam Jaffe. The later film *Soldiers Three* (1951; dir. Tay Garnett) reworks the same material, but Gunga Din does not appear. Yet another movie variation is the comic Western *Sergeants Three* (1961; dir. John Sturges), which had Sammy Davis, Jr in a Gunga Din-like role.

GUNN, BEN   Marooned English sailor who appears as a comparatively minor character in Robert Louis Stevenson's classic adventure tale *Treasure Island* (1883). A demented Robinson CRUSOE, whose main characteristic is his craving for the taste of cheese, Ben Gunn has fascinated later writers. A modern sequel by another hand is *The Adventures of Ben Gunn* (1956) by R. F. Delderfield (see Long John SILVER for mention of other sequels). There has also been a British television series of the same title. In the later TV series entitled 'John Silver's Return to Treasure Island' (1986) Ben Gunn was played by Ken Colley.

GUNN, PETER   Private-eye played by Craig Stevens in the American television series 'Peter Gunn' (1958–61). This semi-humorous series was created by writer/director Blake Edwards. Gunn has been described as 'a Brooks Brothers hero, rich enough not to care who is paying him, and well enough connected to take no stick from the law' (Wicking and Vahimagi in *The American Vein*). Craig Stevens also played the character in a feature film, *Gunn* (1967; dir. Edwards).

GUTHRIE, CHRIS   Heroine of a trilogy of novels, known collectively as *A Scots Quair*, by Lewis Grassic Gibbon (J. Leslie Mitchell). The three titles are *Sunset Song* (1932), *Cloud Howe* (1934) and *Grey Granite* (1935). Chris Guthrie grows up in the east of Scotland, marries three times (one of her husbands is a minister of the church), and becomes involved with the working-class struggle. The BBC television serials of *Sunset Song* (1971), *Cloud Howe* (1982) and *Grey Granite* (1983) all starred Vivien Heilbron as Chris.

H

HACKER, JIM   English politician played by Paul Eddington in the BBC television comedy series 'Yes, Minister' (1980–5) and 'Yes, Prime Minister' (1986). The civil servant who acts as his private secretary is the urbane Sir Humphrey Appleby (Nigel Hawthorne). The two series were scripted by Antony Jay and Jonathan Lynn, and proved very popular – especially with politicians.

HACKETT, TOD   Young painter who is invited to work in Hollywood, where he falls for an attractive starlet called Faye Greener. His blackly humorous story is told in Nathanael West's novel *The Day of the Locust* (1939). In the film of the book (1975; dir. John Schlesinger) Hackett was played by William Atherton.

HAGAR THE HORRIBLE   Comic-strip Viking created by American cartoonist Dik Browne (from 1973). Despite his name, Hagar is a softy, henpecked by his fearsome wife Helga. Browne's strip has been syndicated around the world, and has proved very popular in paperback reprints.

HAJJI BABA   Persian picaroon in James Morier's novels *The Adventures of Hajji Baba of Ispahan* (1824) and *Hajji Baba in England* (1828). Morier served as a British diplomat in Persia, and his rumbustious tales of life in the Middle East were based on his own observations. The books were very popular in their day. A film, *The Adventures of Hajji Baba* (1954; dir. Don Weis), is vaguely inspired by Morier's novels (it probably owes more to *The Arabian Nights*). John Derek played the hero.

HAL 9000   The only computer to achieve the status of a famous fictional character (so far, at any rate). HAL is an artificial intelligence aboard the spacecraft *Discovery*, sent with a three-man crew to locate the origin of an alien monolith found on the Moon. HAL malfunctions, plans to take total control of the

mission, and murders two of the crew members by devious means.
The remaining human, David Bowman, dismantles the
computer's memory, effectively 'killing' HAL. The scene in
which HAL regresses to babbling mental infancy, singing 'Daisy,
Daisy . . .', is oddly poignant. All this is recounted in Arthur C.
Clarke's novel *2001: A Space Odyssey* (1968) and the spectacular
film which was released simultaneously with it (co-scripted,
produced and directed by Stanley Kubrick). Years later Clarke
wrote a sequel, *2010: Odyssey Two* (1982), in which HAL is
reactivated by the crew of another space vessel who are trying to
unravel the mystery of what happened to the *Discovery*. This
in turn was filmed by Peter Hyams (1984).

HALIFAX, JOHN   Hard-working, low-born hero of Mrs Dinah
Craik's novel *John Halifax, Gentleman* (1856). He is apprenticed
to a tanner, and works his way to prosperity and a happy marriage.
It is his moral worth which earns him the title 'Gentleman'. The
novel was extremely successful in Britain and America.

HALLER, HARRY   Man who imagines himself a wolf of the Steppes,
in Hermann Hesse's novel *Steppenwolf* (1927). In fact he is a
sensitive German intellectual who feels thoroughly alienated
from the materialistic modern world. Hesse's novel was surprisingly
popular with the American young during the late 1960s and early
1970s. Like YOSSARIAN and Paul ATREIDES, Harry Haller became
a campus hero. One could call him the thinking man's Lawrence
Talbot (see the WOLF MAN). (The hero of Mayne Reid's
adventure novel *The Rifle Rangers* [1850] is called Captain Henry
Haller.)

HAMBLEDON, TOMMY   Rugged British Intelligence agent whose
international exploits are the subject of a series of thrillers by
Manning Coles (Cyril Henry Coles and Adelaide Frances
Manning). In his earlier adventures Tommy is a great basher of
Nazis. The novels in which he appears are: *Drink to Yesterday*
(1940), *Pray Silence* (1940; vt *A Toast for Tomorrow*), *They Tell
No Tales* (1941), *Without Lawful Authority* (1943), *Green Hazard*
(1945), *The Fifth Man* (1946), *Let the Tiger Die* (1947), *A Brother
for Hugh* (1947; vt *With Intent to Deceive*), *Among Those Absent*
(1948), *Diamonds to Amsterdam* (1949), *Not Negotiable* (1949),

Dangerous by Nature (1950), *Now or Never* (1951), *Alias Uncle Hugo* (1952; vt *Operation Manhunt*), *Night Train to Paris* (1952), *A Knife for the Juggler* (1953; vt *The Vengeance Man*), *Not for Export* (1954; vt *All That Glitters*), *The Man in the Green Hat* (1955), *Basle Express* (1956), *Birdwatcher's Quarry* (1956; vt *The Three Beans*), *Death of an Ambassador* (1957), *No Entry* (1958), *Crime in Concrete* (1960), *Search for a Sultan* (1961) and *The House at Pluck's Gutter* (1963). Tommy Hambledon also features in one collection of short stories, *Nothing to Declare* (1960).

HAMMER, MIKE   Tough, amoral private eye in a series of violent thrillers by Mickey Spillane, beginning with *I, the Jury* (1947). Hammer bulldozes his way through various criminal cases, never hesitating to use violent means. He is brutal towards women, and he has a particular hatred for communists. Spillane's later books about this none too endearing character are *Vengeance is Mine!* (1950), *My Gun is Quick* (1950), *The Big Kill* (1951), *One Lonely Night* (1951), *Kiss Me, Deadly* (1952), *The Girl Hunters* (1962), *The Snake* (1964), *The Twisted Thing* (1966), *The Body Lovers* (1967) and *Survival . . . Zero!* (1970). In the movies Hammer has been played by Biff Elliot in *I, the Jury* (1953; dir. Harry Essex); by Ralph Meeker in *Kiss Me Deadly* (1955; dir. Robert Aldrich); by Robert Bray in *My Gun is Quick* (1957; dir. Phil Victor); by Mickey Spillane (the author!) in *The Girl Hunters* (1963; dir. Roy Rowland); and by Armand Assante in a remake of *I, the Jury* (1982; dir. Richard T. Heffron). The American television series 'Mickey Spillane's Mike Hammer' (1957–9) starred Darren McGavin; and a later series (from 1983) had Stacy Keach. The TV movie *Mickey Spillane's Margin for Murder* (1981; dir. Daniel Haller) starred Kevin Dobson as the macho hero.

HANAUD, INSPECTOR   French policeman who features in crime novels by the English writer A. E. W. Mason, beginning with *At the Villa Rose* (1910). According to Melvyn Barnes, Hanaud is 'one of the indisputably great fictional detectives'. After a gap of fourteen years, Mason revived Inspector Hanaud for *The House of the Arrow* (1924) and three more books: *The Prisoner in the Opal* (1928), *They Wouldn't be Chessmen* (1935) and *The House in Lordship Lane* (1946). Mason also wrote stage adaptations of his own novels *At the Villa Rose* (1920) and *The House of the Arrow* (1928). The first Hanaud book, *At the Villa Rose*, has been filmed at least three times – in 1920, with Teddy Arundell as the Inspector; in 1930, with Austin Trevor; and in 1939, with Keneth Kent. The second novel, *The House of the Arrow*, has been filmed twice – in 1930 (dir. Leslie Hiscott), with Dennis Neilson Terry; and in 1940 (dir. Harold French), with Keneth Kent. A BBC radio adaptation of *The House of the Arrow* (1984) had Richard Pasco as Hanaud.

HANBURY, GEORGE   See under Richard William Chandos

HANNAY, RICHARD   Adventure-seeking hero of John Buchan's novel *The Thirty-Nine Steps* (1915) and its sequels. A stalwart upholder of the British Empire, Hannay has made his fortune in

Richard Hannay (Robert Donat) in the 1935 version of *The Thirty-Nine Steps*

South Africa. At one point he expresses the opinion: 'Perhaps the Scots are better than the English, but we're all a thousand per cent better than anybody else.' He feels a continuing need to test his own courage, and World War I gives him plenty of opportunities. In the affair of the '39 steps' he becomes embroiled with a spy ring and is pursued across the hills of Scotland. His further adventures are recounted by Buchan in *Greenmantle* (1916 – this is the novel in which he meets Sandy ARBUTHNOT), *Mr Standfast* (1919), *The Three Hostages* (1924), *The Runagates Club* (1928 – short stories, not all of which feature Hannay) and *The Island of Sheep* (1936). By the time of this last novel he has become *Sir* Richard Hannay. Jack Smithers's *Combined Forces* (1985) is a pastiche novel in which Hannay and other Buchan characters appear alongside Bulldog DRUMMOND and Jonah MANSEL. Of Buchan's five books about Richard Hannay, only *The Thirty-Nine Steps* has been made into a feature film – three times: in 1935 (dir. Alfred Hitchcock), with Robert Donat; in 1959 (dir. Ralph Thomas), with Kenneth More; and in 1978 (dir. Don Sharp), with Robert Powell. *The Three Hostages* has been made into a BBC TV movie (1977; dir. Clive Donner), with Barry Foster as Hannay.

HANS AND FRITZ   See Hans and Fritz KATZENJAMMER

HARDIN, OLE DEVIL   See under EDGE

HARDING, SEPTIMUS   Good-natured old clergyman in Anthony Trollope's novel *The Warden* (1855). He is Warden of the almshouse known as Hiram's Hospital, home for twelve elderly men, but his position is challenged by an ambitious young doctor who thinks that the funds should be put to better use. The Reverend Harding also appears in subsequent novels of Trollope's 'Barsetshire' sequence (see the entry on Mrs PROUDIE for further details). In the BBC television serial 'The Barchester Chronicles' (1982) Harding was played by Donald Pleasence. In a BBC radio dramatization of *The Warden* (also 1982) he was played by Timothy Bateson.

HARDY, ANDY   Energetic young man played by Mickey Rooney in a series of fifteen Hollywood films, beginning with *A Family Affair*

(1937; dir. George B. Seitz). The Hardys are a typical mid-American family, and in 1942 this sentimental series was awarded a special Oscar for 'furthering the American way of life'. Other movies in the series include *You're Only Young Once* (1938; dir. Seitz), *Love Finds Andy Hardy* (1938; dir. Seitz), *Love Laughs at Andy Hardy* (1946; dir. Willis Goldbeck) and – after a twelve-year hiatus – *Andy Hardy Comes Home* (1958; dir. Howard W. Koch).

HARDY, FRANK AND JOE   The Hardy Boys, America's best-known juvenile detectives. They are the teenage sons of a former police officer turned private detective, and their father has trained them fron infancy to be super-sleuths. Conceived by publisher Edward Stratemeyer (of the 'Stratemeyer syndicate' – see also Nancy DREW), the stories of the Hardy Boys have been written by numerous authors, all using the house name Franklin W. Dixon. The first of these writers was Leslie McFarlane, and early titles in the long-lived series include *The Tower Treasure, House on the Cliff* and *Secret of the Old Mill* (all 1927). Novels about the Hardy Boys have continued to be published under the Dixon byline in the 1970s and 1980s. An American television series, 'The Hardy Boys and Nancy Drew Mysteries' (1977–9), had Parker Stevenson as Frank and Shaun Cassidy as Joe.

HARKAWAY, JACK   Celebrated hero of Victorian boys' fiction ('penny dreadfuls'). Harkaway was invented by S. Bracebridge Hemyng, whose stories first appeared in the magazine *Boys of England* (from 1871). For some thirty years new adventures of Jack Harkaway, and his indistinguishable son and grandson, were published in a variety of magazines and part-works. Initially a schoolboy (his first adventure was entitled *Jack Harkaway's Schooldays*), he later became a world-rover and the star of such exploits as *Jack Harkaway in Search of the Mountain of Gold* and *Jack Harkaway Out West Among the Indians*. In the 1890s he graduated to his own periodical, *Jack Harkaway's Journal for Boys*.

HARKER, KAY   Young hero of John Masefield's novels of the supernatural, *The Midnight Folk* (1927) and *The Box of Delights* (1935). In the first of these Kay goes treasure-hunting at night, with the assistance of some supernaturally-endowed animal friends.

In the second tale he is given a magic box which enables him to shrink in size, travel in time and conjure up people from the past. Other members of the Harker family had already appeared in Masefield's adult adventure novels *Sard Harker* (1924) and *Odtaa* (1926). In the expensively-produced BBC television serial, 'The Box of Delights' (1984), Kay was played by Devin Stanfield.

HARKER, MINA   See under Count DRACULA

HARLETH, GWENDOLEN   English heroine of the novel *Daniel Deronda* (1876) by George Eliot (Mary Ann Evans). She is unhappily married to the rich Henleigh Grandcourt, and later falls in love with the young idealist Daniel Deronda. Harcourt is drowned, but Gwendolen loses Daniel to another woman and to the cause of Jewish nationalism. An anonymous sequel by another hand is entitled *Gwendolen*. In his book *The Great Tradition*, F. R. Leavis has pointed to the strong similarity between Gwendolen Harleth and Henry James's Isabel ARCHER.

HARLOWE, CLARISSA   Virtuous, long-suffering heroine of Samuel Richardson's immense novel *Clarissa, or The History of a Young Lady* (1748–9), a book which set all Europe a-weeping. Clarissa is a middle-class girl of great beauty who is pursued by the aristocratic rake Robert LOVELACE. She resists him constantly; and after he abducts her and rapes her, she refuses his desperate proposal of marriage, falls ill, and dies. *Clarissa* was probably the most popular and influential of all eighteenth-century novels (*Robinson Crusoe* excepted). Kingsley Amis's *Take a Girl Like You* (1960) is a comic recension of the story in a modern setting (Amis's heroine is called Jenny Bunn). The Marxist literary critic Terry Eagleton has written a book entitled *The Rape of Clarissa* (1982); he argues that Richardson's novel is 'the major feminist text of the language . . . It deeply offends the fashionable liberal assumption that virtue is boring, the banality that the devil has all the best tunes.'

HARMON, JOHN   See under Mr and Mrs VENEERING

HAROLD, CHILDE   Wandering, rebellious *persona* of the poet, in Lord Byron's *Childe Harold's Pilgrimage* (1812–18). This long narrative poem was first published in four parts, and it achieved great popularity. The work is essentially a travelogue, with meditations on European history, but readers were particularly attracted by the darkly brooding Harold – the first of a long line of 'Byronic' heroes (for later examples see CONRAD and MANFRED).

HARRIS, ADA   Better known as Mrs 'Arris, a Cockney charlady who travels the world and experiences fairy-tale adventures. She appears in a series of comic novels by Paul Gallico: *Flowers for Mrs Harris* (1958; vt *Mrs 'Arris Goes to Paris*), *Mrs Harris Goes to New York* (1960), *Mrs Harris, M.P.* (1965; vt *Mrs 'Arris Goes to Parliament*) and *Mrs Harris Goes to Moscow* (1974). (Dickens's Sarah GAMP has an imaginary friend called Mrs Harris, whose opinions she quotes at tedious length.)

HART, JONATHAN AND JENNIFER   Rich, glamorous sleuths played by Robert Wagner and Stefanie Powers in the American television movie *Hart to Hart* (1978; dir. Don M. Mankiewicz) and the subsequent series which ran until 1984. The Harts bear more than a passing resemblance to Nick and Nora CHARLES; they also have a certain amount in common with an earlier TV duo, Stewart and Sally McMillan (who appeared in the series 'McMillan and Wife', 1971–7).

HARTMAN, MARY   Soap-opera heroine, a denizen of the crazy town of Fernwood, played by Louise Lasser in the American television series 'Mary Hartman, Mary Hartman' (1976–7). The spoofing tone of this series, which was produced by Norman Lear, endeared Mary Hartman to New York intellectuals – for a brief spell. After Louise Lasser left, the show was retitled 'Forever Fernwood'. (For a slightly later character of similar type see Jessica TATE.)

HARVEY   Invisible six-foot rabbit who befriends the drunken Elwood P. Dowd in Mary C. Chase's amusing play *Harvey* (1944), which won a Pulitzer Prize and ran for years on the New York stage. Dowd claims that Harvey is a 'phouka' (a shape-changing Irish fairy). In the film of the play (1950; dir. Henry Koster) James Stewart starred as Dowd; Harvey was never seen. The imaginary rabbit's name has entered American parlance: in the 1980s the military programme to develop a 'stealth' aircraft was nicknamed 'Project Harvey'.

HARVEY, ALEC   See under Laura JESSON

HAVISHAM, MISS   Eccentric old lady, 'immensely rich and grim', in Charles Dickens's novel *Great Expectations* (1860–61). She lives in a cobwebbed room with permanently shuttered windows, and she has worn her wedding gown and veil since the day she was jilted. Miss Havisham is the guardian of ESTELLA, the girl who is loved by Philip PIRRIP. According to Angus Calder in his introduction to the Penguin edition of the novel (1965), 'Miss Havisham . . . is one of the many Dickens creatures – Pickwick, Quilp, Fagin, Little Nell, Pecksniff – who are as much part of the permanent furniture of the private and public rooms of the Western mind as Ulysses and Sinbad.' In films and on television she has been played by Florence Reed (1934), Martita Hunt (1946) and Margaret Leighton (1975), among others.

HAWK   See under EDGE

HAWKE, DIXON   English detective, a popular competitor with Sexton BLAKE and Nelson LEE in the period between the two world wars. His boy assistant is called Tommy Burke. Dixon Hawke and Tommy first appeared in the boys' paper *Adventure*, published by D. C. Thomson from the early 1920s. Their exploits were chronicled by many authors, among them the remarkable Edwy Searles Brooks (who was also responsible for numerous Sexton Blake and Nelson Lee sagas).

HAWKE, JEFF   Spaceman hero of a strip cartoon which appeared in the *Daily Express* (1954–74). Hawke was a British equivalent of Buck ROGERS or Flash GORDON, involved in much derring-do on the space frontier. The strip was drawn by Sidney Jordan and written by Eric Souster. It was reprinted in book form during the 1980s.

HAWKE, STRINGFELLOW   Pilot of an extremely lethal military helicopter, in which he performs clandestine operations for an American intelligence agency. He was played by Jan-Michael Vincent in the television series 'Airwolf' (from 1984). Hawke, who plays the cello for relaxation, has a grizzled sidekick called Dominic Santini (played by Ernest Borgnine). The series was created by producer Donald P. Bellisario. Children of the 1980s will remember characters like Stringfellow Hawke, Michael KNIGHT and B.A. BARACUS in the same way that those who were young during the 1950s and 1960s have fond memories of Cheyenne BODIE, Marshal Matt DILLON, Bret MAVERICK, and a horde of lesser cowboys. The major difference between today's TV heroes and those of a generation ago is that the current crop seem to be heavily reliant on the most elaborate technological back-up: a six-gun is no longer sufficient.

HAWKEYE   See (1) Natty BUMPPO; (2) Hawkeye PIERCE

HAWKINS, JIM   Youthful narrator of Robert Louis Stevenson's novel *Treasure Island* (1883). He goes to sea aboard the *Hispaniola*, in search of the island where Captain Flint's fabled treasure lies buried. He is befriended by the villainous Long John SILVER, although the marooned sailor Ben GUNN turns out to be a more loyal ally. There have been many film and television adaptations of Jim's adventures. In *Treasure Island* (1934; dir. Victor Fleming) he was played by Jackie Cooper; in the remakes of 1950 (dir. Byron Haskin) and 1971 (dir. John Hough) he was played by Bobby Driscoll and Kim Burfield. A Russian film version (1973; dir. Valeri Bazylev) starred a young actor called Aare Laanemets. The BBC television serialization of the novel (1978) had Ashley Knight as Jim, and the more recent independent TV production called 'John Silver's Return to Treasure Island' (1986) had Christopher Guard. The latter is a sequel to Stevenson's classic yarn, written by John Goldsmith. There have been previous sequels by other hands in book form (see the entries for SILVER and GUNN).

HAWKMOON, DORIAN   See under ELRIC OF MELNIBONÉ and EREKOSË

HAWKS, MAGNOLIA   Actress daughter of Captain Andy Hawks, and wife of the handsome leading man, Gaylord Ravenal, in Edna Ferber's novel *Show Boat* (1926). This story of a Mississippi steamer and its travelling troupe of players was turned into a celebrated stage musical (1927), with music by Jerome Kern and lyrics by Oscar Hammerstein. Film versions were made in 1929; 1936 (dir. James Whale), with Irene Dunne; and in 1951 (dir. George Sidney), with Kathryn Grayson.

HAWKSHAW   Detective who appeared in a nineteenth-century British play, *The Ticket-of-Leave Man* (1863) by Tom Taylor. The character's name became a generic term for a private detective, especially in the United States (for example, Robert Leslie Bellem's hero, Dan TURNER, was billed as 'Hollywood's hottest hawkshaw'). A newspaper comic-strip, *Hawkshaw the Detective* by American cartoonist Gus Mager, ran sporadically from 1913 to the 1940s.

HAWTHORN, JERRY   See TOM AND JERRY

HAZE, DOLORES   See LOLITA

HAZEL   (1) Bossy American housemaid who appeared in *Saturday Evening Post* cartoons by Ted Key. These ran from 1943 until the magazine's demise in 1969, since when they have appeared in various newspapers. The Hazel cartoon panels have been reprinted in paperback under such titles as *Hazel*, *Here's Hazel* and *Hazel Rides Again*. The television series 'Hazel' (1961–6) starred Shirley Booth.
　　(2) Courageous, level-headed rabbit, the hero of Richard Adams's bestselling children's novel *Watership Down* (1972) – a book which soon became the object of a cult among adults. Hazel and his second-sighted brother Fiver lead a small band of rabbits from their doomed warren and go in search of a new home. It is an epic tale, compellingly told. In the animated feature film, *Watership Down* (1978; dir. Martin Rosen), Hazel's voice was provided by John Hurt.

HAZELL, JAMES   Cockney private-eye, an East End avatar of Philip MARLOWE, who has low-life adventures in a series of crime novels by P. B. Yuill (a collaborative pseudonym for the Scottish novelist Gordon Williams and the ex-footballer Terry Venables): *Hazell Plays Solomon* (1974), *Hazell and the Three-Card Trick* (1975) and *Hazell and the Menacing Jester* (1976). He also appeared in a British television series, 'Hazell' (1977–8), where he was played by Nicholas Ball.

HEADROOM, MAX   Pop video presenter played by Matt Frewer in Channel Four Television's 'The Max Headroom Show' (from 1985).

A computer-generated image, he has 'a permanent suntan, improbably white teeth, the squarest of jawbones, a high forehead and the bluest of eyes'. He also stutters. A picture book about the character is entitled *Max Headroom: 20 Minutes Into the Future* (1985).

HEATHCLIFF Brooding hero of Emily Brontë's novel *Wuthering Heights* (1847). He is a 'gypsy' foundling who is adopted by a Yorkshire family. As they grow up together in the remote moorland house known as Wuthering Heights, Heathcliff and Catherine EARNSHAW fall passionately in love. Believing that he has been rebuffed by Catherine, he runs away – and returns three years later after making his fortune. To his rage and sorrow, he discovers that Catherine has married another man. Heathcliff becomes the master of Wuthering Heights, and after Catherine's death in childbirth he lives on for many years, permanently embittered. A modern sequel by another hand is *Heathcliff* (1977) by Jeffrey Caine. In the memorable Hollywood film *Wuthering Heights* (1939; dir. William Wyler) Heathcliff was played by Laurence Olivier. In a British remake (1970; dir. Robert Fuest) he was portrayed by Timothy Dalton. There have been several television serials based on the story, including one made by the BBC (1978) which had Ken Hutchinson as Heathcliff.

HEBBLETHWAITE, GINGER See under BIGGLES

HEEP, URIAH Repulsive, toadying villain, a creature of feigning ''umbleness', in Charles Dickens's novel *David Copperfield* (1850). He blackmails his virtuous employer, Mr Wickfield, but luckily the trusty Wilkins MICAWBER finds him out. In films and on television Uriah Heep has been played by Roland Young (1935), Ron Moody (1970), Martin Jarvis (1975) and Paul Brightwell (1986) among others. (See also David COPPERFIELD.)

HEIDI Little orphan heroine of Johanna Spyri's popular novel *Heidi* (1881). At the age of five she is sent to live in her grandfather's mountain hut, where she melts the stubborn old man's heart. Removed from there by her severe Aunt Dete, Heidi goes to live in Frankfurt. She pines for the mountains and her grandfather, and eventually she is allowed to return. Two English-language sequels by another hand are *Heidi Grows Up* (1938) and *Heidi's Children* (1950) by Charles Tritten. There have been several film adaptations of the original Heidi story. Talkie versions, all entitled *Heidi*, were made in 1937 (dir. Allan Dwan), with Shirley Temple; in 1952 (dir. Luigi Comencini), with Elsbeth Sigmund; in 1965 (dir. Werner Jacobs), with Eva Marie Singhammer; and in 1968 as a TV movie (dir. Delbert Mann), with Jennifer Edwards (Julie Andrews's daughter). The film *Heidi and Peter* (1955; dir. Franz Schnyder), starring Elsbeth Sigmund, is a sequel to the original story, as is *A Gift for Heidi* (1958; dir. George Templeton), with Sandy Descher. There have been many television adaptations, including the TV movie *The New Adventures of Heidi* (1979; dir. Ralph Senensky), which had Katy Kurtzman in the role.

HELM, MATT   Known as 'the American James Bond' – the smooth, tough hero of espionage thrillers by Donald Hamilton: *Death of a Citizen* (1960), *The Wrecking Crew* (1960), *The Removers* (1961), *Murderer's Row* (1962), *The Silencers* (1962), *The Ambushers* (1963), *The Ravagers* (1964), *The Shadowers* (1964), *The Devastators* (1965), *The Betrayers* (1966), *The Menacers* (1968), *The Interlopers* (1969), *The Poisoners* (1971), *The Intriguers* (1973), *The Intimidators* (1974), *The Terminators* (1975), *The Retaliators* (1976), *The Terrorizers* (1977), *The Revengers* (1982) and *The Annihilators* (1983). In the films *The Silencers* (1966; dir. Phil Karlson), *Murderer's Row* (1966; dir. Henry Levin), *The Ambushers* (1967; dir. Levin) and *The Wrecking Crew* (1968; dir. Karlson) Helm was played (for laughs) by Dean Martin. A subsequent television series, 'Matt Helm' (1975–6), starred Tony Franciosa.

HELMER, NORA   Self-deceiving heroine of Henrik Ibsen's play *A Doll's House* (1879). After eight years of marriage she comes to realize that her husband has never taken her seriously as an adult human being, so she leaves him (the famous stage direction 'noise of a door slamming' concludes the action). A sequel by another hand is *Nora's Return* by Mrs E. D. Cheney. Ibsen's play has been filmed a number of times. A silent Russian version was entitled *Her Sacrifice* (1917). More recently, two film versions were released in the same year, 1973 – one with Claire Bloom as Nora (dir. Patrick Garland), and one with Jane Fonda (dir. Joseph Losey).

HENCHARD, MICHAEL   Drunken farmhand who sells his wife and baby daughter to a passing stranger, in Thomas Hardy's novel *The Mayor of Casterbridge* (1886). He suffers guilt, swears never to drink again, and grows prosperous. By the time his wife and child return, eighteen years later, he has risen to be Mayor of Casterbridge. He is publicly disgraced and takes to drink once more. The novel has been dramatized by Dennis Potter for BBC television (1978), with Alan Bates as the unfortunate Henchard.

HENDERSON, MIRIAM   Central character of Dorothy Richardson's twelve-volume *roman fleuve* which is known collectively as *Pilgrimage* (1915–38). At one time famous for its stream-of-consciousness technique, this massive work has been described by Angus Wilson as being about 'the material and spiritual struggles of a young, very gifted, but at the same time utterly underprivileged woman in a world made by men for men' (quoted in *The Oxford Companion to English Literature*). The first novel in the sequence is entitled *Pointed Roofs* (1915) and the last *Dimple Hill* (1938). A pendant volume, *March Moonlight*, was published posthumously in 1967.

HENRY, FREDERIC   Suffering hero of Ernest Hemingway's novel *A Farewell to Arms* (1929). An American army lieutenant in Italy during World War I, he is wounded and subsequently falls in love with his English nurse, Catherine Barkley (who dies in childbirth). Lieutenant Henry was played by Gary Cooper in the first film version of the novel (1932; dir. Frank Borzage), and by Rock Hudson in the remake (1957; dir. Charles Vidor).

HENRY, JOHN   Black American folk hero, possibly based on a real person. Henry is an enormously strong railroad worker of the late nineteenth century. He appears in oral tales and ballads, many of which were collected in the book *John Henry: Tracking Down a Negro Legend* (1931) by Guy B. Johnson. Roark Bradford's novel *John Henry* (1931) has been adapted for the stage.

HERNE THE HUNTER   See under EDGE

HERRIES, FRANCIS   Hero of Hugh Walpole's novel about eighteenth-century Cumberland, *Rogue Herries* (1930). The immediate sequels, *Judith Paris* (1931) and *The Fortress* (1932) tell the story of 'Rogue' Herries's daughter, Judith. Other novels about more distant members of the Herries family are *Vanessa* (1933) and *Bright Pavilions* (1940).

HERZOG, MOSES   Despairing, world-weary protagonist of Saul Bellow's novel *Herzog* (1964). In an effort to make sense of the modern scene (and his own predicament) he writes letters to the quick and the dead, but never posts them. Herzog is named after a minor character in James Joyce's *Ulysses* (1922; see Leopold BLOOM).

HEWITT, MARTIN   One of 'the rivals of Sherlock HOLMES' – a detective invented by Arthur Morrison for various series of short stories which appeared in the *Strand Magazine* and the *Windsor Magazine*. The tales are collected in the books *Martin Hewitt, Investigator* (1894), *Chronicles of Martin Hewitt* (1895), *Adventures of Martin Hewitt* (1896), and *The Red Triangle, Being Some Further Chronicles of Martin Hewitt, Investigator* (1903).

HEXAM, LIZZY   See under Mr and Mrs VENEERING

HIAWATHA   Red Indian hero of Henry Wadsworth Longfellow's narrative poem *The Song of Hiawatha* (1855). Hiawatha is the son of the West Wind; he marries the beautiful Minnehaha before leaving for the Isles of the Blest. The poem is based on genuine Amerindian legends, but Longfellow 'fictionalized' these considerably, borrowing the name Hiawatha from a sixteenth-century Iroquois chief. The hero's exploits have been retold many times, for example in the prose *Stories from 'Hiawatha'* (1910) by Alice M. Chesterton. The movie *Hiawatha* (1952; dir. Kurt Neumann) had Vincent Edwards as the brave. A National Theatre stage version, directed by Michael Bogdanov and starring Frederick Warder, was shown on British television in 1984.

HIGGINS, HENRY   See under Eliza DOLITTLE

HILL, FANNY   Heroine of the most famous English pornographic novel of the eighteenth century, John Cleland's *Memoirs of a Woman of Pleasure* (1748–9; vt *Fanny Hill*). Fanny narrates her story in the epistolary form made fashionable by the novels of

Hiawatha and Minnehaha

Richardson; in contrast to the latter's work, however, this tale of
a fallen woman contains a good deal of explicit sexual detail.
Long suppressed, Cleland's novel was 'rediscovered' and made

freely available in the 1960s. It was turned into a poor film, *Fanny Hill* (1965; dir. Russ Meyer), and it has inspired at least one modern sequel by another hand: Erica Jong's *Fanny, Being the True History of the Adventures of Fanny Hackabout-Jones* (1980). This is the Fanny Hill story reimagined by a modern American feminist writing in mock eighteenth-century style.

HILL, HAROLD   Also known as 'Professor' Hill, a conman who starts a boys' band in a small American town. He is the hero of Meredith Willson's hit stage musical of the 1950s, *The Music Man*. The show was filmed, under the same title (1962; dir. Morton da Costa), with Robert Preston (who had also played the role on stage – 886 times).

HINGE AND BRACKETT   Full names Dr Evadne Hinge and Dame Hilda Brackett, a concert singer and piano accompanist. These middle-aged English gentlewomen are the *personae* of comedians George Logan and Patrick Fyffe. They originally gained fame as a revue act, and have reappeared in the BBC television series 'Dear Ladies' (1983–4) and elsewhere.

HOBSON, HENRY HORATIO   Lancashire bootmaker, a domestic tyrant who comes into conflict with his eldest daughter, Maggie, in Harold Brighouse's popular play of 'the Manchester School', *Hobson's Choice* (1916). A film version (1931; dir. Thomas Bentley) starred James Harcourt. In the later film of the play (1953; dir. David Lean) the fearsome Henry Hobson was played by Charles Laughton. The story has also been Americanized for a TV movie of the same title (1983; dir. Gilbert Cates), with Jack Warden.

HOLLIDAY, HIRAM   Meek, bespectacled journalist, a Clark Kent (see SUPERMAN) without an alter ego who nevertheless has remarkable hidden talents. Hiram was created by Paul Gallico for his books *The Adventures of Hiram Holliday* (1939) and *The Secret Front* (1940). In the American television series 'The Adventures of Hiram Holliday' (1956–7) he was played by Wally Cox.

HOLLY, LUDWIG HORACE   Learned narrator of the novels *She* (1887) and *Ayesha* (1905) by H. Rider Haggard. He accompanies

young Leo Vincey to the lost African city of Kôr, where they both
fall in love with Ayesha, the near-immortal white queen known as
SHE-WHO-MUST-BE-OBEYED. In film versions of *She* Holly has
been played by Nigel Bruce (1935) and Peter Cushing (1965).

HOLMES, MYCROFT   Mysterious brother of Sherlock HOLMES, in
the novels and short stories by Arthur Conan Doyle. Mycroft is very
fat, being averse to physical exercise, and he spends much of his
time in the Diogenes Club, London. He is prodigiously
intelligent, and works for a government department. In the film
A Study in Terror (1965) he was played by Robert Morley; in *The
Private Life of Sherlock Holmes* (1970) Christopher Lee took the
role; and in *The Seven Per Cent Solution* (1976; dir. Herbert
Ross) Charles Gray was Mycroft. Another film, *The Adventure of
Sherlock Holmes' Smarter Brother* (1975; dir. Gene Wilder), is *not*
about Mycroft but concerns a third brother, Sigerson Holmes.
(Gerald Heard wrote a short series of detective novels about a
character called 'Mr Mycroft' – *A Taste of Honey* [1941; vt
A Taste for Murder], *Reply Paid* [1942] and *The Notched Hairpin*
[1949] – but this sleuth has more in common with Sherlock than
Mycroft Holmes.)

HOLMES, SHERLOCK   Consulting detective invented by Arthur
Conan Doyle. Undoubtedly the most famous fictional character
of modern times, Holmes is an unforgettable creation. A lean,
hawk-nosed English gentleman, whose recreations include
playing the violin and consuming cocaine, he has the finest
analytic mind of his age and is capable of solving any mystery.
He lives in rooms in London's Baker Street, and his adventures
arc recounted by his erstwhile lodging companion, the amiable Dr
John WATSON. Other characters of importance in the Holmes
stories are Mycroft HOLMES (his brother), Irene Adler (the
enchantress who almost ensnares him), Mrs Hudson (his
landlady), Inspector LESTRADE (his professional rival) and
Professor James MORIARTY and Colonel Sebastian Moran (a pair
of juicy villains). Holmes and Watson first appeared in Doyle's novel
A Study in Scarlet. This was written in March–April 1886 and
lay unpublished for more than a year. It eventually appeared in
Mrs Beeton's Christmas Annual for 1887, and then as a separate
slim volume in 1888. The publishers, Ward Lock, paid the

Dr Watson (Nigel Bruce) and Sherlock Holmes (Basil Rathbone)
in *The Hound of the Baskervilles* (1939)

unknown Conan Doyle just £25 for all rights. The book was far
from being an immediate success, although the interest of an
American publisher encouraged its author to write a sequel, *The
Sign of Four* (1890). This too seemed to sink without trace. It
was only when Doyle produced a series of short stories about
Holmes for the *Strand Magazine* that the character began to attract
the enormous popularity which has scarcely diminished in the
century since. These stories were collected in *The Adventures of
Sherlock Holmes* (1892) and *The Memoirs of Sherlock Holmes*
(1894). In the last of the sequence, 'The Final Problem', Doyle has
Holmes die at the hands of his arch-enemy, Professor Moriarty.
It was clear that the author had tired of his creation and intended
to write no more about him. There was much distress, and young

men in the City of London wore public mourning for the great detective. The demand for more Holmes stories proved irresistible, and eventually Doyle revived him for the novel *The Hound of the Baskervilles* (1902), followed by a new series of short stories collected in *The Return of Sherlock Holmes* (1905). A final novel about the character is *The Valley of Fear* (1915), and the concluding collections of stories are *His Last Bow* (1917) and *The Case Book of Sherlock Holmes* (1927). Essays, playlets, parodies and other scraps by Doyle which pertain to Holmes are collected in the overlapping volumes *The Final Adventures of Sherlock Holmes* (1981), edited by Peter Haining, and *The Uncollected Sherlock Holmes* (1983), edited by Richard Lancelyn Green.

Critical commentary and exegesis of the Doyle/Holmes 'canon' has grown to vast proportions. Notable volumes include *Sherlock Holmes: Fact or Fiction?* (1932) by T. S. Blakeney; *The Private Life of Sherlock Holmes* (1933) by Vincent Starrett; *Baker Street Studies* (1934) edited by H. W. Bell; *Profile by Gaslight: An Irregular Reader About the Private Life of Sherlock Holmes* (1944) edited by Edgar W. Smith; *My Dear Holmes* (1951) by Gavin Brend; *In the Footsteps of Sherlock Holmes* (1958) by Michael Harrison (and other titles by this author); *Sherlock Holmes: A Biography of the World's First Consulting Detective* (1962) by W. S. Baring-Gould; *The Sherlock Holmes Companion* (1962) by Michael and Mollie Hardwick (and several other books by these authors); *Seventeen Steps to 221B* (1967) edited by James Edward Holroyd; *The Annotated Sherlock Holmes* (1968) edited by W. S. Baring-Gould; *A Sherlock Holmes Commentary* (1972) by D. Martin Dakin; *The World Bibliography of Sherlock Holmes and Dr Watson: A Classified and Annotated List of Materials Relating to Their Lives and Adventures* (1974) by Ronald Burt De Waal; *The Encyclopaedia of Sherlockiana, or, A Universal Dictionary of the State of Knowledge of Sherlock Holmes and His Biographer, John H. Watson, M.D.* (1977) edited by Jack Tracy; *Sherlock Holmes: The Man and His World* (1979) by H. R. F. Keating; *The Quest for Sherlock Holmes: A Biographical Study of Sir Arthur Conan Doyle* (1982) by Owen Dudley Edwards (perhaps the most serious and illuminating of all these books); and the slightly premature *Sherlock Holmes: A Centenary Celebration* by Allen Eyles (1986).

The Sherlock Holmes stage adaptations, films, television

versions, pastiches (see Solar PONS for a good example) and sequels
by other hands have been astonishingly numerous. Sequels by
other hands in book form include *The Misadventures of Sherlock
Holmes* (1944) edited by Ellery Queen; *The Exploits of Sherlock
Holmes* (1954) by Adrian Conan Doyle and John Dickson Carr;
The Seven Per Cent Solution (1974) by Nicholas Meyer (in which
Holmes meets Sigmund Freud); *The Case of the Peerless Peer*
(1974) by Philip José Farmer (wherein he encounters TARZAN);
Sherlock Holmes's War of the Worlds (1975) by Manly Wade
Wellman and Wade Wellman (in which he is pitted against H. G.
Wells's MARTIANS); *The West End Horror* (1976) by Nicholas
Meyer (in which he becomes entangled with the likes of Oscar
Wilde and George Bernard Shaw); *Exit Sherlock Holmes: The
Great Detective's Final Days* (1977) by Robert Lee Hall; *The
Last Sherlock Holmes Story* (1978) by Michael Dibdin (in which
he tackles Jack the Ripper); *Sherlock Holmes Versus Dracula*
(1978) and *Dr Jekyll and Mr Holmes* (1979) by Loren D. Estleman;
Sherlock Holmes: My Life and Crimes (1984), an
'autobiography' by Michael Hardwick; *Ten Years Beyond Baker
Street: Sherlock Holmes Matches Wits with the Diabolical Dr
Fu Manchu* (1984) by Cay Van Ash; and *Sherlock Holmes at the
1902 Fifth Test* (1985), a cricketing novel by Stanley Shaw.

The artist Sidney Paget did more than anyone else to establish
Holmes's physical appearance. He was commissioned by the
Strand Magazine to illustrate the first series of Doyle's short
stories, and was retained for later series. It was Paget who gave
Holmes his famous deerstalker hat. However, another of the great
detective's characteristic garments, the Inverness cape, is thought
to have originated with the American actor-playwright William
Gillette. The latter's play, *Sherlock Holmes*, was first produced on
the New York stage in 1899. It was an immense success around
the world, and Gillette continued to act the part of Holmes in this
play for the next thirty years. Another very successful stage
adaptation was *The Speckled Band* (1910), dramatized by Doyle
himself. The actor most associated with the latter play was H. A.
Saintsbury, who also took the part of Holmes for many years.
Notable stage productions of Holmes's adventures also include
The Return of Sherlock Holmes (1923) by J. E. Harold Terry and
Arthur Rose; *The Holmeses of Baker Street* (1933) by Basil
Mitchell; *The Great Detective* (1953), a ballet with music by Richard

Arnell and choreography by Margaret Dale; and *Baker Street* (1965), a musical play by Jerome Coopersmith, with music and lyrics by Marian Grudneff and Raymond Jessell.

It should come as no surprise to find that Holmes holds the record as the fictional character who has appeared most frequently in films. According to Patrick Robertson's *Guinness Film Facts and Feats* there had been 186 Holmes films produced by 1984 (including early one-reelers and later TV movies, but not including TV series). The earliest film listed is *Sherlock Holmes Baffled*, a tiny movie made in America in 1900. It was followed by *The Adventures of Sherlock Holmes, or Held for a Ransom* (1903; dir. J. Stuart Blackton), with Maurice Costello as the detective. The first actor to play Holmes repeatedly was Viggo Larsen, who portrayed the character in a number of Danish and German films released between 1908 and 1919 (in several of these movies Holmes encounters A. J. RAFFLES and Arsène LUPIN). The first actor to repeat the role in the British cinema was the Frenchman Georges Treville, who in 1912–13 appeared in eight films based on the short stories. One of the first Americans to play Holmes was Francis Ford (brother of the great film director John Ford) who appeared in the silent *A Study in Scarlet* (1914). Other US films made in this period were *Sherlock Holmes* (1916), starring William Gillette (who had specialized in portraying the character on stage); *Black Sherlock Holmes* (1918), starring Sam Robinson, a black actor; and *Sherlock Holmes* (1922; dir. Albert Parker), with the eminent John Barrymore. The longest series of Holmes films starred Eille Norwood – some forty-seven titles were produced in Britain between 1921 and 1923, most of them short but two of them feature-length. Back in Hollywood, Clive Brook took on the role in *The Return of Sherlock Holmes* (1929; dir. Basil Dean) and one other title; and Reginald Owen (the only actor to play both Holmes and Watson) took the lead in *A Study in Scarlet* (1933; dir. Edwin L. Marin). Meanwhile in Britain Holmes was played by Raymond Massey in one film, *The Speckled Band* (1931; dir. Jack Raymond) and by Arthur Wontner in five films beginning with *The Sleeping Cardinal* (1931; dir. Leslie Hiscott) and ending with *Silver Blaze* (1937; dir. Thomas Bentley). Then came Basil Rathbone, perhaps the most fondly remembered of all the screen Holmeses, in *The Hound of the Baskervilles* (1939; dir. Sidney Lanfield) and thirteen subsequent

films, concluding with *Dressed to Kill* (1946; dir. Roy William
Neill). After World War II there was a dearth of Holmes movies
until Peter Cushing took on the part in a remake of *The Hound
of the Baskervilles* (1959; dir. Terence Fisher). Others who have
played the detective since include Christopher Lee in *Sherlock
Holmes and the Deadly Necklace* (1962; dir. Terence Fisher); John
Neville in *A Study in Terror* (1965; dir. James Hill); Robert
Stephens in *The Private Life of Sherlock Holmes* (1970; dir.
Billy Wilder); Nicol Williamson in *The Seven Per Cent Solution*
(1976; dir. Herbert Ross); Peter Cook in an abominable spoof version
of *The Hound of the Baskervilles* (1977; dir. Paul Morrissey);
Christopher Plummer in *Murder by Decree* (1979; dir. Bob Clark);
and Nicholas Rowe, who played the hero as a lad in *Young
Sherlock Holmes and the Pyramid of Fear* (1985).

Radio series about Holmes and Watson are too numerous to
list. Suffice to say that since 1930 scarcely a year has gone by
without someone, somewhere dramatizing a Holmes story on the
air. One particularly notable series of twelve BBC broadcasts in 1954
had John Gielgud as Holmes and Ralph Richardson as Watson
(with a guest appearance by Orson Welles as Moriarty!).
Television series and serials include 'Sherlock Holmes' (BBC,
1951), with Alan Wheatley as Holmes; 'The Adventures of
Sherlock Holmes' (1954–5), made in France and starring Ronald
Howard; 'Sherlock Holmes' (BBC, 1965–6), with Douglas
Wilmer, later replaced by Peter Cushing for a new series (1968);
'Sherlock Holmes and Dr Watson' (Polish-made but featuring
mainly British actors, 1980), with Geoffrey Whitehead; 'Young
Sherlock: The Mystery of the Manor House' (UK, 1982), starring
Guy Henry as the boy Holmes; 'The Hound of the Baskervilles'
(BBC, 1983), with Tom Baker; and 'The Adventures of Sherlock
Holmes' (UK, 1984–5) and 'The Return of Sherlock Holmes' (UK,
1986), with Jeremy Brett as the detective. Television movies
based on the character include *The Hound of the Baskervilles*
(1972; dir. Barry Crane), starring Stewart Granger; *Sherlock Holmes
in New York* (1976; dir. Boris Sagal), with Roger Moore; *The Sign
of Four* and (yet again) *The Hound of the Baskervilles* (both
1983), with Ian Richardson; and *The Masks of Death* (1984; dir.
Roy Ward Baker), with Peter Cushing once more. In the last-
named TV movie the great detective comes out of retirement to
assist his country on the eve of World War I.

HOLT, FELIX Idealistic hero of the novel *Felix Holt, the Radical* (1866) by George Eliot (Mary Ann Evans). He chooses to live and work among the lower classes, and accidentally kills a man while quelling a riot. He is pardoned, and eventually marries his beloved, Esther Lyon. Felix's commitment to social justice is contrasted with the shallow radicalism of his rival, Harold Transome, who runs for Parliament.

HOMILY, POD AND ARRIETY See The Borrowers

HONDO See Hondo Lane

HONEYCHURCH, LUCY English girl who visits Italy, where she falls in love with George Emerson, a young man of lower social status. Later, despite the opposition of her family, she marries him. Their tale is told in E. M. Forster's novel *A Room with a View* (1908). In the film of the novel (1985; dir. James Ivory) Lucy was played by Helena Bonham-Carter.

HOOD, CHARLES British Intelligence operative who poses as a dealer in *objets d'art*. Like Dr Jason Love, he is one of the many 'sons of' James Bond. Hood's adventures are recounted in a series of violent, sexy thrillers by James Mayo (Stephen Coulter): *Hammerhead* (1964), *Let Sleeping Girls Lie* (1965), *Shamelady* (1966), *Once in a Lifetime* (1968; vt *Sergeant Death*), *The Man Above Suspicion* (1969) and *Asking for It* (1971). In the film *Hammerhead* (1968; dir. David Miller) the hero was played by Vince Edwards.

HOOK, JAMES Pirate captain in J. M. Barrie's play *Peter Pan* (1904) and the novel *Peter and Wendy* (1911). Captain Hook's lower right arm has been bitten off by a crocodile and replaced by a wicked steel hook. The crocodile gets the rest of him in the end, after he has done his utmost to make life miserable for Peter Pan, Wendy Darling and the other inhabitants of Never-Never Land. Notable actors who have relished the role of Captain Hook on stage include Gerald du Maurier, Charles Laughton, Alastair Sim and Boris Karloff.

HOOPER, FANNY Illegitimate daughter of a Victorian cabinet minister, in Michael Sadleir's novel *Fanny by Gaslight* (1940). After her mother's death she becomes a servant in her father's home. In the film of the novel (1944; dir. Anthony Asquith) Fanny was played by Phyllis Calvert. The BBC television serial (1981) had Chloe Salaman in the same role.

HOPE, MATTHEW   Florida lawyer who serves as hero in a recent series of crime novels by Ed McBain (Evan Hunter). His cases are named after familiar fairy tales, and they include *Goldilocks* (1978), *Rumpelstiltskin* (1981), *Beauty and the Beast* (1983), *Jack and the Beanstalk* (1984), *Snow White and Rose Red* (1985) and *Cinderella* (1986).

HORNBLOWER, HORATIO   Midshipman, Lieutenant, Captain, Commodore, and later Admiral in the British navy at the time of the Napoleonic Wars. His career is outlined in a series of eleven books by C. S. Forester, beginning with *The Happy Return* (1937; vt *Beat to Quarters*). Hornblower is a taciturn, intelligent commander, an excellent seaman and strategist. His seafaring adventures take him all over the world. The other volumes in the series are: *A Ship of the Line* (1938), *Flying Colours* (1939), *The Commodore* (1945; vt *Commodore Hornblower*), *Lord Hornblower* (1948), *Mr Midshipman Hornblower* (1950), *Hornblower and the Atropos* (1953), *Lieutenant Hornblower* (1954), *Hornblower in the West Indies* (1958), *Hornblower and the Hotspur* (1962) and the posthumous *Hornblower and the Crisis* (1967). Forester also wrote *The Hornblower Companion* (1964), a volume of anecdotes and maps which illuminate the series. A biography of the character, *The Life and Times of Horatio Hornblower* (1970), has been written by C. Northcote Parkinson. The hero was portrayed by the American actor Gregory Peck in the film *Captain Horatio Hornblower RN* (1951; dir. Raoul Walsh) – but the cinema has yet to do justice to this character, whose exploits have inspired emulative series by many other novelists. Hornblower was played by Michael Redgrave in a BBC radio series of the early 1950s.

HORNLEIGH, INSPECTOR   Police officer in the BBC radio series 'Inspector Hornleigh Investigates' (broadcast from 1937). The scriptwriter was Hans Wolfgang Priwin (who later changed his name to John P. Wynn). Hornleigh, played by S. J. Warmington, was always accompanied by the trusty Sergeant Bingham (Ewart Scott). The pair became very popular, and soon appeared in a stage play (1938). In the film *Inspector Hornleigh* (1938; dir. Eugene Forde) the hero was played by Gordon Harker, with Alastair Sim as Bingham. Two more films followed, in 1939 and 1940.

HOULIHAN, HOTLIPS   See under Hawkeye PIERCE

HOUYHNHNMS, THE   See under Lemuel GULLIVER

HOWARD THE DUCK   Rebellious intellectual duck from another dimension of space/time. A 'superhero' created by Steve Gerber for Marvel Comics in the mid-1970s, Howard quickly became a cult figure. He was even thrust forward as a prospective candidate in the 1976 presidential election. The comic-book series was discontinued in the late 1970s when Gerber left Marvel, and a revival of Howard the Duck in 1985 was generally deemed less successful. Howard has been described as 'the single most anarchic and essential character ever created in mainstream comics' (Mick Mercer, *New Musical Express*, 26 October 1985). He has since featured in his own movie, *Howard the Duck* (1986; dir. Willard Huyck; also released as *Howard – A New Breed of Hero*), where he was played by a whole succession of midget actors in duck costumes.

HOWDY DOODY   Puppet cowboy created by Bob Smith for the long-running television show 'Howdy Doody' (1947–60). Howdy became very popular with American kids, and also appeared in his own comic-book from 1949.

HUBBARD, REGINA   Daughter of a rich, corrupt Southern family. She is the fearsome heroine of Lillian Hellman's play *The Little Foxes* (1939). Regina was played by Tallulah Bankhead on the Broadway stage, and by Bette Davis in the celebrated film of the play (1941; dir. William Wyler). Hellman's later play *Another Part of the Forest* (1946) is a 'prequel' to *The Little Foxes*; it shows how the Hubbards developed their rapaciousness and became 'the little foxes who spoil the vines'. It too was filmed (1948; dir. Michael Gordon).

HUDSON, MR   Butler to the Bellamy household, played by the
Scottish actor Gordon Jackson in the popular British television
series 'Upstairs, Downstairs' (1970–75). Set during the first three
decades of the twentieth century, the story-line dealt with the lives
of both masters and servants – but the servants soon gained
dominance in the public eye. Mr Hudson, a figure of moral
rectitude, became the best-known character of the series,
although also important were the cook, Mrs Bridges, and the maid,
Rose. The series was created by Jean Marsh and Eileen Atkins,
and the many paperback novels based on the scripts are mostly
by John Hawkesworth and Mollie Hardwick. The book *Mr
Hudson's Diary* (1973) is by Michael Hardwick. Another
volume, *The Bellamys of Eaton Place* (1976) by John Pearson,
gives a complete history of the Bellamy family and its servants.

HUDSON, MRS   See under Sherlock HOLMES

HUER, DOCTOR   See under Buck ROGERS

HUEY, DEWEY AND LOUIE   See under DONALD DUCK

HUGGETT, JOE AND ETHEL   Ordinary English couple played by
Jack Warner and Kathleen Harrison in the mystery-comedy film
Holiday Camp (1947; dir. Ken Annakin). Ted Willis had a hand
in the script, as did Mabel and Denis Constanduros. Film
sequels, with much the same cast, are *Here Come the Huggetts*
(1948; dir. Annakin), *Vote for Huggett* and *The Huggetts Abroad*.
The characters were revived for a BBC radio comedy series, 'Meet
the Huggetts' (1953–61), where they continued to be played by
Warner and Harrison. Various actors and actresses played their
children, Jane and Bobby Huggett. The family also appears in a series
of books by Mabel and Denis Constanduros.

HUGHES, YOSSER   Stubborn, violent, pitiable unemployed
tarmac-layer played by Bernard Hill in the BBC television drama
series *The Boys from the Blackstuff* (1982). The tele-plays were
written by Alan Bleasdale (who had originally introduced the
characters in his play *The Black Stuff* [1978]). Yosser's catch-
phrase – 'I can do that. Gi'e us a job' – became current throughout
Britain in the latter part of 1982.

HULK, THE   See The INCREDIBLE HULK

HULOT, MONSIEUR   Bumbling, accident-prone *persona* of the
French comic genius Jacques Tati, in a series of films which began
with *Monsieur Hulot's Holiday* (1953). His later appearances are
in *Mon Oncle* (1958), *Playtime* (1968) and *Traffic* (1971), all directed
by Tati. Hulot has been described as 'a gangling, awkward
character whose peculiar gait and odd misadventures set him
apart from the gadget-obsessed world around him. [He is] an island
of sanity and warm humanity surrounded by a sea of antiseptic
modernity' (Ephraim Katz).

HUMAN TORCH, THE   See under Mr FANTASTIC

HUMBERT, HUMBERT   See under LOLITA

HUNCHBACK OF NOTRE DAME, THE   See QUASIMODO

HUNT, LAURA   *Femme fatale* in Vera Caspary's mystery novel
Laura (1943). She is presumed dead at the beginning of the story,
and the policeman who is assigned to investigate her murder
gradually falls in love with her image. The film of the novel
(1944; dir. Otto Preminger) is remembered as one of Hollywood's
most ingenious *films noirs*. It starred Gene Tierney as Laura.
In David Thomson's *Suspects* (1985) Laura Hunt is the sister-in-
law of the book's narrator, George BAILEY.

HURSTWOOD, GEORGE   See under Carrie MEEBER

HUTCHINSON, KEN   See STARSKY AND HUTCH

HYDE, EDWARD   See Henry JEKYLL

I

IBBETSON, PETER   Jailed murderer who reviews his past life, and experiences strange dreams, in George Du Maurier's novel *Peter Ibbetson* (1891). The story was turned into a play by Nathaniel Raphael and an opera by Deems Taylor (1931). A silent movie version of the play (1921; dir. George Fitzmaurice) was entitled *Forever*. The later film *Peter Ibbetson* (1935; dir. Henry Hathaway) starred Gary Cooper; it has been praised by André Breton and Luis Bunuel as a notable piece of cinematic surrealism.

ICHABOD   See Ichabod CRANE

IGNATZ MOUSE   See under KRAZY KAT

IKEY MO   See under Ally SLOPER

IM-HO-TEP   See The MUMMY

INCREDIBLE HULK, THE   Dr Bruce Banner, a meek scientist who every now and again metamorphoses into a huge green-skinned humanoid, apparently brainless and ravening (but curiously law-abiding, since it is usually villains that he stomps on). Banner's career as a part-time monster began during a bomb test when he found himself accidentally 'bathed in the full force of the mysterious gamma rays'. Now, whenever he is possessed by anger he turns into the Hulk, and on reverting to normal shape he has no memory of his actions as the green brute. This modern variation on Dr JEKYLL is one of the most absurdly memorable characters to have sprung from American comic-books. The Hulk was conceived by Stan Lee, and has appeared in the Marvel Comics title *The Incredible Hulk* since 1962. He also appeared in the animated television series 'Marvel Superheroes' (1966–8), and subsequently in his own live-action series which commenced with the TV movie *The Incredible Hulk* (1977; dir. Kenneth Johnson). The latter series, which ran until 1982, starred Bill Bixby as Dr Banner (his forename changed to David) and

muscleman Lou Ferrigno as his green alter ego. Clive James has
described the TV Hulk in memorable terms: he 'has the standard
body-builder's physique, with two sets of shoulders one on top of
the other and wings of lateral muscle that hold his arms out from
his sides as if his armpits had piles. He is made remarkable by his
avocado complexion [and] eyes like plover's eggs.' The series
was very popular with kids the world over, a fact reflected in the
successful merchandising of Hulk dolls, Hulk T-shirts, and
other trivia. There have been several Incredible Hulk novels,
including *Murdermoon* (1979) by Paul Kupperberg – in which
he meets SPIDER-MAN.

INGLESANT, JOHN   Hero of Joseph Henry Shorthouse's popular
historical novel *John Inglesant* (1880). Inglesant is caught up in the
religious disputes of the seventeenth century, sides with King
Charles I in the Civil War, and later travels to Italy.

INGOLDSBY, THOMAS   Supposed narrator of R. H. Barham's
collection of comical verse, *The Ingoldsby Legends, or Myth and
Marvel by Thomas Ingoldsby Esquire* (1840–47). This work, with
its eccentric rhymes and grotesque tales (including the story of
the Jackdaw of Rheims), became very popular in Britain. It was
the particular favourite of H. Rider Haggard's Allan QUATERMAIN.

INJUN JOE   See under Tom SAWYER

INNES, DAVID   Stalwart American who journeys underground in
Abner Perry's wonderful Iron Mole – 'a steel cylinder a hundred feet
long, and jointed so that it may turn and twist through solid rock
if need be. At one end is a mighty revolving drill . . .' Innes and
Perry discover the lost land of Pellucidar, a place of eternal
daylight where time does not exist and dinosaurs still roam. Their
exciting adventure story is to be found in Edgar Rice Burroughs's
novel *At the Earth's Core* (serialized 1914; first published in
book form 1922). The sequels are *Pellucidar* (1923), *Tanar of
Pellucidar* (1929), *Tarzan at the Earth's Core* (1930 – in which David
Innes meets TARZAN, Lord of the Jungle), *Back to the Stone Age*
(1937), *Land of Terror* (1944) and the posthumous *Savage Pellucidar*
(1963). Burroughs's son, John Coleman Burroughs, drew a comic-
strip entitled 'Dave Innes of Pellucidar' (from 1940). The hero has

also appeared in a film, *At the Earth's Core* (1976; dir. Kevin Connor), where he was played by Doug McClure.

INVISIBLE GIRL, THE   See under Mr FANTASTIC

INVISIBLE MAN, THE   Dr Griffin, the scientist who discovers the secret of invisibility and is driven mad by the consequences, in H. G. Wells's novel *The Invisible Man* (1897). The film of the book (1933; dir. James Whale) starred Claude Rains (whose face became visible only at the very end of the picture). A spate of 'invisible man' films followed the success of this adaptation of Wells's original: it included *The Invisible Man Returns* (1940; dir. Joe May), *The Invisible Man's Revenge* (1944; dir. Ford Beebe) and such spoofs as *Abbott and Costello Meet the Invisible Man* (1951; dir. Charles Lamont). There have been two television series called 'The Invisible Man': the first, made in Britain in 1958–9, owed a little to Wells's story; the second, made in America in 1975–6, owed nothing at all. The latter series starred David McCallum as an invisible secret agent, and after a season it was retitled 'The Gemini Man' with Ben Murphy taking over the lead. A faithful version of Wells's novel has since been serialized on BBC television (1984), with Pip Donaghy as the unhappy Dr Griffin.

IOLANTHE   Fairy who marries a mortal and gives birth to a semi-mortal son, Strephon, in W. S. Gilbert and Arthur Sullivan's satirical operetta *Iolanthe, or The Peer and the Peri* (1882).

IRONSIDE, ROBERT   Chief of detectives (in the San Francisco police force) who has the misfortune to be confined to a wheelchair. This does not prevent him from getting his man, again and again. The creation of scriptwriter Collier Young, he was played by Raymond Burr in the long-running television series 'Ironside' (1967–75).

ISAAC OF YORK   See under REBECCA

ISHMAEL   Narrator of Herman Melville's novel *Moby Dick, or, The Whale* (1851). The book opens with the phrase 'Call me Ishmael'. It recounts how Ishmael goes to sea on the whaler *Pequod* under the command of the half-mad Captain AHAB. He befriends the harpooner QUEEQUEG, and learns a humble and humane philosophy in the face of the vasty deep and its mysterious denizens, the great sperm whales. Ahab sails his ship to disaster, but Ishmael survives the wreck, buoyed up by Queequeg's coffin. As the *Pequod* goes under, Ishmael quotes from the Book of Job: 'And only I am escaped alone to tell thee.' A curious sequel by another hand is *The Wind Whales of Ishmael* (1971) by Philip José Farmer, in which Ishmael finds himself translated into a far future world where the oceans have dried up and the whales have taken to the skies. In the film *Moby Dick* (1956; dir. John Huston) Ishmael was played by Richard Basehart.

IVANHOE, SIR WILFRED OF   Knightly hero of Sir Walter Scott's celebrated historical romance *Ivanhoe* (1819). A pure-bred Saxon, Ivanhoe is a staunch supporter of King Richard the

Sir Wilfred of Ivanhoe

Lionheart, whom he accompanies on Crusade. On returning to England he clashes with the villainous Norman henchmen of the usurping Prince John. He is torn between love of the Saxon maiden Rowena and the beautiful Jewess REBECCA, both of whom are threatened by the Normans. With the aid of Robin Hood and King Richard himself, Ivanhoe saves the day and marries Rowena. A comic sequel by another hand is *Rebecca and Rowena* (1849) by W. M. Thackeray, in which Ivanhoe abandons the virtuous Rowena and goes in search of the more alluring Rebecca. Sir Arthur Sullivan wrote an opera entitled *Ivanhoe* (1890); it was his only attempt at a grand opera, and the libretto was by J. Sturgis. The film *Ivanhoe* (1952; dir. Richard Thorpe) starred Robert Taylor as the knight. A British television series of the 1950s had Roger Moore as Ivanhoe, and a TV movie of the same title (1982; dir. Douglas Camfield) starred Anthony Andrews. Scott's Ivanhoe was the second famous character to grace the 'Classics Illustrated' series of comic-books, which began publication in America in 1941 (the first to appear in this gaudy format was D'ARTAGNAN).

JABBERWOCK, THE Monstrous creature, with 'jaws that bite [and] claws that catch', in Lewis Carroll's mock-heroic nonsense poem 'Jabberwocky'. This appears in *Through the Looking Glass and What Alice Found There* (1872; see ALICE). As envisaged in the famous illustration by John Tenniel, the Jabberwock is a winged, dragon-like beast.

JACKAL, THE Assassin who stalks President Charles de Gaulle, in Frederick Forsyth's bestselling thriller *The Day of the Jackal* (1971). In the film of the novel (1973; dir. Fred Zinnemann) the would-be killer was played by Edward Fox.

JACKSON, MIKE See under PSMITH

JACOT, MERIEM See under KORAK

JAN OF THE JUNGLE See under BOMBA

JANE (1) See Jane PORTER
   (2) See Jane TURPIN
   (3) Strip-cartoon heroine who was very popular in Britain during World War II. She had a penchant for losing her clothes in almost every episode of her exotic adventures, and this is said to have boosted the morale of the nation's fighting forces. She was created by artist Norman Pett in 1932 for a *Daily Mirror* strip which was originally entitled 'Jane's Journal – Or the Diary of a Bright Young Thing'. By the war Jane and her dachshund dog Fritz were working as special agents. During the 1940s a successful stage show starred Christabel Leighton-Porter as Jane, and the same actress took the part in a film, *The Adventures of Jane* (1949). The 'Jane' newspaper strip ran until 1959, and has since been reprinted in book form. The character was revived in 1982 for a semi-animated British television series: this starred Glynis Barber, who also took the role in the sequel, 'Jane in the Desert' (1984).

The Return of Jane as drawn by *John M. Burns*
for the *Daily Mirror* in 1985

JANET   See under Doctor FINLAY

JANET AND BRAD   See under Frank N. FURTER

JANSON, HANK   Tough Chicago reporter who becomes involved
in many crime cases. He is the hero and narrator of a long series
of pseudo-American thrillers by the prolific British author 'Hank
Janson' (Stephen Daniel Frances), beginning with such titles as
When Dames Get Tough (1946), *This Woman is Death* (1948),
Gun Moll for Hire (1949) and *Lilies for My Lovely* (1949). The
books appeared as lurid paperback originals, and soon achieved
widespread popularity. S. D. Frances lost control of his creation in
1952, and thereafter most of the Hank Janson novels were written
by other hands. In the mid-1950s the publishers were prosecuted
for obscenity, and lost their case; nevertheless the books
continued to appear. The majority of the later Janson novels were
published by Roberts and Vintner Ltd during the 1960s, and many
of these stories were the work of a writer called Henry Hobson,
who produced them at the rate of one a month. In all, well over
200 Hank Janson titles appeared between 1946 and 1970.

JARNDYCE, JOHN   See under Esther SUMMERSON

JASPER, JOHN   Presumed villain of Charles Dickens's last work, *The Mystery of Edwin Drood* (1870) (see Edwin DROOD for further details). Wilkie Collins, who was a close friend of Dickens, wrote a short story entitled 'John Jasper's Ghost'.

JAVERT   See under Jean VALJEAN

JAWS   Nickname of the great white shark in Peter Benchley's bestselling novel *Jaws* (1974). The film (1975; dir. Steven Spielberg) was even more of a popular success than the book, and the name 'Jaws' entered the language – for example, a metal-fanged villain played by Richard Kiel in the James BOND film *The Spy Who Loved Me* (1977; dir. Lewis Gilbert) was known as Jaws. The sequels to the film *Jaws* were *Jaws 2* (1978; dir. Jeannot Szwarc) and *Jaws 3-D* (1983; dir. Joe Alves), each of which featured yet another monstrous fish intent on snapping off unwary swimmers' legs.

JEAN-CHRISTOPHE   See Jean-Christophe KRAFFT

JEEVES, REGINALD   Dignified, loyal and extremely intelligent manservant to the brainless Bertie WOOSTER, in a series of hilarious stories and novels by P. G. Wodehouse. His first name is rarely used. Jeeves and Bertie made their initial appearance in the short story 'Extricating Young Gussie' (1915). Most of the early tales are included in the collections *My Man Jeeves* (1919), *The Inimitable Jeeves* (1923), *Carry On, Jeeves* (1925) and *Very Good, Jeeves* (1930). The first Jeeves novel was *Thank You, Jeeves* (1934), and it was followed by *Right-Ho, Jeeves* (1934; vt *Brinkley Manor*), *The Code of the Woosters* (1938 – wherein Jeeves and Bertie tangle with Roderick Spode, would-be fascist leader: this is possibly the masterpiece of the series), *Joy in the Morning* (1946), *The Mating Season* (1949), *Ring for Jeeves* (1953; vt *The Return of Jeeves*), *Jeeves and the Feudal Spirit* (1954; vt *Bertie Wooster Sees it Through*), *Jeeves in the Offing* (1960; vt *How Right You Are, Jeeves*), *Stiff Upper Lip, Jeeves* (1963), *Much Obliged, Jeeves* (1971; vt *Jeeves and the Tie That Binds*) and *Aunts Aren't Gentlemen* (1974; vt *The Cat-Nappers*). There is a 'biography' of Jeeves by C. Northcote Parkinson. The films *Thank You, Jeeves* (1936; dir. Arthur Greville Collins) and *Step Lively, Jeeves*

(1937) starred Arthur Treacher as the resourceful manservant. In a British television series called 'The World of Wooster' (1965–8) Jeeves was played by the urbane actor Dennis Price. A stage musical, *Jeeves* (1975), was adapted by Alan Ayckbourn to music by Andrew Lloyd-Webber, but it proved unsuccessful.

JEKYLL, DR HENRY   Virtuous doctor who brews a medicinal potion which transforms him into the villainous Edward Hyde, in Robert Louis Stevenson's novella *The Strange Case of Dr Jekyll and Mr Hyde* (1886). This remarkably Freudian pre-Freudian fantasy of a split personality has become one of the myths of our age. A modern sequel by another hand is *Dr Jekyll and Mr Holmes* (1979) by Loren D. Estleman – wherein Henry Jekyll meets the most famous of his fictional contemporaries. There were various theatrical adaptations of *Dr Jekyll and Mr Hyde* from 1888, followed by seven silent-movie versions made between 1908 and 1921 (the last of these starred John Barrymore). Later films include *Dr Jekyll and Mr Hyde* (1931; dir. Rouben Mamoulian), with Fredric March; a remake of the same title (1941; dir. Victor Fleming), with Spencer Tracy; *Abbott and Costello Meet Dr Jekyll and Mr Hyde* (1953; dir. Charles Lamont), with Boris Karloff; *The Two Faces of Dr Jekyll* (1960), with Paul Massie; the trans-sexual variant *Dr Jekyll and Sister Hyde* (1970; dir. Roy Ward Baker), with Ralph Bates; and many more. A British TV movie of Stevenson's story (1981; dir. Alastair Reid) had David Hemmings as Dr Jekyll.

JELLIPOT, MR   Solicitor who has a flair for solving crimes. He appears in a series of books by the British writer Sydney Fowler (S. Fowler Wright): *The Bell Street Murders* (1931), *The Attic Murder* (1936), *Post-Mortem Evidence* (1936), *Four Callers in Razor Street* (1937), *The Jordans Murder* (1938), *The Murder in Bethnal Square* (1938), *Dinner in New York* (1943), *Too Much for Mr Jellipot* (1945) and *With Cause Enough* (1954).

JENKINS, NICHOLAS   Narrator of Anthony Powell's twelve-volume novel sequence, known collectively as *A Dance to the Music of Time*. The individual novels which make up this major work of modern English fiction are: *A Question of Upbringing* (1951), *A Buyer's Market* (1952), *The Acceptance World* (1955),

At Lady Molly's (1957), *Casanova's Chinese Restaurant* (1960), *The Kindly Ones* (1962), *The Valley of Bones* (1964), *The Soldier's Art* (1966), *The Military Philosophers* (1968), *Books Do Furnish a Room* (1971), *Temporary Kings* (1973) and *Hearing Secret Harmonies* (1975). The volumes span the period from World War I until the late 1960s. We follow Nicholas from Eton and Oxford through his adult life as a writer and army officer. However, he is a very self-effacing narrator and most of the emphasis is on other characters, among them Nicholas's old schoolmates, Charles Stringham, Peter Templer and the beastly Kenneth WIDMERPOOL. A companion to the sequence, which gives full details of its host of characters, is *Invitation to the Dance* (1977) by Hilary Spurling. The novels have been adapted by Frederick Bradnum for BBC radio (1982), with Noel Johnson providing the voice of Nicholas Jenkins.

JENNINGS, JOHN CHRISTOPHER TIMOTHY   Impetuous schoolboy who first appeared on BBC radio's 'Children's Hour' programme in 1948, and has since featured in a series of twenty-two books by Anthony Buckeridge. On the air the character was played by David Page, who was replaced by Glyn Dearman in 1954. Jennings attends Linbury Court preparatory school, where he is constantly getting into comic scrapes. His best friend is a boy named Darbishire, a staid bespectacled foil for Jennings's hilarious antics. In his forty years as 'Britain's most popular schoolboy' Jennings has not aged in the least. The titles of Buckeridge's books about the character are: *Jennings Goes to School* (1950), *Jennings Follows a Clue* (1951), *Jennings' Little Hut* (1951), *Jennings and Darbishire* (1952), *Jennings' Diary* (1953), *According to Jennings* (1954), *Our Friend Jennings* (1955), *Thanks to Jennings* (1957), *Take Jennings, for Instance* (1958), *Jennings, as Usual* (1959), *The Trouble with Jennings* (1960), *Just Like Jennings* (1961), *Leave it to Jennings* (1963), *Jennings, of Course!* (1964), *Especially Jennings!* (1965), *Jennings Abounding* (1967), *Jennings in Particular* (1968), *Trust Jennings!* (1969), *The Jennings Report* (1970), *Typically Jennings!* (1971), *Speaking of Jennings* (1973) and *Jennings at Large* (1977).

JESSON, LAURA   Love-lorn heroine of Noël Coward's play *Still Life* (1935). She has a clandestine affair with a doctor, Alec Harvey, but eventually returns to her staid, suburban husband. The story became more famous as the atmospheric film *Brief Encounter* (1945; dir. David Lean), which starred Celia Johnson as Laura and Trevor Howard as Alec. This was remade as a TV movie (1975; dir. Alan Bridges) with Sophia Loren and Richard Burton miscast as the ever-so-English couple.

JIGGS AND MAGGIE   Working-class American couple who win the Irish sweepstakes, and forever after have problems in adapting to a wealthy life-style. Maggie wishes to be accepted as a member of high society, while the coarse Jiggs just wants to go out drinking with the boys. The embattled pair appear in George McManus's long-running newspaper comic-strip *Bringing Up Father* (from 1913). From its origins in the Hearst papers, the strip went on to worldwide fame and frequent adaptation to other media. Since George McManus's death in 1954, it has been perpetuated by Frank Fletcher, Vernon Greene and other artists. There have been stage plays, animated films and live-action movies about the adventures of Jiggs and Maggie. The silent film *Bringing Up Father* (1928; dir. Jack Conway) had J. Farrell MacDonald as Jiggs and Polly Moran as Maggie. A sound remake of the same title (1946) had Joe Yule (Mickey Rooney's father) and Renie Riano in the parts, and this was followed by such low-budget sequels as *Jiggs and Maggie in Society* (1947), *Jiggs and Maggie in Court* (1948), *Jiggs and Maggie in Jackpot Jitters* (1949) and *Jiggs and Maggie Out West* (1950).

JIM   (1) See NIGGER JIM
   (2) 'Shanghai Jim', the semi-autobiographical hero of J. G. Ballard's phantasmagoric war novel *Empire of the Sun* (1984). Jim is an eleven-year-old English boy living in Shanghai at the time of the Japanese takeover in 1941. Separated from his parents, he wanders the streets of the 'terrible city' and eventually seeks the safety of Japanese custody. He is interned in Lunghua camp, and later suffers great privations when his captors realize that they have lost the war. Jim is a quick-witted survivor, unsentimentally portrayed. Reviewers compared him to Jim HAWKINS, Kimball O'HARA, Tom SAWYER and Oliver TWIST. A film version of his story is promised.

JIM, 'LORD'   Idealistic chief mate aboard a scruffy merchant ship which is carrying pilgrims to Mecca. The officers abandon the ship when it is in danger of sinking, and at the last minute Jim goes with them. The vessel does not sink but Jim is haunted by remorse for his own apparent cowardice. He eventually proves his worth when he offers his life in atonement for the killing of a Malay chief's son by a band of marauding Europeans. Jim is known to the Malays as 'Tuan' (Lord), and his story is narrated by Marlow in Joseph Conrad's novel *Lord Jim* (1900). The book was first filmed in 1926. In a much later movie based on the novel (1964; dir. Richard Brooks) Jim was played by Peter O'Toole. The story has also been dramatized on BBC radio (1985), with Simon Treves as Jim.

JIMSON, GULLEY   Roguish old artist who appears in a trilogy of novels by the Anglo-Irish writer Joyce Carey — *Herself Surprised* (1941), *To Be a Pilgrim* (1942) and *The Horse's Mouth* (1944). The third title is the best known, and is the only one to feature Jimson as the central character. In the film *The Horse's Mouth* (1958; dir. Ronald Neame) he was played by Alec Guinness.

JINGLE, ALFRED   See under Samuel Pickwick

JOAD, TOM   Rebellious hero of John Steinbeck's novel about a family of dust-bowl Okies, *The Grapes of Wrath* (1939). Forced to leave their farm, the Joads travel to California in search of work as poorly-paid fruit-pickers. Tom was played beautifully by Henry Fonda in the moving film of the novel (1940; dir. John Ford). The folk-singer Woody Guthrie wrote a song called 'Tom Joad'.

JOCK   Small brindle terrier, very courageous and loyal, who is the central character of one of the most famous animal stories, Sir Percy Fitzpatrick's *Jock of the Bushveld* (1907). The narrative is set in the Transvaal during the late nineteenth century. It begins with Jock's adoption by the narrator, describes his training and travels, and ends with the dog's death while he is bravely guarding a henhouse. The book has been described by Margery Fisher as 'one of the best canine portraits in literature, for adults or for the young'.

JOHNSON, COFFIN ED   See Grave Digger JONES

JOHNSON, HILDY   Ace reporter in Chicago of the late 1920s. About
to get married and take up a job in advertising, he abandons his
fiancée in order to pursue one last hot story – the escape of a
dangerous 'anarchist'. The hilarious consequences are described
in Ben Hecht and Charles MacArthur's play *The Front Page* (1928).
Hildy Johnson is the archetypal American newspaperman, just
as his boss, Walter Burns, is the archetypal hard-nosed editor. *The
Front Page* has been filmed twice under its proper title – in 1931
(dir. Lewis Milestone), with Pat O'Brien as Hildy; and in 1974
(dir. Billy Wilder), with Jack Lemmon. Perhaps the best film version,
however, is the least faithful: *His Girl Friday* (1940; dir. Howard
Hawks) changes the character's sex – Hildy is played by
Rosalind Russell, and of course Walter Burns (Cary Grant) gets
her in the end. There has also been an American television series
based on *The Front Page* (1949–50), with Mark Roberts as Hildy
Johnson.

JOHNSON, JOHNSON   Painter-cum-spy who appears in a series of
light thrillers by the Scottish writer Dorothy Halliday (Dorothy
Dunnett). He is the owner of a yacht called the *Dolly*. 'Johnson,
whose baggy sweaters and bifocals camouflage a first-rate mind,
owes a great deal to Allingham's early Albert Campion' (according
to Carol Cleveland, in *Twentieth-Century Crime and Mystery
Writers*). The titles in which Johnson Johnson appears are: *Dolly
and the Singing Bird* (1968; vt *The Photogenic Soprano*), *Dolly
and the Cookie Bird* (1970; vt *Murder in the Round*), *Dolly and
the Doctor Bird* (1971; vt *Match for a Murderer*), *Dolly and the
Starry Bird* (1973; vt *Murder in Focus*), *Dolly and the Nanny Bird*
(1976) and *Dolly and the Bird of Paradise* (1983).

JOKER, THE   See under BATMAN

JOLLIFANT, INIGO   Ex-schoolmaster turned musician and
songwriter, in J. B. Priestley's novel *The Good Companions* (1929).
With his friends Jess OAKROYD and Miss Elizabeth Trant, he joins
a group of travelling players known as the Dinky Doos. They become
the Good Companions and have picaresque adventures the length
and breadth of England. The story was turned into a play by

Priestley and Edward Knoblock (1931), and it has been filmed twice: in 1932 (dir. Victor Saville), with John Gielgud as Jollifant; and in 1956 (dir. J. Lee Thompson), with John Fraser. A Radio Luxembourg series of the early 1950s was based on *The Good Companions*: it had Ronald Howard as Jollifant. There have also been a stage musical version (1974), with music by André Previn, and a British television serial (1980), adapted by Alan Plater. The latter had Jeremy Nicholas as Jollifant.

JONES, AMOS   See AMOS AND ANDY

JONES, BARNABY   Ageing private detective played by Buddy Ebsen in the American television series 'Barnaby Jones' (1973–80). He has also appeared in occasional TV movies, for example *Nightmare in Hawaii* (1979; dir. Michael Caffey).

JONES, BRUTUS   Former railway worker and convict who becomes the tinpot dictator of a West Indian island, in Eugene O'Neill's play *The Emperor Jones* (1920). His subjects rebel, and Jones flees into the jungle where he is tormented by atavistic fears. O'Neill's play formed the basis of a successful opera by Louis Gruenberg (1933; libretto by Kathleen de Jaffa). The play has also been filmed (1933; dir. Dudley Murphy), with Paul Robeson in the lead.

JONES, CARMEN   See CARMEN

JONES, GRAVE DIGGER   Black New York police detective who appears with his colleague Coffin Ed Johnson in a series of crime novels by Chester Himes. Jones and Johnson are tough, streetwise and amusing. Although he is an American, Himes's novels were first published in French (he went to live in Paris after completing a prison sentence in the USA). The series consists of *For Love of Imabelle* (1957; vt *A Rage in Harlem*), *The Crazy Kill* (1959), *The Real Cool Killers* (1959), *All Shot Up* (1960), *The Big Gold Dream* (1960), *Cotton Comes to Harlem* (1964), *The Heat's On* (1966; vt *Come Back, Charleston Blue*), *Blind Man with a Pistol* (1968; vt *Hot Day, Hot Night*). In the films *Cotton Comes to Harlem* (1970; dir. Ossie Davis) and *Come Back, Charleston Blue* (1972; dir. Mark Warren) Grave Digger and Coffin Ed were played by Godfrey Cambridge and Raymond St Jacques.

JONES, HALO Post-punk heroine of *The Ballad of Halo Jones*, a science fiction comic-strip by the British writer Alan Moore and artist Ian Gibson. Halo and her friends inhabit a very lived-in future, full of outrageous argot, menacing street-gangs and alien monstrosities. The strip originally appeared in *2000 AD* magazine (from 1984), and was republished in book form in 1986. According to Don Watson (*Observer*, 2 November 1986): Alan Moore's 'stated aim was to make a heroine out of an Everywoman of the future. Remarkably, the results, reminiscent of an all-female, futuristic *Apocalypse Now*, are in turn disturbing and touching . . . Lisa Tuttle, editor of the *Encyclopedia of Feminism*, has commented on his ability to formulate independent female figures, a rare skill in the *Boy's Own* world of comics.'

JONES, INDIANA Whip-cracking archaeologist in a slouch hat. He is the hero of George Lucas's adventure movie *Raiders of the Lost Ark* (1981; dir. Steven Spielberg). Played by the stubbly and laconic Harrison Ford, Jones is a latter-day version of the omnicompetent heroes who featured in the 'B' movies and cinema serials of the 1930s. He reappears in a sequel (actually a prequel), with the rousing title of *Indiana Jones and the Temple of Doom* (1984; dir. Spielberg).

JONES, SETH Hero of the American West. He was invented by the nineteen-year-old Edward Sylvester Ellis, one of a number of hack writers who worked for the pioneering publisher of 'dime novels', Erastus Beadle. Ellis's *Seth Jones, or The Captives of the Frontier* (1860) sold some 400,000 copies, a spectacular figure for its day, and it helped establish the dime-novel format which was to endure for the rest of the century.

JONES, TOM Exuberant young hero of Henry Fielding's novel *The History of Tom Jones, a Foundling* (1749). Tom is an orphan who has been adopted by the benign Squire Allworthy. He falls in love with his neighbour's beautiful daughter, Sophie Western, but is obliged to leave home after a fight with a rival. After many picaresque adventures Tom discovers his true parentage and claims Sophie's hand. The story has been adapted as a comic opera, *Tom Jones* (1907), with music by Edward German and lyrics by

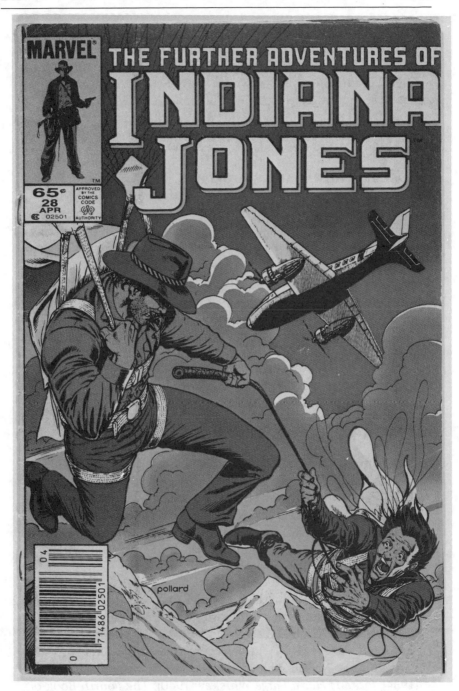

Indiana Jones as he appears in Marvel Comics

Charles H. Taylor. In the successful film of the same title (1963; dir. Tony Richardson) Tom was played by Albert Finney. The later film *The Bawdy Adventures of Tom Jones* (1976; dir. Cliff Owen) is a musical version which starred Nicky Henson. A recent sequel by another hand in book form is *The Later Adventures of Tom Jones* (1986) by Bob Coleman.

JONES, VICTORIA   See under Rodney SAVAGE

JORDACHE, THOMAS AND RUDOLPH   Contrasting brothers, the sons of an immigrant baker, who make their different ways in American society after World War II. One becomes a boxer, the other a businessman. They appear in Irwin Shaw's blockbusting novel *Rich Man, Poor Man* (1970), which was made into an even more successful television mini-series (1975; dir. David Greene and Alex Segal), with Nick Nolte as the rough Tom and Peter Strauss as the smooth Rudy. The TV production of *Rich Man, Poor Man* began the whole vogue for mini-series, or 'novelizations' as they are sometimes crassly called, and so great was its popularity that an even longer sequel followed: *Rich Man, Poor Man: Book Two* (1976). The latter bears no relation to Irwin Shaw's own book sequel, *Beggarman, Thief* (1977), which deals with a younger generation of Jordaches.

JORDAN, HAL   See GREEN LANTERN

JORDAN, ROBERT   American who chooses to take part in the Spanish Civil War, in Ernest Hemingway's novel *For Whom the Bell Tolls* (1940). Fighting on the Republican side, he falls in love with a girl called Maria. Their happiness is short-lived, however, for Jordan is fatally wounded while blowing up a bridge. The novel was a bestseller, and was filmed (1943; dir. Sam Wood) with Gary Cooper and Ingrid Bergman in the leading roles.

JORKENS, JOSEPH   Sometime traveller, now a teller of tall tales. He appears in a series of short stories by Lord Dunsany (Edward Plunkett, 18th Baron Dunsany), collected in *The Travel Tales of Mr Joseph Jorkens* (1931). Jorkens continues to spin his fantastic yarns through four more books: *Mr Jorkens Remembers Africa* (1934), *Jorkens Has a Large Whiskey* (1940), *The Fourth Book of Jorkens* (1948) and *Jorkens Borrows Another Whiskey* (1954).

JORROCKS, JOHN   London grocer and keen amateur sportsman, in Robert Smith Surtees's collection of sketches *Jorrocks' Jaunts and Jollities: The Hunting, Shooting, Racing, Driving, Sailing, Eating, Eccentric and Extravagant Exploits of That Renowned Sporting Citizen, Mr John Jorrocks* (1838). The character reappears in two later books by Surtees, *Handley Cross* (1843) and *Hillingdon Hall* (1845). The stage musical *Jorrocks* (1966) is based on Surtees's original book; it has music by David Heneker.

JOSÉ, DON   See under CARMEN

JUDY   See Judy FOSTER

JULIETTE   See under JUSTINE (1)

JUNGLE JIM   American comic-strip character created by Alex Raymond in the 1930s. The jungle wallah also appeared on the radio and in a cinema serial, *Jungle Jim* (1937; dir. Ford Beebe). He was subsequently played by Johnny Weissmuller (after he had become too fat for the role of TARZAN) in a series of sixteen low-budget feature films, beginning with *Jungle Jim* (1948; dir. William Berke) and ending with *Devil Goddess* (1955; dir. Spencer Bennet).

JURGEN   Middle-aged pawnbroker who is magically restored to the age of twenty-one and then sets out on an adventurous (and amorous) quest through the land of Poictesme and as far afield as Heaven and Hell. This story is told in James Branch Cabell's eccentric work of fantasy, *Jurgen* (1919) – a book which had the good fortune to be charged with obscenity by the New York Society for the Suppression of Vice, as a result of which it became a bestseller and made Cabell's name. The novel is just one of a series which runs to some twenty volumes, all set in the imaginary realm of Poictesme. The principal character of the series is not Jurgen but Dom Manuel, a pig-keeper turned prince. The other titles include *The Cream of the Jest* (1917), *Figures of Earth* (1921), *The High Place* (1923) and *The Silver Stallion* (1926).

JUSTINE   (1) Tortured heroine of the novel *Justine, ou les Malheurs de la Vertu* (1791) and its sequel *La Nouvelle Justine . . . Suivie de L'Histoire de Juliette sa Soeur* (1797). Both were written by

Comte Donatien Alphonse François Sade, better known as the
Marquis de Sade. In these, among the most infamous pornographic
works ever written, 'Justine keeps to the rules laid down by
men, her reward rape and humiliation; Juliette, her monstrous
antithesis, viciously exploits her sexuality in a world where all
tenderness is false, all beds are minefields' (according to the cover
blurb on Angela Carter's study, *The Sadeian Woman*).

(2) Seductive wife of an Egyptian banker in Lawrence Durrell's
'Alexandria Quartet'. The individual novels which comprise
this set are: *Justine* (1957), *Balthazar* (1958), *Mountolive* (1958)
and *Clea* (1960). The first of these books is prefaced by a short
quotation from the Marquis de Sade's *Justine*. In the film *Justine*
(1969; dir. George Cukor) Durrell's *femme fatale* was played by
Anouk Aimée.

K

K., JOSEPH Persecuted protagonist of Franz Kafka's novel *The Trial* (1925). Accused of some uncertain crime, he stumbles through a comic-horrific world of rampant bureaucracy which is part Freudian nightmare, part projection of the Austro-Hungarian Empire in its last days. The land-surveyor in Kafka's other great novel, *The Castle* (1926), is also called K. but we are not told that his first name is Joseph, and he should not necessarily be taken as the same character. In the film *The Trial* (1962; dir. Orson Welles) K. was played by the twitchy and apparently guilt-ridden Anthony Perkins. (Most critics have assumed Kafka's Joseph K. to be 'innocent' but Orson Welles once stated in an interview that his film version of *The Trial* was intended to be the study of a guilty man.)

KAA See under Mowgli

KAI LUNG Chinese sage and tale-teller who is the hero of an amusing series of short stories by the English author Ernest Bramah (E. B. Smith). These abound with mock-Chinese aphorisms, of the type also made popular by Charlie Chan. The tales are collected in *The Wallet of Kai Lung* (1900), *Kai Lung's Golden Hours* (1922), *Kai Lung Unrolls His Mat* (1928), *The Moon of Much Gladness* (1932; vt *The Return of Kai Lung*) and *Kai Lung Beneath the Mulberry Tree* (1940). A later selection of stories from the various Kai Lung books is entitled *The Celestial Omnibus* (1963).

KANE, CHARLES FOSTER Central character of Orson Welles's remarkable film *Citizen Kane* (1941). Reputedly modelled on the American newspaper magnate William Randolph Hearst, Kane is a ruthless over-achiever who eventually immures himself in a grotesque 'castle', his mansion called Xanadu. When he dies he has the word 'Rosebud' on his lips, and the search for the significance of this provides the story with its large element of psychological mystery. The young Orson Welles played Kane with great conviction and bravura; he also directed the film. The script was written by Welles in collaboration with Herman J. Mankiewicz.

KANE, MARTIN New York detective who appeared on the American radio in the 1940s, and in a television series called 'Martin Kane, Private Eye' (1949–54). On TV he was played by various actors, including Lloyd Nolan, Lee Tracy and William Gargan. The last-named repeated the role in a later TV series, 'The New Adventures of Martin Kane' (1957).

KANE, WILL Small-town marshal whose wedding is delayed by the arrival of a noon train carrying gun-slinging villains, in the classic western movie *High Noon* (1952; dir. Fred Zinnemann). The film, which was scripted by Carl Foreman, starred Gary Cooper as Marshal Kane – the man who stands up for justice, all alone in a town full of cowards (the script was clearly intended as an allegory appropriate to America's McCarthy era). A television movie entitled *High Noon, Part Two: The Return of Will Kane* (1980; dir. Jerry Jameson) starred Lee Majors.

KAPLAN, HYMAN Immigrant who has trouble with the American language. He first appeared in a series of humorous sketches by Leonard Q. Ross (Leo Rosten) which were published in the *New Yorker*. These were collected in the book *The Education of Hyman Kaplan* (1937), which has been followed by two sequels, *The Return of Hyman Kaplan* (1938, 1959) and *O Kaplan, My Kaplan* (1979). The books are now published under the name of Leo Rosten.

KARA See SUPERGIRL

KARAMAZOV, DMITRI, IVAN AND ALEXEI Principal characters of Fyodor Dostoevsky's major novel *The Brothers Karamazov* (1879–80). Dmitri is the active hero, Ivan the doubting intellectual, and Alexei (known as 'Alyosha') the calm religious mystic. When their sinful and debauched father is murdered by their half-brother Smerdyakov, Dmitri is accused of the parricide. In fact, Ivan is more to blame, since he has filled the worthless Smerdyakov's head with nihilistic ideas. It is Ivan who invents the notorious 'Legend of the Grand Inquisitor', a story-within-a-story which has long been regarded as Dostoevsky's most forceful parable of religious doubt. *The Brothers Karamazov* has been filmed twice in Germany – in 1921 (dir. Dmitri Buchowetzki), with Emil Jannings in the lead; and in 1930, as *The Murder of Dmitri Karamazov* (dir. Fedor Ozep), with Fritz Kortner. The American film of the novel (1958; dir. Richard Brooks) starred Yul Brynner as Dmitri, Richard Basehart as Ivan and a very young and suitably saintly-looking William Shatner as Alyosha. A Russian remake (1972; dir. Ivan Pyriev) had Mikhail Ulyanov and Kirill Lavrov as Dmitri and Ivan.

KARENINA, ANNA   Heroine of Count Leo Tolstoy's novel *Anna Karenina* (1875–7). She falls in love with an army officer, Alexei Vronsky, and leaves her husband and child in order to live with him. When Vronsky's ardour cools, Anna commits suicide by throwing herself under a train at Moscow station. Anna Karenina ranks with Emma BOVARY as one of the great tragic adulteresses of nineteenth-century fiction. There have been many film versions of her story, including the Hollywood silent *Love* (1928; dir. Clarence Brown) and the talkie remake *Anna Karenina* (1935; dir. Brown), both of which starred Greta Garbo. A later British film of the novel (1948; dir. Jules Duvivier) had Vivien Leigh in the role. The BBC television serial (1978) had Nicola Pagett as Anna. This last was a great success throughout the world, and proved particularly popular in the People's Republic of China where it was the first western TV serial to be shown widely. An American TV-movie version (1985; dir. Simon Langton) starred Jacqueline Bisset.

KARLA   See under George SMILEY

KATO   See under The GREEN HORNET

KATY   See Katy CARR

KATZENJAMMER, HANS AND FRITZ   Tearaway boys, a pair of 'liddle anchels' who speak English with heavy German accents. They are the longest-lived characters in American newspaper comic-strips. The mischievous Katzenjammer Kids were created by Rudolph Dirks for the *New York Journal* in 1897, and they are still up to their crazy antics in the 1980s (Dirks continued to draw them until 1958, when he was replaced by his son John). The inspiration for the Katzenjammers was an earlier duo, 'Max und Moritz', created in 1865 by the German cartoonist Wilhelm Büsch.

KAY, JULIAN   See under Norma DESMOND

KA-ZAR   See under BOMBA

KENNEDY, CRAIG   American 'scientific detective' created by
Arthur B. Reeve for short stories in *Cosmopolitan* magazine in
1910. He uses technological gadgetry as well as up-to-date
psychological methods to solve his cases. His adventures were
subsequently published in *The Poisoned Pen* (1911), *The Silent
Bullet* (1912; vt *The Black Hand*) and twenty-four later books
which appeared before the author's death in 1936. Kennedy was
played by Arnold Daly in the silent cinema serial *The Exploits
of Elaine* (1915) and its sequels *The New Exploits of Elaine* (1915)
and *The Romance of Elaine* (1916). (The 'Elaine' of these films was
played by Pearl White.) Herbert Rawlinson took on the role in
another serial, *The Carter Case: The Craig Kennedy Serial*
(1919). The character was revived in the sound era for *The
Clutching Hand* (1936; dir. Albert Herman), a fifteen-parter
which starred Jack Mulhall; and again in the television era for an
American TV series, 'Craig Kennedy, Criminologist' (1952), which
starred Donald Woods. During the second and third decades of
this century Craig Kennedy was the best-known fictional detective
in the United States, sometimes referred to as 'the American
Sherlock Holmes'.

KENT, CLARK   See SUPERMAN

KENT FAMILY, THE   Philip Kent, son of an English aristocrat but
American by adoption, and his various offspring and descendants
are the central characters in a series of seven novels known as
'The Kent Family Chronicles'. The books were unexpected
super-sellers. Conceived and 'produced' by Lyle Kenyon Engel in
order to cash in on the bicentennial of the United States, they were
written to commission by the former science fiction author John
Jakes, and published in the first instance as paperback originals.
The titles are: *The Bastard* (1974), which describes Philip's arrival
in the American colonies; *The Rebels* (1975), which deals with
the War of Independence; *The Seekers* (1975), which tells of the
war's aftermath; *The Furies* (1976), which deals with the second

generation; *The Titans* (1976), which is about the Civil War; *The Warriors* (1978), which deals, in part, with the West; and *The Lawless* (1978), which brings the series to a close in the year 1877. An associated book is *The Kent Family Chronicles Encyclopedia* (1979) by Robert Hawkins. A television mini-series, *The Bastard* (1978; dir. Lee H. Katzin), was based on the first of the novels. It starred Andrew Stevens.

KERMIT THE FROG   Talkative green-skinned puppet frog, leader of the Muppets. Created by Jim Henson, Kermit first appeared on American television as early as 1957 (in the 'Tonight Show'). However, the engaging little frog did not gain general fame until 1969, when he appeared in the ingenious 'Sesame Street', an educational TV show for young children. The success of this admirable programme eventually led to the long-lived (British-produced) 'Muppet Show' (1976–81), in which Kermit cavorted weekly with his outrageous friends Miss PIGGY, Fozzie Bear, and others. The series entertained adults as well as children, and won several awards. 'This was probably the most widely viewed television program in the world during the late 1970s,' according to Tim Brooks and Earle Marsh. 'Originated by an American and produced in England, it has been seen in more than 100 countries by upward of 235 million people.' Kermit and his associates have since appeared in films – *The Muppet Movie* (1979; dir. James Frawley) and *The Great Muppet Caper* (1981; dir. Jim Henson).

KETTLE, MA AND PA   Hillbilly couple played by Marjorie Main and Percy Kilbride in the film *The Egg and I* (1947; dir. Chester Erskine; based on a book by Betty Macdonald). The Kettles and their huge brood of children proved such popular characters that they went on to star in a series of nine further films, beginning with *Ma and Pa Kettle* (1949; dir. Charles Lamont). After Percy Kilbride left the series it stuttered to an end with *The Kettles in the Ozarks* (1956; dir. Lamont) and *The Kettles on Old Macdonald's Farm* (1957; dir. Virgil Vogel). The spirit of the Kettles lived on in later television series such as 'The Beverly Hillbillies' (from 1962; see Jed CLAMPETT) and 'The Dukes of Hazzard' (from 1978).

KETTLE, OWEN   Seafaring hero of many stories by C. J. Cutliffe Hyne, most of them written for *Pearson's Magazine* (where they proved very popular). Kettle is the skipper of a merchant ship, and he has various adventures around the globe. The short stories are collected in the books *The Paradise Coal-Boat* (1897), *Adventures of Captain Kettle* (1898), *Further Adventures of Captain Kettle* (1899; vt *A Master of Fortune*), *The Derelict* (1901; vt *Mr Horrocks, Purser*), *The Escape Agents* (1911), *Red Herrings* (1918), and *The Reverend Captain Kettle* (1925). The character also appears in the following novels by Hyne: *Honour of Thieves* (1895; vt *The Little Red Captain: An Early Adventure of Captain Kettle*), *Captain Kettle, K.C.B.* (1903), *McTodd* (1903), *Kate Meredith* (1906), *The Marriage of Kettle* (1912), *Firemen Hot* (1914), *Captain Kettle on the War-Path* (1916), *Captain Kettle's Bit* (1918), *President Kettle* (1920), *Mr Kettle, Third Mate* (1931), *Captain Kettle, Ambassador* (1932) and *Ivory Valley: An Adventure of Captain Kettle* (1938). Kettle appeared in some low-budget British films, and his exploits were broadcast on BBC radio between 1937 and the late 1940s. Actors who provided his voice on the air include Abraham Sofaer and Julian Somers.

KEYHOLE KATE   Sharp-nosed schoolgirl whose insatiable curiosity leads to many comic disasters. Created by artist Allan Morley, the keyhole-peeping terror appeared in the weekly British comic *Dandy* from 1937 to 1955. In 1965 she was revived by other hands for a new paper, *Sparky*.

KHARIS   See The MUMMY

KILDARE, JAMES   Young doctor created by the American pulp-magazine writer Max Brand (Frederick Faust) for a series of novels which includes such titles as *The Secret of Dr Kildare, Calling Dr Kildare, Young Dr Kildare* and *Dr Kildare Takes Charge*. Sequels by another hand are *Dr Kildare's Secret Romance* and *Dr Kildare's Finest Hour* (both 1963) by Norman A. Daniels. Kildare works at Blair General Hospital under the supervision of the crusty Dr Gillespie (who is confined to a wheelchair). Kildare's first film appearance was in *Interns Can't Take Money* (1937; dir. Alfred Santell), where he was played by Joel McCrea. There followed a series of nine films starring Lew Ayres as Kildare and Lionel

Barrymore as Gillespie. This began with *Young Dr Kildare* (1938;
dir. Harold S. Bucquet) and ended with *Dr Kildare's Victory* (1942;
dir. W. S. Van Dyke). Later films, such as *Calling Dr Gillespie*
(1942; dir. Harold S. Bucquet) and *Dr Gillespie's Criminal Case*
(1943; dir. Willis Goldbeck) feature the Lionel Barrymore character
without Dr Kildare. A popular television series, 'Dr Kildare'
(1961–6), starred Richard Chamberlain as the intern and
Raymond Massey as his boss. There was an attempt to revive the
characters for a later series, 'Young Dr Kildare' (1972), which had
Mark Jenkins in the title role and Gary Merrill as Dr Gillespie.

KIM   See Kimball O'HARA

KIMBLE, RICHARD   See The FUGITIVE

KING KONG   Gigantic ape discovered on 'Skull Island' in the Pacific
and shipped to America as a circus attraction. Kong breaks his
chains, runs amok in New York, climbs the Empire State Building,
and is eventually killed by the machine-gun fire of fighter planes.
The film *King Kong* (1933; dir. Merian C. Cooper and Ernest B.
Schoedsack) is the most famous beast-fable of the twentieth
century. It starred Fay Wray as the delectable young lady who
softens Kong's heart (he carries her to the top of the skyscraper
in his hairy fist). The story was by Merian Cooper and Edgar
Wallace in collaboration with scriptwriters James Creelman and
Ruth Rose, and the animation of Kong himself was achieved by
special-effects man Willis J. O'Brien. The movie inspired several
'sequels' and imitations, such as *Son of Kong* (1934; dir.
Schoedsack) and *Mighty Joe Young* (1949; dir. Schoedsack). Two
Japanese films about the great ape are *King Kong vs. Godzilla*
(1962) and *King Kong Escapes* (1967). There has also been an
animated television series about Kong's adventures (1966–8). *King
Kong* itself was remade in colour (1976; dir. John Guillermin),
with Jessica Lange in the Fay Wray role. The science fiction author
Philip José Farmer has written a strangely moving short-story
sequel, 'After King Kong Fell' (1974).

KINNISON, KIMBALL   'Lensman' hero of a series of extravagant
space operas by the American writer Edward Elmer Smith
(known familiarly as 'Doc' Smith). Kinnison is a leading member

of an élite military force which has been bred and trained by the Arisians to aid them in their cosmic struggle against the evil Eddorians. Each Lensman wears a super-technological lens on his wrist; this conveys wonderful abilities (rather like the GREEN LANTERN's power-ring). The early Lensman stories were serialized in the magazines *Amazing* and *Astounding* during the 1930s and 1940s. They were republished in book form (with added material) as follows: *Triplanetary* (1948), *First Lensman* (1950), *Galactic Patrol* (1950), *Gray Lensman* (1951), *Second-Stage Lensman* (1953) and *Children of the Lens* (1954). These books proved enormously popular when they were reprinted in paperback during the 1960s and 1970s (and they had a strong influence on George Lucas's *Star Wars* films – see Luke SKYWALKER). A direct sequel by another hand is *New Lensman* (1977) by William B. Ellern.

KIOGA See under BOMBA

KIPPS, ARTHUR Counter-jumping hero of H. G. Wells's comic novel *Kipps* (1905). Kipps is a draper's assistant who inherits some money and attempts to enter fashionable society. A silent movie version (1921) had George K. Arthur as Kipps. In the later film of the book (1941; dir. Carol Reed) he was played by Michael Redgrave. The stage musical *Half a Sixpence* (1963), with music by David Heneker, was based on Wells's novel, and this too has been filmed (1967; dir. George Sidney), with Tommy Steele as Kipps. The original novel has also been serialized on BBC radio (1984), with Michael Straka in the leading role. (The hero of Susan Hill's 'Victorian' ghost story *The Woman in Black* [1983] is also named Arthur Kipps; there appears to be no connection with the Wells character.)

KIRBY, RIP Bespectacled private-eye created by American cartoonist Alex Raymond for a highly successful newspaper comic-strip (from 1946). After Raymond's death the strip was carried on by John Prentice.

KIRK, HOWARD Repulsive, trendy anti-hero of Malcolm Bradbury's novel *The History Man* (1975). Kirk is a sociology lecturer in a new British university; he foments trouble in every area of his life, sexual, political, academic. The story was serialized on British television (1981), with a script by Christopher Hampton. Anthony Sher played the detestable Kirk. This production coincided with the Conservative government's attack on university funding and with a fashionable downgrading of the social sciences in particular; for a while 'History Man' became a catch-phrase used by the right-wing press to denote untrustworthy academics, especially sociologists.

KIRK, JAMES T. Captain of the Starship *Enterprise*, played by William Shatner in the American television series 'Star Trek' (1966–9). With his deputy, the cool Mr Spock, Kirk is in command

Captain James Kirk (right) with Mr Spock and Dr McCoy

of a crew of several hundred persons engaged on a five-year interstellar exploratory mission. Among the more notable members of the crew are Dr Leonard 'Bones' McCoy and the sexy communications officer Lieutenant Uhura. It is their task 'to boldly go where no man has gone before' (or to boldly split infinitives no man has split before, as the British science fiction writer Bob Shaw once quipped). The series and the characters it created have proved remarkably durable; the whole thing was the brainchild of producer Gene Roddenberry, though 'the Star Trek universe' has long since taken on an unstoppable life of its own. A series of animated 'Star Trek' adventures was first broadcast on US television in 1973–4. Numerous novelizations, of both the live-action and the animated TV series, have been written by such sf writers as James Blish and Alan Dean Foster. Moreover, a large number of 'original' novels and stories about Captain Kirk and his crew have now been published – many of them are by amateur writers who are avid fans of the series, a typical example being the book *Star Trek: The New Voyages* (1976) edited by Sondra Marshak and Myrna Culbreath. There is even an underground pornographic literature, known as 'K/S' (for Kirk/Spock), produced in duplicated fanzine format and sold by 'Trekkies' at their numerous conventions around the world.

After rumours of a new TV 'Star Trek' proved unfounded in the late 1970s, a series of cinema feature films was initiated: *Star Trek: The Motion Picture* (1979; dir. Robert Wise), *Star Trek: The Wrath of Khan* (1982; dir. Nicholas Meyer), *Star Trek: The Search for Spock* (1984; dir. Leonard Nimoy) and *Star Trek: The Voyage Home* (1986; dir. Nimoy). William Shatner continued to play Captain Kirk in these big-budget films. On the release of the first of them, one critic remarked on the ageing of the familiar actors' faces, but added that Shatner seemed 'oddly youthened' by contrast: perhaps this is a sign that the character he embodies will be with us for a long time to come.

KLINGER, CORPORAL   See under Hawkeye PIERCE

KNIGHT, MICHAEL   Handsome young man who drives a computerized car which seems to have a mind of its own. (It is a black Pontiac TransAm, armed with missiles, tear-gas and grappling-hooks, and equipped with a built-in talking computer

called KITT.) Michael was played by David Hasselhoff in the
rather juvenile American television series 'Knight Rider'
(1982–6). The series was created by producer Glen Larson, who is
also responsible for the TV adventures of Steve AUSTIN, Buck
ROGERS and many other brawny men of action.

KNIGHTLEY, GEORGE   See under Emma WOODHOUSE

KOJAK, THEO   Tough New York cop played by Telly Savalas in
the very popular television series 'Kojak' (1973–8). The character
first appeared in the downbeat TV movie *The Marcus Nelson
Murders* (1972; dir. Joseph Sargent), and he was the creation of
the writer Abby Mann. Lieutenant Kojak is memorable because
of his bald head and his habit of sucking lollipops. His
adventures have been chronicled in many paperback books, and
he has been revived for a one-off TV movie, *Kojak: The Belarus File*
(1984; dir. Robert Markowitz).

KOOKIE   Full name Gerald Lloyd Kookson III, a petrol-pump
attendant and spare time private-eye played by Edd Byrnes in the
American television series '77 Sunset Strip' (1958–64). Kookie
began life as a minor character in this glamorous series, but soon
his fame overtook that of the programme's leads – Stuart Bailey
(played by Efrem Zimbalist Jr) and Jeff Spencer (played by Roger
Smith). With his greased-back hair, his ever-brandished comb and
his amusing jive talk, Kookie appealed to teenage viewers (he has
been described by TV historians Tim Brooks and Earle Marsh as
'a kind of "Fonzie" of the 1950s' – see The FONZ).

KORAK   Real name Jack Clayton, the son of TARZAN (Lord
Greystoke) and his wife Jane. His adventures begin when he is a
mere babe in arms. In Edgar Rice Burroughs's novel *The Beasts
of Tarzan* (1916) young Jack is kidnapped by an evil Russian,
Nicholas Rokoff, and this action sets in train a particularly
gruelling series of adventures for the boy's father. In *The Son
of Tarzan* (1917) more than a decade has gone by, and Jack has
grown into a muscular lad who senses the call of the jungle in
his blood (although he has been kept ignorant of his father's true
past). He befriends a captured ape, runs away from his over-civilized
home in England and takes ship for Africa, where he spends

several years learning the ways of the wild. He is dubbed Korak (apish for 'Killer') by his great-ape friends. Eventually he is reunited with his family, and marries the beautiful French girl Meriem Jacot. In *Tarzan the Terrible* (1921), Korak returns from World War I just in time to rescue Tarzan, who is in deadly peril in the lost land of Pal-ul-Don. He plays a very minor role in several of the Tarzan novels which follow.

Korak was played by Kamuela Searle in the cinema serial *Son of Tarzan* (1920); unfortunately, the young actor was killed during filming, and Korak made no further appearances in the serials. Later 'sons of Tarzan' who appeared in the movies – for example, Boy, played by Johnny Sheffield in *Tarzan Finds a Son* (1939; dir. Richard Thorpe) and several subsequent films – were actually foundlings taken in by the Lord of the Jungle and his mate. Korak has continued to lead a vigorous independent life in the comic books, however. Philip José Farmer argues in *Tarzan Alive* (1972) that Korak is not really Tarzan's son at all (since Tarzan was born in 1888 it would have been impossible for him to have fathered a son who was old enough to fight in World War I). According to Farmer, Korak is actually the younger brother of Tarzan's cousin, Hugh 'Bulldog' DRUMMOND – he was adopted by the Greystokes in 1912, at the age of fourteen. J. T. Edson accepts this genealogy in his *Bunduki* novels (from 1975), where Korak is referred to as Sir John Drummond-Clayton.

KOWALSKI, STANLEY   See under Blanche DuBOIS

KRAFFT, JEAN-CHRISTOPHE   Musician-hero of Romain Rolland's ten-volume *roman fleuve*, known collectively as *Jean-Christophe* (or *John Christopher* in English). Born of German parents, the young prodigy makes his way to Paris, where he embarks on a glorious career. The sequence, which helped win its author a Nobel Prize for Literature, consists of the following novels: *Dawn, Morning, Youth, Revolt, The Market Place, Antoinette, The House, Love and Friendship, The Burning Bush* and *The New Dawn*, all first published in French between 1904 and 1912. The British edition is compressed into four volumes, entitled *Dawn and Morning, Storm and Stress, John Christopher in Paris* and *Journey's End*.

KRAVITZ, DUDDY   Young Canadian hustler, a would-be hotshot businessman, in Mordecai Richler's novel *The Apprenticeship of Duddy Kravitz* (1959). In the film of the book (1974; dir. Ted Kotcheff) he was played by the energetic Richard Dreyfuss. Duddy has aspirations to become a film producer (like Sammy GLICK before him), but eventually settles for a career in pinball machines and real-estate.

KRAZY KAT   Comic-strip alley-cat invented by the American cartoonist George Herriman in 1910. The adventures of the madcap puss and his friend Ignatz Mouse were syndicated in American newspapers until the artist's death in 1944. In the early 1950s Krazy Kat was revived for a series of comic-books. The beast has also led a long and active life in animated films. The first series of short movies was produced by Gregory La Cava (1916–17), and it was followed by fresh series from various hands in 1919–20, 1926–8, 1936–9 and (for television) in 1963.

KREBS, MAYNARD   See under Dobie GILLIS

KROOK   See under Esther SUMMERSON

KRULL, FELIX   Duplicitous young hero of Thomas Mann's last novel *The Confessions of Felix Krull, Confidence Man* (1954). A German television serialization was shown on the British Channel 4 in 1983. It starred the English actor John Moulder-Brown as Felix.

KUMALO, STEPHEN   Black clergyman from Natal who goes to Johannesburg to look for his erring sister and son. His sister has become a prostitute and his son has been condemned to death for the murder of a white man. The Reverend Kumalo's moving story is told in Alan Paton's novel *Cry, the Beloved Country* (1948). In the film of the novel (1951; dir. Zoltan Korda) he was played by Canada Lee. The story has also been turned into a musical play, *Lost in the Stars* (1949) by Kurt Weill and Maxwell Anderson, and this has been filmed (1974; dir. Daniel Mann) with Brock Peters as Kumalo.

KUNTA KINTE   Eighteenth-century West African who is captured by slavers, is shipped to America, runs away from the plantation, has his toes chopped off, and eventually settles down to found an Afro-American dynasty (and Kunta Kinte begat Kizzy, and Kizzy begat Chicken George, and Chicken George begat Tom Harvey . . .). Allegedly a real-life great-great-great-grandfather of the author Alex Haley, Kunta features in the latter's 'non-fiction' novel *Roots* (1976). This was a massive bestseller (helped by the fact that its publication coincided with the USA's bicentenary) and it formed the basis of a television mini-series (1977; dir. David Greene and others) which also won a very large audience. In the latter production Kunta Kinte was played by LeVar Burton (as a boy) and by John Amos (as a man). The critic Leslie A. Fiedler views Haley's *Roots* as a latter-day recasting of the much-maligned *Uncle Tom's Cabin* (see Uncle TOM): 'It is an anti-anti-Tom book, and appropriately enough, its most memorable, which is to say, its only even approximately mythic character, Kunta Kinte, is an anti-anti-Tom: a noble African who after a symbolic castration and a happy marriage becomes a "good bad nigger", passing on the hope of freedom, but running away no more' (Fiedler, *What Was Literature?*).

KURTZ, MR   Tortured villain of Joseph Conrad's novella 'Heart of Darkness' (1899). The story is narrated by MARLOW, who tells of his journey to a remote part of central Africa (evidently the Belgian Congo, although not named as such in Conrad's text). Kurtz is a successful agent for a company of ivory traders; he enjoys god-like power over his native workers, but this has been bought at a terrible price. He has learned to employ the most barbaric methods, including human sacrifice, and he dies with the words 'The horror! The horror!' on his lips. The character reappears as 'Colonel Kurtz', a crazed American who has created a savage fiefdom in the jungles of Cambodia, in Francis Ford Coppola's remarkable film *Apocalypse Now* (1979). The latter version of Kurtz was played by Marlon Brando.

KURYAKIN, ILLYA   Blond, boyish secret agent played by the British actor David McCallum in the American television series 'The Man from UNCLE' (1964–8), and in the various spin-off movies such as *To Trap a Spy* (1966; dir. Don Medford). See also Napoleon SOLO.

LACY, ALGY See under BIGGLES

LADISLAW, WILL See under Dorothea BROOKE

LAM, DONALD See under Bertha COOL

LAMPTON, JOE Ambitious working-class anti-hero of John Braine's novel *Room at the Top* (1957). He hails from a small Yorkshire town, and in his ruthless pursuit of wealth he abandons an unprofitable mistress in order to marry a rich man's daughter. In the sequel, *Life at the Top* (1962), we learn the consequences of Lampton's material success. In the film *Room at the Top* (1958; dir. Jack Clayton) Joe was played by the appropriately dislikable actor Laurence Harvey, who also took the part in the following film *Life at the Top* (1965; dir. Ted Kotcheff). A British television series, 'Man at the Top' (1971–3), and a spin-off feature film of the same title (1973; dir. Mike Vardy) both starred Kenneth Haigh as the sour Joe Lampton.

LANE, HONDO Hard-riding, hard-fighting hero of Louis L'Amour's Western novel *Hondo* (1953): 'He was a big man, wide-shouldered, with the lean, hard-boned face of the desert rider. There was no softness in him. His toughness was ingrained and deep, without cruelty, yet quick, hard, and dangerous.' Hondo was portrayed by John Wayne in the film of the novel (1954; dir. John Farrow). In a later short-lived television series, also entitled 'Hondo' (1967), the role was taken by Ralph Taeger.

LANE, LOIS Girl reporter on the *Daily Planet* newspaper, in the *Superman* comic-books. She is friendly with her meek, bespectacled colleague Clark Kent, but does not know that he is really SUPERMAN. Lois was played by Phyllis Coates (later replaced by Noel Neill) in the television series 'The Adventures of Superman' (1952–7). In the films, *Superman I, II* and *III* (1978–83), Margot Kidder took the part.

LANGUISH, LYDIA   See under Captain Jack ABSOLUTE

LANYARD, MICHAEL   See The LONE WOLF

LAO, DOCTOR   Aged Chinese circus-master in Charles Finney's fantasy novel *The Circus of Dr Lao* (1935). He tours America with a menagerie of unicorns, sphinxes, werewolves, etc. In the film *The Seven Faces of Dr Lao* (1964; dir. George Pal) he was played by Tony Randall.

LAPHAM, SILAS   Unscrupulous businessman who moves to Boston and attempts to rise in society. He suffers embarrassment and impoverishment, but gains a sense of morality. His tale is told in William Dean Howells's novel *The Rise of Silas Lapham* (1885).

LAPUTA, JOHN   Black African nationalist leader in John Buchan's adventure novel *Prester John* (1910). Laputa is a Christian minister, tall, deep-voiced and most impressive in appearance, whose hidden aim is to lead a bloody revolt against the white rulers of his country. He is foiled by the young Scotsman David CRAWFURD.

LARA   (1) See CONRAD (2) see under Yuri ZHIVAGO

LARINA, TATYANA   See under Eugene ONEGIN

LARKIN, POP AND MA   Farming couple who appear in a series of comic-bucolic novels by H. E. Bates: *The Darling Buds of May* (1958), *A Breath of French Air* (1959), *When the Green Woods Laugh* (1961), *Oh! To Be in England* (1963) and *A Little of What You Fancy* (1970). They have a large brood of children with such names as Zinnia, Petunia and Primrose.

LARKINS, ALF AND ADA   Cockney couple played by David Kossoff and Peggy Mount in the British television comedy series 'The Larkins' (from 1958). They keep a public house, where Ada Larkins rules her weak husband Alf with a rod of iron. The series was created by Fred Robinson, and it later formed the basis of a feature film called *Inn for Trouble*.

LARRY THE LAMB   Wee innocent beastie who appears in a series
of nursery-story books by the artist and toymaker S. G. Hulme
Beaman: *The Road to Toytown* (1925), *Tales of Toytown* (1928)
and others. Larry and his wooden-toy friends, Dennis the
Dachshund and Ernest the Policeman, appeared on BBC radio's
'Children's Hour' from 1929. Larry's voice was provided by
Derek McCulloch, and eventually the little lamb became a
national institution, his adventures continuing to be broadcast until
the demise of 'Children's Hour' in 1964.

LARSEN, WOLF   Ship's captain in Jack London's novel *The Sea-
Wolf* (1904). He is a ruthless man of mystery, somewhat reminiscent
of the legendary Flying Dutchman. His story has been filmed
many times – in 1913, in 1920, in 1925 and in 1930. In the most
memorable film, *The Sea Wolf* (1941; dir. Michael Curtiz), Larsen
was played by Edward G. Robinson. There have been two
remakes entitled *Wolf Larsen* – in 1958 (dir. Harmon Jones), with
Barry Sullivan, and in 1975 (dir. Giuseppe Vari), with Chuck
Connors. The latter version is also known as *Wolf of the Seven
Seas.*

LASSIE   Canine heroine of Eric Knight's novel for children, *Lassie
Come-Home* (1940). Lassie is a bright, courageous collie who is sold
by her impoverished owners, much to the distress of their young
son. She promptly runs away from her new home in Scotland
and travels hundreds of miles to be reunited with the family she
loves. The book formed the basis of a popular Hollywood film of
the same title (1943; dir. Fred M. Wilcox), which starred Roddy
McDowall as the boy and a male dog called Pal as Lassie. Pal
returned to the role in several more films, including *The Courage
of Lassie* (1946; dir. Wilcox) and *The Sun Comes Up* (1949; dir.
Richard Thorpe). Numerous other performing dogs have played
the faithful beast since, notably in the long-running American
television series 'Lassie' (1954–71). There has also been an
animated TV series, 'Lassie's Rescue Rangers' (1973–5), a TV movie,
Lassie: The New Beginning (1978; dir. Don Chaffey), and a musical
feature film, *The Magic of Lassie* (1978; dir. Chaffey). Like the great
RIN TIN TIN before her, Lassie also appeared on American radio
(1947–50).

LASSITER   Gun-slinging hero of Zane Grey's bestselling Western novel *Riders of the Purple Sage* (1912) and its sequel, *The Rainbow Trail*. There is a much later Western novel called *Lassiter* (1967); it is by Jack Slade (Willis Todhunter Ballard) and seems to have no connection with Zane Grey's work. *Riders of the Purple Sage* has been filmed a number of times, most notably with Tom Mix in the leading role (1925; dir. Lynn Reynolds). It was remade as a talkie in 1931 and 1941. The sequel, *The Rainbow Trail*, has also been filmed – in 1925 (dir. Lynn Reynolds), with Tom Mix, and in 1932.

LASZLO, VICTOR   See under Rick BLAINE

LAURA   See Laura HUNT

LAVENGRO   Wandering hero of George Borrow's semi-autobiographical novel *Lavengro, the Scholar, the Gypsy, the Priest* (1851) and its sequel, *The Romany Rye* (1857). 'Lavengro' means 'philologist' in the Romany tongue, and it is a nickname which Borrow says was actually bestowed on him by an old gypsy.

LAWRENCE, FRANCINE   See GIDGET

LAYNE, BRONCO   See under Cheyenne BODIE

LAYTON, SARAH   Principal female character of Paul Scott's tetralogy of novels about the British withdrawal from India, *The Raj Quartet* (1966–75). In the television serial, 'The Jewel in the Crown' (1984), she was played by Geraldine James. Sarah is the sister-in-law of the beastly Ronald MERRICK.

LEAROYD, JOCK   Scottish soldier serving in India. He appears, together with the Irishman Terence MULVANEY and the Cockney Stanley ORTHERIS, in Rudyard Kipling's short story 'The Three Musketeers' (included in *Plain Tales from the Hills*, 1888). Kipling revived the high-spirited trio for many later stories and poems, including some of those collected in *Soldiers Three, and Other Stories* (1890), *Life's Handicap* (1891), *Many Inventions* (1893) and *Actions and Reactions* (1909). The film *Soldiers Three* (1951; dir. Tay Garnett) bears small resemblance to Kipling's tales.

It starred Stewart Granger, David Niven and Robert Newton. (See also GUNGA DIN.)

LEATHERSTOCKING   See Natty BUMPPO

LECOQ   Police detective, a member of the French Sûreté, in the novels of Emile Gaboriau. The books had a great international success, and in Britain (prior to the invention of Sherlock HOLMES) the term 'Gaboriau novel' was often synonymous with 'detective fiction'. Lecoq first appears as a second-string character in *L'Affaire Lerouge* (1866), and he takes a leading role in the succeeding novels: *Le Crime d'Orcival* (1867), *Le Dossier No. 113* (1867) and *Monsieur Lecoq* (1869). He also plays a minor part in the same author's *Les Esclaves de Paris* (1868). A sequel by another hand is *The Old Age of Lecoq, the Detective* by Fortuné du Boisgobey.

LEE, LORELEI   Archetypal gold-digger of the flapper age, in the comic novel *Gentlemen Prefer Blondes* (1925) and its sequel *But Gentlemen Marry Brunettes* (1928) by Anita Loos. The first of these bestselling books (much admired by James Joyce, among others) became a stage play (1925), a silent movie (1928; dir. Mal St Clair), a stage musical (1949) and then a musical film (1953; dir. Howard Hawks). The last-named production starred Marilyn Monroe as Lorelei; her performance of the song 'Diamonds are a Girl's Best Friend' was particularly treasurable.

LEE, NELSON   Detective created by Maxwell Scott (John Staniforth) for the boys' paper *Marvel* in 1894. Later he featured in a series of novellas collectively entitled the *Nelson Lee Library*. A rival of Sexton BLAKE, Lee has an office in Gray's Inn Road, London, where he is assisted by a boy called Nipper. Occasionally Lee and Nipper join forces with Blake and the latter's assistant, Tinker (all four characters belonged to the same publisher, Harmsworth). Lee was to remain popular until the 1930s, and from 1917 onwards he doubled as a schoolmaster at 'St Frank's'. The author who wrote more Nelson Lee stories than any other was Edwy Searles Brooks (who later used the pseudonym Berkeley Gray to create the blithe desperado Norman CONQUEST). It is estimated that Brooks wrote some 900 Nelson Lee adventures between 1917 and 1933.

LEE, TERRY   Juvenile hero of *Terry and the Pirates*, a popular American newspaper strip created in 1934 by Milton Caniff. Terry is a blond-haired American lad who goes treasure-seeking in China and falls foul of a band of pirates led by the infamous Dragon Lady. In the years up until 1946 (when Milton Caniff abandoned Terry) both the character and the storylines matured: Terry grows to manhood and encounters hosts of colourful characters along the way. Terry's chief ally is the manly, pipe-smoking Pat Ryan; another of his friends is a brassy blonde known as Burma (of whom Caniff has said 'I stole the whole character from Sadie Thompson' – see Sadie THOMPSON). Connoisseurs of *bandes dessinées* rate Caniff's *Terry and the Pirates* as one of the finest adventure strips. Drawn by various artists, Terry's Far Eastern exploits continued to appear until 1973. A cinema serial, *Terry and the Pirates* (1940), starred William Tracy.

LEGREE, SIMON   Villainous slave-owner in Harriet Beecher Stowe's novel *Uncle Tom's Cabin* (1851–2). In the climactic scene his men whip poor Uncle TOM to death. A favourite figure of hate in countless stage productions and silent movies based on Mrs Stowe's tale, Legree was played by Herbert Lom in the only recent film version of the book (1965; dir. Geza von Radvanyi).

LEIA ORGANA, PRINCESS   See under Luke SKYWALKER

LEIGH, AMYAS   Hero of Charles Kingsley's rousing historical novel *Westward Ho!* (1855). Reared in Devon, he goes to sea with Sir Francis Drake. Later, he has adventures in Central America, marries the Indian princess Ayacanora, and is blinded.

LEIGH, AURORA   Heroine of Elizabeth Barrett Browning's 'novel in verse', *Aurora Leigh* (1857). A penniless orphan, she becomes a writer in order to support herself, and eventually marries her idealistic cousin, Romney Leigh. According to the critic Elaine Showalter: 'Aurora's struggle to become an artist is complicated by the self-hatred in which she has been educated, by her internalized convictions of her weakness and narcissism, and by the gentle scorn of her suitor Romney. She defies him, however . . . and succeeds as a poet.'

LEITHEN, EDWARD   Lawyer and politician, narrator of several
novels by John Buchan. He is a friend of Richard HANNAY and Sandy
ARBUTHNOT. The books in which Sir Edward Leithen plays a
prominent role are *The Power-House* (1913), *John McNab* (1925),
The Dancing Floor (1926), *The Gap in the Curtain* (1932), *The
Runagates Club* (1928) and the posthumous *Sick Heart River*
(1941; vt *Mountain Meadow* – in which Leithen goes to meet his
death in the wastes of northern Canada). He also appears briefly
in *The Moon Endureth* (1912) and *A Prince of the Captivity* (1933).

LENNOX, MARY   Central character of Frances Hodgson Burnett's
fine children's novel *The Secret Garden* (1911). She is an
unhealthy and unattractive little girl, sent home to England by
her parents in India. At an old manor house in Yorkshire she
begins to regain her health, especially when she discovers the
secret garden, an area which has been walled off since its owner's
death ten years before. As Mary brings the neglected garden to
life she is simultaneously curing her own ills. She makes new
friends – Dickon, a boy with 'green fingers', and Colin, a crippled
child given to tantrums. Under the influence of Mary, and in the
magical environment of their little garden, Colin learns to walk.
It is a touching story, and it has formed the basis of a film, *The
Secret Garden* (1949; dir. Fred M. Wilcox), with Margaret O'Brien
as Mary, and a BBC television serial (1970s), with Sarah Hollis
Andrews.

LESCAUT, MANON   Bewitching heroine of the Abbé Prévost's novel
L'Histoire du Chevalier des Grieux et de Manon Lescaut (1731;
usually abbreviated to *Manon Lescaut*). The book tells how a
young man, Des Grieux, becomes obsessed by a lower-class beauty,
Manon, for whom he abandons his studies, steals money and
fights a duel. They are exiled from France to America, where
Manon dies while they are wandering in a desert. The story has
formed the basis of no fewer than four operas – *Manon Lescaut*
(1856) by Daniel Auber, *Manon* (1884) by Jules Massenet, *Manon
Lescaut* (1893) by Giacomo Puccini, and *Boulevard Solitude* (1952)
by Hans Werner Henze. The film *Manon* (1949; dir. H. G. Clouzot)
is a modernized version of Prévost's tale, with Cécile Aubry in the
leading role. The novel has also been adapted as a three-part mini-
series for French television (1984; dir. Jean Delannoy). This version

had a script by Jean Anouilh and starred Fanny Cottesco as Manon.
There have been several ballets based on Prévost's story, a
recent example being Kenneth MacMillan's *Manon* (1974).

LESSWAYS, HILDA   See under Edwin CLAYHANGER

LESTER, JEETER   Feckless Georgia cotton-farmer in Erskine
Caldwell's novel *Tobacco Road* (1932). He lives in a tumbledown
shack with his careworn wife and their two remaining children,
the brainless Dude and the disfigured Ellie May. The novel was
adapted into an astonishingly successful play by Jack Kirkland:
from 1933 it ran for seven and a half years in New York. Henry
Hull was the first actor to play Jeeter Lester on stage. The part
was later re-created by Charley Grapewin in the film *Tobacco Road*
(1941; dir. John Ford).

LESTRADE, INSPECTOR   Scotland Yard policeman who is a foil
to Sherlock HOLMES, in the novels and short stories by Arthur
Conan Doyle. The assiduous but dim-witted Lestrade makes his
appearance in the very first Holmes novel, *A Study in Scarlet*
(1888). Sequels by another hand, in which Lestrade appears as the
hero, are *The Adventures of Inspector Lestrade* (1985), *Brigade*
(1986) and *Lestrade and the Hallowed House* (1987), all by M. J.
Trow. In films the inspector has been played by Phillip Hewland,
in *The Sleeping Cardinal* (1931) and *The Missing Rembrandt*
(1932); by Alan Mowbray, in *Sherlock Holmes* (1932) and *A Study
in Scarlet* (1933); by Charles Mortimer, in *The Triumph of Sherlock
Holmes* (1935); by John Turnbull, in *Silver Blaze* (1937); by
Dennis Hoey, in six of the Basil Rathbone movies of the 1940s; and
by Frank Finlay, in *A Study in Terror* (1965). On television he has been
played by Bill Owen, in the first BBC Sherlock Holmes series (1951);
by Archie Duncan, in the series produced in France for American
TV (1954); and by Colin Jeavons, in the recent British series which
starred Jeremy Brett as Holmes (1984–6).

LESTRANGE, DICK AND EMMELINE   See under PAUL AND
VIRGINIA

LEVERKÜHN, ADRIAN   Composer whose brilliant but tragic career
parallels the fate of Germany during the first half of the

twentieth century. His demonic story is told in Thomas Mann's great novel *Doktor Faustus* (1947). The book is narrated by Leverkühn's friend Serenus Zeitblom, a man of normal intelligence who is unable fully to comprehend Leverkühn's flights of genius but who nevertheless feels a deep human sympathy for the tortured composer.

LEVI, DOLLY   Marriage broker in turn-of-the-century New York, who appears in Thornton Wilder's comical play *The Merchant of Yonkers* (1938 – later retitled *The Matchmaker*). In the film *The Matchmaker* (1958; dir. Joseph Anthony) she was portrayed by Shirley Booth. The play was turned into a stage musical, *Hello, Dolly!*, with lyrics and music by Jerry Herman. Carol Channing played Dolly on stage in this version of the story. In the film of the musical (1969; dir. Gene Kelly) she was replaced by Barbra Streisand. The title song, 'Hello, Dolly!', was sung by Louis Armstrong and became a worldwide hit.

LEVINE, JACK   New York private-eye in the novels *The Big Kiss-Off of 1944* (1974) and *Hollywood and LeVine* (1976) by Andrew Bergman. Although bald and thick-set, he is very much a wisecracking shamus in the mould of Philip MARLOWE. (Another, similar, character who also operates in a 'period' setting is Mike Dime, hero of two novels by British writer Barry Fantoni: *Mike Dime* [1980] and *Stickman* [1982].)

LEWIS, JOHN   Young Welsh librarian, central character of Kingsley Amis's second novel *That Uncertain Feeling* (1955). He is seduced by a glamorous older woman, but eventually settles for a quiet married life. The film *Only Two Can Play* (1962; dir. Sidney Gilliatt) was based on the novel, with Peter Sellers taking the part of Lewis. A BBC television serialization, under the original title (1986), starred Denis Lawson.

LIAR, BILLY   See Billy FISHER

LIDENBROCK, OTTO   Eccentric German professor who undertakes a *Journey to the Centre of the Earth*, in Jules Verne's famous novel of that title (1864). With his enthusiastic nephew, Axel, and a stalwart guide, Hans, he descends a volcanic crater in

Iceland, discovers a vast subterranean world inhabited by prehistoric beasts, and eventually makes his way back to the surface via an eruption of Mount Stromboli in Sicily. In the Hollywood film of the novel (1959; dir. Henry Levin) the Professor was played by James Mason (the character's name was changed to 'Oliver Lindenbrook'). There has also been an American television cartoon series entitled 'Journey to the Center of the Earth' (1967).

LIGEIA   Dark-haired wife to the narrator of Edgar Allan Poe's macabre short story 'Ligeia' (1838). She sickens and dies, as does her fair-haired successor, Rowena. The narrator imagines that Ligeia's spirit takes over Rowena's corpse, and that the former is reborn. The story was filmed as *The Tomb of Ligeia* (1964; dir. Roger Corman), with Elizabeth Shepherd (and Vincent Price).

LIGHT, CHRISTINA   See The Princess CASAMASSIMA

LIKELY LADS, THE   Bob Ferris and Terry Collier, two young men-about-Tyneside in the BBC television comedy series 'The Likely Lads' (1965–9), scripted by Dick Clement and Ian La Frenais. Bob was played by Rodney Bewes and Terry by James Bolam. The characters were revived for a later series, 'Whatever Happened to the Likely Lads?' (1973), and for a feature film, *The Likely Lads* (1976; dir. Michael Tuchner) which also starred Bewes and Bolam.

LI'L ABNER   Handsome, hulking hillbilly created by American newspaper cartoonist Al Capp (Alfred G. Caplin) in 1934. With his dumb-blonde girlfriend, Daisy Mae, he hails from the dead-end town of Dogpatch. A *Li'l Abner* movie was released in 1940, with Granville Owen as the hero, and in the same decade there were also some short cinema cartoons about the character. Later, Abner's adventures were turned into a stage musical by Johnny Mercer and Gene de Paul, and this in turn became a film, *Li'l Abner* (1959; dir. Norman Panama and Melvin Frank), starring Peter Palmer as Abner. Al Capp continued to produce his comic-strip until the 1970s.

LILLIPUTIANS, THE   Miniature people who inhabit the land of Lilliput, in Jonathan Swift's satire *Gulliver's Travels* (1726). A sequel

Li'l Abner (Peter Palmer) in the 1959 film

by another hand is *Mistress Masham's Repose* (1947) by T. H. White, wherein the young heroine discovers a colony of Lilliputians who have been living for centuries on an island in an English lake. (See also Lemuel GULLIVER.)

LIME, HARRY   Fascinating villain who runs a medical racket in post-war Vienna. He was played by Orson Welles in the film *The Third Man* (1949; dir. Carol Reed), which was scripted by Graham Greene. Lime does not appear until over half-way through the movie, yet when Welles died in 1985 all the obituary notices, seemingly without fail, mentioned his characterization of Harry Lime. Graham Greene subsequently published *The Third Man* as a novella (1950). The BBC radio series 'The Lives of Harry Lime' (from 1951) also starred Orson Welles (who wrote some of the scripts). An Anglo-American television series, 'The Third Man' (1959–62), had Michael Rennie as a Harry Lime who bore little relation to the Graham Greene/Orson Welles character. The authentic Harry Lime is evoked in David Thomson's book *Suspects* (1985; see under George BAILEY), where he is depicted as a South London wide boy who makes a killing from a crooked salvage business during the Blitz before going to Vienna to meet his end in the city's sewers, 'sunk in the dark flow of sewage'.

LINDENBROOK, OLIVER   See Otto LIDENBROCK

LINGARD, TOM   See under Kaspar ALMAYER

LINTON, EDGAR   See under Catherine EARNSHAW

LINUS   See under Charlie BROWN

LITTLE BLACK SAMBO   Indian boy who appears in Helen Bannerman's picture book for very young children, *Little Black Sambo* (1899). A late sequel by the same author is *Sambo and the Twins* (1938). Bannerman's original book has stayed in print ever since its first publication, despite recent protests in Britain and America that the story helps perpetuate racial stereotypes.

LITTLE CAESAR   See Rico BANDELLO

LITTLE COLONEL, THE   See Lloyd SHERMAN

LITTLE EM'LY   See under David COPPERFIELD

LITTLE EVA   Full name Evangeline St Clare, the girl-child whose death moved a million readers to tears, in Harriet Beecher Stowe's novel *Uncle Tom's Cabin* (1951–2). She is the daughter of Uncle TOM's owner, Augustine St Clare. In film versions of the book Little Eva has been played by Marie Eline (1914), Marguerite Clark (1918), Virginia Grey (1927) and Gertrud Mittermayer (1965), among others.

LITTLE MERMAID, THE   Youngest daughter of the Mer-King, in Hans Christian Andersen's latter-day fairy story 'The Little Mermaid' (1836). She saves a human prince from drowning, falls in love with him, and longs to join him on dry land. At the price of losing her tongue, she has her fishtail changed into human legs by the Sea Witch. The Danish fabulist Hans Andersen differs from earlier collators of fairy tales, such as Charles Perrault and the Brothers Grimm, in that most of his works were freshly invented fictions rather than reworkings of oral traditions. Although a few of Andersen's stories were based on genuine folk tales, 'The Little Mermaid' is largely his own creation (even if it does bear some resemblance to 'Undine' [1811] by the Baron de la Motte Fouqué, and to earlier French and Italian tales about underwater temptresses). Later stories about mermaids include H. G. Wells's novel *The Sea Lady: A Tissue of Moonshine* (1902); the British film *Miranda* (1947; dir. Ken Annakin), which was based on a play by Peter Blackmore; and the American movie *Splash!* (1984; dir. Ron Howard). The last-named, which starred Daryl Hannah as a very sexy mermaid, followed the outlines of Andersen's fable quite closely.

LITTLE NELL   Full name Nell Trent, the girl whose untimely death set the world weeping, in Charles Dickens's novel *The Old Curiosity Shop* (1841). She lives with her grandfather in his 'curiosity shop'. They are persecuted by the dwarfish Daniel QUILP, who has loaned money to the old man and who eventually forecloses on the debt and claims the shop. Nell and her grandfather

wander, homeless, until they are given a cottage; both of them
are worn out by their ordeal and soon die. Little Nell's death scene
was much admired in Dickens's day, but it has incurred adverse
criticism since. Oscar Wilde once quipped, cruelly, that one must
have a heart of stone to read it without laughing. In the film *The
Old Curiosity Shop* (1934; dir. Thomas Bentley) Nell was played by
Elaine Benson. In the musical film *Mr Quilp* (1975; dir. Michael
Tuchner) the part was taken by Sarah-Jane Varley.

LITTLE NEMO   Small boy who falls asleep to dream wonderful
dreams, in Winsor McCay's comic strip *Little Nemo in Slumberland*
(1905–14). This phantasmagorical strip was published in the *New
York Herald*. Little Nemo also appeared in early animated films
(from 1911), and was revived for a comic-book (drawn by McCay's
son) in the 1930s.

LITTLE ORPHAN ANNIE   Archetypal American waif in Harold
Gray's newspaper comic-strip *Little Orphan Annie* (from 1924).
She is adopted by a billionaire businessman, Daddy Warbucks,
but continues to have many adventures during his frequent absences
from home. Two films about Little Orphan Annie were made in
the 1930s (they starred Mitzi Green and Ann Gillis), and the
character also appeared on the radio for many years. Latterly, the
strip has been turned into a long-running stage musical, *Annie*
(1977), with music by Charles Strouse and lyrics by Martin
Charnin. The latter has been filmed (1982; dir. John Huston), with
Aileen Quinn as the waif. There is a poem entitled 'Little Orphant
Annie' (1885) by James Whitcomb Riley, the 'Hoosier poet'.

LIU   See under Princess TURANDOT

LLOYD, COLONEL   See under Lloyd SHERMAN

LOAM, LORD   See under Bill CRICHTON

LOCKE, ALTON   Apprentice tailor who turns to Chartism (and to
poetry) in Charles Kingsley's novel *Alton Locke, Tailor and Poet:
An Autobiography* (1850). Alton spends three years in prison, and
eventually becomes a devout Christian Socialist (like his creator).
Kingsley stated: 'The moral of my book is that the working-class

man who tries to get on, to desert his class and rise above it, enters into a lie, and leaves God's path for his own . . .'

LOLA-LOLA   Night-club singer played by Marlene Dietrich in the film *The Blue Angel* (1930; dir. Josef von Sternberg). A middle-aged German professor falls for her, and Lola-Lola makes a fool of him. This was the role which first established Dietrich's mystique. The story is based on Heinrich Mann's novel *Professor Unrat* (1905), although the *femme fatale* in the book has a different name. Sternberg's Lola owes something to Wedekind's (and Pabst's) LULU. In the inferior remake of *The Blue Angel*

Lola-Lola (Marlene Dietrich) in *The Blue Angel*

(1959; dir. Edward Dmytryk) Lola was played by May Britt. The German film *Lola* (1982; dir. Rainer Werner Fassbinder) is an updated version of the story with Barbara Sukowa in the main part.

LOLITA Full name Dolores Haze, a twelve-year-old 'nymphet' beloved of the middle-aged Humbert Humbert in Vladimir Nabokov's risqué but brilliant novel *Lolita* (1955). In the film of the book (1962; dir. Stanley Kubrick) she was played by Sue Lyon (who was slightly too old for the part). Nabokov's novel has also been adapted for the stage by Edward Albee (1980). Lolita merits a chapter in David Thomson's book *Suspects* (1985; see under George BAILEY), where she appears as Dolly Schiller, a seventeen-year-old bride who is doomed to die in childbirth.

LOMAN, WILLY Central character of Arthur Miller's play *Death of a Salesman* (1949). The hard-driving materialistic life of a travelling salesman drives him to despair and suicide. In the film of the play (1951; dir. Laslo Benedek) he was portrayed by Fredric March. Among the numerous actors who have played Loman on stage are Lee J. Cobb, Warren Mitchell and Dustin Hoffman. The last-named also appeared in the TV movie version (1985; dir. Volker Schlondorff).

LONE RANGER, THE Real name John Reid, a masked adventurer of the American West, who rides a white stallion called Silver. (The Ranger's cry, 'Hi-ho, Silver, awaaaaay!', became a catch-phrase for at least two generations of kids.) A former Texas Ranger turned freelance law-enforcer, he is exceptionally clean-living and well-spoken. He uses special silver bullets and shoots only to wound. He rights wrongs with the help of his faithful Indian friend, Tonto (who addresses him as 'Kemo Sabe'). The Ranger and Tonto were originally invented in 1933 by producer George W. Trendle and scriptwriter Fran Striker for an American radio series which was destined to run until 1954. The actors who gave voice to the Lone Ranger over the years were Jack Deeds, George Seaton, Brace Beemer and Earle W. Graser. The Ranger has proved to be the most durable of all radio 'originals'. Fran Striker wrote seventeen Lone Ranger novels between 1936 and 1957, and there was a pulp magazine devoted to the hero which had a short run in 1937. He also appeared in 'Big Little Books' during the 1940s, and in numerous Lone Ranger comic-strips and comic-books. The character soon re-emerged in cinema serials: *The Lone Ranger* (1938), starring Lee Powell, and *The Lone Ranger Rides Again* (1939), with Robert Livingston. After World War II he graduated to television: Clayton Moore took the role in almost 200 episodes of the TV series (1949–57), with Jay Silverheels, a genuine Indian, as Tonto. A couple of spin-off films, also starring Moore, are *The Lone Ranger* (1956; dir. Stuart Heisler) and *The Lone Ranger and the Lost City of Gold* (1958; dir. Lesley Selander). A series of animated TV cartoons was made in 1966–9, and more recently there has been a new full-length movie, *The Legend of the Lone Ranger* (1981; dir. William A. Frakar) featuring Klinton Spilsbury as the masked hero.

LONE WOLF, THE   Real name Michael Lanyard, a gentleman thief created by Louis Joseph Vance for his book *The Lone Wolf* (1914). Sequels include *The False Faces* (1918), *Red Masquerade* (1921), *Alias the Lone Wolf* (1921), *The Lone Wolf Returns* (1923), *The Lone Wolf's Son* (1931), *Encore the Lone Wolf* (1933) and *The Lone Wolf's Last Prowl* (1934). In the film *The Lone Wolf Returns* (1935; dir. Roy William Neill) he was played by Melvyn Douglas. It was followed by thirteen more films, in which the character was played by Francis Lederer – in *The Lone Wolf in Paris* (1938; dir. Albert S. Rogell); by Warren William – in *The Lone Wolf Spy Hunt* (1939; dir. Peter Godfrey) and seven others; by Gerald Mohr – in *The Lone Wolf in London* (1947; dir. Leslie Goodwins); and by Ron Randell – in *The Lone Wolf and His Lady* (1949; dir. John Hoffman), the last of the series.

   Mike Barry (Barry Malzberg) has also created a character who is known as the Lone Wolf: Burton Wulff, an aggressor in the mould of Don Pendleton's THE EXECUTIONER, appeared in some fourteen hastily-written novels, beginning with *Bay Prowler* (1973) and ending with *Philadelphia Blowup* (1975).

LONG, LAZARUS   Tough hero of Robert A. Heinlein's science fiction novel *Methuselah's Children* (serialized 1941; revised for book publication 1958). Lazarus has lucky genes: he is extremely long-lived, a nineteenth-century rugged individualist who has survived into the twenty-first century. Heinlein takes

Lazarus even further into the future in the later novel *Time Enough for Love, or the Lives of Lazarus Long* (1973). A series of apothegms from this book were republished separately in a small illustrated volume called *The Notebooks of Lazarus Long* (1978) – Lazarus is nothing if not a mouthpiece for Heinlein's often cranky social and political beliefs. Endlessly talkative and opinionated, he reappears in smaller roles in later Heinlein novels, *The Number of the Beast* (1980) and *The Cat Who Walks Through Walls* (1985).

LONGARM   See under EDGE

LONGSTOCKING, PIPPI   Gawky, red-headed extremely athletic young girl in the Swedish novel for children *Pippi Longstocking* (1945) by Astrid Lindgren (the character is known as Pippi Langstrump in the original). Pippi is an orphan who believes that her father is a South Sea cannibal king. She is so strong that she can heft horses and policemen; she is also very untidy, and wears mismatching stockings. In the words of critic Marcus Crouch she 'embodies all the dreams of small children who weave fantasies about total freedom from adult supervision, enormous physical strength, [and] escape from the conventions of a civilization invented by grownups'. Sequels, also by Astrid Lindgren, are *Pippi Goes on Board* (1946) and *Pippi in the South Seas* (1948). Pippi has appeared in four Swedish films (1969–71; dir. Olle Hellblom), where she was played by Inger Nilsson.

LONIGAN, STUDS   Working-class Irish-American whose tragic life-story is told in a trilogy of novels by James T. Farrell: *Young Lonigan: A Boyhood in Chicago Streets* (1932), *The Young Manhood of Studs Lonigan* (1934) and *Judgment Day* (1935). The film *Studs Lonigan* (1960; dir. Irving Lerner) had Christopher Knight as the suffering Studs, and the television mini-series of the same title (1979; dir. James Goldstone) starred Harry Hamlin.

LOOBY LOO   See under ANDY PANDY

LORD, TRACY SAMANTHA   Erring heiress who returns to her estranged husband after almost marrying another, in Philip Barry's witty play *The Philadelphia Story* (1939). Tracy was played on stage by Katharine Hepburn, who repeated the role in the

much-acclaimed film of the play (1940; dir. George Cukor) –
'Hollywood's most wise and sparkling comedy', according to Leslie
Halliwell. The story was recast as a musical film, *High Society*
(1956; dir. Charles Walters), with music and lyrics by Cole
Porter, and with Grace Kelly in the role of Tracy Samantha Lord.
The Porter version has since been performed on stage. It has been
suggested that the recent general popularity of the forenames
'Tracy' and 'Samantha' owes much to *High Society*.

LORING, SIR NIGEL   Hero of Arthur Conan Doyle's historical
novels *The White Company* (1890) and *Sir Nigel* (1906). The latter
novel tells of Sir Nigel's youth in fourteenth-century England and
France. In the first book he is a man of mature years serving
under the Black Prince during the Hundred Years War.

LOS   See under URIZEN

LOTHAR   See under MANDRAKE THE MAGICIAN

LOVE, JASON   British medical doctor who is recruited as a
government agent and proceeds to have roving adventures of
the James BOND type. He appears in a series of thrillers by James
Leasor: *Passport to Oblivion* (1964; vt *Where the Spies Are*),
Passport to Peril (1966; vt *Spylight*), *Passport in Suspense* (1967;
vt *The Yang Meridian*), *Passport for a Pilgrim* (1968), *A Week of
Love: Being Seven Adventures of Jason Love* (1969), *Love-All*
(1971), *Host of Extras* (1973) and *Love and the Land Beyond*
(1979). David Niven played Dr Jason Love in the film *Where the
Spies Are* (1965; dir. Val Guest).

LOVEJOY   Antiques dealer who doubles as an amateur detective,
in a series of violent, amusing mystery novels by the British writer
Jonathan Gash (John Grant). Lovejoy, who narrates his own
adventures, has not divulged his first name. Titles in the series
include: *The Judas Pair* (1977), *Gold from Gemini* (1978), *The
Grail Tree* (1979), *Spend Game* (1980), *The Vatican Rip* (1981),
Firefly Gadroon (1982), *The Sleepers of Erin* (1983), *The Gondola
Scam* (1984) and *The Tartan Ringers* (1986). The character has
also appeared in a British TV series of the mid-1980s, although
there is a 'difference between the reasonably raunchy original and

the sanitized version shown on television' (according to T. J. Binyon, *The Times Literary Supplement*, 8 August 1986).

LOVELACE, ROBERT   Would-be seducer of Clarissa HARLOWE, in Samuel Richardson's great novel *Clarissa* (1748–9). Lovelace is an upper-class libertine, a man of great charm whose irresistible force cannot overcome the immovable object of Clarissa's virtue. According to Leslie Fiedler, 'Lovelace is an archetypal figure: just as Hamlet signifies finally only "hamletism" or Don Quixote "the quixotic", so Lovelace represents a complex that only his name fully defines.'

LOVEWELL, LILLUMS   See under Harold TEEN

LUCIA   Full name Mrs Emmeline Lucas, the insufferable heroine of a series of comic novels by E. F. Benson, beginning with *Queen Lucia* (1920). Lucia is a snob and a schemer, who is forever meddling in the affairs of her friends and rivals – Georgie Pillson, Daisy Quantock, Miss Elizabeth Mapp, and other inhabitants of the fictional towns of Riseholme and Tilling. The later books in the series are *Lucia in London* (1927), *Mapp and Lucia* (1931), *Lucia's Progress* (1935; vt *Worshipful Lucia*) and *Trouble for Lucia* (1939). Sequels by another hand are *Lucia in Wartime* (1985) and *Lucia Triumphant* (1986) by Tom Holt. Nancy Mitford once described Benson's heroine as 'the splendid creature, the great, the wonderful Lucia' (among her other notable admirers were Noël Coward and W. H. Auden). In the television series 'Mapp and Lucia' (1985) Mrs Lucas was played by Geraldine McEwan (with Prunella Scales as the redoubtable Miss Mapp). Benson's *Lucia in London* was dramatized on BBC radio (1985), with Barbara Jefford in the title role.

LUCKETT, SAYWARD   Heroine of a trilogy of novels by Conrad Richter, known collectively as *The Awakening Land*: *The Trees* (1940), *The Fields* (1946) and *The Town* (1950). The Luckett family settles in Ohio during the 1790s; the mother dies, and young Sayward takes charge of domestic affairs. The trilogy depicts a developing community over many decades, and ends with Sayward's death. A television mini-series, 'The Awakening Land' (1979; dir. Boris Sagal), starred Elizabeth Montgomery.

LUCKY   See under VLADIMIR AND ESTRAGON

LUCKY JIM   See Jim DIXON

LUCY   See under Charlie BROWN

LUDLOW, JOHNNY   Hero and narrator of a dozen volumes of short
stories set in the neighbourhood of Worcester. These tales are by
Mrs Henry Wood (Ellen Price), the author who is best remembered
for her lachrymose novel *East Lynne* (see Lady Isabel VANE).
The Ludlow stories were published in book form, as *Johnny
Ludlow Papers*, between 1874 and 1889. According to E. F.
Bleiler, 'about half the stories in the Johnny Ludlow series deal
with matters criminal and mysterious . . . Today Mrs Wood is
undeservedly forgotten. She was a skilled craftsman, despite
sentimental quirks common to the period . . . Her contemporaries
rated her Johnny Ludlow stories highest, and in this I would
concur.'

LULU   German *femme fatale* in Frank Wedekind's plays *Earth-
Spirit* (1895) and *Pandora's Box* (1902). She breaks the hearts of
many lovers, including the wealthy newspaper editor Dr Schön,
his son Alwa, and the lesbian Countess Geschwitz. She is
imprisoned for the murder of Dr Schön, but escapes and flees to
Paris and London, where finally she sinks into prostitution and
is killed by Jack the Ripper. Both plays formed the basis of a
remarkable silent film, *Pandora's Box* (1928; dir. G. W. Pabst),
which starred the American actress Louise Brooks as the curiously
innocent enchantress. The composer Alban Berg used the same
material as the basis of his opera *Lulu* (1937). Wedekind's Lulu
plays were revived by the American Repertory Theater Company
in the 1980s, with the action transposed to a modern New York
setting.

LUMPKIN, TONY   Coarse, good-for-nothing young man who
spends his time carousing at the Three Jolly Pigeons tavern. He
appears in Oliver Goldsmith's comic play *She Stoops to Conquer,
or the Mistakes of a Night* (1773).

LUND, ILSA   See under Rick BLAINE

LUNN, JOE   Faintly rebellious school teacher who eventually
settles down to become a stolid middle-class citizen, in William
Cooper's novels *Scenes from Provincial Life* (1950), *Scenes from
Married Life* (1961), *Scenes from Metropolitan Life* (1982) and
Scenes from Later Life (1983). (William Cooper is a pseudonym
for Harry Summerfield Hoff.) Anthony Burgess describes Joe Lunn
as 'the first of the British anti-heroes . . . a small good-hearted
rebel, too feeble to make his protest against society seem more than
a clown's gesture'. Nevertheless he paved the way for other
provincial anti-heroes such as Jim Dixon, Joe Lampton and
Arthur Seaton.

LUPIN, ARSÈNE   Master thief turned master detective, in the
stories and novels of Maurice Leblanc, beginning with *The
Seven of Hearts* (1907; vt *The Exploits of Arsène Lupin*). He is
very much the French version of both Raffles and Sherlock
Holmes – wrapped up in one person. In fact the latter character
actually appears in some of the Lupin stories, in the guise of
'Herlock Sholmès' (usually translated as 'Holmlock Shears',
although one of Leblanc's books appeared in America under the title
Sherlock Holmes Versus Arsène Lupin [1910]). English-language
editions of the Lupin stories have borne many different titles, but
volumes published in Britain include: *Arsène Lupin versus
Holmlock Shears* (1909), *Arsène Lupin* (1909), *The Fair-Haired Lady*
(1909), *The Arrest of Arsène Lupin* (1911), *The Confessions of
Arsène Lupin* (1913), *The Teeth of the Tiger* (1914) and *The
Golden Triangle* (1917). Recent sequels by other hands have been
produced by the French writing team of Pierre Boileau and
Thomas Narcejac.

Films about the 'gentleman *cambrioleur*' began with a series of
five German-made movies under the general title of *Arsène Lupin
Contra Sherlock Holmes* (1910–11), all starring Paul Otto as
Lupin. Later films include a 1917 silent starring Earle Williams,
and the talkies *Arsène Lupin* (1932; dir. Jack Conway), with John
Barrymore; *Arsène Lupin Returns* (1938), with Melvyn Douglas;
Enter Arsène Lupin (1944), with Charles Korvin; *The Adventures
of Arsène Lupin* (1957; dir. Jacque Becker), with Robert
Lamoureux; and the strangely-titled *Arsène Lupin Contre Arsène
Lupin* (1962), with Jean-Claude Brialy. A French television series
of the 1970s also featured Lupin.

LUVAH   See under URIZEN

LYNDON, BARRY   Irish rogue in W. M. Thackeray's novel *The Luck of Barry Lyndon* (1844; vt *The Adventures of Barry Lyndon, Esquire, by Himself*). His real name is Redmond Barry. He leaves Ireland after a duel, becomes a soldier of fortune and a professional gambler, and marries the rich Countess of Lyndon. A bawdy sequel by another hand is Christopher Wood's *The Further Adventures of Barry Lyndon, by Himself* (1976). In the film *Barry Lyndon* (1975; dir. Stanley Kubrick) the Irish adventurer was played by Ryan O'Neal.

LYON, ESTHER   See under Felix HOLT

M

M   See under James BOND

MABUSE, DR   Evil mastermind played by Rudolf Klein-Rogge in the two-part German film, *Doktor Mabuse, der Spieler* (1922; dir. Fritz Lang). The movie was based on a novel by Norbert Jacques. The villainous Dr Mabuse made a considerable impact in his day, and was later revived for sound films, including *The Testament of Dr Mabuse* (1933; dir. Lang), with Klein-Rogge, and *The Thousand Eyes of Dr Mabuse* (1960; dir. Lang), with Wolfgang Preiss.

MAC THE KNIFE   See Captain MACHEATH

McCANN, TERRY   Tough but good-natured bodyguard to the Cockney crook Arthur DALEY, in the amusing British television series 'Minder' (1979–85). Terry is a one-time boxer and former jailbird whose pugilistic skills prove extremely useful in protecting the cowardly Arthur from the consequences of his shady deals. Terry was played by Dennis Waterman, and the series was created by Leon Griffiths.

McCARTHY, CHARLIE   Wisecracking puppet character invented by American ventriloquist Edgar Bergen in the 1920s. He became extremely popular on the vaudeville circuit, then on the radio and in short films. Full-length movies in which Charlie McCarthy (and Bergen) appear include *The Goldwyn Follies* (1938; dir. George Marshall), *Charlie McCarthy, Detective* (1939; dir. Frank Tuttle) and *Look Who's Laughing* (1941; dir. Allan Dwan). In the last-named film Charlie meets Fibber and Molly McGEE. Edgar Bergen gained a special Academy Award in 1937, and eventually gave his puppet to the Smithsonian Institution.

McCLOUD, SAM   Country cop who is assigned to duty in New York City, and has to prove to his urban colleagues that he is no mere hick. He was played by Dennis Weaver in the television movie

Who Killed Miss USA? (1969; dir. Richard A. Colla) and in the subsequent TV series 'McCloud' (1970–77).

McCOY, LEONARD   See under James T. KIRK

McCOY FAMILY, THE   See under Jed CLAMPETT

McGARRETT, STEVE   Honolulu police detective played by Jack Lord in the American television series 'Hawaii Five-O' (1968–80). This has been described as 'the longest continuously running police show in the history of television' (Tim Brooks and Earle Marsh). McGarrett's favourite foe was a Hawaiian 'criminal genius' known as Wo Fat.

McGEE, FIBBER AND MOLLY   Man and wife who live at 79 Wistful Vista, somewhere in the USA. Fibber has earned his nickname because he constantly stretches the truth and is taken for a compulsive liar. The radio comedy series 'Fibber McGee and Molly' was popular for many years in America (1935–57). The characters also appeared in at least two films, *Look Who's Laughing* (1941; dir. Allan Dwan) and *Here We Go Again* (1942; dir. Dwan), where they were played by Jim and Marian Jordan. A television series, also entitled 'Fibber McGee and Molly' (1959–60), starred Bob Sweeney and Cathy Lewis. Among the characters who originally appeared alongside Fibber and Molly on the radio were the black maid, BEULAH, and one Throckmorton P. Gildersleeve who later graduated to a radio series of his own, 'The Great Gildersleeve'.

McGEE, TRAVIS   Freelance 'salvage expert' who lives on a Florida houseboat, frequently venturing out to set the world to rights. A sort of latter-day, Americanized version of The SAINT, McGee makes his living from extra-legal (if fundamentally noble) activities, most of which involve salvaging the property, or honour, of various attractive young women. As a sideline, he is also an unlicensed sexual therapist, expert at gently piecing together the shattered personalities of his beautiful clients. McGee was invented by crime writer John D. MacDonald for the paperback-original novel *The Deep Blue Goodbye* (1964). Within a few years the McGee books had garnered critical acclaim as well as high sales, and they graduated to the dignity of hard covers. The rest of the series consists of: *Nightmare in Pink* (1964), *A Purple Place for Dying* (1964), *The Quick Red Fox* (1964), *A Deadly Shade of Gold* (1965), *Bright Orange for the Shroud* (1965), *Darker Than Amber* (1966), *One Fearful Yellow Eye* (1966), *Pale Grey for Guilt* (1968), *The Girl in the Plain Brown Wrapper* (1968), *Dress Her in Indigo* (1969), *The Long Lavender Look* (1970), *A Tan and Sandy Silence* (1971), *The Scarlet Ruse* (1973), *The Turquoise Lament* (1973), *The Dreadful Lemon Sky* (1975), *The Empty Copper Sea* (1978), *The Green Ripper* (1979), *Free Fall in Crimson* (1981), *Cinnamon Skin* (1982) and *The Lonely Silver Rain* (1985). One of the books has been made into a feature film – *Darker Than Amber* (1970; dir. Robert Clouse), starring Rod Taylor – and another has formed the basis of a TV movie – *Travis McGee – The Empty Copper Sea* (1982; dir. Andrew V. McLaglen), with Sam Elliott.

MACHEATH, CAPTAIN   Highwayman in John Gay's musical play *The Beggar's Opera* (1728) and its sequel *Polly* (1729). He secretly marries Polly PEACHUM (the daughter of a criminal confederate),

Captain Macheath with Polly Peachum and Lucy

is betrayed by the girl's father, and ends up in Newgate prison. The character was revived by Bertolt Brecht for *The Threepenny Opera* (1928), a musical play he wrote in collaboration with the composer Kurt Weill. The well-known song 'Mac the Knife' was written for this production and refers to Macheath. Brecht also wrote *The Threepenny Novel*, an adaptation of his own play based upon Gay's original story. The film, *The Threepenny Opera* (1931; dir. G. W. Pabst) starred Rudolph Forster as Macheath. Other films in which Macheath appears include *The Beggar's Opera* (1952; dir. Peter Brook), with Laurence Olivier, and a remake of *The Threepenny Opera* (1965; dir. Wolfgang Staudte), with Curt Jurgens. A National Theatre production of *The Beggar's Opera*, with Paul Jones as Macheath, has been broadcast on Channel 4 Television (1983; dir. Richard Eyre).

MACHIN, DENRY   Full name Edward Henry Machin, the amusing trickster hero of Arnold Bennett's novel *The Card* (1911; vt *Denry the Audacious*). Despite his blatant cheating, conniving and practical-joking, he does well in life. He founds the Five Towns Universal Thrift Club, earns a fortune, and is elected Mayor. Bennett's *The Regent* is a sequel. In the film *The Card* (1952; dir. Ronald Neame; released in America as *The Promoter*) Denry was played by Alec Guinness. There has also been a stage musical based on Bennett's story.

McHUGH, DRAKE   See under Parris MITCHELL

McINTYRE, TRAPPER JOHN   See under Hawkeye PIERCE

MACISTE   Muscleman hero of popular Italian films. He is supposed to have been invented by Gabriele D'Annunzio, who collaborated on the script of the lavish silent film *Cabiria* (1914; dir. Giovanni Pastrone). In this epic production (which had 'an enormous international box-office success and in the US influenced the work of both Cecil B. De Mille and D. W. Griffith', according to Ephraim Katz) Maciste was portrayed as a loyal slave, but he developed later into an all-purpose strong-arm hero fit to vie with Hercules or Samson. The first actor to play him was Bartolomeo Pagano. The character recurred in such rousing films as *The Marvelous Maciste* (1915) and *Maciste in Hell* (1926). A latter-day example of the genre is *Maciste – The Mighty* (1960; dir.

Carlo Campogalliani), starring Mark Forrest. Other films dubbed
into English during the 1960s include *Maciste, Strongest Man in
the World* (1961; dir. Antonio Leonviola), with Mark Forrest (this
film is also known by the wonderful title of *Mole Men Against
the Son of Hercules*); *Maciste Against Hercules in the Vale of
Woe* (1962; dir. Mario Mattoli), with Kirk Morris; *Maciste in King
Solomon's Mines* (1964; dir. Martin Andrews), with Reg Park; and
so on. In some English-language releases, Maciste's name was
changed to 'Atlas' or 'Goliath'.

MacIVOR, FERGUS AND FLORA   See under Edward WAVERLEY

MacKENZIE, BARRY   Known to his friends as Bazza, a rough-and-
ready Australian at large among the poms of England. He was
created by comedian Barry Humphries and artist Nicholas
Garland for a comic-strip which first appeared in *Private Eye*
and was later collected in the books *The Wonderful World of
Barry MacKenzie* and *Bazza Pulls It Off!* (both 1972). He soon
graduated to films: *The Adventures of Barry MacKenzie* (1972;
dir. Bruce Beresford), which starred Barry Crocker; and *Barry
MacKenzie Holds His Own* (1974).

MacKENZIE, CONSTANCE AND ALLISON   Mother and daughter
who appear in Grace Metalious's bestselling novel about the
seamy side of American small-town life, *Peyton Place* (1956). In
the film of the book (1957; dir. Mark Robson) they were played
by Lana Turner and Diane Varsi. The follow-up novel by
Metalious, *Return to Peyton Place* (1960), has also been filmed
(1961; dir. José Ferrer), with Eleanor Parker and Carol Lynley in
the leading roles. However, the characters achieved their greatest
popularity when they were played by Dorothy Malone and Mia
Farrow in the television series 'Peyton Place' (1964–9). The success
of this soap-opera series, which was masterminded by producer
Paul Monash, has led to many spin-offs; these include the daytime
television serial 'Return to Peyton Place' (1972) and the TV movies
Murder in Peyton Place (1977; dir. Bruce Kessler) and *Peyton
Place: The Next Generation* (1985; dir. Larry Elikaan). There have
also been several paperback novels about the TV versions of the
characters, including such titles as *Again Peyton Place* and
Carnival at Peyton Place, both by Roger Fuller.

McMILLAN, STEWART AND SALLY   See under Jonathan and
Jennifer HART

McMURPHY, RANDALL PATRICK   Rebellious hero of Ken Kesey's
novel *One Flew Over the Cuckoo's Nest* (1962). After various
criminal transgressions, he is committed to a mental hospital but
refuses to be sedated. He befriends the other patients and
becomes the ring-leader of a hospital revolt. Eventually the
exasperated authorities destroy his spirit by lobotomizing him.
In the multi-Oscar-winning film based on the book (1975; dir.
Milos Forman) McMurphy was played by Jack Nicholson.

MacNEIL, REGAN   Young girl who is possessed by evil in William
Peter Blatty's horror novel *The Exorcist* (1971). Named after
one of King Lear's ungrateful daughters, Regan gradually changes
from a sweet child to an obscenely murderous fury. It takes all the
saintly power of a pair of self-sacrificing Jesuit priests to bring her
under control. In the film of the novel (1973; dir. William
Friedkin) Regan was played by Linda Blair (with Mercedes
McCambridge providing the deep voice of her possessing demon).
Both the novel and the film were spectacularly successful and led
to a spate of emulations (see, for example, Damien THORN). In the
sequel film, *Exorcist II: The Heretic* (1977; dir. John Boorman),
Linda Blair played Regan as a teenager.

MACQUART, GERVAISE   See under NANA and ROUGON- MACQUART

MacTAGGART, GEORDIE   Scottish teenager who tires of being
called 'Wee Geordie' and decides to become a muscleman. After
much strenuous body-building he wins an Olympic medal for the
shot-put. He appears in David Walker's novel *Geordie* (1950) and
its delayed sequel *Come Back, Geordie* (1966). In the film *Geordie*
(1955; dir. Frank Launder) he was played by Bill Travers.

McTEAGUE   Disbarred dentist who murders his wife for her money
and dies while on the run through Death Valley, in Frank
Norris's grimly naturalistic novel *McTeague* (1899). The book
formed the basis of Erich von Stroheim's mammoth film *Greed*
(1923), an eight-hour silent epic which was slashed to just two
hours in length. Gibson Gowland played McTeague.

M'TURK AND BEETLE   See under Arthur CORKRAN

MAD HATTER, THE   See under ALICE

MAD MAX   Violent leading man of futuristic Australian films: *Mad Max* (1980; dir. George Miller), *Mad Max II (The Road Warrior)* (1982; dir. Miller) and *Mad Max: Beyond the Thunderdome* (1985; dir. Miller and George Ogilvie). In an oil-thirsty world, he drives an armour-plated automobile and fights off attacks by groups of motorcycle barbarians. Max was played by Mel Gibson in all three movies.

MADDISON, PHILLIP   Hero of Henry Williamson's fifteen-part *roman fleuve* known collectively as *A Chronicle of Ancient Sunlight*. Phillip grows up in the England of the 1900s, becomes a keen naturalist, then goes off to fight in World War I and has traumatic experiences in the trenches. In the inter-war years Phillip becomes interested in fascism (his creator was at one time a keen supporter of Adolf Hitler). The titles of the individual novels are: *The Dark Lantern* (1951), *Donkey Boy* (1952), *Young Phillip Maddison* (1953), *How Dear is Life* (1954), *A Fox Under My Cloak* (1955), *The Golden Virgin* (1957), *Love and the Loveless* (1958), *A Test to Destruction* (1960), *The Innocent Moon* (1961), *It Was the Nightingale* (1962), *The Power of the Dead* (1963), *The Phoenix Generation* (1965), *A Solitary War* (1966), *Lucifer Before Sunrise* (1967) and *The Gale of the World* (1969).

MADISON, OSCAR   See under Felix UNGER

MAGGIE   See JIGGS AND MAGGIE

MAGNOLIA   See Magnolia HAWKS

MAGNUM, THOMAS   Likable private-eye played by Tom Selleck in the American television series 'Magnum, P.I.' (since 1980). He is a veteran of the Vietnam War, and now resides in Hawaii, where he solves crimes against a backdrop of palm trees, beaches and beautiful girls. The series was conceived (as a replacement for 'Hawaii Five-O' – see Steve McGARRETT) by Donald P. Bellisario and Glen Larson.

MAGOO, QUINCY   Irascible and extremely short-sighted cartoon character, the creation of animators John Hubley and Robert Cannon. The incompetent Mr Magoo appeared in films and on American television from the late 1940s. His voice was provided by Jim Backus. Mr Magoo 'starred' as Ebenezer Scrooge in a TV cartoon version of *A Christmas Carol* (1962). In the subsequent TV series 'The Famous Adventures of Mr Magoo' (1964–5) he played the parts of various other celebrated fictional characters, including Frankenstein, Dr Jekyll, Long John Silver, Dr Watson and Rip Van Winkle.

MAGWITCH, ABEL   Escaped prisoner who terrifies young Philip Pirrip, In Charles Dickens's novel *Great Expectations* (1861). He later becomes Pip's secret benefactor. A recent sequel by another hand, which tells of the character's life in Australia, is *Magwitch* (1985) by Michael Noonan. In the definitive film version of Dickens's original story (1946; dir. David Lean) Magwitch was played by Finlay Currie. A television-movie remake (1975; dir. Joseph Hardy) had James Mason in the part. See also under Estella.

MAHON, CHRISTY   Young peasant who believes he has killed his father, in John Millington Synge's celebrated stage comedy *The Playboy of the Western World* (1907). Pegeen Mike and the other County Mayo villagers protect Christy from the law and elevate him to hero's status – before it is discovered that his bullying father is still alive. The play provoked riots when it was first performed at the Abbey Theatre in Dublin, but has since become established as a classic of modern Irish literature.

MAHONEY, RICHARD   Young Irish doctor who settles in Australia, where he marries, builds a career, and eventually meets with tragedy. His story is told in a trilogy of powerful novels by Henry Handel Richardson (Ethel Florence Lindesay Richardson): *The Fortunes of Richard Mahoney* (1917; vt *Australia Felix*), *The Way Home* (1925) and *Ultima Thule* (1929). The books have been reprinted in one volume, under the first title, and have come to be regarded as a major contribution to Australian fiction. 'In its epic sweep it is at once the history of a man, a marriage, and a continent,' according to *The Oxford Companion to English Literature*.

MAIGRET, JULES Pipe-smoking police detective who is the hero of a very long series of stories and novellas by one of the world's most prolific writers, Georges Simenon. Maigret was conceived in 1929, and some eighteen books about him appeared in France in the period up until 1933, when Simenon tired of the character and put him aside for more 'serious' fiction. Returning to Maigret in 1942, Simenon wrote a further sixty-eight books about the detective before finally retiring in 1972. The first Maigret titles to be published in Britain were *Introducing Inspector Maigret* (1933), *Inspector Maigret Investigates* (1933) and *The Triumph of Inspector Maigret* (1934). Each of them contains two short novels, a practice which Simenon's British publishers continued until the mid-1950s, after which the stories began to appear singly. The last new title to come out in the UK was *Maigret and the Coroner* (1980). The English author Julian Symons has written a Maigret story which appears in his book *The Great Detectives* (1981), alongside similar treatments of Sherlock HOLMES and several others. Maigret has appeared in many French, German and Italian films, as well as in the Hollywood movie *The Man on the Eiffel Tower* (1949; dir. Burgess Meredith), where he was played by Charles Laughton. A later French film is *Maigret Sets a Trap* (1957; dir. Jean Delannoy), with Jean Gabin. He also appeared in a popular BBC television series, 'Maigret' (late 1950s to early 1960s), in which Rupert Davies took the leading role.

MAINWARING, CAPTAIN Officer of the Home Guard during World War II. As played by Arthur Lowe in the BBC television comedy series 'Dad's Army' (1967–77), Captain Mainwaring is a fussy, self-important little man whose military ambitions are continually thwarted by the inefficiency and ineptitude of the volunteers with whom he is obliged to work. The series was created by writers David Croft and Jimmy Perry. A feature-film spin-off, *Dad's Army* (1971; dir. Norman Cohen) also starred Arthur Lowe as Mainwaring.

MAISIE Vivacious showgirl played by Ann Sothern in a series of Hollywood 'B' movies which began with *Maisie* (1939; dir. Edwin L. Marin; based on a novel called *Dark Dame*, by Wilson Collison). The sequel *Congo Maisie* (1940; dir. H. C. Potter) is a remake of the

steamy safari love story *Red Dust* (1932; dir. Victor Fleming).
There were eight more Maisie films, concluding with
Undercover Maisie (1947; dir. Harry Beaumont).

MAITLAND, ANTONY   English barrister who has appeared in a
series of more than thirty crime novels by Sara Woods,
beginning with *Bloody Instructions* (1962). He is, more or less, a
British equivalent of Perry MASON. Other titles in which he appears
include: *Malice Domestic* (1962), *The Taste of Fear* (1963), *Error
of the Moon* (1963), *The Windy Side of the Law* (1965), *Knives
Have Edges* (1968), *Serpent's Tooth* (1971), *Enter the Corpse*
(1973), *A Show of Violence* (1975), *The Law's Delay* (1977), *This
Fatal Writ* (1979), *Dearest Enemy* (1981) and *Enter a
Gentlewoman* (1982).

MAITLAND, DOROTHY   See DIMSIE

MALAPROP, MRS   Character in Richard Brinsley Sheridan's play
The Rivals (1775). She is the aunt of Lydia Languish, who is
courted by Captain Jack ABSOLUTE. Her conversation is rendered
hilarious by the fact that she frequently uses the wrong or
inappropriate word – hence the term 'malapropism'.

MALDOROR   Protagonist of *Les Chants de Maldoror* (1868–74), a
long prose poem by the Comte de Lautréamont (Isidore-Lucien
Ducasse). 'Maldoror, the half-man, half-beast hero . . . wanders
day and night without rest or respite, troubled by horrible
nightmares and by phantoms that hover about his bed and trouble
his sleep' (Anna Balakian, *Surrealism: The Road to the
Absolute*, 1959). This strange dream-like work was recognized by
the twentieth-century Surrealist poets and painters as a forerunner
of their own fantastic creations.

MALLOY, TERRY   Inarticulate young bruiser who works as strong-
arm man for a corrupt dockland union boss, in the memorable
film *On the Waterfront* (1954; dir. Elia Kazan). The script was by
Budd Schulberg (who turned the story into a novel, published the
following year), and the rebellious Terry was played by Marlon
Brando.

MALONE, EDWARD   See under George Edward CHALLENGER

MALONE, JERRY   Medical hero of the long-running American radio soap opera 'Young Doctor Malone' (1939–60). Over the years he was voiced by Alan Bunce and Sandy Becker. The character made the transition to television, where he appeared for several years in a daytime serial (from 1958).

MALONE, JOHN J.   See under Hildegarde WITHERS

MAME, AUNTIE   Eccentric lady who adopts many roles in life, much to the astonishment of her orphaned nephew, Patrick. She appears in Patrick Dennis's novel *Auntie Mame* (1955) and its sequel *Around the World with Auntie Mame* (1958). The first of these books was adapted to the stage, then made into a film, *Auntie Mame* (1958; dir. Morton DaCosta), starring Rosalind Russell. The story was then transformed into a Broadway musical, *Mame*, with music and lyrics by Jerry Herman. This in turn was filmed (1974; dir. Gene Saks), with Lucille Ball replacing Angela Lansbury in the title part.

MAN FROM ATLANTIS, THE   See under SUB-MARINER

MAN FROM UNCLE, THE   See Illya KURYAKIN and Napoleon SOLO

MAN IN THE IRON MASK, THE   See under D'ARTAGNAN

MAN WITH NO NAME, THE   Mysterious avenger of the American West played by Clint Eastwood in a series of stylish Italian films, the so-called 'spaghetti Westerns'. The nameless one wears a poncho, smokes a cheroot and says very little. The movie which started the trend was *A Fistful of Dollars* (1964; dir. Sergio Leone), and its direct sequels are *For a Few Dollars More* (1965; dir. Leone) and *The Good, the Bad and the Ugly* (1966; dir. Leone). There have been many imitations, including a couple in which Eastwood plays essentially the same character: *Hang 'Em High* (1968; dir. Ted Post) and *High Plains Drifter* (1973; dir. Eastwood).

The Man with No Name (Clint Eastwood)

MANETTE, LUCIE   See under Sydney CARTON

MANDERS, BUNNY   See under A. J. RAFFLES

MANDRAKE THE MAGICIAN   Hypnotist hero of a comic-strip, written by Lee Falk and drawn by Phil Davis, which enjoyed a very long run in American newspapers from 1934. Mandrake has learned all manner of secret powers from a Tibetan guru; with the help of his black African sidekick Lothar, he uses his magical abilities to trap numerous villains. He became the hero of a cinema serial (1939), which starred Warren Hull, and also featured in various short-lived comic-books of the 1950s and 1960s. A television series, 'Mandrake' (1954), had Coe Norton in the leading role. The TV movie *Mandrake the Magician* (1978; dir. Harry Falk) was an unsuccessful attempt to revive the character. It starred Anthony Herrera as Mandrake.

MANFRED (1) Hero-villain of Horace Walpole's *The Castle of Otranto* (1765; published under the pseudonym of Onuphrio Muralto), a short novel which is regarded as the first of the Gothic tales of terror. Manfred is the Prince of Otranto in medieval Italy. His son, Conrad, is crushed by a gigantic helmet which apparently falls from the sky, and this supernatural wonder is the first link in a nightmarish chain of events which leads to Manfred's downfall.

(2) Lonely Faustian hero of Lord Byron's verse drama *Manfred* (1817). He lives in a castle high in the crags of the Alps. Tortured by his forbidden love for his sister, he seeks death, but is prevented from ending his own life by various supernatural powers.

MANNERING, GUY English army officer who dabbles in astrology. He is the titular hero of Sir Walter Scott's novel *Guy Mannering, or The Astrologer* (1815). The plot mainly concerns the fortunes of Harry Bertram, a Scottish laird's son who is kidnapped at a tender age and who subsequently marries Guy Mannering's daughter. Notable characters who appear in the novel include the farmer Dandie Dinmont (who has given his name to a breed of terrier dogs) and the gypsy queen Meg MERRILIES. The story was adapted for the stage many times in the nineteenth century.

MANNERING, JOHN See The BARON

MANNIX, JOE Technological detective played by Mike Connors in the American television series 'Mannix' (1967–75). He starts out as the employee of an investigative agency known as Intertect. However, 'despite the fact that the company was dedicated to the use of computers and other advanced scientific detection aids, Mannix seemed happiest when working with no implements other than his own intuition and fists' (in the words of Tim Brooks and Earle Marsh). The series was created by Richard Levinson and William Link.

MANON   See Manon LESCAUT

MANSEL, JONAH   Gentleman adventurer, much enamoured of open-top Rolls-Royce motorcars, who appears in a series of romantic thrillers by Dornford Yates (Cecil William Mercer). Jonah is a member of the 'White Ladies' group (see Berry PLEYDELL) and the book *Jonah and Co.* (1922) is named for him, but he has also enjoyed a number of thrilling adventures away from Berry and Co. Most, but not all, of the novels about these exploits are narrated by Jonah's friend Richard ('Bill') CHANDOS. They include *Blind Corner* (1927), *Perishable Goods* (1928), *She Fell Among Thieves* (1935), *Gale Warning* (1939), *Shoal Water* (1940), *An Eye for a Tooth* (1943), *Red in the Morning* (1946) and *Cost Price* (1949). Jonah also appears, with his spiritual brethren Bulldog DRUMMOND and Richard HANNAY, in the novel *Combined Forces* (1985) by Jack Smithers. In the British television film *She Fell Among Thieves* (1978; dir. Clive Donner) Jonah Mansel was played by Michael Jayston.

MANSON, ANDREW   Idealistic young doctor in A. J. Cronin's bestselling novel *The Citadel* (1937). He works among the miners of South Wales, strays briefly into the richer medical pastures of fashionable London, then dedicates himself once more to improving the health of the poor. In the film of the novel (1937; dir. King Vidor) he was played by Robert Donat (with a faltering Scottish accent). The BBC television serialization (1983) starred Ben Cross.

MANUEL   (1) See under JURGEN; (2) see under Basil FAWLTY

MAPP, ELIZABETH   See under LUCIA

MARCH, AUGIE   Hero of Saul Bellow's first major novel, *The Adventures of Augie March* (1953). Augie, a discontented young man from Chicago, travels to Mexico and France in order to escape his lot. According to Leslie A. Fiedler, Augie March is 'a renegade from respectability and belongingness,' like Huckleberry FINN and many other American heroes before him.

MARCH, JO   Boyish heroine of Louisa M. Alcott's well-loved domestic novel *Little Women* (1868). She lives with her sisters, Meg, Beth and Amy, and their beloved 'Marmee', in a Massachusetts town at the time of the American Civil War. Jo is the most creative of the girls, and hopes to be a writer (the narrative is clearly based on Louisa Alcott's own life-story). In the sequel, originally published as *Little Women, Part II* but now known as *Good Wives* (1869), Jo marries Professor Friedrich Bhaer and helps him set up a boys' school. Further sequels are *Little Men: Life at Plumfield with Jo's Boys* (1871) and *Jo's Boys and How They Turned Out* (1886). Films based on the books include *Little Women* (1933; dir. George Cukor), starring Katharine Hepburn as Jo; *Little Men* (1940; dir. Norman Z. McLeod), with Kay Francis; a remake of *Little Women* (1949; dir. Mervyn Le Roy), with June Allyson; and a two-part TV movie of the same title (1978; dir. David Lowell Rich), with Meredith Baxter Birney. The short-lived television series 'Little Women' (1979) had Jessica Harper as Jo.

MARCHMAIN, LORD   See under Sebastian FLYTE

MARIUS   See under FANNY

MARKER   Seedy private dick played by Alfred Burke in the British television series 'Public Eye' (1969–73). A later series about the character was simply entitled 'Marker'.

MARLEY, JACOB   See under Ebenezer SCROOGE

MARLOW   Narrator and part-hero of a number of works by Joseph Conrad. He first appears in the story 'Youth' (1898). Conrad introduces him again in the novella 'Heart of Darkness' (1899) – where he has a terrible encounter with Mr KURTZ in Central Africa – and the novels *Lord Jim* (1900) and *Chance* (1913).

MARLOW, KEEN   See under The DESTROYER

MARLOWE, PHILIP   Californian private-eye in the stories and
novels of Raymond Chandler. He is undoubtedly the most
famous of all fictional private-eyes, a curiously noble figure who
moves incorruptibly through the 'mean streets' of America's West
Coast underworld. The first Marlowe novel was *The Big Sleep*
(1939), and it was followed by *Farewell, My Lovely* (1940), *The High
Window* (1942), *The Lady in the Lake* (1943), *The Little Sister*
(1949), *The Long Goodbye* (1953) and *Playback* (1959). Marlowe
also appears in a number of short stories which have been collected
in such volumes as *The Simple Art of Murder* (1950) and *The
Smell of Fear* (1965). This gumshoe has had many imitators – see
for example Lew ARCHER, James HAZELL and Jack LEVINE. An
apocryphal Marlowe story appears in Julian Symons's book *The
Great Detectives* (1981).
    The films in which Marlowe appears as the named central
character are: *Murder My Sweet* (1944; dir. Edward Dmytryk),
starring Dick Powell; *The Big Sleep* (1946; dir. Howard Hawks),
with Humphrey Bogart – much the most famous Marlowe,
although Bogart only played him in the one film; *Lady in the
Lake* (1946; dir. Robert Montgomery), with Robert Montgomery;
The Brasher Doubloon (1947; dir. John Brahm), with George
Montgomery; *Marlowe* (1969; dir. Paul Bogart), with James Garner;
The Long Goodbye (1973; dir. Robert Altman), with Elliot Gould;
Farewell, My Lovely (1975; dir. Dick Richards), with Robert
Mitchum; and *The Big Sleep* (1977; dir. Michael Winner), again
with Mitchum. Philip Carey played him in the American television
series 'Philip Marlowe' (1959–60). A surprisingly authentic British
TV series, 'Marlowe' (1984), was written, produced and directed
by David Wickes, and starred Powers Boothe as the detective.

MARMELADOVA, SONYA   See under RASKOLNIKOV

MARNER, SILAS   Miserly weaver who becomes stepfather to a
golden-haired little girl, Eppie Cass. The experience of caring
for her transforms him into a saintly figure. He appears in George
Eliot's moving novel *Silas Marner, or the Weaver of Raveloe*
(1861). A recent BBC television film (1985; dir. Giles Foster)
starred the excellent Ben Kingsley as Silas.

MARPLE, JANE   Spinster detective who is the heroine of Agatha Christie's *Murder at the Vicarage* (1930) and subsequent books: *The Tuesday Club Murders* (1933; vt *The Thirteen Problems*), *The Regatta Mystery* (1939), *The Body in the Library* (1942), *The Moving Finger* (1942), *The Mousetrap and Other Stories* (1950; vt *Three Blind Mice*), *A Murder is Announced* (1950), *Murder with Mirrors* (1952; vt *They Do It with Mirrors*), *A Pocket Full of Rye* (1954), *What Mrs McGillicuddy Saw* (1957; vt *4:50 from Paddington*), *Double Sin and Other Stories* (1961), *The Mirror Crack'd from Side to Side* (1962), *A Caribbean Mystery* (1964), *At Bertrams Hotel* (1965), *Nemesis* (1971) and the posthumously published *Sleeping Murder* (1976) and *Miss Marple's Final Cases* (1979). Like Jules MAIGRET and Philip MARLOWE, Miss Marple also appears in Julian Symons's volume of pastiches, *The Great*

Miss Jane Marple (Margaret Rutherford)

Detectives (1981). A recent full-length 'biography' of the character is *The Life and Times of Miss Jane Marple* (1986) by Anne Hart.

Miss Marple has been played by Margaret Rutherford in four British films: *Murder She Said* (1962; dir. George Pollock), *Murder at the Gallop* (1963; dir. Pollock), *Murder Most Foul* (1964; dir. Pollock) and *Murder Ahoy!* (1964; dir. Pollock). She has been played by Angela Lansbury in a more recent movie, *The Mirror Crack'd* (1980; dir. Guy Hamilton). The elderly female sleuth has also appeared frequently on television, where Gracie Fields portrayed her in a dramatization of *A Murder is Announced* (1956). Later TV movies of Miss Marple's adventures include *A Caribbean Mystery* (1983; dir. Robert Lewis) and *Murder with Mirrors* (1985; dir. Dick Lowry), both with Helen Hayes; and several BBC mini-series under the collective title *Miss Marple* (1984–7), with Joan Hickson.

MARTIANS, THE   Monstrous aliens who invade Earth with their three-legged fighting machines and heat-rays, in H. G. Wells's novel *The War of the Worlds* (1898). 'Those who have never seen a Martian can scarcely imagine the strange horror of their appearance. The peculiar V-shaped mouth with its pointed upper lip, the absence of brow ridges, the absence of a chin beneath the wedge-like lower lip, the incessant quivering of this mouth, the Gorgon group of tentacles, the tumultuous breathing of the lungs in a strange atmosphere, the evident heaviness and painfulness of movement, due to the greater gravitational energy of the earth – above all, the extraordinary intensity of the immense eyes – culminated in an effect akin to nausea. There was something fungoid in the oily brown skin, something in the clumsy deliberation of their tedious movements unspeakably terrible.' These frightful beings, with their vast, cool and unsympathetic intellects, are eventually defeated by God's humblest creatures, our planet's disease bacteria. Wells's book is one of the great, fundamental tales of science fiction, and it has been emulated by many later writers. Direct sequels by other hands include *Sherlock Holmes's War of the Worlds* (1975) by Manly Wade Wellman and Wade Wellman, *The Second War of the Worlds* (1976) by George H. Smith, and *The Space Machine* (1976) by Christopher Priest. The most famous adaptation of the original story, and one which caused a major public panic in

America, is Orson Welles's radio version (1938) – when broadcast, its verisimilitude caused many listeners to believe that the United States really was being invaded by monsters from outer space. The film version (1953; dir. Byron Haskin) was rather less effective.

MARTIN, JACK   See under Ralph ROVER

MARVEL, CAPTAIN   Affectionately known as 'the Big Red Cheese', one of the most popular of all the costumed superheroes who have appeared in American comic-books. At times his adventures used to outsell SUPERMAN's, and indeed the owners of the latter character, DC Comics, brought a lawsuit against Fawcett, Captain Marvel's publishers, which succeeded in suppressing the character for many years. It was alleged that the Captain was altogether too similar to Superman. He first appeared in Fawcett's *Whiz Comics* in 1940. From 1941 to 1953 (when he was suppressed) he had his own comic-book, *Captain Marvel Adventures*. The artist responsible was C. C. Beck, and the stories were scripted by science fiction writer Otto Binder, among others. Captain Marvel's real name is Billy Batson. A scrawny youth who sells newspapers for a living, he meets a wizard who promises him 'the wisdom of Solomon, the strength of Hercules, the stamina of Atlas, the power of Zeus, the courage of Achilles and the speed of Mercury'. All he has to do is pronounce the word which is an acronym of these heroes' names – 'Shazam'. This he does, repeatedly transforming himself into the red-suited, mighty-muscled Captain Marvel. The character was revived (by his old enemies, DC Comics) in 1972, and has pursued his colourful crime-fighting career ever since. A movie serial, *The Adventures of Captain Marvel* (1941; dir. William Witney and John English), starred Tom Tyler as the Captain. A much later television series, 'Shazam!' (1974), had Jackson Bostwick as Marvel (later replaced by John Davey). There has also been a TV cartoon series based on the character.

MARVIN THE PARANOID ANDROID   See under Arthur DENT

MARY ANN   See Mary Ann SHAUNESSY

MASON, PERRY   Investigating lawyer who appears in a series of
eighty-nine crime novels by Erle Stanley Gardner, beginning with
The Case of the Velvet Claws (1933). Much of the action takes
place in the courtroom, and Mason is assisted throughout the series
by his legman Paul Drake and secretary Della Street. Later titles
include *The Case of the Sulky Girl* (1933), *The Case of the
Curious Bride* (1934), *The Case of the Caretaker's Cat* (1935), *The
Case of the Dangerous Dowager* (1937), *The Case of the Silent
Partner* (1940), *The Case of the Golddigger's Purse* (1945), *The
Case of the Negligent Nymph* (1950), *The Case of the Duplicate
Daughter* (1960) and *The Case of the Postponed Murder* (1973 –
last in the series). Six Perry Mason films appeared soon after the
character's creation: they include *The Case of the Howling Dog*
(1934; dir. Alan Crosland) and *The Case of the Curious Bride*
(1935; dir. Michael Curtiz), both of which starred Warren William
as the lawyer. Ricardo Cortez took the lead in *The Case of the
Black Cat* (1936; dir. William McGann) and Donald Woods played
the role in *The Case of the Stuttering Bishop* (1937). From 1943
to 1955 a Perry Mason series was broadcast on American radio.
The first actor to play Perry on the air was Bartlett Robinson,
and the series was sponsored by Procter and Gamble (soap
manufacturers, whose line of business gave rise to the term 'soap
opera'). The character made a successful transition to television,
where he was played by Raymond Burr (1957–66). A later TV series,
'The New Adventures of Perry Mason' (1973–4), starred Monte
Markham. An ageing Raymond Burr was persuaded to take on
the role once more for the TV movie *Perry Mason Returns* (1985;
dir. Ron Satlof).

MASON, RANDOLPH   Wily lawyer who is adept at finding legal
loopholes which will allow his criminal clients to go free. He
appears in several series of short stories by the American writer
Melville Davisson Post (creator of Uncle ABNER). These were
collected in the books *The Strange Schemes of Randolph Mason*
(1896), *The Man of Last Resort; or The Clients of Randolph
Mason* (1897) and *The Corrector of Destinies* (1908). By the third
volume Mason had become a reformed character, working within
the spirit as well as the letter of the law.

MASTERSON, SKY   Full name Obadiah Masterson, a New York
gambler and petty crook who falls for a Salvation Army girl.
Their love affair is described in Damon Runyon's short story 'The
Idyll of Miss Sarah Brown' (collected in *Runyon à la Carte*,
1946). The story is also known as 'Guys and Dolls', a title which
is in fact borrowed from an earlier Runyon volume (1931) which
features stories about some of the same characters. 'Of all the
high players this country ever sees, there is no doubt but that
the guy they call The Sky is the highest . . .' Among The Sky's
acquaintances are Nathan DETROIT and Miss Adelaide. A
successful stage musical, *Guys and Dolls* (1950), was based on
the story. It has music and lyrics by Frank Loesser, and a 'book' by
Jo Swerling and Abe Burrows. In the film of the same title (1955;
dir. Joseph L. Mankiewicz) Sky Masterson was played by Marlon
Brando.

MATHO   See under SALAMMBÔ

MATURIN, STEPHEN   See under Jack AUBREY

MATZERATH, OSKAR   Dwarfish narrator of Günter Grass's
remarkable novel *The Tin Drum* (1959). Born in Danzig in the
1920s, Oskar disapproves of the world he has entered and decides
to stay a child for ever: 'I remained the three-year-old, the gnome,
the Tom Thumb, the pigmy, the Lilliputian, the midget, whom
no one could persuade to grow.' In this state of arrested
development he lives through the horrors of the Nazi era, banging
his little tin drum. The film of the novel (1979; dir. Volker
Schlondorff) had child-actor David Bennent as Oskar.

MAUBERLEY, HUGH SELWYN   Minor poet who is the central
character of Ezra Pound's long poem *Hugh Selwyn Mauberley*
(1920). He is frequently regarded as an autobiographical *persona*,
although Pound once stated: 'Of course I'm no more Mauberley
than Eliot is Prufrock' (see J. Alfred PRUFROCK). The Canadian
novelist Timothy Findley has used the name Hugh Selwyn
Mauberley for the narrator of his novel *Famous Last Words* (1981),
which concerns a Nazi plot to place the Duke and Duchess of
Windsor on the throne of a European empire.

MAUDE   See under Archie BUNKER

MAVERICK, BRET   Charming but cowardly gambler played by
James Garner in the television Western series 'Maverick'
(1957–62). Maverick's brother Bart (played by Jack Kelly) and his
cousin Beau (played by Roger Moore) also featured in the series,
which was produced by Roy Huggins. James Garner returned to
play Bret in the TV movies *The New Maverick* (1978; dir. Hy
Averback) and *Bret Maverick* (1981; dir. Stuart Margolin) – and
in the subsequent series also called 'Bret Maverick' (1981–2).

MAX UND MORITZ   See under Hans and Fritz KATZENJAMMER

MAYFAIR, ANDREW BLODGETT   See under Doc SAVAGE

MAYO, ASEY   Plain-speaking Yankee detective, an inhabitant of
Cape Cod, Massachusetts, who is sometimes known as the
'Codfish Sherlock' or the 'Homespun Sleuth'. He appears in a
series of humorous mystery novels and short-story collections by
Phoebe Atwood Taylor: *The Cape Cod Mystery* (1931), *Death
Lights a Candle* (1932), *The Mystery of the Cape Cod Players* (1933),
The Mystery of the Cape Cod Tavern (1934), *Sandbar Sinister*
(1934), *The Tinkling Symbol* (1935), *Deathblow Hill* (1935), *The
Crimson Patch* (1936), *Out of Order* (1936), *Figure Away* (1937),
Octagon House (1937), *The Annulet of Gilt* (1938), *Banbury
Bog* (1938), *Spring Harrowing* (1939), *The Criminal C.O.D.* (1940),
The Deadly Sunshade (1940), *The Perennial Boarder* (1941),
The Six Iron Spiders (1942), *Three Plots for Asey Mayo* (1942),
Going, Going, Gone (1943), *Proof of the Pudding* (1945), *The
Asey Mayo Trio* (1946), *Punch with Care* (1946) and *Diplomatic
Corpse* (1951).

MAYO, DIANA   See under The SHEIK

MEAULNES, AUGUSTIN   Adolescent boy who discovers a dream-
world deep in the woods, in Henri Alban Alain-Fournier's
haunting novel *Le Grand Meaulnes* (1913; sometimes published
in English as *The Lost Domain*). He falls in love with Yvonne, a girl
who lives in the mysterious house he finds there. The story has
been filmed as *The Wanderer* (1967; dir. Jean-Gabriel Albicocco).

MEGGS, GINGER Young red-headed sporting hero of Australia's most popular comic-strip. The plucky, anti-authoritarian 'Ginge' was created by cartoonist Jimmy Bancks for a Sydney paper in 1921, and after Bancks's death in 1952 was perpetuated by Ron Vivian and other artists. The original *Ginger Meggs* newspaper strips have been supplemented by Australian comic-book reprints.

MEEBER, CARRIE Heroine of Theodore Dreiser's grimly realistic novel *Sister Carrie* (1900). She moves from the country to the town, where she is rescued from poverty by a friendly salesman. She meets a respectable restaurant-manager, George Hurstwood, who becomes infatuated by her and abandons his family in order to take her to New York. Carrie becomes successful as an actress, while Hurstwood falls into disgrace and destitution. In the film *Carrie* (1952; dir. William Wyler) she was played by Jennifer Jones (with Laurence Olivier as Hurstwood).

MEGAPHONE MARK See under DOONESBURY

MEISTER, WILHELM Young hero of Johann Wolfgang von Goethe's *Bildungsroman*, *Wilhelm Meister's Apprenticeship* (1795–6). He joins a theatrical troupe, where he meets the entrancing MIGNON, but suffers disillusionment and gradually learns to accept a less romantic view of life. His story is continued in Goethe's late sequel to the original story, *Wilhelm Meister's Travels* (1821; revised 1829).

MEKON, THE A 'Treen' from the planet Venus, deadly foe of spaceman Dan DARE in the comic-strip created by Frank Hampson for the *Eagle* in 1950. The Mekon is green-skinned, slit-eyed, small of body and vast of head. Like most villains of space opera, he is intent on conquering the human race. In his foreword to the book *Dan Dare, Pilot of the Future, in the Man from Nowhere* (1979) Kit Pedler says of the Mekon: 'His tiny wizened body showed you that he was far too clever to need muscles and his enormous vaulted cranium meant that inside was a cold, clinical, chess-playing brain entirely devoted to plotting universal domination. His face too had both machine-like and lizard-like qualities, and his overall appearance suggested a monstrously talented human foetus – with the added menace that we knew

he was horribly and totally alien.' In 1979–80 the prominent British
Conservative politician Angus Maude was dubbed 'The Mekon'
by his junior parliamentary colleagues – because of an alleged
physical similarity.

MELLORS, OLIVER   See under Lady Constance CHATTERLEY

MELMOTH, JOHN   Long-lived but doomed hero of *Melmoth the
Wanderer* (1820), a Gothic novel by the Irish clergyman Charles
Maturin. Melmoth has sold his soul to the devil in return for an
extended life on earth; he is tortured by remorse and wanders the
world attempting to find someone who will take the curse of
longevity from him. According to Alethea Hayter (in her
introduction to the Penguin edition of the novel, 1977), Maturin's
Melmoth, 'human but exempt from death, a lost soul and a tempter,
is descended from both Faust and Mephistopheles, from the Flying
Dutchman and the Wandering Jew of European legends'. The great
French novelist Honoré de Balzac was moved to write a sequel,
Melmoth Reconciled (1835). Another admirer of Maturin's novel
was Oscar Wilde; after his release from prison in 1897 Wilde
assumed the name 'Sebastian Melmoth'.

MENDOZA, LUIS   Mexican-American police detective, a
connoisseur of sports cars and pussy cats, who has featured in a long
series of crime novels by Dell Shannon (Elizabeth Linington). The
series began with *Case Pending* (1960), and among the later
titles are *The Ace of Spades* (1961), *Extra Kill* (1962), *Mark of
Murder* (1964), *Chance to Kill* (1967), *Unexpected Death* (1970), *No
Holiday for Crime* (1973), *Streets of Death* (1976), *Felony at
Random* (1979), *The Motive on Record* (1982), *Destiny of Death*
(1984) and *Chaos of Crime* (1985). Mendoza works for the Los
Angeles police department, and is an expert card-player.

MERLYN, JOSS   See under Mary YELLAN

MERRICK, DIANA   See Iris FENWICK

MERRICK, RONALD   Villainous British officer who appears in Paul
Scott's series of novels about the last days of English rule in India,
known collectively as *The Raj Quartet*. The individual novels are

Ronald Merrick (Tim Pigott-Smith) in *The Jewel in the Crown*

The Jewel in the Crown (1966), *The Day of the Scorpion* (1968),
The Towers of Silence (1971) and *A Division of the Spoils* (1975).
Merrick was played memorably by Tim Pigott-Smith in the
British television adaptation of the quartet, 'The Jewel in the
Crown' (1984). 'Clutching his swagger-stick as if it were a
talisman to ward off feelings of class discomfiture, Tim Pigott-
Smith brings out the way Merrick is a man trying to exorcize a
sense of social inferiority by exercising a sense of racial superiority,
as well as a homosexual spurred by guilt into sadism, avidly
humiliating males who awake the impulses that humiliate him'
(Peter Kemp, *The Times Literary Supplement*, 6 April 1984).

MERRILIES, MEG Fearsome, six-foot-tall gypsy prophetess in Sir Walter Scott's novel *Guy Mannering, or the Astrologer* (1815). She is described by one of the characters as 'harlot, thief, witch, and gypsy'. John Keats wrote a poem about Meg Merrilies which begins: 'Old Meg she was a Gypsy, And liv'd upon the Moors:/ Her bed it was the brown heath turf,/And her house was out of doors.' Meg was a leading character in stage versions of Scott's novel produced in 1816 and 1821; also in French opera versions such as François Boïeldieu's *La Dame Blanche* (1825). See also Guy MANNERING.

MERRIVALE, SIR HENRY Barrister, physician and amateur detective created by Carter Dickson (John Dickson Carr) for his novel *The Plague Court Murders* (1934). Known to his friends as 'HM', Merrivale is supposed to have been modelled on Sir Winston Churchill. The other titles in the series, most of them ingenious 'locked-room' mysteries, are: *The White Priory Murders* (1934), *The Red Widow Murders* (1935), *The Unicorn Murders* (1935), *The Magic-Lantern Murders* (1936; vt *The Punch and Judy Murders*), *The Ten Teacups* (1937; vt *The Peacock Feather Murders*), *The Judas Window* (1938), *Death in Five Boxes* (1938), *The Reader is Warned* (1939), *And So to Murder* (1940), *Murder in the Submarine Zone* (1940; vt *Nine – and Death Makes Ten*), *Seeing is Believing* (1941), *The Gilded Man* (1942), *She Died a Lady* (1943), *He Wouldn't Kill Patience* (1944), *Lord of the Sorcerers* (1945; vt *The Curse of the Bronze Lamp*), *My Late Wives* (1946), *The Skeleton in the Clock* (1948), *A Graveyard to Let* (1949), *Night at the Mocking Widow* (1950), *Behind the Crimson Blind* (1952) and *The Cavalier's Cup* (1953).

MERRIWELL, FRANK American school and college sporting hero invented by Gilbert Patten. His adventures appeared in Street & Smith's *Tip Top Weekly* from 1896, and continued to be published for half a century. In 1955 there was an attempt to revive him in a comic-book, *Frank Merriwell at Yale*, but this soon failed.

MERTEUIL, MARQUISE DE See under Vicomte de VALMONT

MERTON, TOMMY See SANDFORD AND MERTON

METROLAND, LADY MARGOT   Society lady in the novels of Evelyn Waugh. She first appears as Margot Beste-Chetwynde in *Decline and Fall* (1928), where she comes close to marrying the hapless Paul PENNYFEATHER. (It transpires that she is the owner of a chain of Latin American brothels.) Following her marriage to Lord Metroland, she reappears as Lady Margot in Waugh's *Vile Bodies* (1930), *Scoop* (1938) and other books. In the film *Decline and Fall* (1968; dir. John Krish) she was played by Genevieve Page.

MEURSAULT   Cold, affectless narrator of Albert Camus's disturbing short novel *L'Étranger* (1942; sometimes translated as *The Outsider*). He is a Frenchman who lives under the hot sun of Algeria. He shows no emotion when his mother dies, and later he is sentenced to death for killing an Arab. In the film of the novel, known in English as *The Stranger* (1967; dir. Luchino Visconti), Meursault was played by Marcello Mastroianni.

MICAWBER, WILKINS   Grandiloquent, improvident, but kind-hearted gentleman in Charles Dickens's novel *David Copperfield* (1850). He is penurious but ever convinced that 'something will turn up' – so much so that his name is now synonymous with 'an incurable optimist', according to Brewer's *Dictionary of Phrase and Fable*. He was played memorably by the American comedian W. C. Fields in the movie *David Copperfield* (1935; dir. George Cukor). Ralph Richardson played him in a 1970 TV-movie adaptation, and Arthur Lowe took the part in a BBC television serial version (1975). The most recent BBC serial (1986) had Simon Callow in the role. See also David COPPERFIELD and Uriah HEEP.

MICKEY MOUSE   Squeaky-voiced hero of cartoon films produced by Walt Disney. The most famous rodent in the world, Mickey is known by many names (for instance in Italy he is called Topolino). To many people outside the United States he is as familiar a symbol of America as the Coca-Cola bottle. Mickey first appeared in the short silent film *Plane Crazy* (1928), and this was swiftly followed by *Steamboat Willie* (1928), another black-and-white cartoon with simple sound effects. The artist Ub Iwerks collaborated with Disney on the animation; Disney provided the mouse's voice himself. A spate of Mickey Mouse films

appeared in the late 1920s and early 1930s, and they were soon
supplemented by comic-strips, toys and wrist-watches which bore
the character's image. Disney's creation had assumed the
proportions of a mythical hero, and was extravagantly praised by
writers and artists the world over. The great Soviet film-maker
Sergei Eisenstein described the adventurous mouse as
'America's most original contribution to culture'. Mickey's
principal friends were Minnie Mouse and the clumsy dog, Pluto.
These were joined in the mid-1930s by another canine hero,
Goofy, and by the very popular DONALD DUCK. Mickey Mouse
made his first feature-film appearance in Disney's *Fantasia* (1940;
dir. Ben Sharpsteen), where he played the Sorcerer's Apprentice. He
has since appeared in many more films and on television, and he
frequently performs 'live' at Disneyland and Disney World and in
other amusement parks around the world.

Mickey Mouse   *copyright Walt Disney Productions*

MIDNIGHT, CAPTAIN   Real name Captain Jim 'Red' Albright, an American radio hero created by Robert M. Burtt and Wilfred G. Moore. The Captain is a daredevil pilot, commander of the Secret Squadron. His anti-Nazi and crime-busting adventures enlivened the air-waves from 1940 to 1953. During this period he was voiced by various actors, including Ed Prentiss, Billy Bouchey and Paul Barnes. He was also played by Dave O'Brien in the cinema serial *Captain Midnight* (1942), and by Richard Webb in a television series of the same title (1954–6). There were Captain Midnight comic-books and newspaper strips in the 1940s. The movie *On The Air Live with Captain Midnight* (1979) is not actually about the ace pilot but concerns a disc jockey who takes on the well-known name as an alias.

MIGHTY MOUSE   Flying mouse who has appeared in American animated films since 1942. Originally known as 'Supermouse', he is an absurd cross between SUPERMAN and MICKEY MOUSE. Over seventy short cartoons in the Terrytoons series featured Mighty Mouse, who was drawn by animator Isidore Klein and voiced by actor Roy Halee. The character has also appeared in comic-books, and in an animated television series (*circa* 1955–62).

MIGNON   Mysterious girl who captivates young Wilhelm MEISTER, in Johann Wolfgang von Goethe's novel *Wilhelm Meister's Apprenticeship* (1795–6). Wilhelm rescues Mignon from a cruel master, but she eventually dies while dreaming of her birthplace in sunny Italy. The popular opera *Mignon* (1866), by Ambroise Thomas, is based on Goethe's story.

MILES AND FLORA   See under Peter QUINT

MILLER, DAISY   Lively, flirtatious American girl who tours Europe. She comes to a sad end, dying of fever in Rome. Her story is told in Henry James's novella *Daisy Miller: A Study* (1878). The author wrote an unsuccessful three-act stage version, in which he completely changed the ending, bringing Daisy to a happy dénouement. In the film of the book (1974; dir. Peter Bogdanovich) she was played by Cybill Shepherd. *Daisy Miller* has also been dramatized on British television as part of a series of James adaptations collectively entitled 'Affairs of the Heart' (1975).

MILTON, GEORGE   See under Lennie SMALL

MILTON, HENRY ARTHUR   See The RINGER

MILVAIN, JASPER   See under Edwin REARDON

MIMI   See under RODOLFO

MING THE MERCILESS   Emperor of the planet Mongo, in the
celebrated *Flash Gordon* comic-strip created by artist Alex
Raymond in 1934. An alien of distinctly Oriental appearance,
Ming was to become the best-known villain in the Hollywood
movie serials of the 1930s and 1940s. Like many of the nastiest
characters, he is blessed with a beautiful daughter (Princess
Aura). He was played by Charles Middleton in the three Flash
GORDON serials produced by Universal (1936, 1938 and 1940).
Decades later he was impersonated afresh by no less an actor than
Max von Sydow, in the wide-screen epic *Flash Gordon* (1980;
dir. Mike Hodges).

MINIVER, CAROLINE   Middle-class English housewife in Jan
Struther's book *Mrs Miniver* (1939). She was played by Greer
Garson in the famous Hollywood film of the same title (1942; dir.
William Wyler) – a movie which has been credited with helping the
Allies to win World War II – and in its sentimental sequel *The
Miniver Story* (1950; dir. H. C. Potter). In the latter film Mrs Miniver
suffers from cancer.

MINNEHAHA   See under HIAWATHA

MINNIE MOUSE   See under MICKEY MOUSE

MINNIE THE MINX   Aggressive little female created by comic-strip
artist Leo Baxendale for the children's weekly paper *The Beano*
(from 1953). She is rather more than a distaff version of DENNIS
THE MENACE, as Baxendale was to point out many years later in a
letter to the *Guardian* newspaper (13 October 1982): 'In creating
Minnie the Minx, I produced a girl of demonic energy and
boundless ambition . . . I had Minnie deploying her limitless
energy, entire lack of inhibition, her physical prowess, resource

and self-confidence to destroy streets full of little boys; intricate scenes with boys' teeth flying everywhere and Minnie triumphant in the midst . . . By the late Fifties and early Sixties I had Minnie constructing medieval war engines with six-foot spikes to demolish her hordes of schoolboy enemies (all this apart from her ceaseless undermining of the entire adult world).'

MITCHELL, DENNIS See DENNIS THE MENACE (1)

MITCHELL, PARRIS Young midwesterner who grows up to become a psychiatrist, in Henry Bellamann's steamy novel of small-town sin, *Kings Row* (1940). A sequel, completed by Bellamann's wife Katherine, is *Parris Mitchell of Kings Row* (1948). In the film *Kings Row* (1941; dir. Sam Wood) Parris was played by Robert Cummings (with Ronald Reagan as his friend Drake McHugh). A short-lived television series, 'Kings Row' (1955–6), starred Jack Kelly.

MITTY, WALTER Daydreaming hero of James Thurber's funny short story 'The Secret Life of Walter Mitty', first published in *The New Yorker* in 1939 (collected in the book *My World – and Welcome to It*, 1942). Mitty works as a magazine proofreader; inspired by the pulp fiction which he reads for a living, he spins extravagant fantasies within his own mind, projecting himself as a daring sea captain, pilot, Western outlaw, and so on. In the film *The Secret Life of Walter Mitty* (1947; dir. Norman Z. McLeod) he was played by Danny Kaye.

MOBY DICK Great white whale in Herman Melville's novel *Moby Dick* (1851). AHAB, one-legged captain of the *Pequod*, pursues the whale that cost him a limb. Among his crew are ISHMAEL and QUEEQUEG. The book is part sea yarn, part religious allegory, part mock-Elizabethan tragedy. It is also an accurate handbook of mid-nineteenth-century whaling lore. In his critical study, *Herman Melville* (1929), Lewis Mumford wrote: '*Moby Dick* . . . is one of the first great mythologies to be created in the modern world, created, that is, out of the stuff of that world, its science, its exploration, its terrestrial daring, its concentration upon power and dominion over nature, and not out of ancient symbols, Prometheus, Endymion, Orestes, or medieval folk-legends like Dr Faustus.'

MOCK TURTLE, THE   See under ALICE

MOLE   See under TOAD OF TOAD HALL

MOLE, ADRIAN   Self-styled 'intellectual' schoolboy in Sue
Townsend's humorous novel *The Secret Diary of Adrian Mole,
Aged 13¾* (1982) and its sequel *The Growing Pains of Adrian Mole*
(1984). The books were bestsellers in Britain, and Master Mole
soon appeared on the stage and on television. Adrian was played
by Gian Sammarco in two TV series based on the books
(1985–87).

MOLESWORTH, NIGEL   Inky schoolboy, 'the curse of St Custard's',
created by writer Geoffrey Willans and artist Ronald Searle in the
1950s. Nigel's adventures, all of which are recounted in his
atrocious spelling, have been reprinted in the omnibus volume *The
Compleet Molesworth* (1984). A sequel by another hand is
Molesworth Rites Again (1983) by Simon Brett.

MOND, MUSTAPHA   World controller, a relatively benign
equivalent of Orwell's BIG BROTHER, in Aldous Huxley's
dystopian novel *Brave New World* (1932). The novel formed the
basis of a lengthy but unsatisfactory television movie (1979;
dir. Burt Brickerhoff).

MONTE CRISTO, THE COUNT OF   Real name Edmond Dantès, the
vengeful hero of Alexandre Dumas's long novel *The Count of
Monte Cristo* (1844–5). Dantès is a young sea captain who is
unjustly imprisoned in a French island-fortress, the Château d'If.
After fourteen years of incarceration he escapes by the hair-raising
method of having himself trussed up as a corpse and thrown into
the sea. He finds a great treasure, assumes the identity of 'Monte
Cristo' and sets out to track down his enemies. Termed 'the
greatest *story* in the world' by the critic Maurice Baring, Dumas's
novel has been dramatized, filmed and televised countless
times. Films made in the silent era include a fifteen-part serial
version (1922), with Leon Mathot as Dantès; and a Hollywood
feature, *Monte Cristo* (1923), with John Gilbert. Sound versions
of *The Count of Monte Cristo* were made in 1934 (dir. Rowland V.
Lee), with Robert Donat; in 1954 (dir. Robert Vernay), with Jean

Marais; and in 1961 (dir. Claude Autant-Lara), with Louis Jourdan. A TV movie (1975; dir. David Greene) starred Richard Chamberlain. There has also been a film called *The Son of Monte Cristo* (1940; dir. Rowland V. Lee), with Louis Hayward; and a British television series, 'The Count of Monte Cristo' (1955), with George Dolenz. James O'Neill, father of the playwright Eugene O'Neill, is said to have acted the part of Monte Cristo on stage more than 5,000 times.

MONTGOMERY, ELLEN   Heroine of the weepy novel *The Wide, Wide World* (1850) by Elizabeth Wetherell (Susan Bogert Warner). Separated from her parents, she goes to live on a farm with her stern Aunt Fortune, who teaches her stoical virtues. Ellen's story was astonishingly popular throughout the second half of the nineteenth century, vying with *Uncle Tom's Cabin* for the status of America's favourite novel.

MONTONI   Satanic hero-villain of Mrs Radcliffe's Gothic novel *The Mysteries of Udolpho* (1794). He persecutes the heroine, Emily de St Aubert, who eventually escapes his clutches and marries her chosen lover. The apparently supernatural horrors which Emily endures in Montoni's castle of Udolpho are all shown to have rational explanations. The novel was extremely popular and influential.

MONTRAVILLE   See under Charlotte TEMPLE

MOOMINTROLL   Bland-faced little creature, vaguely reminiscent of a pigmy hippopotamus, who lives with his Moominpappa and Moominmamma in the Valley of the Moomins, somewhere in northern Scandinavia. The story of Moomintroll has been told by the Finnish writer Tove Jansson in a series of illustrated books which have been published since 1946. In English, the titles include *Finn Family Moomintroll* (1950), *Comet in Moominland* (1951) and at least nine others. The characters have gained worldwide popularity, and have appeared in newspaper comic-strips and on television.

MOOR, KARL   Hero of Friedrich Schiller's very influential romantic play *The Robbers* (1781). He is 'an angel-outlaw' (in the words

of critic Mario Praz), and a Byronic hero-villain before the fact
(see CONRAD and Childe HAROLD). Karl Moor also has affinities
with Robin Hood and with Milton's Satan.

MOPP, MRS   Charlady played by Dorothy Summers in the BBC
radio comedy series 'It's That Man Again' (1939–49; better known
as 'ITMA'). Mrs Mopp appeared with comedian Tommy Handley
and the other stars of this favourite show from 1941. Later she
was awarded her own series, 'The Private Life of Mrs Mopp' (from
1946). She became a British institution, and her exit line, 'TTFN'
(ta-ta for now), entered the language. Her creator was scriptwriter
Ted Kavanagh.

MORAN, SEBASTIAN   See under Sherlock HOLMES

MORBIUS, DOCTOR   See under ROBBY THE ROBOT

MOREAU, ANDRÉ-LOUIS   See SCARAMOUCHE

MOREAU, DOCTOR   Scientist who endeavours to turn animals
into men, in H. G. Wells's gruesome novel *The Island of Dr Moreau*
(1896). A modern sequel by another hand is *Moreau's Other Island*
(1980) by Brian Aldiss. In the film *The Island of Lost Souls*
(1932; dir. Erle C. Kenton) Moreau was played by Charles
Laughton. A later version, entitled *The Island of Dr Moreau* (1977;
dir. Don Taylor), starred Burt Lancaster.

MOREAU, FRÉDÉRIC   Youthful protagonist of Gustave Flaubert's
novel *L'Education Sentimentale* (1869). Like Emma BOVARY,
he is influenced by his reading of romantic literature. He hopes
to conquer Paris, has several affairs, and falls hopelessly in love
with Madame Marie Arnoux.

MOREL, PAUL   Nottingham miner's son with artistic aspirations,
in D. H. Lawrence's semi-autobiographical novel *Sons and
Lovers* (1913). Paul rejects his coarse father, but remains
somewhat unhealthily attached to his sensitive mother. In the film
of the novel (1960; dir. Jack Cardiff) he was played by Dean
Stockwell. There has also been a BBC television serial based on the
book (1981).

MORGAN, HANK Resourceful Yank who travels through time as a result of a blow to the head and finds himself a member of King Arthur's Round Table at Camelot. He is the hero of Mark Twain's amusing novel *A Connecticut Yankee at the Court of King Arthur* (1889). A silent movie version of the story was made in 1921; in the first talkie version, *A Connecticut Yankee* (1931; dir. David Butler) Hank the Yank was played by American folk-hero Will Rogers; in the musical remake, *A Connecticut Yankee at King Arthur's Court* (1949; dir. Tay Garnett) he was embodied (and given a crooning voice) by Bing Crosby.

MORGAN, HARRY American fishing-boat captain who plies his trade out of Key West, in Ernest Hemingway's novel *To Have and Have Not* (1937). Made desperate by financial hardship, he turns to smuggling people and booze. Morgan is one of Hemingway's most macho heroes. The book has formed the basis of at least three films: *To Have and Have Not* (1944; dir. Howard Hawks; part-scripted by William Faulkner), with Humphrey Bogart in the lead; *The Breaking Point* (1950; dir. Michael Curtiz), with John Garfield – this is the version which is most faithful to the novel; and *The Gun Runners* (1958; dir. Don Siegel), with Audie Murphy.

MORGAN, HUW Young hero of Richard Llewellyn's lyrically Welsh novel *How Green Was My Valley* (1940). The book tells of life in a coal-mining town during the late nineteenth and early twentieth centuries. Llewellyn returned to the character many years later and wrote three sequels: *Up, Into the Singing Mountain* (1960), which deals with Huw's life as an immigrant in Argentina, *Down Where the Moon is Small* (1966) and *Green, Green My Valley Now* (1975). The Oscar-winning Hollywood film *How Green Was My Valley* (1941; dir. John Ford) starred Roddy McDowall as the boy Huw. The novel has since been turned into a BBC television serial (1976).

MORGAN, JET World-saving spaceman hero of the popular BBC radio serial 'Journey Into Space' (1953–5), written by Charles Chilton. 'The programme reached five million listeners, the largest UK radio audience ever, and deservedly so, since no previous sf radio drama had equalled its narrative vigour' (*Encyclopedia of Science Fiction*). The series was sold to fifty-eight countries, and Chilton based three novels on the scripts: *Journey Into Space* (1954), *The Red Planet* (1956) and *The World in Peril* (1960). There was also a Jet Morgan comic-strip in *Express Weekly* (1956–7).

MORGENSTERN, RHODA   Sharp-witted New York lady played by Valerie Harper in the television comedy series 'The Mary Tyler Moore Show' (1970–4) and 'Rhoda' (1974–8). The latter series dealt with the story of her marriage and divorce.

MORIARTY, DEAN   Tearaway character in Jack Kerouac's 'Beat' novel *On the Road* (1957). He is said to be based on the real-life Neal Cassady, a man who inspired much of Kerouac's work.

MORIARTY, JAMES   Brilliant mathematician who turns to the bad, becoming a 'Napoleon of Crime' and the arch-enemy of Sherlock HOLMES. Professor Moriarty was created by A. Conan Doyle as a worthy nemesis for the great detective in 'The Final Problem' (1893), the story with which Doyle intended to finish Holmes's career. Moriarty is the ultimate villain, a man who bends his considerable intellect to the management of an international crime syndicate. Holmes catches up with Moriarty at the Reichenbach Falls in Switzerland; the two men struggle and apparently both topple to their deaths in the cataract. Several years later Doyle revived Holmes, but Moriarty remained safely dead (he appears in a few of the later Holmes short stories and the novel *The Valley of Fear* [1915], but these are all imagined as taking place *before* the incident at Reichenbach). The stage and film adaptors of Doyle's work gave Moriarty eternal life, however. He is prominent as the villain in William Gillette's play *Sherlock Holmes* (1899), and he also appears in the ballet *The Great Detective* (1953) and the stage musical *Baker Street* (1965). In the Holmes movies Moriarty has been played by Ernest Maupin (1916), Gustav von Seyffertitz (1922), Harry T. Morey (1929), Ernest Torrence (1932), Lyn Harding (1935), George Zucco (1939), Lionel Atwill (1942), Henry Daniell (1945), Hans Söhnker (1962) and many others. In *The Seven Per Cent Solution* (1976; dir. Herbert Ross) he was played by Laurence Olivier, and in the TV movie *Sherlock Holmes in New York* (1976; dir. Boris Sagal) John Huston took the part. The reptilian Professor has also appeared in

numerous sequels by other hands, notably two novels by John
Gardner: *Moriarty* (1974; vt *The Return of Moriarty*), where he
is billed as 'the Godfather of the Gaslight', and *The Revenge of
Moriarty* (1975). Another recent novel in which he looms large is
The Infernal Device (1978) by Michael Kurland. (An 'arch
criminal' called Moriarty also appeared on BBC radio's 'The
Goon Show' [1952–60], where he was voiced by Spike Milligan.)

MORLAND, CATHERINE   Young woman whose imagination is
inflamed by the reading of Gothic romances (of the *Mysteries of
Udolpho* type – see MONTONI). She appears in Jane Austen's novel
Northanger Abbey (1818). The plot concerns the comedy of
errors which ensues when Catherine is invited to Mr Henry
Tilney's imposing ancestral home. Catherine has something in
common with both Don QUIXOTE and Emma BOVARY, in that her
perception of reality is unbalanced by her avid consumption of
fiction. The BBC television film of the novel (1987; dir. Giles
Foster) had Katharine Schlesinger in the leading role.

MORLOCKS, THE   See under The TIME TRAVELLER

MORNINGSTAR, MARJORIE   Jewish-American heroine of Herman
Wouk's bestselling novel *Marjorie Morningstar* (1955). She has
show-biz aspirations, but is seduced into humdrum housewifery.
In the inevitable film of the novel (1958; dir. Irving Rapper)
Marjorie was played by Natalie Wood. Leslie A. Fiedler comments,
in his *Love and Death in the American Novel*: 'Only one
fundamental revision has been made in the mythos of seduction
between *Charlotte Temple* and *Marjorie Morningstar* (their
very titles indicate their kinship): the newer genteel
Sentimentalism will not let the fallen woman die. That Marjorie in
losing her virginity has been permanently maimed, incapacitated
for the full enjoyment of marriage, Mr Wouk does not doubt;
yet he insists on marrying her off into a bitter-sweet happy
ending.' (See also Charlotte TEMPLE.)

MORRIS, DINAH   See under Adam BEDE

MORTIMER, MEG   See Meg RICHARDSON

MORVILLE, GUY   Self-sacrificing hero of Charlotte M. Yonge's popular novel *The Heir of Redclyffe* (1853). He nurses his priggish cousin Philip, when the latter is laid low by fever, catches the disease himself, and dies, allowing Philip to become heir to the estate of Redclyffe. According to the critic Elaine Showalter, 'Guy Morville is the grand master of guilt . . . Philip, we are assured, can look forward to a life that is totally blighted and haunted by guilty memory.' Another writer, Rachel Anderson, views *The Heir of Redclyffe* as the first of the English romantic novels, and reports that the book 'was an enormous success with all levels of readers. It was read by young ladies, by undergraduates, by soldiers fighting in the Crimean War, by parsons and high church officials and by members of the Pre-Raphaelite Movement, who saw its insipid young hero, Sir Guy, as "the spirit of the modern crusader".'

MOSEBY, HARRY   See under George BAILEY

MOTO, I. O.   Japanese detective and secret agent invented by John P. Marquand for his books *Ming Yellow* (1935; vt *No Hero*), *Thank You, Mr Moto* (1936), *Think Fast, Mr Moto* (1937), *Mr Moto is So Sorry* (1938), *Mr Moto Takes a Hand* (1940), *Last Laugh, Mr Moto* (1942) and *Stopover: Tokyo* (1957; vt *The Last of Mr Moto*). Most of the Moto stories were serialized in the *Saturday Evening Post*. The hero was played by Peter Lorre in a series of eight low-budget films, commencing with *Think Fast, Mr Moto* (1937; dir. Norman Foster) and ending with *Mr Moto Takes a Vacation* (1939; dir. Foster). Henry Silva played the character in an unsuccessful revival, *The Return of Mr Moto* (1965; dir. Ernest Morris).

MOWGLI   Boy raised by wolves in the forests of India. Prior to TARZAN (who resembles Mowgli in several ways) he is the most celebrated feral child in modern fiction. Rudyard Kipling first invented him for his short story 'In the Rukh' (1892), collected in the book *Many Inventions* (1893). In this Mowgli appears as an adult, but there are passing references to his childhood in the jungle. Kipling went on to write a number of stories about Mowgli's strange upbringing, and these were included in *The Jungle Book* (1894) and *The Second Jungle Book* (1895). Neither volume is

Mowgli (Sabu) in the 1942 film of *The Jungle Book*

devoted entirely to Mowgli, and several decades went by before the
tales of the wolf-boy were collected in one book as *All the Mowgli
Stories* (1933). Mowgli (which means 'Frog') is saved by the
wolves after he and his parents have been attacked by Shere Khan
the tiger. He is reared as a wolf cub, and later learns the Law of the
Jungle from Baloo the bear. His other main allies are Bagheera the
panther and Kaa the python, and with the help of these beasts he
survives many dangers, including several renewed encounters
with the mighty Shere Khan. Eventually Mowgli reaches
adulthood and returns, sadly, to the world of human beings.

Kipling's vividly-written tales have been immensely popular
and influential. Lord Baden-Powell's cub scouts took their
language and lore from the Mowgli stories. There have been a
couple of attempts to film Mowgli's adventures, neither of which
really succeeds in capturing the magic of Kipling's original. *The
Jungle Book* (1942; dir. Zoltan Korda) had Sabu as Mowgli. A

Disney-produced animated film of the same title (1967; dir. Wolfgang Reitherman) depends mainly on its jazzy musical score, and comes a very long way after Kipling. There have also been stage renditions of *The Jungle Book*.

MUAD'DIB   See Paul ATREIDES

MUFFIN, CHARLIE   Bolshie British spy, more in the tradition of Harry PALMER than of James BOND, who appears in a series of thrillers by Brian Freemantle. The titles include: *Charlie Muffin* (1977; vt *Charlie M*), *Clap Hands, Here Comes Charlie* (1978; vt *Here Comes Charlie M*), *The Inscrutable Charlie Muffin* (1979), *Charlie Muffin's Uncle Sam* (1980; vt *Charlie Muffin USA*) and *Madrigal for Charlie Muffin* (1981). The British television film *Charlie Muffin* (1979; dir. Jack Gold) starred David Hemmings.

MUFFIN THE MULE   Children's puppet character who became very popular on BBC television during the 1950s. Muffin was presented by Annette Mills, who also wrote books about the little mule. Along with LARRY THE LAMB and other well-loved characters, Muffin appeared in the weekly paper *TV Comic* (from 1951).

MUGG, MATTHEW   See under John DOLITTLE

MULVANEY, TERENCE   Irishman in the Indian army, one of Rudyard Kipling's 'Soldiers Three'. See also Jock LEAROYD and Stanley ORTHERIS.

MUMMY, THE   Revivified Egyptian corpse in the celebrated American horror film *The Mummy* (1932; dir. Karl Freund), starring Boris Karloff in wrinkly make-up. The movie was written by John L. Balderston. The idea, if not precisely the same character, has been used in many films since – for example, *The Mummy's Hand* (1940; dir. Christy Cabanne), *The Mummy's Tomb* (1942; dir. Harold Young), *Abbott and Costello Meet the Mummy* (1955; dir. Charles Lamont), and *The Mummy* (1959; dir. Terence Fisher). The last-named, British-made, film has Christopher Lee in the eponymous role. In the original Boris Karloff movie the Mummy's name is Im-ho-Tep; in most of the

later films he is known as Kharis. A children's book in the
'Ladybird Horror Classics' series, *The Mummy* (1985), is based on
short stories by A. Conan Doyle (although he never actually
wrote a story entitled 'The Mummy').

MUNSTER, HERMAN   Amiable, peace-loving lookalike of
FRANKENSTEIN's monster, played by Fred Gwynne in the US
television comedy series 'The Munsters' (1964–6). Herman is the
head of a hilariously ghoulish family, all based on characters
from 1930s horror films. The series was conceived and produced
by Joe Connelly and Bob Mosher (probably in imitation of the
ADDAMS FAMILY). Subsequent TV movies featuring Herman
Munster and friends are *Munster Go Home* (1966; dir. Earl
Bellamy) and *The Munsters' Revenge* (1981; dir. Don Weis).

MUTT AND JEFF   Pair of buffoons, one short, one tall, who became
very popular in American newspaper comic-strips. Mutt and
Jeff were conceived and drawn by Bud Fisher from 1907, and they
subsequently appeared in short animated films (from 1916). The
characters reached their greatest heights of fame in the 1920s.

MYCROFT, MR   See under Mycroft HOLMES

MYSHKIN, PRINCE   Unworldly, Christ-like hero of Fyodor
Dostoevsky's novel *The Idiot* (1868–9). Myshkin is a quixotic
innocent who inherits a Russian fortune, with tragic
consequences for himself and his friends, the proud Natasha
Filippovna and the jealous Rogozhin. When Rogozhin murders
Natasha, Myshkin loses his sanity. Dostoevsky declared that this
was his favourite among his novels (although some critics have
argued that Alexei KARAMAZOV is a more effective portrait of a
saintly man than Prince Myshkin). There have been several
notable movie versions of the story, including a French one
(1946; dir. Georges Lampin), with Gérard Philipe, and a Japanese
one (1951; dir. Akira Kurosawa), with Masayuki Mori. In the
Russian-made film *The Idiot* (1958; dir. Ivan Pyriev) Myshkin
was played by Yuri Yakovlev. There has been a ballet version of the
story (1952), with music by Hans Werner Henze and choreography
by Tatjana Gsovsky. The novel has also been adapted for the English
stage by Simon Gray (1970).

NAMOR, PRINCE   See Sub-mariner

NANA   Full name Anna Coupeau, a prostitute who appears in one of Emile Zola's best known novels, *Nana* (1880). The book is part of the multi-volume Rougon-Macquart series, and Nana makes her first appearance as a young girl in the preceding novel, *L'Assommoir* (1877) – which has been filmed as *Gervaise* (1956;

Nana (Ann Sten) in the 1934 film, with Phillips Holmes

dir. René Clément). It is her parents' dissipation by drink which causes Nana to take to the boulevards, thus demonstrating Zola's conviction that our lives are shaped by heredity and environment. The silent movie *Nana* (1926; dir. Jean Renoir) had Catherine Hesseling as the heroine. The Hollywood film of the same title (1934; dir. Dorothy Arzner) starred Anna Sten. The story has been adapted for BBC television (1968), with Katharine Schofield as Nana. There has also been a French TV version (1983), with Véronique Genest in the leading role.

NANCY See under Bill SIKES

NANKI-POO Son of the Mikado (ruler of a never-never land which bears some small resemblance to Japan). He courts Yum-Yum, the Lord High Executioner's ward, in the comic opera *The Mikado, or the Town of Titipu* (1885) by W. S. Gilbert and Arthur Sullivan. This has long been the most popular of the Gilbert-and-Sullivan operettas, and has been translated into many languages. British film versions were released in 1939 and 1966.

NATASHA See Natasha ROSTOVA

NAUGHTON, CLAUDIA Girl-wife of architect David Naughton, in a series of popular domestic novels by American writer Rose Franken. *Claudia: The Story of a Marriage* (1939) was followed by *Claudia and David* (1940), *Another Claudia* (1943), *Young Claudia* (1946), *The Marriage of Claudia* (1948), *From Claudia to David* (1960), *The Fragile Years* and *The Return of Claudia*. The first of these novels was turned into a successful stage play in 1941, and this was subsequently filmed (1943; dir. Edmund Goulding) with Dorothy McGuire as Claudia. A film sequel is *Claudia and David* (1946; dir. Walter Lang), which also starred McGuire. Claudia also appeared on the radio during the 1940s. The television series 'Claudia, the Story of a Marriage' (1952) had Joan McCracken in the title role.

NEMO, CAPTAIN Master of the submarine *Nautilus*, an Indian prince turned super-technological pirate in Jules Verne's novel *20,000 Leagues Under the Sea* (1870). Nemo was embittered by Britain's crushing of the Indian Mutiny in 1857, and he used his immense wealth to build his submarine in utmost secrecy; he now roams the seas, occasionally surfacing to sink an 'enemy' warship. In Verne's semi-sequel to this story, *The Mysterious Island* (1875), the *Nautilus* is crippled and Nemo hides away in a cavern beneath an uncharted island. He becomes a Prospero figure for the castaways there, working scientific wonders which enable them to survive. At the end of the novel he drowns in the sunken *Nautilus*. A modern sequel by another hand is *The Secret Sea* (1979) by Thomas F. Monteleone, in which Nemo sails his wondrous vessel into parallel worlds.

The Captain has appeared in many films, including *Mysterious Island* (1929; dir. Lucien Hubbard), in which he was played by Lionel Barrymore; *20,000 Leagues Under the Sea* (1954; dir. Richard Fleischer), starring James Mason; *Mysterious Island* (1961; dir. Cy Endfield), with Herbert Lom; and *Captain Nemo and the Underwater City* (1969; dir. James Hill), with Robert Ryan. There has also been an American television series, 'The Return of Captain Nemo' (1978), which starred José Ferrer.

NEWCOME, THOMAS Upright, honourable, but somewhat unworldly and quixotic British colonel, in W. M. Thackeray's novel *The Newcomes* (1853–5). Colonel Newcome's son Clive is an artist, and the plot of the novel largely concerns Clive's thwarted love for his cousin, Ethel Newcome. The narrator is Arthur PENDENNIS. According to one critic, Colonel Thomas Newcome 'remains to the end an innocent, untouchable by the Great World, yet Thackeray manages in his case to achieve the effect of skilful sentimentality, especially in the famous death scene' (Seymour Betsky, in *The Pelican Guide to English Literature*).

NEWSOME, CHAD See under Lambert STRETHER

NEWTON, CURT See Captain FUTURE

NICKLEBY, NICHOLAS Young man who makes his way in the harsh world of early nineteenth-century England. He is the central character of Charles Dickens's novel *The Life and Adventures of Nicholas Nickleby* (1839). Left penniless on the death of his father, Nicholas works as an usher at Dotheboys Hall, a terrible school run by the infamous Mr Wackford Squeers. He befriends an unfortunate urchin called SMIKE, and together they escape to join an acting troupe. As with other early Dickens novels, notably *The Pickwick Papers* and *Oliver Twist, Nicholas Nickleby* attracted plagiarisms and sequels by other hands. A book of the latter type is *Scenes from the Life of Nickleby Married* (1840) by 'Guess'. According to Louis James, this 'takes up the story of Nicholas where Dickens left off . . . While far short of Dickens, the writing is lively, and the quite incredible plot is partly compensated for by the vivid pictures of London low life; its music halls, fortune tellers, thieves, and labyrinths of dirty back streets.' The film *Nicholas Nickleby* (1947; dir. Alberto Cavalcanti) had Derek Bond as Nicholas. In the 1980s the Nickleby story has become one of the best-known of all Dickens's works, thanks to a remarkable nine-hour stage adaptation by David Edgar. As performed by the Royal Shakespeare Company in Britain and America since 1981, this has had a huge critical success. The play was televised in two parts on Channel Four in 1982, with Roger Rees in the role of Nicholas.

NIGGER JIM   Runaway slave who becomes a fast friend of Huckleberry FINN in Mark Twain's novel *The Adventures of Huckleberry Finn* (1884). Jim accompanies Huck on a raft-voyage down the Mississippi, eventually gaining his freedom from slavery. In his controversial essay of the 1950s, 'Come Back to the Raft Ag'in, Huck Honey', Leslie A. Fiedler argued that the relationship between Huck and Jim is chastely 'homoerotic,' making *Huckleberry Finn* a leading example of his nation's 'favourite books, in which a white and coloured American male flee from civilization into each other's arms' (Fiedler, *Love and Death in the American Novel* – for other examples of this phenomenon in American fiction see Natty BUMPPO and CHINGACHGOOK, and ISHMAEL and QUEEQUEG).

NINOTCHKA   Unsmiling lady commissar played by Greta Garbo in Ernst Lubitsch's celebrated comedy film *Ninotchka* (1939). She comes to Paris to help the cause of the Russian Revolution, and ends up falling in love with a decadent westerner (and learning how to smile). The movie, which was publicized as the one in which 'Garbo laughs', was scripted by Charles Brackett, Billy Wilder and Walter Reisch from an original three-sentence outline

by Melchior Lengyel. The story was subsequently turned into
a stage musical, *Silk Stockings*, with music and lyrics by Cole
Porter; this in turn was filmed in 1957 by Rouben Mamoulian,
with Cyd Charisse playing the part of Ninotchka. (Mrs Margaret
Thatcher's meeting with Mr Mikhail Gorbachev in 1987 was
described by one witty journalist as 'Ninotchka in reverse'.)

NIPPER   See under Nelson LEE

NO, DOCTOR   See under James BOND

NOBLE, MARY   Heroine of one of the longest-running American
radio soap-operas, 'Backstage Wife' (1935–59). According to the
programme's epigraph, this series was about 'Mary Noble, a little
Iowa girl, who married Larry Noble, handsome matinee idol,
dream sweetheart of a million other women, and her struggle to
keep his love in the complicated atmosphere of backstage life'
(quoted in R. W. Stedman, *The Serials*). The story was one of
many conceived by the Blackett-Sample-Hummert advertising
agency (see also Ma PERKINS and Helen TRENT). Mary Noble was
voiced by Vivian Fridell, and later by Claire Niesen.

NODDY   Little pixie who lives in Toyland and drives a bright-red
motorcar. His friends include Big Ears, a bearded gnome, and Mr
Plod, a policeman. This apparently inoffensive nursery-story
character has been much reviled by critics, teachers and
librarians, but nevertheless remains popular. Noddy was created
by Enid Blyton for her book *Little Noddy Goes to Toyland*
(1949), and she continued to write small books of his adventures
almost until her death in 1968. For the first five years they were
illustrated by the Dutch artist Harmsen van der Beek. Blyton also
wrote a musical stage show, *Noddy in Toyland* (1954), which
proved a success. Noddy soon became the centre of a considerable
merchandising industry, his figure appearing on numerous nursery
products. A remarkably vehement critical reaction set in, and
some libraries ceased stocking Noddy books. Margery Fisher's
views are typical of many others when she refers to Noddy as
'this monotonously infantile character . . . put together from the
weakest and least desirable attributes of childhood. It is hard to

explain the persistent popularity of these trivial, repetitive stories with their small, retarded, masochistic hero.'

NOLAN, FRANCIE   Irish-American slum child whose early life with her drunken father and long-suffering mother is described in Betty Smith's popular novel *A Tree Grows in Brooklyn* (1943). In the film of the novel (1945; dir. Elia Kazan) young Francie was played by Peggy Ann Garner. The TV movie remake (1974; dir. Joseph Hardy) had Pamela Ferdin in the role.

NOLAN, GYPO   Irishman who betrays his IRA comrade to the police for 'twenty pieces of silver', in Liam O'Flaherty's novel *The Informer* (1925). In the Academy Award-winning film of the same title (1935; dir. John Ford) he was played by Victor McLaglen (who won an Oscar for his portrayal of the stumbling, bemused, half-moronic Nolan). A later movie, *Up Tight* (1968; dir. Jules Dassin), steals the plot of O'Flaherty's book but transfers it to a black American setting.

NOON, ED   New York private detective, a lover of old movies, who appears in a series of more than thirty mystery novels by Michael Avallone. Titles include: *The Spitting Image* (1953), *Dead Game* (1954), *Violence in Velvet* (1956), *The Case of the Violent Virgin* (1957), *Meanwhile Back at the Morgue* (1960), *The Bedroom Bolero* (1963; vt *The Bolero Murders*), *The Fat Death* (1966), *Assassins Don't Die in Bed* (1968), *Death Dives Deep* (1971), *Shoot it Again, Sam* (1972; vt *The Moving Graveyard*), *The X-Rated Corpse* (1973), *The Big Stiffs* (1977) and *Dark on Monday* (1978). The prolific Mr Avallone has also used the pseudonym 'Edwina Noone' for a series of Gothic romances.

NORA   See Nora HELMER

NORRIS, ARTHUR   Shady character who intrigues the narrator of Christopher Isherwood's novel *Mr Norris Changes Trains* (1935; vt *The Last of Mr Norris*). He professes to be a communist, and has mysterious dealings with the criminal underworld in Berlin. In a BBC radio adaptation of the novel (1984) Norris was played by David March. Isherwood originally intended that *Mr Norris Changes Trains* and *Goodbye to Berlin* should both be

incorporated in a long novel to be called *The Lost* (see also Sally
Bowles).

NORTH, HUGH   American army Intelligence officer who appears
in a long series of thrillers by F. Van Wyck Mason, beginning with
Seeds of Murder (1930). The first few books, including *The Vesper
Service Murders* (1931) and *The Yellow Arrow Murders* (1932),
are straightforward detective novels in which Hugh North
stumbles across various bodies. As the series progresses, however,
the novels become tales of international intrigue, with Captain
(later Colonel) North playing the role of secret agent on behalf
of the US government. Among the later titles are *The Shanghai
Bund Murders* (1933; vt *The China Sea Murders*), *The Budapest
Parade Murders* (1935), *The Hongkong Airbase Murders* (1937),
The Bucharest Ballerina Murders (1940), *Saigon Singer* (1946),
Himalayan Assignment (1952), *The Gracious Lily Affair* (1957),
Secret Mission to Bangkok (1960), *Maracaibo Mission* (1965) and
The Deadly Orbit Mission (1968). (It is amusing to note that a
real-life 'Colonel North' [Oliver North] became notorious
during the so-called 'Irangate' scandal of 1986.)

NORTH, JERRY AND PAM   Detective couple created by the
husband-and-wife writing team Richard and Frances Lockridge.
The Norths began life in a series of stories published in the *New
Yorker* magazine, and soon became successful in book form.
The volumes in the series are *Mr and Mrs North* (1936), *The
Norths Meet Murder* (1940) and almost thirty others – including
Murder Out of Turn (1941), *Killing the Goose* (1944), *Murder is
Served* (1948), *Dead as a Dinosaur* (1952), *Voyage Into Violence*
(1956) and *The Judge is Reversed* (1960), and ending with *Murder
by the Book* (1963). In the film *Mr and Mrs North* (1941; dir.
Robert B. Sinclair) Jerry and Pam were played by William Post
and Gracie Allen. The Norths also appeared on American radio
during the 1940s, and on BBC radio in the early 1950s (where they
were played by the Canadian couple Bernard Braden and Barbara
Kelly). The US television series 'Mr and Mrs North' (1952–4)
starred Richard Denning and Barbara Britton.

NOSFERATU   See under Count Dracula

NOSTROMO Flamboyant, charismatic Italian dock-worker, a 'Man of the People'. He becomes involved in a counter-revolution in the imaginary Latin-American country of Costaguana. The story of his heroism, and of his eventual corruption by a hoard of silver, is told in Joseph Conrad's most ambitious novel, *Nostromo: A Tale of the Seaboard* (1904). Another of the principal characters is Charles Gould, owner of Costaguana's silver mine and the unwitting agent of Nostromo's downfall. Nostromo's real name is Gian Battista Fidanza. The novel has been serialized on BBC radio (1986).

NUGENT, FRANK See under Harry WHARTON

NUMBER-ONE SON See under Charlie CHAN

NUMBER SIX See The PRISONER

NYOKA See under BOMBA

OAK, GABRIEL See under Bathsheba EVERDENE

OAKROYD, JESS Carpenter, and a member of the travelling concert party, in J. B. Priestley's picaresque novel *The Good Companions* (1929). He was revived by Priestley for a radio play, *The Return of Jess Oakroyd* (1941). In films of *The Good Companions* Oakroyd has been played by Edmund Gwenn (1932) and Eric Portman (1956). In the Radio Luxembourg series *The Good Companions* (from 1952) he was played by Wilfred Pickles. In Alan Plater's television adaptation of the original novel (1982) John Stratton took the part of Oakroyd. (See also Inigo JOLLIFANT.)

OAKES, BOYSIE Cowardly secret agent in a series of comedy thrillers by John Gardner: *The Liquidator* (1964), *The Understrike* (1965), *Amber Nine* (1966), *Madrigal* (1968), *Founder Member* (1969), *Traitor's Exit* (1970), *The Airline Pirates* (1970; vt *Air Apparent*), *The Champagne Communist* (1971) and *A Killer for a Song* (1975). Gardner has described his hero as 'the picture of what most of us are like – luxury-loving, lecherous and a mass of neuroses'. In the film *The Liquidator* (1965; dir. Jack Cardiff) Boysie was played by Rod Taylor.

OBELIX See under ASTERIX

OBLOMOV, ILYA Slothful Russian landowner in Ivan Goncharov's novel *Oblomov* (1859). He is given to reclining all day in his dressing-gown and slippers, while his estate suffers from neglect. The novel provoked much discussion in nineteenth-century Russia, and various explanations for Oblomov's 'malady' were put forward by earnest participants in the debate. A BBC radio dramatization of the novel (1984) had James Fox as the indolent Oblomov.

O'BRIEN See under Winston SMITH

OCHILTREE, EDIE   See under Jonathan OLDBUCK

O'FERRAL, TRILBY   Young model who is groomed as a singer by
the sinister, manipulative SVENGALI. Their story is told in George
Du Maurier's popular novel *Trilby* (1894). In the film *Svengali*
(1931; dir. Archie Mayo) Trilby O'Ferral was played by Marian
Marsh. In the remake of the same title (1954; dir. Noel Langley)
she was played by Hildegarde Neff. Trilby has given her name to a
type of soft felt hat.

OGILVIE, JAMES   Captain of the 114th Highlanders, the Queen's
Own Royal Strathspeys, in a series of historical novels by Duncan
MacNeil (Philip McCutchan). Ogilvie's adventures take place
mainly on the North-West Frontier of India in the 1890s. The
titles are: *Drums Along the Khyber* (1969), *Lieutenant of the Line*
(1970), *Sadhu on the Mountain Peak* (1971), *The Gates of
Kunarja* (1972), *The Red Daniel* (1973), *Subaltern's Choice* (1974),
By Command of the Viceroy (1975), *The Mullah from Kashmir*
(1976), *Wolf in the Fold* (1977), *Charge of Cowardice* (1978), *The
Restless Frontier* (1979), *The Train at Bundarbar* (1981) and
A Matter for the Regiment (1982).

O'HARA, KIMBALL   Youthful hero of Rudyard Kipling's finest
novel, *Kim* (1901). Kim is an orphan who passes as a native boy
in India. He attaches himself to a wise old Tibetan lama, and later
becomes a secret agent on behalf of the British government,
playing the 'Great Game' on the North-West Frontier. In the
Hollywood film version of the novel (1951; dir. Victor Saville) Kim
was played by Dean Stockwell. In the British TV movie version
(1984; dir. John Davies) he was played by an Indian actor, Ravi Sheth.

O'HARA, SCARLETT   Headstrong southern belle who is wooed by
Rhett BUTLER in Margaret Mitchell's romantic novel of the
American Civil War, *Gone With the Wind* (1936). In the 1939
film of the novel (dir. Victor Fleming), perhaps the most popular
movie Hollywood has ever produced, Scarlett was played by the
English actress Vivien Leigh. There has since been a stage
musical version of *Gone With the Wind*, which opened in Britain
in 1972 with June Ritchie in the role of Scarlett O'Hara (or
'Harlot Mascara', as someone once quipped).

Scarlett O'Hara (Vivien Leigh), the cynosure of all their eyes,
in *Gone With the Wind* (1939)

OKONKWO   Hero of *Things Fall Apart* (1958), a novel written in
English by the Nigerian novelist Chinua Achebe. Set in pre-colonial
Nigeria, the story deals with the conflict between African and
European cultures, and in particular with Okonkwo's heroic
but perhaps misguided stand against change. The novel was
dramatized on BBC radio (1984), with Hugh Quarshie as
Okonkwo.

O-LAN   See under WANG LUNG

OLD MAN IN THE CORNER, THE   See Bill OWEN

OLD SHATTERHAND   See under WINNETOU

OLDBUCK, JONATHAN   Laird of Monkbarns in Scotland: he is the
eponymous character of Sir Walter Scott's novel *The Antiquary*

(1816). Oldbuck, who is versed in curious lore, is in some ways a self-portrait of the author. Another notable character who appears in this novel is Edie Ochiltree, a garrulous old 'bedesman'.

OLSEN, JIMMY   Cub reporter on the *Daily Planet* newspaper in the city of Metropolis. He is a friend of SUPERMAN and Lois LANE. He first appeared in the *Superman* comic-book in 1941, since when he has become the star of his own publication, *Jimmy Olsen*, and has occasionally been transformed into 'Elastic Lad' and other minor-league superheroes. Jack Larson played him in the American television series 'The Adventures of Superman' (1952–7). In the films *Superman I, II* and *III* (1978–83), Jimmy was played by Marc McClure.

OLYMPIA   See under Dr COPPELIUS

O'MALLEY, CHARLES   Soldier-hero and narrator of Charles James Lever's picaresque novel *Charles O'Malley* (1841). This was one of many stories of Irish life written by Lever, who was one of the most popular novelists of his day. Other titles include *The Confessions of Harry Lorrequer* (1839) and *Jack Hinton the Guardsman* (1843).

O'MALLEY, FATHER CHUCK   Catholic priest in a tough area of New York. He was played by Bing Crosby in two schmaltzy but exceedingly popular movies written and directed by Leo McCarey, *Going My Way* (1944) and *The Bells of St Mary's* (1945). The character was revived for the inevitable television series, 'Going My Way' (1962–3), with Gene Kelly.

O'MALLEY, MR   See under BARNABY

OMNIUM, DUKE OF   See Plantagenet PALLISER

ONEGIN, EUGENE   Bored aristocratic hero of Alexander Pushkin's long narrative poem *Eugene Onegin* (1831). He spurns the love of a romantic girl, Tatyana Larina, but regrets this some time later after he learns that she has married another. He approaches her once more, but it is now Tatyana's turn to spurn him. The story forms the basis of Pyotr Ilyich Tchaikovsky's greatest opera, *Eugene Onegin* (1879), which has a libretto by the composer and K. S. Shilovsky. Onegin has frequently been described as a 'Byronic' hero (see Childe HAROLD).

OOGIE   See under Judy FOSTER

OOLA   See under ALLEY OOP

OOMPA-LOOMPAS, THE   See under Willy WONKA

OOR WULLIE   Shock-headed little boy who wears dungarees and sits on an upturned pail. His strip-cartoon adventures, scripted in broad Scots dialect, have appeared in the *Sunday Post* for many years. The strips are collected in annual volumes. Wullie first appeared in 1936, drawn by Dudley D. Watkins, and has since become a part of Scotland's national mythology.

ORC   See under URIZEN

ORDWAY, ROBERT   See The CRIME DOCTOR

O'REILLY, RADAR   See under Hawkeye PIERCE

ORLAC, STEPHEN   Pianist who loses his hands and has those of a murderer grafted on in their stead. He first appeared in a novel, *Les Mains d'Orlac* (1920) by Maurice Renard, but has become best known as a character in horror films. *The Hands of Orlac* (1925; dir. Robert Wiene) starred Conrad Veidt; *Mad Love* (1935; dir. Karl Freund) had Colin Clive (and Peter Lorre); *The Hands of Orlac* (1960; dir. Edmond T. Gréville) had Mel Ferrer; and *Hands of a Stranger* (1962; dir. Newton Arnold) had Paul Lukather.

ORTHERIS, STANLEY   Cockney soldier in the nineteenth-century Indian army – one of Rudyard Kipling's 'Soldiers Three'. See also Jock LEAROYD and Terence MULVANEY.

ORVILLE, LORD   See under Evelina ANVILLE

ORWELL, HARRY   Policeman turned private-eye in the American television series 'Harry O' (1974–6). He was played by David

Janssen, and the series was produced by Jerry Thorpe. Harry Orwell has been described as 'one of TV's more bohemian private eyes' (Tim Brooks and Earle Marsh).

OSBALDISTONE, FRANCIS English hero of Sir Walter Scott's novel *Rob Roy* (1817), which is set at the time of the Jacobite rebellion of 1715. A would-be poet, scornful of business, he is banished by his father to his uncle's house, where he falls in love with Diana Vernon. When he and Diana are threatened by a rascally Jacobite, Osbaldistone travels to the Scottish highlands to seek the help of the wild clansman Rob Roy Macgregor (an historical character, now best remembered for his appearance in this novel). Another notable character is Andrew Fairservice, Osbaldistone's untrustworthy manservant.

OSBORNE, 'OZ' Loud-mouthed, ill-mannered but nevertheless very cherishable Geordie bricklayer in the British television comedy series 'Auf Wiedersehen, Pet' (1982), created by scriptwriters Dick Clement and Ian La Frenais. He is one of a group of English workers on a building site in Germany. The inimitable Oz was played by Jimmy Nail. A later series with the same cast (1986) showed Oz and his friends ('the magnificent seven') at work in Spain.

OSKAR See Oskar MATZERATH

OSMOND, GILBERT See under Isabel ARCHER

OWEN, BILL Known as 'the Old Man in the Corner', a brilliant armchair detective invented by Baroness Orczy for a long series of short stories which she published in the *Royal Magazine* from 1901. Bill Owen solves crimes at a distance, without stirring from his favourite café seat. The stories were collected in *The Case of Miss Elliott* (1905), *The Old Man in the Corner* (1909) and *Unravelled Knots* (1925).

OYL, OLIVE Girlfriend of POPEYE the Sailor-Man. She was actually created long before him – in 1919 – by newspaper cartoonist Elzie Crisler Segar, for his continuing series known as *Thimble Theatre*. Olive Oyl appears in numerous short animated films

produced by Max Fleischer and others after 1933. In the feature
film, *Popeye* (1980; dir. Robert Altman), she was played, very
appropriately, by the scrawny, big-eyed actress Shelley Duvall.

OZ   See 'Oz' OSBORNE

OZ, THE WIZARD OF   Ruler of the Land of Oz in L. Frank Baum's
children's novel *The Wonderful Wizard of Oz* (1900) and its many
sequels. In fact he is a charlatan who has arrived in the magical
country of Oz by balloon. He befriends Dorothy GALE, the little
girl from Kansas, although he is unable to help her to find her
way home. In the famous musical film *The Wizard of Oz* (1939; dir.
Victor Fleming) the Wizard was played by Frank Morgan. The
title of John Boorman's odd science fiction film *Zardoz* (1973) is a
veiled reference to 'the Wiz', but it is hard to see a purpose in the
allusion.

P

P.C.49 Police Constable Archibald Berkeley-Willoughby, an implausibly upper-crust English copper who was voiced by Brian Reece in the popular BBC radio series 'The Adventures of P.C.49' (1949–53). The creator of P.C.49 was scriptwriter Alan Stranks. The likeable policeman also appeared in two minor British films, including *A Case for P.C.49* (1951).

PADDINGTON BEAR Little Peruvian bear who is found by the Brown family on Paddington Station in London. They discover that he can speak perfect English and has a passion for marmalade sandwiches. Paddington was invented by Michael Bond for his book *A Bear Called Paddington* (1958). There have been many sequels, all engagingly illustrated by Peggy Fortnum. Paddington Bear toys have become very popular in Britain, and the little animal has also appeared in an animated television series.

PAGET, JEAN Heroine of Nevil Shute's most popular novel, *A Town Like Alice* (1950). Captured by the Japanese in Malaya during World War II, she undergoes many privations but is eventually reunited with the man she loves in Alice Springs, Australia. In the film of the book (1956; dir. Jack Lee) Jean was played by Virginia McKenna. In the Australian-produced television mini-series (1981) Helen Morse took the lead.

PALADIN Well-dressed, well-educated gunslinger, played by Richard Boone in the American television series *Have Gun, Will Travel* (1957–63). A veteran of the Civil War, he sets himself up as a private investigator and troubleshooter in old San Francisco. The smooth, black-clad and mysterious Paladin became one of the most popular Western heroes on TV – even at the height of the Western 'boom', when series such as 'Wagon Train', 'Cheyenne' (see Cheyenne BODIE), 'Rawhide', 'Maverick' (see Bret MAVERICK), 'Bronco' and 'Gunsmoke' (see Matt DILLON) were all jostling for space on the airwaves.

PAL JOEY   American nightclub singer. He is the cynical anti-hero of short stories by the *New Yorker* writer John O'Hara, collected in the book *Pal Joey* (1940). These tales formed the basis of a popular stage musical of the same title, with music by Richard Rodgers and lyrics by Lorenz Hart. This was filmed (1957; dir. George Sidney), with Frank Sinatra as the wheeling-and-dealing Joey.

PALLISER, PLANTAGENET   English politician whose career is described in a series of novels by Anthony Trollope: *Can You Forgive Her?* (1864–5), *Phineas Finn* (1869), *The Eustace Diamonds* (1873), *Phineas Redux* (1874), *The Prime Minister* (1876) and *The Duke's Children* (1880). He is the heir of the Duke of Omnium (acceding to that title in the fourth novel), and eventually he becomes Prime Minister. A BBC television series, 'The Pallisers' (1975), scripted by Simon Raven, had Philip Latham as Plantagenet Palliser and Susan Hampshire as his wife, Lady Glencora. A descendant of Palliser's, one of the later Dukes of Omnium, appears in some of Angela Thirkell's twentieth-century 'Barsetshire' novels. See also Phineas FINN.

PALMER, HARRY   Lower-class British spy played by Cockney actor Michael Caine in the films based on the novels of Len Deighton – *The Ipcress File* (1965; dir. Sidney J. Furie), *Funeral in Berlin* (1966; dir. Guy Hamilton), and *Billion Dollar Brain* (1967; dir. Ken Russell). Palmer is insubordinate and bloody-minded, but he nevertheless serves his Queen and country well. In the novels the hero remains nameless; nevertheless he is recognizable as the central character of five of Deighton's espionage thrillers: *The Ipcress File* (1962), *Horse Under Water* (1963), *Funeral in Berlin* (1964), *Billion Dollar Brain* (1966) and *An Expensive Place to Die* (1967).

PALOOKA, JOE   Big, blond, simple-minded boxer, in an American comic-strip drawn by Ham Fisher from 1928 (with help from Al Capp, the creator of LI'L ABNER). Palooka became the most popular sporting hero in the United States, with his adventures reprinted in comic-books and adapted for the cinema. Ham Fisher once claimed that President Truman had told him he was a regular reader of the strip. The movie *Palooka* (1934; dir. Benjamin Stoloff) had Stuart Erwin as the boxer; it was followed a decade later by a short series of films which starred Joe Kirkwood.

PAMELA See Pamela ANDREWS

PAN, PETER See PETER PAN

PANCHO See under The CISCO KID

PANGLOSS, DOCTOR Eternal optimist who gives voice to the
famous opinion that 'all is for the best in this best of all possible
worlds'. He is the tutor of CANDIDE, in Voltaire's satirical novella
Candide, ou L'Optimisme (1759).

PARAGOT, BERZELIUS NIBBIDARD Wandering Bohemian, a
gentleman in rags, who plays the violin and cultivates
philosophy. He is the title character of William J. Locke's
bestselling novel *The Beloved Vagabond* (1906). Paragot's real
name is Gaston de Nérac. In the film of the novel (1936; dir.
Curtis Bernhardt) he was played by Maurice Chevalier.

PARIS, JUDITH See under Francis HERRIES

PARKER Tough criminal anti-hero of a series of stripped-down
novels by Richard Stark (Donald E. Westlake), beginning with *The
Hunter* (1962; vt *Point Blank*). No one knows his first name.
There have been at least sixteen Parker thrillers, and the later
titles are: *The Man with the Getaway Face* (1963; vt *The Steel
Hit*), *The Outfit* (1963), *The Mourner* (1963), *The Score* (1964;
vt *Killtown*), *The Jugger* (1965), *The Seventh* (1966, vt *The Split*),
The Handle (1966; vt *Run Lethal*), *The Rare Coin Score* (1967),
The Green Eagle Score (1967), *The Black Ice Score* (1968), *The
Sour Lemon Score* (1969), *Deadly Edge* (1971), *Slayground* (1971),
Plunder Squad (1972) and *Butcher's Moon* (1974). In the film
Point Blank (1967; dir. John Boorman) Parker was played by Lee
Marvin.

PARKER, LYNDON See under Solar PONS

PARKER, PETER See SPIDER-MAN

PATTERNE, SIR WILLOUGHBY Self-regarding character referred
to in the title of George Meredith's novel *The Egoist* (1879). Sir

Willoughby has health, wealth and looks, and he thinks the world of himself. As the result of a complex comedy of embarrassment, he learns a little humility and wins the hand of Laetitia Dale.

PATTERSON, SIR LES   Australian 'attaché for cultural affairs', a gross figure of fun who is forever swilling alcohol and dribbling down his tie. He is a memorable *persona* of the comedian Barry Humphries (see also Edna EVERAGE), and has appeared on television frequently during the 1970s and 1980s. The revolting Sir Les has written a book, *The Traveller's Tool*, and has also released an LP of songs, *Twelve Inches of Sir Les* (both 1985).

PAUL AND VIRGINIA   Boy and girl who grow up in pastoral solitude on the island of Mauritius; chaste lovers, they turn their surroundings into a happy garden, but are separated forever when Virginia is compelled to take ship for France and is drowned. They figure in the novel *Paul et Virginie* (1788) by Jacques-Henri Bernardin de Saint-Pierre. According to critic Peter Ackroyd (*Sunday Times*, 12 September 1982): 'It made the world weep. It was Emma Bovary's favourite reading, and indeed 19th-century fiction is awash with sentimental memories of this story of "naive love" . . . *Paul and Virginia* . . . went through hundreds of editions in its native French and, before 1900, some 85 printings in the English language. Bernardin had created, by chance or instinct, an authentic myth.' A much later bestseller which uses a similar story is *The Blue Lagoon* (1908) by H. de Vere Stacpoole (his children are called Dick and Emmeline Lestrange).

PEACHUM, POLLY   Leading lady of John Gay's satirical musical play *The Beggar's Opera* (1728). She falls in love with Captain MACHEATH, the highwayman, and marries him in secret. Gay wrote a sequel, *Polly* (1729), which was suppressed for several decades. In the film *The Beggar's Opera* (1952; dir. Peter Brook) she was played by Dorothy Tutin. Polly also appears in Bertolt Brecht's updated version of the story, *The Threepenny Opera* (1928).

PECKSNIFF, SETH   Architect whose surname has become a byword for canting hypocrisy. He appears, with his two long-suffering daughters, Charity and Mercy, in Charles Dickens's

novel *The Life and Adventures of Martin Chuzzlewit* (1843–4).
Although the eponymous Martin CHUZZLEWIT is the hero of the
story, Mr Pecksniff is in some ways the most important
character. According to John Forster's *Life of Dickens*, 'the notion
of taking Pecksniff for a type of character was really the origin of
the book, the design being to show, more or less by every person
introduced, the number and variety of humours and vices that have
their root in selfishness' (quoted by R. C. Churchill in *The Pelican
Guide to English Literature* Volume 6).

PEEL, EMMA   Elegant, athletic, black-garbed heroine of the British
television series 'The Avengers' (1961–8). She assists secret agent
John STEED in his various bizarre cases. Mrs Peel was played by
Diana Rigg. She entered the show in its second series, replacing
a similar character, Mrs Gale, who was played by Honor
Blackman.

PEGEEN MIKE   See under Christy MAHON

PEGGOTTY, DANIEL   See under David COPPERFIELD

PELHAM, HENRY   Fashionable young Englishman who appears in
Bulwer-Lytton's novel *Pelham, or The Adventures of a Gentleman*
(1828), a work which is a leading example of the so-called 'Silver-
Fork School' of early nineteenth-century fiction. According to *The
Oxford Companion to English Literature*, the author's 'tone of
sparkling cynicism captivated contemporary readers and made
his hero's name a catch-phrase.'

PENDENNIS, ARTHUR   Known as 'Pen' for short – the likeable,
erring young man whose growth to wisdom, a happy marriage, and
a career as a writer is described in William Makepeace Thackeray's
novel *The History of Pendennis* (1848–50). He reappears as a
comparatively minor character in a couple of later novels by
Thackeray, *The Newcomes* (1853–5) and *The Adventures of Philip*
(1861–2). *Pendennis* has been dramatized for BBC radio (1986),
with Dominic Guard as the hero.

PENDLETON, JERVIS   See under Judy ABBOTT

PENNYFEATHER, PAUL   Hero of Evelyn Waugh's comic novel *Decline and Fall* (1928). An innocent student of theology, he is sent down from Oxford for 'indecent behaviour' (the victim of a debagging), becomes a schoolmaster, has an affair with the dangerous Margot METROLAND, is imprisoned as a white slave-trafficker, and eventually returns to Oxford in the pretence of being his own distant cousin. The film of the novel (1968; dir. John Krish) had Robin Phillips in the lead part.

PENROD   See Penrod SCHOFIELD

PÉPÉ LE MOKO   Parisian gangster who takes refuge in the Casbah at Algiers, in the novel *Pépé Le Moko* by Roger d'Ashelbe (Henri La Barthe). In the French film of the book (1936; dir. Julien Duvivier) he was played by Jean Gabin. The movie was remade in an American version entitled *Algiers* (1938; dir. John Cromwell), with Charles Boyer as Pépé (this film has become famous for the apocryphal line: 'Come with me to the Casbah'). The musical remake, *Casbah* (1948; dir. John Berry), starred Tony Martin.

PEPPONE   See under Don CAMILLO

PERKINS, MA   Matriarch played by Virginia Payne in one of American radio's longest-running soap operas, 'Ma Perkins' (1933–60). She is a widow who runs a lumber-yard, solving friends' and neighbours' problems in her spare time.

PERRIN, REGINALD   Frustrated businessman who attempts to remake his life by faking suicide and starting afresh, in David Nobbs's comic novels *The Death of Reginald Perrin* (1975), *The Return of Reginald Perrin* (1977) and *The Better World of Reginald Perrin* (1978). In the BBC television series 'The Fall and Rise of Reginald Perrin' (1976–80) he was played by Leonard Rossiter.

PERRIN, VINCENT   Middle-aged, conservative schoolmaster in Hugh Walpole's novel *Mr Perrin and Mr Traill* (1911). He becomes jealous of the younger teacher, Archie Traill, but fails in an attempt to murder him, and is drowned. A rewritten American

edition of the book, entitled *The Gods and Mr Perrin*, has a more
sentimental ending in which Perrin is redeemed. In the film *Mr
Perrin and Mr Traill* (1948; dir. Lawrence Huntington) he was
played by Marius Goring.

PERRY, ABNER   See under David INNES

PETER PAN   Boy who never grows up. As a baby, he befriends the
fairies in Kensington Gardens and they come to accept him as
more-or-less one of their own. In Peter's best-known adventure
he carries Wendy DARLING and her two little brothers away to
Never-Never Land, where they encounter the villainous Captain
HOOK. Peter was invented by J. M. Barrie in his novel *The Little
White Bird* (1902), the relevant chapters of which were later
republished as a children's book with illustrations by Arthur
Rackham, *Peter Pan in Kensington Gardens* (1906). Barrie's
imagination was seized by the magical figure of the elfin boy, and
he used him as the central character of an astonishingly elaborate
stage play, *Peter Pan, or The Boy Who Wouldn't Grow Up* (1904).
It was in this production that Barrie introduced the Darling
children and their dog Nana, the fairy Tinker Bell, and the pirate
leader Captain Hook. He later turned the play into a novel, *Peter
and Wendy* (1911), which contained much new material.
Because of its length and complexity the book has often been
abridged or 'retold' by other authors – just as the stage play has been
through many adaptations during its frequent revivals.
   The first film of the play was made in 1924, and starred Betty
Bronson as Peter (it has become traditional practice for the boy
to be played by an actress). Following this, J. M. Barrie added to the
Peter Pan myth by writing his own film scenario (never produced)
and by publishing a new book version of the play (1928), both
of which contained fresh details that have been incorporated into
later stage productions (notably, a Royal Shakespeare Company
version of 1982 which was described by one critic as 'a national
masterpiece'). The best-known film is the Walt Disney animated
feature, *Peter Pan* (1953; dir. Wilfred Jackson, Clyde Geronimi
and Hamilton Luske). There have also been an American
television production (1955; dir. Michael Kidd), starring Mary
Martin, and a British TV movie (1976; dir. Dwight Hemion), with
Mia Farrow. A statue of Peter Pan, erected at Barrie's expense in

1912, still stands in Kensington Gardens. In recent years, Peter
Pan has become a fruitful subject for psychologists and
psychologizing literary critics; he has lent his name to at least
one 'syndrome', and the critic Jacqueline Rose worries about him
at length in her book *The Case of Peter Pan, or The Impossibility
of Children's Fiction* (1984).

PETER RABBIT   Very small and harmless rabbit – the best-known
of the many characters created by Beatrix Potter for her nursery
tales. Her tiny illustrated book, *The Tale of Peter Rabbit*, first
appeared in 1901. Other Potter creations include Mrs Tiggy-Winkle,
Tabitha Twitchett, Pigling Bland, Jemima Puddle-Duck and
Squirrel Nutkin. A ballet film, *Tales of Beatrix Potter* (1971;
dir. Reginald Mills), features all these animal characters.

PETERSON, CARL   See under Bulldog DRUMMOND

PETRIE, DOCTOR   See under Denis Nayland SMITH

PETROVNA, NATALYA   Bored heroine of Ivan Turgenev's play
A Month in the Country (1850 – but not performed until 1872). The
wife of a Russian landowner, she falls fruitlessly in love with her
son's tutor. The play has been adapted as a ballet by Sir Frederick
Ashton (1976; with music by Frédéric Chopin).

PHANTOM, THE   Real name Kit Walker (or perhaps Christopher
Standish), a costumed superhero of American newspaper comic-
strips. He was created by writer Lee Falk and artist Ray Moore in
1936, and his adventures are still being published today. Also
known as the Ghost Who Walks, the Phanton was the first of the
masked-and-suited comic-strip heroes, an obvious inspiration
for BATMAN and many others who have followed. The
contemporary Phantom is supposed to be the heir to a 400-year
line. A sixteenth-century ancestor was marooned in the land of
'Bangalla'; protected by a tribe of pygmies, he created a secret
home for himself in Skull Cave. From there he and his long line
of sons have ventured forth as the Phantom, pursuing
wrongdoers around the world. A cinema serial, *The Phantom*
(1943), starred Tom Tyler as the hero. The Phantom has also
appeared in comic-books, and in a series of twelve novels by Frank

S. Shawn and Lee Falk, beginning with *The Story of the Phantom* (1972).

PHANTOM OF THE OPERA, THE Erik, the man with a hideous skull-like face who lives in furtive seclusion beneath a Paris opera house. In love with a beautiful singer, he masks his deformity and commits various murders in order to attain his ends – but nevertheless fails to get the girl. His story is told in Gaston Leroux's novel *The Phantom of the Opera* (1911), which was filmed in 1925 with Lon Chaney, 'the man of a thousand faces', in the leading role. Since then it has become a standard part of the cinema's horror repertoire, with remakes appearing in 1943 (dir. Arthur

Erik, the Phantom of the Opera (Lon Chaney) in the 1925 film

Lubin), starring Claude Rains, and 1962 (dir. Terence Fisher), with
Herbert Lom. A later version, entitled *The Phantom of the
Paradise* (1974; dir. Brian de Palma), had Paul Williams in an
updated story with a rock-music setting. There has also been a
TV movie *Phantom of the Opera* (1983; dir. Robert Markowitz),
with Maximilian Schell. Leroux's hoary old tale has recently been
given a new lease of life as a stage musical by Andrew Lloyd
Webber (1986).

PHIBES, DOCTOR   Disfigured villain played by Vincent Price in
the spoof horror film *The Abominable Dr Phibes* (1971; dir. Robert
Fuest). Embittered by the death of his wife, he plans and carries
out a number of ghastly murders which are inspired by an
ancient Pharaoh's curses. He returns to his nefarious work in *Dr
Phibes Rises Again* (1972; dir. Fuest)

PICAROON, THE   In British crime fiction there have been two
daredevil heroes known as 'The Picaroon'. The Picaroon Mark I is
featured in a series of thrillers by Herman Landon. Titles include:
The Green Shadow (1928), *The Picaroon Does Justice* (1929),
Buy My Silence (1931), *The Picaroon Resumes Practice* (1931),
Picaroon in Pursuit (1932), *The Elusive Picaroon* (1932),
Picaroon: Knight Errant and *The Trailing of the Picaroon*. The
Picaroon Mark II, alias Ludovic Saxon, is the hero of a later thriller
series by John Cassells (W. Murdoch Duncan): *Enter the Picaroon*
(1954), *The Avenging Picaroon* (1956), *Beware! The Picaroon* (1956),
Meet the Picaroon (1957), *The Engaging Picaroon* (1958), *The
Enterprising Picaroon* (1959), *Salute the Picaroon* (1960), *The
Picaroon Goes West* (1962), *Prey for the Picaroon* (1963),
Challenge for the Picaroon (1964), *The Benevolent Picaroon* (1965),
Plunder for the Picaroon (1966), *The Audacious Picaroon* (1967),
The Elusive Picaroon (1968), *Night of the Picaroon* (1969), *Quest
for the Picaroon* (1970), *The Picaroon Collects* (1970), *Profit for
the Picaroon* (1972), *The Picaroon Laughs Last* (1973), *Action
for the Picaroon* (1975) and *The Picaroon Gets the Run-Around*
(1976). Ludovic Saxon is a laughing desperado of much the same
type as Simon Templar, The SAINT.

PICKLE, PEREGRINE   Rascally young man who undertakes an
educational Grand Tour, in Tobias Smollett's novel *The*

Adventures of Peregrine Pickle (1751). Peregrine has many love-affairs, dissipates his money, and at one point is imprisoned in the Bastille. The only figure of authority whom he holds in esteem is his half-mad uncle, the one-eyed Commodore Hawser Trunnion.

PICKWICK, SAMUEL Rotund and orotund hero of Charles Dickens's *The Posthumous Papers of the Pickwick Club* (better known as *The Pickwick Papers*), first published in weekly parts in 1836–7 under the pseudonym 'Boz'. Originally Dickens had been commissioned to write the text for a series of 'sporting' illustrations by 'Phiz' (H. K. Browne), but Mr Pickwick soon took on a vigorous life of his own and became one of the great characters of English literature. He and his friends, Tracy Tupman, Augustus Snodgrass and Nathaniel Winkle, set themselves up as a 'corresponding society' – to travel the country and report back to their club on the state of English life and manners. There follows a long series of comical adventures, in which the well-meaning Pickwick frequently finds himself in dire difficulties. He is assisted throughout by his resourceful Cockney manservant, Sam WELLER. Other characters of note include Mrs Bardell, who takes Pickwick to court for breach of promise, and Alfred Jingle, a fast-talking rogue. The adjective 'Pickwickian' has entered the language, as in the phrase 'in a Pickwickian sense' (applied to insults which are not meant to carry full force but are intended more as terms of endearment). Dickens's book enjoyed enormous popularity: 'By the fifteenth number it was selling 40,000 copies an issue. One met *Pickwick* everywhere – one rode in "Boz" cabs, wore Pickwick coats and hats and smoked Pickwick cigars' (according to Louis James).

Dickens revived Mr Pickwick and Sam Weller for his short-lived periodical *Master Humphrey's Clock* (1840–42). Prior to this, however, there had been several unofficial sequels by other hands. The publisher Edward Lloyd issued a plagiarism called *The Penny Pickwick* (1837–9) by 'Bos' (the author is thought to have been Thomas Peckett Prest), which ran to 112 weekly parts and sold very well indeed. The *Monthly Magazine* serialized *Pickwick Abroad, or The Tour in France* (1837–8) by G. W. M. Reynolds; unlike *The Penny Pickwick*, this was a true sequel, and its author justified himself by saying: 'If the talented "Boz" has not chosen to

enact the part of Mr Pickwick's biographer in his continental
tour, it is not my fault . . . it is now my duty to compile and
put in order the notes taken by him abroad.' Other plagiarisms
and sequels include *Pickwick in America*, *Pickwick in India* and
Pickwick Married. A later sequel by another hand is *Mr
Pickwick's Second Time on Earth* by C. G. Harper. There were also
many stage adaptations of Dickens's original story, including *The
Peregrinations of Pickwick* (1836) by William Leman Rede, a
play which was written and staged before Dickens had even
finished his book. The film *The Pickwick Papers* (1952; dir.
Noel Langley) starred James Hayter as Mr Pickwick. A stage
musical, *Pickwick* (1963), had music by Cyril Ornadel and lyrics by
Leslie Bricusse. The most recent BBC television serial version
(1985) had Nigel Stock as Pickwick.

PIERCE, HAWKEYE   Full name Benjamin Franklin Pierce – a
madcap American military doctor in the Korean War, created
by Richard Hooker (H. Richard Hornberger) for his novel
M∗A∗S∗H (1968) and over a dozen sequels. (The acronym stands
for Mobile Army Surgical Hospital.) Later titles include *M∗A∗S∗H
Goes to Maine* (1972) and a number of volumes written by Hooker
in collaboration with William E. Butterworth: *M∗A∗S∗H Goes to
Hollywood*, *M∗A∗S∗H Goes to London*, *M∗A∗S∗H Goes to
Miami*, *M∗A∗S∗H Goes to San Francisco*, *M∗A∗S∗H Goes to
Vienna*, *M∗A∗S∗H Goes to Montreal* and so on. The film
M∗A∗S∗H (1970; dir. Robert Altman) starred Donald Sutherland
and Elliot Gould as Hawkeye Pierce and his bosom buddy,
Trapper John McIntyre. It was a popular and critical success, but
its fame was later surpassed by that of the hit television series
of the same title (1972–83). The series was produced by Larry
Gelbart and Gene Reynolds, and starred Alan Alda (who also
directed many of the episodes). One critic wrote: 'Without Alan
Alda as Hawkeye, they have no show. Millions love him. I love
him, and I even know why I love him. I love his realistic approach
to sex, stimulants and survival. I love his wit, intelligence and
stamina. In every crisis, he is resourceful, pragmatic and self-
mocking. I hope he goes on forever' (Myles Palmer, *New Society*,
22 September 1977). Among the other characters who became
household names are Hotlips Houlihan (played by Loretta Swit),
Corporal Radar O'Reilly (Gary Burghoff) and Corporal Maxwell

Klinger (Jamie Farr). When the 251st and last episode of the TV 'M*A*S*H' was shown in early 1983 it is estimated that some 125 million American viewers tuned in to say farewell to Hawkeye Pierce and his friends.

PIERCE, MILDRED   Hardworking American mother who builds a small business empire but is betrayed by her ungrateful daughter, in James M. Cain's novel *Mildred Pierce* (1941). In the memorable film of the story (1945; dir. Michael Curtiz) Mildred was played by Joan Crawford.

PIERRE   See Pierre BEZUKHOV

PIGGY, MISS   Extremely vain little pig with long hair and fluttery eyelashes. The most unlikely sex-symbol of the 1970s, she is the girlfriend of KERMIT THE FROG in television's 'The Muppet Show' (1976–81). Her creators are Frank Oz and Jim Henson. She has also appeared in films, such as *The Muppet Movie* (1979; dir. James Frawley).

PIGLET   See under WINNIE-THE-POOH

PIGLING BLAND   See under PETER RABBIT

PILGRIM, BILLY   Battered innocent, the hero of Kurt Vonnegut's bestselling novel *Slaughterhouse-5, or The Children's Crusade* (1969). He shuttles backwards and forwards in space and time between the fire-bombing of Dresden in 1945 and the planet Tralfamadore in the far future. Billy is a great fan of the seedy science-fiction writer Kilgore TROUT. In the film *Slaughterhouse Five* (1972; dir. George Roy Hill) Pilgrim was played by Michael Sacks.

PILLSON, GEORGIE   See under LUCIA

PINK, MELINDA   Mountain-climbing lady detective, a justice of the peace, who has appeared in a series of crime novels by the British writer Gwen Moffat: *Lady with a Cool Eye* (1973), *Miss Pink at the Edge of the World* (1975), *Over the Sea to Death* (1976), *A Short Time to Live* (1976), *Persons Unknown* (1978),

The Buckskin Girl (1982), *Miss Pink's Mistake* (1982), *Die Like a Dog* (1982), *Last Chance Country* (1983) and *Grizzly Trail* (1984).

PINK PANTHER, THE   See under Jacques CLOUSEAU

PINKERTON, B. F.   See under Madame BUTTERFLY

PINKERTON, MISS   See Hilda ADAMS

PINKIE   Young scarfaced hoodlum in Graham Greene's 'entertainment' *Brighton Rock* (1938). In order to conceal a murder he woos an innocent young waitress. Despite his crimes Pinkie is a believing Catholic, and knows that he is condemned to eternal suffering. In the film of the novel (1947; dir. John Boulting) he was played by Richard Attenborough.

PINOCCHIO   Wooden puppet who eventually becomes a real flesh-and-blood boy, in the well-loved classic of Italian children's

Pinocchio with Jiminy Cricket in the 1939 Disney cartoon
copyright Walt Disney Productions

literature *The Adventures of Pinocchio* (1883) by Carlo Collodi
(Carlo Lorenzini). Pinocchio is carved by an old carpenter,
Gepetto. Since he has been made from an enchanted piece of
wood, he comes to life before Gepetto has even finished his shaping
task. Pinocchio is infinitely mischievous and most reluctant to
attend school. In a famous scene the good fairy who watches over
the puppet causes his wooden nose to grow longer every time he
tells a lie. After running off and having many frightening adventures,
Pinocchio mends his ways and is transformed into a real boy. The
story has proved very popular in English translation, and has been
adapted to the stage, film and television innumerable times. The
most celebrated version is Walt Disney's animated feature film
Pinocchio (1939; dir. Ben Sharpsteen and Hamilton Luske). A TV
movie of the same title (1976; dir. Ron Field and Sidney Smith)
had Sandy Duncan as Pinocchio. On the celebration of Pinocchio's
centenary a few years ago it was reported that some 60,000 visitors
a month were drawn to the Pinocchio Monumental Park in the
village of Collodi, Tuscany.

PIRRIP, PHILIP   Known as Pip – orphan hero of Charles Dickens's
novel *Great Expectations* (1860–1). As a boy, he is frightened into
giving food to an escaped convict, Abel MAGWITCH. Years later
he is repaid most generously, but Pip mistakenly believes his
benefactor to be the eccentric Miss HAVISHAM. He falls in love
with the beautiful ESTELLA, Miss Havisham's ward, and eventually
his love is returned. The book is one of Dickens's most memorable
works, and it has been adapted frequently. A Hollywood film,
Great Expectations (1934; dir. Stuart Walker), starred Phillips
Holmes as Pip. The British remake (1946; dir. David Lean), with
John Mills, is regarded as the classic film version. The TV movie
(1975; dir. Joseph Hardy), with Michael York, is less satisfactory.
There have also been a number of television serials based on the
story.

PLASTIC MAN   See under Mr FANTASTIC

PLEYDELL, BERRY   Laughing hero of a series of magazine stories
and 'light' novels by Dornford Yates (Cecil William Mercer).
The character made his initial appearance in the *Windsor
Magazine* in 1911. Tales of Berry (full name Bertram Pleydell) first

appeared in book form in *The Brother of Daphne* (1914). He leads
a leisured existence at his Hampshire country home, White Ladies,
or on motoring holidays in the south of France. Like his friend
and relative Jonah MANSEL, he is a clubman, sportsman and
wit, as well as a connoisseur of good food and Rolls-Royce cars.
Later books about Berry and his carefree circle of cousins,
Daphne and 'Boy', Jonah and Jill, include *The Courts of Idleness*
(1920), *Berry and Co.* (1920), *Jonah and Co.* (1922), *Adèle and
Co.* (1931), *And Berry Came Too* (1936), *The House That Berry
Built* (1945), *The Berry Scene* (1947), *As Berry and I Were Saying*
(1952) and *B-Berry and I Look Back* (1958). Berry also makes guest
appearances in *And Five Were Foolish* (1924), *Maiden Stakes*
(1928) and the Richard CHANDOS thriller *Perishable Goods* (1928).

PLOD, MR   See under NODDY

PLURABELLE, ANNA LIVIA   Wife to Humphrey Chimpden
EARWICKER, in James Joyce's *Finnegans Wake* (1939). She
represents the eternal feminine, and is identified with the river
Liffey. A section of Joyce's massive 'Work in Progress', entitled
Anna Livia Plurabelle, was first published as a booklet in 1928.
When this was reissued by Faber in 1930, Joyce wrote a small
verse for the dust-jacket: 'Buy a book in brown paper/From Faber
and Faber/To see Annie Liffey trip, tumble and caper./
Sevensinns in her singthings,/Plurabelle on her prose,/Seashell
ebb music wayriver she flows.'

PLUTO   See under MICKEY MOUSE

POGO   Cartoon opossum who first appeared as a minor character
in a comic book called *Animal Comics* (1942). Within a few years
he grew to fame, and Walt Kelly's *Pogo* strip was published in
American newspapers from 1948 until the artist's death in 1973.
An innocent little creature, Pogo lives in Okefenokee Swamp
with his friend Albert the Alligator and others. In 1952 his
many campus fans urged Pogo to run for President of the United
States (HOWARD THE DUCK was to receive similar promptings
decades later). It was Pogo (or Walt Kelly) who invented the motto:
'We have met the enemy and he is us' – with reference to
environmental pollution.

POINDEXTER, JEFF See under Billy PRIEST

POIROT, HERCULE Belgian detective, small of stature with a
waxed moustache, 'patent-leather hair' and a slightly comical
manner. He was created by Agatha Christie for her first detective
novel, *The Mysterious Affair at Styles* (1920), and has appeared in
about forty subsequent titles, including: *The Murder on the Links*
(1923), *Poirot Investigates* (1925), *The Murder of Roger Ackroyd*
(1926), *The Big Four* (1927), *The Mystery of the Blue Train* (1928),
Peril at End House (1932), *Thirteen at Dinner* (1933; vt *Lord
Edgware Dies*), *Murder on the Orient Express* (1934), *Murder in
Three Acts* (1934), *Death in the Air* (1935; vt *Death in the Clouds*),
The A.B.C. Murders (1935), *Murder in Mesopotamia* (1936), *Death
on the Nile* (1938), *Evil Under the Sun* (1941), *The Labours of
Hercules* (1947), *Mrs McGinty's Dead* (1952; vt *Blood Will Tell*),
Hickory Dickory Death (1955), *The Clocks* (1963), *Elephants Can
Remember* (1972) and the posthumous *Curtain: Poirot's Last
Case* (1975; written many years earlier). A biography of the hero
appears in Julian Symons's book *The Great Detectives* (1981).
Poirot has been portrayed in numerous films. Among them are
three British titles which had Austin Trevor as the little detective:
Alibi (1931; dir. Leslie Hiscott), *Black Coffee* (1931; dir. Hiscott)
and *Lord Edgware Dies* (1934; dir. Henry Edwards). Later films
include: *The Alphabet Murders* (1966; dir. Frank Tashlin), with
Tony Randall; *Murder on the Orient Express* (1974; dir. Sidney
Lumet), with Albert Finney; *Death on the Nile* (1978; dir. John
Guillermin), with Peter Ustinov; and *Evil Under the Sun* (1982;
dir. Guy Hamilton), also with Peter Ustinov. In the TV movies
Agatha Christie's Thirteen at Dinner (1985; dir. Lou Antonio)
and *Agatha Christie's Dead Man's Folly* (1986; dir. Clive Donner)
Ustinov took the role yet again. Ian Holm made a convincing
Poirot in Nick Evans's television play 'Murder by the Book'
(1986).

POLDARK, ROSS Cornish landowner of the late eighteenth
century, hero of a series of historical novels by Winston
Graham. The titles are: *Ross Poldark: A Novel of Cornwall
1783–1787* (1945; vt *The Renegade*), *Demelza: A Novel of
Cornwall 1788–1790* (1946; vt *Elizabeth's Story*), *Jeremy Poldark:
A Novel of Cornwall 1790–1791* (1950; vt *Venture Once More*),

Warleggan: A Novel of Cornwall 1792–1793 (1953; vt *The Last Gamble*), *The Black Moon: A Novel of Cornwall 1794–1795* (1973), *The Four Swans; A Novel of Cornwall 1795–1797* (1976), *The Angry Tide: A Novel of Cornwall 1798–1799* (1977), *The Stranger from the Sea: A Novel of Cornwall 1810–1811* (1981), *The Miller's Dance: A Novel of Cornwall 1812–1813* (1982) and *The Loving Cup* (1985). The successful BBC television series 'Poldark' (1976–7) starred Robin Ellis as Ross. Winston Graham has also written a non-fiction book entitled *Poldark's Cornwall* (1983).

POLLIFAX, EMILY   Elderly female spy in Dorothy Gilman's novel *The Unexpected Mrs Pollifax* (1966; vt *Mrs Pollifax, Spy*), and its sequels: *The Amazing Mrs Pollifax* (1970), *The Elusive Mrs Pollifax* (1971), *A Palm for Mrs Pollifax* (1973), *Mrs Pollifax on Safari* (1977) and *Mrs Pollifax on the China Station* (1983). In the film *Mrs Pollifax – Spy* (1970; dir. Leslie Martinson) Rosalind Russell played the matronly CIA agent.

POLLY, ALFRED   Rebellious shopkeeper in H. G. Wells's comic novel *The History of Mr Polly* (1910). He sets his home on fire, and is supposed dead. This frees him to roam the countryside, and eventually to build a new life for himself with the landlady of a cosy pub. In the film of the novel (1949; dir. Anthony Pelissier) Polly was portrayed by John Mills.

POLLYANNA   See Pollyana WHITTIER

POLYNESIA THE PARROT   See under John DOLITTLE

PONDEROVO, GEORGE   Narrator of H. G. Wells's novel *Tono-Bungay* (1909). He is apprenticed to his pharmacist uncle, Edward Ponderovo, who invents a wonderful (but worthless) medicine called Tono-Bungay. George and his uncle grow rich, and the former uses some of the money to set himself up as an aircraft and ship designer.

PONS, SOLAR   Consulting detective who lives at 7B Praed Street, London, and is accompanied in all his adventures by his faithful friend Dr Lyndon Parker. The nineteen-year-old American author August Derleth invented Solar Pons in 1928, after he had written

to Sir Arthur Conan Doyle begging for more Sherlock HOLMES
stories and had received a disappointing reply. The Solar Pons series
has turned out to be the most sustained of all the Holmes
pastiches, for Derleth wrote some seventy episodes, and since
the author's death in 1971 the character has been perpetuated by
another hand. The Pons stories are collected in the following books:
'In Re: Sherlock Holmes' – The Adventures of Solar Pons (1945),
The Memoirs of Solar Pons (1951), Three Problems for Solar Pons
(1952), The Return of Solar Pons (1958), The Reminiscences of
Solar Pons (1961), The Casebook of Solar Pons (1965), Praed
Street Papers (1965), The Adventure of the Unique Dickensians
(1968) and The Chronicles of Solar Pons (1973). Derleth also
wrote one novel which featured the detective: Mr Fairlie's Final
Journey (1968). Most of these books were first published by the
appropriately-named 'Mycroft and Moran', an imprint of Derleth's
own Sauk City (Wisconsin) publishing company, Arkham
House. Sequels by another hand are four books by Basil Copper:
The Dossier of Solar Pons (1979), The Further Adventures of Solar
Pons (1979), The Secret Files of Solar Pons (1979) and Some
Uncollected Cases of Solar Pons (1980).

PONTIFEX, ERNEST   Unhappy hero of Samuel Butler's semi-
autobiographical novel The Way of All Flesh (1903 – but written
two decades earlier). Bullied by his clergyman father, Ernest is
briefly jailed as the result of a foolish mistake. He then marries
unwisely but is released by the discovery that his wife is a
bigamist. Eventually he inherits some money from an aunt and
settles down to become a writer.

POOH   See WINNIE-THE-POOH

POOTER, CHARLES   Insignificant clerk who secretly recounts his
life in The Diary of a Nobody (1892), written and illustrated by
George and Weedon Grossmith. The book was initially serialized
in Punch, and is regarded as one of the enduring classics of English
humour. The respectable Mr Pooter and his wife Carrie live in
'The Laurels', Brickfield Terrace, Holloway. Recent sequels by
another hand are Mrs Pooter's Diary (1983) and The Collected
Letters of a Nobody, Including Mr Pooter's Advice to His Son (1986)
by Keith Waterhouse. Mr Pooter's original adventures have been

dramatized for BBC television, in 1964 (dir. Ken Russell) with Bryan
Pringle, and in 1980 as a longer serial. They have also been adapted
to the stage (1986) by Keith Waterhouse.

POPEYE   Pugilistic sailor-man with an inimitable way of talking.
He turns into a superhero whenever he eats a can of spinach, and
is able to pound the living daylights out of his perennial enemy,
the hulking Bluto (also known as Brutus). His girlfriend is the
scrawny and screechy Olive OYL. Popeye, a great figure in
twentieth-century American mythology, was the happy
creation of newspaper strip-cartoonist Elzie Crisler Segar. The
character first appeared in Segar's already well-established strip
Thimble Theater, in 1929. He soon became its leading figure.
From 1933 onwards he appeared in some 234 animated films
produced by Max Fleischer. Noted for their vigour and
inventiveness, most of these films were short, though one,
Popeye the Sailor Meets Sinbad the Sailor (1936), was almost
feature-length. Jack Mercer was the longest-serving of the actors
who gave voice to Popeye. Later (much inferior) series of Popeye
cartoons were made for American television in the 1960s and 1970s.
There were also Popeye comic-books from the 1930s to the 1970s,
as well as a series of 'Big Little Books' about the sailor's antics.
The rather ponderous live-action film *Popeye* (1980; dir. Robert
Altman) starred Robin Williams.

POPPINS, MARY   Children's nanny who is gifted with magical
powers, including the ability to slide *up* banisters. She appears in
the book *Mary Poppins* (1934) by P. L. Travers, and its sequels:
Mary Poppins Comes Back (1935), *Mary Poppins Opens the Door*
(1944), *Mary Poppins in the Park* (1952) and *Mary Poppins in
Cherry Tree Lane* (1982). In the highly successful musical film
Mary Poppins (1964; dir. Robert Stevenson) she was played by
Julie Andrews, who was suitably charming but rather too young
for the part.

PORGY   Crippled black hero of DuBose Heyward's novel about the
Deep South, *Porgy* (1925). Heyward and his wife Dorothy turned
the story into a play (1927), which in turn formed the basis of a
celebrated stage musical (or 'folk opera'), *Porgy and Bess* (1935).
The latter had music and lyrics by George and Ira Gershwin. The

The magical Mary Poppins

film musical *Porgy and Bess* (1959; dir. Otto Preminger) starred Sidney Poitier.

PORTER, JANE Beloved of TARZAN, in Edgar Rice Burroughs's novel *Tarzan of the Apes* (1914) and its sequels. She is the daughter

of Professor Archimedes Q. Porter of Baltimore, USA. In the
Weissmuller/Tarzan films of the 1930s (where she is wrongly
named Jane *Parker*) she was played by Maureen O'Sullivan.
Numerous other actresses have portrayed her before and since,
including Joan Burroughs (the author's daughter) who gave voice
to Jane on the radio. She is immortalized in the apocryphal
phrase 'Me Tarzan, you Jane'.

PORTER, JIMMY   Voluble young man in John Osborne's play *Look
Back in Anger* (1956). The action of the play concerns his uneasy
relationship with his wife Alison, but what made the piece so
memorable and influential were the rebellious opinions that
Jimmy utters. He castigates the hidebound English society of the
1950s and its traditional middle-class values to such an extent that
critics promptly hailed him as the symbol of a new literary
movement – the Angry Young Men. The play was subsequently
filmed (1959; dir. Tony Richardson) with Richard Burton in the
leading role.

PORTHOS   See under D'ARTAGNAN

PORTNOY, ALEXANDER   Jewish-American hero of Philip Roth's
very funny novel about motherhood, masturbation and male
anxieties, *Portnoy's Complaint* (1969). Portnoy narrates his life
story from the psychiatrist's couch. His name swiftly became
a byword for guilt-ridden sexual licentiousness. In the
unsuccessful film of the novel (1972; dir. Ernest Lehman) Portnoy
was played by Richard Benjamin.

POSTE, FLORA   Young woman who visits her rural relatives, the
gloomy Starkadder family, in deepest darkest Sussex. Her unlikely
adventures are recounted in Stella Gibbons's very funny novel
Cold Comfort Farm (1932). The book has been described as 'a
brilliant parody of the novel of rustic pessimism . . . [which]
virtually put an end to a widely popular genre' (William Rose
Benét). Sequels by Gibbons include *Christmas at Cold Comfort
Farm* (1940) and *Conference at Cold Comfort Farm* (1948). In
the BBC television serial 'Cold Comfort Farm' (1968) Flora was
played by Sarah Badel.

POYSER, RACHEL   See under Adam BEDE

POZZO   See under VLADIMIR AND ESTRAGON

PRAY, ADDIE   Little girl who becomes an accomplished con artist, as she travels 1930s Kansas in the company of her erring father, the 'Bible salesman' Moses Pray. Their story is told in Joe David Brown's novel *Addie Pray*. This was turned into an attractive movie, *Paper Moon* (1973; dir. Peter Bogdanovich), which starred Tatum O'Neal (and her real-life father, Ryan O'Neal). A subsequent television series, also called 'Paper Moon' (1974–5), had Jodie Foster as Addie.

PRICE, FANNY   Virtuous heroine of Jane Austen's novel *Mansfield Park* (1814). Her parents are impoverished and she goes to live in the household of an uncle, Sir Thomas Bertram. There she grows to be much loved and eventually marries her cousin, Edmund Bertram. During Sir Thomas's absence the young people of the house indulge in amateur theatricals and flirtatious behaviour, of which Fanny disapproves. Readers have found her to be something of a killjoy, and consequently *Mansfield Park* is often regarded as Jane Austen's 'problem' novel. Sequels by other hands are *Susan Price* by Mrs F. Brown and *Mansfield Revisited* (1985) by Joan Aiken.

PRICE, WILLIE   See under Anna TELLWRIGHT

PRIEST, BILLY   Small-town judge, a warm lovable sage, who appears in short stories of the Old South by Irvin S. Cobb. The books about the Judge and his black servant Jeff include *Old Judge Priest* (1915), *J. Poindexter, Colored* (1922), *Down Yonder with Judge Priest and Irvin S. Cobb* (1932) and *Judge Priest Turns Detective* (1937). In the film *Judge Priest* (1934; dir. John Ford) he was played by America's favourite cracker-barrel philosopher, Will Rogers. In John Ford's curiously moving reprise of the same cornball material, *The Sun Shines Bright* (1953), the part of old Billy Priest was taken by Charles Winninger.

PRIESTLEY, LANCELOT   Scientific detective invented by the British writer John Rhode (Cecil John Charles Street) for a very long series of crime novels which were published over a period of some forty years. The middle-aged, dispassionate Dr Priestley has certain qualities in common with R. Austin Freeman's Dr John THORNDYKE. The first novel in the Lancelot Priestley series was *The Paddington Mystery* (1925), and among the scores of titles which followed were *Dr Priestley's Quest* (1926), *The Murders in Praed Street* (1928), *The House on Tollard Ridge* (1929), *Peril at Cranbury Hall* (1930), *Dead Men at the Folly* (1932), *The Motor Rally Mystery* (1933), *The Corpse in the Car* (1935), *Death Pays a Dividend* (1939), *Men Die at Cyprus Lodge* (1943), *Death in Harley Street* (1946), *Up the Garden Path* (1949; vt *The Fatal Garden*), *Death in Wellington Road* (1952), *Death of a Godmother* (1955; vt *Delayed Payment*), *Death Takes a Partner* (1958) and *The Vanishing Diary* (1961).

PRIMROSE, CHARLES   Sweet-natured, quixotic hero of Oliver Goldsmith's novel *The Vicar of Wakefield* (1766). Dr Primrose and his family suffer many misfortunes, up to and including imprisonment for debt, but the vicar bears his troubles stoically, and everything turns out well in the end. In his 'Advertisement' to the book Goldsmith wrote: 'The hero of this piece unites in himself the three greatest characters upon earth; he is a priest, an husbandman, and the father of a family.'

PRINCE, DIANA   See WONDER WOMAN

PRINGLE, GUY AND HARRIET   Central characters of a series of sensitive novels by Olivia Manning known as 'The Balkan Trilogy' and 'The Levant Trilogy'. Guy and Harriet are a newly-married British couple living in Rumania at the outbreak of World War II. Fleeing the German advance, they move to Greece and then to Egypt. According to *The Oxford Companion to English Literature*, the books add up to 'a fine portrait of the tragi-comedy of war and of its effects on civilian life, and give a vivid sense of place and period'. The first trilogy consists of *The Great Fortune* (1960), *The Spoilt City* (1962) and *Friends and Heroes* (1965); the second consists of *The Danger Tree* (1977), *The Battle Lost and Won* (1978) and *The Sum of Things* (1980). Harriet Pringle is the centre of consciousness, but Guy Pringle provides the dominating presence. Anthony Burgess has described the latter as 'a complex

character, big, cultured, quixotic, vital, often foolish, demanding
– indeed, one of the most fully created male leads in
contemporary fiction.'

PRINGLE, OOGIE   See under Judy FOSTER

PRISONER, THE   Known as 'Number Six', the nameless hero of a
most unusual television series, 'The Prisoner' (1967). He was
played by Patrick McGoohan, who also produced and co-wrote
the series. Number Six is a former secret agent (possibly John
DRAKE of 'Danger Man'?) who awakes to find himself a prisoner
in a strange environment which resembles a luxury holiday camp.
He makes repeated attempts to escape, but is constantly thwarted
by hidden surveillance, technological gadgetry, brainwashing
techniques, and the like. His captors remain mysterious, their
almost disembodied malevolence lending an air of Kafkaesque
nightmare to the entire series. A novel based on the scripts is *The
Prisoner* (1969) by Thomas M. Disch. The series was not a great
success on its first airing, but it has been repeated many times
and has gained a cult following.

PROUDIE, MRS   Ambitious evangelical wife of the Bishop of
Barchester, in Anthony Trollope's 'Barsetshire' novels. She is
the real power behind her husband's high office. The books in the
sequence are: *The Warden* (1855), *Barchester Towers* (1857), *Doctor
Thorne* (1858), *Framley Parsonage* (1861), *The Small House at
Allington* (1864) and *The Last Chronicle of Barset* (1867). In the
second of these novels Mrs Proudie vies with the repulsive
chaplain, Obadiah Slope, to make life miserable for the long-
suffering Reverend Septimus HARDING. She dies in the final book
of the series. The novelist Angela Thirkell has also written a lengthy
'Barsetshire' sequence, which purports to be about the twentieth-
century descendants of Trollope's characters. In the BBC
television serial 'The Barchester Chronicles' (1982) Mrs Proudie
was played by Geraldine McEwan.

PRUFROCK, J. ALFRED   Narrator of T. S. Eliot's intensely ironic
poem 'The Love Song of J. Alfred Prufrock' (1915 – reprinted in
Prufrock and Other Observations, 1917). He is a timid,
conventional middle-aged man who longs for emotional and

spiritual fulfilment but cannot break out of the sterile round of his dull daily life.

PRYNNE, HESTER   Heroine of Nathaniel Hawthorne's novel about seventeenth-century New England, *The Scarlet Letter* (1850). She commits adultery with a young minister, Arthur Dimmesdale, and is condemned by the Puritan clergy to wear the embroidered letter 'A' on her breast. Despite her emotional torment she guards the secret of her lover's name, although Dimmesdale is eventually exposed by Hester's monstrously vengeful husband. Many film versions of the novel appeared in the silent-movie era, including one (1926; dir. Victor Sjöström) which starred Lillian Gish as Hester. A recent television serialization of the book (1986) had Meg Foster in the leading role.

PSAMMEAD, THE   Sand fairy, created by E. Nesbit for her delightful children's books *Five Children and It* (1902) and *The Story of the Amulet* (1906). The Psammead is a remarkably ugly creature with a fat furry body, bat-like ears and eyes on stalks. It is also ill-tempered, but it has the wonderful gift of being able to grant wishes. In the first book this results in comic mayhem; in the second novel the Psammead's magical abilities allow the children to travel backwards in time to ancient Egypt and Babylon.

PSMITH   Full name Ronald Eustace Rupert Smith (the 'P' is an affectation), an endearing schoolboy eccentric created by P. G. Wodehouse. Psmith has been to Eton; he is grandiloquent and mischievous, wears a monocle, professes to be a socialist, and calls everyone 'Comrade'. He first appeared in a serial which Wodehouse contributed to a boys' paper, the *Captain*, in 1908. This was published in book form as *Mike* (1909), and subsequently split into two volumes, *Mike at Wrekyn* and *Mike and Psmith*. It is in the latter half of the story that Psmith arrives as a new friend for the cricket-loving hero Mike Jackson. He soon dominates the scene, and becomes the leading character in three sequels: *Psmith in the City* (1910), *Psmith Journalist* (1915) and *Leave it to Psmith* (1923). In the last of these he visits Blandings Castle, and makes the acquaintance of Lord EMSWORTH. All of the Psmith stories have since been combined in an omnibus, *The World of Psmith* (1974). *Leave it to Psmith* has been turned into a play (1930), and has also been adapted for BBC radio (1981, with Simon Ward as Psmith).

PUDDLE-DUCK, JEMIMA   See under PETER RABBIT

PULVER, FRANK   See under Douglas ROBERTS

PUREHEART, OSRIC   See under ECCLES

PUREHEART THE POWERFUL   See ARCHIE

PYE, HAROLD   Eccentric hero of Mervyn Peake's fantasy novel *Mr Pye* (1953). Harold Pye arrives in the Island of Sark determined to convert all its inhabitants to his religion of love. A dramatized version on British independent television (1986) had Derek Jacobi in the leading role.

PYLE, GOMER   Rustic nitwit who joins the United States Marine Corps. He was played by Jim Nabors in the television comedy series 'The Andy Griffith Show' (1960–64) and 'Gomer Pyle USMC' (1964–9).

PYM, ARTHUR GORDON   Hero of Edgar Allan Poe's seafaring novel, *The Narrative of A. Gordon Pym* (1838). Pym stows away aboard a Nantucket whaler and has sundry alarming adventures which end, mysteriously and abruptly, at the South Pole. Because of the unfinished quality of Pym's narrative more than one writer has been tempted to write a sequel. The most notable is Jules Verne, whose 'further adventures of A. Gordon Pym', *Le Sphinx des Glaces* (1897), has been translated as *An Antarctic Mystery*.

PYNCHEON, JAFFREY   Villainous judge in Nathaniel Hawthorne's novel *The House of the Seven Gables* (1851). He commits a murder in order to gain control of the family fortune – and sends another man to prison for the crime. The film of the novel (1940; dir. Joe May) starred George Sanders.

Q

QUANTOCK, DAISY See under Lucia

QUARLES, PHILIP Novelist whose novel-within-a-novel
'counterpoints' the work in which he is a character: Aldous Huxley's
long novel about contemporary English literary and artistic life,
Point Counter Point (1928). Among the other characters in the
book is one Mark Rampion – evidently a fictionalized portrait of
Huxley's friend D. H. Lawrence. *Point Counter Point* has been
serialized on British television.

QUASIMODO Hideously deformed but good-hearted bell-ringer in
Victor Hugo's romantic historical novel *Notre Dame de Paris* (1831).
Deafened by the bells at the Cathedral of Notre Dame where he
has worked since childhood, Quasimodo is a grotesque figure
of fun, and is incapable of normal human intercourse.
Nevertheless he falls in love with a beautiful gypsy girl,
Esmeralda, and offers her a hiding-place when she is unjustly
accused of witchcraft by the lustful archdeacon, Claude Frollo.
This richly-coloured variation on the Beauty-and-the-Beast theme
has moved many generations and has frequently been adapted to
the stage and screen. Theatrical versions of the nineteenth century
were often entitled *Esmeralda*, although one, an opera by
Edward Fitzball (1836), was called *Quasimodo*. Film versions
include *The Hunchback of Notre Dame* (1923; dir. Wallace
Worsley), starring Lon Chaney, and two remakes of the same title
– in 1939 (dir. William Dieterle), with Charles Laughton, and in
1956 (dir. Jean Delannoy), with Anthony Quinn. Quasimodo has
also been impersonated by Warren Clarke (1978) and Anthony
Hopkins (1982) in British television versions of the story.

QUATERMAIN, ALLAN Grizzled hunter who is known to the
natives of southern Africa as 'Macumazahn' – 'in vulgar English, he
who keeps his eyes open'. He is the hero and narrator of a series
of adventure novels by Henry Rider Haggard, beginning with
the ever-popular *King Solomon's Mines* (1885). With his guide,

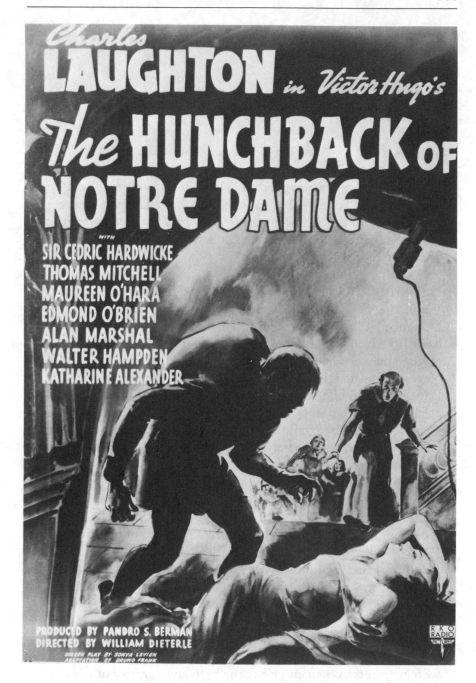

Quasimodo and Esmeralda in a poster for the 1939 film

the majestic UMBOPA, and his companions, the sterling Englishmen
Sir Henry Curtis and Captain John Good, Quatermain penetrates
an unexplored region of Africa in search of the lost diamond
mines of the Biblical king. In the sequel, entitled *Allan
Quatermain* (1887), he visits the frowning city of Zu-Vendis in
the company of the heroic Zulu warrior UMSLOPOGAAS. At the
very end of the second novel the 'editor' reports that Allan has died.
Despite this early killing-off of his best-loved hero, Haggard went
on to write a further twelve books about Quatermain's
adventures. Many of them are supernatural in flavour. The titles
are: *Maiwa's Revenge* (1888), *Allan's Wife* (1889), *Marie* (1912),
Child of Storm (1913), *The Holy Flower* (1915), *The Ivory Child*
(1916), *Finished* (1917), *The Ancient Allan* (1920 – in which
Quatermain 'dreams' himself back to the Egypt of the Pharaohs),
She and Allan (1921), *Heu-Heu* (1924), *The Treasure of the Lake*
(1926) and *Allan and the Ice Gods* (1927 – another time-travel
tale, which Rudyard Kipling helped Haggard to plot).
    The first Allan Quatermain novel has been continuously in
print for over a hundred years, though most of the others are now
little read. In the film of *King Solomon's Mines* (1937; dir. Robert
Stevenson) Quatermain was played by Cedric Hardwicke. In a 1950
remake (dir. Compton Bennett) he was impersonated none too
convincingly by Stewart Granger. The disappointing centenary
remake (1985) starred an even less convincing Richard
Chamberlain – Allan Quatermain reimagined as an American
adventurer in the mould of Indiana JONES. A recent sequel to the
last film is *Allan Quatermain and the Lost City of Gold* (1986),
also starring Chamberlain.

QUATERMASS, BERNARD   Professor who made a speciality of
tackling threats from outer space, in three hugely successful
BBC television serials written by Nigel Kneale: 'The Quatermass
Experiment' (1953), 'Quatermass II' (1955) and 'Quatermass and
the Pit' (1958–9). The actors who played Quatermass in these
three productions were Reginald Tate, John Robinson and André
Morell. All three stories were subsequently filmed: *The
Quatermass Experiment* (1955; dir. Val Guest), with Brian
Donlevy; *Quatermass II* (1957; dir. Guest), with Donlevy; and
Quatermass and the Pit (1967; dir. Roy Ward Baker), with
Andrew Keir. Nigel Kneale revived the Professor for a new

television serial called simply 'Quatermass' (1979). This starred John Mills, but was received with less enthusiasm than the classic serials of the 1950s.

QUEEG, CAPTAIN Cowardly skipper of an American minesweeper during World War II. He provokes revolt among his crew, in Herman Wouk's novel *The Caine Mutiny* (1951). The author turned the latter part of his book into a play, *The Caine Mutiny Court Martial* (1953), which had a considerable success. In the film of the novel (1954; dir. Edward Dmytryk) Queeg was played by Humphrey Bogart.

QUEEN, ELLERY Both a famous fictional character and a famous pseudonym, Ellery is the suave New York detective hero of a series of novels which Manfred B. Lee and Frederick Dannay wrote under the name 'Ellery Queen'. To confuse matters, they also signed a number of *other* books with the same name, although these do not concern Ellery Queen the detective. There is also an *Ellery Queen Mystery Magazine*, published in the United States since 1941. The first of the novels about Ellery was *The Roman Hat Mystery* (1929). The hero is presented as a youthful amateur (his father, Richard Queen, is a police inspector). The other books in the series are: *The French Powder Mystery* (1930), *The Dutch Shoe Mystery* (1931), *The Greek Coffin Mystery* (1932), *The Egyptian Cross Mystery* (1932), *The American Gun Mystery* (1933), *The Siamese Twin Mystery* (1933), *The Adventures of Ellery Queen* (1934), *The Chinese Orange Mystery* (1934), *The Spanish Cape Mystery* (1935), *Halfway House* (1936), *The Door Between* (1937), *The Devil to Pay* (1938), *The Four of Hearts* (1938), *The Dragon's Teeth* (1939), *The New Adventures of Ellery Queen* (1940), *Calamity Town* (1942), *There Was an Old Woman* (1943), *The Case Book of Ellery Queen* (1945), *The Murderer is a Fox* (1945), *Ten Days' Wonder* (1948), *Cat of Many Tails* (1949), *Double, Double* (1950), *The Origin of Evil* (1951), *Calendar of Crime* (1952), *The King is Dead* (1952), *The Scarlet Letters* (1953), *Q.B.I.: Queen's Bureau of Investigation* (1955), *Inspector Queen's Own Case* (1956 – this one is about Ellery's father) and *The Finishing Stroke* (1958). Thereafter it appears that the books issued under the 'Ellery Queen' byline were not by Manfred Lee and Frederick Dannay. The series about Ellery Queen the detective

was resumed after a five-year hiatus, each of the titles
ghost-written (mainly by professional science fiction writers, who
seem to be able to turn their hand to anything): *The Player on
the Other Side* (1963 – by Theodore Sturgeon, as is evident to
anyone who knows his distinctive style), *And on the Eighth Day*
(1964 – said to be by Avram Davidson), *The Fourth Side of the
Triangle* (1965 – also by Davidson), *Queens Full* (1965), *A Study
in Terror* (1961; vt *Sherlock Holmes Meets Jack the Ripper* –
the novelization of a film script in which Ellery tackles HOLMES,
at a distance), *Face to Face* (1967), *The House of Brass* (1968), *Q.E.D.:
Queen's Experiments in Detection* (1968), *The Last Woman in
His Life* (1970) and *A Fine and Private Place* (1971).

A series of nine Ellery Queen films began with *The Spanish
Cape Mystery* (1935; dir. Lewis D. Collins), which starred
Donald Cook as Ellery. The detective was subsequently played
by Eddie Quillan (one film), by Ralph Bellamy (four films) and by
William Gargan (three films, concluding with *Enemy Agents Meet
Ellery Queen* [1942; dir. James Hogan]). The exploits of Ellery Queen
also ran on American radio from 1939 to 1948. There have been
no fewer than four television series entitled 'Ellery Queen' (or
'The Adventures of Ellery Queen'): the first was in 1950–52, with
Richard Hart in the lead; the second was in 1954, with Hugh
Marlowe (who had played Ellery on the radio); the third was in
1958–9, with George Nader; and the fourth was in 1975–6, with Jim
Hutton. There has also been a TV movie, *Ellery Queen: Don't
Look Behind You* (1971; dir. Barry Shear), which starred Peter
Lawford.

QUEEQUEG   Fearsome-looking but good-natured Polynesian
harpooner who becomes a good friend of ISHMAEL'S, in the novel
Moby Dick (1851) by Herman Melville. It is Queequeg's
intricately carved coffin which saves Ishmael's life when MOBY
DICK destroys their ship at the end of the story.

QUEST, MARTHA   Heroine of a series of novels by Doris Lessing,
beginning with *Martha Quest* (1952). Like her creator, she
grows up in colonial Rhodesia, rebels against her parents' values,
joins the Communist Party, has love affairs with various would-be
revolutionaries, seeks restlessly for new wisdom, and eventually
leaves Africa for London. The overall title of the five-novel sequence

is 'The Children of Violence' and the other volumes are *A Proper Marriage* (1954), *A Ripple from the Storm* (1958), *Landlocked* (1965) and *The Four-Gated City* (1969). In the last of these Martha's story moves into the future and up to the end of the twentieth century.

QUESTED, ADELA   See under Doctor Aziz

QUILLER   Tough British secret agent who features in a series of thrillers by Adam Hall (Elleston Trevor). 'Quiller' is his code-name. The titles are: *The Berlin Memorandum* (1965; vt *The Quiller Memorandum*), *The Ninth Directive* (1966), *The Striker Portfolio* (1969), *The Warsaw Document* (1971), *The Tango Briefing* (1973), *The Mandarin Cypher* (1975), *The Kobra Manifesto* (1976), *The Sinkiang Executive* (1978), *The Scorpion Signal* (1980), *The Peking Target* (1982) and *Northlight* (1985). George Segal played the spy in the film *The Quiller Memorandum* (1966; dir. Michael Anderson). The BBC television series 'Quiller' (1975) starred Michael Jayston.

QUILP, DANIEL   Deformed villain in Charles Dickens's novel *The Old Curiosity Shop* (1841). He turns LITTLE NELL and her grandfather out of their home. The film of the novel (1934; dir. Thomas Bentley) starred Hay Petrie as Quilp. The musical remake, entitled *Mister Quilp* (1975; dir. Michael Tuchner), had Anthony Newley in the part.

QUINT, PETER   Villainous ghost in Henry James's frightening novella 'The Turn of the Screw' (1898). The story concerns two children, Miles and Flora, who are haunted by their former governess and her lover (the manservant, Quint). The story was dramatized by William Archibald as *The Innocents* (1950), and filmed under that title (1961; dir. Jack Clayton) with Peter Wyngarde as Quint. A later film version, entitled *The Nightcomers* (1972; dir. Michael Winner), starred Marlon Brando. James's tale has also formed the basis of an opera, *The Turn of the Screw* (1954), by Benjamin Britten.

QUIRT, SERGEANT   See FLAGG AND QUIRT

QUONG LEE   Chinese sage who lives in the Limehouse district of
London. He was invented by the British writer Thomas Burke
for a series of short stories which were collected in the books
Limehouse Nights: Tales of Chinatown (1916), *The Pleasantries
of Old Quong* (1931; vt *A Tea-Shop in Limehouse*) and elsewhere.
There is also a volume of verse by Burke entitled *The Song Book of
Quong Lee of Limehouse* (1920). D. W. Griffith's celebrated silent
film *Broken Blossoms* (1919) was based on 'The Chink and the
Child', one of the pieces from Burke's *Limehouse Nights*.

R

R2-D2 See under Luke SKYWALKER

RABBIT See Harry ANGSTROM

RACE, ROY Known as 'Roy of the Rovers', the leading sports hero of British comics. He has been player-manager of Melchester Rovers football club since he first appeared in the boys' paper *Tiger* in 1954. In 1976 there appeared the first issue of his own weekly publication, *Roy of the Rovers*, and this was still being published a decade later. According to Denis Gifford, Roy was 'the first character in British comics to fall in love, get married and raise a family'.

RADAMES See under AÏDA

RAFFLES, A. J. Cricket-playing gentleman crook invented by Ernest William Hornung for a series of short stories published in the *Strand* and other popular British magazines of the 1890s. Raffles was considered a rather shocking creation (not least by Hornung's brother-in-law, Conan Doyle) as he is a clear-cut example of the criminal as hero. He is a very upper-crust criminal, however – a clubman, a sportsman and a patriot. Raffles's adventures are recounted by his former public-school 'fag', the slavishly admiring Bunny Manders. The stories were collected in the books *The Amateur Cracksman* (1899) and *The Black Mask* (1901), later combined in one volume as *Raffles, The Amateur Cracksman* (1906). More tales were included in *A Thief in the Night* (1905), at the end of which Raffles dies a hero's death in the Boer War. Hornung's only full-length novel about the character, *Mr Justice Raffles* (1909), is concerned with an earlier episode in the life of England's most charming thief. Hornung also wrote two Raffles plays in collaboration with others: *Raffles, The Amateur Cracksman* (with Eugene W. Presbury, 1903) and *A Visit from Raffles* (with Charles Sanson, 1909).

The Raffles tales have inspired numerous sequels by other

A. J. Raffles (David Niven) in the 1940 film

hands. In 1932 Barry Perowne (Philip Atkey) began a series of
short stories about Raffles in the pages of *Thriller* magazine.
After World War II he contributed further episodes to such
publications as *Ellery Queen's Mystery Magazine* and the *Saint
Mystery Magazine*. Perowne's stories have been collected in many
volumes, among them *Raffles After Dark* (1933; vt *The Return
of Raffles*), *Raffles in Pursuit* (1934), *Raffles Under Sentence*
(1936), *She Married Raffles* (1936), *Raffles' Crime in Gibraltar*
(1937; vt *They Hang Them in Gibraltar*), *Raffles vs. Sexton Blake*
(1937), *The A.R.P. Mystery* (1939), *Raffles and the Key Man* (1940),
Raffles Revisited (1974), *Raffles of the Albany* (1976) and *Raffles
of the M.C.C.* (1979). Graham Greene has written a comic play
called *The Return of A. J. Raffles* (1975), and Peter Tremayne has
published a novel entitled *The Return of Raffles* (1981). The first
screen Raffles seems to have been Holger Madsen, who played
the character in a couple of Sherlock HOLMES films made in
Denmark in 1908. He was followed by John Barrymore in a silent
American movie (1917). The cricket-loving crook was played very
effectively by Ronald Colman in *Raffles* (1930; dir. George
Fitzmaurice) and by David Niven in the remake of the same
title (1940; dir. Sam Wood). Raffles was voiced by Frank Allenby
on BBC radio during the 1940s; a more recent radio series (1985)
had Jeremy Clyde in the part. Anthony Valentine made an
excellent hero in the British television film *Raffles* (1975; dir.
Christopher Hodson) and in the subsequent thirteen-episode
series.

RAMAGE, NICHOLAS   Son of the tenth Earl of Blazey, and a hero
of Nelson's navy in the series of seafaring yarns by Dudley Pope
which begins with *Ramage* (1965). The later titles are *Ramage
and the Drumbeat* (1967), *Ramage and the Freebooters* (1969; vt
The Triton Brig), *Governor Ramage, R.N.* (1972), *Ramage's Prize*
(1974), *Ramage and the Guillotine* (1975), *Ramage's Diamond*
(1976), *Ramage's Mutiny* (1977), *Ramage and the Rebels* (1978),
The Ramage Touch (1979), *Ramage's Signal* (1980), *Ramage and
the Renegades* (1981), *Ramage's Devil* (1982), *Ramage's Trial*
(1984), *Ramage's Challenge* (1985) and *Ramage at Trafalgar* (1986).

RAMBO, JOHN   Hero of David Morrell's violent thriller *First Blood*
(1972). A tough veteran of the Vietnam War, he runs into trouble

with a small-town sheriff, takes to the hills, and ends up massacring an entire National Guard unit single-handed. In the film of the novel (1982; dir. Ted Kotcheff) he was played by the muscular Sylvester Stallone. In the follow-up film, *Rambo: First Blood, Part II* (1985), which was 'novelized' by David Morrell, Rambo is sent back to Vietnam to rescue some American prisoners – which he does, amidst much slaughter. The character's name became a household word when President Reagan saw fit to commend this second film in one of his speeches. 'Rambo' promptly entered the vocabulary of politicians and journalists the world over as a designation for Reagan himself, particularly when referring to his policy of overseas military intervention.

RAMPION, MARK   See under Philip QUARLES

RANDALL, REBECCA   Plucky little girl, almost a female Tom SAWYER, who is sent to live with her aunts in the town of Riverboro, Maine. She raises money by selling soap door to door, becomes assistant editor of a school magazine, and engages in other enterprising schemes. She appears in Kate Douglas Wiggin's novel *Rebecca of Sunnybrook Farm* (1903) and its sequel *More About Rebecca* (1907). Mary Pickford played Rebecca in the film of the first title (1917), and Shirley Temple played her in a talkie version (1938; dir. Allan Dwan) which had very little to do with the original novel.

RANDOM, RODERICK   Scottish rogue whose adventures are described in Tobias Smollett's picaresque novel *The Adventures of Roderick Random* (1748). After killing a man in a duel, he goes to sea as a surgeon's mate and, after many vicissitudes, finds his long-lost father in South America. The book was much influenced by Alain-René Lesage's *Gil Blas* (1715–35), which Smollett translated into English. (The science fiction author John Sladek has written two very funny novels about an innocent little robot named Roderick. The titles of these books are *Roderick* [1980] and *Roderick at Random* [1983].)

RANSOM, BASIL   See under Olive CHANCELLOR

RAQUIN, THÉRÈSE   Adulterous heroine of Emile Zola's early novel in the low-life, naturalistic vein, *Thérèse Raquin* (1867). The story has been filmed at least twice – in 1928 (dir. Jacques Feyder), with Gina Manès; and in 1953 (dir. Marcel Carné), with Simone Signoret giving a notable performance – and has also been adapted as a serial for BBC television (1980), with Kate Nelligan in the title role.

RASKOLNIKOV   Tortured protagonist of Fyodor Dostoevsky's great novel *Crime and Punishment* (1866). As a poverty-stricken student, he kills an old woman pawnbroker for her money. He tries to justify his act as that of an incipient Napoleonic superman, and feels no immediate remorse. The slow workings of conscience and the urgings of his girlfriend, Sonya Marmeladova, eventually force him to confess, whereupon he is sent to Siberia. In the Hollywood film *Crime and Punishment* (1935; dir. Josef von Sternberg) Raskolnikov was played by Peter Lorre. A French-made film version (1935; dir. Pierre Chenal) had Harry Baur in the part. The novel has also been serialized on British television, with John Hurt in the leading role.

RASSELAS   Young man who escapes from the Happy Valley where he has been confined by his father, only to discover that the world has nothing better to offer him. His story is told in Dr Samuel Johnson's philosophical fable *The History of Rasselas, Prince of Abyssinia* (1759). Johnson wrote this short novel at top speed in order to pay his mother's funeral expenses.

RASSENDYLL, RUDOLF   Red-headed hero of the adventure story *The Prisoner of Zenda* (1894) and its sequel *Rupert of Hentzau* (1898) by Anthony Hope (Anthony Hope Hawkins). He travels to the central European kingdom of 'Ruritania' for the coronation of its monarch, a distant cousin. There he becomes embroiled in the courtly intrigue which surrounds the new king. Because of a strong family resemblance, Rassendyll is able to impersonate the king when the latter is drugged by his enemies. He saves the day by doing so, and wins the heart of the beautiful Princess Flavia. *The Prisoner of Zenda* has been adapted to the stage several times since the first dramatization in 1896, and silent film versions were made in 1913 and 1922. In the definitive talkie version (1937;

Rudolf Rassendyll (Ronald Colman – right) tangles with Rupert of Hentzau (Douglas Fairbanks Jr) in the 1937 version of *The Prisoner of Zenda*

dir. John Cromwell) Rassendyll was played by Ronald Colman. It was remade less successfully in 1952 (dir. Richard Thorpe), with Stewart Granger; and in 1979 (dir. Richard Quine), with Peter Sellers. Rassendyll was played by Julian Glover in the BBC radio dramatizations of both novels, and by Malcolm Sinclair in the 1984 BBC television serial of 'The Prisoner of Zenda'.

RASTIGNAC, EUGÈNE DE   Law student who makes his fortune in Paris and decides to rise in society. Ruthlessly ambitious, he becomes the lover of one of Père GORIOT's daughters. Rastignac appears in several of Honoré de Balzac's novels in the *Comédie Humaine* sequence, including *La Peau de Chagrin* (1831), *Le Père Goriot* (1834), *La Maison Nucingen* (1838) and *La Cousine Bette* (1846).

RAT   See under TOAD OF TOAD HALL

RAVENAL, GAYLORD   See under Magnolia HAWKS

RAVENSWOOD, EDGAR   See under Lucy ASHTON

READE, FRANK   Hero of a long series of stories in American boys'
papers and dime novels, beginning with *Frank Reade and His
Steam Man of the Plains* by 'Noname' (actually a plagiarism of
an earlier dime novel, *The Steam Man of the Prairies* [1868], by
Edward S. Ellis). The writer who is credited with the creation of
Frank Reade is one Harry Enton. The inventive hero and his
indistinguishable son, Frank Reade, Jr, appeared in over 180
novellas published between 1876 and the 1900s, most of which
were written by Luis P. Senarens, an extremely prolific writer
known as 'the American Jules Verne'.

READY, MASTERMAN   Trusty English sailor who serves the
shipwrecked Seagrave family in Captain Frederick Marryat's
'improving' novel for young people *Masterman Ready* (1841).
Ready dies while saving the family from savages. The book is
yet another variation on the myth of Robinson CRUSOE; and in
some ways the character of Ready prefigures that of Bill CRICHTON
in J. M. Barrie's play *The Admirable Crichton* (1902).

REARDON, EDWIN   Honest English novelist who struggles to
make a living in the uncaring literary marketplace. His tragic story
is told in George Gissing's novel *New Grub Street)* (1891), where
his career is contrasted with that of the ambitious but facile
critic Jasper Milvain.

REBECCA   (1) Beautiful daughter of Isaac of York, in Sir Walter
Scott's novel *Ivanhoe* (1819). She falls in love with the stalwart Sir
Wilfred of IVANHOE, who champions her when she is accused of
witchcraft. However, Ivanhoe marries the fair Saxon girl, Rowena.
Their story is continued in W. M. Thackeray's burlesque sequel
Rebecca and Rowena (1850). The critic Edgar Rosenberg remarks
that Rebecca is 'one of those literary creations who assume a sort
of suprapersonal significance the moment the book is out on the
market'. Indeed, Rebecca was celebrated from the first, the
reviewer in *Blackwood's Magazine* declaring: 'The true interest
of this romance is placed . . . in the still, devoted, sad and
unrequited tenderness of a Jewish damsel – by far the most romantic
creation of female character the author has ever formed – and

Rebecca, daughter of Isaac of York

second, we suspect, to no creature of female character whatever that is to be found in the whole annals either of poetry or of romance' (quoted in Rosenberg's *From Shylock to Svengali*). In films and television adaptations the heroine has been played by Elizabeth Taylor (1952) and Olivia Hussey (1982), among others.

(2) See Rebecca De Winter

REBECCA OF SUNNYBROOK FARM   See Rebecca RANDALL

RED SHADOW, THE   See Pierre BIRABEAU

RED SKULL, THE   See under Captain AMERICA

REEDER, JOHN G.   Unassuming middle-aged detective who works for the Public Prosecutor's office. 'I see wrong in everything,' he says. 'That is my curious perversion – I have a criminal mind!' Thanks to this peculiar gift he is able to solve the most baffling crimes. He was invented by Edgar Wallace for a series of novels and short stories. The best-known book to feature the character is the story-collection *The Mind of Mr J. G. Reeder* (1925; vt *The Murder Book of Mr J. G. Reeder*). Other books by Wallace about Mr Reeder are *Room 13* (1924), *Terror Keep* (1927), *Red Aces* (1929), and *Mr J. G. Reeder Returns* (1934). Unlikely as it may seem, Mr Reeder has been resurrected long after his creator's death by J. T. Edson, a writer of Western novels, who has used the character in such titles as *'Cap' Fog, Texas Ranger, Meet Mr J. G. Reeder* and *The Return of Rapido Clint and J. G. Reeder*. A film, *The Mind of Mr Reeder* (1939; dir. Jack Raymond), starred Will Fyffe. A sixteen-episode British TV series, 'The Mind of J. G. Reeder' (1971), had Hugh Burden in the leading role.

REGAN   See Regan MACNEIL

REGAN, JACK   Tough detective from Scotland Yard's flying squad, played by John Thaw in the television series 'The Sweeney' (1974–8; preceded by the feature-length pilot film *Regan*). His sidekick is a younger, gentler policeman called Carter. The series was conceived by Troy Kennedy Martin. The title refers to a famous fictional character, Sweeney TODD (= flying squad in Cockney rhyming slang). The feature film *Sweeney!* (1976; dir. David Wickes) also starred John Thaw. A series of paperback novels based on the Sweeney TV series tends to have Regan's name prominent in the titles – for example, *Regan and the Deal of the Century* and *Regan and the Lebanese Shipment*.

REID, BRITT   See The GREEN HORNET

REID, JOHN   See The LONE RANGER

REINHART, CARLO   Average American whose life story is told in
a series of darkly-comic novels by Thomas Berger: *Crazy in Berlin*
(1958), *Reinhart in Love* (1962), *Vital Parts* (1970) and *Reinhart's
Women* (1981). Reinhart has been described as 'an American
Schweik' (see Josef SVEJK).

REMO   See The DESTROYER

REMUS, UNCLE   Old cotton-plantation slave who tells wonderful
folk tales, blending African myth with American topography. His
stories are animal fables, and involve such recurring characters
as Brer Rabbit and Brer Fox. Remus was invented by Joel Chandler
Harris for his books *Uncle Remus: His Songs and His Sayings*
(1880; vt *Uncle Remus and His Legends of the Old Plantation*),
Nights with Uncle Remus (1883), *Uncle Remus and His Friends*
(1892), *The Tar-Baby and Other Rhymes of Uncle Remus* (1904),
Told by Uncle Remus (1905), *Uncle Remus and Brer Rabbit*
(1907), *Uncle Remus and the Little Boy* (1910), and *Uncle Remus
Returns* (1918). Remus was played by Edric Connor in the BBC
radio series 'Cabin in the Cotton' (1947). The character also
appeared in the semi-animated Walt Disney film *Song of the
South* (1947; dir. Harve Foster) where he was played by James
Baskett.

RENWICK, JOHN   See under Doc SAVAGE

RHODA   See Rhoda MORGENSTERN

RHODAN, PERRY   Spaceman hero created by Clark Darlton
(Walter Ernesting) and Karl-Herbert Scheer for a vast series of
cheap science fiction novellas published in West Germany since
1961. Rhodan's adventures span the galaxy, 'the ultimate series
incorporating everything that was ever thought of in science
fiction written into one interminable sequence' (according to critic
Franz Rottensteiner). There have been many hundreds of episodes,
making this one of the longest fictional series ever penned. Other
authors who have contributed to the saga include Kurt Brand, H. G.
Ewers and Kurt Mahr. The stories have been widely translated, and

have appeared in English since 1969. By 1981 more than 750 million copies of the Rhodan tales had been sold in Germany alone.

RICARDO, LUCY   Wacky suburban housewife played by the red-headed comedienne Lucille Ball, in the American television series 'I love Lucy' (1951–7). This programme was one of the earliest to be produced on film, rather than broadcast 'live', and it has been reshown endlessly since the time of its first huge success (which TV critics Tim Brooks and Earle Marsh have described as 'unparalleled in the history of television'). It co-starred Desi Arnaz (Ms Ball's real-life spouse) as Lucy's husband, Ricky Ricardo. The same characters reappeared in an occasional series known variously as 'The Lucille Ball–Desi Arnaz Show' or 'The Lucy–Desi Comedy Hour' (late 1950s to mid-1960s). Another very popular series which starred Lucille Ball, 'The Lucy Show' (1962–74; known in its later years as 'Here's Lucy'), did not feature the Ricardos.

RICE, ARCHIE   Ageing music-hall comedian in John Osborne's tragi-comic play *The Entertainer* (1957). He was portrayed on stage by Laurence Olivier, who also took the role in the film (1960; dir. Tony Richardson). 'Olivier's bravura performance is one of the most brilliant and exciting ever filmed', according to Steven H. Scheuer. In the TV movie of the same title (1976; dir. Donald Wrye) the action was moved from England to America, and Jack Lemmon played Archie.

RICHARDS, MARY   See under Lou GRANT

RICHARDS, REED   See Mr FANTASTIC

RICHARDSON, MEG   Widowed motel-owner in British independent television's long-running soap opera 'Crossroads' (from 1964). She has a crippled son, Sandy, and a daughter, Jill. She remarried briefly and her name changed to Meg Mortimer. Actress Noele Gordon played the role for seventeen years until she was ditched from the serial amidst some public acrimony in 1981. 'Crossroads' was 'devised' by Hazel Adair and Peter Ling. A book which treats the programme with great seriousness is *Crossroads: The Drama of a Soap Opera* (1982) by Dorothy Hobson. See also BENNY.

RIDD, JOHN   See under Lorna Doone

RIGBY, ELEANOR   One of 'the lonely people' in Paul McCartney's song 'Eleanor Rigby'. It was included on the Beatles' LP *Revolver* (1966), and later was used to good effect in the animated film *Yellow Submarine* (1968; dir. George Dunning).

RIGOLETTO   Hunchbacked jester to the Duke of Mantua, in Giuseppe Verdi's opera *Rigoletto* (1851). In order to impress the mocking courtiers he allows them to believe that his beautiful daughter, Gilda, is his mistress. This deception leads to tragedy. The libretto, by Maria Piave, is based on the play *Le Roi S'amuse* (1832) by Victor Hugo. In the latter work the principal character is called Triboulet, not Rigoletto.

RIGSBY, MR   Ever suspicious, ever complaining landlord played by Leonard Rossiter in the British television comedy series 'Rising Damp' (1974–8), written by Eric Chappell. A feature film, *Rising Damp* (1980; dir. Joe McGrath), was based on the series and also starred Rossiter.

RILEY, CHESTER A.   Irish-American aircraft riveter played by William Bendix in the popular radio series 'The Life of Riley' (from 1943). When the series was transferred to television in 1949–50, Bendix was temporarily unavailable, and the role of Riley was taken by Jackie Gleason. The latter failed to create a new following for the character. However, Bendix returned to the part of the beefy but soft-hearted Chester Riley when the TV series was successfully revived (1953–8).

RILEY, OLD MOTHER   Voluble old washerwoman created by British music-hall comedian Arthur Lucan. With her daughter Kitty (played by Lucan's wife), Old Mother Riley raised many laughs from British audiences between the wars. After years on stage, the characters appeared in some fourteen low-budget films from 1937 to 1952, and in various BBC radio series. Among their film titles were *Old Mother Riley in Paris* (1938), *Old Mother Riley's Circus* (1941), *Old Mother Riley's Jungle Treasure* (1949) and *Mother Riley Meets the Vampire* (1952). A rather sad play, *On Your Way, Riley!* by Alan Plater, appeared on Channel

Four television in 1985. Brian Murphy played Arthur Lucan (and Old Mother Riley), and Maureen Lipman played his wife Kitty McShane.

RIMA   Full name Riolama, a South American jungle girl in W. H. Hudson's romance *Green Mansions* (1904). The hero, Guevez de Argensola Abel, falls in love with this 'bird girl' and tries to help find her mother. They become separated, and Rima is sacrificed by Indians. The film *Green Mansions* (1959; dir. Mel Ferrer) starred Audrey Hepburn as the jungle waif. A famous statue of Rima, by Jacob Epstein, stands in London's Hyde Park.

RINGER, THE   Real name Henry Arthur Milton, a master criminal who is a supreme expert in the art of disguise. He appears in Edgar Wallace's novel *The Gaunt Stranger* (1925; vt *The Ringer*) and in its highly successful adaptation as a stage play, *The Ringer* (produced 1926; published in book form 1929). A subsequent collection of short stories is entitled *Again the Ringer* (1929; vt *The Ringer Returns*). There have been several film versions of Wallace's original tale, including *The Ringer* (1931) with Patrick Curwen; *The Gaunt Stranger* (1938; dir. Walter Forde) with Sonnie Hale; and *The Ringer* (1952; dir. Guy Hamilton) with Donald Wolfit.

RINK, JETT   Ranch-hand who grows rich. He is the resentful anti-hero of Edna Ferber's novel about the Texas oil-fields, *Giant* (1952). In the film of the book (1956; dir. George Stevens) Jett was played by the brooding James Dean (shortly before that actor's untimely death).

RIN TIN TIN   Talented German shepherd dog who became a star of Hollywood movies in the 1920s. Strictly speaking, Rin Tin Tin (or 'Rinty') is not a fictional character. The original dog which bore the name was found in Europe by Lee Duncan, an American soldier during World War I. Duncan named the beast, took it to Los Angeles, and trained it for a successful career in Warner Brothers films. Among the many adventure movies which featured Rin Tin Tin were *The Man from Hell's River* (1922), *Clash of the Wolves* (1925), *Jaws of Steel* (1927) and *Rinty of the Desert* (1928). It is said that Rinty earned over a million dollars, and received some

10,000 fan letters a week at the height of his fame. Although the original animal died in 1932, he has been perpetuated as a 'fictional character' in a radio series (1931–4), in such films as *The Return of Rin Tin Tin* (1947), and in a television series entitled 'The Adventures of Rin Tin Tin' (1954–9).

RIPLEY, TOM   Hero-villain of a series of psychological crime novels by Patricia Highsmith, beginning with *The Talented Mr Ripley* (1955). Ripley is a 'charming psychopath' who commits several murders. He has been described as 'likeable and monstrous at the same time, comic and frightening . . . a proper hero for dark comedy in suspense fiction' (Mary Helen Becker, in *Twentieth-Century Crime and Mystery Writers*). The later titles are *Ripley Underground* (1970), *Ripley's Game* (1974) and *The Boy Who Followed Ripley* (1980). Alain Delon played Ripley in the French film *Plein Soleil* (1960; dir. René Clément; adapted from *The Talented Mr Ripley*). Dennis Hopper also played a version of Ripley in the film *The American Friend* (1977; dir. Wim Wenders).

ROBBY THE ROBOT   Vaguely humanoid artificial entity in the science fiction film *Forbidden Planet* (1956; dir. Fred M. Wilcox). Robby resembles a 1950s jukebox on bulbous legs. He is servant to Dr Morbius, who presides like Prospero over the lonely planet Altair-4 (in this refashioning of *The Tempest* Robby plays the part of Ariel). He helps Dr Morbius and a party of explorers from Earth to fight the local equivalent of Caliban, the Monster from the Id. The film was scripted by Cyril Hume from an original story by Irving Block and Allen Adler. The 'novel of the film', *Fobidden Planet* (1956), is by W. J. Stuart. Robby proved very popular, and he was brought back as the 'star' of a later film, *The Invisible Boy* (1957; dir. Herman Hoffman). This is not really a sequel to *Forbidden Planet* but an entirely different story about a boy who builds his own robot.

ROBERTS, DOUGLAS   American naval lieutenant in Thomas Heggen's novel *Mr Roberts* (1946). He becomes a hero to the bored crew of a World War II navy cargo ship. The novel formed the basis of a very successful play by Joshua Logan (1948). Henry Fonda became identified with the part on stage, and he repeated the role for the film (1955; dir. John Ford and Mervyn Le Roy). A

Robby the Robot in a gallant pose with a young friend

film sequel, which deals with the subsequent career of Roberts's subordinate Frank Pulver, is *Ensign Pulver* (1964; dir. Joshua Logan). An American television series, 'Mr Roberts' (1965–6), starred Roger Smith.

ROBIN   See under BATMAN

ROBINSON, HYACINTH   See under The Princess CASAMASSIMA

ROBINSON, MRS   See under Benjamin BRADDOCK

ROBUR   Airship captain who holds the world to ransom, in Jules Verne's novel *Robur the Conqueror* (1886; also known in English as *The Clipper of the Clouds*) and its sequel *Master of the World* (1904). Initially a benign aeronautical version of Captain NEMO, Robur develops into 'a dangerous madman, blasphemous and uncontrollable, [whose] excesses – like those of Wells's Dr Moreau – seem to represent the excesses of an unfettered development of the implications of scientific "progress" ' (according to John Clute in *The Encyclopedia of Science Fiction*). In the Hollywood film *Master of the World* (1961; dir. William Witney) Robur was played by Vincent Price. Verne's Robur was one of the last characters to appear in the 'Classics Illustrated' series of American comic-books, which ceased publication in the early 1960s.

ROCHESTER, EDWARD   Moody, saturnine master of Thornfield Hall in Charlotte Brontë's novel *Jane Eyre* (1847). His servant, young Jane EYRE, falls in love with him despite his strange ways (he resembles a Gothic hero-villain). They are about to be married when it is revealed that Rochester already has a wife, a madwoman whom he has kept imprisoned in an attic. The house burns down, the mysterious Mrs Rochester dies, Edward Rochester is blinded, and he and Jane are eventually reconciled. The story of Rochester's earlier life is told in a remarkable 'prequel' by Jean Rhys, *Wide Sargasso Sea* (1966). This recounts how Antoinette Cosway, a beautiful Creole heiress, meets and marries the young Mr Rochester while he is on an extended visit to the West Indies. He hears rumours of madness in her family and comes to believe that she is insane; on returning to England to claim his

inheritance, he locks her in the attic of Thornfield Hall . . .
Brontë's original novel has been filmed several times. The first
talkie *Jane Eyre* (1934) starred Colin Clive. In the most notable
version (1943; dir. Robert Stevenson), Rochester was played by
Orson Welles. A later TV movie (1971; dir. Delbert Mann) starred
George C. Scott.

ROCKET J. SQUIRREL   See under BULLWINKLE

ROCKFORD, JIM   Californian private-eye, amiably played by James
Garner in the American television series 'The Rockford Files'
(1974–80). He lives impecuniously in a trailer park near Los
Angeles.

ROCKY   See Rocky BALBOA

RODERICK   See under Roderick RANDOM

RODNEY, STELLA   Widowed Englishwoman who falls in love with
a spy, during the wartime blitz on London. Her unhappy story is
told in Elizabeth Bowen's sensitive novel *The Heat of the Day*
(1949). According to Anthony Burgess, 'no novel has better caught
the atmosphere of London during the Second World War'.

RODOLFO   Parisian poet who falls in love with the doomed Mimi,
in Giacomo Puccini's great opera *La Bohème* (1896). The
character first appeared (as 'Rodolphe') in Henri Murger's novel
Scènes de la Bohème (1847–9), which was turned into a
successful play entitled *Scènes de la Vie Bohème*. The librettists
for Puccini's opera were Giuseppe Giacosa and Luigi Illica. (Ruggero
Leoncavallo also wrote an opera called *La Bohème* at much the
same time as Puccini's, but this version has been completely
overshadowed.) Rodolfo was subsequently played by John Gilbert
in the silent(!) film *La Bohème* (1926; dir. King Vidor).

ROGERS, BUCK   Spaceman hero created by Philip Francis Nowlan
for his magazine serial 'Armageddon: 2419' (*Amazing Stories*,
1928–9). The cartoonist Dick Calkins seized on this space opera
as the subject matter for his newspaper strip *Buck Rogers in
the 25th Century*, which became an immense success and ran

continuously from 1929 until the late 1960s. The strip became so well known that at one time the entire science fiction genre in America was stigmatized as 'that Buck Rogers stuff'. In 1932 Buck made the transition to the radio: 'What Dick Calkins did not imagine for his newspaper strip, writer Jack Johnstone did for the air shows. While planets waged war against each other with death rays, gamma bombs, incendiary missiles, and massed flights of space ships, Buck, his lovely co-pilot Wilma Deering, and the brilliant Dr Huer spent week after week trying to save the universe from total destruction' (according to Raymond William Stedman). Later, Buck appeared in a cinema serial (1939; dir. Ford Beebe and Saul A. Goodkind) which starred Buster Crabbe (who had already played the similar character Flash GORDON). A cheaply-made television series, also entitled 'Buck Rogers in the 25th Century' (1950–51), starred Kem Dibbs. Nearly thirty years later, an elaborate TV movie of the same title, which was also released as a cinema feature film (1979; dir. Daniel Haller), had Gil Gerard as Buck Rogers, and this gave rise to a new TV series which ran for two seasons in 1979–81.

ROGERS, STEVE   See Captain AMERICA

ROGOZHIN   See under Prince MYSHKIN

ROJACK, STEPHEN RICHARD   Television commentator, a former war hero, who murders his wife and becomes involved with the underworld, in Norman Mailer's novel *An American Dream* (1965). This work was described by *Life* magazine as 'a devil's encyclopedia of our secret visions and desires'. In the film of the book (1966; dir. Robert Gist) Rojack was played by Stuart Whitman.

ROKOFF, NICHOLAS   See under KORAK

ROLAND RAT   Rather nauseating rodent puppet who became a 'superstar' on British television during the 1980s. He is credited with saving the commercial breakfast television company TV-am: its fortunes were failing, but after the company imported Roland Rat as a star attraction the ratings began to rise again. Roland is the creation of puppeteer Dave Claridge.

ROLLISON, RICHARD   See The TOFF

ROLLO   Little boy who appears in numerous books of moral tales by the nineteenth-century American children's writer Jacob Abbott: *The Little Scholar Learning to Talk* and *Rollo Learning to Read* (both 1835), and such sequels as *Rollo at Work, Rollo at Play, Rollo at School, Rollo's Vacation, Rollo's Museum, The Rollo Code of Morals* and *The Rollo Philosophy*.

ROME, TONY   Private-eye in the novel *Miami Mayhem* (1960; vt *Tony Rome*) by 'Anthony Rome' (Marvin H. Albert), and its sequels: *The Lady in Cement* (1961) and *My Kind of Game* (1962). The character was played by Frank Sinatra in the movies *Tony Rome* (1967; dir. Gordon Douglas) and *Lady in Cement* (1968; dir. Douglas).

RON AND ETH   See The GLUM FAMILY

ROQUENTIN, ANTOINE   Existentialist narrator of Jean-Paul Sartre's novel *La Nausée* (1938; initially translated into English as *The Diary of Antoine Roquentin* but subsequently known as *Nausea*). He is overcome by a sense of the absurdity of existence, the apparent meaninglessness of time and space, objects and people. He eventually finds solace in the possibility of creating an artistic masterpiece.

ROSEMARY   See Rosemary WOODHOUSE

ROSS, MATTIE   See under Rooster J. COGBURN

ROSTOVA, NATASHA   Heroine of a novel which contains over 500 well-realized characters – Leo Tolstoy's *War and Peace* (1864–9). Against the background of the Napoleonic Wars, the story follows Natasha's life from girlhood to motherhood, centring on her engagement to Prince Andrei Bolkonsky and her subsequent marriage to Pierre BEZUKHOV. Although the book is long and complex, there have been many attempts to adapt it to the stage, opera, film and television. Sergei Prokofiev's opera *War and Peace*, with a libretto by the composer and Mira Mendelson, was first performed in 1946, with an extended version in 1955. The

Natasha Rostova (Audrey Hepburn) with Pierre Bezukhov (Henry Fonda)
in the 1956 version of *War and Peace*

principal Hollywood movie of the novel (1956; dir. King Vidor)
starred Audrey Hepburn. An extremely long (and faithful) Russian
film (1967; dir. Sergei Bondarchuk) had Lyudmila Savelyeva as
Natasha. The BBC television serial (1972; dir. John Howard Davies)
had Morag Hood.

ROUGIERRE, MADAME DE LA   See under Silas RUTHYN

ROUGON-MACQUART   Family whose fortunes are described in a
series of twenty naturalistic novels by Emile Zola, beginning
with *La Fortune des Rougons* (1871) and ending with *Le Docteur
Pascal* (1893). Zola described his saga as 'the natural and social
history of a family under the Second Empire', and he used it to
show the validity of his deterministic theories of heredity and
environment. The common ancestress of the Rougons and the

Macquarts is Adelaïde Fouque, an eighteenth-century Provençal woman who marries a peasant called Rougon and has a son by him. When Rougon leaves her she takes up with a violent drunkard called Macquart, by whom she has two more children. Thus the two branches of the family are founded. One of Adelaïde Fouque's granddaughters is the alcoholic Gervaise Macquart, who marries a man called Coupeau and gives birth to their daughter, NANA. Among the best-known books in the Rougon-Macquart series are *L'Assommoir* (1877), *Nana* (1880), *Germinal* (1885), *La Terre* (1887), *La Bête Humaine* (1890) and *La Débâcle* (1892). Notable films which have been based on the fortunes of the Rougon and Macquart families include *La Bête Humaine* (1938; dir. Jean Renoir) and *Gervaise* (1956; dir. René Clément).

ROULETABILLE, JOSEPH   Cub reporter on a Paris newspaper who doubles as a private detective. He is the hero of Gaston Leroux's celebrated crime novel *The Mystery of the Yellow Room* (1907). Rouletabille's later cases are recounted in *The Perfume of the Lady in Black* (1909) and *The Slave Bangle* (1923), and in a number of other novels which appear not to have been translated into English: *Rouletabille Chez le Tsar* (1913), *Le Château Noir* (1916), *Les Étranges Noces de Rouletabille* (1916), *Rouletabille Chez Krupp* (1920), and *Rouletabille Chez les Bohémiens* (1923).

ROVER, RALPH   Youthful narrator of R. M. Ballantyne's novel of adventure, *The Coral Island* (1858). With his friends Jack Martin and Peterkin Gray, he is cast away on a South Sea island. In true Robinson CRUSOE fashion, they struggle to survive, and not only do they meet with natural privations but with cannibals and pirates as well. Like junior Victorian imperialists, they prevail. In an unpleasant sequel, *The Gorilla Hunters* (1861), Ralph and his companions go to darkest Africa to slaughter great apes. The first of these books has become a perennial children's classic. William Golding produced an ironic inversion of it in his novel *Lord of the Flies* (1954), where one of the central characters is also named Ralph. A British television serial of *The Coral Island* (1983), adapted by James Andrew Hall, had Richard Gibson as Ralph.

ROWENA   See under Sir Wilfred of IVANHOE

ROY OF THE ROVERS   See Roy RACE

ROXTON, LORD JOHN   See under George Edward CHALLENGER
and The SPIDER

RUBASHOV, NICOLAS SALMANOVICH   Former 'Commissar of the
People' who is arrested, interrogated, and persuaded to admit
to crimes he did not commit, in Arthur Koestler's powerful
anti-Stalinist novel *Darkness at Noon* (1940). The author stated in
a preface: 'The characters in this book are fictitious. The historical
circumstances which determined their actions are real. The life
of the man N. S. Rubashov is a synthesis of the lives of a number
of men who were victims of the so-called Moscow Trials.'
Although his experiences are closely based on such fact, Rubashov
has much in common with Kafka's Joseph K. and Orwell's
Winston SMITH.

RUBBLE, BARNEY AND BETTY   See under Fred and Wilma
FLINTSTONE

RUDGE, BARNABY   Half-wit who is caught up in the Gordon riots
of 1780, in Charles Dickens's historical novel *Barnaby Rudge* (1841).
He has a devoted mother, a villainous father, and a pet raven
called Grip. This novel remains the least known of Dickens's
longer works, despite the vigour of its depiction of the
anti-Catholic riots.

RUFTY-TUFTY   See under The GOLLIWOGG

RUGGLES, MARMADUKE   English butler adrift in the Wild West.
He appears in Harry Leon Wilson's humorous novel *Ruggles of Red
Gap* (1915). The sequels are *Somewhere in Red Gap* and *Ma
Pettengill*. In the film *Ruggles of Red Gap* (1935; dir. Leo McCarey)
he was played by Charles Laughton. The remake entitled *Fancy
Pants* (1950; dir. George Marshall) starred Bob Hope.

RUMPOLE, HORACE   Crusty but lovable old barrister invented by
lawyer-playwright John Mortimer for a BBC television drama in
1976. Played by the excellent Leo McKern, Rumpole has a vast
understanding of human frailties and a sharp (if bulbous) nose for

hidden truths. He refers to himself as an 'Old Bailey Hack' and to his wife as 'She Who Must Be Obeyed'. Mortimer reintroduced Rumpole as the hero of an independent TV series 'Rumpole of the Bailey' (1978–9). The character later appeared in the TV movie *Rumpole's Return* (1981), and in another series of shorter episodes (1983–4). Rumpole's cases have also been published in book form, in a series of volumes by John Mortimer based on his own TV scripts. These include *Rumpole of the Bailey* (1978), *The Trials of Rumpole* (1979), *Rumpole's Return* (1980), *Rumpole for the Defence* (1982) and *Rumpole and the Golden Thread* (1983). There will be more episodes, on TV and in book form. The critic Clive James has stated: 'In Rumpole, it is by now clear, John Mortimer has created one of the truly durable television figures.'

RUPERT BEAR   Small bear, invariably clad in check trousers, red pullover and scarf, who has magical adventures in an English rural setting. He is the most enduring newspaper comic-strip character in Britain, first created by Mary Tourtel for the *Daily Express* in 1920. Books of Tourtel's drawings and stories about Rupert began to appear in the mid-1920s, but it was not until 1936 that the much-lauded and unbroken series of Rupert Annuals began. These were almost entirely the work of the outstanding artist Alfred Bestall, who had taken over responsibility for Rupert from the ailing Mary Tourtel in 1935. For some thirty years Bestall wrote and drew the bulk of the Rupert stories which appeared in the daily newspaper strip, the annual volumes and quarterly pamphlets. He created a world of enchantment, centred on the cosy village of 'Nutwood' but ranging as far as the South Sea islands and the North Pole. Rupert's friends include Bill Badger, Algy Pug, Edward Trunk, Bingo the Brainy Pup, and a host of eccentric characters such as the Wise Old Goat and the Chinese Conjuror. At its height of popularity, in the 1950s, the Rupert Annual sold one and a half million copies. Since the mid-1960s Rupert has been perpetuated by artists Alex Cubie, John Harrold and others. He also made an unauthorized and scandalous appearance in the 'underground' paper *Oz*, which was prosecuted for obscenity.

Rupert's name and figure have long been exploited in merchandising, and millions of Rupert dolls, mugs, towels and the like have been sold. In 1970 British commercial television began an animated Rupert series which lasted for seven years. A

short animated film, *Rupert and the Frog Song* (1984; dir. Geoffrey
Dunbar) was produced by Paul McCartney, one of the little
bear's most influential admirers. In the 1980s, Rupert's standing
has never been higher. This is indicated by the publication of the
celebratory book *Rupert: A Bear's Life* (1985) by George Perry,
and by a long-drawn-out correspondence which appeared in the
Guardian newspaper towards the end of 1985; this last concerned
the important subject of what Rupert's father did for a living, and
it culminated in an authoritative letter from the ninety-three-
year-old Alfred Bestall – the artist who had done so much
to make Rupert one of the best-loved children's heroes of the
twentieth century.

RUSSELL, CHARLES   British security chief, in the espionage novels
of William Haggard (Richard Henry Michael Clayton). Colonel
Russell is very much a conservative, Establishment figure (Donald
McCormick describes him as '*a pukka sahib*', and says 'Buchan
would have approved of him'). Russell made his fictional debut
in Haggard's *Slow Burner* (1958), and has reappeared in *Venetian
Blind* (1959), *The Arena* (1961), *The Unquiet Sleep* (1962), *The
High Wire* (1963), *The Antagonists* (1964), *The Powder Barrel*
(1965), *The Hard Sell* (1965), *The Power House* (1966), *The
Conspirators* (1967), *A Cool Day for Killing* (1968), *The Doubtful
Disciple* (1969), *The Hardliners* (1970), *The Bitter Harvest* (1971;
vt *Too Many Enemies*), *The Old Masters* (1973; vt *The Notch on
the Knife*), *The Scorpion's Tail* (1975), *Yesterday's Enemy* (1976),
The Poison People (1978), *Visa to Limbo* (1978) and *The Median
Line* (1979).

RUTHERFORD, MARK   Narrator of the *The Autobiography of
Mark Rutherford, Dissenting Minister* (1881), a novel by William
Hale White. The story concerns a young man's loss of faith in his
church. In the sequel *Mark Rutherford's Deliverance* (1885) he
finds a renewed purpose in social service. Neither of these novels
carried the author's name; White continued to use 'Mark
Rutherford' as a pseudonym for most of his other books, both
fiction and non-fiction.

RUTHYN, SILAS   Tall, white-haired villain of J. Sheridan Le Fanu's
novel *Uncle Silas* (1864). The orphaned heiress Maud Ruthyn

is sent to live with her mysterious uncle at his home, Bartram-Haugh. Silas attempts to marry her to his unprepossessing son, but Maud refuses. He then instigates a dastardly plot to kill Maud and obtain her money. The girl is tormented by Madame de la Rougierre, a French governess who is in Silas's employ, but eventually she escapes. In the film *Uncle Silas* (1947; dir. Charles Frank) the wicked uncle was played by Derrick de Marney.

RYAN, PAT   See under Terry LEE

RYDER, CHARLES   Narrator and hero of Evelyn Waugh's biliously class-conscious novel *Brideshead Revisited* (1945). Ryder makes friends with the aristocratic Sebastian FLYTE while both are undergraduates at Oxford; he is invited to the ancestral home, where he falls in love with the architecture, the ambience and the daughter of the house, Julia. Adapted by John Mortimer, the novel became a hugely successful television serial in 1981, with Jeremy Irons in the role of the pining and repining Charles Ryder. A posthumous fragment by Waugh entitled 'Charles Ryder's Schooldays' was first published in 1982.

RYMER, HUXTON   See under Sexton BLAKE

SABRE, MARK   Talkative, opinionated, liberal-minded Englishman, known affectionately as 'Old Puzzlehead'. He is the hero of A. S. M. Hutchinson's bestselling novel *If Winter Comes* (1921). It is Sabre's curse to be able to see both sides of every question, and this gets him into deep trouble when he offers hospitality to a lower-class girl who has given birth to an illegitimate child. In the film of the novel (1947; dir. Victor Saville) the philosophical Mark Sabre was played by Walter Pidgeon. (A television character of the 1950s was named 'Mark Saber'. In the first 'Mark Saber' series [1951–4] he was a British cop working for an American police force. Tom Conway played him. In the second series [1955–60] Saber was a one-armed private-eye working in London. In this incarnation he was played by Donald Gray.)

SAD SACK   Comic-strip GI, a lugubrious little man, created during World War II by artist George Baker for an American army magazine. The humorous adventures of Sad Sack soon became popular in civilian newspapers, and the character also appeared in his own comic-books from 1949. Typical titles are *Sad Sack and the Sarge* and *Sad Sack's Army Life* (both published by Harvey Comics in the 1950s).

SAINT, THE   Debonair hero, 'the Robin Hood of modern crime', created by the Anglo-Chinese thriller-writer Leslie Charteris for a long series of short stories, novellas and novels which have appeared in British and American magazines and have been reprinted in book form around the world. 'The Saint' is his criminal alias (his symbol is a haloed stick-figure), and his actual name is Simon Templar. Although he lives outside the law, he is a gallant and honourable English gentleman, a righter of wrongs, a saver of damsels and a merry prankster. He is always blithe and witty and immaculately dressed. The first Saint novel was *Meet the Tiger* (1928; vt *The Saint Meets the Tiger*). It was followed by *The Last Hero* (1930; vt *The Saint Closes the Case*), *Enter the Saint* (1930), *Knight Templar* (1930; vt *The*

The Saint (Roger Moore) as he appeared in the 1960s TV series

Avenging Saint), *Featuring the Saint* (1931), *Alias the Saint* (1931), *She Was a Lady* (1931; vt *The Saint Meets His Match*), *The Holy Terror* (1932; vt *The Saint Versus Scotland Yard*), *Getaway* (1932; vt *The Saint's Getaway*) and about thirty more titles over the next several decades. Particularly notable novels in the series include *The Saint in New York* (1935), *The Saint Overboard* (1936) and *The Saint in Miami* (1940). From the mid-1960s, some (possibly all) of the new Saint books were not actually written by Leslie Charteris. Although the novel *Vendetta for the Saint* (1964) carries his name it was in fact ghost-written by science fiction writer Harry Harrison. *The Saint on TV* (1968), *The Saint Returns* (1969), *The Saint and the Fiction Makers* (1970) and *The Saint and the People Importers* (1970) were based on TV scripts, adapted to book form by Fleming Lee. Later Saint novels, which bear the Charteris byline once more, are *The Saint in Pursuit* (1971;

based on an old comic-strip) and *Salvage for the Saint* (1983).
There have been numerous short stories about the character.
The Fantastic Saint (1982; edited by Martin H. Greenberg and
Charles G. Waugh) is a collection of all the Charteris/Saint
stories which contain apparently supernatural elements.

The first film version of a Saint story was *The Saint in New York*
(1938; dir. Ben Holme). It starred the South African-born actor
Louis Hayward, who was not judged to be a success in the part.
The smoothly English George Sanders took over the role for *The
Saint Strikes Back* (1938; dir. John Farrow) and four subsequent
films. He in turn was replaced by Hugh Sinclair in *The Saint's
Vacation* (1940; dir. Leslie Fenton) and one other film. After a hiatus
of some years Louis Hayward was restored to the part in the
British-made *The Saint's Return* (1953; dir. Seymour
Friedmann). There have also been a few French-made Saint films
starring Jean Marais. A series of Saint adaptations was broadcast
on American radio during the latter half of the 1940s; among the
actors who gave him voice were Brian Aherne, Vincent Price and
Tom Conway (George Sanders's brother). The Saint has also been
played by Terence De Marney on BBC radio. In addition, there has
been a Saint comic-strip and a *Saint Mystery Magazine* (1958–67).
In 1963 there came a successful British TV series, 'The Saint',
starring an appropriately handsome and debonair Roger Moore.
The series was renewed over several seasons, coming to an end in
1968. Ten years later, a fresh series, 'The Return of the Saint',
starred Ian Ogilvy as the ever-youthful buccaneering hero.

ST AUBER, EMILY DE   See under MONTONI

ST CLARE, EVANGELINE   See LITTLE EVA

ST CLAIR, AMBER   Beautiful, promiscuous heroine of Kathleen
   Winsor's bestselling novel *Forever Amber* (1944). She has sundry
   adventures among the royalty and aristocracy of Restoration
   England. In the film of the novel (1947; dir. Otto Preminger)
   she was played by Linda Darnell.

SALAMMBÔ   Priestess-princess of ancient Carthage, daughter of
   the great Hamilcar, in Gustave Flaubert's exotic historical novel
   Salammbô (1862). She is loved by the rebel soldier Matho (who

comes to a gory end at the hands of the Carthaginian citizenry).
The novel has been described as 'a superb pageant, glowing with
colour, alive with movement, clamorous with the shock and
din of weapons, reeking with pungent perfumes and fetid odours.
The focus of interest is not Salammbô but Carthage; the real
drama lies not in Matho's passion but in the fate of the city on
the hill. Handled by a great artist like Flaubert, this conflict between
Carthaginian and Barbarian becomes the theme of a mighty
symphony whose orchestration is wonderfully rich in colour and
sonority' (F. C. Green, introduction to the Everyman edition,
1931). Although many of the characters are actual historical
persons, Salammbô herself is fictional.

SALLUST, GREGORY   Military adventurer and secret agent in a
series of World War II thrillers by Dennis Wheatley. The central
sequence consists of the novels *The Scarlet Impostor* (1940), *Faked
Passports* (1940), *The Black Baroness* (1941), *V for Vengeance* (1942),
Come Into My Parlour (1946), *Traitor's Gate* (1958) and *They
Used Dark Forces* (1964). Sallust also appears in several quite
unrelated books: a smuggling adventure, *Contraband* (1936), and
the fantastic novels *Black August* (1934), *The Island Where
Time Stands Still* (1954) and *The White Witch of the South Seas*
(1968).

SAMBO   See LITTLE BLACK SAMBO

SAMMLER, ARTUR   See under Colonel BRAMBLE

SAMSA, GREGOR   Young man who awakes one morning to find
himself transformed into a large insect, in Franz Kafka's
disturbing short story 'The Metamorphosis' (1916). The
horrifyingly matter-of-fact tone of this psychological allegory has
had a large effect on the subsequent literature of the fantastic –
witness such stories as J. G. Ballard's 'The Drowned Giant' (1964).
Kit Reed's short story 'Sisohpromatem' (1967) is a neat inversion
of Kafka's tale: it is about a bug which changes into a human.
The Kafka story has been turned into a stage play by Steven
Berkoff (1969). A ballet by David Bintley is also based on 'The
Metamorphosis'; it was performed at Sadler's Wells in 1984.

SANDERS, MR COMMISSIONER   British District Commissioner of
a region in West Africa. 'Sandi' (as he is known) rules the black
natives with a kindly but firm hand: 'He governed a people three
hundred miles beyond the fringe of civilization. Hesitation to
act, delay in awarding punishment, either of these two things
would have been mistaken for weakness . . .' His adventures,
along with those of Bones (Lt Augustus Tibbets), Bosambo and
associated characters, are recounted by Edgar Wallace in a long
series of short stories which appeared in various magazines from
1909. The tales are collected in the following books: *Sanders of the
River* (1911), *The People of the River* (1912), *Bosambo of the River*
(1914), *Bones* (1915), *The Keepers of the King's Peace* (1917),
Lieutenant Bones (1918), *Bones in London* (1921), *Sandi the King
Maker* (1922), *Bones of the River* (1923), *Sanders* (1926; vt *Mr
Commissioner Sanders*) and *Again Sanders* (1928). After Wallace's
death Francis Gerard wrote three more books about Sanders:
The Return of Sanders of the River (1938), *The Law of the River*
(1939) and *The Justice of Sanders* (1951). More recently, in his
novel *Bunduki* (1975), J. T. Edson has made the claim that Sanders
was actually the unnamed British official who divulged the story of
TARZAN to Edgar Rice Burroughs.

   The British-made film *Sanders of the River* (1935; dir. Zoltan
Korda) had Leslie Banks as the stiff-upper-lipped hero (completely
overshadowed by Paul Robeson in the role of Bosambo). A comedy
entitled *Old Bones of the River* (1938; dir. Marcel Varnel) had
Wyndham Goldie as Sanders (and Will Hay as Bones). Two
much later films, *Death Drums Along the River* (1963; vt *Sanders*)
and *Coast of Skeletons* (1964), starred Richard Todd as an updated
Sanders. The character also appeared on BBC radio during the
1930s and 1940s. The Sanders books are not reprinted frequently
nowadays, perhaps because of their overt racism. A left-wing
critic, Bob Dixon, has said: 'With the possible exception of *The
Black Gang* by "Sapper", *Sanders of the River* is the most odious
fictional work I've ever read.'

SANDFORD AND MERTON   Harry Sandford and Tommy Merton
are two boys of opposite natures who appear in Thomas Day's
instructional story-book, *The History of Sandford and Merton, a
Work Intended for the Use of Children* (1783–9). This became
the standard English children's book of its day, and its characters

became household names. A parodic sequel by another hand is *The New History of Sandford and Merton* (1872) by F. C. Burnand.

SANGER, TESSA Sensitive and sickly teenage heroine of Margaret Kennedy's very popular novel *The Constant Nymph* (1924). She falls in love with Lewis Dodd, a 'brilliant' musician who is much older than herself, but their affair comes to grief. The novel was turned into a stage play in 1926, and has been filmed at least three times: in 1928 (dir. Adrian Brunel), with Mabel Poulton; in 1923 (dir. Basil Dean), with Victoria Hopper; and in 1943 (dir. Edmund Goulding), with Joan Fontaine.

SANTINI, DOMINIC See under Stringfellow HAWKE

SARN, PRUDENCE Hare-lipped country lass, in Mary Webb's novel *Precious Bane* (1925). 'The dour figure of Gideon Sarn is set against that of his gentle sister, Prudence, who tells the tale. She is a woman flawed with a hare-shotten lip and cursed in the eyes of the neighbours until her soul's loveliness is discerned by Kester Woodseaves, the weaver.' The novel became a huge bestseller after it was commended by the British Prime Minister of the day, Stanley Baldwin (who wrote the foregoing piece of plot-description in a preface to a later edition of the book). Mary Webb's dark tale of rustic passions is said to have inspired Stella Gibbons to write her comic novel *Cold Comfort Farm* (1932) – see Flora POSTE.

SARTORIS, JOHN Confederate army colonel who founds a Yoknapatawpha County dynasty, in the novels and short stories of William Faulkner (see also Quentin COMPSON, Temple DRAKE, Flem SNOPES and Gavin STEVENS). Colonel Sartoris figures prominently in the story-cycle which is collected in *The Unvanquished* (1938). His descendants, particularly the doomed World War I pilot Bayard Sartoris, appear in the novel *Sartoris* (1929) and elsewhere.

SAURON See under Frodo BAGGINS and GANDALF

SAVAGE, DOC Full name Clark Savage, Jr – a brilliant young scientist who is trained by his father to become a muscular

crime-fighter. With The SHADOW, he is the best known of the
American pulp-magazine superheroes of the 1930s. He appeared
in 181 issues of *Doc Savage Magazine*, published between 1933
and 1949. All of the magazine's novellas carried the house
byline 'Kenneth Robeson' but in fact 165 of them were written
by the veteran pulpsmith Lester Dent (including the very first,
entitled 'The Man of Bronze'.) Most of the stories were reprinted
in paperback during the 1960s and 1970s, and met with
considerable renewed success. Some of the most evocative titles
of these slim volumes are: *The Thousand-Headed Man* (1964),
The Mystic Mullah (1965), *Land of Always-Night* (1966) and *The
Czar of Fear* (1967). Doc Savage has the benefit of a perfect physique
and a sharp, analytical brain. He uses many technological gadgets
in his fight against villainy, and he is assisted by a team of comrades
who include the enormous engineer Col. John Renwick ('Renny'),
the thick-set chemist Lt Col. Andrew Blodgett Mayfair ('Monk'),
and the well-dressed lawyer Brig. Gen. Theodore Marley Brooks
('Ham'). He also has a lady friend, his cousin, the resourceful
Patricia Savage. Normally, Doc resides in a vast apartment at the
top of New York's tallest skyscraper (presumably the Empire
State Building), though he also has a 'Fortress of Solitude' on an
Arctic island (where he is wont to perform brain surgery on
criminals). Many of his adventures are fantastic in the extreme,
in the realm of science fiction rather than the conventional crime
thriller.

   Doc Savage appeared briefly on the radio (1934) and in
comic-books (1940–43; and again in 1972–5). The film *Doc
Savage: The Man of Bronze* (1975; dir. Michael Anderson) starred
Ron Ely (a former television TARZAN) as the well-muscled hero.
The Doc also appears, under the pseudonym 'Doc Caliban', in two
novels by Philip José Farmer: *A Feast Unknown* (1969) and *The
Mad Goblin* (1970; vt *The Keepers of the Secrets*). Farmer has
also written a detailed biography of the character, *Doc Savage:
His Apocalyptic Life* (1973), in which he describes the
golden-eyed hero as 'the Archangel of Technopolis'. In an
addendum entitled 'The Fabulous Family Tree of Doc Savage
(Another Excursion into Creative Mythography)', Farmer goes on
to suggest that the Doc's forebears and blood relations include
Captain BLOOD, Allan QUATERMAIN, the SCARLET PIMPERNEL,
Sam SPADE and many others, including of course Sherlock

HOLMES, TARZAN and James BOND. Earlier details of this complex
family tree were given in Farmer's *Tarzan Alive* (1972).

SAVAGE, RODNEY   British Army colonel in India at the time that
country gains its independence. He falls in love with a beautiful
Anglo-Indian, Victoria Jones. Their story is told in John Masters's
novel *Bhowani Junction* (1954) and its sequel *To the Coral
Strand* (1962). Both novels belong to a series which chronicles the
fortunes of the Savage family in India since the seventeenth century.
The other titles are *The Nightrunners of Bengal* (1951), *The
Deceivers* (1952), *The Lotus and the Wind* (1953), *Coromandel!*
(1955) and *Far, Far, the Mountain Peak* (1957). In the film *Bhowani
Junction* (1956; dir. George Cukor) Colonel Savage was played by
Stewart Granger. Four of the 'Savage' novels were serialized on
BBC radio in 1984, under the title 'Masters' India'.

SAWYER, TOM   Plucky youngster, a 'good bad boy', who lives with
his Aunt Polly in the nineteenth-century town of St Petersburg,
Missouri. Tom is given to telling tall tales, particularly when
trying to impress his girlfriend Becky Thatcher. Nevertheless
he enjoys some genuinely hair-raising adventures on the river
Mississippi with his disreputable friend Huckleberry FINN,
becomes embroiled with the villainous Injun Joe, and finally
locates hidden treasure in a cave. The novel *The Adventures of Tom
Sawyer* was first published in 1876 and gradually became accepted
as an American classic. It is by Mark Twain (Samuel Langhorne
Clemens). Twain revived the characters for another book, *The
Adventures of Huckleberry Finn (Tom Sawyer's Comrade)* (1884) –
one of the rare examples in literature of a sequel which is
indubitably greater than the work which it follows. Tom also
appears in two later, much inferior, sequels, *Tom Sawyer Abroad*
(1894) and *Tom Sawyer, Detective* (1896). A sequel by another hand
is *Tom Sawyer Grows Up* by C. Wood.

There have been many film versions of Tom's adventures. A
couple of silent movies featured Jack Pickford in the role. In the
sound period, films about the character have included *Tom Sawyer*
(1930; dir. John Cromwell), starring Jackie Coogan; *The
Adventures of Tom Sawyer* (1938; dir. Norman Taurog), with
Tommy Kelly; and the musical *Tom Sawyer* (1973; dir. Don
Taylor), with Johnnie Whitaker. There have been various television

Tom Sawyer (Tommy Kelly) in the 1938 film

series as well as a 1975 TV movie (dir. James Neilson) based on the original novel. In the TV series 'Huckleberry Finn and His Friends' (early 1980s) Tom was played by Sammy Snyders.

SAYER, ROSE   See under Charlie ALLNUTT

SCARAMOUCHE   Real name André-Louis Moreau, the cloak-and-dagger hero of Rafael Sabatini's novel *Scaramouche* (1921), set at the time of the French Revolution. His assumed name derives from the Italian 'Scaramuccia', a braggart soldier who was a stock character of the seventeenth-century *commedia dell'arte*. A sequel, also by Sabatini, is *Scaramouche, the Kingmaker* (1931). Sabatini's hero has been portrayed in films by Ramon Novarro, in *Scaramouche* (1923); by Stewart Granger, in a remake of the same title (1952; dir. George Sidney); and by Gerard Barray, in *The Adventures of Scaramouche* (1964; dir. Antonio Isamendi).

SCARECROW, THE   See under Dorothy GALE

SCARLET PIMPERNEL, THE   Sir Percy Blakeney, an apparently worthless English fop who is really one of the most courageous men of his day. A master of disguise and an inspiring leader, he rescues condemned aristocrats from the guillotine during the aftermath of the French Revolution. His great enemy is Citizen Chauvelin, one of Robespierre's most cunning agents. The piece of doggerel with which Sir Percy mocks the baffled Chauvelin was once known to every schoolboy in England: 'They seek him here, they seek him there,/Those Frenchies seek him everywhere./Is he in heaven or is he in hell,/That demned elusive Pimpernel?' This gay hero was created by the Hungarian-born Emmuska, Baroness Orczy for her bestselling novel *The Scarlet Pimpernel* (1905). In collaboration with her husband, Montague Barstow, she also turned the story into a very popular stage play (which was first performed in 1903, before the novel's publication). The first Pimpernel book was followed by ten more: *I Will Repay* (1906), *The Elusive Pimpernel* (1908), *Eldorado* (1913), *Lord Tony's Wife* (1917), *The League of the Scarlet Pimpernel* (1919), *The Triumph of the Scarlet Pimpernel* (1922), *Sir Percy Hits Back* (1927), *Adventures of the Scarlet Pimpernel* (1929), *The Way of the*

Scarlet Pimpernel (1933), *Sir Percy Leads the Band* (1936) and
Mam'zelle Guillotine (1940). In addition, there is a biography
of the Scarlet Pimpernel: *A Gay Adventurer* (1930) by 'John
Blakeney' (possibly Baroness Orczy). The film *The Scarlet
Pimpernel* (1934; dir. Harold Young) starred Leslie Howard as Sir
Percy. Later, less successful, movies are *The Return of the Scarlet
Pimpernel* (1937; dir. Hans Schwarz), with Barry K. Barnes; and
The Elusive Pimpernel (1950; dir. Michael Powell and Emeric
Pressburger), with David Niven in the role. Leslie Howard played
a character who bears a strong resemblance to Sir Percy in the World
War II film *Pimpernel Smith* (1941; dir. Howard). A Radio
Luxembourg series, 'The New Adventures of the Scarlet
Pimpernel' (early 1950s), had Marius Goring as the hero. Goring
also starred in a BBC television series based on the character
(1954). A much later TV movie (1983; dir. Clive Donner) had
Anthony Andrews as the hero. (The Pimpernel's beautiful wife,
Lady Marguerite, has enjoyed many adventures of her own – see
Marguerite BLAKENEY.)

SCARLETT, SYLVIA   Young actress who makes her first appearance
in the second half of Compton Mackenzie's two-part novel
Sinister Street (1914), where she befriends Michael FANE. She
recurs in the novels *Sylvia Scarlett* (1918) and *Sylvia and Michael*
(1919). In the film *Sylvia Scarlett* (1935; dir. George Cukor) she
was played by Katharine Hepburn.

SCARPIA, BARON   See under Floria TOSCA

SCHEDONI   Sinister, suffering monk, described as 'a man with a
hatred of truth but a profound love of disputation and argument'.
He commits various crimes and ends as a victim of the Inquisition.
Schedoni is the hero-villain of Mrs Ann Radcliffe's Gothic novel
The Italian, or The Confessional of the Black Penitents (1797).

SCHILLER, DOLLY   See LOLITA

SCHOFIELD, PENROD   Midwestern boy in novels by American
writer Booth Tarkington, commencing with *Penrod* (1914). He
is supposedly 'the worst boy in town' but in reality he is very
much a Good Bad Boy in the tradition of Tom SAWYER. Sequels

by Tarkington are *Penrod and Sam* (1916) and *Penrod Jashber* (1929); the volume *Penrod: His Complete Story* (1931) is an omnibus. Penrod was played by Gordon Griffith and Ben Alexander in silent films of the 1920s. Talkies about the character include *Penrod and Sam* (1931; dir. William Beaudine), with Leon Janney; a remake of the same title (1937; dir. William McGann), with Billy Mauch; and two sequels, *Penrod's Double Trouble* and *Penrod and His Twin Brother* (both 1938), also starring Mauch.

SCHON, ALWA   See under Lulu

SCHTROUMPFS, THE   See The Smurfs

SCOBIE, HENRY   British assistant police commissioner in West Africa during World War II. He is the central character of Graham Greene's moody novel *The Heart of the Matter* (1948). Scobie is a believing Catholic who suffers from an excess of pity for the various women with whom he becomes involved. In the film of the novel (1953; dir. George More O'Ferrall) he was played by Trevor Howard. There has also been a German-produced television serial based on Greene's book (1983; dir. Marco Leto), with Jack Hedley as Scobie amidst a mainly German cast.

SCOTT, ALAN   See The Green Lantern

SCOTT, SHELL   Tough private-eye, an ex-marine working in Hollywood, who has appeared in many paperback thrillers by the American writer Richard S. Prather. Titles include *Case of the Vanishing Beauty* (1950), *Bodies in Bedlam* (1951), *Way of a Wanton* (1952), *Always Leave 'em Dying* (1954), *Take a Murder, Darling* (1958), *Dig That Crazy Grave* (1961), *Kill the Clown* (1962), *The Kubla Khan Caper* (1966), *The Shell Scott Sampler* (1969) and *The Sure Thing* (1975).

SCROOGE, EBENEZER   Miser who mends his ways, in Charles Dickens's well-loved fable *A Christmas Carol* (1843). Certainly the most famous skinflint in fiction, Scrooge is haunted by the chain-rattling ghost of his late business partner, Jacob Marley. He is shown the terrible future which awaits him if he remains selfish and heartless; he repents, showers gifts on everybody he knows, and

Ebenezer Scrooge confronts the ghost of Jacob Marley

leads the Christmas revels. Other important characters in this
heart-warming story are Scrooge's good-natured clerk, Bob Cratchit,
and the latter's crippled son, Tiny Tim. There have been numerous
stage adaptations of the tale, including an opera by Thea
Musgrave (shown on British television in 1982, with Frederick
Burchinal as Scrooge). There were at least seven silent movie
versions (usually entitled *Scrooge*). Sound films include *Scrooge*
(1935; dir. Henry Edwards), with Seymour Hicks in the title role;
A Christmas Carol (1938; dir. Edwin L. Marin), starring Reginald
Owen; a remake of the same name (1951; dir. Brian Desmond Hurst),
with Alastair Sim; and the musical *Scrooge* (1970; dir. Ronald
Neame), in which Albert Finney gave a memorable performance in
the title part. In addition, there has been an animated film version,
A Christmas Carol (1971; dir. Richard Williams), in which Alastair
Sim once more provided Scrooge's voice (this short production
won an Academy Award). The TV movie *An American
Christmas Carol* (1979; dir. Eric Till) had Henry Winkler as an
updated version of Scrooge. There has also been a Walt Disney
cartoon version, *Mickey's Christmas Carol* (1983; dir. Burny
Mattinson), in which Scrooge becomes 'Scrooge McDuck', and Bob
Cratchit is played by MICKEY MOUSE.

SCULLY, FRANNY   Liverpool schoolboy who gets into comic
  scrapes. He appears in radio plays and novels by Alan Bleasdale,
  including the books *Scully* (1975) and *Who's Been Sleeping in My
  Bed?* (1977). A British independent television series based on
  Scully's adventures (1984) featured Andrew Schofield as the hero.

SEAGOON, NEDDIE   See under BLUEBOTTLE and ECCLES

SEAGRAVE FAMILY, THE   See under Masterman READY

SEATON, ARTHUR   Rebellious working-class anti-hero of Allan
  Sillitoe's novel *Saturday Night and Sunday Morning* (1958). Seaton
  works in a Nottingham bicycle factory, and spends most of his
  free time drinking and pursuing women. His surly
  bloody-mindedness made him one of the archetypal 'angry young
  men' of English postwar fiction. He was played very effectively
  by Albert Finney in the influential film of the novel (1960; dir.
  Karel Reisz).

SEBRILL, ALAN   English school teacher, poet and Marxist, whose life-story is told in a trilogy of novels by Edward Upward: *In the Thirties* (1962), *The Rotten Elements* (1969) and *No Home But the Struggle* (1977). The books have been republished in one volume under the overall title *The Spiral Ascent*. Anthony Burgess has described Sebrill as 'a less than compelling character with whom it is no pleasure to identify ourselves' (*The Novel Now*).

SEDLEY, AMELIA   See under Becky SHARP

SEREBRYAKOV, ALEXANDER   See under Ivan Petrovitch VOYNITSKY

SÉVERIN   Narrator of Leopold von Sacher-Masoch's perverse nineteenth-century novel *Venus in Furs*. Severin is in love with the fur-clad Wanda . . . and her whip. His creator unwittingly gave us the word 'masochism' (coined by Baron Richard von Krafft-Ebing in his *Psychopathia Sexualis* [1886]). The cool blonde heroine of Luis Bunuel's film *Belle de Jour* (1967; based on a novel by Joseph Kessel) is named 'Séverine'. Played by Catherine Deneuve, she overcomes her frigidity by working in a brothel for a few hours every day. The allusion to Sacher-Masoch is intentional. The science fiction writer Gene Wolfe calls the far-future hero of his four-part novel *The Book of the New Sun* (1980–83) 'Severian': again, the allusion is quite deliberate, since Wolfe's Severian begins his career as a (somewhat reluctant) member of the Torturers' Guild.

SHADOW, THE   Alias Lamont Cranston (or Kent Allard), a cloaked-and-hatted crime fighter, who has the power to 'cloud men's minds' and render himself effectively invisible. Originally created in 1930 for a Sunday-night radio series, 'Detective Story', he featured in more than 280 novellas written by Maxwell Grant (Walter B. Gibson) for *The Shadow* magazine, a pulp periodical issued by Street & Smith from 1931 to 1949 (many of these stories have been reprinted as slim paperback books since the 1960s). The house pseudonym Maxwell Grant was also used by a few other writers who added about forty more tales to the saga at times when the prolific Gibson's inspiration flagged. The Shadow also appeared in his own radio show, to great acclaim, between the years

1936 and 1954. A generation of American listeners became familiar with the repeated homilies: 'Who knows what evil lurks in the hearts of men? The Shadow knows'; and 'The weed of crime bears bitter fruit.' For a few remarkable months in 1937–8 The Shadow was played on the air by Orson Welles. The character also featured in films, beginning with *The Shadow Strikes* (1937; dir. Lynn Shores), in which he was portrayed by Rod La Rocque. A cinema serial, *The Shadow* (1940; dir. James Horne) starred Victor Jory, and later serials, including *The Shadow Returns* (1946), had Kane Richmond in the role. There was also a comic-book devoted to the penumbral sleuth. The Shadow is the best remembered of all the pulp-magazine and radio superheroes of the 1930s, remaining a cult figure to this day. As critic Otto Penzler has written: 'A hero of the Great Depression, The Shadow has outlived his time . . . The old radio programs are successfully revived in syndication . . . and nostalgia buffs covet the fragile comic books, magazines, toys, games, radio premiums and books that are so avidly collected today – at prices that numb the soul . . . The Shadow has not lost his ability to cloud men's minds.'

SHAFT, JOHN   Black private-eye, a denizen of Harlem, created by novelist and screenwriter Ernest Tidyman. Shaft is tough, selfish and amoral, and exceedingly sexist. He is much like Mike HAMMER. He appears in the books *Shaft* (1970), *Shaft Among the Jews* (1972), *Shaft's Big Score* (1972), *Shaft Has a Ball* (1973), *Good-bye, Mr Shaft* (1973), *Shaft's Carnival of Killers* (1974) and *The Last Shaft* (1977), all by Tidyman; and in the films *Shaft* (1971; dir. Gordon Parks), *Shaft's Big Score* (1972; dir. Gordon Parks) and *Shaft in Africa* (1973; dir. John Guillermin), where he was played by Richard Roundtree. The same actor took the part of Shaft in a short-lived television series (1973–4).

SHANDY, TOBY   Uncle to Tristram SHANDY (see following entry). An amiable old soldier, he suffers from a war-wound in his thigh and from the amorous attentions of his neighbour, the Widow Wadman. But he is uninterested in love and prefers to play war games, reconstructing Marlborough's military campaigns on a lawn. His companion and servant is the talkative Corporal Trim. The essayist William Hazlitt referred to Sterne's depiction of Uncle Toby as 'one of the finest compliments ever paid to human nature'.

SHANDY, TRISTRAM   Narrator of Laurence Sterne's eccentric
novel *The Life and Opinions of Tristram Shandy, Gentleman*
(1759–67). One of the work's eccentricities rests in the fact that
its 'hero' is not born until Volume Three; most of the narrative
concerns the doings of Tristram's father, Walter Shandy, his Uncle
Toby (Captain Toby SHANDY), Parson Yorick, the 'man-midwife' Dr
Slop, and other memorable comic characters. The novel has been
adapted to the stage by Peter Buckman (1986).

SHANE   Romantic loner who rights wrongs in the American West,
the hero of Jack Schaefer's novel *Shane* (1949). He assists a family
of homesteaders who are being persecuted by cattlemen. In the
celebrated film of the novel (1953; dir. George Stevens) Shane
was played by the diminutive actor Alan Ladd. A television series
of the same title (1966) starred lanky David Carradine.

SHARP, BECKY   Young, scheming heroine of William Makepeace
Thackeray's greatest work, *Vanity Fair: A Novel Without a Hero*
(1847–8). An artist's daughter, she is educated at an academy for
young ladies; however, being a penniless orphan, she has to
make her way in the world by her wits. She becomes a governess
and marries her employer's son, Rawdon Crawley, but this does not
put a stop to her *amours*. Throughout the novel her behaviour is
contrasted with that of her virtuous and beautiful friend, Amelia
Sedley, who eventually marries the equally virtuous William
Dobbin. In the Hollywood film, *Becky Sharp* (1935; dir. Rouben
Mamoulian), Becky was played by Miriam Hopkins. The novel
has also been adapted as a stage musical, *Vanity Fair* (1962),
with music by Julian Slade. A BBC television serialization of the
novel (1969) had Susan Hampshire in the role of Becky.

SHARPE, RICHARD   British army captain in the war against
Napoleon. His adventures are recounted in a series of historical
novels by Bernard Cornwell: *Sharpe's Eagle: The Talavera
Campaign, 1809* (1980), *Sharpe's Gold: The Destruction of Almeida,
1810* (1981), *Sharpe's Company: The Siege of Badajoz, 1812*
(1982), *Sharpe's Sword* (1983), *Sharpe's Enemy* (1984), *Sharpe's
Honour* (1985) and *Sharpe's Siege* (1987).

SHARPLES, ENA   Formidable, hair-netted busybody played by
Violet Carson in British independent television's long-running
soap opera of northern working-class life, 'Coronation Street'
(from 1960). The serial was devised by Tony Warren, and other
characters who became household names in Britain include Ken
Barlow, Len Fairclough, Elsie TANNER, Annie Walker and Bet Lynch.
The scriptwriter and producer H. V. Kershaw has written a book
about the series entitled *The Street Where I Live* (1981).

SHAUNESSY, MARY ANN   Working-class heroine of Catherine
Cookson's popular novels set in Tyneside: *A Grand Man* (1954),
The Lord and Mary Ann (1956), *The Devil and Mary Ann* (1958),
Love and Mary Ann (1961), *Life and Mary Ann* (1962), *Marriage
and Mary Ann* (1964), *Mary Ann's Angels* (1965) and *Mary Ann
and Bill* (1967).

SHAWCROSS, JOHN HAMER   Labour Party politician who
gradually abandons his early socialist ideals, becomes a Cabinet
minister, and ends with a seat in the House of Lords. He appears
in the novel *Fame is the Spur* (1940) by Howard Spring. The film of
the same title (1949; dir. John and Roy Boulting) starred Michael
Redgrave. The book was later serialized by Elaine Morgan for
BBC television (1982), with Tim Pigott-Smith in the role of
Shawcross. It has also been adapted for BBC radio (1984), with
Ian McKellen in the lead.

SHAYNE, MIKE   Private detective who operates out of an office in
Miami – created by Brett Halliday (Davis Dresser) for his novel
Dividend on Death (1939) and no fewer than sixty-five sequels.
Later Halliday/Shayne titles include *The Private Practice of
Michael Shayne* (1940), *Murder is My Business* (1945), *A Taste
for Violence* (1949), *When Dorinda Dances* (1951), *Murder by
Proxy* (1962), *A Redhead for Mike Shayne* (1964) and *At the Point
of a .38* (1974). The character was played by Lloyd Nolan in
seven films beginning with *Michael Shayne, Private Detective*
(1940; dir. Eugene Forde), and by Hugh Beaumont in five more
films commencing with *Murder is My Business* (1946; dir. Sam
Newfield). Shayne has also appeared on the radio, where he was
voiced by Jeff Chandler, and on television (1960–61), where he
was acted by Richard Denning. The detective has had a periodical

named after him, *Mike Shayne's Mystery Magazine*, and this
continued to publish new novellas about Shayne even after his
creator's death in 1977.

SHE-WHO-MUST-BE-OBEYED Ayesha, the long-lived white
queen of the lost city of Kôr in central Africa – created by H. Rider
Haggard in his bestselling novel *She* (1887). The story is narrated
by Ludwig Horace HOLLY, scholar and explorer. Ayesha's love
for the Englishman Leo Vincey causes her to re-enter the flame
of life in order to persuade him of its power to bestow
immortality. The flame will not accept her twice; she withers
and dies in moments. This potent tale of supernatural romance
provoked numerous emulations, parodies and sequels – including
three more books by Haggard himself: *Ayesha* (1905), in which She
is reincarnated in central Asia; *She and Allan* (1921), in which a
slightly younger Ayesha meets Allan QUATERMAIN and
UMSLOPOGAAS; and *Wisdom's Daughter* (1923), which tells of
Ayesha's early life in the Egypt of some 2,000 years ago.
    Sequels by other hands include *The King of Kôr, or She's
Promise Kept* (1903) by Sidney J. Marshall and *The Vengeance
of She* (1978) by Peter Tremayne. The most famous parody was
He (1887) by Andrew Lang and Walter H. Pollock. There were
stage adaptations of the original story and at least seven silent
movie versions between 1899 and 1925. Sound films include
She (1935; dir. Irving Pichel and Lansing C. Holden), which starred
Helen Gahagen as Ayesha; and a Hammer Films remake of 1965
with Ursula Andress in the leading role.

SHEENA Real name Janet Ames, a jungle girl who appeared in
American comic-books from 1938. She is very much the female
equivalent of TARZAN – a white foundling reared by members of
an African tribe who teach her martial arts and shamanistic
skills. Sheena was created by Will Eisner and S. M. Iger for *Jumbo
Comics*. A television series, 'Sheena, Queen of the Jungle' (1955–6),
starred Irish McCalla as the tree-swinging heroine. A feature film,
Sheena (1984; dir. John Guillermin), had Tanya Roberts in the part.

SHEIK, THE Ahmed Ben Hassan, the dusky-skinned ravisher of
English girl Diana Mayo in E. M. Hull's semi-pornographic romance
The Sheik (1919). He throws her across his horse and carries her

off into the desert to enjoy several weeks of ardent love. As in so many popular novels of the period, the authoress cheats on the miscegenation theme by revealing that her 'Sheik' is in fact the long-lost son of a British aristocrat and a Spanish noblewoman. Diana may marry him with a clear conscience. A sequel, also by E. M. Hull, is *The Sons of the Sheik* (1925). The silent films based on these two novels (1921, 1926) starred the doomed Rudolph Valentino as Ahmed, and were immensely popular.

SHELTON, DICK   Youthful hero of Robert Louis Stevenson's *The Black Arrow* (1888), an historical novel about the Wars of the Roses. The villainous Sir Daniel Brackley attempts to rob him of his birthright, but Dick wins through and eventually takes his place on the battlefield alongside the future King Richard III. In the film of the novel (1948; dir. Gordon Douglas) Dick was played by Louis Hayward. The Disney-produced TV movie (1985; dir. John Hough) starred Stephan Chase.

SHERE KHAN   See under MOWGLI

SHERMAN, LLOYD   Fiery-tempered little girl who comes to live in Kentucky where she annoys her grandfather, the old Confederate soldier Colonel Lloyd, by playing with the local black children. She appears in Annie Fellows Johnston's novel *The Little Colonel* (1895) and its sequels, which include *The Little Colonel at Boarding School* (1903) and *The Little Colonel's Christmas Vacation* (1905). In the film *The Little Colonel* (1935; dir. David Butler) the heroine was played by Shirley Temple.

SHIRLEY, ANNE   Red-haired orphan heroine of *Anne of Green Gables* (1908) and other novels by the Canadian children's writer Lucy Maude Montgomery. Anne is a rather precocious, outspoken girl; taken on by an elderly couple, she soon learns how to make herself useful around the farm. Mark Twain, none other than the creator of Tom SAWYER and Huckleberry FINN, once described Anne as 'the dearest and most lovable child in fiction since the immortal Alice' (see ALICE). The other books in the series by L. M. Montgomery are *Anne of Avonlea* (1909), *Chronicles of Avonlea* (1912), *Anne of the Island* (1915), *Anne's House of Dreams* (1917), *Rainbow Valley* (1919), *Further*

Chronicles of Avonlea (1920), *Rilla of Ingleside* (1921), *Anne of Windy Poplars* (1936; vt *Anne of Windy Willows*) and *Anne of Ingleside* (1939). Anne's adventures have been adapted for stage, film and television a number of times. A silent film of *Anne of Green Gables* (1919) starred Mary Miles Minter. Sound movies include a remake of that title (1934; dir. George Nicholls), with 'Anne Shirley' (actress Dawn Paris, alias Dawn O'Day, who was to retain the name of this fictional character for the rest of her career), and *Anne of Windy Poplars* (1940; dir. Jack Hively), also with Anne Shirley. A Canadian TV mini-series, 'Anne of Green Gables' (1985; dir. Kevin Sullivan), starred Megan Fellows; it was a great popular success.

SHOCK-HEADED PETER   See STRUWWELPETER

SHOESTRING, EDDIE   Unusual British private-eye – he is the employee of a local commercial radio station, and is called upon to solve listeners' mysteries. He was played by Trevor Eve in the BBC television series 'Shoestring' (1979–80), conceived by Robert Banks Stewart. The novels based on the series are by Paul Ableman.

SHORE, JEMIMA   She who investigates, in a series of crime novels by Antonia Fraser, beginning with *Quiet as a Nun* (1977). Jemima is a high-flying television reporter who becomes involved in various mysteries. Later titles are *The Wild Island* (1978), *A Splash of Red* (1981), *Cool Repentance* (1982), *Oxford Blood* (1985), the short-story collection *Jemima Shore's First Case* (1986) and *Your Royal Hostage* (1987). The character has also appeared in a British TV series, 'Jemima Shore Investigates' (1983), where she was played by Patricia Hodge.

SIKES, BILL   Dastardly murderer in Charles Dickens's novel *Oliver Twist* (1838). He kills the unfortunate Nancy, and ends by accidentally hanging himself while attempting to escape from justice. Sikes's grisly comeuppance has always featured large in stage and film adaptations of the novel. Actors who have played him in the cinema include Robert Newton (1948) and Oliver Reed (1968). See also Oliver TWIST.

SILAS, UNCLE   See Silas RUTHYN

SILENCE, JOHN   Investigator of occult events, in short stories by
the British writer of ghostly tales, Algernon Blackwood. Dr Silence's
cases are collected in the books *John Silence, Physician
Extraordinary* (1908) and *Day and Night Stories* (1917; vt *Tales of
the Mysterious and Macabre*). According to Julia Briggs, Silence
is 'very much an Englishman, a gentleman who loves outdoor
life' but is also familiar with 'the black arts, the Egyptian Book
of the Dead, and Eliphas Lévi'. A somewhat similar character,
created slightly later, is W. H. Hodgson's CARNACKI, the
ghost-finder.

SILVER, LONG JOHN   One-legged pirate who masquerades as a
sea-cook aboard the *Hispaniola*. Silver is perhaps the best-loved
villain in modern fiction. With his pet parrot, Captain Flint, and
his rich seaman's vocabulary, he is an oddly endearing character,
even if he makes a very untrustworthy father-figure for young Jim
HAWKINS. He was created by Robert Louis Stevenson for his novel
Treasure Island (1883), and has loomed large in adaptations of the
story ever since. Recent sequels by other hands are *Flint's Island*
(1972) by Leonard Wibberley, *The Adventures of Long John Silver*
by Denis Judd, and *Silver's Revenge* (1979) by Robert Leeson. In
films of *Treasure Island* Long John Silver has been played by
Wallace Beery (1934), Robert Newton (1950) and Orson Welles
(1972). Newton's rolling-eyed performance is the one that
everyone remembers, and indeed the actor was invited to
perpetuate the character in a follow-up film, *Long John Silver*
(1953; dir. Byron Haskin) and in an Australian-made television
series, 'The Adventures of Long John Silver' (1955). Alfred Burke
played the character in the BBC television serial 'Treasure
Island' (1978). A more recent TV series was the British-made 'John
Silver's Return to Treasure Island' (1986), which starred Brian
Blessed.

SILVER, MAUD   Retired schoolmistress who becomes a
professional detective, in the novels of Patricia Wentworth (Dora
Amy Elles). Miss Silver first appeared in *Grey Mask* (1929) and
was revived eight years later for *The Case is Closed* (1937).
However, the bulk of her cases appeared during and after World
War II. They include: *Lonesome Road* (1939), *In the Balance* (1941;
vt *Danger Point*), *The Chinese Shawl* (1943), *The Key* (1944), *She*

Long John Silver with his parrot, Cap'n Flint

Came Back (1945; vt *The Traveller Returns*), *Pilgrim's Rest* (1946; vt *Dark Threat*), *The Case of William Smith* (1948), *Miss Silver Comes to Stay* (1949), *The Brading Collection* (1950), *Ladies' Bane* (1952), *Poison in the Pen* (1955), *The Fingerprint* (1956) and *The Girl in the Cellar* (1961). Miss Silver bears some resemblance to Agatha Christie's Miss Jane MARPLE, although she maintains a more professional demeanour.

SILVER SURFER, THE   Silver-coated alien being who rides a thought-controlled flying surf-board. An ally of Mr FANTASTIC and the Fantastic Four, the Surfer is probably the weirdest of the superheroes unleashed on the world by Marvel Comics' writer Stan Lee and artist Jack Kirby (from 1966). According to Jeff Rovin, 'while he seems quaintly pretentious in retrospect, the Silver Surfer was, during the '60s, a popular philosopher on matters of war, peace, and power'.

SIMON, MARIA   Née Maria Wiegand, a German peasant woman who is the central character of Edgar Reitz's remarkable sixteen-hour film *Heimat* (1984). Abandoned by her husband, who emigrates to America in the 1920s, Maria rears her children with the help of her mother-in-law and other members of the extended Simon and Wiegand families, all of whom inhabit the village of Schabbach in the Hunsrück district of West Germany. They live relatively unscathed through the Nazi era, World War II and the postwar reconstruction. Maria dies in 1982, by which time she has seen one of her sons become an affluent businessman and another develop into a composer of avant-garde music. Maria was played throughout the film by a twenty-eight-year-old actress, Marita Breuer. 'With *Heimat*, it seemed, the cinema had discovered the equivalent of the great nineteenth-century novel' (according to David Robinson, *Radio Times*, 19 April 1986). The film was shown in cinemas and on television throughout Europe, and proved to be a great popular and critical success.

SIMONIN, SUZANNE   Innocent girl who is placed in a convent against her will; once beyond the reach of outside help, she is persecuted, tortured and sexually molested by the Mother Superior. Her story is told in Denis Diderot's novel *La Religieuse* (written 1760, but not published in full until 1796). The book has been filmed as *The Nun* (1965; dir. Jacques Rivette), with Anna Karina as Suzanne.

SINGH, RAM   See under The SPIDER

SINGH, HURREE JAMSET RAM   See under Harry WHARTON

SINGLETON, ROBERT   Seafarer, pirate and explorer. His travels are described in Daniel Defoe's novel *The Adventures of Captain Singleton* (1720), wherein his main exploit is the crossing of darkest Africa from east to west. According to Martin Green (in his interesting study *Dreams of Adventure, Deeds of Empire*), Defoe's *Captain Singleton* is the archetypal English adventure story, an even clearer precursor of the Victorian imperial romances than its great predecessor, *Robinson Crusoe.*

SIX MILLION DOLLAR MAN   See Steve AUSTIN

SKEETER   See under TAILSPIN TOMMY

SKIMPOLE, HAROLD   See under Esther SUMMERSON

SKINNER, SKIPPY   All-American boy in the newspaper comic-strip *Skippy*, created by Percy L. Crosby in 1925. Skippy subsequently appeared in his own comic book (from 1934), and in the Oscar-winning movie *Skippy* (1931; dir. Norman Taurog) where he was played by Jackie Cooper.

SKYWALKER, LUKE   Youthful hero of the most successful adventure story of recent times – the *Star Wars* trilogy. Luke grows up on a far planet, and on reaching manhood finds himself sucked into a revolutionary war against the interstellar Empire. He trains to become a 'Jedi knight', and befriends the beautiful Princess Leia Organa, the roughneck space pilot Han SOLO, and the comical but talented robots C-3PO and R2-D2. Eventually, by using his Jedi skills and by tapping 'the Force' (a sort of spiritual ether), he overcomes his arch-enemy, the black-clad and heavy-breathing Darth VADER. All this was conceived by film-maker George Lucas. On its release in 1977 his movie *Star*

Wars achieved phenomenal popularity, a success which was helped
by superb special effects and a rousing musical score by John
Williams. The movie's sequels, *The Empire Strikes Back* (1980;
dir. Irvin Kershner) and *Return of the Jedi* (1983; dir. Richard
Marquand), have been just as popular as the original. Mark Hamill
played Luke Skywalker in all three films. A publishing and
merchandising industry has grown up around *Star Wars*. As well as
the bestselling novelizations of the film scripts, there have been
other novels about Skywalker and his confederates. An example
is the book *Splinter of the Mind's Eye: From the Adventures of
Luke Skywalker* (1978) by Alan Dean Foster. There have also been
an American radio series and a comic-book devoted to the *Star
Wars* characters.

SLARTIBARTFAST   See under Arthur DENT

SLICK, SAM   Caricature Yankee created by the Canadian writer
Thomas Chandler Haliburton. The sketches of his adventures
were collected in *The Clockmaker, or The Sayings and Doings of
Samuel Slick of Slickville* (1837), and in such later volumes as *The
Attaché, or Sam Slick in England* (1843–4) and *Sam Slick's Saws
and Modern Instances* (1853). According to William Rose Benét:
'Sam Slick became the best-known character in the field of Yankee
humour and had many imitators. A shrewd, ruthless trader, ready
to trick his customers at every opportunity, Sam is full of wise
saws and has an unfailing supply of humorous stories.'

SLOP, DOCTOR   See under Tristram SHANDY

SLOPE, OBADIAH   See under Mrs PROUDIE

SLOPER, ALLY   Bulbous-nosed, impecunious but ever-inventive
hero of Victorian comic-strips. He first appeared, with his friend
Isaac Moses (better known as Ikey Mo), in the pages of *Judy*
magazine in 1867. Ally, who bears the initials F.O.M. ('Friend of
Man') after his name, was the creation of Charles Henry Ross,
although he was to become more famous under the penmanship
of W. G. Baxter. It was the latter who drew the characters for *Ally
Sloper's Half-Holiday*, a penny comic which became
exceedingly popular during the 1880s. (This was the first weekly

comic paper, and it ran from 1884 to 1923.) According to Victor
E. Neuburg, its 'success gave rise to further publications, and the
founder's son claimed that Sloper publications of all kinds
amounted to over 52 million copies in the 1890s. Ally Sloper
became a household word, and on to the market came Ally Sloper
umbrellas, walking sticks, pipes, watches, toys, sweets, kites,
fireworks. Ally Sloper was played as a character in a Drury Lane
pantomine, *The Forty Thieves*, and there was a set-piece Ally
Sloper display in fireworks at the Crystal Palace.' There was a
latter-day attempt to revive the character in 1976, when Denis
Gifford produced four issues of a comic called *Ally Sloper*. The actor
Chris Harris has recently created a one-man touring show entitled
Ally Sloper's Half-Holiday (1987).

SLOPER, CATHERINE   Plain, long-suffering heroine of Henry
James's novel *Washington Square* (1881). Her rich and
tyrannical father, Dr Austen Sloper, prevents her from marrying
her only suitor, Morris Townsend (who is clearly a fortune
seeker), and she becomes resigned to a lonely life of needlework.
The novel was turned into a successful play, *The Heiress*, by
Ruth and Augustus Goetz, and this in turn was filmed (1949; dir.
William Wyler), with Olivia de Havilland in the role of
Catherine.

SMALL, DAVID   Massachusetts rabbi who doubles as an amateur
detective. His knowledge of the Talmud and other Jewish lore assists
him in the solution of various crimes. Rabbi Small's adventures
are described in a series of novels by Harry Kemelman: *Friday
the Rabbi Slept Late* (1964), *Saturday the Rabbi Went Hungry*
(1966), *Sunday the Rabbi Stayed Home* (1969), *Monday the
Rabbi Took Off* (1972), *Tuesday the Rabbi Saw Red* (1973),
Wednesday the Rabbi Got Wet (1976), *Thursday the Rabbi Walked
Out* (1978) and *Someday the Rabbi Will Leave* (1985). An
appendage to the series is *Conversations with Rabbi Small* (1981).
The character has also appeared in the TV movie *Lanigan's Rabbi*
(1976; dir. Lou Antonio), which was based on one of
Kemelman's novels.

SMALL, LENNIE   Gentle, half-witted giant who comes to a tragic
end in John Steinbeck's novella *Of Mice and Men* (1937).

Lennie's friend George Milton shoots him in order to keep him from a lynch-mob. The story formed the basis of a stage play, as well as a film (1939; dir. Lewis Milestone) which provided Lon Chaney, Jr with the best acting role of his career. The TV movie *Of Mice and Men* (1981; dir. Reza Badiyi) had Randy Quaid as Lennie.

SMALLEY, TUSKER AND LUCY   Ageing servants of the British Raj in Paul Scott's novel *Staying On* (1977). Tusker and his wife Lucy remain in India after Independence, for they can imagine no other life. After twenty-five years, reduced economic circumstances and reminders of mortality have caught up with them. The Smalleys also played a small role in Scott's earlier novel sequence, *The Raj Quartet* (1966–75). In the TV movie based on *Staying On* (1980; dir. Silvio Narizzano) Tusker was played by Trevor Howard and Lucy by Celia Johnson.

Tusker and Lucy Smalley (Trevor Howard and Celia Johnson) in the 1980 TV movie of *Staying On*

SMART, MAXWELL   Incompetent secret agent (Agent Number 86) who is always apologizing for his mistakes. His female sidekick is the glamorous 'Agent 99', and the pair work for a US agency known as C.O.N.T.R.O.L. Smart was played by Don Adams in the American television series 'Get Smart' (1964–70), created by scriptwriters Mel Brooks and Buck Henry.

SMERDYAKOV   See under Dmitri, Ivan and Alexei KARAMAZOV

SMIKE   Starved, half-witted, rickety urchin, a figure of great pathos in Charles Dickens's novel *The Life and Adventures of Nicholas Nickleby* (1839). After being rescued by Nicholas from the atrocious conditions of Dotheboys Hall, Smike eventually dies of consumption. In David Edgar's 1981 stage adaptation of the book Smike was originally played by David Threlfall.

SMILEY, GEORGE   British Intelligence chief who features in various novels by John Le Carré (David Cornwell), beginning with *Call for the Dead* (1961) and *A Murder of Quality* (1962). Smiley plays a relatively small part in Le Carré's early espionage stories, *The Spy Who Came in From the Cold* (1963) and *The Looking Glass War* (1965), but he comes to the fore in *Tinker, Tailor, Soldier, Spy* (1974) and its immediate sequels, *The Honourable Schoolboy* (1977) and *Smiley's People* (1980). In the last of these books Smiley's deadly enemy is a Russian master-spy known as Karla. The novels have been praised as imaginative literature of high quality, and Smiley is now a British myth-figure appropriate to the age of Burgess, MacLean, Philby and Blunt. In the film *The Spy Who Came in from the Cold* (1966; dir. Martin Ritt) he was played by Rupert Davies. In the BBC television serial 'Tinker, Tailor, Soldier, Spy' (1979) Smiley was played with great subtlety by Alec Guinness, who repeated the role in a later serial, 'Smiley's People' (1982). According to Blake Morrison (*The Times Literary Supplement*, 11 April 1986): 'Smiley is [Le Carré's] best known and best loved character because he is a still point in the turn-around world, a figure of stability amid so much that is confused and provisional.' The book *Smiley's Circus* (1986) by David Monaghan is a guide to Le Carré's (and Smiley's) labyrinthine 'secret world'.

SMITH, DENIS NAYLAND   Robust hero of Sax Rohmer's *The Mystery of Dr Fu Manchu* (1913) and all the subsequent novels about the machinations of the Devil Doctor (see FU MANCHU for more details). His companion and amanuensis is one Dr Petrie. In films Nayland Smith has been played by Lewis Stone (1932), Nigel Green (1965) and Douglas Wilmer (1966), among others. He was played by Lester Matthews in the American television series 'The Adventures of Fu Manchu' (1955–6).

SMITH, HARRIET   See under Emma WOODHOUSE

SMITH, JOHN 'HANNIBAL'   See under B. A. BARACUS

SMITH, NEVADA   Former cowboy, a violent half-breed, who appears as one of the lesser characters in Harold Robbins's steamy novel *The Carpetbaggers* (1960). In the film of the book (1964; dir. Edward Dmytryk) he was played by Alan Ladd. Smith's early life in the turbulent days of the Old West is the subject of another film, *Nevada Smith* (1966; dir. Henry Hathaway), which starred Steve McQueen. The character has also been revived for a TV movie (1975; dir. Gordon Douglas), pilot for a projected *Nevada Smith* series starring Cliff Potts.

SMITH, RONALD EUSTACE RUPERT   See PSMITH

SMITH, WINSTON   Unhappy protagonist of George Orwell's chilling dystopian novel *Nineteen Eighty-Four* (1949). Smith is a minor bureaucrat in the future totalitarian state known as Airstrip One. He rebels against the Thought Police, but eventually his spirit is crushed by the interrogator, O'Brien, and he learns to 'love' the state's unseen leader, BIG BROTHER. In the famous BBC television production of 'Nineteen Eighty-Four' (1954) Winston Smith was played by Peter Cushing. In the subsequent feature film (1955; dir. Michael Anderson) he was portrayed, rather less satisfactorily, by Edmond O'Brien. In the far superior remake (1984; dir. Mike Radford) John Hurt took the part.

SMURFS, THE   Race of pixie-like beings invented by the Belgian comic-strip artist Peyo (Pierre Culliford). In the French-language original the Smurfs are known as 'Les Schtroumpfs'. They first appeared in Peyo's strip *Johan et Pirlouit* in 1957, and were given a strip of their own from 1960. Since then they have become popular throughout Europe, have appeared in books and television series, and have been much used in merchandising.

SNEERWELL, LADY   See under Charles and Joseph SURFACE

SNODGRASS, AUGUSTUS   See under Samuel PICKWICK

SNOOPY   Daydreaming beagle, in Charles M. Schulz's *Peanuts* (from 1950) – reputedly the world's most successful comic-strip (see also Charlie BROWN). Ruthven Tremain says, in *The Animal's Who's Who*: 'With his image on everything from nightshirts to telephones . . . Snoopy is surely the most famous dog in the world.' He stars in the animated movie *Snoopy, Come Home* (1972; dir. Bill Melendez).

SNOPES, FLEM   Head of a low-born family on the make in William Faulkner's Snopes Trilogy (part of his 'Yoknapatawpha County' cycle of books): *The Hamlet* (1940), *The Town* (1957) and *The Mansion* (1959). Flem, who rises to become a bank president, is a vulgar, materialistic representative of the New South – as opposed to the aristocratic Old South which is embodied in the declining Sartoris and Compson families (see John SARTORIS and Quentin COMPSON). Flem Snopes is eventually murdered by his cousin. Other Snopeses appear in various short stories and novels by Faulkner (including *Sanctuary* – see Temple DRAKE), and they are notable for their odd forenames: for example, Mink, Byron, Lump, Eck and Wallstreet Panic Snopes. *The Hamlet* formed the basis of a film, *The Long Hot Summer* (1958; dir. Martin Ritt), which starred Orson Welles and Paul Newman. This in turn became a television series (1965), with Edmond O'Brien and Roy Thinnes in the leading roles. Twenty years later *The Long Hot Summer*

was remade as a TV mini-series (1985; dir. Stuart Cooper), with Jason Robards and Don Johnson.

SNOWE, LUCY   Impoverished English girl who becomes a teacher in the town of Villette (a fictionalized Brussels). She falls in love with a handsome English doctor, but this love is not returned and eventually she forms an affection for her employer's cousin, Professor Paul Emmanuel. Lucy's story is told in Charlotte Brontë's novel *Villette* (1853).

SNOWY   See under TIN-TIN

SNUDGE   See BOOTSIE AND SNUDGE

SOLNESS   Central character of Henrik Ibsen's symbolic play *The Master Builder* (1892). The ageing architect Solness suffers from vertigo; nevertheless he climbs the newly-built spire of his house, whence he falls to his death. It is clear that Ibsen intended Master-Builder Solness to symbolize the Artist.

SOLO, HAN   Rough, tough space pilot played by Harrison Ford in the films *Star Wars* (1977), *The Empire Strikes Back* (1980) and *Return of the Jedi* (1983), all conceived by George Lucas. He assists Luke SKYWALKER and Princess Leia in their struggle against Darth VADER and the evil Empire. Solo's further adventures have been recounted in a series of novels by Brian C. Daley: *Han Solo at Star's End* (1979), *Han Solo's Revenge* (1979) and *Han Solo and the Lost Legacy* (1980).

SOLO, NAPOLEON   American secret agent played by Robert Vaughn in the camp television series 'The Man from UNCLE' (1964–8). Solo's sidekick is a Russian-born agent, Illya KURYAKIN, and the organization they work for is the ominous-sounding United Network Command for Law and Enforcement. 'The Man from UNCLE' and a companion series, 'The Girl from UNCLE' (1966), enjoyed a considerable vogue during the second half of the 1960s. Several cinematic feature films were cobbled together from episodes of the series, and in 1983 there came *The Return of the Man from UNCLE*, a TV movie which also starred Robert Vaughn.

SOMMERS, JAIME   Super-lady played by Lindsay Wagner in the American TV series 'The Bionic Woman' (1976–8 – a spin-off from 'The Six Million Dollar Man'). Like her friend Steve AUSTIN, she is 'rebuilt' after an accident and hence is able to run like the wind, lift huge weights, and so on – all in the cause of catching various crooks and spies.

SOOTY   Small black-eared bear who has enjoyed a long career on British television. He was created by glove-puppeteer Harry Corbett in the 1950s, and has been perpetuated to the present day by the originator's son, Matthew Corbett. Along with LARRY THE LAMB and MUFFIN THE MULE, Sooty was one of the characters featured in the weekly paper *TV Comic*. He has also appeared in children's books.

SOREL, JULIEN   Ambitious, amoral young Frenchman, an admirer of Napoleon, who aims to ascend the social pyramid by way of the church and a series of love-affairs. The story of his rise (and fall) is told in *Le Rouge et le Noir* (1830; translated variously as *The Red and the Black* or *Scarlet and Black*) by Stendhal (Marie Henri Beyle). Sorel has been described as 'the distant progenitor of all anti-heroes' (Anthony Burgess, *Ninety-Nine Novels*). In the film of the novel (1954; dir. Claude Autant-Lara) Julien was played by Gérard Philipe.

SORREL, HETTY   Flighty heroine of George Eliot's novel *Adam Bede* (1859). She spurns the love of the worthy Adam BEDE, and is seduced by the local squire's grandson, Arthur Donnithorne. She agrees to marry Adam Bede, but runs away when she discovers that she is pregnant by her lover. The baby dies, Hetty is convicted of infanticide, and is transported overseas.

SORRELL, STEPHEN   Middle-class Englishman who struggles against poverty and unemployment in the aftermath of World War I, raises his son single-handedly, and eventually dies in noble fashion. He appears in Warwick Deeping's sentimental and class-conscious bestseller *Sorrell and Son* (1925). The films of the novel (1927 and 1934) both starred H. B. Warner (best remembered for his role as Christ in Cecil B. de Mille's *The King of Kings*).

This dated story was revived for a British television serial (1984), with Richard Pasco in the role of Stephen Sorrell.

SPADE, SAM   San Francisco-based private-eye in Dashiell Hammett's novel *The Maltese Falcon* (1930) and three short stories which are included in *The Adventures of Sam Spade and Other Stories* (1944). His cases are narrated in a tough, laconic manner which has made him seem the archetypal hero of the 'hardboiled school' of crime fiction. Unlike the CONTINENTAL OP, he does not carry a gun. In the film *The Maltese Falcon* (1931; dir. Roy del Ruth) he was played by Ricardo Cortez. This was remade as *Satan Met a Lady* (1936; dir. William Dieterle), with Warren William in the lead. The definitive film version, *The Maltese Falcon* (1941; dir. John Huston), had Humphrey Bogart as Spade. A BBC radio dramatization (1984) had Tom Wilkinson as the hero.

SPALANZANI   See under Doctor COPPELIUS

SPENCER, FRANK   Gormless young man played by Michael Crawford in the BBC television comedy series 'Some Mothers Do 'Ave 'Em' (1974–9). Frank is accident-prone in the extreme, and is always getting into desperate scrapes. The series was written by Raymond Allen. 'The central character is so consistently developed that the audience take it for granted the house will fall down only a few weeks after he has started to live in it' (Clive James, *The Crystal Bucket*). Thanks to his mincing and apparently brainless mannerisms, Frank Spencer became a favourite butt of mimics and stand-up comics during the 1970s.

SPENCER, JEFF   See under KOOKIE

SPENLOW, DORA   See under David COPPERFIELD

SPENSER   Boston-based private-eye who does not divulge his first name. He appears in the crime novels of Robert B. Parker. Somewhat academically inclined, Spenser is the American equivalent of a British 'donnish' detective. His adventures are recounted in *The Godwulf Manuscript* (1973), *God Save the Child* (1974), *Mortal Stakes* (1975), *Promised Land* (1976), *The Judas*

Goat (1978), *Looking for Rachel Wallace* (1980), *Early Autumn* (1981), *A Savage Place* (1981), *Ceremony* (1982), *The Widening Gyre* (1983), *Valediction* (1984) and *A Catskill Eagle* (1985). Spenser has been played by Gary Waldhorn in a BBC radio adaptation of *The Godwulf Manuscript* (1984). In the American television series 'Spenser: For Hire' (1985) he was played by Robert Urich.

SPIDER, THE   Real name Richard Wentworth, a pulp-magazine hero invented by R. T. M. Scott. *The Spider Magazine* ran from 1933 to 1943, and most of the 118 novellas it published were written by Norvell Page (under the house name 'Grant Stockbridge'). The Spider is a mysterious avenger in a similar vein to the Shadow: he wears a black mask, he carries a fine silk cord which is useful for climbing walls, and he stamps his dead enemies' foreheads with a red spider-shaped seal. His servant is Ram Singh, who assists the Spider with his many disguises. Two movie serials starred Warren Hull as the hero: *The Spider's Web* (1938) and *The Spider Returns* (1941). Philip José Farmer, the leading expert on the genealogy of fictional characters, once argued that the Spider, the Shadow and G-8 were one and the same person. In the addendum to his book *Doc Savage: His Apocalyptic Life* (1973), Farmer withdraws this suggestion, saying that 'Wentworth was far more bloodthirsty than the Shadow, and he would have scorned Doc Savage's thesis that the best way to handle criminals was to capture and then rehabilitate them. The only good crook was a dead crook, according to Wentworth, and he saw to it that the streets and the backrooms of New York City were littered with good crooks.' Farmer goes on to assert that Richard Wentworth was in fact the son of Lord John Roxton, one of the leading characters in A. Conan Doyle's novel *The Lost World* (1912).

SPIDER-MAN   Real name Peter Parker, one of the best-known costumed superheroes of the 1960s. As a youth, Parker is bitten by a mutant spider which somehow imparts its arachnid skills to him. Discovering that he now has enormous strength and awesome climbing ability, Parker decides to become a crime-fighter, for which purpose he adopts the persona of Spider-Man. Clad in a red and blue uniform decorated with black webbing, and armed with a 'webshooter', he pursues baddies

Spider-Man

wherever they may lead him – which usually means up and down the sheer faces of New York skyscrapers. 'Spidey' was created by scriptwriter Stan Lee and artist Steve Ditko, and has appeared in various Marvel Comics titles since 1962. He has also appeared in at least two animated television series, and in the live-action TV movie *Spider-Man* (1977; dir. E. W. Swackhamer) and the subsequent series, where he was played by Nicholas Hammond. Spider-Man's exploits have been recounted in the novels *Mayhem in Manhattan* (1978) by Len Wein and Marv Wolfman, and *Crime Campaign* (1979) and *Murdermoon* (1979) by Paul Kupperberg.

SPOCK, MR   Alien, pointy-eared, supposedly emotionless crew-member of the Starship *Enterprise*, played by Leonard Nimoy in the American television series 'Star Trek' (1966–9). He became the most famous character of the series, much loved by the fans known as 'Trekkies' who regularly hold conventions to honour

'Star Trek'. (One of their amusements of the mid-1980s, in Britain at any rate, was the performance of an illicit comic-pornographic play, *Spock in Manacles*.) The TV series was conceived and produced by Gene Roddenberry. Mr Spock features prominently in the novelizations of the series by James Blish (who wrote eleven volumes between 1967 and his death in 1975) and many other writers. Blish's book *Spock Must Die!* (1970) is an original novel about the character (not based on a script). *Spock, Messiah!* (1976) by Theodore R. Cogswell and Charles A. Spano is another such original book – its title is perhaps revealing of many fans' attitude to Mr Spock. Leonard Nimoy has continued to play Spock in the feature films based on the TV series: *Star Trek: The Motion Picture* (1979; dir. Robert Wise), *Star Trek: The Wrath of Khan* (1982; dir. Nicholas Meyer), *Star Trek: The Search for Spock* (1984; dir. Nimoy) and *The Voyage Home: Star Trek IV* (dir. Nimoy).

SPODE, RODERICK   See under Reginald JEEVES

SPRATT, SIR LANCELOT   Senior surgeon at St Swithin's general hospital, in a series of humorous novels by Richard Gordon beginning with *Doctor in the House* (1952). Sir Lancelot is 'a surgeon of the grand old school', referred to behind his back as 'that bloody old butcher'. It is said that he earned his knighthood 'by performing a small but essential operation on a cabinet minister that allowed him to take his seat in the House with greater ease'. He is absent from the second novel in the series, *Doctor at Sea* (1953), but he reappears in the later volumes: *Doctor at Large* (1955), *Doctor in Love* (1957), *Doctor and Son* (1959), *Doctor in Clover* (1960), *Doctor on Toast* (1961), *Doctor in the Swim* (1962), *The Summer of Sir Lancelot* (1963), *Love and Sir Lancelot* (1965), *Doctor on the Boil* (1970), *Doctor on the Brain* (1972), *Doctor in the Nude* (1973), *Doctor on the Job* (1976) and *Doctor in the Nest* (1979). Played by the bearded Scottish actor James Robertson Justice, he also looms large in the films based on the books – *Doctor in the House* (1954; dir. Ralph Thomas), *Doctor at Sea* (1955; dir. Thomas), *Doctor at Large* (1957; dir. Thomas), *Doctor in Love* (1960; dir. Thomas), *Doctor in Distress* (1963; dir. Thomas), *Doctor in Clover* (1966; dir. Thomas) and *Doctor in Trouble* (1970; dir. Thomas). A British television series, 'Doctor in the House' (1970–73), was also based on Richard Gordon's books; however, it did not feature Sir Lancelot Spratt.

SPRING-HEELED JACK Bogeyman of uncertain origins who features in many 'penny bloods' of the Victorian period – for example, the anonymous *Spring-Heeled Jack, the Terror of London* (1870s). According to E. S. Turner, Jack 'traversed the countryside in giant bounds, as a man might do on the moon; he could clear stage-coaches, haystacks or cottages with contemptuous ease'. Stories about the mysterious Spring-Heeled Jack, who usually turned out to be a virtuous young man equipped with extraordinary mechanical springs, continued to appear until the Edwardian era.

SQUEERS, WACKFORD See under Nicholas NICKLEBY

SQUIRREL NUTKIN See under PETER RABBIT

STAHR, MONROE Hollywood film producer, the tragic central figure of F. Scott Fitzgerald's unfinished novel *The Last Tycoon* (1941). It is commonly supposed that Stahr is based on the real-life producer Irving Thalberg, although it has also been pointed out that he embodies much of Fitzgerald's own self-image as an under-appreciated artist in the crass world of movie-making. In the film *The Last Tycoon* (1976; dir. Elia Kazan; screenplay by Harold Pinter) Stahr was played by Robert De Niro.

STAINLESS STEEL RAT, THE Also known as Slippery Jim diGriz, an interstellar crook-turned-policeman who appears in humorous science fiction novels by the American writer Harry Harrison (Henry Maxwell Dempsey). The titles are: *The Stainless Steel Rat* (1961), *The Stainless Steel Rat's Revenge* (1970), *The Stainless Steel Rat Saves the World* (1972), *The Stainless Steel Rat Wants You!* (1978), *The Stainless Steel Rat for President* (1982) and *A Stainless Steel Rat is Born* (1985).

STALKY See Arthur CORKRAN

STANDISH, TIGER The Honourable Timothy Overbury Standish, a gentleman-adventurer from the same mould as Bulldog

DRUMMOND. He was invented by the prolific Sydney Horler for his thrillers *Tiger Standish* (1932) and *Tiger Standish Comes Back* (1934). Later books about Standish include *The Mystery of the Seven Cafés* (1935), *The Grim Game* (1936), *Tiger Standish Takes the Field* (1939), *Tiger Standish Steps on It* (1940), *Tiger Standish Does His Stuff* (1941), *The Lady with the Lamp* (1944), *Exit the Disguiser* (1948), *They Thought He was Dead* (1949) and *The House of Jackals* (1951). Sydney Horler once described Standish as having 'all the attributes of a thoroughly likable fellow . . . he likes his glass of beer, he is a confirmed pipe smoker, he is always ready to smile back into the face of danger'. The character was played by Norman Shelley in a BBC radio serial (1935). (Sapper, Bulldog Drummond's creator, also introduced a character called Standish. Sapper's private detective Ronald Standish appears in various novels and short stories, including some of the later Bulldog Drummond titles.)

STANLEY, ANN VERONICA   'New Woman' who chooses to live openly with the man she loves. She is the heroine of H. G. Wells's feminist novel *Ann Veronica* (1909), a book which was considered scandalous in its day. A stage musical version of the novel (1969), with music by Cyril Ornadel, was not a great success.

STARDUST, ZIGGY   'Hero' of David Bowie's glitter-rock record album *Ziggy Stardust and the Spiders from Mars* (1972). The mercurial Mr Bowie is frequently referred to as 'Ziggy Stardust' to this day. A cinema film, also entitled *Ziggy Stardust and the Spiders from Mars* (1982; dir. D. A. Pennebaker), is centred round a 1973 concert performance by Bowie.

STARK, WILLIE   Demagogic governor of a Southern state, in Robert Penn Warren's novel *All the King's Men* (1946). Stark is a fictional portrait of the real-life politician Huey Long. He was played by Broderick Crawford in the film of the novel (1949; dir. Robert Rossen).

STARKADDER FAMILY, THE   See under Flora POSTE

STARR, BRENDA   Comic-strip newspaperwoman created by artist Dale Messick in 1940. Her far-fetched adventures were perpetuated in the Columbia cinema serial, *Brenda Starr, Reporter* (1945). In the TV movie *Brenda Starr, Girl Reporter* (1975; dir. Mel Stuart) she was played by Jill St John.

STARSKY AND HUTCH   Dave Starsky and Ken Hutchinson, an appealing pair of plainclothes American cops played by Paul Michael Glaser and David Soul in the very successful television series 'Starsky and Hutch' (1975–9). They are forever leaping in and out of fast cars.

STAVROGIN, NIKOLAI   Well-born young Russian who is haunted by nihilism. He commits various crimes before joining a revolutionary group and failing to find satisfaction in political activity. Eventually, tortured by the memory of a young woman who committed suicide on his account, he hangs himself. Stavrogin's story is told in Fyodor Dostoevsky's novel *The Possessed* (1871–2; vt *The Devils*).

STEED, JOHN   Suave, bowler-hatted adventurer, a perfect English gentleman, played by Patrick MacNee in the popular British television series 'The Avengers' (1961–8). The programme evolved from an earlier series called 'Police Surgeon' (1960), and its principal creator was Sydney Newman. For several years Steed's assistant was the redoubtable Mrs Emma PEEL. Various novelizations of the TV scripts, with such titles as *The Afrit Affair*, *The Drowned Queen* and *The Gold Bomb* (all 1968) were written by the American science fiction author Keith Laumer. A later, Canadian-produced, series called 'The New Avengers' (1976–7) also starred MacNee.

STEELE, ADAM   See under EDGE

STEERFORTH, JAMES   See under David COPPERFIELD

STEERPIKE   Sinister young revolutionary who upsets the cobwebby world of Gormenghast, in Mervyn Peake's novel *Titus Groan* (1946). He begins as a persecuted kitchen-boy, and ends as 'His Infernal Slyness, the Arch-fluke Steerpike'. His story continues in the sequel, *Gormenghast* (1950), which concludes with

Steerpike's death at the hands of the castle's rightful heir, the youthful Titus GROAN. In Brian Sibley's BBC radio adaptations of the two books (1984) Steerpike was played by the pop-singer Sting (who has bought the movie rights to Peake's novels and has promised us film versions of them soon).

STEPHENS, SAMANTHA   Beautiful, domesticated witch played by Elizabeth Montgomery in the American television comedy series 'Bewitched' (1964–72). An ordinary suburban housewife much of the time, she summons her magic powers by twitching her nose. This popular series was created by producers William Dozier and Harry Ackerman, and it has been reshown in Britain in the 1980s. A spin-off series, 'Tabitha' (1977–8), was about the adventures of Samantha's equally talented daughter.

STEPTOE, HAROLD AND ALBERT   Rag-and-bone man with middle-class aspirations, and his down-to-earth tetchy old Dad. They live in a dilapidated London house which is brimming with cast-off junk. Harry H. Corbett was Harold and Wilfred Brambell was his Dad in the deservedly popular BBC television series 'Steptoe and Son' (1964–73). The very funny scripts were by Ray Galton and Alan Simpson, and the series was subsequently Americanized as 'Sanford and Son' (1972–6). Two feature films, *Steptoe and Son* (1972; dir. Cliff Owen) and *Steptoe and Son Ride Again* (1973), also starred Corbett and Brambell.

STEVENS, GAVIN   Southern lawyer-cum-detective created by William Faulkner for a series of short stories which first appeared in the *Saturday Evening Post*. He is attorney for Yoknapatawpha County, Mississippi, and his cases are collected in the book *Knight's Gambit* (1949). He also appears in the novels *Intruder in the Dust* (1948), *Requiem for a Nun* (1951), *The Town* (1957) and *The Mansion* (1959).

STIG   Cave-boy who inhabits an old chalk-pit, in Clive King's popular novel for children *Stig of the Dump* (1963). Stig is discovered by the eight-year-old Barney, and the two become fast friends. The novel has been serialized for British television (1981), with Keith Jayne as Stig.

STONE, FLEMING   Hero of many detective stories by the prolific American novelist Carolyn Wells. Stone first appeared in a short story published in 1906. Novels in which he plays the lead role include *The Clue* (1909), *The Gold Bag* (1911), *Anybody But Anne* (1914), *The Curved Blades* (1916), *The Diamond Pin* (1919), *Feathers Left Around* (1923), *Prilligirl* (1924), *All at Sea* (1927), *The Ghosts' High Noon* (1930), *The Clue of the Eyelash* (1933), *The Wooden Indian* (1935), *The Radio Studio Murder* (1937), *The Importance of Being Murdered* (1939) and *Who Killed Caldwell?* (1942).

STONE, KAREN   Wealthy, widowed actress who becomes infatuated with a young Italian gigolo, in Tennessee Williams's novella *The Roman Spring of Mrs Stone* (1950). In the film version (1961; dir. José Quintero) Karen Stone was played by Vivien Leigh.

STORM, SUE AND JOHNNY   See under Mr Fantastic

STRANGE, DOCTOR   Full name Stephen Strange, a comic-book hero who is gifted with supernatural powers and a Cloak of Levitation. He is known as 'The Master of the Mystic Arts'. Dr Strange was created by artist Steve Ditko and writer Stan Lee for Marvel Comics in 1963. The character has also appeared in a television movie, *Dr Strange* (1978; dir. Philip de Guere), which starred Peter Hooten, and in a novel, *Nightmare* (1979), by William Rotsler.

STRANGELOVE, DOCTOR   Military scientist, a former Nazi now working for the USA, who was played by Peter Sellers in the satirical film *Dr Strangelove, or How I Learned to Stop Worrying and Love the Bomb* (1963; dir. Stanley Kubrick). Strangelove, inventor of the ultimate doomsday weapon, is an utter madman who cannot stop his right arm from rising in an involuntary Nazi salute. The script, by Kubrick and Terry Southern, was based on the novel *Two Hours to Doom* (1958; vt *Red Alert*) by Peter Bryant (Peter George). Strangelove does not appear in the original novel, which is a sober, admonitory work; however, he does feature in Peter George's completely rewritten version of the book, *Dr Strangelove* (1963).

STRANGEWAYS, NIGEL   Private detective who features in the donnish crime novels of Nicholas Blake (Cecil Day-Lewis). The series consists of *Question of Proof* (1935), *Thou Shell of Death* (1936), *There's Trouble Brewing* (1937), *The Beast Must Die* (1938), *The Smiler With the Knife* (1939), *Malice in Wonderland* (1940; vt *Summer Camp Mystery*), *The Case of the Abominable Snowman* (1941; vt *Corpse in the Snowman*), *Minute for Murder* (1947), *Head of a Traveller* (1949), *The Dreadful Hollow* (1953), *Whispers in the Gloom* (1954), *End of a Chapter* (1957), *Widow's Cruise* (1959), *The Worm of Death* (1960), *Sad Variety* (1964) and *The Morning After Death* (1966). A BBC radio adaptation of *The Smiler With the Knife* (1986) had Simon Cadell as Nigel Strangeways.

STREET, DELLA   See under Perry MASON

STRETHER, LAMBERT   Middle-aged native of New England who goes to Paris in order to persuade a wayward young man, Chad Newsome, to return home. He fails, and is himself converted to *la vie Parisienne*. Strether's story is told in Henry James's subtle novel *The Ambassadors* (1903). An unsuccessful musical version, *The Ambassador*, was staged in Britain in 1971, with Howard Keel in the role of Strether.

STRICKLAND, CHARLES   English stockbroker who abandons his job and family to become a painter in Tahiti, where he dies of leprosy. The story of this Gauguin-like character is told in W. Somerset Maugham's novel *The Moon and Sixpence* (1919). In the film (1943; dir. Albert Lewin) Strickland was portrayed by George Sanders. He has also been played by Patrick Allen in a BBC radio dramatization of the book (1984).

STRIDER   See under Frodo BAGGINS

STRINGHAM, CHARLES   See under Nicholas JENKINS

STRULDBRUGS, THE   See under Lemuel GULLIVER

STRUWWELPETER   Known in English as Shock-Headed Peter, a long-nailed wild boy who appears in the title story of Heinrich

Hoffmann's children's book *Struwwelpeter* (1845), a collection of hair-raising cautionary tales and pictures. This work was immensely successful in German, English and other languages, and it has been adapted in numerous forms (one of its translators was Mark Twain). Over six hundred editions have appeared in the original language alone. The stories have been adapted to the stage, and there has been at least one comic opera about Struwwelpeter (1900).

STUBBS, HORATIO Randy young man created by Brian Aldiss in his comic novel *The Hand-Reared Boy* (1970). Stubbs grows to manhood in the late 1930s, his imagination totally obsessed by sex. Book reviewers regarded him as the English version of Alex PORTNOY, though Aldiss protested that his novel had been written before Philip Roth's came out (publication of *The Hand-Reared Boy* was delayed because an elderly and eminent member of a certain publishing house took strong exception to it). Aldiss recounts Stubbs's subsequent adventures as a soldier in the Far East in *A Soldier Erect* (1971) and *A Rude Awakening* (1978). The three novels have subsequently been republished in one volume as *The Horatio Stubbs Saga*.

SUB-MARINER Prince Namor of sunken Atlantis, a comic-book superhero who is able to swim at speeds of sixty miles an hour. Drawn by Bill Everett, Sub-Mariner first appeared in *Marvel Comics* No. 1 (1939) and he has continued to lead a healthy existence ever since. Like many of the great comic-book heroes, he appeared in an animated television series during the 1960s. (Other submersible characters who bear a strong resemblance to Prince Namor include the comic-book Aquaman [from 1940] and the TV adventurer the Man from Atlantis [1977–8].)

SUMMERSON, ESTHER Heroine and part-narrator of Charles Dickens's novel *Bleak House* (1852–3). Unaware of her true parentage, she goes to live as a companion to the ward of Mr John Jarndyce at Bleak House. Her employers are involved in the endless law suit of 'Jarndyce and Jarndyce', a case which has blighted the lives of all concerned. The plot of the novel – which contains a host of other characters, such as Sir Leicester and Lady Dedlock, Inspector BUCKET (an early Scotland Yard detective), the importunate Harold Skimpole, and the rag-and-bone man Krook (who dies by spontaneous combustion) – is taken up with the unhappy outcome of this litigation, and with the discovery of Esther Summerson's parents. In the highly-praised BBC television serialization of the novel (1985) Esther was played by Suzanne Burden.

SUMURU   Exotic lady villain invented by Sax Rohmer (Arthur Sarsfield Ward) at a comparatively late stage in his blood-and-thunder writing career. This attempt at a female substitute for Dr Fu MANCHU appeared in five novels: *Nude in Mink* (1950; vt *Sins of Sumuru*), *Sumuru* (1951; vt *Slaves of Sumuru*), *The Fire Goddess* (1952; vt *Virgin in Flames*), *Return of Sumuru* (1954; vt *Sand and Satin*) and *Sinister Madonna* (1956).

SUPERGIRL   Real name Kara, alias Linda Lee Danvers. Like her cousin, SUPERMAN, she hails from the planet Krypton. Arriving on Earth somewhat later than the Man of Steel, she is adopted by a couple called Danvers, goes to college and subsequently works for a TV station. Meanwhile she is trained in the use of her super-powers by her mighty cousin: like him, she is invulnerable, has super senses, and can fly. Supergirl first appeared in *Action Comics* in 1959. She has since become a member of the Legion of Super-Heroes. In the film *Supergirl* (1984; dir. Jeannot Szwarc) she was played by Helen Slater.

SUPERMAN   Costumed superhero who can fly, is invulnerable, has X-ray vision, and is capable of moving mountains single-handedly. A refugee from the planet Krypton, he has been raised on Earth by loving foster-parents in the town of Smallville. In daily life he is the 'mild-mannered' newspaper reporter Clark Kent; but when the occasion demands he removes his suit and spectacles, and soars into the sky fully resplendent in blue tights and a red cape. His day-to-day friends and colleagues on the *Daily Planet* newspaper include Lois LANE and Jimmy OLSEN. Superman is surely the most omnipotent hero ever invented (although he can be weakened by the mysterious element Kryptonite), and certainly the most famous character to emerge from American comic-books. He was created by Jerome Siegel and Joe Schuster, a pair of juvenile science

fiction fans who first concocted the character in the early 1930s.
A prototype of Superman appeared in their amateur fanzine,
but when they tried to sell the idea to newspapers they met with
failure. It was not until June 1938 that Superman found a home, in
the first issue of a new publication called *Action Comics*. He
became a huge success, and the progenitor of a whole line of
outlandishly-costumed heroes (his immediate 'descendants'
include BATMAN and Captain MARVEL). From the summer of
1939 Superman had his own comic-book, the first of a complex
family which includes such later titles as *Superboy* (the adventures
of Superman as a lad) and *Supergirl* (the adventures of Superman's
lovely cousin from Krypton; see SUPERGIRL). And before long the
Man of Steel was a considerable hit on the radio, in cartoons and
in cinema serials.

Siegel and Schuster soon lost control of their creation. The
individual who was most responsible for developing Superman,
over a period of several decades, was comic-book editor Mort
Weisinger. One of Weisinger's innovations was to give the character
the power of time travel, 'making it possible for our hero to go
into the past and introduce Hercules, Samson and Atlas into the
adventures, or to reach into the future to foil a menace that would
not arrive for 1,000 years' (according to Sam Moskowitz).
Weisinger also rewrote the story of Superman's origins,
introducing super-villains from the planet Krypton, alternate
time-lines and other refinements which helped keep the saga from
becoming too predictable.

Clayton 'Bud' Collyer was the actor who gave voice to Superman
on the radio, from 1940. (He indicated that the character was
taking flight by use of the repeated phrase 'Up, up, and
awa-a-a-ay!') Collyer also worked on the sound-tracks of seventeen
short animated films about Superman produced by Max Fleischer
(1941–3). Others who have incarnated the hero include Kirk Alyn
in the film serials *Superman* (1948) and *Atom Man vs. Superman*
(1950); and George Reeves in the feature film *Superman and
the Mole Men* (1951) and the television series 'The Adventures of
Superman' (1952–7). There has also been a stage musical entitled
It's a Bird, It's a Plane, It's Superman (a catch-phrase from the
radio series), and this was turned into a TV movie (1975), with David
Wilson in the leading part. Latterly, there have been various
animated series on TV, including 'The New Adventures of

Superman' (1966) and 'Super Friends' (1973–4) (in which
Superman joins forces with BATMAN and WONDER WOMAN).
Superman has gained a new lease of life in the past decade through
the big-budget feature films about his exploits. *Superman* (1978;
dir. Richard Donner), *Superman II* (1980; dir. Richard Lester) and
Superman III (1983; dir. Lester) all starred Christopher Reeve as the
Man of Steel. These films adhere quite faithfully to the spirit of
the comic-books, and Reeve makes a satisfactorily muscular
and good-looking hero – even if he is at his most effective when
he plays the bumbling and diffident Clark Kent. According to
television historians Tim Brooks and Earle Marsh, there is a
Superman museum in Illinois and there have been 'endless nostalgia
books about the Man of Steel. He will no doubt be seen on
videodisks and holographic TV in the year 2000.'

SURFACE, CHARLES AND JOSEPH   Contrasting brothers in
Richard Brinsley Sheridan's great comedy *The School for Scandal*
(1777). Charles Surface, a likeable but apparently good-for-nothing
young man, is in love with Maria, Sir Peter Teazle's ward. His
hypocritical brother, Joseph Surface, is also in pursuit of Maria,
and creates havoc by pretending to make love to Lady Teazle, Sir
Peter's young wife. After many complications, Joseph stands
revealed as the villain of the piece, and the good-hearted Charles
wins Maria. Other notable characters who appear in this play
include Sir Benjamin Backbite and Lady Sneerwell.

SUTPEN, THOMAS   See under Quentin COMPSON

SVEJK, JOSEF   Often transliterated as 'Schweik', a meek but
cunning soldier created by the Czech writer Jaroslav Hasek for a
series of short stories which were published in book form as *The
Good Soldier Svejk and Other Strange Stories* (1912). This was
followed by *The Good Soldier Svejk in Captivity* (1917) and by
Hasek's four-volume masterpiece *The Good Soldier Svejk and His
Fortunes in the World War* (1920–23). The last-named novel was
still incomplete at the time of Hasek's death in 1923, and it
was finished by his friend Karel Vanek – although this conclusion
is usually omitted from modern translations. The critic Kenneth
McLeish describes Svejk as 'an amiable, self-proclaimed
simpleton who uses wide-eyed innocence as a devastating

mirror for the venal, arrogant and deadly fools he finds on every side. He is a medieval rogue strayed into the modern world, a *Simplex Simplicissimus* of the War that was to End War.' Josef Lada's illustrations to the Svejk story appeared with a much-modified text as a newspaper 'comic-strip' in 1924. The German dramatist Bertolt Brecht subsequently wrote a play, *Schweik in the Second World War* (c. 1945), in which the good soldier Svejk meets Hitler. A later sequel by another hand is H. Putz's novel *The Adventures of Good Comrade Schweik* (1969), a satire on communism. There have been several films based on the character, including a British production, *Schweik's New Adventures* (1943; dir. Karel Lamac), which starred Lloyd Pearson.

SVENGALI   Deep-dyed villain of George du Maurier's bestselling novel *Trilby* (1894). He is a musician who uses his sinister hypnotic ability to exert an unwholesome influence over the young singer Trilby O'FERRAL. Under Svengali's guidance, she becomes a famous performer, but loses her voice when he dies. Svengali's name has entered the language as a synonym for any mentor who wields a dark, mesmeric power over his pupil. However, in common with Dickens's FAGIN, this character may be viewed as a pernicious racial stereotype, as Edgar Rosenberg has noted: 'Like Dracula and Frankenstein's monster, Svengali has been so vastly diffused and generalized by the public media that he has passed into the popular consciousness as something of a household name, with the result that one has difficulty in remembering his exact credentials . . . Svengali has thus managed to horrify and amuse several million people who are apt to forget that the real Svengali is in the first instance a Jew, and that his Jewishness provides the source of all his horrific and comic endowments.' The novel was turned into a successful stage play in 1895, with Beerbohm Tree playing the part of Svengali. It also formed the basis of many silent films. Two talkie versions are *Svengali* (1931; dir. Archie Mayo), with John Barrymore in the main role; and a remake of the same title (1954; dir. Noel Langley), with Donald Wolfit. In the TV movie *Svengali* (1983; dir. Anthony Harvey) Peter O'Toole played an updated version of the character.

SWANN, CHARLES   Elegant man-about-town who falls in love with and marries the courtesan Odette de Crécy. They have a daughter,

Gilberte, who becomes an object of affection for the narrator of
Marcel Proust's great *roman fleuve, A la Recherche du Temps Perdu*
(1913–27 – known in English as *Remembrance of Things Past*).
The novel is split into seven parts, of which the first, *Du Côté de
Chez Swann* (1913; translated as *Swann's Way*), deals principally
with Swann and his *grand amour*. In the film *Swann in Love*
(1984; dir. Volker Schlondorff) Swann was played by the English
actor Jeremy Irons.

SWIFT, TOM   Inventive boy-hero of a long series of scientific
romances for children, beginning with *Tom Swift and His Motor
Cycle* (1910) and *Tom Swift and His Electric Rifle* (1911). He is
very much in the mould of his dime-novel predecessor Frank
READE. Swift was the creation of publisher Edward L. Stratemeyer.
All the stories appeared under the house name 'Victor
Appleton', although most of the first series was written by Howard
R. Garis. The original series came to an end in 1935, but from
1954 to 1971 a second series appeared: these concerned the
adventures of 'Tom Swift, Jr' and some of them were written by
Harriet S. Adams (Stratemeyer's daughter). A critical work which
deals with the hero is *Tom Swift and Company: Boys' Books by
Stratemeyer and Others* (1982) by John T. Dizcr.

SWISS FAMILY ROBINSON, THE   See under Robinson CRUSOE

SYLVESTER   Spluttering pussy cat (or 'puddy tat') who pursues the
canary Tweety Pie, in a long series of animated films produced by
Warner Brothers. Sylvester first appeared (without Tweety Pie) in
a short cartoon called *A Tale of Two Kitties* (1942). He was voiced
by Mel Blanc (master of such expletives as 'sufferin' succotash!')
and the animators who were primarily responsible for his antics
included Friz Freleng and Chuck Jones. A comic-book entitled
Tweety and Sylvester was published in the 1960s. 'American
essayist S. J. Perelman held Tweety Pie personally responsible for
what he regarded as a reprehensible British habit of referring to all
felines as "puddy tats".' (Patrick Robertson, *Guinness Film Facts
and Feats*.)

SYN, DOCTOR   Eighteenth-century vicar of Dymchurch in Kent –
a pious and broadminded man, with as great a taste for good

Virginian tobacco and a glass of something hot as for the penning of long sermons' – who is in reality the notorious Captain Clegg, pirate and smuggler, sometimes known as The Scarecrow. Like his near-contemporary the SCARLET PIMPERNEL, he leads a double life full of danger and derring-do. He was invented by Russell Thorndike for the novel *Doctor Syn* (1915). Years later Thorndike returned to the character and wrote half a dozen 'prequels': *Dr Syn Returns* (1935; vt *The Scarecrow Rides*,) *The Further Adventures of Dr Syn* (1936), *Dr Syn on the High Seas* (1936), *The Amazing Quest of Dr Syn* (1938), *The Courageous Exploits of Dr Syn* (1939) and *The Shadow of Dr Syn* (1944). A British film, *Dr Syn* (1937; dir. Roy William Neill), starred George Arliss as the notorious parson-cum-pirate. A Disney made-for-TV version, *Dr Syn Alias the Scarecrow* (1962; dir. James Neilson), had Patrick McGoohan in the leading role. Yet another film version of the original novel, this time entitled *Captain Clegg* (1962; dir. Peter Graham Scott), had Peter Cushing in the main part.

SYNTAX, DOCTOR Simple-minded clergyman who appears in several series of humorous illustrations by Thomas Rowlandson, published in English magazines from 1809. They were reissued in book form, with verses by William Combe, as *Tours of Dr Syntax* (1812–21). According to Denis Gifford, Dr Syntax was 'the first continuing cartoon hero' and a 'cult figure, inspiring such merchandising spin-offs as Syntax hats, coats and wigs'. (A schoolmaster called Syntax makes an appearance in Tobias Smollett's novel *The Adventures of Roderick Random* [1748].)

TABU DICK British boy who grows up in the African jungle and becomes a tree-swinging athlete in the tradition of TARZAN. In order to protect him from 'savage natives' the boy's dying father declares Dick to be taboo. The story is told in Patrick Greene's novel *Tabu Dick* (1935). This was originally written for the author's nephews, who had wanted 'a jungle character who could give . . . Tarzan a good fight and that he should be white, unhampered by love affairs and have adventures with elephants, leopards, crocodiles and savage warriors' (quoted in Brian V. Street, *The Savage in Literature*). For mention of other characters in this mould see under BOMBA.

TADZIO See under Gustave von ASCHENBACH

TAILSPIN TOMMY Daredevil pilot who appeared in American newspaper strips from 1928 to 1942. His creators were artist Hal Forrest and writer Glen Chaffin. Tommy, who had a sidekick called Skeeter, was the first hero from the adventure strips to appear in a Hollywood movie serial – *Tailspin Tommy* (1934; dir. Louis Friedlander), with Maurice Murphy in the lead. Five more serials followed, the last four of which starred John Trent as the intrepid Tommy.

TALBOT, LAWRENCE See The WOLF MAN

TALBOYS, GEORGE See under Lady Lucy AUDLEY

TALLEYRAND See under Hildergarde WITHERS

TANNER, ELSIE Leading lady of the long-running British television soap opera 'Coronation Street' (from 1960). An earthy northerner, at one time glamorous but later a matronly figure, she was played by Patricia Phoenix until 1983. The programme which she dominated for so long has been celebrated in the book *Coronation Street: 25 Years, 1960–1985* (1985) edited by Graham Nown. (See also Ena SHARPLES.)

TANNER, JOHN Freethinking hero of George Bernard Shaw's play
Man and Superman: A Comedy and a Philosophy (1903). He is the
author of the 'Revolutionist's Handbook' (which is appended to
the play in its published form). The plot involves Tanner's efforts
to escape the attentions of a young woman, Ann Whitefield, who
nevertheless captures him in the end. The famous Act Three,
'Don Juan in Hell', is often omitted from stage performances since
it is really a play within a play: Tanner becomes Don Juan, and
argues with the devil about human reason, evolution and the Life
Force.

TANQUERAY, PAULA Woman who is driven to suicide by the
prejudices of her new husband's family and friends, in Sir Arthur
Wing Pinero's once-scandalous play *The Second Mrs Tanqueray*
(1893). This sad story of a wife with a 'past' was a great success on
the stage, and has been filmed (1952; dir. Dallas Bower) with
Pamela Brown in the leading role.

TAPLEY, MARK See under Martin CHUZZLEWIT

TARKA An otter who lives in a riverbank in north Devon. The
story of his life, and of how he is eventually hunted to death,
is movingly told in Henry Williamson's *Tarka the Otter* (1927).
The book is one of the most acutely-observed animal stories
ever written, and is not intended for children. A later work of
similar type by the same author is *Salar the Salmon* (1935).
Tarka the Otter has been filmed (1978; dir. David Cobham), with
Peter Ustinov narrating.

TARNOPOL, PETER See under Nathan ZUCKERMAN

TARRANT, VERENA See under Olive CHANCELLOR

TARTARIN Gentleman of Provence who is much given to
exaggerating his own exploits. He believes himself to be a Don
Quixote in a Sancho Panza body. He appears in Alphonse Daudet's
comic novels *Tartarin of Tarascon* (1872), *Tartarin on the Alps*
(1885) and *Port Tarascon* (1890). In the French film *Tartarin de
Tarascon* (1934) the character was played by Raimu (once
described by Orson Welles as 'the greatest actor who ever lived').

TARZAN   Also known as John Clayton, Lord Greystoke: an English
foundling who is reared in the African jungle by 'great apes'. A
hero of enormous strength, agility and intelligence, he communes
with animals, rescues damsels in distress (beginning with his first
love, Jane PORTER), and discovers sundry lost civilizations.
Created by Chicago-born novelist Edgar Rice Burroughs in 1912,
Tarzan first appeared in *All-Story* magazine, since when he has
become perhaps the most famous of all twentieth-century
fictional characters – a universal hero sprung from popularized
versions of Rousseau's and Darwin's ideas. His adventures have
featured in every medium – magazines, books, films, newspaper
strips, radio, comic-books and television series (both live-action and
animated) – but essentially there have been three major
incarnations: the book Tarzan, the movie Tarzan, and the
comic-strip Tarzan.

The twenty-four books by Edgar Rice Burroughs are: *Tarzan
of the Apes* (1914), *The Return of Tarzan* (1915), *The Beasts of
Tarzan* (1916), *The Son of Tarzan* (1917 – chiefly about the
adventures of Tarzan Junior, alias KORAK the Killer), *Tarzan and
the Jewels of Opar* (1918), *Jungle Tales of Tarzan* (1919), *Tarzan the
Untamed* (1920), *Tarzan the Terrible* (1921), *Tarzan and The
Golden Lion* (1923), *Tarzan and the Ant Men* (1924), *Tarzan,
Lord of the Jungle* (1928), *Tarzan and the Lost Empire* (1929),
Tarzan at the Earth's Core (1930 – in which he visits an
underground world), *Tarzan the Invincible* (1931), *Tarzan
Triumphant* (1932), *Tarzan and the City of Gold* (1933), *Tarzan and
the Lion Man* (1934), *Tarzan and the Leopard Men* (1935),
Tarzan's Quest (1936), *Tarzan and the Forbidden City* (1938),
Tarzan the Magnificent (1939), *Tarzan and the 'Foreign Legion'*
(1947), *Tarzan and the Madman* (1964) and *Tarzan and the
Castaways* (1965). The last two titles are posthumous. Sequels
by other hands include an illicit series of five novels by 'Barton
Werper' (Peter T. Scott and Peggy O. Scott). These are: *Tarzan
and the Silver Globe, Tarzan and the Cave City, Tarzan and the
Snake People* (all 1964), and *Tarzan and the Abominable
Snowmen* and *Tarzan and the Winged Invaders* (both 1965). A
sequel which was actually authorized by the Edgar Rice Burroughs
estate is *Tarzan and the Valley of Gold* (1966) by Fritz Leiber
(loosely based on a film script by Claire Huffaker). A more unusual
piece of 'apocrypha' is *The Adventure of the Peerless Peer* (1974) by

Tarzan, in a recent Marvel Comics incarnation

Philip José Farmer, in which Tarzan meets Sherlock HOLMES.
Tarzan appears, in various guises, in a number of other books
by Farmer, including the pornographic *A Feast Unknown* (1969)
where he is called 'Lord Grandrith' and does battle with 'Doc
Caliban' (DOC SAVAGE). Farmer has also written *Tarzan Alive:
A Definitive Biography of Lord Greystoke* (1972), which contains a
fascinating family tree linking Tarzan to numerous other modern
fictional characters. Taking his cues from Farmer, J. T. Edson
(writer of Western stories) has produced a short series of novels,
beginning with *Bunduki* (1975), about the jungle adventures of
Tarzan's adopted son.

The film *Tarzan of the Apes* (1918) starred strong-man Elmo
Lincoln as the hero, and there were various other silent movie
and serial versions througout the 1920s. *Tarzan the Ape Man* (1932;

dir. W. S. Van Dyke) was the first talkie to feature the hero – and the first to star Olympic swimming champion Johnny Weissmuller, who played Tarzan in a further twelve films, perhaps the best of which is *Tarzan and His Mate* (1934; dir. Cedric Gibbons). Meanwhile other film production companies were in competition: Buster Crabbe starred in *Tarzan the Fearless* (1933), and Herman Brix (Bruce Bennett) featured in *The New Adventures of Tarzan* (1935) and a sequel. Lex Barker was a handsome lead in *Tarzan's Magic Fountain* (1949) and four subsequent films, while Gordon Scott was an over-muscled incarnation of the ape-man in *Tarzan's Hidden Jungle* (1955) and the five later movies. Jock Mahoney was a lean and mature hero in *Tarzan Goes to India* (1962) and one other film, while Mike Henry played the protagonist as a hulking brute in *Tarzan and the Valley of Gold* (1966) and two sequels. Ron Ely was an amiable TV Tarzan in an American series made in 1966–9. Miles O'Keefe played Tarzan as a pretty-boy nonentity in the remade *Tarzan the Ape Man* (1981), while Christopher Lambert was splendid in the leading role of *Greystoke: The Legend of Tarzan, Lord of the Apes* (1984; dir. Hugh Hudson). This last is the only film which comes close to doing justice to Burroughs's conception of Tarzan. In addition to all these English-language movies, there have been many Indian films based on the character. They include such intriguing titles as *Tarzan and Delilah* (1964), starring Azad, *Tarzan and King Kong* (1965), starring Dara Singh, and *Tarzan in Fairy Land* (1968), starring Azad once again (apparently this actor has played Tarzan more often than Johnny Weissmuller did). Inevitably, there have also been pornographic additions to the Tarzan saga – for example, the little-known movie *Tarzan and the Valley of Lust* (1976).

The newspaper comic-strip adventures of Tarzan began in 1929, and were initially the work of leading American artist Hal Foster. However, the strips reached their greatest aesthetic heights under the pen of Burne Hogarth, who took over in 1937. Hogarth's Tarzan is magnificently vital, and truer to the character than anything which appeared in films prior to 1984. Hogarth ceased working on the strip in 1950, though Russ Manning and numerous other artists have perpetuated the hero in strips and comic-books to the present day. Some of Hogarth's work is collected in the book *Tarzan, Jungle Lord* (1968), together with an essay by the artist in which he describes Tarzan as 'a shimmering figment of myth and dream'. In 1972 Hogarth published his *Tarzan of the Apes*, a deluxe comic-book version of the first half of Burroughs's novel. The actor James H. Pierce, Edgar Rice Burroughs's son-in-law, played Tarzan on the radio for many years. An animated television series, 'Tarzan, Lord of the Jungle' (1976), featured the voice of Robert Ridgely. The town of Tarzana, near Los Angeles, has been named after Burroughs's creation. In his book *Tarzan and Tradition: Classical Myth in Popular Literature* (1981) the classics professor Erling B. Holtsmark asserts: 'The power that makes us respond to the wanderings of Odysseus is also at work in Burroughs' Tarzan, and the two great popular heroes speak openly to our most cherished fantasies.'

TATE, JESSICA   Scatty leading lady played by Katherine Helmond in the American television comedy series 'Soap' (1977–81). Jessica has been described as 'a spaced-out fluttery idiot' (Tim Brooks and Earle Marsh). Dreadful things are forever happening to the various members of her crazy family. The series, which was intended as the ultimate send-up of soap operas, was created by scriptwriter Susan Harris. A spin-off series, 'Benson' (1979–83), concerned the further career of Benson DuBois, the Tates' black servant.

TEAZLE, SIR PETER AND LADY   See under Charles and Joseph Surface

TEEN, HAROLD   Comic-strip youngster created for the *Chicago Tribune* by cartoonist Carl Ed (from 1919). Harold became famous as America's first 'teenager', a walking lexicon of juvenile slang. His girlfriend was known as Lillums Lovewell. The strip endured for forty years, until Carl Ed's death in 1959. In the silent movie *Harold Teen* (1928; dir. Mervyn Le Roy) the hero was played by Arthur Lake (who later impersonated another comic-strip favourite, Dagwood Bumstead – see Blondie). In the talkie of the same title (1934; dir. Murray Roth) Hal LeRoy took the role of Harold.

TELLWRIGHT, ANNA   Repressed heroine of Arnold Bennett's novel *Anna of the Five Towns* (1902). Daughter of a mean-minded Nonconformist preacher, she grows up in the industrial 'Potteries'

of northern England. She becomes engaged to marry a respectable businessman – but really loves another man, Willie Price. Her inability to oppose her father's will leads to tragedy. The novel has been serialized on BBC television (1985), with Linsey Beauchamp as Anna.

TEMPLAR, SIMON   See The SAINT

TEMPLE, CHARLOTTE   Heroine of Mrs Susanna Haswell Rowson's sentimental novel *Charlotte: A Tale of Truth* (1791; vt *Charlotte Temple*), which has been through more than 200 editions. She is seduced by a dashing British officer, Montraville, and comes to grief. In the words of Leslie A. Fiedler, this was 'the first book by an American to move American readers' and it provoked many imitations and emulations. Mrs Rowson's own sequel to the story is the posthumously-published *Lucy Temple* (1828; vt *Charlotte's Daughter, or The Three Orphans*).

TEMPLE, PAUL   English novelist-detective created by Francis Durbridge for the radio serial 'Send for Paul Temple' (1938) and its many sequels which were broadcast over a period of thirty years. The first actor to play Temple was Hugh Morton. The character soon reappeared in novels, also written by Durbridge. Book titles include *Send for Paul Temple* (1938), *Paul Temple and the Front Page Men* (1939), *News of Paul Temple* (1940), *Paul Temple Intervenes* (1944), *Send for Paul Temple Again!* (1948), *Paul Temple and the Kelby Affair* (1970), *Paul Temple and the Harkdale Robbery* (1970), *The Geneva Mystery* (1971) and *The Curzon Case* (1972). There are also two novels, co-written by Francis Durbridge and Douglas Rutherford, which carry the byline 'Paul Temple' and are supposedly written by the character: *The Tyler Mystery* (1957) and *East of Algiers* (1959). Temple became the leading fictional detective on BBC radio during the 1940s, and then graduated to films. Movies include *Calling Paul Temple* (1948; dir. Maclean Rogers), *Paul Temple's Triumph* (1950) and *Paul Temple Returns* (1952), all of which starred John Bentley. The hero was also played by Francis Matthews in a British television series of the 1960s.

TEMPLER, PETER   See under Nicholas JENKINS

TERRY AND THE PIRATES   See Terry LEE

TESMAN   See under Hedda GABLER

TEVYE   Impoverished village milkman who wishes to find good husbands for his daughters. He and his family live in the pre-revolutionary Ukraine, where they are threatened by a pogrom. Tevye first appeared in short stories by the Yiddish writer Sholem Aleichem (Solomon J. Rabinowitz), who died in 1916. He became world-famous as the leading character of Joseph Stein's stage musical *The Fiddler on the Roof* (1964), which has music and lyrics by Jerry Bock and Sheldon Harnick. Tevye was played on the Broadway stage by Zero Mostel. The play has been filmed (1971; dir. Norman Jewison), with the Israeli actor Chaim Topol in the role of Tevye.

THATCHER, BECKY   See under Tom SAWYER

THATCHER, JOHN PUTNAM   Wall Street banker who is also an amateur detective. He is the hero of a series of crime novels by Emma Lathen (Mary J. Latis and Martha Hennissart). Thatcher's creators have said 'there is nothing on God's earth a banker can't get into'. The titles are: *Banking on Death* (1961), *A Place for Murder* (1963), *Accounting for Murder* (1964), *Murder Makes the Wheels Go Round* (1966), *Death Shall Overcome* (1966), *Murder Against the Grain* (1967), *A Stitch in Time* (1968), *Come to Dust* (1968), *When in Greece* (1969), *Murder to Go* (1969), *Pick Up Sticks* (1970), *Ashes to Ashes* (1971), *The Longer the Thread* (1971), *Murder Without Icing* (1972), *Sweet and Low* (1974), *By Hook or by Crook* (1975), *Double, Double, Oil and Trouble* (1978), *Going for the Gold* (1981) and *Green Grow the Dollars* (1982).

THING, THE   See under Mr FANTASTIC

THINKING MACHINE, THE   Real name Professor Augustus S. F. X. Van Dusen, an intellectual detective invented by American writer Jacques Futrelle for his famous short story 'The Problem of Cell 13' (1905). Futrelle (who died on board the *Titanic* in 1912) wrote another forty stories about the character, and these are collected in *The Thinking Machine* (1907; vt *The Problem of*

Cell 13), *The Thinking Machine on the Case* (1908; vt *The Professor on the Case*) and the posthumous volumes *Best Thinking Machine Detective Stories* (1973) and *Great Cases of the Thinking Machine* (1976). The Professor also appears in one novel, *The Chase of the Golden Plate* (1906).

THOMPSON, SADIE   Attractive young woman of loose morals who arrives on a South Sea island during the rainy season. She drives a sexually repressed Scottish missionary into a frenzy which ends with his suicide. Sadie Thompson appears in the short story 'Rain' (1921) by W. Somerset Maugham, which was turned into a successful play by John Colton and Clemence Randolph. It was filmed as *Sadie Thompson* (1928; dir. Raoul Walsh), with Gloria Swanson in the title role. Later film versions of the story include *Rain* (1932; dir. Lewis Milestone), with Joan Crawford, and *Miss Sadie Thompson* (1953; dir. Curtis Bernhardt), with Rita Hayworth.

THORN, DAMIEN   Satanic child who kills his various guardians in the horror film *The Omen* (1976; dir. Richard Donner) and its sequels *Damien: Omen II* (1978; dir. Don Taylor) and *The Final Conflict* (1981; dir. Graham Baker). In the first of these the angelic little Antichrist was played by child actor Harvey Stephens. The script was by David Seltzer, who has also written the novels of the films.

THORNDYKE, JOHN   Scientific detective invented by R. Austin Freeman for a series of novels and short stories, beginning with *The Red Thumb Mark* (1907). He is a doctor of law as well as an expert in medicine, and he sometimes works as an investigator for an assurance company. Known as the 'Great Fathomer', Dr Thorndyke is meticulous in his application of forensic methods to the bizarre mysteries that he encounters. His later ratiocinations are described in *John Thorndyke's Cases* (1909), *The Eye of Osiris* (1911; vt *The Vanishing Man*), *The Mystery of 31, New Inn* (1912), *The Singing Bone* (1912), *A Silent Witness* (1914), *Helen Vardon's Confession* (1922), *Dr Thorndyke's Case Book* (1923; vt *The Blue Scarab*), *The Cat's Eye* (1923), *The Mystery of Angelina Frood* (1924), *The Shadow of the Wolf* (1925), *The Puzzle Lock* (1925), *The D'Arblay Mystery* (1926), *The Magic Casket* (1927), *A*

Certain Dr Thorndyke (1927), As a Thief in the Night (1928), Mr Pottermack's Oversight (1930), Pontifex, Son and Thorndyke (1931), When Rogues Fall Out (1932; vt Dr Thorndyke's Discovery), Dr Thorndyke Intervenes (1933), For the Defence: Dr Thorndyke (1934), The Penrose Mystery (1936), Felo de Se? (1937; vt Death at the Inn), The Stoneware Monkey (1938), Mr Polton Explains (1940) and The Jacob Street Mystery (1942; vt The Unconscious Witness). It seems there have been no films based on Thorndyke's adventures, but he did appear in the British television series 'The Rivals of Sherlock Holmes' (1972–3), which took its inspiration from a pair of anthologies edited by Sir Hugh Greene. It is evident from Sir Hugh's introduction to the first of these books that Dr Thorndyke is his favourite among the many 'Rivals'.

THREE JUST MEN, THE   See The FOUR JUST MEN

THREEPWOOD, CLARENCE   See Lord EMSWORTH

THURSBY, ROGER   Green young barrister in the humorous novels Brothers in Law (1955), Friends at Court (1956) and Sober as a Judge (1957) by the English comic writer Henry Cecil. In the film Brothers in Law (1957; dir. Roy Boulting) Thursby was played by Ian Carmichael. A BBC television series of the same title (early 1960s) was scripted by Denis Norden and Frank Muir; it had Richard Briers in the lead role.

TIBBS, VIRGIL   Black police detective who overcomes white racial prejudice in a small Southern town. He appears in John Ball's award-winning mystery novel In The Heat of the Night (1964), and its sequels: The Cool Cottontail (1966), Johnny Get Your Gun (1969), Five Pieces of Jade (1972), The Eyes of the Buddha (1976) and Then Came Violence (1980). In the Heat of the Night was made into an Oscar-winning film (1967; dir. Norman Jewison) starring Sidney Poitier. Two film sequels, also starring Poitier, are They Call Me Mr Tibbs (1970; dir. Gordon Douglas) and The Organization (1971; dir. Don Medford).

TIETJENS, CHRISTOPHER   Edwardian Englishman of high ideals who goes off to fight in World War I. His story is told in Ford Madox

Ford's tetralogy of novels, known collectively as *Parade's End*: *Some Do Not* (1924), *No More Parades* (1925), *A Man Could Stand Up* (1926) and *Last Post* (1928). Anthony Burgess has written: 'Tietjens is, for all his static monolithic qualities, one of the great characters of modern English fiction and might be – if he were better known – one of the great myths of a society that seems to be losing its bearings.'

TIGE   See under Buster BROWN

TIGER TIM   Inoffensive little tiger, leader of the Bruin Boys. He has the distinction of being the oldest British comic-strip character still in existence, having first appeared in the *Daily Mirror* in 1904. He was the creation of artist Julius Stafford Baker. For a long time Tim and his friends appeared in the children's paper *Rainbow*. Since 1956 he has appeared in *Jack and Jill* and in numerous annuals.

TIGGER   See under WINNIE-THE-POOH

TIGGY-WINKLE, MRS   See under PETER RABBIT

TIK-TOK   See under Dorothy GALE

TILNEY, HENRY   See under Catherine MORLAND

TIME TRAVELLER, THE   Nameless hero of H. G. Wells's memorable short novel *The Time Machine* (1895). He builds his own machine for travelling the time stream, returns from a trip to the year 802,701 to recount his terrifying experiences to a group of friends, then disappears once more into far futurity. The open ending to the tale has provoked a number of people into writing sequels. For example, the German writer Egon Friedell published his *The Return of the Time Machine* in 1946. Later sequels by other hands include *The Space Machine* (1976) by Christopher Priest (in which the Time Traveller visits Mars) and *Morlock Night* (1979) by K. W. Jeter (in which the evil Morlocks from 802,701 invade the London of the 1890s). A film, *The Time Machine* (1960; dir. George Pal), starred Rod Taylor as the Time Traveller. The TV movie of the same title (1978; dir. Henning Schellerup) bears little resemblance to Wells's story.

TIN-TIN   Plucky young adventurer, a Francophile equivalent of
Terry LEE, in comic-strips by the Belgian artist Hergé (Georges
Rémi). Tin-Tin is a cub reporter who has a quiff of red hair, and
is accompanied in all his travels by a faithful dog, Milou (called
Snowy in the English translations). He was invented by Hergé in
1929, and his exploits have been reprinted around the world in book
form. The last new title to be published was *Tin-Tin et les Picaros*
(1976). The character has also appeared in a French animated
television series and in at least two feature-length cartoon films,
Tin-Tin and the Temple of the Sun (1969) and *Tin-Tin and the Lake
of Sharks* (1972).

TIN WOODMAN   See under Dorothy GALE

TINKER   See under Sexton BLAKE

TINKER BELL   See under PETER PAN

TINY TIM   See under Ebenezer SCROOGE

TIP   See under Dorothy GALE

TISCHBEIN, EMIL   Boy hero of Erich Kästner's classic juvenile
novel *Emil and the Detectives* (1929). The villainous Herr
Grundeis steals Emil's money while he is on a train journey, and
Emil enlists the help of a resourceful band of young Berliners in
order to catch the criminal. A whole genre of children's detective
fiction was established by this book, which has been very popular
in English translation. Kästner himself wrote a sequel, *Emil and
the Three Twins* (1934). The original novel was filmed in
Germany in 1931 (dir. Gerhard Lamprecht), with a script by Billy
Wilder. Later film versions include one made in Britain in 1934 (dir.
Milton Rosmer) and another made in West Germany in 1954 (dir.
R. A. Stemmle). The most recent movie, a Disney production,
was made in 1964 (dir. Peter Tewksbury).

TOAD OF TOAD HALL   Perhaps the best known of the animal
characters in Kenneth Grahame's well-loved children's novel,
The Wind in the Willows (1908). Toad, who drives a motor car
and lives in the 'finest house on the whole river', has adventures

Toad, as drawn by *E. H. Shepard*

with his friends Mole, Rat and Badger. The book was turned into a musical play, *Toad of Toad Hall* (1930) by A. A. Milne, and has gained enduring popularity on the stage and British radio. Recent sequels by other hands are the books *Wild Wood* (1981) by Jan Needle and *A Fresh Wind in The Willows* by Dixon Scott (1983). An animated film version of *The Wind in the Willows* was made by the Walt Disney company as half of the two-part feature *Ichabod and Mr Toad* (1949; dir. Ben Sharpsteen). Another animated version was broadcast on British television in 1983, and led to a subsequent series based on the characters (1984–5), with David Jason giving voice to Toad. A BBC radio play, *The Killing of Mr Toad* (1984) by David Gooderson, concerned the domestic life of Toad's creator, Kenneth Grahame.

TOBY, UNCLE See Toby SHANDY

TODD, SWEENEY 'Demon barber' who slits his customers' throats and disposes of their bodies by having them made into meat pies. Now regarded as a comic/horrific figure of British folklore, the ghastly Mr Todd is said to be based on a French murderer of fourteenth-century legend. Under his present name, the character first appeared in Thomas Peckett Prest's ninety-two-part novel *The String of Pearls, or The Barber of Fleet Street* (about 1840). This was subsequently adapted into the most famous of all Victorian stage melodramas, *A String of Pearls, or The Fiend of Fleet Street* (1847; later known as *Sweeney Todd, The Demon Barber of Fleet Street*) by George Dibdin Pitt. There were countless retellings and adaptations of Prest's (and Pitt's) delightfully gruesome tale throughout the nineteenth century, and several film versions were made in the early years of the present century – culminating in a 1936 talkie which starred the appropriately-named Tod Slaughter as the evil Sweeney. Latterly, the hoary melodrama has formed the basis of an ambitious stage musical, *Sweeney Todd* (1979), with music by Stephen Sondheim and lyrics by Hugh Wheeler (this successful production was inspired by a recent stage adaptation of the Sweeney Todd story by Christopher Bond).

TOFF, THE   Real name the Honourable Richard Rollison, a young man 'down from Cambridge with half a million and a hatred of dullness'. He is the suave roguish hero of *Introducing the Toff* (1938), *The Toff Steps Out* (1939), *The Toff Goes On* (1939),*The Toff Breaks In* (1940), *Here Comes The Toff* (1940), *The Toff Goes to Market* (1942), *The Toff on Ice* (1947), *Call the Toff* (1953), *Vote for the Toff* (1971) and many other crime novels by John Creasey. He first appeared in *The Thriller* magazine in 1933 (where he served as a stand-in for the SAINT), and later featured in more than fifty books which continued to appear until Creasey's death in 1973. There have been a couple of low-budget British films about the character: *Salute the Toff* (1951) and *Hammer the Toff* (1952).

TOM   Young chimney-sweep who is ill-treated by his master, Mr Grimes. Shamed by the unexpected sight of himself in a mirror, Tom runs away, dives into a river and is transformed into a 'water-baby'. He travels out to sea, where he visits the magical Isle of St Brendan and meets the perfect teacher, Mrs Doasyouwouldbedoneby. Tom's fantastic story is recounted in Charles Kingsley's *The Water-Babies, a Fairy Tale for a Land Baby* (1863). Inspired by Kingsley's Christian Socialism, the book became extremely popular and influential. It helped put an end to the practice of using children as chimney-sweeps. There have

been many stage adaptations and several film versions of Tom's
adventures. The most recent movie, *The Water Babies* (1978;
dir. Lionel Jeffries), had Tommy Pender in the leading role.

TOM AND JERRY   There are two famous sets of characters known
as Tom and Jerry. The original pair were young bloods in the
novel *Life in London, or the Day and Night Scenes of Jerry
Hawthorn Esq. and His Elegant Friend Corinthian Tom* (1820–21)
by Pierce Egan. According to the critic Louis James, the book 'had
an immense popularity – some sixty-seven derivative publications
have been recorded.' A sequel by Egan himself is *The 'Finish' to
the Adventures of Tom and Jerry* (1828).

   The twentieth-century Tom and Jerry are a cartoon cat and
mouse in a long series of short animated films produced for MGM
by Fred Quimby. The first cartoon to feature the pair was entitled
Puss Gets the Boot (1937). The artists who originally drew these
very successful films were William Hanna and Joe Barbera. During
the 1940s and 1950s the series won a number of Academy
Awards, although it has also been criticized for its violence. There
has been an insipid television version, 'The Tom and Jerry Show'
(from 1975).

TOM, UNCLE   Old black slave, the saintly hero of the world's
bestselling propaganda novel, *Uncle Tom's Cabin, or Life
Among the Lowly* (1851–2) by Harriet Beecher Stowe. He befriends
his owner's daughter, LITTLE EVA, who dies in one of the novel's
most lachrymose scenes. Other females who play an important
part in Tom's life are the quadroon ELIZA and the little black
girl TOPSY. Later Tom refuses to reveal the whereabouts of some
runaway slaves, and is whipped to death by the henchmen of
his villainous new master Simon LEGREE. The novel's unparalleled
popularity led to countless stage versions which became a genre in
their own right – the so-called 'Tom plays'. There were also a
number of sequels by other hands, books which bore such titles as
Uncle Tom's Cabin As It Is and *Uncle Tom in England, or Proof
that White's Black*. Many silent film versions of Stowe's novel
appeared in the early years of the American cinema, but there has
been a surprising reluctance to film the story since the coming
of the talkies (the exception is a German production made in
1965). The black American novelist Richard Wright entitled his

first book of short stories *Uncle Tom's Children* (1938). Latterly, Uncle Tom's name has been turned into a term of abuse among black people – it is applied to those who show subservience to whites – and this usage has been reinforced by James Baldwin's angry essay, 'Everybody's Protest Novel', which describes *Uncle Tom's Cabin* as 'a very bad novel . . . [a work of] self-righteous, virtuous sentimentality'.

TOMMY Deaf, dumb and blind kid who develops extra-sensory abilities which enable him to play 'a mean pinball'. He appears in the 'rock opera' *Tommy* (1970) by Pete Townshend and The Who. Conceived as a long-playing record and a stage show, it was later filmed by Ken Russell (1975), with Roger Daltrey in the role of Tommy.

TONTO See under The LONE RANGER

TOOTSIE See under Judy FOSTER

TOPAZE Honest French schoolmaster who falls in with some crooked businessmen, in Marcel Pagnol's very successful play *Topaze* (1928). The story has been filmed at least five times: in 1932 (dir. Louis Gasnier); in 1933 (dir. Harry d'Abbadie d'Arrast), with John Barrymore; in 1936 (dir. Marcel Pagnol); in 1951 (dir. Pagnol), with Fernandel; and in 1961 (as *Mr Topaze*; vt *I Like Money*; dir. Peter Sellers), with the director in the starring role. (None of these should be confused with Alfred Hitchcock's thriller movie *Topaz* [1969], which is based on a novel by Leon Uris and bears no relation to the Pagnol play.)

TOPOLINO See MICKEY MOUSE

TOPPER, COSMO Staid banker who is the hero of Thorne Smith's humorous novels *Topper* (1926; vt *The Jovial Ghosts*) and *Topper Takes a Trip* (1932). His life is transformed when he meets two mischievous ghosts. The film *Topper* (1937; dir. Norman Z. McLeod) starred Roland Young. It was followed by *Topper Takes a Trip* (1939; dir. McLeod) and *Topper Returns* (1941; dir. Roy Del Ruth), also with Young. The American television series 'Topper' (1953–4) had Leo G. Carroll in the lead role, and a TV movie of the same title (1979; dir. Charles Dubin) had Jack Warden.

TOPSY   Little orphan slave-girl in Harriet Beecher Stowe's *Uncle Tom's Cabin* (1851–2). She is famous for her assertion: 'Never was born, never had no father, nor mother, nor nothin'. I 'spect I growed.' Hence the common expression 'like Topsy, [he, she or it] just growed.' See also ELIZA, Uncle TOM, Simon LEGREE and LITTLE EVA.

TORRANCE, JACK   Alcoholic writer in Stephen King's horror novel *The Shining* (1977). He takes a temporary job as caretaker of a lonely mountain hotel, and goes to spend a winter there with his wife and young son. The hotel is 'haunted' by the memories of old murders, and Jack's alcoholism returns with a vengeance, threatening his sanity and the lives of his family. In the film of the novel (1980; dir. Stanley Kubrick) Torrance was played by Jack Nicholson. David Thomson devotes a chapter of his book *Suspects* (1985; see under George BAILEY) to the unfortunate Jack Torrance.

TOSCA, FLORIA   Italian singer, the tragic heroine of Victorien Sardou's historical play *La Tosca* (1887). She murders Baron Scarpia, the police chief who is responsible for condemning her lover, the painter Mario Cavaradossi, to death. This play formed the basis of Giacomo Puccini's great opera of the same title (1900; libretto by Giuseppe Giacosa and Luigi Illica).

TOWNSEND, MORRIS   See under Catherine SLOPER

TRACY, DICK   Newspaper comic-strip detective created by Chester Gould (from 1931). By the late 1930s Gould's strip was widely syndicated and also appearing in comic-book reprints. In his heyday Tracy was undoubtedly the best-known hardboiled 'dick' in the USA. He was played by Ralph Byrd in four cinema serials produced by Republic studios: *Dick Tracy* (1937), *Dick Tracy Returns* (1938), *Dick Tracy's G-Men* (1939) and *Dick Tracy vs. Crime, Inc.* (1941). Morgan Conway played him in two feature films, *Dick Tracy, Detective* (1945; dir. William Berke) and *Dick Tracy vs. Cueball* (1946; dir. Gordon Douglas), before the redoubtable Ralph Byrd returned to the role in two more movies, *Dick Tracy's Dilemma* (1947; dir. John Rawlins) and the spendidly-titled *Dick Tracy Meets Gruesome* (1947; dir. Rawlins). Byrd continued to play the hero in the short-lived television

series 'Dick Tracy' (1950–51). This was followed by an animated
TV series (1960). Tracy also appeared on the American radio
between the mid-1930s and late 1940s, and in a stage musical,
Dick Tracy (1970), by Michael Colicchio. To cap it all, it was
announced in the 1970s that the animator Ralph Bakshi intended
to make a feature film entitled *Dick Tracy, Frozen, Fried, and
Buried Alive*, but it seems this project has not come to fruition.

TRAILL, ARCHIE   See under Vincent PERRIN

TRAMPAS   See under The VIRGINIAN

TRANSOME, HAROLD   See under Felix HOLT

TRANT, ELIZABETH   See under Inigo JOLLIFANT

TRENCHARD, JOHN   Teenage narrator of J. Meade Falkner's
adventure novel *Moonfleet* (1898). The story is set on the Dorset
coast, where young Trenchard and the innkeeper Elzevir Block
become involved with a gang of smugglers. The film of the novel
(1955; dir. Fritz Lang) is a none-too-faithful rendition, with Jon
Whiteley as the boy hero. In the BBC television version (1984) John
Trenchard was played by Adam Godley.

TRENT, HELEN   Resourceful heroine of one of American radio's
longest-running soap operas, 'The Romance of Helen Trent'
(1933–60). Helen is a glamorous and apparently unageing widow
of thirty-five, who constantly fends off ardent suitors. She was
voiced by Virginia Clark until 1943, and by Julie Stevens thereafter.

TRENT, NELL   See LITTLE NELL

TRENT, PHILIP   Painter turned amateur detective in E. C.
Bentley's mischievously-titled novel *Trent's Last Case* (1912).
Although earlier cases are referred to they have not been recorded.
Trent's later exploits are to be found in the novel *Trent's Own
Case* (1936; written by Bentley in collaboration with H. Warner
Allen) and in the collection of short stories *Trent Intervenes* (1938).
In the film *Trent's Last Case* (1952; dir. Herbert Wilcox) the hero
was played by Michael Wilding. A BBC radio dramatization of
the same novel (1986) had Martin Jarvis as Trent.

TRIBOULET See RIGOLETTO

TRIFFIDS, THE The most celebrated vegetables in fiction. Giant
ambulatory plants equipped with lethal stings, they feature in *The
Day of the Triffids* (1951; vt *Revolt of the Triffids*), a science
fiction novel by John Wyndham (John Beynon Harris). After the
majority of the human race has been blinded by mysterious
'fireworks' in outer space, the Triffids come into their own,
driving the hero and his small group of friends to a refuge on the
Isle of Wight. The novel has been filmed (1963; dir. Steve Sekely)
and serialized on BBC television (1981).

TRILBY See Trilby O'FERRAL

TRIM, CORPORAL See under Toby SHANDY

TROS Sword-swinging hero of a series of fantastic historical
adventures by the English-born American writer Talbot Mundy
(William Lancaster Gribbon). Tros, who is a literary cousin of
CONAN the Barbarian, first appeared in a serial which ran in
Adventure magazine in 1925–6 (published in book form as *Tros
of Samothrace* [1934]). He reappears in the sequels *Queen Cleopatra*
(1929) and *Purple Pirate* (1935). These books have been reprinted
in paperback under various titles during the 1960s and 1970s.

TROTWOOD, BETSEY See under David COPPERFIELD

TROUT, KILGORE Decrepit, impecunious science fiction writer
who has wonderful ideas even though he cannot write for sour
apples. He first appears as a minor character in Kurt Vonnegut's
novel *God Bless You, Mr Rosewater* (1965): 'Trout, the author
of eighty-seven paperback books, was a very poor man, and
unknown outside the science-fiction field.' He reappears in
Vonnegut's best-known work, *Slaughterhouse-5* (1969), where he
is the favourite living author of that novel's hero, Billy PILGRIM. He
goes on to play a leading role in *Breakfast of Champions* (1973)
and a more retiring one in *Jailbird* (1979). In *Galapagos* (1985) –
which is narrated by his son, Leon Trout – he features briefly as
a ghost. In 1975 there appeared an amusing science-fiction novel,
Venus on the Half-Shell, which carried the byline 'Kilgore Trout'.

Many readers believed this to be by Kurt Vonnegut, but in fact it was revealed to be the work of that arch-trickster Philip José Farmer. The latter has also written an 'interview' with the great man, 'The Obscure Life and Hard Times of Kilgore Trout' (1973).

TROWBRIDGE, DOCTOR   See under Jules DE GRANDIN

TROY, FRANCIS   See under Bathsheba EVERDENE

TRUNNION, HAWSER   See under Peregrine PICKLE

TUBBS, RICARDO   See under Sonny CROCKETT

TUBBS, WASHINGTON   See under Captain EASY

TUGBOAT ANNIE   Tough female skipper created by writer Norman Reilly Raine for a long series of stories which appeared in the *Saturday Evening Post*. In the film *Tugboat Annie* (1933; dir. Mervyn Le Roy) she was played by Marie Dressler. Later films are *Tugboat Annie Sails Again* (1940), with Marjorie Rambeau, and *Captain Tugboat Annie* (1945), with Jane Darwell. A Canadian television series, *The Adventures of Tugboat Annie* (1956), starred Minerva Urecal.

TULKINGHORN   See under Inspector BUCKET

TULLIVER, MAGGIE   Heroine of *The Mill on the Floss* (1860), a novel by George Eliot (Mary Ann Evans). A spirited and intelligent girl, she grows up with her beloved but unimaginative brother Tom at Dorlcote Mill on the river Floss. As the result of an ill-judged love-affair, she quarrels with Tom and is barred from his house. When the river floods she attempts to rescue her brother, and the two are reconciled briefly before both are drowned. The novel was filmed (1937; dir. Tim Whelan), with Geraldine Fitzgerald in the lead. It has also been serialized on British television.

TUPMAN, TRACY   See under Samuel PICKWICK

TURANDOT, PRINCESS   Beautiful but bloodthirsty daughter of the Emperor of China, in Giacomo Puccini's unfinished opera

Turandot (1926). Her heart is melted by Calaf, the Unknown Prince, but not before Liu, a loyal slave-girl, has died to protect him. The libretto is by Giuseppe Adami and Renato Simoni, based on a play by Count Carlo Gozzi (1762). Gozzi's drama had already formed the basis of a musical play by Friedrich von Schiller and Carl Maria von Weber (1809) and of an opera by Ferruccio Busoni (1917). But it is Puccini's version (completed by Franco Alfano) which is now regarded as definitive, despite the fact that 'the story is perhaps the most repulsive that any opera audience is regularly called on to enjoy . . . The love-triumph of Turandot and Calaf is a triumph based on the acceptance of the torture and death of Liu, the only character of the story who shows any positive action for good' (according to Arthur Jacobs and Stanley Sadie, *The Pan Book of Opera*). There is also a ballet, *Princess Turandot* (1944), with music by Gottfried von Einem and choreography by Tatjana Gsovsky.

TURNER, DAN   Private-eye who is known as 'Hollywood's hottest hawkshaw'. He specializes in working for movie-industry clients, and is a master of slang, sexual innuendo and the wisecrack. Turner was invented by Robert Leslie Bellem for a series of short stories which appeared in the pulp magazine *Spicy Detective* from 1934. Later the character graduated to his own magazine, *Dan Turner, Hollywood Detective*, which ran from 1942 to 1950. Bellem wrote many hundreds of Dan Turner stories for these publications, and some of them are collected in the posthumous volume *Dan Turner, Hollywood Detective* (1983; edited by John Wooley).

TURPIN, JANE   Anarchic little girl who appears in a series of comic novels for children by the British writer Evadne Price: *Just Jane* (1928), *Meet Jane* (1930), *Enter – Jane* (1932), *Jane the Fourth* (1937), *Jane the Sleuth* (1939), *Jane the Unlucky* (1939), *Jane the Popular* (1939), *Jane the Patient* (1940), *Jane Gets Busy* (1940) and *Jane at War* (1947). According to the critic Mary Cadogan, 'Jane is the quintessential, unscholarly outdoor child who manages always to make exciting things happen all around her' (*Book and Magazine Collector*, June 1985). Evadne Price's Jane has frequently been described as a female equivalent of Richmal Crompton's William BROWN.

TUTT, EPHRAIM   Shrewd American lawyer who appears in a series
of short stories and novels by Arthur Train (former Attorney-General
for Massachusetts). Many of the tales were first published in the
Saturday Evening Post, and are collected in the following volumes:
Tutt and Mr Tutt (1920), *The Hermit of Turkey Hollow* (1921),
Tut, Tut! Mr Tutt (1923), *Page Mr Tutt* (1926), *When Tutt Meets
Tutt* (1927), *The Adventures of Ephraim Tutt* (1930), *Tutt for Tutt*
(1934), *Mr Tutt Takes the Stand* (1936), *Old Man Tutt* (1938), *Mr
Tutt Comes Home* (1941), *Yankee Lawyer – Autobiography of
Ephraim Tutt* (1943), *Mr Tutt Finds a Way* (1945) and the
posthumous *Mr Tutt at His Best* (edited by Harold R. Medina,
1961). An omnibus volume of Mr Tutt's cases became required
reading in some American law schools during the 1930s and
1940s.

TWEETY PIE   See under SYLVESTER

TWIST, OLIVER   Young orphan hero of Charles Dickens's
celebrated novel *Oliver Twist* (1838). Raised in a workhouse,
Oliver falls into the hands of the wily FAGIN, master of a band of
London pickpockets. He comes under the influence of the even
more villainous Bill SIKES, before his true parentage is discovered
and all ends happily. This has always been the best known of
Dickens's tales – the scene where Oliver asks for more gruel is a
part of British childhood folklore – and the plagiarisms,
adaptations and sequels have been numerous, ranging from an
anonymous 'Oliver Twiss' of 1839 (twice as long as Dickens's
original) to a recent book, *The Further Adventures of Oliver Twist*
(1980) by David Butler and David Snodin. There were many
stage versions of the story in Dickens's own lifetime – indeed,
Dickens himself made the death of Bill Sikes one of his principal
performance pieces when he undertook dramatized readings late
in his career. The very first feature films to be made in Britain
and America (if one defines a feature film as a movie more than
one hour in length) were versions of *Oliver Twist* (both 1912). Later
silent films were made in 1916 and 1922. The first talkie
adaptation (1933; dir. William Cowan) had Dickie Moore in the lead
role. The definitive film version (1948; dir. David Lean) starred
John Howard Davies as Oliver and Alec Guinness as Fagin. Since
then the novel has been adapted by Lionel Bart as a long-running

stage musical, *Oliver!* (1960), and this in turn has been filmed (1968; dir. Carol Reed) with Mark Lester as Oliver and Ron Moody as Fagin. There have been a number of serial versions of *Oliver Twist* on British television (the most recent in 1985, with Ben Rodska as Oliver), and an animated version has been made for American TV (1975).

TWITCHETT, TABITHA   See under PETER RABBIT

TWO-SHOES, MARGERY   See under GOODY TWO-SHOES

TYLER, TIM   Plucky juvenile hero of an American newspaper comic-strip drawn by Lyman Young (with the uncredited assistance of Alex Raymond and Nat Edson). The strip *Tim Tyler's Luck* ran for many years from 1928. It formed the basis of one of the most exciting cinema serials, also entitled *Tim Tyler's Luck* (1937; dir. Ford Beebe), which had Frank Thomas, Jr as the boy searching for his missing father in the African jungle.

TYLER, TOBY   Orphan who runs away from the home of his authoritarian uncle and tries to make a new life with the members of a travelling circus. He appears in James Otis Kaler's novel *Toby Tyler, or Ten Weeks with a Circus* (1881), a popular American classic of children's literature. The story was filmed by the Walt Disney company (1960; dir. Charles Barton), with Kevin Corcoran as Toby.

TYRONE, JAMES   Ageing actor who is driven to despair by his wife's drug addiction and his own inadequacies, in Eugene O'Neill's massive play *Long Day's Journey into Night* (written *circa* 1941; first performed 1956). The action is set on a single day in 1912, and the characters are based on the playwright's own parents, James and Ella O'Neill. In the film of the play (1961; dir. Sidney Lumet) Tyrone was played by Ralph Richardson. Memorable stage productions have starred Laurence Olivier and Jack Lemmon. (O'Neill also used the name James Tyrone for a character in another play, *A Moon for the Misbegotten* [1947].)

U

UBU   Grotesque anti-hero of Alfred Jarry's surrealistic play *Ubu Roi* (1896) and its sequel *Ubu Enchainé* (1899). Ubu is supposedly based on an authoritarian schoolmaster, and the first of these plays caused a scandal in France. In the words of the critic Kenneth McLeish, Ubu is 'a monstrous bourgeois vulgarian, a figure of gargantuan stupidity and scatological excess, the beast in humankind made flesh'. There has been a cartoon film, *Ubu Roi* (1976), by the distinguished Polish animator Jan Lenica.

UHURA, LIEUTENANT   See under James T. KIRK

UKRIDGE, STANLEY FEATHERSTONEHAUGH   Selfish rogue created by P. G. Wodehouse. He first appears as the owner of a poultry farm in the early novel *Love Among the Chickens* (1906). Wodehouse revived him almost two decades later for the series of short stories collected in *Ukridge* (1924). Other stories about this appalling man are included in *Lord Emsworth and Others* (1937), *Eggs, Beans and Crumpets* (1940), *Nothing Serious* (1950), *A Few Quick Ones* (1959) and *Plum Pie* (1966). All the stories are reassembled in the omnibus *The World of Ukridge* (1975). According to Richard Usborne: 'Ukridge is a thief, a blackmailer, a liar and a sponge.' He is also very funny.

UMBOPA   Stalwart black servant and guide to Sir Henry Curtis and Allan QUATERMAIN in H. Rider Haggard's novel of adventure *King Solomon's Mines* (1885). He carries the birthmark which eventually proves him to be the long-lost king of the Kukuanas (guardians of Solomon's legendary treasure mines). Umbopa is frequently confused with UMSLOPOGAAS. They are not the same person. In the best film of *King Solomon's Mines* (1937; dir. Robert Stevenson) Umbopa was played by Paul Robeson.

UMSLOPOGAAS   Mighty Zulu warrior who carries a battle-axe called 'Woodpecker', with which he taps men's skulls. Umslopogaas first appeared in H. Rider Haggard's exciting lost-race novel *Allan Quatermain* (1887), wherein he dies heroically in the culminating battle scene. Haggard then went back to tell of the character's early life in *Nada the Lily* (1892). Finally, he revived Umslopogaas once more for his late novel *She and Allan* (1921), in which he brings together the noble but bloodthirsty Zulu, the white hunter Allan QUATERMAIN, and the near-immortal queen who is known as SHE-WHO-MUST-BE-OBEYED. In his essay 'Rider Haggard's Secret' (1951), Graham Greene stated that the image of Umslopogaas single-handedly holding the queen's stairway in Milosis had stayed in his mind for thirty years (the reference is to the great battle in *Allan Quatermain*).

UNDERSHAFT, BARBARA   Salvation Army Officer, daughter of an arms-manufacturer, in George Bernard Shaw's play *Major Barbara* (1905). She suffers a crisis of conscience when her father gives some of his 'tainted moncy' to the church. Barbara is engaged to the scholar Adolphus Cusins, and with his help she comes to accept the nature of her father's trade. In the film of the play (1941; dir. Gabriel Pascal) Barbara was played by Wendy Hiller.

UNDINE   See under The LITTLE MERMAID

UNGER, FELIX   New York photographer, one half of the eponymous pair in Neil Simon's very funny play *The Odd Couple* (1965). After separating from his wife, Felix moves in with his best friend, the sportswriter Oscar Madison, but he soon becomes irritated by Oscar's sloppy ways. In the film of the play (1968; dir. Gene Saks) Jack Lemmon starred as the prim Felix, with Walter Matthau as his shaggy house-mate. The subsequent television series (1970–75) had Tony Randall as Felix and Jack Klugman as Oscar. This was revived under the title 'The New Odd Couple' (1982–3), with black actors Ron Glass and Demond Wilson as Felix and Oscar.

URFE, NICHOLAS   Rootless, footloose young Englishman who goes to work as a school teacher on an obscure Greek island, in John Fowles's cult novel *The Magus* (1966; revised 1977). He meets a mysterious recluse called Conchis who inducts him into the 'Godgame', a series of bizarre psychodramas through which

Nicholas learns some of life's deeper truths. In the unsatisfactory film of the novel (1968; dir. Guy Green) Nicholas is played by Michael Caine, with Anthony Quinn as Conchis (a deeper, darker version of ZORBA the Greek).

URIZEN God-figure in the eccentric but forceful religious mythology evolved by the poet and artist William Blake. Urizen is a law-giver, the awesome god of reason: in a famous engraving in one of his 'prophetic books' Blake portrays him as a god-like scientist, creating the Earth with the aid of a giant pair of compasses. Blake first mentioned Urizen in *The Book of Thel* (1789), but dealt with him at length in *The Book of Urizen* (1794), *The Song of Los* (1795) and other works. Related figures in Blake's personal mythology include Enitharmon, Los, Luvah and Orc. (Philip José Farmer uses several of these names, to trivial effect, for the immortal alien characters in his science fiction novel *The Gates of Creation* [1966] and its sequels.)

USHER, RODERICK Morbid proprietor of the doomed mansion in Edgar Allan Poe's most famous short story, 'The Fall of the House of Usher' (1839). He believes that his dead sister, entombed below the house, still lives. He dies when she (or her ghost) appears before him. Their mansion then sinks into the waters of an adjacent tarn. The story has been filmed at least three times – in 1928 (dir. Jean Epstein and Luis Bunuel); in 1949 (dir. Ivan Barnett); and in 1960 (dir. Roger Corman), with Vincent Price as Usher.

VADER, DARTH   Heavy-breathing, black-clad villain of the space-opera films *Star Wars* (1977), *The Empire Strikes Back* (1980) and *Return of the Jedi* (1983), all of which were dreamed up by writer-producer-director George Lucas. Vader was formerly a Jedi knight, Annakin Skywalker (father of the young hero Luke SKYWALKER), but he has been seduced by 'the dark side of the Force' and now serves the evil Emperor. In the films he was played by stuntman David Prowse, although his voice was provided by James Earl Jones.

VALENTINE, JIMMY   Gentleman crook who uses his safe-cracking ability to rescue a trapped child. He features in the short story 'A Retrieved Reformation' (collected in *Roads of Destiny*, 1909) by O. Henry (William Sydney Porter). The character became famous when the story was turned into a stage play, *Alias Jimmy Valentine* (1910), by Paul Armstrong. Two silent films were based on the play – in 1915, with Robert Warwick in the lead; and in 1920, with Bert Lytell. There have also been several talkies: *Alias Jimmy Valentine* (1928; dir. Jack Conway), with William Haines (this production was notable for being MGM's first all-talking picture); *The Return of Jimmy Valentine* (1936), with Roger Pryor; and *Affairs of Jimmy Valentine* (1942), with Dennis O'Keefe. Valentine has also appeared on American radio and television.

VALIANT, PRINCE   Hero of a celebrated American comic-strip conceived and drawn by Hal Foster (from 1937). Valiant is a young adventurer in the days of King Arthur. His travels take him from his birthplace, 'Thule', to Arthur's Britain, and later across the sea to the mysterious New World. Prince Val is notable for being one of the few comic-strip characters who has aged over the decades; in later episodes his son Arn takes the leading role. The film *Prince Valiant* (1954; dir. Henry Hathaway) starred Robert Wagner.

VALJEAN, JEAN   Fugitive hero of Victor Hugo's great romantic novel *Les Misérables* (1862). Valjean steals some food and is

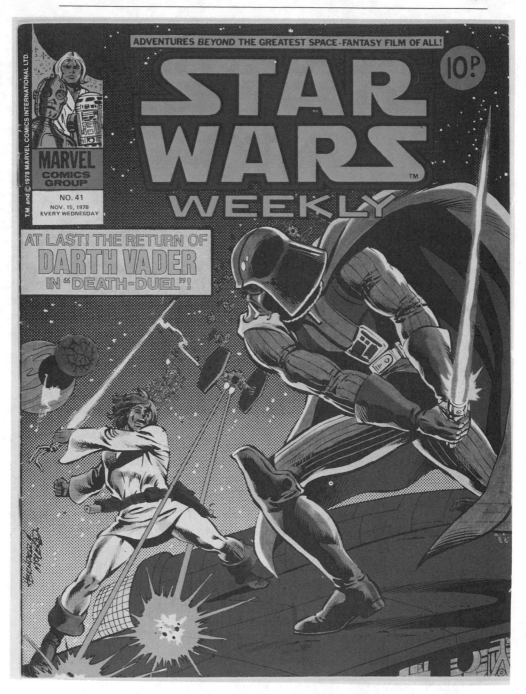

Darth Vader duels with Luke Skywalker on a Marvel Comics cover

unjustly sentenced to penal servitude in the galley-ships. After
years of suffering he tries to build a new life for himself under an
assumed name, but he is recognized and pursued by a sadistic
policeman called Javert. The novel was adapted to the
nineteenth-century stage, and in the present century it has been
filmed and televised a great many times. Two film versions were
made in 1909, a French one which was feature-length and an
American one which consisted of four separate short films. Later
silent versions appeared in 1913, 1917 and 1923. In the sound era,
it was remade in 1929 (as *The Bishop's Candlesticks*), with Walter
Huston as Valjean; in 1934 (French-made), with Harry Baur; in
1935 (dir. Richard Boleslawski), with Fredric March – this is
usually regarded as the classic version; in 1946 (Italian-made),
with Gino Cervi; in 1952 (dir. Lewis Milestone), with Michael
Rennie; in 1957 (dir. Jean Paul Le Chancois), with Jean Gabin;
and in 1978 as a TV movie (dir. Glenn Jordan), with Richard Jordan
as the harried ex-convict. In 1980 the story of Jean Valjean formed
the basis of a spectacular stage musical, with music by
Claude-Michel Schonberg and lyrics by Alain Boublil. In 1985
this was staged in Britain by the Royal Shakespeare Company and
received much praise.

VALMONT, VICOMTE DE   Amoral, licentious hero-villain of the
once scandalous novel *Les Liaisons Dangereuses* (1782) by Pierre
Choderlos de Laclos. Valmont and his mistress, the Marquise de
Merteuil, conspire to corrupt various innocents. The novel is
written in the epistolary style of Samuel Richardson (see Clarissa
HARLOWE) but its subject-matter has more in common with that of
the Marquis de Sade (see JUSTINE). Recently, the story has been
successfully adapted to the English stage by Christopher
Hampton (1985).

VAMPIRELLA   Gorgeous, scantily-clad female vampire who
appeared in an American comic-book drawn by Frank Frazetta and
written by Forrest J. Ackerman (from 1969). The strip has been
'novelized' in a series of paperback books by Ron Goulart:
Bloodstalk (1975), *On Alien Wings* (1975), *Deadwalk* (1976),
Blood Wedding (1976), *Deathgame* (1976) and *Snakegod* (1976).
(The British novelist Angela Carter has written a radio play
entitled *Vampirella* [1976]; there appears to be no connection.)

VANCE, PHILO Immaculate playboy detective created by American crime novelist S. S. Van Dine (Willard Huntington Wright) for *The Benson Murder Case* (1926) and eleven other books. Vance is a sleuth of the same languid and erudite upper-class school as Lord Peter WIMSEY and the young Ellery QUEEN. Although the character was very popular in his day, the poet Ogden Nash was moved to write a damaging couplet: 'Philo Vance/Needs a kick in the pance.' The other books about Philo Vance are: *The Canary Murder Case* (1927), *The Greene Murder Case* (1928), *The Bishop Murder Case* (1929), *The Scarab Murder Case* (1930), *The Kennel Murder Case* (1933), *The Dragon Murder Case* (1933), *The Casino Murder Case* (1934), *The Garden Murder Case* (1935), *The Kidnap Murder Case* (1936), *The Gracie Allen Murder Case* (1938) and *The Winter Murder Case* (1939). Vance has appeared in many films. William Powell took the part in *The Canary Murder Case* (1929; dir. Malcolm St Clair) and three subsequent films, concluding with the much-praised *The Kennel Murder Case* (1933; dir. Michael Curtiz). Basil Rathbone played Vance in *The Bishop Murder Case* (1930; dir. Nick Grinde and David Burton); Warren William in *The Dragon Murder Case* (1934; dir. H. Bruce Humberstone) and one other film; Paul Lukas in *The Casino Murder Case* (1935; dir. Edwin L. Marin); Edmund Lowe in *The Garden Murder Case* (1936; dir. Marin); Wilfrid Hyde-White in *The Scarab Murder Case* (1936; dir. Michael Hankinson); Grant Richards in *Night of Mystery* (1937; dir. E. A. Dupont); James Stephenson in *Calling Philo Vance* (1940; dir. William Clemens); William Wright in *Philo Vance Returns* (1947; dir. William Beaudine); and Alan Curtis in *Philo Vance's Gamble* (1948; dir. Basil Wrangell) and one other film.

VAN DER VALK, PIET Dutch detective in a series of *romans policiers* by the British-born writer Nicolas Freeling (F. R. E. Nicholas), beginning with *Love in Amsterdam* (1962). After ten years and ten books, Freeling killed Van der Valk in the middle of his last case (since when there have been a few books about the character's widow, Arlette). The other Van der Valk novels are *Because of the Cats* (1963), *Gun Before Butter* (1963; vt *A Question of Loyalty*), *Double Barrel* (1964), *Criminal Conversation* (1965), *King of the Rainy Country* (1966), *Strike Out Where Not Applicable* (1965), *Tsing-Boom* (1969), *The Lovely Ladies* (1971) and

A Long Silence (1972; vt *Auprès de Ma Blonde*). The film
Amsterdam Affair (1968; dir. Gerry O'Hara) had Wolfgang Kieling
as Van der Valk. The British television series 'Van der Valk' (1972
and 1977) starred Barry Foster. The character has also been
played by Frank Finlay for German television.

VAN DUSEN, AUGUSTUS S. F. X.   See The THINKING MACHINE

VANE, HARRIET   See under Lord Peter WIMSEY

VANE, LADY ISABEL   Central character of Mrs Henry Wood's
  weepy Victorian novel *East Lynne* (1861). She leaves her husband
  and children but later suffers remorse and returns to them in
  disguise. She acts as a nurse to her own unsuspecting offspring
  for several years before her identity is revealed. The story was
  dramatized for the stage, and is now regarded as the archetypal
  nineteeth-century tear-jerker. The most famous line from the play
  is: 'Dead – and never called me "Mother"!' *East Lynne* was
  filmed several times during the silent movie era: a version in 1916
  starred Theda Bara, and one in 1925 had Alma Rubens. A talkie
  version (1931; dir. Frank Lloyd) had Ann Harding as Lady Isabel.
  Much more recently, the story has been serialized on BBC television
  (1982), with Lisa Eichhorn in the principal part.

VAN HELSING, ABRAHAM   Dedicated vampire-hunter, in Bram
  Stoker's novel *Dracula* (1897). In the many film adaptations of
  this famous story, not to mention the sequels and quasi-sequels,
  Van Helsing is the most frequently recurring character, apart from
  Count DRACULA himself. The most notable actor to have played
  Van Helsing on screen is Laurence Olivier, in *Dracula* (1979; dir.
  John Badham).

VAN RYN, REX   See under Duke DE RICHLEAU

VAN WINKLE, RIP   Colonial who falls asleep in the Catskill
  mountains, after drinking a dwarf's magic potion, and awakes
  twenty years later to find himself a citizen of the United States.
  He appears in the story 'Rip Van Winkle', in Washington Irving's
  Sketch Book of Geoffrey Crayon, Gent. (1819). Allegedly based
  on a folk tale from the Orkneys, Rip's story has become a part of

American lore. It was adapted to the stage many times in the nineteenth century: one actor, Joseph Jefferson, played Rip Van Winkle for nigh on forty years, from the 1860s to the 1900s. The tale has also formed the basis of three operas – by G. F. Bristow (1855); by Robert Planquette (1882); and by Henry Louis Reginald de Koven (1920).

VANYA, UNCLE   See Ivan Petrovitch VOYNITSKY

VARNEY, SIR FRANCIS   Villain of the anonymous *Varney the Vampire, or The Feast of Blood* (1847), a long novel issued in parts. The authorship has often been attributed to J. M. Rymer, though some experts believe it is the work of Thomas Peckett Prest (see Sweeney TODD). This precursor of *Dracula* is one of the most famous among early-Victorian 'penny dreadfuls'. According to E. S. Turner: 'The incomparable Rymer kept his tale going for 220 chapters. He gloated on the lustrous eyes and rosy cheeks of the happy, well-fed vampire; on the shot vampire reviving in the first rays of moonlight; on the impaling of suspected corpses of young women with a wooden stake . . .' The near-immortal Varney eventually disposes of himself by jumping into the crater of Mount Vesuvius.

VATHEK   Caliph who sells his soul to Eblis (the Devil) in William Beckford's Gothic romance *Vathek, an Arabian Tale* (1786). He is permitted to enter the underground halls of Eblis and view the treasures there, but is condemned to suffer ever more when his heart bursts into flame. Beckford wrote several more episodes which were included in a French edition of the story (1815), and these were first published in English a century later as *The Episodes of Vathek* (1912). One of Beckford's more famous admirers, Lord Byron, called *Vathek* his 'Bible'.

VAUTRIN   Real name Jacques Collin, a hero-villain who features in Honoré de Balzac's massive sequence of novels known collectively as *La Comédie Humaine* (see also Père GORIOT, Eugénie GRANDET and Eugène de RASTIGNAC). Vautrin is a criminal who turns policeman (much like the real-life Vidocq), and he says of himself: 'In every million men there are ten who put themselves above everything, even the law, and I am one of them.'

He first appears in *Le Père Goriot* (1834), and recurs in such titles as *Les Splendeurs et Misères des Courtisanes* (1843), *Le Député d'Arcis* (1847) and *La Dernière Incarnation de Vautrin* (1847). A play, *The Crimes of Vautrin* by Nicholas Wright, was staged in Britain in 1983.

VEGA, DIEGO   See ZORRO

VELVET   See Velvet BROWN

VENEERING, MR AND MRS   *Noveau riche* couple who appear in Charles Dickens's novel *Our Mutual Friend* (1864–5). They are comparatively minor characters in a complex plot which mainly concerns the fortunes of the disinherited young man John Harmon, the villain Silas Wegg, and the boatman's daughter Lizzy Hexam. Mr and Mrs Veneering are notable for living in a 'bran-new' house, with 'bran-new' furniture and servants. A sequel by another hand is *The Veneerings* (1922) by Sir Harry Johnston. In a BBC radio adaptation of *Our Mutual Friend* (1984) Mr and Mrs Veneering were played by Geoffrey Collins and Jane Wenham.

VENNER, ELSIE   Mysterious young woman whose sad, fated life is described in the novel *Elsie Venner: A Romance of Destiny* (1861) by Oliver Wendell Holmes. Her mother is supposed to have been bitten by a snake during pregnancy, and so to have passed on serpentine traits to her daughter. Elsie wears a gold necklace to hide a telltale birthmark. Holmes's purpose in the novel was to discredit the Calvinist doctrine of predestination.

VERLOC, MR   Double agent who keeps a London shop as a 'front', in Joseph Conrad's novel *The Secret Agent* (1907). Verloc's wife turns against him after her retarded brother is killed when he attempts to plant a terrorist bomb at Verloc's instigation. Alfred Hitchcock's film *Sabotage* (1936) is based on the Conrad novel and stars Oscar Homolka (this should not be confused with Hitchcock's later movie *Saboteur*, nor with his film entitled *The Secret Agent*; the latter is based on Somerset Maugham's ASHENDEN stories).

VERNON, DIANA   See under Francis OSBALDISTONE

VERRELL, RICHARD   See BLACKSHIRT

VIDEO, CAPTAIN   Spacefaring hero of the twenty-second century, in the American television series 'Captain Video' (1949–55). With his Video Rangers, he patrols the solar system in a spaceship called the *Galaxy*. The first actor to play Captain Video was Richard Coogan, but he was soon replaced by Al Hodge, who took the part for the bulk of the series. The character was also embodied by Judd Holdren in a cinema serial, *Captain Video* (1952). There was a Captain Video comic-book in the early 1950s, and an animated TV series, 'Captain Video's Cartoons' (1956–7).

VINCEY, LEO   See under Ludwig Horace HOLLY and SHE-WHO-MUST-BE-OBEYED

VIOLETTA AND ALFREDO   See under CAMILLE

VIRGINIAN, THE   Nameless cowboy hero of the book which is widely regarded as the first 'serious' Western, Owen Wister's *The Virginian* (1902). Set in Wyoming, it involves a feud between the hero and a villain named Trampas. When he is insulted by the latter, the Virginian delivers his famous line: 'When you call me that, *smile!*' Films of the novel were released in 1914 (starring Dustin Farnum); in 1929 (dir. Victor Fleming) with Gary Cooper; and in 1946 (dir. Stuart Gilmore) with Joel McCrea. A long-running television series entitled 'The Virginian' (1962–71) starred James Drury as the black-clad hero: it bore little resemblance to the novel.

VITELLI, POPEYE   See under Temple DRAKE

VLADIMIR AND ESTRAGON   Argumentative tramps who are the central characters of Samuel Beckett's influential absurdist play *Waiting for Godot* (1952; originally published in French). They spend most of their time sitting under a tree, anticipating the imminent coming of the mysterious Godot. The other characters who appear on stage are named Pozzo and Lucky. Needless to say, Godot never arrives.

VOSS, JOHANN   Nineteenth-century German explorer of Australia in Patrick White's ambitious historical novel *Voss* (1957). He sets

out to cross the continent, but dies in the attempt. The novel
forms the basis of an opera (1986), with music by Richard Meale
and a libretto by David Malouf.

VOYNITSKY, IVAN PETROVITCH   Known as 'Uncle Vanya', an
estate manager for his brother-in-law, Professor Alexander
Serebryakov, in Anton Chekhov's play *Uncle Vanya: Scenes from
Country Life in Four Acts* (1899). Voynitsky comes to realize
that the self-satisfied Professor is not the great scholar he has
always believed him to be; frustrated and jealous, Vanya makes a
bungled attempt to kill Serebryakov, before finally becoming
reconciled to his lot. An earlier, unsuccessful, version of the play
was called *The Wood Demon*.

VRONSKY, ALEXEI   See under Anna KARENINA

VYE, EUSTACIA   See under Clym YEOBRIGHT

W

WACO See under E<small>DGE</small>

WADMAN, WIDOW See under Toby S<small>HANDY</small>

WALDO THE WONDER MAN See under Sexton B<small>LAKE</small>

WALKER, COALHOUSE Ragtime pianist in early twentieth-century New York who is driven to political terrorism after a gang of racists damage his prized Model T Ford. He appears, alongside many celebrated characters drawn from real life (from Sigmund Freud to Harry Houdini), in E. L. Doctorow's bestselling novel *Ragtime* (1975). According to the *New York Times Book Review*: 'In this excellent novel, silhouettes and rags not only make fiction out of history but also reveal the fictions out of which history is made.' In the film of the book (1981; dir. Milos Forman) Coalhouse was played effectively by Howard E. Rollins, Jr.

WALKER, KIT See The P<small>HANTOM</small>

WALKER, RIDDLEY Youth who lives in a post-nuclear England some thousands of years hence. In the debased but curiously poetic language of this barbarous future, he narrates the story of his meagre life. The account forms the text of Russell Hoban's novel *Riddley Walker* (1980). Hoban has since written a stage version of his cautionary fable (1986).

WALKER FAMILY, THE John, Susan, Titty and Roger Walker, with their parents and baby sister, are the principal characters of Arthur Ransome's celebrated novel for young readers, *Swallows and Amazons* (1930). While on holiday in the English Lake District the children go boating in a dinghy named the *Swallow*. They encounter another craft, the *Amazon*, which is crewed by the sisters Nancy and Peggy Blackett. The two groups of children soon nickname themselves the 'Swallows' and the 'Amazons' and go hunting for buried treasure. The book was a *succès d'estime*, though not an immediate bestseller, and Ransome went on to write eleven sequels: *Swallowdale* (1931), *Peter Duck* (1932), *Winter Holiday* (1933), *Coot Club* (1934 – in which the Walkers do not actually appear), *Pigeon Post* (1936), *We Didn't Mean to Go to Sea* (1937), *Secret Water* (1939), *The Big Six* (1940), *Missee Lee* (1941), *The Picts and the Martyrs* (1943) and *Great Northern?* (1947). A number of these novels have been dramatized for BBC radio and for television. The film *Swallows and Amazons* (1974; dir. Claude Whatham) had Virginia McKenna and Ronald Fraser in the adult roles. A later TV series was entitled 'Swallows and Amazons Forever!' (1982).

WALLINGFORD, J. RUFUS   Sharp businessman who appears in a series of short stories by George Randolph Chester, collected as *Get-Rich-Quick Wallingford* (1908). The sequels are *Young Wallingford* (1910), *Wallingford in His Prime* (1913), *Wallingford and Blackie Daw* (1913) and *Son of Wallingford* (1921). According to William Rose Benét, Wallingford's name 'has become part of American folklore'. Some of his misadventures were successfully dramatized by George M. Cohan (1910). The character appeared in several silent movies, including *Get-Rich-Quick Wallingford* (1921; dir. Frank Borzage) where he was played by Sam Hardy. A talkie entitled *The New Adventures of Get-Rich-Quick Wallingford* (1931; dir. Sam Wood) starred William Haines.

WALTER   Described by his mother as 'one of Jesus's mistakes', a mentally-retarded man who has a great love for pigeons. After his mother's death he is institutionalized and suffers cruel privations. His story unfolds in David Cook's novel *Walter* (1978) and its sequel *Winter Doves* (1979). Both books were adapted as British television films, *Walter* (1982; dir. Stephen Frears) and *Walter and June* (1983; dir. Frears), with Ian McKellen giving outstanding performances as the uncomprehending hero.

WALTON FAMILY, THE   Rural American family of the Depression era who first appeared in Earl Hamner, Jr's novel *Spencer's Mountain*. This was filmed (1963; dir. Delmer Daves) with Henry Fonda and Maureen O'Hara as the adult leads and James MacArthur as their son. The family reappeared in a television movie, *The*

Homecoming: A Christmas Story (1971; dir. Fielder Cook), with Edgar Bergen and Patricia Neal heading the cast – and Richard Thomas as the son, John-Boy Walton. A subsequent very successful TV series 'The Waltons' (1972–81) starred Ralph Waite (Dad), Michael Learned (Mom), Richard Thomas (John-Boy), Will Geer (Grandpa) and Ellen Corby (Grandma). The Waltons have been described as 'the seventies equivalent of the Hardy family' (Leslie Halliwell – see Andy HARDY).

WANG LUNG Long-suffering Chinese peasant, in Pearl S. Buck's novel *The Good Earth* (1931). He marries the beautiful O-lan, and grows rich, but disaster strikes his family. The story is continued in two sequels, *Sons* (1932) and *A House Divided* (1935). In the big-budget film *The Good Earth* (1937; dir. Sidney Franklin) Paul Muni starred as Wang Lung, with Luise Rainer as O-lan.

WAPSHOT, LEANDER New England patriarch who captains a ferry boat, in John Cheever's humorous bestseller *The Wapshot Chronicle* (1957). A sequel, which deals with members of the same family, is *The Wapshot Scandal* (1964).

WARBUCKS, DADDY See under LITTLE ORPHAN ANNIE

WARING, MICHAEL See The FALCON

WARREN, VIVIE Young heroine of George Bernard Shaw's controversial play *Mrs Warren's Profession* (1898). She discovers that her mother, the 'Mrs Warren' of the title, has only been able to raise her in comfort as a result of immoral earnings. Because it deals candidly with prostitution, Shaw's play caused a public outcry, and it was not produced on stage in England until 1925. A sequel in novel form is *Mrs Warren's Daughter* (1920) by Sir Harry Johnston.

WARWICK, DIANA Née Diana Merion, the beautiful Irish-born heroine of George Meredith's most popular novel, *Diana of the Crossways* (1885). Unhappily married to the respectable Augustus Warwick, she plans to set up home with the young politician Percy Dacier – but because of a minor political scandal the affair comes to nothing.

WATERS, ESTHER   Pious working-class girl who becomes pregnant
and insists on rearing her own child, despite terrible hardships.
George Moore's naturalistic novel *Esther Waters* (1894) was
considered scandalous in its day. In the film of the book (1947; dir.
Ian Dalrymple and Peter Proud) Esther was played by Kathleen Ryan.

WATSON, JOHN H.   Stolid English doctor, friend and amanuensis
to Sherlock HOLMES in the novels and short stories by A. Conan
Doyle. Because Holmes is so eminent among modern fictional
characters, Watson has the distinction of being the most famous of
all supporting characters. The good, unimaginative doctor has
joined the immortals, appearing in countless stage and film
adaptations and sequels by other hands. One such sequel is a BBC
television play by Kingsley Amis, 'Dr Watson and the Darkwater
Hall Mystery' (1974), which starred Edward Fox as Watson in an
adventure without Holmes; another is the book entitled *The Private
Life of Dr Watson* (1985) by Michael Hardwick. The BBC radio
play *221B* (1986) by M. J. Read, in which the character was
voiced by Nigel Stock, dealt with Watson's life after the supposed
death of Holmes at the hands of Professor MORIARTY. Actors who
have played Watson on film or television include: Hubert Willis
(in the Eille Norwood series of Holmes films, 1921–3); Roland
Young (in the John Barrymore *Sherlock Holmes*, 1922); H. Reeves
Smith (in *The Return of Sherlock Holmes*, 1929); Ian Fleming
(in most of the films starring Arthur Wontner, 1931–7); Reginald
Owen (in the Clive Brook *Sherlock Holmes*, 1932); Nigel Bruce
(opposite Basil Rathbone in many films from 1939); Raymond
Francis (in the first BBC television series, 1951); Howard Marion
Crawford (in the series made in France for American TV, 1954);
André Morell (in *The Hound of the Baskervilles*, 1959); Thorley
Walters (in *Sherlock Holmes and the Deadly Necklace*, 1962);
Donald Houston (in *A Study in Terror*, 1965); Nigel Stock (in the
BBC's 'Sherlock Holmes' series, 1965–6, and in the radio play
mentioned above); Colin Blakely (in *The Private Life of Sherlock
Holmes*, 1970); Robert Duvall (in *The Seven Per Cent Solution*,
1976); Patrick MacNee (in the TV movie *Sherlock Holmes in
New York*, 1976); James Mason (in *Murder by Decree*, 1979);
Donald Pickering (in the Polish-made TV series 'Sherlock
Holmes and Dr Watson', 1980); John Mills (in the TV movie *The
Masks of Death*, 1984); David Burke (in the British TV series

'The Adventures of Sherlock Holmes', 1984–5); and Edward
Hardwicke (in the TV 'Return of Sherlock Holmes', 1986).

WATTS, ANGIE AND DEN Landlady and landlord of a London pub,
in the BBC television soap opera 'EastEnders' (from 1985).
Played by Anita Dobson and Leslie Grantham, they soon emerged
as the leading figures of a large cast. Because of his wandering
affections, Den Watts quickly became known as 'Dirty Den' to
the British popular press.

WAVERLEY, EDWARD Hero of Sir Walter Scott's first novel,
Waverley, or 'Tis Sixty Years Since (1814). He subsequently lent his
name to all Scott's works of prose fiction, which were known
collectively as 'the Waverley novels'. Edward is a young man of
romantic leanings. He joins the army in 1745, the year of the
Jacobite rebellion, and is posted to Scotland. There he meets
the highlander Fergus MacIvor and his beautiful sister Flora, and
is persuaded to join them in the doomed Jacobite cause. After
the defeat of Bonnie Prince Charlie, Edward gains a pardon as a
result of having saved the life of an English officer.

WAYNE, BRUCE See BATMAN

WEARY WILLIE AND TIRED TIM Comical tramps,
one fat, one thin, invented by cartoonist Tom
Browne in 1896 for Harmsworth's weekly
Illustrated Chips. The adventures of the
'World-Famous Tramps' continued on the front
page of this paper until it ceased publication in
1953. In later decades the strip was drawn by
Percy Cocking.

WEGG, SILAS See under Mr and Mrs VENEERING

WEIR, ARCHIE Unhappy young Scotsman who is the central
character of Robert Louis Stevenson's last, unfinished, novel
Weir of Hermiston (1896). His authoritarian father banishes him
to the village of Hermiston, where he falls in love with a girl called
Christina Elliott. The story has been adapted as a serial for British
television.

WELBY, MARCUS American television doctor who differs from Doctors CASEY and KILDARE in that he is a man of mature years. He was played by Robert Young in the TV movie *Marcus Welby MD* (1968; dir. David Lowell Rich) and in the subsequent long-running series (1969–76). According to Tim Brooks and Earle Marsh, the programme won an Emmy Award and 'was held in very high esteem by medical groups, with Young serving offscreen as honorary chairman of numerous national fund drives and observances'. The creator of the series was producer David Victor. Robert Young played the part once more in the TV movie *The Return of Marcus Welby* (1984; dir. Alexander Singer).

WELLER, SAM Servant and companion to Mr PICKWICK, in Charles Dickens's *The Pickwick Papers* (1836–7). Sam is a cheerful Cockney with a vast knowledge of life. Fond of telling comic/horrific anecdotes (which became known as 'Wellerisms'), he acts as an earthy Sancho Panza to Pickwick's Don Quixote. Along with Mr Pickwick, Sam Weller was revived briefly by Dickens for the periodical *Master Humphrey's Clock* (1840–41). In the film *The Pickwick Papers* (1952; dir. Noel Langley) he was played by Harry Fowler. In the BBC television adaptation of the novel (1985) Phil Daniels took the part.

WENDY See Wendy DARLING

WENTWORTH, A. J. Accident-prone schoolmaster in hilarious sketches by H. F. Ellis which first appeared in *Punch*. His adventures are collected in two books, *The Papers of A. J. Wentworth, B.A.* (1949) and *The Papers of A. J. Wentworth, B.A. (Ret'd.)* (1962). These have since been combined in one volume. A British television series, 'A. J. Wentworth, B.A.' (1982), was scripted by Basil Boothroyd and starred Arthur Lowe.

WENTWORTH, FREDERICK See under Anne ELLIOT

WENTWORTH, RICHARD See The SPIDER

WERTHER Suicidal hero of Johann Wolfgang von Goethe's very influential novel of sentiment *The Sorrows of Young Werther* (1774). Werther is a lovelorn young artist, much given to exquisite suffering. His example had an alarming effect on the intellectual youth of Europe: they not only imitated his dress (a blue coat and yellow breeches), but some are said to have killed themselves in emulation of their hero. The novel's vogue spread far beyond Germany. According to *The Oxford Companion to English Literature*, 'the term "Wertherism" became current in English to describe a man's early self-indulgent moods of melancholy'. Jules Massenet based his opera *Werther* (1893) on Goethe's tale (the libretto was by Edouard Blau, Paul Milliet and Georges Hartmann).

WEST, ROGER   Scotland Yard policeman who appears in many crime novels by the remarkably prolific John Creasey (see also The BARON, George GIDEON and The TOFF). Titles in the series include: *Inspector West Takes Charge* (1942), *Inspector West Leaves Town* (1943), *Inspector West at Home* (1944), *Inspector West Regrets –* (1945), *Holiday for Inspector West* (1946), *Battle for Inspector West* (1948), *Inspector West Kicks Off* (1949; vt *Sport for Inspector West*), *Inspector West Cries Wolf* (1950; vt *The Creepers*), *Inspector West at Bay* (1952; vt *The Blind Spot*), *Inspector West Makes Haste* (1955; vt *The Gelignite Gang*), *Accident for Inspector West* (1957; vt *Hit and Run*), *Murder on the Line* (1960), *Policeman's Dread* (1962), *Look Three Ways at Murder* (1964), *So Young to Burn* (1968), *Alibi* (1971) and *The Extortioners* (1974).

WESTENRA, LUCY   See under Count DRACULA

WESTERN, SOPHIE   See under Tom JONES

WESTON, EDWARD   See under Agnes GREY

WEXFORD, REGINALD   Rural police inspector who appears in a series of detective novels by Ruth Rendell: *From Doon with Death* (1965), *A New Lease of Death* (1967; vt *Sins of the Fathers*), *Wolf to the Slaughter* (1968), *The Best Man to Die* (1969), *A Guilty Thing Surprised* (1970), *Secret House of Death* (1970), *No More Dying Then* (1971), *Murder Being Once Done* (1972), *Some Lie and Some Die* (1973), *Shake Hands Forever* (1975), *A Sleeping Life* (1978), *Means of Evil* (1979), *Put On by Cunning* (1981; vt *Death Notes*),

The Speaker of Mandarin (1983) and *An Unkindness of Ravens* (1985). A Wexford series is due to appear on British television in 1987.

WHARTON, HARRY   Energetic schoolboy hero, leader of the 'Famous Five' at Greyfriars School. He and his friends appear in the stories of Frank Richards (Charles Hamilton), written for the boys' paper *Magnet* from 1908. The best-known character of the series is Billy BUNTER, but Harry Wharton actually preceded him as a creation. The other members of Wharton's inner circle of friends are Frank Nugent, Bob Cherry, Johnny Bull and the more exotic Hurree Jamset Ram Singh, youthful Nabob of Bhanipur. Unlike Bunter, Wharton is brave, athletic, and has all the conventional virtues of a young leading man. In her book *The Heirs of Tom Brown* Isabel Quigly says: 'The pop school story grew up in spite of, not because of, the reality of the public schools.' A fictional institution such as Greyfriars is 'a cloud-cuckoo-land, an all-purpose repository of dreams for those who had never been there'. Because of the posthumous fame of his prolific creator, Charles Hamilton, the resourceful Harry Wharton seems destined to live on much longer than most fantasy schoolboys of the early twentieth century.

WHITE, CARRIE   Adolescent girl with a fanatically religious mother, in Stephen King's bestselling horror novel *Carrie* (1974). Carrie develops telekinetic abilities which enable her to avenge herself on her mocking schoolmates and her monstrous mother. Stephen King says, in his book *Danse Macabre*: 'For me, Carrie White is a sadly misused teenager, an example of the sort of person whose spirit is so often broken for good in that pit of man- and woman-eaters that is your normal suburban high school. But she's also Woman, feeling her powers for the first time.' In the gory film of the novel (1976; dir. Brian de Palma) Carrie was played by Sissy Spacek.

WHITE FANG   Part wolf, part dog. He is adopted by Canadian Indians, then sold to a cruel white man who consigns him to the fighting pits. After a savage fight which leaves him badly wounded, White Fang is bought by a kinder master who nurses the animal and wins his trust. Jack London's novel *White Fang*

(1906) is one the best-known dog stories in the world. The Italian-made film, *White Fang* (1972; dir. Lucio Fulci) is an effective rendering of the tale.

WHITE RABBIT, THE   See under ALICE

WHITEFIELD, ANN   See under John TANNER

WHITEOAK, RENNY   Canadian landowner who is the linchpin character in Mazo de la Roche's sixteen 'Jalna' novels. The series covers a hundred years in the history of Renny's family, from pioneering days through to the mid-twentieth century. In order of publication, which does not correspond to the chronological sequence, the books are: *Jalna* (1927), *Whiteoaks of Jalna* (1929), *Finch's Fortune* (1931), *The Master of Jalna* (1933), *Young Renny* (1935), *Whiteoak Harvest* (1936), *Whiteoak Heritage* (1940), *Wakefield's Course* (1941), *The Building of Jalna* (1944 – Renny has yet to be born at the time of this story), *Return to Jalna* (1946), *Mary Wakefield* (1949), *Renny's Daughter* (1951), *Whiteoak Brothers* (1953), *Variable Winds at Jalna* (1954), *Centenary at Jalna* (1958) and *Morning at Jalna* (1960). In the film *Jalna* (1935; dir. John Cromwell) Renny was played by Ian Hunter. De la Roche's characters have also featured in a Canadian television series, 'The Whiteoaks of Jalna' (1972).

WHITTIER, POLLYANNA   Sunny heroine of Eleanor H. Porter's novel *Pollyanna* (1913). Known as the 'glad girl', she is determined to remain optimistic no matter what happens. Orphaned at the age of eleven, she goes to live with a formidable aunt, but soon succeeds in melting the hearts of all the crusty old folks she meets. In Eleanor Porter's sequel, *Pollyanna Grows Up* (1915), she finds a husband. There have also been a few sequels by other hands and stage adaptations. The first film version of *Pollyanna* (1920; dir. Paul Powell) starred Mary Pickford. The Disney studios' remake (1960; dir. David Swift) had Hayley Mills. There has also been a BBC television serial (1973), with Elizabeth Archard as the little ray of sunshine.

WHO, DOCTOR   Benign Time Lord, hero of 'Doctor Who', a children's science fiction series on BBC television from 1963. He

travels through time and space in a vehicle known as the Tardis
(disguised on the outside to resemble a London police telephone
box). Doctor Who was created by Sydney Newman and Donald
Wilson, and the first of many scriptwriters was Anthony Coburn.
The most celebrated of the scriptwriters has been Terry Nation,
who introduced the Doctor's deadly enemies, the alien DALEKS.
The series has been astonishingly long-lived, and a number of
actors have played the Doctor over the years. The first was
William Hartnell, who portrayed the mysterious Time Lord as a
rather irascible old man. He was followed by several younger
actors – Patrick Troughton, Jon Pertwee, Tom Baker (whose
characterization was the most memorable: he played the Doctor
as a tousle-headed weirdo who sported an extremely long scarf),
Peter Davison and Colin Baker. At the height of the series'
popularity 'the youth of Starship Britain would watch Hartnell or
Troughton or Pertwee or Baker – the loner, the individualist,
the eccentric – triumph over pan-galactic evil armed only with
the eccentricities of the wardrobe department, his brains and a sonic
screwdriver' (comedian Alexei Sayle, in an article entitled 'Why
I Should Have Been the New Doctor Who: The Case for a Marxist
in the Tardis', *Foundation*, November 1984).

The Doctor has appeared in two cinematic feature films:
Doctor Who and the Daleks (1965; dir. Gordon Flemyng) and
Daleks: Invasion Earth 2150 AD (1966; dir. Flemyng). Both starred
Peter Cushing. Although he originated on TV, Doctor Who has
been especially popular in novel form, with over eight million
books in print by 1985. The hundredth account of his adventures,
Doctor Who: The Two Doctors by Robert Holmes, appeared in that
year. The preceding ninety-nine volumes included many titles by
Terry Nation and Terrance Dicks. In addition, there have been
such books as *Doctor Who: The Key to Time – A Year-by-Year
Record* (1984) by Peter Haining, published to celebrate the
twenty-first anniversary of the character's first appearance. A
serious critical study of the TV series is *Doctor Who: The Unfolding
Text* (1983) by John Tulloch and Manuel Alvarado.

WICKFIELD, AGNES   See under David COPPERFIELD

WIDMERPOOL, KENNETH   Sinister, clownish power-seeker
whose life becomes entangled with that of the narrator Nicholas

JENKINS in Anthony Powell's drily humorous novel sequence
A Dance to the Music of Time (1951–75). Over several decades
Widmerpool progresses from being the laughing-stock of his
public school to the eventual attainment of a life peerage. The critic
John Bayley says of Widmerpool: 'He is toady, spoilsport and
sneak – the boy the school loves to hate; but he grows to have heroic
qualities as anarch, potential tyrant and lord of misrule . . .
Inspiring revulsion, pursued by contempt, with mishaps
constantly engineered for him, he bounces back, his outrages of
survival a kind of passive equivalent of Falstaff's wit or Quilp's
malignant relish' (*The Times Literary Supplement*, 12 September
1975). In a BBC radio adaptation of the novels, broadcast in
1982, Widmerpool was played by Brian Hewlett.

WIEGAND, MARIA   See Maria SIMON

WIGGAR   See under Peter CLANCY

WIGGS, MRS   Kentucky shanty-town widow, mother of many
children, who appears in Alice Hegan Rice's popular novel *Mrs
Wiggs of the Cabbage Patch* (1901) and its sequel *Lovey Mary*
(1903). A film of the first title was released in 1934 (dir. Norman
Taurog), with Pauline Lord as Mrs Wiggs, and remade in 1942
(dir. Ralph Murphy), with Fay Bainter. The character also
appeared in an American radio series (1934–7), where she was
voiced by Betty Garde.

WILDE, JONAS   Known as the Eliminator, billed as the 'most
dangerous man in the world'. Wilde is a British secret agent (yet
another in the mould of James BOND) who appears in a series of
slightly tongue-in-cheek thrillers by Andrew York (Christopher
Nicole): *The Eliminator* (1966), *The Co-Ordinator* (1967), *The
Predator* (1968), *The Deviator* (1969), *The Dominator* (1969),
The Infiltrator (1971), *The Expurgator* (1972), *The Captivator*
(1973) and *The Fascinator* (1975).

WILDEVE, DAMON   See under Clym YEOBRIGHT

WILKES, ASHLEY   See under Rhett BUTLER

WILKINS, PETER   Shipwrecked sailor in Robert Paltock's novel *The Life and Adventures of Peter Wilkins, a Cornishman* (1751). His adventures resemble Robinson CRUSOE's and Lemuel GULLIVER's, and he is also regarded as an early hero of science fiction. He discovers a lost land in the Antarctic which is inhabited by flying people, one of whom he marries.

WILLIAM   See William BROWN

WILLIAMS, CALEB   Hero and narrator of William Godwin's Gothic thriller *Things as They Are, or The Adventures of Caleb Williams* (1794; the book is commonly known as *Caleb Williams*). Caleb is secretary to the wealthy Falkland; he finds evidence that his master is a murderer, flees from him, and is pursued and persecuted by Falkland's agents. Godwin's novel proved popular and influential, and it was dramatized for the stage by George Colman as *The Iron Chest* (1796). Much more recently, the story has been serialized as an Anglo-German television production (under the title 'Caleb Williams', 1983), with Mick Ford in the leading role.

WILLIAMS, ERIC   Schoolboy in F. W. Farrar's infamous novel *Eric, or Little By Little* (1858). Eric is a proud, well-set-up lad who comes under bad influences at his public school and gradually goes to ruin. He is expelled after arriving at evening prayers in a state of drunkenness. Although he promises to reform, his author hardly gives him a chance: he is wrongly accused of theft, runs away, suffers as a cabin boy aboard a merchant ship, and dies. This moral tale of terror was widely read and very influential in its day (it appeared within a year of the much sunnier *Tom Brown's Schooldays* by Thomas Hughes). According to Margery Fisher: 'Farrar was writing to expose the brutalities and moral dangers of public school life as he knew it, and with a reforming zeal as strong as that of Dr Arnold and as strong a belief in the discipline of Christian life.'

WILLIAMS, RACE   Gun-toting private-eye invented by Carroll John Daly for *Black Mask* magazine in 1923. He is commonly regarded as the first of the 'hard-boiled' detective heroes, the immediate ancestor of Sam SPADE and Philip MARLOWE. Race Williams adventures continued to appear in pulp magazines for some thirty

years, and he also features in Daly's novels *The Snarl of the Beast*
(1927), *The Hidden Hand* (1929), *The Tag Murders* (1930), *Tainted
Power* (1931), *The Third Murderer* (1931), *The Amateur Murderer*
(1933), *Murder from the East* (1935) and *Better Corpses* (1940).

WILLIAMS, REMO   See The DESTROYER

WILSON, JEM   See under Mary BARTON

WILSON, WILLIAM   Man who is haunted by his *doppelgänger*, in
Edgar Allan Poe's macabre short story 'William Wilson' (1839).
Driven to desperation, he eventually murders his alter ego.

WILT, HENRY   College lecturer in the comic novel *Wilt* (1976) by
Tom Sharpe. He teaches Liberal Studies (later known as
'Communication Skills and Expressive Attainment') at the
Fenland Tech, Ipford. Sequels are *The Wilt Alternative* (1979) and
Wilt on High (1984). The accident-prone Henry Wilt has been
described as 'a sane and rational voice in a nightmarishly comic
universe of stupidity, greed and malevolent coincidence' (T. O.
Treadwell, *The Times Literary Supplement*, 12 October 1984).

WIMSEY, LORD PETER   Second son of the Duke of Denver, and
the aristocrat of private detectives. He was created by Dorothy
L. Sayers for her crime novel *Whose Body?* (1923). Like Bertie
WOOSTER (whom he resembles in some of his mannerisms), Lord
Peter has a devoted manservant (called Mervyn Bunter), a private
income, and a large circle of acquaintances among the idle rich.
Unlike Wooster, he is also a shrewd amateur investigator. His
girlfriend, whom he eventually marries, is Harriet Vane, a writer
of mystery stories. The later Wimsey books are: *Clouds of Witness*
(1926), *Unnatural Death* (1927; vt *The Dawson Pedigree*), *The
Unpleasantness at the Bellona Club* (1928), *Lord Peter Views the
Body* (1928), *Strong Poison* (1930 – it is in this book that Lord Peter
first meets Harriet, who is accused of murder), *The Five Red
Herrings* (1931; vt *Suspicious Characters*), *Have His Carcase* (1932),
Murder Must Advertise (1933), *Hangman's Holiday* (1933), *The
Nine Tailors* (1934), *Gaudy Night* (1935), *Busman's Honeymoon:
A Love Story with Detective Interruptions* (1937), *In the Teeth of
the Evidence* (1939 – only two of the stories in this volume feature

Wimsey) and the posthumous *Lord Peter: A Collection of All the Lord Peter Stories* (1972). A slim book which delves into Lord Peter's antecedents is *The Wimsey Family: A Fragmentary History Compiled from Correspondence with Dorothy L. Sayers* (1977) by C. W. Scott-Giles. Two films about Wimsey were made in Britain: *The Silent Passenger* (1935; dir. Reginald Denham), with Peter Haddon, and *Busman's Honeymoon* (1940; dir. Arthur Woods), with Robert Montgomery. In the BBC television series 'Lord Peter Wimsey' (early 1970s) the hero was played by Ian Carmichael. In several recent BBC mini-series (1987) he was played by Edward Petherbridge

WINE, MOSES   Sixties' student radical turned private-eye, in a short series of novels by Roger L. Simon: *The Big Fix* (1973), *Wild Turkey* (1975) and *Peking Duck* (1979). In the film *The Big Fix* (1978; dir. Jeremy Paul Kagan) the hip Mr Wine was played by Richard Dreyfuss.

WING, ISADORA   Liberated American woman, a female equivalent of Alex PORTNOY, who goes in search of 'the zipless fuck'. How she fares is described in Erica Jong's bestselling novel *Fear of Flying* (1973) and its sequel *How To Save Your Own Life* (1977).

WINGRAVE, OWEN   Pacifist hero of one of Henry James's lesser-known short stories of the 1890s, 'Owen Wingrave'. Benjamin Britten chose to base an opera on the tale. His *Owen Wingrave*, commissioned by the BBC and first performed in 1971, has a libretto by Myfanwy Piper.

WINKLE, NATHANIEL   See under Samuel PICKWICK

WINNETOU   Hero of Wild West novels by the popular German writer Karl May. *Winnetou* first appeared in three volumes in 1893. The American actor Lex Barker (a former screen TARZAN) became a big star in Germany when he played Winnetou in three films (1963–5); he also played the lead in *Old Shatterhand* (1964), based on another of Karl May's novels.

WINNIE-THE-POOH   Bear of very little brain. Originally called Edward Bear, he appeared in A. A. Milne's nursery verses from 1924.

Winnie-the-Pooh and his friend Piglet

In Milne's story books, *Winnie-the-Pooh* (1926) and *The House at Pooh Corner* (1928), he has mild adventures with the boy Christopher Robin, and their animal friends Eeyore, Piglet and Tigger. The books were illustrated by Ernest Shepard and soon became exceedingly well known. They are now established as oft-quoted children's classics. The little bear's adventures have been translated into Latin, and there have also been two mock-scholarly studies of Winnie-the-Pooh: *The Pooh Perplex: A Freshman Casebook* (1963) by Frederick C. Crews, and *The Tao of Pooh* (1982) by Benjamin Hoff. Pooh has appeared frequently on radio and television. Several short animated films produced by the Disney studios have been collected in the feature-length release known as *The Many Adventures of Winnie-the-Pooh* (1977; dir. Wolfgang Reitherman).

WINSLOW, DON   Lieutenant Commander in the United States Naval Intelligence, hero of Frank V. Martinek's newspaper comic-strip *Don Winslow of the Navy* (1934–55). Winslow became successful in other media, including comic-books, juvenile novels, a radio series, and two cinema serials (1941 and 1943, with Don Terry as the hero).

WINTERBOURNE, GEORGE   Young Englishman whose apparently carefree life is shattered by World War I. The experience of trench warfare robs him of all illusions, and he finally dies in

action in 1918. The story is told in Richard Aldington's bitter
novel *Death of a Hero* (1929).

WISE OLD GOAT, THE   See under RUPERT BEAR

WITHERS, HILDEGARDE   Spinster schoolmarm who doubles as a
very effective amateur detective. She wears outrageous hats and
has a pet poodle called Talleyrand. Miss Withers appears in a
series of crime novels by Stuart Palmer, beginning with *The
Penguin Pool Murder* (1931). Her later cases include *Murder on
Wheels* (1932), *Murder on the Blackboard* (1932), *The Puzzle of the
Pepper Tree* (1933), *The Puzzle of the Silver Persian* (1934), *The
Puzzle of the Red Stallion* (1936; vt *The Briar Pipe*), *The Puzzle of
the Blue Banderilla* (1937), *The Puzzle of the Happy Hooligan*
(1941), *Miss Withers Regrets* (1947), *Four Lost Ladies* (1949), *The
Green Ace* (1950; vt *At One Fell Swoop*), *Nipped in the Bud* (1951;
vt *Trap for a Redhead*), *Cold Poison* (1954; vt *Exit Laughing*)
and *Hildegarde Withers Makes the Scene* (1969 – written with
Fletcher Flora). She also appears in several volumes of short stories,
and in *The People vs. Withers and Malone* (1963), written by
Stuart Palmer in collaboration with Craig Rice (in which Miss
Withers joins forces with Rice's hero, lawyer John J. Malone). In
the movie *The Penguin Pool Murder* (1932; dir. George
Archainbaud) she was played by Edna May Oliver. A few other
films followed. Miss Withers has also been played by Eve Arden
in the TV movie *A Very Missing Person* (1972; dir. Russell Mayberry).

WO FAT   See under Steve MCGARRETT

WOLF MAN, THE   Lawrence Talbot, the man who sprouts hair and
fangs whenever the moon is full: 'Even a man who is pure in
heart/And says his prayers by night/Can become a wolf when the
wolfbane blooms/And the moon is shining bright.' He was played
by Lon Chaney, Jr in several Hollywood werewolf movies,
beginning with *The Wolf Man* (1941; dir. George Waggner). His
tragi-comic story continues in *Frankenstein Meets the Wolf Man*
(1943; dir. Roy William Neill), *House of Frankenstein* (1944;
dir. Erle C. Kenton), *House of Dracula* (1945; dir. Erle C. Kenton)
and *Abbott and Costello Meet Frankenstein* (1948; dir. Charles
Barton). An earlier film, *Werewolf of London* (1935; dir. Stuart

Walker) starred Henry Hull as a similar lycanthrope. The much
more recent *An American Werewolf in London* (1981; dir. John
Landis) helped give new life to the old myth.

WOLFE, NERO   Heavyweight orchid-loving detective created by
American crime novelist Rex Stout for his *Fer-de-Lance* (1934), *The
League of Frightened Men* (1935), *The Rubber Band* (1936) and
subsequent books. Wolfe is a marvellously eccentric character.
A connoisseur of all the finer things in life (especially *haute
cuisine*), he rarely ventures from his New York brownstone
house. He solves crimes at a distance, using the eyes, ears and
legs of his faithful servant and amanuensis, the tough Archie
Goodwin. Despite his physical torpor, Wolfe is probably
America's greatest fictional detective—a brilliant intellect, and
a worthy son of Sherlock HOLMES. The claim that Wolfe is 'in
fact' Holmes's son is made by W. S. Baring-Gould in his biography
of the character, *Nero Wolfe of West Thirty-Fifth Street* (1969). A
recent novel which embodies the same thesis is *Son of Holmes* (1986)
by John T. Lescroart, in which the young Nero Wolfe is clearly
recognizable under the alias 'Auguste Lupa'. Wolfe also appears
in a pastiche interview, 'In Which Archie Goodwin Remembers',
included in Julian Symons's book *The Great Detectives* (1981).

Rex Stout's later novels about Wolfe are *The Red Box* (1937),
Too Many Cooks (1938), *Some Buried Caesar* (1939), *Over My Dead
Body* (1940), *Where There's a Will* (1940), *The Silent Speaker*
(1946), *Too Many Women* (1947), *And Be a Villain* (1948; vt
More Deaths Than One), *The Second Confession* (1949), *In the
Best Families* (1950), *Murder by the Book* (1951), *Prisoner's Base*
(1952; vt *Out Goes She*), *The Golden Spiders* (1953), *The Black
Mountain* (1954 – an unusual volume in which Wolfe bestirs himself
to travel as far as Yugoslavia in order to revisit his home patch,
Montenegro), *Before Midnight* (1955), *Might as Well be Dead* (1956),
If Death Ever Slept (1957), *Champagne for One* (1958), *Plot it
Yourself* (1959; vt *Murder in Style*), *Too Many Clients* (1960), *The
Final Deduction* (1961), *Gambit* (1962), *The Mother Hunt* (1963),
A Right to Die (1964), *The Doorbell Rang* (1965 – in which
Wolfe goes up against the FBI), *Death of a Doxy* (1966), *The Father
Hunt* (1968), *Death of a Dude* (1969), *Please Pass the Guilt* (1973)
and *A Family Affair* (1975). There have also been over a dozen
collections of short stories about Wolfe.

The character has appeared in films rarely. Two movies were made before World War II, but Rex Stout apparently was displeased with them and forbade any more. They are *Meet Nero Wolfe* (1936; dir. Herbert Biberman), starring Edward Arnold, and *The League of Frightened Men* (1937; dir. Alfred E. Green), with Walter Connolly. A radio series, 'The Adventures of Nero Wolfe', was a success from 1943 onwards. In later episodes Wolfe's voice was provided by actor Sydney Greenstreet (one cannot help feeling he would have made a good Nero Wolfe in films – but Orson Welles would have been even better). A TV movie, *Nero Wolfe* (1977; dir. Frank Gilroy), was based on *The Doorbell Rang* and had Thayer David as the hero. A US television series, made in 1981 (several years after Stout's death) featured William Conrad as the corpulent detective.

WOMBLES, THE   Small, hairy bear-like creatures who live beneath Wimbledon Common. They are dedicated conservationists, and they make ingenious use of the litter left by human beings. These cuddly creatures first appeared in Elisabeth Beresford's book *The Wombles* (1968). They soon became cult figures on BBC children's television, appearing in short animated films with puppets designed by Ivor Wood. In the mid-1970s the cult became a craze, when a Wombles pop group, clad in absurd hairy costumes, sang: 'The Wombles of Wimbledon Common are we . . .' Later books by Elisabeth Beresford include *The Wandering Wombles* (1970) and *The Wombles at Work* (1973).

WONDER WART-HOG   Real name Philbert Desenex, a costumed anti-hero of the comic-strips, and one of the first 'underground' cult figures. Philbert periodically consumes a small capsule of drugs which transforms him into the grotesquely ugly Hog of Steel; armed with powers of flight and super-strength, he struggles to save America from communists and other subversives. In this patriotic chore he is supported by his friends of the Bacon Brigade. Wonder Wart-Hog's adventures were written and drawn by Gilbert Shelton from 1961. They originally appeared in a University of Texas student paper, later in *Help!* magazine.

WONDER WOMAN   Also known as Diana Prince, an Amazon from Paradise Island in the Bermuda Triangle. Armed with various

super-powers, a magical lasso, and a pair of 'Feminium' bracelets
which repel bullets, she goes to the United States in order to
help that country win World War II. Wonder Woman has been
the most successful of all the comic-book superheroines. She
first appeared in *All-Star Comics* in 1941, and has pursued her
career as a fighter for peace and justice ever since. Since 1960
she has been a member of the Justice League of America, along
with BATMAN and SUPERMAN. She appeared in the animated
television series 'Super Friends' (1973) and its various follow-ups.
She has also appeared as a live-action character in the TV movies
Wonder Woman (1974; dir. Vincent McEveety), starring Cathy
Lee Crosby; and *The New Original Wonder Woman* (1975; dir.
Leonard Horn), with Lynda Carter. The subsequent TV series
(1976–9) also starred Lynda Carter.

WONG, JAMES LEE   Oriental sleuth created by crime-story writer
Hugh Wiley. Like his fellow Asiatic detectives, Charlie CHAN
and Mr MOTO, he also appeared in a series of Hollywood second
features. *Mr Wong, Detective* (1938; dir. William Nigh) was
followed by four more films, all of which starred Boris Karloff. A
sixth movie, *Phantom of Chinatown* (1941; dir. Nigh), had Keye
Luke as the hero.

WONKA, WILLY   Owner of the chocolate factory in Roald Dahl's
very popular children's book *Charlie and the Chocolate Factory*
(1964). He wears a top hat and goatee beard, and carries a cane.
Mr Wonka's sweet factory is a wonderful and mysterious place for
the young Charlie Bucket, winner of a competition set by Wonka.
It is crammed with eccentric machinery, and staffed by a tribe
of African pygmies known as the Oompa-Loompas. In the sequel,
Charlie and the Great Glass Elevator (1973), Mr Wonka takes
Charlie and his long-suffering family into outer space. The
musical film, *Willy Wonka and the Chocolate Factory* (1971;
dir. Mel Stuart), had Gene Wilder as the madcap factory-owner-
cum-inventor.

WOODHOUSE, EMMA   Beautiful, high-spirited but erring heroine
of Jane Austen's great novel *Emma* (1816). She 'adopts' Harriet
Smith, a young woman of lowly birth, and her attempts to find a
partner for Harriet lead to many comic misunderstandings. Emma

gradually learns by her embarrassing mistakes, and in the end
Harriet marries a local farmer, while Emma is betrothed to a
most eligible and level-headed land-owner, the aptly-named Mr
George Knightley. Among the other important characters in the
novel are Emma's valetudinarian father, Mr Woodhouse, and the
dull but well-meaning old maid, Miss Bates. Emma's story has
been serialized on BBC radio and television.

WOODHOUSE, ROSEMARY   Unfortunate young woman who gives
birth to the Devil's child, in Ira Levin's horror novel *Rosemary's
Baby* (1967). 'The strength of the book lies not only in its weaving
of a dreadful spell but in the strong, sweet character of the
pregnant heroine' (according to Cherry Wilder in *Twentieth-
Century Science-Fiction Writers*, edited by Curtis C. Smith). In
the highly successful film of the book (1968; dir. Roman
Polanski) sweet Rosemary was played by Mia Farrow. A TV-movie
sequel, *Look What's Happened to Rosemary's Baby* (1976; dir.
Sam O'Steen) starred Patty Duke Astin.

WOODRUFF, SARAH   Young lady with a mysterious past, in John
Fowles's novel of nineteenth-century Dorset, *The French
Lieutenant's Woman* (1969). She was played memorably by Meryl
Streep in the film of the novel (1981; dir. Karel Reisz).

WOODSEAVES, KESTER   See under Prudence SARN

WOODY WOODPECKER   Animated bird with a famously manic
laugh. He was created by Walter Lantz in the late 1930s, and
subsequently moved from the cinema to television. 'The Woody
Woodpecker Song' became a hit record in the late 1940s. Woody's
voice was provided by Grace Stafford, Walter Lantz's wife. Woody
Woodpecker also appeared in his own comic-book from 1947.

WOOSTER, BERTIE   Amiable but brainless young man-about-
town who has comic adventures with his manservant
JEEVES, in a long series of short stories and novels by P. G.
Wodehouse. Bertie is the narrator of these frothy comedies
(apart from the novel *Ring for Jeeves* [1953]), and in some respects
he is a greater creation than his brilliant servant. His apparently
idiotic speech, full of the 'Knut' slang of pre-1914 days, is laced

with poetry. The authority-figures who mar Bertie's otherwise idyllic life are his dreadnought aunts. Aunt Agatha – 'who eats broken bottles and wears barbed wire next to the skin', according to Bertie's memorable hyperbole – and the equally meddlesome Aunt Dahlia are responsible for precipitating many hilarious crises. Bertie was played by David Niven in the film *Thank You, Jeeves* (1936). A British television series, 'The World of Wooster' (1965–8), starred Ian Carmichael as the irrepressible chucklehead. The book *Wooster's World* (1967) by Geoffrey Jaggard is a handy guide to the stories about Bertie and his urbane servant.

WORTH, MARY   Wise, middle-aged heroine of a long-running American comic-strip – a newspaper equivalent of such radio soap-opera figures as Ma PERKINS. She first appeared in 1932, in a strip known as *Apple Mary* created by Mary Orr. The strip was retitled *Mary Worth's Family* in 1940, when artist Dale Conner and writer Allen Saunders took charge. It has been perpetuated by other hands, and a number of the strips have been reprinted in paperback.

WOYZECK   German soldier who kills his common-law wife, in Georg Büchner's powerful, radical play *Woyzeck* (first published 1879, although its author had died at the age of twenty-three in 1837). The opera *Wozzeck* (1925), by Alban Berg, is an adaptation of Büchner's story. The play has also been filmed at least twice: in 1950 (dir. Georg C. Klaren), with Kurt Meisel; and in 1979 (dir. Werner Herzog), with Klaus Kinski.

WU FANG   Chinese master criminal, a 'son of' Dr FU MANCHU, who was created by the British thriller writer Roland Daniel. The series includes the books *Wu Fang* (1929), *Wu Fang's Revenge* (1934), *The Son of Wu Fang* (1935) and *The Return of Wu Fang* (1937). There was also an American pulp magazine called *The Mysterious Wu Fang* (from 1935). This contained novellas by Robert J. Hogan (creator of G-8).

WU LING, PRINCE   See under Sexton BLAKE

WULFF, BURTON   See under The LONE WOLF

X

X-9 Hero of a newspaper comic-strip, *Secret Agent X-9*, initially drawn by Alex Raymond and written by Dashiell Hammett (from 1934). Hammett's biographer, William F. Nolan, has claimed that 'Hammett combined the [Continental] Op and Sam Spade in the character of X-9. He was cool, efficient, quick with a gun or a wisecrack and, like the Op, was a man without a name.' Hammett was involved with the strip for barely a year, to be replaced by Lesle Charteris among other writers. The strip was still running as late as 1967, by which time the hero had been given a name, Phil Corrigan, and the title was changed to *Secret Agent Corrigan*.

Y

YAHOOS, THE See under Lemuel GULLIVER

YEATES, SINCLAIR Resident magistrate in a benighted district of
Ireland. He has many mishaps with the wily locals in the
amusing series of stories by Edith Somerville and Martin Ross
(Violet Martin), collected as *Some Experiences of an Irish R.M.*
(1899). The sequels are *Further Experiences of an Irish R.M.* (1908)
and *In Mr Knox's Country* (1915). Major Yeates has been played by
Peter Bowles in a British television series, 'The Irish R.M.' (1983–4).

YELLAN, MARY Heroine of Daphne du Maurier's romantic
historical novel *Jamaica Inn* (1936). After her parents' death
Mary goes to live with her aunt at the lonely Jamaica Inn, in the
midst of Bodmin Moor, Cornwall. There she meets the
villainous Joss Merlyn, leader of a band of smugglers. In the film
of the novel (1939; dir. Alfred Hitchcock) Mary was played by
Maureen O'Hara. The British television mini-series (1983; dir.
Lawrence Gordon Clarke) was scripted by Derek Marlowe and
starred Jane Seymour.

YELLOW KID, THE See under Buster BROWN

YEOBRIGHT, CLYM West-country schoolmaster who marries the
passionate Eustacia Vye, in Thomas Hardy's novel *The Return of
the Native* (1878). The setting is the barren but mysteriously
beautiful Egdon Heath, whence Yeobright has returned after
living in Paris. Clym's eyesight fails, obliging him to give up his
teaching, and become a furze cutter. Tragedy ensues when
Eustacia turns once more to a former lover, Damon Wildeve.

YOGI BEAR Ursine denizen of 'Jellystone Park' who starred in the
animated television series 'Yogi Bear' (1958–63), produced by
Hanna-Barbera. His best friend was a glum little bear called
Boo-Boo. Yogi was perhaps the most popular of all the American
TV cartoon characters in his day, and he was revived for a later

series, 'Yogi's Gang' (1973–7). There have been a Yogi Bear
comic-book and a feature-length cartoon film, *Hey There! It's
Yogi Bear!* (1964; dir. William Hanna and Joseph Barbera).

YORICK, PARSON   See under Tristram SHANDY

YOSSARIAN   Cunning anti-hero of Joseph Heller's blackly comic
novel about American airmen during World War II, *Catch-22* (1961).
He is a born survivor in a paradoxical world of military
bureaucracy, madness and sudden death. One of the other characters
says of him: 'That crazy bastard may be the only sane one left.'
In the film of the book (1970; dir. Mike Nichols) Yossarian was
played by Alan Arkin.

YOSSER   See Yosser HUGHES

YSABEL KID, THE   See under EDGE

YUM-YUM   See under NANKI-POO

YVONNE, MADEMOISELLE   See under Sexton BLAKE

Z

ZADIG Ancient Babylonian hero of the satirical novella *Zadig, ou La Destinée* (1748) by Voltaire (François Marie Arouet). In search of happiness and prosperity for all, he eventually learns that good cannot exist without evil, and evil cannot exist without good. Armed with this wisdom, he becomes a benign king. (See also CANDIDE and RASSELAS.)

ZAZA Parisian music hall singer in the play *Zaza* by Pierre Berton and Charles Simon. She was played by Gloria Swanson in the silent movie *Zaza* (1923; dir. Allan Dwan), and by Claudette Colbert in the talkie remake (1939; dir. George Cukor).

ZAZIE Impish little heroine of Raymond Queneau's novel *Zazie Dans le Métro* (1959; known in English as *Zazie*). 'Some critics maintain that Zazie is related to Lolita; certainly, her precociousness has made her the talk of France, America . . . and now Great Britain' (according to the blurb on an English paperback edition). In the film of the book (1960; dir. Louis Malle) the scamp was played by Catherine Demongeot.

ZEBEDEE See under DOUGAL

ZEITBLOM, SERENUS See under Adrian LEVERKÜHN

ZENITH THE ALBINO See under Sexton BLAKE

ZERO, MR Frustrated anti-hero of Elmer Rice's satirical play *The Adding Machine* (1923). Threatened with replacement by an office machine, he kills his boss, is executed for the murder and goes to the afterlife, where he does penance before being granted another boring life on earth. In the British film of the play (1968; dir. Jerome Epstein) the part of Mr Zero was taken by Milo O'Shea.

Yuri Zhivago (Omar Sharif) in the 1965 film

ZHIVAGO, YURI   Central character of Boris Pasternak's novel *Doctor Zhivago* (1957). He is a young doctor and poet at the time of the Russian Revolution. During the civil war he is separated from his beloved mistress, Lara, and suffers intense privations. Certain anti-Marxist sentiments expressed by Zhivago caused the book to be banned in the Soviet Union until recently, but it was a great success in the West and earned its author a Nobel Prize for Literature. In the somewhat disjointed but very popular film of the novel (1965; dir. David Lean) Zhivago was played by the Egyptian actor Omar Sharif.

ZORBA, ALEXIS   Hero of the novel *Zorba the Greek* (1946) by Nikos Kazantzakis. 'Vigorous and passionate . . . [he]

personifies the Dionysian approach to life that fascinated his creator' (according to *The Reader's Encyclopedia*). In the film of the novel (1964; dir. Michael Cacoyannis) the larger-than-life Zorba was played by Anthony Quinn.

ZORBA, DOCTOR   See under Ben CASEY

ZORRO   Black-masked and caped avenger of old California created by writer Johnston McCulley for his 1919 serial 'The Curse of Capistrano' (*All-Story* magazine) and its sequel 'The Further Adventures of Zorro'. He is a master swordsman, and is in the habit of leaving his sign, a slashed 'Z', on the clothing or the skin of his foes. Zorro (Spanish for 'fox') is really Don Diego de la Vega, an apparently foppish aristocrat who secretly takes up his sword on behalf of the disinherited and the downtrodden. He has much in common with Robin Hood and the SCARLET PIMPERNEL (not to mention such later characters as BATMAN, SPIDER-MAN, et al.). The character made a swift transition from the written word to the cinema screen. The athletic Douglas Fairbanks played him in *The Mark of Zorro* (1920; dir. Fred Niblo), a film which proved to be one of the star's most popular vehicles. He also played the role in the sequel, *Don Q, Son of Zorro* (1925). Sound films about Zorro include *The Bold Caballero* (1937), starring Robert Livingston, and the remade *The Mark of Zorro* (1940; dir. Rouben Mamoulian), with Tyrone Power. There were several Zorro serials, beginning with *Zorro Rides Again* (1937), starring John Carroll. The best of the serials is reckoned to be *Zorro's Fighting Legion* (1939), with Reed Hadley. It was followed by *Son of Zorro* (1947), with George Turner, and *Ghost of Zorro* (1949), with Clayton Moore. A 'Zorro' television series was made by the Walt Disney company in 1957–9; it starred Guy Williams, and segments of it were also released as feature films. There has also been a TV-movie remake of *The Mark of Zorro* (1974; dir. Don McDougall), with Frank Langella as the black-clad swordsman. In addition, there have been various foreign-language films based on the character and featuring such actors as Sean Flynn, Gordon Scott and Alain Delon. The spoof movie, *Zorro, the Gay Blade* (1981; dir. Peter Medak), had George Hamilton as an effeminate version of the hero. A Zorro comic-book appeared regularly from the late 1940s until the 1960s, and an animated TV series was made in

1981. A live-action TV comedy series, 'Zorro and Son' (1983), had Henry Darrow as the ageing Don Diego and Paul Regina as his son, Zorro Jr.

ZUCKERMAN, NATHAN   Jewish-American novelist, an alter ego of his creator, who appears in Philip Roth's serio-comic novels *My Life as a Man* (1974), *The Ghost Writer* (1979), *Zuckerman Unbound* (1981), *The Anatomy Lesson* (1983), *The Prague Orgy* (1985) and *The Counterlife* (1986). In the first of these books he features merely as a 'fictional character', a figment invented by the novel's protagonist, Peter Tarnopol (also a writer). In the later books, however, Roth presents Nathan Zuckerman as 'real' – and loads him with many of the problems suffered by the real-life Philip Roth, including the embarrassment of having written a literary novel which everyone takes to be pornographic (see Alexander PORTNOY). *The Ghost Writer*, in which the young Zuckerman searches desperately for a literary father-figure, has been adapted as a television movie (1984; dir. Tristram Powell).

BIBLIOGRAPHY

This bibliography is limited to the principal non-fiction works consulted. Primary texts (novels, plays, etc.) are not listed, apart from a few anthologies of short material which contain useful introductions or appendices. Nor are newspaper and periodical articles listed here – I have given citations for these, where appropriate, in the body of the book.

Aldiss, Brian W. with David Wingrove. *Trillion-Year Spree: The History of Science Fiction*. New York: Atheneum, 1986.

Amis, Kingsley. *The James Bond Dossier*. New York: Mysterious Press, 1987.

Amis, Kingsley. *What's Become of Jane Austen? and Other Questions*. London: Cape, 1970.

Amos, William. *The Originals: Who's Really Who in Fiction*. Boston: Little, Brown, 1986.

Anderson, Rachel. *The Purple Heart Throbs: The Sub-Literature of Love*. London: Hodder and Stoughton, 1974.

Ashley, Mike. *Who's Who in Horror and Fantasy Fiction*. New York: Taplinger, 1978.

Baring-Gould, W. S. *Nero Wolfe of West Thirty-Fifth Street*. New York: Viking, 1969.

Baring-Gould, W. S. *Sherlock Holmes: A Biography of the World's First Consulting Detective*. New York: C.N. Potter, 1962.

Barnes, Melvyn. *Best Detective Fiction: A Guide from Godwin to the Present*. Hamden, CT: Linnet Books, 1975.

Barron, Neil (ed.). *Anatomy of Wonder: A Critical Guide to Science Fiction*. 2nd edition. New York: Bowker, 1981.

Beauman, Nicola. *A Very Great Profession: The Woman's Novel 1914–39*. London: Virago, 1983.

Belton, John. *The Hollywood Professionals, Volume 3: Howard Hawks, Frank Borzage, Edgar G. Ulmer*. New York: A.S. Barnes, 1974.

Benét, William Rose (ed.). *The Reader's Encyclopedia*. 2nd edition. New York: T.Y. Crowell, 1965.

Bogdanovich, Peter. *Allan Dwan: The Last Pioneer*. New York: Praeger, 1971.

Bold, Alan and Robert Giddings. *True Characters: Real People in Fiction*. London: Longman, 1984.

Brandreth, Gyles. *Superheroes*. London: Knight Books, 1984.

Briggs, Julia. *Night Visitors: The Rise and Fall of the English Ghost Story*. London: Faber and Faber, 1977.

Brooks, Tim, and Earle Marsh. *The Complete Directory to Prime Time Network TV Shows, 1946–Present*. 3rd edition. New York: Ballantine Books, 1985.

Brosnan, John. *Future Tense: The Cinema of Science Fiction*. New York: St Martin's Press, 1978.

Buchanan-Brown, J. (ed.). *Cassell's Encyclopaedia of World Literature*. Revised edition. 3 volumes. New York: Morrow, 1973.

Buckman, Peter. *All for Love: a Study in Soap Opera*. London: Secker and Warburg, 1984.

Burgess, Anthony. *Ninety-Nine Novels: The Best in English Since 1939*. New York: Summit, 1984.

Burgess, Anthony. *The Novel Now: A Student's Guide to Contemporary Fiction*. New edition. London: Faber and Faber, 1971.

Butler, William Vivian. *The Durable Desperadoes*. London: Macmillan, 1973.

Cadogan, Mary, and Patricia Craig. *Women and Children First: The Fiction of Two World Wars*. London: Gollancz, 1978.

Calder, Jenni. *There Must be a Lone Ranger: The Myth and Reality of the American West*. New York: Taplinger, 1975.

Canham, Kingsley. *The Hollywood Professionals, Volume 1: Michael Curtiz, Raoul Walsh, Henry Hathaway*. New York: A.S. Barnes, 1973.

Carpenter, Humphrey. *The Inklings: C. S. Lewis, J. R. R. Tolkien, Charles Williams, and Their Friends*. New York: Ballantine, 1981.

Carpenter, Humphrey and Mari Prichard. *The Oxford Companion to Children's Literature*. New York: Oxford University Press, 1984.

Carr, John Dickson (ed. by Douglas G. Greene). *The Door to Doom and Other Detections*. New York: Harper & Row, 1980.

Carter, Angela. *The Sadeian Woman: An Exercise in Cultural History*. London: Virago, 1979.

Carter, Lin. *Lovecraft: A Look Behind the 'Cthulhu Mythos'*. New York: Ballantine, 1972.

Carter, Lin. *Imaginary Worlds: The Art of Fantasy*. New York: Ballantine, 1973.

Cawelti, John G. *Adventure, Mystery and Romance: Formula Stories as Art and Popular Culture*. Chicago: University of Chicago Press, 1976.

Charney, Maurice. *Sexual Fiction*. New York: Methuen, 1981.

Cockburn, Claud. *Bestseller: The Books That Everyone Read 1900–1939*. London: Sidgwick and Jackson, 1972.

Craig, Patricia and Mary Cadogan. *The Lady Investigates: Women Detectives and Spies in Fiction*. London: Gollancz, 1981.

Daniell, David. *The Interpreter's House: A Critical Assessment of John Buchan*. London: Nelson, 1975.

Denton, Clive and Kingsley Canham. *The Hollywood Professionals, Volume 5: King Vidor, John Crowell, Mervyn Le Roy*. New York: A.S. Barnes, 1976.

Denton, Clive, Kingsley Canham and Tony Thomas. *The Hollywood Professionals, Volume 2: Henry King, Lewis Milestone, Sam Wood*. New York: A.S. Barnes, 1974.

Disher, Maurice Willson. *Blood and Thunder: Mid-Victorian Melodrama and its Origins*. Brooklyn, NY: Haskell, 1974.

Dixon, Bob. *Catching Them Young 1: Sex, Race and Class in Children's Fiction*. London: Pluto Press, 1977.

Dixon, Bob. *Catching Them Young 2: Political Ideas in Children's Fiction*. London: Pluto Press, 1977.

Dorfman, Ariel. *The Empire's Old Clothes: What the Lone Ranger, Babar, and Other Innocent Heroes Do to Our Minds*. New York: Pantheon, 1983.

Drabble, Margaret (ed.). *The Oxford Companion to English Literature*. 5th edition. New York: Oxford University Press, 1985.

Drinkrow, John. *The Vintage Musical Comedy Book*. Reading: Osprey, 1974.

Edwards, Owen Dudley. *The Quest for Sherlock Holmes: A Biographical Study of Sir Arthur Conan Doyle*. Totowa, NJ: Barnes & Noble Books, 1983.

Ellman, Richard. *James Joyce*. Oxford University Press, 1959.

Enser, A. G. S. *Filmed Books and Plays: A List of Books and Plays from which Films Have Been Made, 1928–1967*. Revised edition. London: Deutsch, 1971.

Evans, Ivor H. (ed.). *Brewer's Dictionary of Phrase and Fable*. Centenary edition. New York: Harper & Row, 1981.

Farmer, Philip José. *Doc Savage: His Apocalyptic Life*. Garden City, NY: Doubleday, 1973.

Farmer, Philip José (ed.). *Mother Was a Lovely Beast: A Feral Man Anthology*. New York: Pyramid Books, 1976.

Farmer, Philip José. *Tarzan Alive: A Definitive Biography of Lord Greystoke.* Garden City, NY: Doubleday, 1972.

Feiffer, Jules. *The Great Comic Book Heroes.* New York: Dial Press, 1965.

Fiedler, Leslie A. *Cross the Border – Close the Gap.* New York: Stein and Day, 1972.

Fiedler, Leslie A. *Love and Death in the American Novel.* 2nd edition. New York: Stein and Day, 1975.

Fiedler, Leslie A. *The Return of the Vanishing American.* New York: Stein and Day, 1968.

Fiedler, Leslie A. *What Was Literature: Class Culture and Mass Society.* New York: Simon and Schuster, 1982.

Fisher, Margery. *Who's Who in Children's Books: A Treasury of the Familiar Characters of Childhood.* New York: Harper & Row, 1975.

Folsom, James K. (ed.). *The Western: A Collection of Critical Essays.* Englewood Cliffs, NJ: Prentice-Hall, 1979.

Ford, Boris (ed.) *The New Pelican Guide to English Literature.* Volumes 4 to 7. New York: Penguin, 1982–84.

Freeman, William. *Everyman's Dictionary of Fictional Characters.* 3rd edition, revised by Fred Urquhart. Boston: Writer, 1974.

Frye, Northrop. *Anatomy of Criticism: Four Essays.* Princeton, NJ: Princeton University Press, 1957.

Frye, Northrop. *The Secular Scripture: A Study of the Structure of Romance.* Cambridge, MA: Harvard University Press, 1976.

Gifford, Denis. *The Golden Age of Radio: An Illustrated Companion.* London: Batsford, 1985.

Gifford, Denis. *The International Book of Comics.* London: Hamlyn/W. H. Smith, 1984.

Goulart, Ron. *The Adventurous Decade.* New Rochelle, NY: Arlington House, 1975.

Goulart, Ron. *An Informal History of the Pulp Magazine.* New York: Ace Books, 1973.

Green, Martin. *Dreams of Adventure, Deeds of Empire.* New York: Basic Books, 1979.

Green, Martin. *The English Novel in the Twentieth Century: The Doom of Empire.* University Park, PA: Pennsylvania State University Press, 1987.

Greenblatt, Stephen Jay. *Three Modern Satirists: Waugh, Orwell, and Huxley.* New Haven, CT: Yale University Press, 1965.

Greene, Graham. *Collected Essays.* New York: Viking, 1969.

Greene, Hugh (ed.). *The Rivals of Sherlock Holmes: Early Detective Stories.* London: Bodley Head, 1970.

Greene, Hugh, (ed.). *More Rivals of Sherlock Holmes: Cosmopolitan Crimes.* London: Bodley Head, 1971.

Halliwell, Leslie. *Halliwell's Film Guide,* 4th edition. New York: Scribner, 1985.

Halliwell, Leslie. *Halliwell's Filmgoer's Companion.* 8th edition. New York: Scribner, 1985.

Halliwell, Leslie with Philip Purser. *Halliwell's Television Companion.* 3rd edition. London: Grafton, 1986.

Harry, Bill. *Heroes of the Spaceways.* London: Omnibus Press. 1981.

Hibbert, Christopher. *The Making of Charles Dickens.* New York: Harper & Row, 1967.

Hicken, Marilyn E. *Sequels. Volume 1: Adult Books.* 7th edition. London Association of Assistant Librarians, 1982.

Holtsmark, Erling B. *Tarzan and Tradition: Classical Myth in Popular Literature.* Westport, CT: Greenwood Press, 1981.

Horn, Maurice (ed.). *The World Encyclopedia of Cartoons.* New York: Chelsea House, 1980.

Husband, Janet. *Sequels: An Annotated Guide to Novels in Sequence.* Chicago: American Library Association, 1982.

Jacobs, Arthur and Stanley Sadie. *The Limelight Book of Opera.* Enlarged edition. New York: Limelight Editions, 1985.

James, Clive. *Visions Before Midnight: Television Criticism from the Observer 1972–76.* London: Cape, 1977.

James, Clive. *The Crystal Bucket: Television Criticism from the Observer 1976–79.* London: Cape, 1981.

James, Clive. *Glued to the Box: Television Criticism from the Observer 1979–82.* London: Cape, 1983.

James, Louis. *Fiction for the Working Man 1830–50: A Study of the Literature Produced for the Working Classes in Early Victorian Urban England.* New York: Oxford University Press, 1963.

Katz, Ephraim. *The Film Encyclopedia.* New York: T.Y. Crowell, 1979.

Keating, H. R. F. (ed.). *Crime Writers: Reflections on Crime Fiction.* London: BBC, 1978.

Keating, H. R. F. (ed.). *Whodunit?: A Guide to Crime, Suspense and Spy Fiction.* New York: Van Nostrand Reinhold Co., 1982.

King, Stephen. *Danse Macabre.* New York: Everest House, 1981.

Kittredge, William and Steven M. Krauzer (eds.). *The Great American Detective.* New York: New American Library, 1978.

Koegler, Horst. *The Concise Oxford Dictionary of Ballet.* New York: Oxford University Press, 1977.

Lambert, Gavin. *The Dangerous Edge.* New York: Grossman Publishers, 1976.

Leavis, F. R. *The Great Tradition: George Eliot, Henry James, Joseph Conrad.* New York: G.W. Stewart, 1948.

Lee, Stan. *Origins of Marvel Comics.* New York: Simon and Schuster, 1974.

Lofts, W. O. G. and Derek Adley. *The British Bibliography of Edgar Wallace.* London: Howard Baker, 1969.

Lofts, W. O. G. and Derek Adley. *The Saint and Leslie Charteris.* London: Hutchinson, 1971.

Lupoff, Dick and Don Thompson (eds). *All in Color for a Dime.* New York: Ace Books, 1970.

Lupoff, Richard A. *Edgar Rice Burroughs: Master of Adventure.* Revised edition. New York: Ace Books, 1968.

McCarthy, Mary. *The Writing on the Wall and Other Literary Essays.* New York: Harcourt Brace Jovanovich, 1971.

McCormick, Donald. *Who's Who in Spy Fiction.* London: Elm Tree, 1977.

Macdonald, Dwight. *Against the American Grain: Essays on the Effects of Mass Culture.* New York: Vintage Books, n.d. (1964?).

McLeish, Kenneth. *The Penguin Companion to the Arts in the Twentieth Century.* New York: Penguin Books, 1986.

McNally, Raymond T. and Radu Florescu. *In Search of Dracula: A True History of Dracula and Vampire Legends.* Greenwich, CT: New York Graphic Society, 1972.

Maltin, Leonard (ed.). *TV Movies 1983–84 Edition.* New York: New American Library, 1982.

Mann, Jessica. *Deadlier Than the Male: Why Are Respectable English Women So Good at Murder?* New York: Macmillan, 1981.

Marcus, Steven. *The Other Victorians: A Study of Sexuality and Pornography in Mid-Nineteenth Century England.* New York: Basic Books, 1966.

Moskowitz, Sam. *Seekers of Tomorrow: Masters of Modern Science Fiction.* New York: Ballantine Books, 1967.

Neuburg, Victor E. *The Batsford Companion to Popular Literature.* London: Batsford, 1982.

Neuburg, Victor E. *Popular Literature: A History and Guide from the Beginning of Printing to the Year 1897.* Harmondsworth: Penguin Books, 1977.

Nicholls, Peter (ed.). *The Encyclopedia of Science Fiction: An Illustrated A to Z.* London: Granada, 1979.

Nicholls, Peter. *World of Fantastic Films Illustrated Survey.* New York: Dodd, Mead, 1984.

Orwell, George. *The Penguin Essays of George Orwell.* Harmondsworth: Penguin Books, 1984.

Palmer, Jerry. *Thrillers: Genesis and Structure of a Popular Genre.* New York: St. Martin's Press, 1979.

Parker, Derek and Julia. *The Story and the Song: A Survey of English Musical Plays, 1916-78.* New York: Chappell, 1979.

Pate, Janet. *The Black Book of Villains.* Newton Abbot: David and Charles, 1975.

Parkinson, C. Northcote. *The Life and Times of Horatio Hornblower.* Boston: Little, Brown, 1971.

Pawling, Christopher (ed.). *Popular Fiction and Social Change.* New York: St. Martin's Press, 1984.

Payton, Geoffrey. *Payton's Proper Names.* New York: Warne, 1969.

Penzler, Otto. *The Private Lives of Private Eyes, Spies, Crimefighters, and Other Good Guys.* New York: Grosset and Dunlap, 1977.

Pointer, Michael. *The Public Life of Sherlock Holmes.* New York: Drake Publishers, 1975.

Pointer, Michael. *The Sherlock Holmes File.* Newton Abbot: David and Charles, 1976.

Praz, Mario. *The Hero in Eclipse in Victorian Fiction.* New York: Oxford University Press, 1956.

Praz, Mario. *The Romantic Agony.* 2nd edition. New York: Oxford University Press, 1970.

Priestley, J. B. *The English Comic Characters.* 2nd edition. Staten Island, NY: Phaeton, 1972.

Punter, David. *The Literature of Terror: A History of Gothic Fictions from 1765 to the Present Day.* New York: Longman, 1980.

Quigly, Isabel. *The Heirs of Tom Brown: The English School Story.* London: Chatto and Windus, 1982.

Ray, Sheila G. *The Blyton Phenomenon: The Controversy Surrounding the World's Most Successful Children's Writer.* London: Deutsch, 1982.

Reilly, John M. *Twentieth-Century Crime and Mystery Writers.* 2nd edition. Chicago and London: St James Press, 1985.

Robertson, Patrick. *Guinness Film Facts and Feats.* Revised edition. London: Guinness Superlatives, 1985.

Rosenberg, Edgar. *From Shylock to Svengali: Jewish Stereotypes in English Fiction.* Stanford, CA: Stanford University Press, 1960.

Rovin, Jeff. *The Encyclopedia of Superheroes.* New York: Facts on File, 1985.

Rovin, Jeff. *The Fantasy Almanac.* New York: Dutton, 1979.

Sandison, Alan. *The Wheel of Empire: A Study of the Imperial Idea in Some Late Nineteenth and Early Twentieth-Century Fiction.* London: Macmillan, 1967.

Scheuer, Steven H. (ed.). *Movies on TV 1984–1985.* New York: Bantam, 1983.

Scholes, Percy A. *The Concise Oxford Dictionary of Music.* 2nd edition. New York: Oxford University Press, 1964.

Scott-Giles, C. W. *The Wimsey Family: A Fragmentary History Compiled from Correspondence with Dorothy L. Sayers.* New York: Avon Books, 1979.

Seymour-Smith, Martin (ed.). *Novels and Novelists: A Guide to the World of Fiction.* London: Windward, 1980.

Showalter, Elaine. *A Literature of Their Own: British Women Novelists from Brontë to Lessing.* Revised edition. Princeton, NJ: Princeton University Press, 1977.

Slung, Michele B. (ed.). *Crime on Her Mind: Fifteen Stories of Female Sleuths from the Victorian Era to the Forties.* New York: Pantheon, 1975.

Smith, Curtis C. *Twentieth-Century Science Fiction Writers.* 2nd edition. Chicago and London: St James Press, 1986.

Smith, Henry Nash. *Virgin Land: The American West as Symbol and Myth.* Cambridge, MA: Harvard University Press, 1950.

Stedman, Raymond William. *The Serials: Suspense and Drama by Installment.* Norman, OK: University of Oklahoma Press, 1971.

Stewart, R. F. *. . . And Always a Detective: Chapters on the History of Detective Fiction.* North Pomfret, VT: David and Charles, 1980.

Street, Brian V. *The Savage in Literature: Representations of 'Primitive' Society in English Fiction 1858–1920.* Boston: Routledge and Kegan Paul, 1975.

Street, Douglas (ed.). *Children's Novels and the Movies.* New York: Frederick Ungar, 1983.

Sutherland, John. *Bestsellers: Popular Fiction of the 1970s.* Boston: Routledge and Kegan Paul, 1981.

Symons, Julian. *Bloody Murder: From the Detective Story to the Crime Novel, A History.* New York: Viking, 1985.

Symons, Julian. *The Great Detectives: Seven Original Investigations.* London: Orbis Publishing, 1981.

Thomson, David. *Suspects.* New York: Knopf, 1985.

Tompkins, J. M. S. *The Popular Novel in England 1770–1800.* Lincoln, NE: University of Nebraska Press, 1961.

Tremain, Ruthven. *The Animal's Who's Who: 1,146 Celebrated Animals in History, Popular Culture, Literature, and Lore.* London: Routledge and Kegan Paul, 1982.

Tropp, Martin. *Mary Shelley's Monster: The Story of Frankenstein.* Boston: Houghton Mifflin, 1976.

Turner, E. S. *Boys Will Be Boys: The Story of Sweeney Todd, Deadwood Dick, Sexton Blake, Billy Bunter, Dick Barton, et al.* 3rd edition. London: Michael Joseph, 1975.

Tymn, Marshall B. (ed.). *Horror Literature: A Core Collection and Reference Guide.* New York: Bowker, 1981.

Usborne, Richard. *Clubland Heroes: A Nostalgic Study of Some Recurrent Characters in the Romantic Fiction of Dornford Yates, John Buchan and Sapper.* Revised edition. London: Barrie and Jenkins, 1974.

Usborne, Richard. *Wodehouse at Work to the End.* Revised edition. London: Barrie and Jenkins, 1976.

Van Ash, Cay and Elizabeth Sax Rohmer. *Master of Villainy: A Biography of Sax Rohmer.* Bowling Green, OH: Bowling Green University Popular Press, 1972.

Vidal, Gore. *On Our Own Now: Collected Essays 1952–1972.* London: Heinemann, 1974.

Wallace, Irving. *The Fabulous Originals: Lives of Extraordinary People Who Inspired Memorable Characters in Fiction.* New York: Knopf, 1955.

Watt, Ian. *The Rise of the Novel: Studies in Defoe, Richardson and Fielding.* Berkeley, CA: University of California Press, 1957.

Wicking, Christopher and Tise Vahimagi. *The American Vein: Directors and Directions in Television.* London: Talisman Books, 1979.

Wilson, Edmund. *Axel's Castle: A Study in the Imaginative Literature of 1870–1930.* New York: Scribner, 1954.

Zipes, Jack. *Breaking the Magic Spell: Radical Theories of Folk and Fairy Tales.* Austin, TX: University of Texas Press, 1979.

PICTURE CREDITS

Pinocchio © Walt Disney Productions *BFI*

Mary Poppins drawn by Mary Shepard

Quasimodo played by Charles Laughton in
'The Hunchback of Notre Dame' RKO
Radio Pictures 1939 *Kobal Collection*

A. J. Raffles, played by David Niven in the
Samuel Goldwyn film 1940 *BFI*

Rudolf Rassendyll (right) and Rupert of
Hentzau, played by Ronald Colman and
Douglas Fairbanks Jr in 'The Prisoner of
Zenda' David O. Selznick 1937 *Kobal
Collection*

Rebecca *Mansell Collection*

Robby the Robot in 'The Forbidden Planet'
MGM 1956 *BFI*

Natasha Rostova, played by Audrey
Hepburn in 'War and Peace' Vistavision
1956 *BFI*

The Saint, played by Roger Moore in the
ATV series (1960's) *Kobal Collection*

Tom Sawyer, played by Tommy Kelly in

'The Adventures of Tom Sawyer' David
O. Selznick 1938 *Kobal Collection*

Ebenezer Scrooge *Mansell Collection*

Long John Silver *Mary Evans Picture
Library*

Tusker and Lucy Smalley, played by
Trevor Howard and Celia Johnson in
'Staying On' 1980 *Granada TV*

Snoopy © 1958 United Feature
Syndicate, Inc.

Spider-Man © *Marvel Comics Group*

Tarzan © *Marvel Comics Group*

Toad of Toad Hall drawn by E. H. Shepard

Darth Vader © *Marvel Comics Group*

Weary Willie and Tired Tim © Tom
Browne

Winnie-the-Pooh drawn by E. H. Shepard

Yogi Bear © Hanna Barbera *Kobal
Collection*

Yuri Zhivago, played by Omar Sharif in
'Dr Zhivago' MGM 1965 *Kobal Collection*